String Trimmer and Blower

SERVICE MANUAL ■ 2ND EDITION

Intertec Publishing Corporation

P.O. Box 12901 ■ Overland Park, KS 66282-2901

© Copyright 1992 by Intertec Publishing Corp. Printed in the United States of America.
Library of Congress Catalog Card Number 92-73675

This book can be recycled. Please remove cover.

Cover photo courtesy of McCulloch Corporation

String Trimmer and Blower

SERVICE MANUAL ■ 2ND EDITION

String Trimmer and Blower Manufacturers:

- Alpina
- Black & Decker
- Bunton
- John Deere
- Echo
- Elliot
- Green Machine
- Hoffco

- Homelite
- Husqvarna
- IDC
- Jonsered
- Kaaz
- Lawn Boy
- Maruyama

- McCulloch
- Olympyk
- Pioneer/Partner
- Poulan
- Redmax
- Robin
- Roper/Rally
- Ryan

- Ryobi
- Sachs-Dolmar
- Sears
- Shindaiwa
- SMC
- Snapper
- Stihl

- Tanaka (TAS)
- Toro
- TML (Trail)
- Wards
- Weed Eater
- Western Auto
- Yard Pro
- Yazoo

String Trimmer and Blower Gasoline Engines:

- John Deere
- Echo
- Efco
- Fuji
- Homelite

- Husqvarna
- IDC
- Kawasaki
- Kioritz

- Komatsu
- McCulloch
- Mitsubishi
- Piston Powered Products

- Poulan
- Sachs-Dolmar
- Shindaiwa
- Stihl

- Tanaka (TAS)
- Tecumseh
- TML (Trail)

INTERTEC PUBLISHING CORP.

President
Jack Hancock

Group Vice President
Bill Wiesner

**The following books and guides are published
by Intertec Publishing Corp.**

CONTENTS

─────────────── **BLOWER SERVICE SECTIONS** ───────────────

DUAL DIMENSIONS

This service manual provides specifications in both the U.S. Customary and Metric (SI) systems of measurement. The first specification is given in the measuring system perceived by us to be the preferred system when servicing a particular component, while the second specification (given in parenthesis) is the converted measurement. For instance, a specification of "0.011 inch (0.28 mm)" would indicate that we feel the preferred measurement, in this instance, is the U.S. system of measurement and the metric equivalent of 0.011 inch is 0.28 mm.

GENERAL MAINTENANCE AND REPAIR

TRIMMER INFORMATION

Line trimmers and brush cutters are manufactured for every use from the smallest home lawn to large scale commercial landscaping and grounds-care operation.

The drive may be electrical from rechargeable batteries, from 110 volt AC current delivered through an extension cable or by a two-stroke air-cooled gasoline engine.

Battery powered trimmers are fine for light trimming, but can't handle heavy grass, weeds or brush. Most models must be recharged after about 45 minutes of operation. A full recharging may require 15 to 24 hours.

Electrical units operating on 110 volt AC current may have more power reserve than battery powered units, however, extension cord length should not exceed 100 feet even when using 14 gage or larger wire.

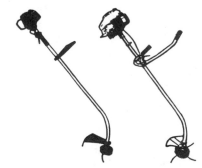

Gasoline engine powered trimmers may be used virtually anywhere that an operator can walk, but usually require more maintenance than a similar electrical unit.

Monofilament spin trimmers use spinning monofilament line (or lines) that is 0.050 to 0.130 inch in diameter. It's not fishing line, which requires high-tensile

strength compared with trimmer line that must resist bending against plants. Spinning monofilament line actually breaks off plants rather than cutting them, much like breaking a plant by striking the stem with a stick.

Depending on head design, trimmers may have one, two, three, or even four lines extended for cutting at the same time. As the line wears back or breaks off, more line may be extended manually or automatically. Manual models require trimmer engine to be stopped. Loosening a lock knob or screw and rotating a housing advances new line. On semi-automatic trimmer heads, line is advanced by tapping the trimmer head on the ground with engine running at full rpm while others require quick adjustment of throttle speed. A cutoff blade on the trimmer shield prevents automatic extenders from letting out too much line, which would then overload the trimmer and reduce cutting efficiency. The motor or engine must be stopped before line is manually extended on other trimmers.

Tall, tough weeds require a weed blade that can replace the monofilament head on some heavier gasoline-powered trimmers. Some of the strongest heavy-duty units can be equipped with brush or saw blade for cutting saplings, brush and low, small tree limbs. Only trimmers designed for such use should be equipped with weed or brush blades. To avoid trimmer damage and possibly serious accidents, only the recommended weed or brush blades should be used. A blade that is too large overloads the trimmer, and the speed of some trimmers is too fast for safe blade operation.

On some power trimmers, the cutting head is attached directly to the output shaft of the engine or motor that is mounted at the lower end of the machine. This eliminates the driveshaft, bearings, etc., required if the power source is attached at the upper end of the trimmer.

A lower engine location exposes the engine to more dust, dirt and debris than is found at the upper position. Placing the engine at the cutting head also shifts most of the weight to that position and operator must support the weight while cutting, increasing operator fatigue.

Trimmers with engine at the upper end expose the operator to more engine noise and heat, but weight of such trimmers is better balanced and the engine is easier to keep clean. Trimmers with a curved shaft drive the cutting head directly from the engine through a flexible shaft. This provides a simple, economical drive.

Straight shaft trimmers have a set of bevel gears in a case atop the cutting head which changes direction of power flow and can change head speed in rela-

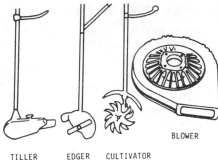

TILLER   EDGER   CULTIVATOR   BLOWER

tion to engine speed if desired. The lower, straight shaft makes it easier to trim farther under low tree limbs, fences and other obstacles.

On some trimmers, a centrifugal clutch (similar to those on chain saws) engages the trimmer head when the engine is accelerated and is disengaged when engine speed is reduced. This improves trimmer safety and makes it easier to start the engine by not having to spin the trimmer head or blade also.

A trimmer that "feels fine" in the store may feel very heavy after long use in the hot sun. Both total weight and balance of a trimmer can affect how fast the operator becomes tired. For instance, some smaller gas trimmers weigh less than 8 pounds while bigger models weigh 25 pounds or more. (Electric models weigh approximately 2 to 10 pounds.)

Smaller trimmers may require more time to complete a given task, but operators with moderate strength may be able to use a smaller trimmer with fewer rest breaks and finish in about the same time as they would when using a trimmer that's too big.

Weed and brush blade should never be used without a shoulder harness on models fully supported by the operator. An approved shoulder harness will be designed to prevent the trimmer head from accidentally swinging back and possibly injuring the operator if the blade kicks against a solid object or if the operator slips. A correctly-adjusted shoulder harness also reduces fatigue and makes trimmer operation much easier.

The cutting head can be removed easily from some trimmers and replaced by other attachments. A blower attachment can remove leaves and grass clippings from sidewalks, driveways, etc. A power edger provides a neat appearance between lawns and sidewalks, driveways or other paved areas. And, a power hoe can weed gardens or flower beds and loosen soil for better infiltration of moisture.

Such attachments eliminate the need to buy separate power units for each tool and, thus, can save considerable money. However, they are usually best for smaller lawns and gardens, particularly if two or more attachments must be used simultaneously.

OPERATING SAFETY

Edger and trimmers are cutting tools and must be operated with great care to reduce the chance of injury. Dangers include electrical shock, burning, muscle strain and being hit by projectile thrown by rotating unit. The operator should exercise caution and observe the following checklist.

Observe the following check list **in addition to STANDARD SAFETY PRACTICES.**

1. Remove debris from working area.
2. Keep people and animals well away from working area. (At least 20 feet from trimmer.)
3. Maintain proper balance and footing at all times. Don't overreach.
4. Be extremely careful of kick back, especially when using a hard blade cutter.
5. Cut only with discharge aimed at a safe direction, away from operator, windows, etc.
6. Use weed and brush blades only on edger/trimmers designed for their use. If the operator carries the full weight of the unit, an attached harness designed to prevent accidental injury to operator must be used.

If the edger/trimmer is powered by a gasoline engine, check fuel requirement

before filling tank. The engines of spin trimmers which are carried by the operator, are lubricated by oil which should be mixed with the gasoline before filling tank. Overheating, rapid wear and serious damage will result if tank of 2 stroke engines requiring gasoline and oil mix is filled with only gasoline. Recommended ratio of oil to fuel is often marked on cap of fuel tank, but operator's manual should be checked for recommended type and amount oil.

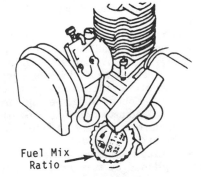

Fuel Mix Ratio

SETTING UP THE UNIT

Key to setting up and operating is the direction of rotation at the cutter. Cutting should only occur in the segment of the cutting plane that will discharge cuttings away from the operator or to the side. The cutter of some models rotates clockwise while the cutter of others turns counter-clockwise.

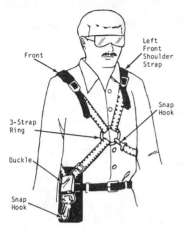

On models so equipped, put the shoulder harness on and adjust size to the user's body. Adjust position of hip guard so that suspension hook will be correct height for easy control of edger/trimmer. The harness plates on back and chest should be level. Make final adjustment so that pressure is even on both shoulders.

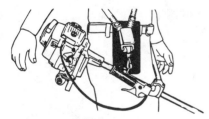

Trimmer should hang freely in front when operator stands squarely with feet about shoulder distance apart. Change balance by moving the hook eye on the drive shaft tube. When fuel tank is empty, trimmer head should float slightly above ground.

Adjust handle bar position for comfortable convenient operation while edger/trimmer is hanging from shoulder strap or harness.

Adjust for trim **mowing**, by positioning the cutting head horizontal, parallel to the ground. Adjust for **trimming** around trees, sidewalks, driveways, curbs, lawn furniture, etc., by turning the cutting head at about 30 degree angle from horizontal. Adjust for **edging** by positioning cutting head vertical (90 degrees from surface to be trimmed).

Adjusting the cutting angle should be accomplished by turning the cutting head or by relocating the handle. Forcibly holding the unit at an uncomfortable angle is only suggested if a change is for a very short time.

On gasoline powered models, fill fuel tank with correct type or mixture of fuel as specified by manufacturer.

Vibration, heat and noise of the operating unit may increase fatigue, decrease operator control and impair hearing. Nonslip gloves, properly adjusted shoulder strap (or harness), ear protection and appropriate protective clothing will help reduce the danger to the operator.

On all models, inspect area to cut and remove all debris that may clog or damage cutting head and all debris which could be damaged or thrown by cutter. Wire, string, rope, vines and cords can wrap around rotating head causing damage or possible injury. Rocks, cans, bottles, sticks and similar items can be thrown by cutter causing damage to property or injury to humans or animals.

STARTING ENGINE

DANGER: Before starting the edger/trimmer, make sure that all other people and animals are at least 20 feet away and that all parts are in place and tight.

On gasoline powered models, lay the edger/trimmer down on flat, clear area away from tall grass or brush. Operate primer or choke, move ignition switch to "ON" position; then, open fuel shut-off valve and open fuel tank cap vent. Squeeze and hold throttle trigger to ½ speed position, hold trimmer to ground as convenient and pull rewind starter

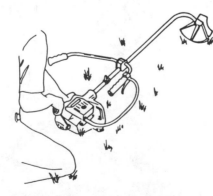

handle smartly. Do not let cord snap back because starter may be damaged.

On models with primer, it may be necessary to operate primer to keep engine running after first starting. On 2 stroke engines with choke, push choke in, then attempt to start after engine has tried to start.

On all models, engine should warm enough to idle smoothly without operating primer or with choke open soon after starting. If equipped with automatic clutch, cutting head should not rotate at idle speed.

MOWING

Trim mowing is very much like having a very narrow rotary lawn mower for places where a regular mower is too wide. String trimmers are also used to mow areas too rough for a standard rotary mower, such as some rocky places.

Cut only in segment of the cutting plane that is away from the operator as indicated by the shaded area in the illustration. Discharge will then be away from operator. When mowing, the cutting head must be kept parallel to the ground. The cut height of the grass should be maintained as if cut with a regular mower. Smooth even cutting will be im-

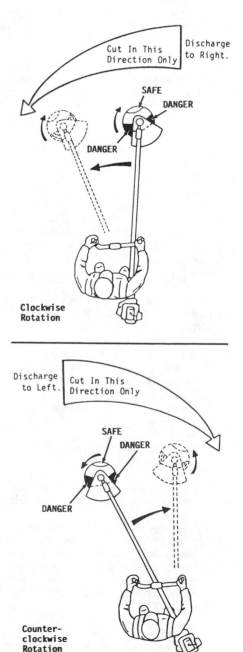

possible if cutting head is angled while attempting to mow.

TRIMMING

The cutting head should be about 30 degrees to the horizontal when trimming around sidewalks, driveways, curbs, lawn furniture, etc. The lower edge should be next to the sidewalk, etc., and should taper upward to the regular cut height of the grass.

WARNING: Always cut so that discharge is away from operator. Never operate with discharge toward feet or legs.

It is possible to forcibly hold the trimmer at the 30 degree angle; however, operator fatigue is increased unnecessarily and safety is compromised. Handle, hook eye or cutting head angles are easily adjusted so that correct 30 degree angle is the natural, easy position of trimmer.

Adjust angle so that the cutting plane is higher on discharge side. Confine cutting to the segment of the cutting plane away from operator so that discharge will be away from operator.

CAUTION: Be careful when trimming around objects such as small pipes, rods or fencing. Trimmer string will wrap around small objects and damage end of trimmer string.

String that is frayed from use is more gentle for trimming around trees and plants than line that has been recently extended and cut. Be careful not to damage bark of trees while trimming.

SCALPING

It's sometimes desirable to remove all grass from certain areas. This scalping is accomplished in much the same way as trimming, except much closer.

Adjust the cutting head so that cutting plane is about 30 degrees from horizontal and discharge is away from operator. Adjust handle, hook eye or cutting head as required so that trimmer will easily assume the desired angle naturally.

Confine cutting to the segment of the cutting plane so that discharge will be away from operator.

Begin scalping area around object, by first cutting perimeter. After establish-

ing outer limits, scalp inside by working in direction necessary to discharge grass toward perimeter.

When cutting next to trees or plants, frayed ends of trimmer string will be more gentle than if the line is recently extended and cut. Trees can be damaged or killed if bark is removed from circumference of tree.

CAUTION: Be careful when cutting around objects such as pipes or rods. Trimmer string may wrap around small objects which can't be moved and are too strong to be cut.

EDGING

The cutter head should be turned so that cutting plane is vertical, perpendicular to part being edged and so that discharge is toward front away from operator.

DANGER: Cut grass, dirt, stones, etc., will be discharged violently when edging, because of the position of the cutting head. Always wear protective glasses or goggles when operating edger. Be especially cautious of the discharge and make sure other people, animals, automobiles, etc., will not be affected by discharge.

Adjust position of handle, hook eye or cutting head angle so that edger is in a natural easy position for comfortable control.

WEED, BRUSH AND CLEARING BLADES

Some edgers and trimmers can be equipped with hard plastic or metal blades for cutting weeds, brush or small trees.

WARNING: Rigid blades should be used only on units supported by wheels or suspended from operator by a harness.

Monofilament string trimmers are designed for safe, easy operation while cutting light grass. Blades may be available to replace the string cutting head; however, make sure that replacement blade is for specific model and is recommended by the manufacturer.

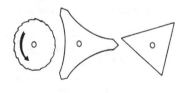

DANGER: Be careful of kick back. Harnesses are designed to minimize danger of injury, but be extremely careful to maintain control at all times when using rigid blades.

Cutting blades that are hard are more dangerous to use than a monofilament string, even though general operation is similar. Blades may be metal or hard plastic, but the rigid design is used to force the cutting edge through the object to be cut. If the object can't be moved or cut by the blade, something else will happen, often with undesirable results. Three results are: The blade breaks apart; The blade stops turning; The cutting head kicks back pushing blade away from object to be cut. Even when used properly, rigid blades impose heavy shock loads to the blade and drive. Stop engine and check condition of blade frequently. Never operate unit if condition of blade, any part of drive or control is cracked, broken or slipping.

DANGER: Always stop engine before inspecting condition or removing debris from around blade. NEVER depend upon clutch to keep blade from turning while engine is running.

Consult dealer for tools and instructions for sharpening blade. Install new blade if condition is questioned. The cost of a new blade is much less costly than injury.

Blades with 3 to 8 widely spaced large teeth or cutter bars are available for some models. This blade is designed for cutting larger grass/weeds and may be made of either ridged plastic or metal. Install blade with sharp cutting edge toward direction of rotation.

DANGER: Kick back is able to occur more easily with wide tooth spacing. Do not swing cutter into hard to cut areas. Check area to be cut carefully and remove or mark anything that would impair cutting or trip operator.

These blades are highly effective for cutting large unrestricted areas, but violent kick back is likely to occur if used near fences, walls or similar firm objects. Blades with more than three teeth are not recommended for use around objects which could cause kick back, but blade can sometimes be installed upside down to reduce kick back. Remove and install blade correctly, with sharp cutting edge toward direction of rotation as soon as practical.

Circular saw blades and clearing blades made especially for specific models can be used to cut brush, including small trees. This type of blade should be used only at ground level; never overhead.

Install blade with sharp cutting edge toward direction of rotation for normal cutting.

WARNING: Blade and drive parts will be damaged by hitting blade against trees, rocks or other solid objects.

Always cut by moving the cutting head, twisting your whole body opposite the rotation of the cutting head. Do not just swing the unit with your arms and hands. Do not cut during the return swing. Cuts should be a series of wedge shaped arcs as shown.

Work stops are provided on some models for cutting larger (but still small) trees. The heavier stop is usually at the rear and is preferred. Do not attempt to cut with work on opposite side of stop.

BASIC OPERATING CHECK LIST
Electric Powered Edger/Trimmers

Check for proper line length or blade for sharpness and condition before use. Stop, disconnect extension cord and check condition frequently during use.

Check cooling air filters for cleanliness and condition before using. Stop and clean cooling air filter frequently, especially when operating in dirty conditions.

Lubricate as recommended by manufacturer. Most use permanently lubricated bearings and require no lubrication; however some require periodic oiling.

Check for proper length extension cord to reach all areas without exceeding safe limit. Attach extension cord and check for operation.

Notice any irregularities during operation, especially vibration or speed. Check for blade or line damage and overheating.

Remove and clean cooling air filter at the end of each working day. Install new filter if damaged.

Clean all accumulated grass, dirt and other debris from motor and cutter.

Inspect cutting blade or line and service if required. Rigid blades can be sharpened. Consult dealer for sharpening tools and instruction.

Gasoline Powered Edger/Trimmers

Check for proper line length or blade for sharpness and condition before use. Stop engine and check condition frequently during use, especially if engine speed increases or unit begins to vibrate.

Check cooling air passages for cleanliness. Grass and dirt should have been cleaned after use, but regardless, don't start off with unit dirty. Also, birds or insects may have built nests in cooling passages since last use.

Check for sufficient amount of fuel to finish anticipated work that day. Be sure that fuel for models requiring gasoline and oil blend is mixed in proper ratio.

Clean around fuel filler cap before removing cap for filling.

Fill fuel tank with required type of gasoline and oil mix. Always leave some room for expansion in tank. Some manufacturers suggest ¾ full.

Start engine and check for proper engine operation. Accelerate and check operation of clutch (if so equipped) and cutter. If binding, overloading or vibration is evident, stop, and repair cause.

At the end of each working day, clean air passages, clean engine air filter and sharpen blade, if equipped with rigid blade.

Fill gear box with approved lubricant at end of each working day. Lithium grease is used for most models with gear box at lower end of drive shaft.

After each 20 hours of operation, remove, clean and lubricate drive shaft, then reinstall, reversing ends to equalize wear.

BLOWER OPERATION

TYPES

Blowers are classified as either backpack blowers or hand-held blowers. Backpack models have a blower power assembly in a unit that is carried on the back of the operator. A flexible blower or vacuum tube extends from the blower to be directed by the operator. Handheld units have a power unit that is carried in the operator's hand and a rigid blower or vacuum tube attached to the blower.

Two major advantages of the handheld blower are ease of use and compact design. But these benefits are offset by a requirement for light weight, which may mean less power, to lessen operator fatigue. Backpack blowers offer greater operator comfort, more power and greater versatility, but are generally heavier and more complex than handheld units.

Some blowers are capable of operating as a vacuum by attaching or reconfiguring tubing. Blowers also can function as sprayers or misters, either using gravity or a pump to supply the solution to the spray head.

OPERATING SAFELY

Blowers are designed to move objects using air as the moving force. Air can be propelled by a blower to approxi-

MAINTENANCE

mately 120 mph, sufficient speed to harm people and damage property. The operator should observe the following safety points as well as accepted safety procedures related to the operation of gasoline powered equipment:

• Do not operate blower in an enclosed or poorly ventilated area.
• Do not point blower towards people, animals or objects, such as cars and buildings that may be damaged.
• Do not blow debris to a location that may create a hazard or hide a potential hazard.
• Do not operate blower in a potential fire hazard area unless the unit is equipped with fire-prevention devices that function properly, *i.e.*, a spark arrestor.

The operator should wear proper clothing, safety eyewear, ear plugs and dust mask.

Before using a backpack blower, the operator should check the fit of the backpack and perform adjustments as needed to obtain a comfortable position. This should be done with the engine stopped. Be sure there is no loose clothing that can contact the muffler or be sucked into the impeller. (If operator has long hair, be sure it cannot reach impeller.)

STARTING ENGINE

DANGER: Start blower engine away from refueling area and away from bystanders.

To start blower, position unit squarely on ground with blower hose pointing in a safe direction. Open fuel valve and close choke. If so equipped, set fast-idle button or latch. If so equipped, operate primer button. Move ignition switch to "ON" position and operate rewind starter smoothly but rapidly. Do not fully extend starter rope or allow rope to

snap back into starter, otherwise starter may be damaged.

When engine is cold, it may be necessary to operate primer or leave the choke on until the engine is sufficiently warm to run with a normal mixture. Disengage the fast-idle device when the engine will idle at normal idle speed. Turn off choke when engine will idle smoothly at normal idle speed and accelerate cleanly without hesitation from idle to full throttle.

The engine will usually start easily if started shortly after the engine was stopped. If the engine was stopped while hot and sits for an extended period, the fuel may have percolated from the fuel passages. It may be necessary to operate the choke for a short period to get fuel to the engine, but do not overchoke or flooding will occur.

Each model requires certain techniques to start a cold or hot engine easily. These techniques usually are learned only by operation of the equipment.

ROUTINE MAINTENANCE

Three key elements for good maintenance are:

1. Keep the electric motor or gasoline engine cool.
2. Keep dirt and debris out of the rotating parts, especially engine parts.
3. Keep parts lubricated.

Attention to these items will result in equipment that will perform when needed for its designed service life.

COOLING SYSTEM

The electric motor or gasoline engine used to power the trimmers, brush cutters and blowers in this manual are cooled by air passing by the motor or engine. Excess heat ruins both electric motors and gasoline engines. This destructive heat is produced when a motor or engine is overloaded or its cooling system is clogged with debris. Motors and engines that are located low, near the ground, will get dirtier than those mounted higher.

The electric motors found on trimmers, brush cutters and blowers are equipped with a fan to circulate cool air around the motor. The motor may be equipped with a filter to prevent the entrance of dirt, grass and debris from passing around the motor. Usually the filter is an open cell pad that is easily accessible for cleaning or replacement. Clean the filter with mild soap and water only. Dry filter before reinstalling.

Check condition of filter and discard if it is damaged or cannot be cleaned.

WARNING: Never operate electric equipment without filters in place. If motor overheats and flammable debris is ingested, a fire may result.

Cooling air for gasoline powered equipment must flow freely through the engine fan and across the cooling fins. Grass, leaves and dust can build up and block the flow of cool air causing the engine to overheat. The shrouds and baffles that cover the fan and form the cooling system air passages should be removed at least once a year so all debris can be cleaned out. More frequent cleaning may be necessary depending on usage. Trimmers with low-mounted engines should be cleaned more often. Clean any unit that has noticeable buildup. Use a brush, compressed air and a nonmetallic scraper to remove grass, dirt, leaves and any crusty deposits from fan and fins.

CAUTION: Cover openings to carburetor, exhaust, fuel tank vent and other engine openings when cleaning the cooling passages to prevent entrance of dirt and debris.

Excessive heat can ruin gasoline engines by breaking down the oil film that separates moving engine parts. Heat also damages seals and distorts components beyond design limits. Minor overheating may cause lowered engine per-

formance; extreme overheating may result in seizure. Overheating is usually a result of inadequate cooling or overloading, and sometimes it is a combination of both. Proper maintenance and operating procedures will prevent most overheating occurrences.

CAUTION: Never attempt to cool an overheated engine or part by plunging it into water or by spraying on water. Rapid cooling may cause parts to break or become brittle. Uneven cooling may increase distortion and damage.

OVERLOADING

Overloading can be a problem for trimmers and brush cutters. Dirt or trash may wrap around the rotating parts and overload the drive system and engine. String trimmers with trimmer line too long for the cutting job will cause overloading. Dull cutting blades or attempting to cut beyond the equipment's capability will overload the engine and drive system.

Overloading the engine forces it to rotate at reduced speed. Engine output (and heat) is high, but reduced cooling air flow due to reduced cooling fan speed causes heat buildup and possible damage. An overloaded electric motor generally smells hot due to overheated wiring or smokes. Overloaded air-cooled engines may smell when overheated, but usually the only sign before seizure may be a drop in performance due to damaged parts. If the motor or engine is overheated, it should be inspected, as well as any nearby parts that may be damaged by heat, before equipment is operated again.

LUBRICATION

Lubrication of moving parts in motors and engines is necessary for their operation. Maintaining the presence of lubricating oil and grease at required points is important to obtain a long service life for all motors and engines. Most electric motors are equipped with no-maintenance bearings and bushings, which do not require lubrication. All gasoline engines use an oil system that provides lubricating oil to moving parts.

Two-stroke engines used on trimmers, brush cutters and blowers are lubricated by oil mixed with gasoline. The oil is specially formulated to mix with gasoline and lubricate internal engine parts when ingested with the fuel. Refer to service sections for the oil recommended by the manufacturer and the correct fuel:oil mixing ratio.

Do not allow dirt or debris to enter fuel or fuel tank when refueling engine. Dirt can also contaminate oil in a two-stroke engine when carried by air passing through the carburetor. A clean air filter prevents dirt from entering the engine. Service the air filter as needed and renew if it is damaged or cannot be cleaned.

STRING TRIMMER LINE

String trimmer cutting heads are constructed in a wide variety of designs, but all use a monofilament line for cutting.

The line is extended from many self-feeding heads by operating the unit while tapping the head against the ground. Centrifugal force draws the line out of the spool and a cutter blade on the protective shield cuts the line to the desired length. If the line is too short for centrifugal force to pull it out (usually less than 3 inches), the line must by pulled out manually. With engine stopped, or motor unplugged, depress center of hub while pulling out approximately 3-4 inches of line. Repeat as needed until sufficient line is extended. If line is not visible, spool may be empty or line may be broken or tangled inside hub. Disassembly is required to fix problem.

Cutting line is extended on some models by accelerating engine speed, slowing engine to idle, then accelerating engine to high speed. Proper line extension depends on size and weight of line, engine speed and tension of springs in cutting head. If line will not feed, stop engine and check the cutting head. If line is too short, centrifugal force will be insufficient to extend line and line must be extended manually. Remove cover, turn spool to extend line approximately 4 inches from eyelet and reassemble. If line is not visible, spool may be empty or line may be broken or tangled inside hub. Disassembly is required to fix problem.

CAUTION: The cutting head must be equipped with the correct string for proper operation. Refer to service section for recommended string dimensions.

Spools on most models can be refilled. Be sure to use the correct type and size of line as recommended by trimmer manufacturer. Some common line diameters are 0.051 inch (1.3 mm), 0.065 inch (1.6 mm), 0.080 inch (2.0 mm), 0.095 inch (2.4 mm) and 0.130 inch (3.3 mm). Cutting heads may contain a single cutting line or several lines. When renewing the spool, be sure the correct spool is reinstalled. When installing cutting line on spool, note arrow on spool that indicates direction to wind line around spool.

DRIVE SHAFT

Trimmers and brush cutters are equipped with a drive shaft that transmits power from the engine to the cutting head. Two types of drive shaft are used: flexible or solid. Flexible shafts are used on models with a curved housing while a solid shaft is used on models with a straight housing. Solid shafts do not generally require maintenance, but most flexible shafts must be lubricated periodically. Refer to trimmer service section for manufacturer's recommended service interval. If not indicated, service shaft after every 20 hours of operation.

To service a flexible drive shaft, remove and clean shaft. The shaft can be pulled from housing on most models after separating housing from cutter head or engine. Removal of the cutter head assembly from the drive shaft housing is generally easier. After cleaning shaft, apply lithium grease to shaft. Reverse ends of shaft during installation to relocate wear points and extend shaft life.

CAUTION: Be sure drive shaft and housing properly engage cutting head or engine during assembly. Misalignment can cause damage.

OTHER ADJUSTMENTS, SERVICES AND REPAIRS

ON-OFF IGNITION SWITCH

Electric Powered Units

Electric powered trimmers and blowers are equipped with a spring-loaded, trigger-type on-off switch. The trigger is usually located on the handle (Fig. 10) and spring-loaded as a safety feature so the motor stops when the trigger is released.

To renew the trigger switch, first disconnect the electrical lead to the unit. On most models, the switch is accessible by removing handle screws (Fig. 11).

Note position of pieces and switch during disassembly (Fig. 12). Disconnect switch leads and remove switch.

Gasoline Powered Units

Gasoline powered units may be equipped with a simple spring-loaded ignition grounding switch (Fig. 13), an "on-off" toggle switch (Fig. 14) or a slider type switch (Fig. 15). The switch may be located on the engine cover/handle assembly, on a bracket attached to the engine or on the drive shaft housing tube.

Before renewing switch, check switch, wires and connections with an electrical tester. Be sure any ground wires are properly attached. Before disconnecting switch, check parts supplier to determine if switch is available individually or as part of a wired assembly.

On most models, it is necessary to remove cover or housing for access to switch. Note position of any wires during disassembly. When reinstalling cover or housing, be sure wires are not pinched, contacting exhaust system or will rub against moving components.

ENGINE CHOKE/PRIMER

Gasoline Powered Units

Gasoline powered units may be equipped with a choke or primer mechanism to enrich fuel starting mixture.

The choke may be a simple plunger that, when turned, closes off the carburetor opening (Fig. 16), or a more complex system using a choke plate activated by pulling a choke lever. The choke plate is usually connected to the choke lever by a wire control rod. Refer to the carburetor paragraphs in the appropriate engine service section of this manual for choke information.

Primer systems consist of a primer bulb (Fig. 18) located on the carburetor or, on engines with a full engine cover, it may be located at an external location and connected to the carburetor by a fuel tube. The primer bulb is compressed to provide a rich initial fuel charge for engine starting. Refer to the carburetor paragraphs in the appropriate engine service section of this manual for primer information.

ENGINE THROTTLE

Gasoline Powered Units

All gasoline powered units are equipped with a spring-loaded throttle trigger assembly. The throttle trigger is spring-loaded so the throttle will return to idle when released. The throttle trigger is usually connected to the carburetor throttle lever by either a solid control rod or by a wire cable. The trigger may be located on the engine cover, on a handle, on the drive shaft housing, or on blower tube.

The throttle cable on models so equipped should be lubricated after every 20 hours of operation. Apply SAE 30 oil to each end of inner wire. Throttle cable service and adjustment information is outlined in service sections in this manual.

ENGINE REMOVAL

Gasoline Powered Trimmers

The engine can be separated from the drive shaft housing tube of most models after loosening clamp bolt or bolts (Fig. 19). The drive shaft will separate from the drive shaft adapter or clutch adapter when the engine is removed. When reconnecting engine and drive shaft, be certain drive shaft engages adapter fully.

CAUTION: Be sure drive shaft and housing properly engage engine and drive shaft adapter during assembly. Misalignment can cause damage.

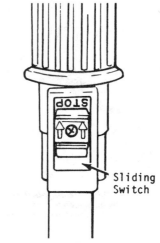

Fig. 14—A toggle switch is used for the ignition switch on many models.

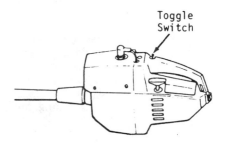

Fig. 10—View showing typical location for the spring loaded trigger type on-off switch used on electric trimmer models.

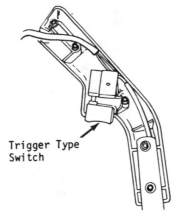

Fig. 12—Trigger assembly is trapped inside handle on many models.

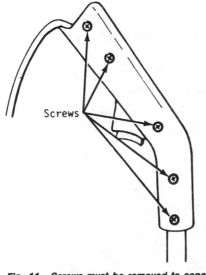

Fig. 11—Screws must be removed to separate handle for access to spring loaded trigger type switch used on many models.

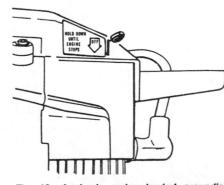

Fig. 13—A simple spring loaded grounding switch is used to stop engine on many models. Push spring down and hold switch lever until engine stops completely.

Fig. 15—Some models are equipped with a sliding type ignition switch.

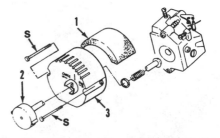

Fig. 16—Choke assembly on some models is a simple plunger(2) which rotates on a ramp and plugs carburetor opening.

Some models are equipped with a threaded collar that screws onto the engine adapter housing as shown in Fig. 20. Unscrew collar and separate engine from drive shaft housing tube. Drive shaft will separate from drive shaft adapter or clutch adapter when engine is removed. When reconnecting engine and drive shaft, be certain drive shaft engages adapter fully (see previous CAUTION).

On some models with a solid drive shaft, the clutch drum is threaded on the drive shaft. On these models, separate engine at adapter/clutch housing by removing screws securing housing to engine (Fig. 21).

Gasoline Powered Blowers

Removing the engine from a gasoline powered blower generally requires disassembly of surrounding shrouds and panels, which is apparent after inspecting the unit. In many cases, the engine can be separated from the blower assembly after detaching the blower impeller from the engine. Some means is necessary to secure the piston while unscrewing the impeller retaining nut.

This may be accomplished using a special piston stop tool installed in spark plug hole. Some manufacturers recommend inserting a nylon or non-fraying rope through the spark plug hole, then rotating the piston against the rope.

DRIVE SHAFT ADAPTER/CLUTCH

Gasoline Powered Trimmers

Direct drive trimmer models (models without a clutch) are equipped with a drive shaft adapter that is threaded onto the crankshaft as shown in Fig. 22. The adapter may be an integral part of the flywheel nut. These models are equipped with a flexible drive shaft and the adapter is machined to engage the squared drive shaft end. When installing drive shaft, make certain squared end of drive shaft engages adapter fully to prevent drive shaft damage.

Models equipped with a clutch use an adapter that is attached to the clutch drum (Fig. 23). Models with a flexible drive shaft have an adapter that is machined to engage the squared end of the drive shaft. Models using a solid drive shaft may have an adapter

machined to engage a splined drive shaft end, or the adapter may be threaded for use with a threaded drive shaft end (see Fig. 24).

When installing drive shaft on models equipped with a squared or splined end, be sure drive shaft end properly engages clutch adapter fully to prevent damage to drive shaft. On models with threads on the drive shaft end, apply locking compound to threads prior to connecting to clutch adapter.

BEARING HEAD/GEAR HEAD REMOVAL

All Trimmers

On most models equipped with a bearing head or gear head, the head may be removed by removing the clamp bolt or bolts and locating screw (Fig. 25). The drive shaft will separate from the drive shaft adapter when the shaft and adapter are disconnected. On models with the clutch mounted at the lower end of the

Fig. 20—Clutch housing or engine cover on some models are equipped with threads which engage a threaded collar on drive shaft housing tube to secure engine to drive shaft housing tube.

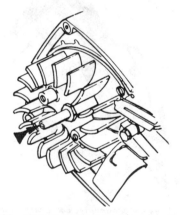

Fig. 22—Most direct drive models are equipped with a drive shaft adapter which also serves as the flywheel retaining nut.

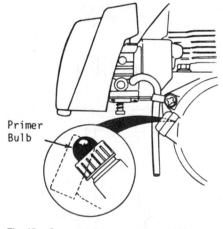

Fig. 18—Some models are equipped with a primer bulb which, when squeezed, injects a measured amount of fuel into carburetor.

Fig. 21—On some models equipped with solid drive shaft which is threaded onto clutch drum, engine must be separated from clutch housing by removing clutch housing bolts.

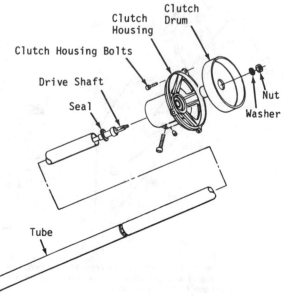

Fig. 19—A clamp (32) and bolt assembly secures engine to drive shaft housing tube on many models.

shaft, refer to appropriate service section for service information. On all models, refer to appropriate service section for service information on the bearing head or gear head.

DRIVE SHAFT HOUSING LINERS/BUSHINGS

All Trimmers

Models equipped with a flexible drive shaft in a curved drive shaft housing may be equipped with a drive shaft housing liner (2—Fig. 26). The liner may be renewed by separating the drive shaft housing tube from the bearing head and engine assemblies. Pull drive shaft (3) out of housing and liner. Mark location of liner (2) in housing (1) and pull liner out of housing. Install a new liner at the old liner location. Lubricate the drive shaft with lithium-base grease and install the shaft.

Models equipped with a solid drive shaft may have drive shaft support bushing (3—Fig. 25) located at intervals inside drive shaft housing (4). To renew bushings, separate the drive shaft housing tube from the trimmer head and engine assemblies. Mark locations of old bushings before removal. Install new bushings at locations of old bushings. A bushing installation tool is offered by some manufacturers and is indicated in trimmer service sections of this manual. Lubricate the drive shaft with lithium-base grease and install the shaft.

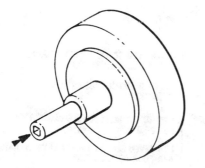

Fig. 23—Clutch drum on models equipped with a centrifugal clutch is equipped with a drive shaft adapter.

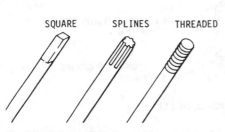

SQUARE   SPLINES   THREADED

Fig. 24—Drive shaft ends may be square, equipped with splines or threaded.

GENERAL CARBURETOR SERVICE

TROUBLE-SHOOTING. Normally encountered difficulties resulting from carburetor malfunction, along with possible causes of difficulty, are as follows:

A. CARBURETOR FLOODS. Could be caused by:

• Dirt or foreign particles preventing inlet fuel needle from seating.

• Diaphragm lever spring not seated correctly on diaphragm lever.

• Improperly installed metering diaphragm. Also, when fuel tank is located above carburetor, flooding can be caused by leaking fuel pump diaphragm.

B. ENGINE RUNS LEAN. Could be caused by:

• Fuel tank vent plugged.

• Leak in fuel line or fittings between fuel tank and carburetor.

• Filter screen in carburetor or filter element in fuel pickup head plugged.

• Fuel orifice plugged.

• Hole in fuel metering diaphragm.

• Metering lever not properly set.

• Dirt in carburetor fuel channels or pulse channel to engine crankcase plugged.

• Leaky gaskets between carburetor and crankcase intake port. Also, check for leaking crankshaft seals, porous or cracked crankcase or other cause for air leak into crankcase. When fuel tank or fuel lever is below carburetor, lean operation can be caused by hole in fuel pump diaphragm or damaged valve flaps on pump diaphragm. On Walbro series SDC carburetor with diaphragm-type accelerating pump, a leak in accelerating pump diaphragm will cause lean operation.

C. ENGINE WILL NOT ACCELERATE SMOOTHLY. Could be caused by:

Fig. 25—Exploded view of a typical solid drive shaft and housing.

1. Adapter	7. Snap ring
2. Adapter	8. Bearing
3. Bushing	9. Bearing
4. Drive shaft housing	10. Input shaft & gear
5. Drive shaft	11. Gear head housing
6. Snap ring	12. Clamp shim

• Inoperative accelerating pump, on carburetors so equipped, due to plugged fuel channel, leaking diaphragm, stuck piston, etc.

• Idle or main fuel mixture too lean on models without accelerating pump.

• Incorrect setting of metering diaphragm lever.

• Diaphragm gasket leaking.

• Main fuel orifice plugged.

D. ENGINE WILL NOT IDLE. Could be caused by:

• Incorrect adjustment of idle fuel and/or idle speed stop screw.

• Idle discharge or air mixture ports clogged.

• Fuel channel clogged.

• Dirty or damaged main orifice check valve.

• Welch (expansion) plug covering idle ports not sealing properly allowing engine to run with idle fuel needle closed.

• Throttle shutter not properly aligned on throttle shaft causing fast idle.

E. ENGINE RUNS RICH. Could be caused by:

• Plug covering main nozzle orifice not sealing.

• When fuel level is above carburetor, leak in fuel pump diaphragm; worn or damaged adjustment needle and seat.

Refer to Fig. 28 for service hints on diaphragm-type carburetors and to following section for pressure testing procedure.

PRESSURE TESTING

DIAPHRAGM-TYPE CARBURETORS. With engine stopped and cool, first adjust carburetor low-speed and high-speed mixture screws to recommended initial settings. Remove fuel tank cap and withdraw fuel line out tank opening. If so equipped, detach

Fig. 26—Flexible drive shaft (3) on some models is supported in drive shaft housing tube (1) in a renewable liner (2).

strainer from end of fuel line and connect a suitable pressure tester to inlet end of fuel line as shown in Fig. 29. Pressurize system until 7 psi (48 kPa) is indicated on gage. Pressure reading must remain constant. If not, remove components as needed and connect pressure tester directly to carburetor inlet fitting as shown in Fig. 30. Pressurize system until 7 psi (48 kPa) is indicated on pressure gage. If pressure reading now remains constant, the fuel line is defective. If pressure reading decreases, the carburetor must be removed for further testing.

Connect pressure tester directly to carburetor inlet fitting and submerge carburetor assembly into a suitable container filled with a nonflammable solution or water as shown in Fig. 31. Pressurize system until 7 psi (48 kPa) is indicated on gage. Observe carburetor and note location of leaking air bubbles. If air bubbles escape from around jet needles or venturi, then inlet needle or metering mechanism is defective. If air bubbles escape at impulse opening, then pump diaphragm is defective. If air bubbles escape from around fuel pump cover, then cover gasket or pump diaphragm is defective.

To check inlet needle and metering mechanism, first rotate low- and high-speed mixture screws inward until

seated. Pressurize system until 7 psi (48 kPa) is indicated on pressure gage. Use a suitable length and thickness of wire, and reach through vent hole in metering diaphragm cover. Slowly depress metering diaphragm. A slight drop in pressure reading should be noted as metering chamber becomes pressurized. If no drop in pressure reading is noted, then inlet needle is sticking. If pressure does not hold after a slight drop, then a defective metering mechanism or leaking high- or low-speed Welch plugs is indicated. To determine which component is leaking, submerge carburetor as previously outlined. Pressurize system until 7 psi (48 kPa) is indicated on pressure gage, then depress metering diaphragm as previously outlined. If bubbles escape around metering diaphragm cover, then metering diaphragm or gasket is defective. If bubbles escape from hole in metering diaphragm cover, then metering diaphragm is defective. If bubbles escape from within venturi, then determine which discharge port the air bubbles are escaping from to determine which Welch plug is leaking.

If low- or high-speed running problems are noted, the passage beneath the respective Welch plug may be restricted. To test idle circuit, adjust low-speed mixture screw to recommended initial setting and rotate high-speed mixture

Fig. 29—View showing connection of pressure tester to fuel tank fuel line. Refer to text.

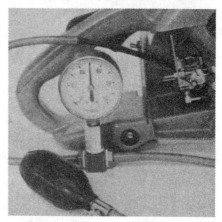

Fig. 30—View showing connection of pressure tester directly to carburetor inlet fitting. Refer to text.

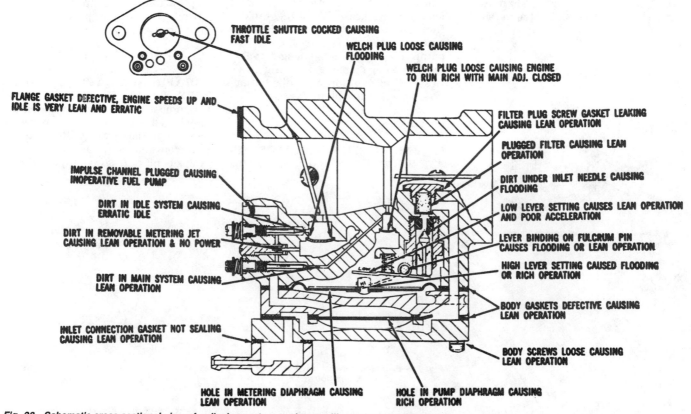

Fig. 28—Schematic cross-sectional view of a diaphragm-type carburetor illustrating possible causes of malfunction. Refer to appropriate engine repair section for adjustment information and for exploded and/or cross-sectional view of specific carburetor used.

screw inward until seated. Pressurize system until 7 psi (48 kPa) is indicated on pressure gage. Depress metering diaphragm as previously outlined. If pressure reading does not drop off or drops off very slowly, then a restriction is indicated. To test high-speed circuit, adjust high-speed mixture screw to recommended initial setting and rotate low-speed mixture screw inward until seated. Pressurize system and depress metering diaphragm as previously outlined and note reading on pressure gage. If pressure reading does not drop off or drops off very slowly, then a restriction is indicated.

Refer to specific carburetor service section in ENGINE SERVICE section and repair defect or renew defective component.

PRESSURE TEST CRANKCASE. Defective gaskets and oil seals or a crack in castings are the usual causes of crankcase leaks. A leak will allow supplementary air to enter the engine and thus upset the desired fuel:air mixture. An improperly sealed crankcase can cause:

A. Hard starting
B. Erratic running
C. Low power
D. Overheating

To test crankcase for leakage, remove muffler. Fabricate a seal using gasket paper or thin metal plate that will cover the exhaust port. Install the seal and muffler. Remove carburetor and fabricate an adapter plate with a fitting to which a rubber hose can be attached that will cover the intake port. Install adapter plate in place of carburetor. Connect a hand pump and pressure gage to adapter plate as shown in Fig. 32. Set piston at top dead center. Actuate hand pump to pump air into crankcase until gage indicates pressure of 7 psi (48 kPa). The pressure should remain constant for at least 10 seconds. If constant pressure cannot be maintained, use a soap and water solution to check crankcase seals, gaskets and castings for evidence of leakage.

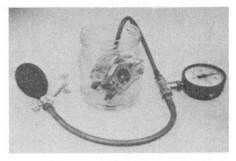

Fig. 31—Submerge carburetor into a suitable container filled with a nonflammable solution or water and pressure test as outlined in text.

Fig. 32—Engine crankcase can be pressure tested for leaks by blocking off exhaust port and applying air pressure to intake port as shown. Refer to text.

SERVICE SHOP TOOL BUYER'S GUIDE

This listing of service shop tools is solely for the convenience of users of the manual and does not imply endorsement or approval by Intertec Publishing Corporation of the tools and equipment listed. The listing is in response to many requests for information on sources for purchasing special tools and equipment. Every attempt has been made to make the listing as complete as possible at time of publication and each entry is made from the latest material available.

Special engine service tools such as drivers, pullers, gages, etc., which are available from the engine manufacturer are not listed in this section of the manual. Where a special service tool is listed in the engine service section of this manual, the tool is available from the central parts or service distributors listed at the end of most engine service sections, or from the manufacturer.

NOTE TO MANUFACTURERS AND NATIONAL SALES DISTRIBUTORS OF ENGINE SERVICE TOOLS AND RELATED SERVICE EQUIPMENT. To obtain either a new listing for your products, or to change or add to an existing listing, write to Intertec Publishing Corporation, Book Division, P.O. Box 12901, Overland Park, KS 66282-2901.

Engine Service Tools

Ammco Tools, Inc.
Wacker Park
North Chicago, Illinois 60064
Valve spring compressor, torque

wrenches, cylinder hones, ridge reamers, piston ring compressors, piston ring expanders.

Bloom, Inc.
Highway 939 West
Independence, Iowa 50644
Engine repair stand with crankshaft straightening attachment.

Brush Research Mfg. Co., Inc.
4642 East Floral Drive
Los Angeles, California 90022
Cylinder hones.

E-Z Lok
P.O. Box 2069
Gardena, California 90247
Thread repair insert kits.

Fairchild Fastener Group
3000 W. Lomita Blvd.
Torrance, California 90505
Thread repair insert kits
(Keenserts) and installation tools.

Foley-Belsaw Company
Outdoor Power Equipment Parts
Div.
6301 Equitable Road
P.O. Box 419593
Kansas City, Missouri 64141
Crankshaft straightener and repair
stand, valve refacer, valve seat
grinder, parts washer, cylinder
hone, ridge reamer, piston ring
expander and compressor, flywheel
puller, torque wrench.

Frederick Manufacturing Corp.
4840 E. 12th Street
Kansas City, Missouri 64127
Piston groove cleaner,
compression tester, piston ring
expander and compressor, valve
spring compressor, valve seat
grinder, valve refacer, cylinder
hone, flywheel puller, flywheel
wrench, flywheel holder, starter
spring rewinder, condenser pliers.

Heli-Coil
Shelter Rock Lane
Danbury, Connecticut 06810
Thread repair kits, thread inserts,
installation tools.

K-D Tools
3575 Hempland Road
Lancaster, Pennsylvania 17604
Thread repair kits, valve spring
compressors, reamers,
micrometers, dial indicators,
calipers.

Keystone Reamer & Tool Co.
South Front Street
P.O. Box 308
Millersburg, Pennsylvania 17061
Valve seat cutter and pilots,
reamers, screw extractors, taps
and dies.

Ki-Sol Corporation
100 Larkin Williams Ind. Ct.
Fenton, Missouri 63026
Cylinder hone, ridge reamer, ring
compressor, ring expander, ring
groove cleaner, torque wrenches,
valve spring compressor, valve
refacing equipment.

K-Line Industries, Inc.
315 Garden Avenue
Holland, Michigan 49424
Cylinder hone, ridge reamer, ring
compressor, valve guide tools,
valve spring compressor, reamers.

K.O. Lee Company
200 South Harrison
P.O. Box 1416
Aberdeen, South Dakota 57402
Valve refacers, valve seat grinders,
valve seat insert tools, valve guide
tools.

Kwik-Way Mfg. Co.
500 57th Street
Marion, Iowa 52302
Cylinder boring equipment, valve
facing equipment, valve seat
grinding equipment.

Lisle Corporation
807 East Main
Clarinda, Iowa 51632
Cylinder hones, ridge reamers,
ring compressors, valve spring
compressors.

Microdot, Inc.
P.O. Box 3001
Fullerton, California 92634
Thread repair insert kits.

Mighty Midget Mfg. Co.,
Div. of Kansas City Screw
Thread Co.
2908 E. Truman Road
Kansas City, Missouri 64127
Crankshaft straightener.

Neway Manufacturing, Inc.
1013 N. Shiawassee
Corunna, Michigan 48817
Valve seat cutters.

OTC
655 Eisenhower Drive
Owatonna, Minnesota 55060
Valve tools, spark plug tools, piston
ring tools, cylinder hones.

Power Lawnmower Parts, Inc.
1920 Lyell Avenue
P.O. Box 60860
Rochester, New York 14606-0860
Flywheel pullers, starter wrench,
flywheel holder, gasket cutter tool,
gasket scraper tool, crankshaft
cleaning tool, ridge reamer, valve
spring compressor, valve seat
cutters, thread repair kits, valve
lifter, piston ring expander.

Precision Manufacturing & Sales
Co., Inc.
2140 Range Road
Clearwater, Florida 34625
Cylinder boring equipment,
measuring instruments, valve
equipment, hones, hand tools, test
equipment, threading tools,
presses, parts washers, milling machines, lathes, drill presses, glass
beading machines, dynos, safety
equipment.

Sioux Tools, Inc.
2901 Floyd Blvd.
P.O. Box 507
Sioux City, Iowa 51102
Valve refacing and seat grinding
equipment.

Sunnen Product Company
7910 Manchester Avenue
St. Louis, Missouri 63143
Cylinder hones, rod reconditioning,
valve guide reconditioning.

Test Equipment and Gages

AW Dynamometer, Inc.
P.O. Box 428
Colfax, Illinois 61728
Engine test dynamometer.

B.C. Ames Company
131 Lexington
Waltham, Massachusetts 02254
Micrometers, dial gages, calipers.

Dixson, Inc.
287 27 Road
Grand Junction, Colorado 81503
Tachometer, compression gage,
timing light.

Foley-Belsaw Company
Outdoor Power Equipment Parts
Div.
6301 Equitable Road
P.O. Box 419593
Kansas City, Missouri 64141
Cylinder gage, amp/volt testers,
condenser and coil tester, magneto
tester, ignition testers, tachometers,
spark testers, compression gages,
timing lights and gages,
micrometers and calipers,
carburetor testers, vacuum gages.

Frederick Manufacturing Corp.
4840 E. 12th Street
Kansas City, Missouri 64127
Ignition tester, tachometer,
compression gage

Graham-Lee Electronics, Inc.
4220 Central Avenue N.E.
Minneapolis, Minnesota 55421
Coil and condenser tester.

K-D Tools
3575 Hempland Road
Lancaster, Pennsylvania 17604
Diode tester and installation tools,
compression gage, timing light,
timing gages.

Ki-Sol Corporation
100 Larkin Williams Ind. Ct.
Fenton, Missouri 63026
Micrometers, telescoping gages,
compression gages, cylinder
gages.

K-Line Industries, Inc.
315 Garden Avenue
Holland, Michigan 49424
Compression gage, leakdown
tester, micrometers, dial gages.

**Merc-O-Tronic Instruments
Corporation**
215 Branch Street
Almont, Michigan 48003
Ignition analyzers for conventional,
solid-state and magneto systems,
electric tachometers, electronic
tachometer and dwell meter, power
timing lights, ohmmeters,
compression gages, mechanical
timing devices.

OTC
655 Eisenhower Drive
Owatonna, Minnesota 55060
Feeler gages, hydraulic test gages.

Power Lawnmower Parts, Inc.
1920 Lyell Avenue
P.O. Box 60860
Rochester, New York 14606-0860
Compression gage, cylinder gage,
magneto tester, compression gage,
condenser and coil tester.

**Prestolite Electronic Div.
An Allied Company**
4 Seagate
Toledo, Ohio 43691
Magneto test plug.

Simpson Electric Company
853 Dundee Avenue
Elgin, Illinois 60120
Electrical and electronic test
equipment.

L.S. Starrett Company
121 Crescent St.
Athol, Massachusetts 01331
Micrometers, dial gages, bore
gages, feeler gages.

Stevens Instrument Company
P.O. Box 193
Waukegan, Illinois 60079
Ignition analyzers, timing lights,
volt-ohm meter, tachometer, spark
checkers, CD ignition testers.

Stewart-Warner Corporation
580 Slawin Ct.
Mt. Prospect, Illinois 60056
Compression gage, ignition
tachometer, timing light, ignition
analyzer.

Shop Tools and Equipment

**AC Delco Division
General Motors Corp.**
3031 W. Grand Blvd.

P.O. Box 33115
Detroit, Michigan 48232
Spark plug tools.

Black & Decker Mfg. Co.
626 Hanover Pike
Hampstead, Maryland 21074
Electric power tools.

**Champion Pneumatic Machinery
Co.**
1301 N. Euclid Avenue
Princeton, Illinois 61356
Air compressors.

Champion Spark Plug Company
P.O. Box 910
Toledo, Ohio 43661
Spark plug cleaning and testing
equipment, gap tools and
wrenches.

Chicago Pneumatic Tool Co.
2200 Bleecker St.
Utica, New York 13501
Air impact wrenches, air hammers,
air drills and grinders, nut runners,
speed ratchets.

Cooper Tools
P.O. Box 728
Apex, North Carolina 27502
Chain type engine hoists and
utility slings

E-Z Lok
P.O. Box 2069
Gardena, California 90247
Thread repair insert kits.

Fairchild Fastener Group
3000 W. Lomita Blvd.
Torrance, California 90505
Thread repair insert kits
(Keenserts) and installation tools.

**Foley-Belsaw Company
Outdoor Power Equipment Parts
Div.**
6301 Equitable Road
P.O. Box 419593
Kansas City, Missouri 64141
Torque wrenches, parts washers,
micrometers and calipers.

Frederick Manufacturing Corp.
4840 E. 12th Street
Kansas City, Missouri 64127
Torque wrenches, gear pullers.

G&H Products, Inc.
P.O. Box 770
St. Paris, Ohio 43027
Equipment lifts.

General Scientific Equipment Co.
525 Spring Garden St.
Philadelphia, Pennsylvania 19122
Safety equipment.

Graymills Corporation
3705 N. Lincoln Avenue
Chicago, Illinois 60613
Parts washing equipment.

Heli-Coil
Shelter Rock Lane
Danbury, Connecticut 06810
Thread repair kits, thread inserts,
installation tools.

Ingersoll-Rand
253 E. Washington Avenue
Washington, New Jersey 07882
Air and electric impact wrenches,
electric drills and screwdrivers.

Jaw Manufacturing Co.
39 Mulberry St.
P.O. Box 213
Reading, Pennsylvania 19603
Files for repair or renewal of damaged threads, rethreader dies,
flexible shaft drivers and
extensions, screw extractors,
impact drivers.

**Jenny Division of Homestead
Ind., Inc.**
700 Second Avenue
Coraopolis, Pennsylvania 15108
Steam cleaning equipment,
pressure washing equipment.

K-Line Industries, Inc.
315 Garden Avenue
Holland, Michigan 49424
Pullers, crack detectors, gloves,
aprons, eyewear,

Keystone Reamer & Tool Co.
South Front Street
P.O. Box 308
Millersburg, Pennsylvania 17061
Adjustable reamers, twist drills,
taps, dies.

Microdot, Inc.
P.O. Box 3001
Fullerton, California 92634
Thread repair insert kits.

OTC
655 Eisenhower Drive
Owatonna, Minnesota 55060
Bearing and gear pullers, hydraulic
shop presses.

Power Lawnmower Parts, Inc.
1920 Lyell Avenue
P.O. Box 60860
Rochester, New York 14606-0860
Flywheel pullers, starter wrench,

Shure Manufacturing Corp.
1601 S. Hanley Road
St. Louis, Missour 63144
Steel shop benches, desks, engine
overhaul stand.

Sioux Tools, Inc.
2901 Floyd Blvd.
P.O. Box 507
Sioux City, Iowa 51102
Air and electric impact tools, drills, grinders.

Sturtevant Richmont
3203 N. Wolf Rd.
Franklin Park, Illinois 60131
Torque wrenches, torque multipliers, torque analyzers.

Mechanic's Hand Tools

Channellock, Inc.
1306 South Main St.
P.O. Box 519
Meadville, Pennsylvania 16335

John H. Graham & Company
P.O. Box 739
Oradell, New Jersey 07649

Jaw Manufacturing Co.
39 Mulberry St.
P.O. Box 213
Reading, Pennsylvania 19603

K-D Tools
3575 Hempland Road
Lancaster, Pennsylvania 17604

K-Line Industries, Inc.
315 Garden Avenue
Holland, Michigan 49424

OTC
655 Eisenhower Drive
Owatonna, Minnesota 55060

Snap-On Tools
2801 80th Street
Kenosha, Wisconsin 53140

Triangle Corporation-Tool Division
P.O. Box 1807
Orangeburg, South Carolina 29115

Shop Supplies (Chemicals, Metallurgy Products, Seals, Sealers, Common Parts Items, etc.)

Clayton Manufacturing Co.
4213 N. Temple City Blvd.
El Monte, California 91731
Steam cleaning compounds and solvents.

E-Z Lok
P.O. Box 2069
Gardena, California 90247
Thread repair insert kits.

Eutectic+Castolin
40-40 172nd Street
Flushing, New York 11358
Specialized repair and maintenance welding alloys.

Fairchild Fastener Group
3000 W. Lomita Blvd.
Torrance, California 90505
Thread repair insert kits (Keenserts) and installation tools.

**Foley-Belsaw Company
Outdoor Power Equipment Parts Div.**
6301 Equitable Road
P.O. Box 419593
Kansas City, Missouri 64141
Parts washers, cylinder head rethreaders, micrometers, calipers, gasket material, nylon rope, oil and grease products, bolt, nut, washer and spring assortments.

Frederick Manufacturing Corp.
4840 E. 12th Street
Kansas City, Missouri 64127
Thread repair kits.

Graymills Corporation
3705 N. Lincoln Avenue
Chicago, Illinois 60613
Parts cleaning fluids.

Heli-Coil
Shelter Rock Lane
Danbury, Connecticut 06810
Thread repair kits, thread inserts, installation tools.

K-Line Industries, Inc.
315 Garden Avenue
Holland, Michigan 49424
Machining lubricants, solvents, cleaning solutions.

Loctite Corporation
705 North Mountain Road
Newington, Connecticut 06111
Compounds for locking threads, retaining bearings and securing machine parts; sealants and adhesives.

Microdot, Inc.
P.O. Box 3001
Fullerton, California 92634
Thread repair insert kits.

Permatex Industrial
30 Tower Lane
Avon Park South
Avon, Connecticut 06001
Cleaning chemicals, gasket sealers, pipe sealants, adhesives, lubricants, thread locking and forming compounds.

Power Lawnmower Parts, Inc.
1920 Lyell Avenue
P.O. Box 60860
Rochester, New York 14606-0860
Grinding compound paste, gas tank sealer stick, shop aprons, eyewear.

Radiator Specialty Co.
1900 Wilkinson Blvd.
Charlotte, North Carolina 28208
Cleaning chemicals (Gunk) and solder seal.

ALPINA

GASOLINE POWERED STRING TRIMMER

Model	Engine Manufacturer	Engine Model	Displacement
160	Tanaka	....	22.6 cc
180	Tanaka	....	30.5 cc
200	Tanaka	....	37.4 cc

ENGINE INFORMATION

All Models

Tanaka (TAS) two-stroke air-cooled gasoline engines are used on all listed Alpina line trimmers and brush cutters. Identify engine by engine displacement and refer to the TANAKA (TAS) ENGINE SERVICE section of this manual.

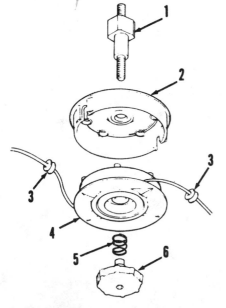

Fig. AL10—Exploded view of dual strand manual feed trimmer head available for most models.
1. Drive shaft adapter
2. Housing
3. Line guides
4. Spool
5. Spring
6. Lock knob

STRING TRIMMER

All Models

A dual strand manual feed trimmer head is available for most models (Fig. AL10). To extend line, loosen lock knob (6) until line may be pulled from housing. Pull line to desired length and tighten lock knob (6).

To renew line, remove lock knob (6), spring (5) and spool (4). Remove any remaining old line and install new line on spool. Wind line in direction indicated by arrow on spool and insert line ends through line guides (3). Install spool, spring and lock knob.

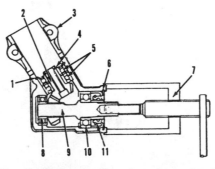

Fig. AL12—Cross-section view of gear head used on most models.
1. Snap ring
2. Input shaft & gear
3. Housing
4. Snap ring
5. Bearings
6. Snap ring
7. Puller
8. Bearing
9. Arbor shaft & gear
10. Bearing
11. Seal

BLADE

All Models

All models may be equipped with a four cutting edge grass, weed and brush blade, an eight cutting edge blade or a saw blade. Always make certain cup washer above blade and adapter plate below blade are centered and fit flat against surface of blade when installing blade.

All Models

All models are equipped with a solid drive shaft supported in a straight drive shaft housing tube. Drive shaft is supported in bushings located in drive shaft housing tube. Drive shaft requires no regular maintenance however, if drive shaft is removed, lubricate shaft with lithium base grease before reinstallation.

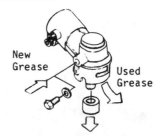

Fig. AL13—A good quality lithium base grease should be pumped into gear head housing through filler opening until grease appears at arbor shaft seal. Refer to text.

GEAR HEAD

All Models

All models are equipped with a gear head similar to the one shown in Fig. AL12. Gear head should be lubricated

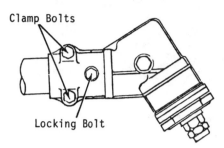

Clamp Bolts

Locking Bolt

Fig. AL14—To separate gear head from drive shaft housing, remove clamp bolts and locking (head locating) bolt.

at 50 hour intervals of use. To lubricate, remove trimmer head or blade assembly. Remove grease plug from side of gear head housing. Pump lithium base grease into housing through plug opening until grease appears at bearing seal (Fig. AL13).

To disassemble gear head, remove clamp bolts and head locking bolt (Fig. AL14). Separate head from drive shaft and housing. Remove snap ring (6-Fig. AL12). Install suitable puller as illustrated in Fig. AL12 and remove oil seal, bearing and arbor shaft assembly. Remove gear (9) from housing. Remove snap ring (1). Insert suitable puller bolt through input shaft and thread a nut on bolt against input gear (Fig. AL15). Remove input shaft and bearing assembly. Remove snap ring (4-Fig. AL12) and press bearings from input shaft. To remove bearing (8), heat gear head

housing to 212° F (100° C) and tap housing against wooden block.

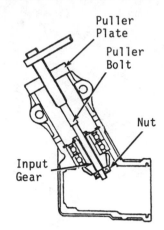

Puller Plate

Puller Bolt

Nut

Input Gear

Fig. AL15—To remove input shaft, gear and bearing assembly, install puller as shown.

BLACK & DECKER
ELECTRIC STRING TRIMMERS

Model	Volts	Amps	Swath	Diameter	Cutting Line RPM
82205	120	1.4	9 in.	0.050 in.	10,500
82209	120	1.4	9 in.	0.050 in.	10,500
82210	120	1.5	10 in.	0.050 in.	9,500
82212	120	3.9	12 in.	0.065 in.	10,000
82214	120	4.3	14 in.	0.065 in.	8,500
82230	120	2.5	10 in.	0.050 in.	10,000
82232	120	3.2	12 in.	0.050 in.	9,500
82234	120	4.3	14 in.	0.050 in.	10,000

ELECTRICAL REQUIREMENTS

All models require electrical circuits with 120-volt alternating current. Extension cord length should not exceed 100 feet (30.5 m). Make certain all circuits and connections are properly grounded at all times.

STRING TRIMMER

Model 82205

Model 82205 is equipped with a manual advance line trimmer head designed to cut a 9 inch (229 mm) swath with 0.050 in. (1.3 mm) monofilament line. To extend line, disconnect power cord. Pull line up out of line slot (2-Fig. BD1) and pull line around spool in direction indicated by arrow and "UNWIND

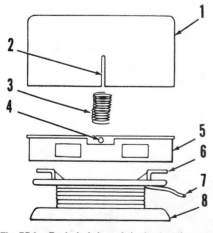

Fig. BD1—Exploded view of single strand manual trimmer head used on Model 82205.

1. Housing
2. Line slot
3. Spring
4. Line hole
5. Line retainer
6. Lock tabs
7. Line
8. Spool

LINE" printed on spool. To renew line, push spool (8) in while turning in direction indicated by arrow and "REMOVE SPOOL" printed on spool. Remove spool, plastic line retainer (5) and any remaining old line. Insert one end of new line in hole in lower side of spool and wind new line onto spool in direction indicated by arrow on upper surface of spool. Insert line end through hole (4) in line retainer and install line retainer over spool. Install spool in housing and push spool in while turning spool to lock tabs (6) in housing (1).

Models 82209, 82210, 82212 And 82214

Models 82209, 82210, 82212 and 82214 are equipped with a single strand semi-automatic trimmer head shown in Fig. BD2. Models 82209 and 82210 are equipped with 0.050 inch (1.3 mm) line and Models 82212 and 82214 are equipped with 0.065 inch (1.6 mm) line. On all models, to extend line with trimmer motor off, push bump button (7) in while pulling on line end. Procedure may have to be repeated until desired line length has been obtained. To extend line with trimmer motor running, tap bump button (7) on the ground. Each time bump button is tapped on the ground a measured amount of new line will be advanced.

To renew line, disconnect power cord. Remove cover (8), button (7) and spool (6). Clean all parts thoroughly and remove any remaining old line from spool. Wind new line onto spool in direction indicated by arrow on spool. Insert line end through line guide opening in drum (1) and install spool, button and cover.

Models 82230, 82232 And 82234

Models 82230, 82232 and 82234 are equipped with a push button line feed system equipped with 0.050 inch (1.3 mm) line. Line is advanced by pushing button on secondary handle with trimmer motor running. Each time button is pushed, approximately 5/8 inch (16 mm) of line is advanced.

To renew line, disconnect power cord.

Fig. BD2—Exploded view of single strand semi-automatic head similar to the one used on Models 82209, 82210, 82212 and 82214.

1. Housing
2. Line guide
3. Spring
4. Spring adapter
5. Drive adapter
6. Spool
7. Bump button
8. Cover

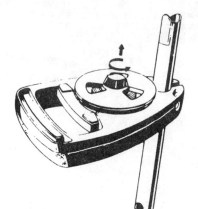

Fig. BD3—Turn spool nut in direction indicated to remove.

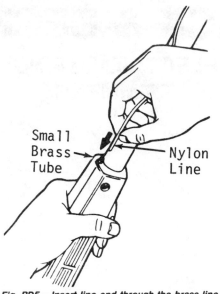

Small Brass Tube

Nylon Line

Fig. BD5—Insert line end through the brass line tube and work line down through tube until line is extending from line guide opening in trimmer head.

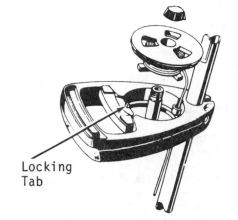

Locking Tab

Fig. BD4—Insert line end through line hole as shown and install spool in bail.

Remove spool nut as shown in Fig. BD3. Lift spool out of handle assembly. Remove remaining old line and clean spool and bail assemblies. Wind new line onto spool leaving 3 feet (0.9 m) of line unwound from spool. Insert line end down through hole in bail handle assembly that is closest to handle tube (Fig. BD4). Install spool in bail assembly and install spool nut. Insert line end into line tube (Fig. BD5) and work entire length of free line through tube. At this point trimmer line should be extending from trimmer head line guide (Fig. BD6). If no line is at trimmer head, remove line spool and advance more free line before installing spool again.

Fig. BD6—Line must extend from line guide opening in trimmer head after line installation.

BLACK & DECKER
GASOLINE POWERED
STRING TRIMMER

Model	Engine Manufacturer	Engine Model	Displacement
8271-04	Kioritz	....	16.0 cc
8289-04	Kioritz	....	21.2 cc
82255	McCulloch	....	21.2 cc
82257	McCulloch	....	21.2 cc
82267	McCulloch	...	21.2 cc

ENGINE INFORMATION

All Models

Early models are equipped with Kioritz two-stroke air-cooled gasoline engines and later models are equipped with McCulloch two-stroke air-cooled gasoline engines. Identify engine model by engine manufacturer and engine displacement. Refer to KIORITZ ENGINE SERVICE or McCULLOCH ENGINE SERVICE section of this manual.

FUEL MIXTURE

All Models

Manufacturer recommends mixing regular grade gasoline (unleaded is an acceptable substitute) with a good quality two-stroke air-cooled engine oil at a 25:1 ratio. Do not use fuel containing alcohol.

STRING TRIMMER

Model 8271-04

Model 8271-04 is equipped with a single strand semi-automatic trimmer head shown in Fig. BD10. Line may be manually advanced with engine stopped by pushing in on housing (9) while pulling on line. Procedure may have to be repeated to obtain desired line length. To advance line with engine running, operate engine at full rpm and tap housing (9) on the ground. Each time housing is tapped on the ground, a measured amount of trimmer line will be advanced.

To renew trimmer line, remove cotter key (10) and twist housing (9) counterclockwise to remove housing. Remove foam pad (6) and any remaining line on spool (3). Clean spool and inside of housing. Cut off approximately 25 feet (7.6 m) of 0.080 inch (2 mm) monofilament line and tape one end of line to spool (Fig. BD12). Wind line on spool in direction indicated by arrow on spool (Fig. BD13). Install foam pad with line end protruding from between foam pad and spool as shown in Fig. BD13. Insert line end through line guide and install housing and spring assembly on spool.

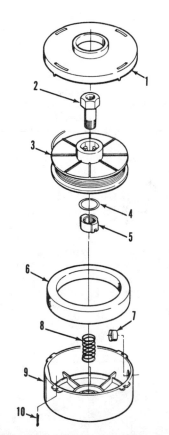

Fig. BD10—Exploded view of single strand semi-automatic trimmer head used on Model 8271-04.

1. Cover	6. Foam pad
2. Drive adapter	7. Line guide
3. Spool	8. Spring
4. "O" ring	9. Housing
5. Drive adapter nut	10. Cotter pin

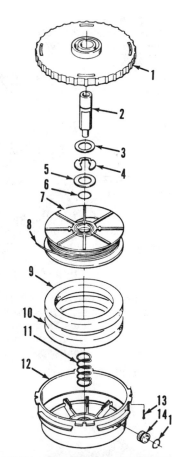

Fig. BD11—Exploded view of single strand semi-automatic trimmer head used on Models 8289-04, 82255, 82257 and 82267.

1. Cover	9. Foam pad
2. Drive adapter	10. Foam pad
3. Washer	11. Spring
4. Retainer	12. Housing
5. Washer	13. Cotter pin
6. Retainer ring	14. Line guide
7. Spool	15. Retainer
8. Line	

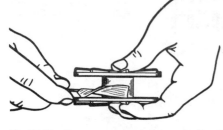

Fig. BD12—Tape one end of new line to center of spool as shown.

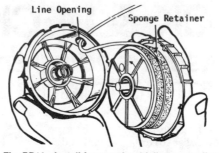

Fig. BD14—Install foam pads with line protruding from between pads. Wind line in direction indicated by arrow on spool.

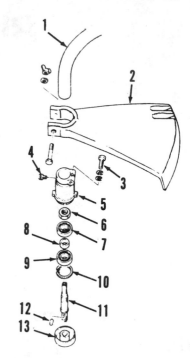

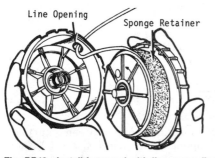

Fig. BD13—Install foam pad with line protruding between pad and spool as shown. Wind line in direction indicated by arrow on spool.

Push in on housing and twist housing to lock into position. Install cotter key through hole in housing and cover.

Model 8289-04, 82255, 82257 And 82267

A single strand semi-automatic trimmer head shown in Fig. BD11 may be used on these models. Line may be manually advanced with engine off by pushing in on housing (12) while pulling on line. Procedure may have to be repeated until desired line length is obtained. To advance line with engine running, operate trimmer engine at full rpm and tap housing (12) on the ground. Each time housing is tapped on the ground, a measured amount of trimmer line is advanced.

To renew trimmer line, remove cotter pin (13). Twist housing (12) counterclockwise and remove housing. Remove foam pads (9 and 10) and any remaining line from spool (7). Clean spool and

inner area of housing. Cut off approximately 25 feet (7.6 mm) of 0.080 inch (2 mm) monofilament line and tape one end of line to spool (Fig. BD12). Wind line on spool in direction indicated by arrow on spool (Fig. BD14). Install foam pads (9 and 10—Fig. BD11) so line is protruding from center of foam pads (Fig. BD14). Insert end of line through line guide and install spool, housing and spring. Push in on housing and twist housing in clockwise direction to lock in position and install cotter pin (13—Fig. BD11).

DRIVE SHAFT

All Models

All models are equipped with a flexible drive shaft enclosed in the drive shaft housing tube. Drive shaft has squared ends which engage adapters at each end. Drive shaft should be removed for maintenance at 50 hour intervals of use. Remove screw (4—Fig. BD15) and bolt (3) at bearing head housing and separate bearing head from drive shaft housing. Pull flexible drive shaft from housing. Lubricate drive shaft with lithium base grease and reinstall in drive shaft housing with end which was previously at clutch end toward bearing head. Reversing drive shaft ends extends drive shaft life. Make certain ends of drive shaft are properly located into upper and lower square drive adapters when installing.

Fig. BD15—Exploded view of bearing head used on all models. Bearings (7 and 9) are sealed bearings and require no regular maintenance.

1. Drive shaft housing
2. Shield
3. Bolt
4. Screw
5. Housing
6. Nut
7. Bearing
8. Spacer
9. Bearing
10. Snap ring
11. Arbor (output) shaft
12. Pin
13. Cup washer

BEARING HEAD

All Models

All models are equipped with the bearing head shown in Fig. BD15. Bearing head is equipped with sealed bearings and requires no regular maintenance. To disassemble bearing head, remove trimmer head assembly and cup washer (13). Remove screw (4) and bolt (3) and separate bearing head from drive shaft housing tube. Remove snap ring (10) and use a suitable puller to remove arbor shaft (11) and bearing assembly. Remove nut (6) and press bearings (7 and 9) and spacer (8) from arbor shaft as required.

BUNTON

GASOLINE POWERED STRING TRIMMER

Model	Engine Manufacturer	Engine Model	Displacement
LBF18K	Kawasaki	TD-18	18.4 cc
LBS24K	Kawasaki	TD-24	24.1 cc
LBS33K	Kawasaki	TD-33	33.3 cc

ENGINE INFORMATION

All Models

All models are equipped with a two-stroke air-cooled gasoline engine manufactured by Kawasaki. Refer to appropriate KAWASAKI ENGINE SERVICE section of this manual.

FUEL MIXTURE

All Models

Manufacturer recommends mixing a good quality two-stroke air-cooled engine oil with regular grade gasoline of at least 87 octane rating. Mix gasoline and oil at a 25:1 ratio. Unleaded regular gasoline is an acceptable substitute.

STRING TRIMMER

All Models

All models may be equipped with a dual strand manual trimmer head as shown in Figs. BT10 and BT11. To install trimmer head, refer to Fig. BT10 for assembly sequence for Model LBF18K and to Fig. BT11 for assembly sequence for Models LBS24K and LBS33K. Note that trimmer head retaining nut on all models has left-hand thread. On all models, line may be extended (with engine stopped) by loosening lock knob on underside of trimmer head and rotating spool in direction which will advance line. Tighten lock knob.

To renew line, remove lock knob and spool. Remove any remaining old line and install new line on spool. Wind line in direction indicated by arrow on spool Insert line ends through line guide openings in housing and install spool and lock knob.

BLADE

All Models

All models may be equipped with an eight blade weed and grass blade. Blade is installed on Model LBF18K as shown in Fig. BT12. Blade is installed on Models LBS24K and LBS33K as shown in

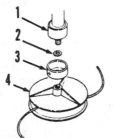

Fig. BT10—Trimmer head parts assembly sequence for trimmer head installation on Model LBF18K.

1. Drive shaft housing	3. Cup washer
2. Spacer	4. Trimmer head

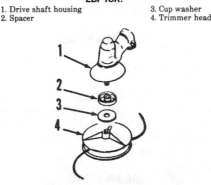

Fig. BT11—Trimmer head parts assembly sequence for trimmer head installation on Models LBS24K and LBS33K.

1. Gear head	3. Washer
2. Cup washer	4. Trimmer head

Fig. BT13. Make certain adapter plate (7) is centered and seated squarely on blade during installation.

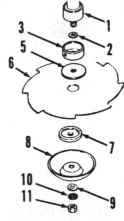

Fig. BT12—Parts assembly sequence for blade installation on Model LBF18K.

1. Drive shaft housing	7. Adapter plate
2. Spacer	8. Cover
3. Cup washer	9. Washer
5. Washer	10. Lock washer
6. Blade	11. Nut (LH)

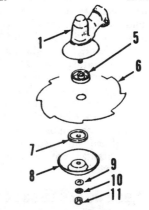

Fig. BT13—Parts assembly sequence for blade installation on Models LBS24K and LBS33K.

1. Gear head	8. Cover
5. Cup washer	9. Washer
6. Blade	10. Lock washer
7. Adapter plate	11. Nut (LH)

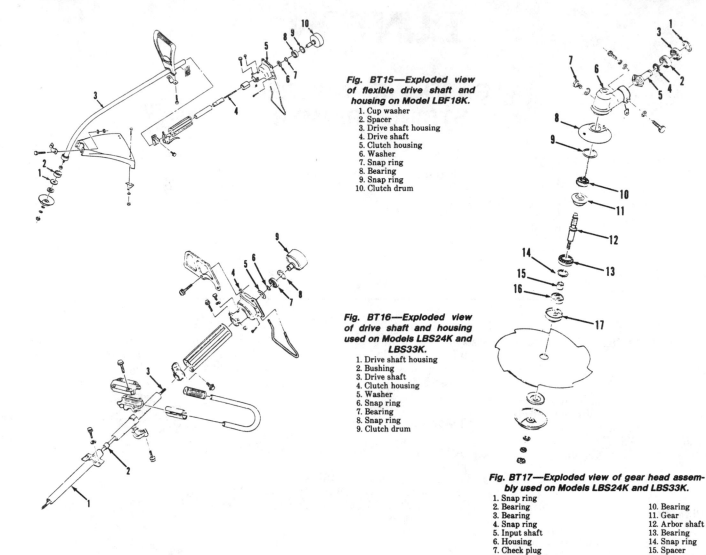

Fig. BT15—Exploded view of flexible drive shaft and housing on Model LBF18K.
1. Cup washer
2. Spacer
3. Drive shaft housing
4. Drive shaft
5. Clutch housing
6. Washer
7. Snap ring
8. Bearing
9. Snap ring
10. Clutch drum

Fig. BT16—Exploded view of drive shaft and housing used on Models LBS24K and LBS33K.
1. Drive shaft housing
2. Bushing
3. Drive shaft
4. Clutch housing
5. Washer
6. Snap ring
7. Bearing
8. Snap ring
9. Clutch drum

Fig. BT17—Exploded view of gear head assembly used on Models LBS24K and LBS33K.
1. Snap ring	
2. Bearing	10. Bearing
3. Bearing	11. Gear
4. Snap ring	12. Arbor shaft
5. Input shaft	13. Bearing
6. Housing	14. Snap ring
7. Check plug	15. Spacer
8. Anti-wrap cover	16. Seal
9. Snap ring	17. Cup washer

DRIVE SHAFT

Model LBF18K

Models LBF18K is equipped with a flexible drive shaft (Fig. BT15) enclosed in the tube housing (3). Drive shaft has squared ends which engage clutch drum (10) adapter at engine end and head adapter at head end. Drive shaft should be removed for maintenance at 30 hour intervals. Remove and clean drive shaft after marking end positions. Inspect for damage. Coat with lithium base grease and make certain drive shaft is installed with ends in opposite locations. Alternating drive shaft squared ends between clutch and trimmer head ends will extend drive shaft life.

Models LBS24K And LBS33K

Models LBS24K and LBS33K are equipped with a solid drive shaft (3—Fig. BT16) supported in drive shaft housing (1) in bushings (2) and at gear head

and clutch housing ends in sealed bearings. Drive shaft requires no regular maintenance however, if drive shaft is removed, lubricate drive shaft with lithium base grease before reinstallation. Drive shaft bushings (2) may be renewed. Mark locations of old bushings in drive shaft tube before removing. Install new bushings at old bushing locations in tube.

BEARING HEAD

Model LBF18K

Model LBF18K is equipped with a bearing head which is an integral part of drive shaft housing. If bearing head is worn or damaged, renew entire drive shaft housing.

GEAR HEAD

Models LBS24K And LBS33K

Models LBS24K and LBS33K are

equipped with the gear head shown in Fig. BT17. At 30-hour intervals of use, remove trimmer head or blade assembly and install a grease fitting at check plug (7) opening. Pump lithium base grease into housing until new grease appears at seal (16) and spacer (15).

To disassemble gear head, remove trimmer head or blade assembly. Remove cup washer (17). Remove snap ring (1) and use a suitable puller to remove input shaft (5) and bearing assembly. Remove snap ring (4) and press bearings (2 and 3) from input shaft as required. Remove seal (16) and spacer (15). Remove snap ring (14) and use a suitable puller to remove arbor shaft (12) and bearing assembly as required. Press bearing (13) from arbor shaft. If bearing (10) stays in housing, heat housing to 140° F (60° C) and tap housing on wooden block to remove bearing.

JOHN DEERE

GASOLINE POWERED
STRING TRIMMERS

Model	Engine Manufacturer	Engine Model	Displacement
80G	Kioritz	...	21.2 cc
82G	Poulan	...	26.2 cc
83G	Poulan	...	26.2 cc
85G	Tecumseh	AV520	85.0 cc
90G	Kioritz	...	30.1 cc
100G	Kioritz	...	16.0 cc
110G	Kioritz	...	21.2 cc
200G	Kioritz	...	21.2 cc
210G	Kioritz	...	21.2 cc
220G	Kioritz	...	21.2 cc
240G	Kiortiz	...	21.2 cc
250G	Kiortiz	...	21.2 cc
260G	Kioritz	...	21.2 cc
300G	Kioritz	...	24.4 cc
350G	Kioritz	...	30.1 cc
450G	Kioritz	...	40.2 cc

FUEL MIXTURE

The manufacturer recommends mixing regular-grade gasoline, leaded or unleaded, with a high-quality two-stroke engine oil. The use of gasohol or other alcohol blended fuels are not approved by manufacturer.

On Models 110G, 210G, 220G, 240G, 250G, 260G, 300G, 350G and 450G, recommended fuel:oil ratio is 50:1 when using John Deere 2-Cycle Engine Oil. Fuel:oil ratio should be 32:1 when using any other two-stroke oil, regardless of recommended ratio on oil container. On Models 90G, 100G and 200G, recommended fuel:oil ratio is 40:1 when using John Deere 2-Cycle Engine Oil. Fuel:oil ratio should be 32:1 when using any other two-stroke oil. On Model 85G, recommended fuel:oil ratio is 24:1. On Models 82G and 83G, recommended fuel:oil ratio is 32:1 when using John Deere 2-Cycle Engine Oil. Fuel:oil ratio should be 16:1 when using any other two-stroke oil. On Model 80G, recommended fuel:oil ratio is 32:1 when using John Deere 2-Cycle Engine Oil. Fuel:oil ratio should be 20:1 when using any other two-stroke oil.

STRING TRIMMER

Model 80G

Model 80G is equipped with the manual advance, single-strand trimmer head

shown in Fig. JD10. To adjust line length, loosen knob (5) and pull out line.

To install new line, remove knob (5) and spool (4). Wind approximately 40 feet (12.2 m) of 0.080 inch (2 mm) diameter line in direction indicated by arrow on spool. Install spool in housing (2) with ribbed side visible and projections (P) positioned in line slots (L) of housing. Be sure line guides (3) are in place.

Model 82G

Model 82G is equipped with a single-strand, semi-automatic head with 40

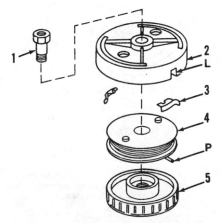

Fig. JD10—Exploded view of manual advance, single-strand trimmer head used on Model 80G.
1. Adapter
2. Housing
3. Line guide
4. Spool
5. Knob

feet (12.2 m) of 0.080 inch (2 mm) diameter line. Early models are equipped with the head assembly shown in Fig. JD11. Later models are equipped with

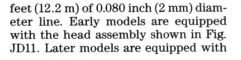

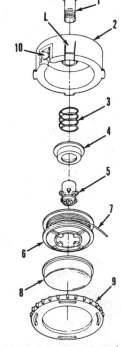

Fig. JD11—Exploded view of semi-automatic, single-strand trimmer head used on Model 82G.
1. Adapter
2. Drum
3. Spring
4. Spring adapter
5. Drive cam
6. Spool
7. Line
8. Button
9. Cover
10. Line guide

a similar head that is identified by grooves on top of drum (2); early models are smooth.

To adjust line length with engine stopped, depress button (8) and pull out line until it stops. Repeat procedure to extract more line. To extend line with engine running, operate trimmer at full throttle and tap button against ground.

To install new line, engine must be stopped. Depress latch (L—Fig. JD11) and rotate cover (9) counterclockwise to

remove cover. Remove button (8) and spool (6). Inspect teeth on inner cam (5) and spool (6). Excessive wear indicates unnecessary pressure on button during operation. Remove any remaining old line and note direction of arrow on spool. Wind approximately 40 feet (12.2 m) of 0.080 inch (2 mm) diameter line in direction indicated by arrow on spool. Install spool in drum (2) with arrow side visible. Install button (8) and cover (9). Rotate cover clockwise until it locks.

Models 83G and 90G

Models 83G and 90G trimmers are equipped with dual-strand, manual advance trimmer heads (Fig. JD12) that have double-grooved spools wound with approximately 50 feet (15.2 m) of 0.080 inch (2 mm) diameter line.

To adjust line length, depress release button (1) and pull out line from both line openings until line stops. Repeat procedure until at least 6 inches (15.2 cm) of line extends from both openings. Each line must be 6 inches (15.2 cm)

long measured from line opening, if not, cut line. Do not operate trimmer with line extended beyond recommended length.

To install new line, hold trimmer head and remove screw (9). Remove cover (8), spring (6) and spool (7). Each side of double spool will hold approximately 25 feet (7.6 m) of 0.080 inch (2 mm) line. Insert ends of new line in spool holes and wrap line around spool in direction indicated by arrow on spool. Make certain that line guides (3) are in position and place spool in housing (2). Install spool so side marked "THIS SIDE IN" is toward housing. Install spring and cover. Tighten cover screw (9) and cut line to proper length.

Model 85G

Model 85G is equipped with the manual advance, four-strand trimmer head shown in Fig. JD13. To extend line, depress top of each spool (3) and pull out line. Release spool being sure square portion of spool properly indexes with square hole in housing (1).

To install new line, remove Allen screw (7), cover (6), springs (5) and spools (3). Clean components. Each spool holds approximately 20 feet (6.1 m) of 0.080 inch (2 mm) diameter line. Wind line around spool in direction of arrow on spool. Note that there should be approximately the same amount of line on each spool so head is balanced. Insert line ends through line guides and assemble components.

Early 100G and Early 200G Models

Early 100G and early 200G models are equipped with a single-strand, semi-automatic trimmer head shown in Fig. JD14. The trimmer head will hold approximately 45 feet (13.7 m) of 0.080 inch (2 mm) diameter line. Line may be manually advanced with engine stopped by pushing in on housing (12) while pulling on line. Repeat procedure until desired line length is obtained. To advance line with engine running, operate trimmer engine at full rpm and tap housing (12) on ground. Each time housing is tapped, a measured amount of line is advanced.

To install new line, remove cotter pin (13). Twist housing (12) counterclockwise and remove housing. Remove foam pads (9 and 10) and any remaining line from spool (7). Clean spool and inner area of housing. Tape one end of new line to spool (Fig. JD15). Wind line on spool in direction indicated by arrow on spool (Fig. JD16). Install foam pads so line is protruding from center of pads as shown in Fig. JD16. Insert end of line

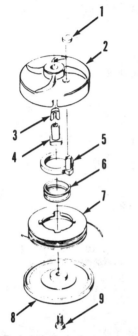

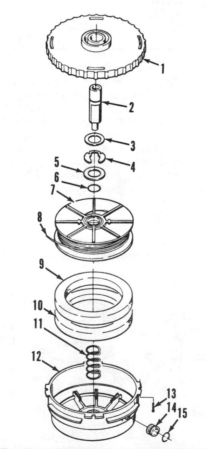

Fig. JD12—Exploded view of manual advance, dual-strand trimmer head used on Models 83G and 90G.

1. Release button
2. Housing
3. Line guide
4. Adapter
5. Lock ring
6. Spring
7. Spool
8. Cover
9. Screw

Fig. JD14—Exploded view of semi-automatic, single-strand trimmer head used on early 100G and early 200G models.

1. Cover
2. Adapter
3. Washer
4. Retainer
5. Washer
6. Retainer
7. Spool
8. Line
9. Foam pad
10. Foam pad
11. Spring
12. Housing
13. Cotter pin
14. Line guide
15. Retainer

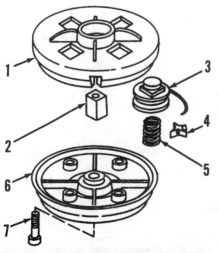

Fig. JD13—Exploded view of manual advance, four-strand trimmer head used on Model 85G.

1. Housing
2. Post
3. Spool
4. Retainer
5. Spring
6. Cover
7. Allen screw

through line guide and install spool, housing and spring. Push housing in and twist in clockwise direction to lock in position, then install cotter pin (13—Fig. JD14).

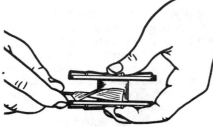

Fig. JD15—Tape end of new line to center of spool as shown.

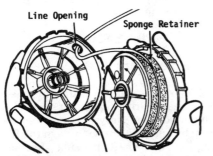

Fig. JD16—Install foam pads with line protruding from between pads. Wind line in direction indicated by arrow on spool.

Later 100G, 110G, Later 200G, 210G and 220G Models

These models are equipped with a dual-strand, semi-automatic trimmer head. To manually advance line with engine stopped, push in button at bottom of head and pull on each line. To extend line with engine running, operate trimmer at full operating rpm and tap button on ground. Line will automatically advance a measured amount.

To install new line, press against tab marked "PUSH" and remove cover (8—Fig. JD17), button (7) and spool (6). Clean and inspect all parts. New line should be 0.080 inch (2 mm) diameter and 15 feet (4.6 m) long. Insert end of line through eye of spool as shown in Fig. JD18 so approximately 1 inch (25 mm) extends past eye. Wrap line on spool in clockwise direction as viewed from top side of spool (note arrow on spool). Install spool while directing line end through eye of drum (2—Fig. JD17). Install button and cover. Cover should snap into place after locking tabs of cover engage tabs on drum next to eye hole. Trim line so approximately 3 inches (75 mm) extend from drum.

If trimmer head retaining nut (4) must be unscrewed, prevent shaft rotation by inserting a pin through hole provided in bearing head to lock shaft.

Models 240G, Later 250G, 260G, 300G, Later 350G and Later 450G

These models are equipped with the dual-strand, semi-automatic trimmer head shown in Fig. JD19. To manually advance line with engine stopped, push in button at bottom of head and pull on each line. Procedure may have to be repeated to obtain desired line length. To extend line with engine running, operate trimmer at full operating rpm and tap button on ground. Line will automatically advance a given amount.

To install new line, hold drum firmly and turn spool in direction shown in Fig. JD20 to remove slack. Twist with a hard snap until plastic peg is between holes and separate spool from drum. Remove old line from spool. Spool will hold approximately 20 feet (6 m) of 0.095 inch (2.4 mm) diameter line. Insert one end of new line through hole on spool (Fig. JD21) and pull line through until line is the same length on both sides of hole. Wind both ends of line at the same time in direction indicated by arrow on spool. Wind tightly and evenly from side-to-side and do not twist line. Insert ends of line through line guide openings, align pegs on drum with slots in spool and push spool into drum. Hold drum firmly, twist spool quickly in direction shown in Fig. JD22 so peg enters hole

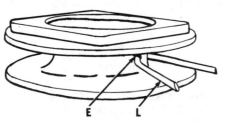

Fig. JD18—Insert end of line (L) through eye (E) of spool as shown so approximately 1 inch (25 mm) extends past eye.

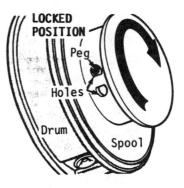

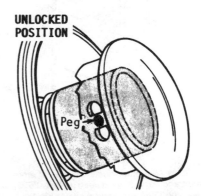

Fig. JD20—To remove spool, hold drum firmly and turn spool in direction shown to take up slack, then twist with a sudden snap until plastic peg is between holes as shown in lower view.

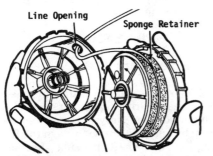

Fig. JD17—Exploded view of semi-automatic, dual-strand trimmer head used on later 100G, 110G, later 200G, 210G and 220G models.

1. Adapter
2. Housing
3. Line guide
4. Nut
5. Spring
6. Spool
7. Button
8. Cover

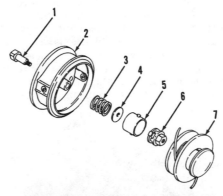

Fig. JD19—Exploded view of semi-automatic, dual-strand trimmer head used on 240G, later 250G, 260G, 300G, later 350G and later 450G models.

1. Adapter
2. Housing
3. Spring
4. Washer
5. Outer cam
6. Inner cam
7. Spool

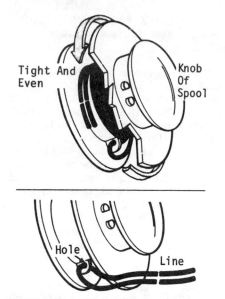

Tight And Even ... Knob Of Spool

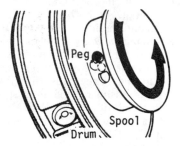

Hole ... Line

Fig. JD21—End of line must be inserted through hole on spool as shown in lower view. Wind line tightly in direction indicated by arrow on spool.

Peg ... Spool ... Drum

Fig. JD22—Hold drum firmly and twist suddenly to lock spool in position.

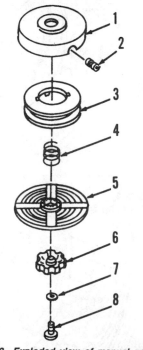

Fig. JD23—Exploded view of manual advance, dual-strand trimmer head used on early 250G, early 350G and early 450G models.

1. Housing	5. Cover
2. Eyelet	6. Knob
3. Spool	7. Washer
4. Spring	8. Screw

with a click and locks spool in position. Cut off lines to approximately 6 inches (15 cm).

If trimmer head inner drive cam (6—Fig. JD19) must be unscrewed, prevent shaft rotation by inserting a pin through hole located in bearing head. Cam has left-hand threads.

Early 250G, Early 350G and Early 450G Models

Early Models 250G, 350G and 450G are equipped with the manual advance, dual-strand trimmer head shown in Fig. JD23. To pull out line, stop engine and loosen knob (6) approximately 1½ turns clockwise (knob has left-hand threads). Line length should be approximately 5 inches (12.7 cm).

To install new line, remove screw (8) and washer (7). Unscrew knob (L.H. threads) and remove cover (5), spring (4) and spool (3). New line should be 0.095 inch (2.4 mm) diameter. Each line is 12 feet (3.7 m) long. Insert line end through slot and into hole on opposite side of spool. Line end should protrude ¼ inch (6.4 mm). Without twisting lines, tightly wrap lines around spool in a counterclockwise direction as viewed from slotted side of spool. Install spool with slotted side out while directing line ends through eyelets in drum. Install spring (4), cover (5), knob (6), washer (7) and screw (8). Be sure dogs (D—Fig. JD24) on spool properly engage slots (S) in cover. Cut line on each side so line length is 6 inches (15 cm).

BLADE

Models 83G, 90G, 240G, 250G, 260G, 300G, 350G and 450G

Model 83G may be equipped with a four-tooth blade or a saw blade. Model 90G may be equipped with an eight-tooth blade. Models 240G, 250G, 260G, 300G, 350G and 450G may be equipped with an eight-tooth blade or a saw blade. When installing blade, make certain all adapter washers are centered and square with blade surface. Note that blade retaining nut has left-hand threads. Install blade so cutting surfaces

will cut when blade rotates clockwise as viewed from ground side of blade.

DRIVE SHAFT HOUSING

All Models

REMOVE AND REINSTALL. The drive shaft housing may be separated from the engine clutch housing by unscrewing the housing clamp screws. If marks do not exist, place marks on clutch housing and drive shaft housing so the housings can be mated in their original positions.

Most models are equipped with a locating screw (S—Fig. JD25) that must be removed before separating lower end of drive shaft housing from gear head or bearing housing.

DRIVE SHAFT

Models 80G and 85G

Models 80G and 85G are equipped with flexible drive shafts that should be lubricated after every 10 hours of operation by injecting grease through the fitting on the shaft housing. Recommended lubricant is SAE high-temperature EP grease. Do not inject more than ½ teaspoon (2.5 mL) of grease as overlubrication may force grease into clutch of trimmer head.

Models 82G, 100G and 200G

Models 82G, 100G and 200G are equipped with flexible drive shafts. Drive shafts should be removed from drive shaft housing, cleaned and installed with ends reversed after every 10 hours of operation.

To remove drive shaft, separate drive shaft housing from clutch housing. Mark drive shaft end and pull drive shaft from housing. Clean and lubricate drive shaft then install with end that was at clutch end, now at trimmer head end. Reversing drive shaft ends extends drive shaft life.

Models 110G and 210G

Models 110G and 210G are equipped

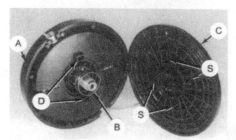

Fig. JD24—Dogs (D) on spool must engage slots (S) in cover (C).

Fig. JD25—Most models have a locating screw (S) that retains and positions the bearing housing or gear head on the drive shaft housing tube.

Illustrations for Fig. JD21, Fig. JD22, Fig. JD23, Fig. JD24 and Fig. JD25 reproduced by permission of Deere & Company. Copyright Deere & Company.

with flexible drive shafts that ride in renewable bushings. Drive shaft should be removed from drive shaft housing, cleaned and installed with ends reversed after every six months.

To remove drive shaft, separate drive shaft housing from bearing housing. Mark drive shaft end and pull drive shaft from housing. Clean and lubricate drive shaft, then install with end that was at clutch end, now at trimmer head end. Reversing drive shaft ends extends drive shaft life.

Models 240G and 260G

Models 240G and 260G are equipped with flexible drive shafts that ride in renewable bushings. Drive shaft should be removed from drive shaft housing, cleaned and lubricated annually.

To remove drive shaft, separate drive shaft housing from gear head.

Models 83G, 90G, 220G, 250G, 300G, 350G and 450G

These models are equipped with solid shafts that ride in bushings in the drive shaft housing. Drive shaft requires no regular maintenance. However, if drive shaft is removed, it should be lubricated with lithium-base grease before installation.

Manufacturer does not recommend renewal of bushings in drive shaft housing.

BEARING HEAD

Later Models 80G and 82G

Later Models 80G and 82G are equipped with the bearing head shown in Fig. JD26, which has sealed bearings and requires no maintenance.

To disassemble bearing head, remove trimmer head. Remove clamp bolt (2) and locating screw (3). Separate bearing head assembly from drive shaft housing. Remove shield (6) and bracket (5), if so equipped. Remove cup washer (13) and washer (12). Carefully press drive shaft adapter (1) out of bearings. Remove snap rings (7 and 11), then press bearings (8 and 10) and spacer (9) out of housing.

Models 85G, 100G, 200G and 220G

Models 85G, 100G, 200G and 220G are equipped with the bearing head shown in Fig. JD27, which has sealed bearings that do not require regular maintenance.

To disassemble bearing head, remove screw (1) and clamp screw (2) and slide bearing head off drive shaft housing.

Remove adapter plate (10) and snap ring (8). Use a suitable puller or press and force shaft and bearing assembly out of housing (3). Unscrew nut (4) and remove bearings and spacer as required. Note that nut (4) has left-hand threads.

Models 110G and 210G

The bearing housings on Models 110G and 210G have no serviceable components and must be serviced as unit assemblies. No lubrication is required.

Model 83G

Lubricant level in gear housing should be checked after every 10 hours of operation. To check lubricant level, remove plug in side of gear housing. Gear housing should be two-thirds full of lubricant. Recommended lubricant is lithium-base grease.

The gear housing on Model 83G has no serviceable components and must be serviced as a unit assembly.

Model 90G

Lubricant level in gear housing should be checked after every 10 hours of operation. To check lubricant level, remove plug (20—Fig. JD28) in side of gear housing. Gear housing should be two-thirds full of lubricant. Recommended lubricant is lithium-base grease.

Before disassembly, note position of all spacers or shims so they can be reinstalled in their original position. Remove blade or trimmer head and separate gear head from drive shaft housing tube. Remove snap ring (19) and use a suitable puller to extract input shaft and bearing assembly from gear head. Remove plug (1) and snap ring (4). Remove seal (10) and snap ring (9). Press arbor (12) and bearing assembly out of gear head.

Inspect components and renew if excessively worn or damaged. Shims (15) may be installed to establish gear position and backlash. Gears should rotate smoothly without binding.

Models 240G, Later 250G and 260G

Lubricant level in gear housing should be checked after every 10 hours of operation. To check lubricant level, remove plug (11—Fig. JD29) in side of gear housing. Gear housing should be nearly full of lubricant while leaving room for expansion. Recommended lubricant is lithium-base grease.

Before disassembly, note position of all spacers or shims so they can be reinstalled in their original position. Remove blade or trimmer head and separate

gear head from drive shaft housing tube. Remove snap ring (17) and use a suitable puller to extract input shaft and bearing assembly from gear head. Remove adapter plate (9). Remove snap ring (8) and seal (7). Use a suitable puller to extract arbor (4), bearing (5) and gear (3) assembly. If bearing (2) is not free, heat housing and tap lightly to dislodge bearing. Inspect components and renew if excessively worn or damaged. Shims (15) may be installed to establish gear position and backlash. Gears should rotate smoothly without binding.

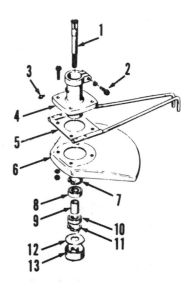

Fig. JD26—Exploded view of bearing head used on Models 80G and 82G.

1. Adapter	
2. Clamp bolt	8. Bearing
3. Locating screw	9. Spacer
4. Housing	10. Bearing
5. Bracket (if equipped)	11. Snap ring
6. Shield	12. Washer
7. Snap ring	13. Drive disc

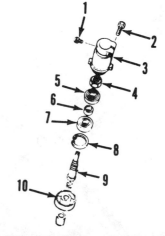

Fig. JD27—Exploded view of bearing head used on Models 100G, 200G and 220G. Model 85G is similar.

1. Locating screw	6. Spacer
2. Clamp screw	7. Bearing
3. Housing	8. Snap ring
4. Nut	9. Shaft
5. Bearing	10. Adapter plate & key

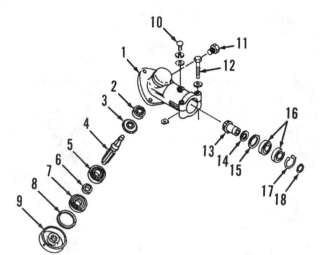

Fig. JD28—Exploded view of gear head used on Model 90G.

1. Plug
2. "O" ring
3. Nut
4. Snap ring
5. Bearing
6. Gear
7. Spacer
8. Housing
9. Snap ring
10. Seal
11. Keys
12. Arbor
13. Input gear
14. Washer
15. Shim
16. Bearing
17. Bearing
18. Snap ring
19. Snap ring
20. Plug
21. Washer
22. Locating screw
23. Clamp bolt

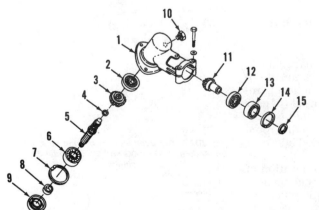

Fig. JD29—Exploded view of gear head used on Models 240G, later 250G and 260G.

1. Housing
2. Bearing
3. Gear
4. Arbor
5. Bearing
6. Washer
7. Seal
8. Snap ring
9. Adapter plate
10. Locating screw
11. Plug
12. Clamp bolt
13. Input gear
14. Washer
15. Shim
16. Bearings
17. Snap ring
18. Snap ring

Fig. JD30—Exploded view of gear head used on early 250G and all 300G models.

1. Housing
2. Bearing
3. Gear
4. Snap ring
5. Arbor
6. Bearing
7. Snap ring
8. Washer
9. Seal
10. Plug
11. Input gear
12. Bearing
13. Bearing
14. Snap ring
15. Snap ring

Early 250G and 300G

Lubricant level in gear housing should be checked after every 10 hours of operation. To check lubricant level, remove plug (10—Fig. JD30) in side of gear housing. Gear housing should be nearly full of lubricant while leaving room for expansion. Recommended lubricant is lithium-base grease.

To disassemble gear head, remove blade or trimmer head and separate gear head from drive shaft housing tube. Remove snap ring (14) and use a suitable puller to extract input shaft and bearing assembly from gear head. Remove adapter plate. Remove seal (9) and snap ring (7). Use a suitable puller to extract arbor (5), bearing (6) and gear (3) assembly. If bearing (2) is not free, heat housing and tap lightly to dislodge bearing. Inspect components and renew if excessively worn or damaged.

Model 350G

Lubricant level in gear housing should be checked after every 10 hours of operation. To check lubricant level, remove plug (11—Fig. JD31) in side of gear housing. Gear housing should be nearly full of lubricant while leaving room for expansion. Recommended lubricant is lithium-base grease.

Before disassembly, note position of all spacers or shims so they can be reinstalled in their original position. Remove blade or trimmer head and separate gear head from drive shaft housing tube. Remove snap ring (19) and use a suitable puller to extract input shaft and bearing assembly from gear head. Pull adapter plate (10) off shaft. Remove seal (9) and snap ring (8). Use a suitable puller to extract arbor (4), bearing (7) and gear (3) assembly. If bearing (2) is not free, heat housing and tap lightly to dislodge bearing.

Inspect components and renew if excessively worn or damaged. Shims (16) may be installed to establish gear position and backlash. Gears should rotate smoothly without binding.

Model 450G

Lubricant level in gear housing should be checked after every 10 hours of operation. To check lubricant level, remove plug (11—Fig. JD32) in side of gear housing. Gear housing should be nearly full of lubricant while leaving room for expansion. Recommended lubricant is lithium-base grease.

Remove blade or trimmer head and separate gear head from drive shaft housing tube. Unscrew and separate input shaft housing (17) from gear housing (1). Detach snap ring (12) and force gear and bearing assembly out of housing by tapping on end of gear shaft. Detach snap ring (16) and separate bearings from shaft. To remove arbor shaft assembly, remove adapter plate from shaft and detach snap ring (9). Remove spacer (10) and use a suitable puller to remove shaft assembly. Disassemble shaft assembly as needed.

Inspect components for damage and excessive wear. Note during reassembly that sealed side of bearing (15) must be toward end of gear shaft.

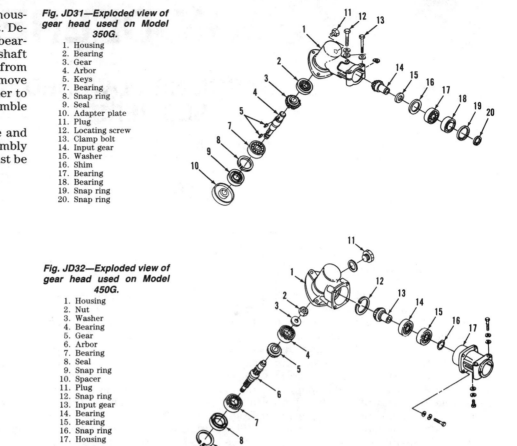

Fig. JD31—Exploded view of gear head used on Model 350G.

1. Housing
2. Bearing
3. Gear
4. Arbor
5. Keys
6. Bearing
7. Bearing
8. Snap ring
9. Seal
10. Adapter plate
11. Plug
12. Locating screw
13. Clamp bolt
14. Input gear
15. Washer
16. Shim
17. Bearing
18. Bearing
19. Snap ring
20. Snap ring

Fig. JD32—Exploded view of gear head used on Model 450G.

1. Housing
2. Nut
3. Washer
4. Bearing
5. Gear
6. Arbor
7. Bearing
8. Seal
9. Snap ring
10. Spacer
11. Plug
12. Snap ring
13. Input gear
14. Bearing
15. Bearing
16. Snap ring
17. Housing

JOHN DEERE

GASOLINE POWERED
BLOWERS

Model	Engine Manufacturer	Engine Model	Displacement
2E	Kioritz	...	21.2 cc
3E	Kioritz	...	30.8 cc
4E	Kioritz	...	39.7 cc
5E	Kioritz	...	44.0 cc

FUEL MIXTURE

Manufacturer recommends mixing regular-grade gasoline, leaded or unleaded, with a high-quality, two-stroke engine oil with a BIA or NMMA certification for TC-W service. Recommended fuel:oil ratio is 50:1 when using John Deere 2-Cycle Engine Oil. Fuel:oil ratio should be 32:1 when using any other two-stroke oil, regardless of recommended ratio on oil container. Gasohol or other alcohol blended fuels are not approved by manufacturer.

ENGINE

Engine removal and installation procedures are outlined below. Refer to appropriate Deere engine service section for engine service procedures and specifications.

Model 2E

R&R ENGINE. To remove engine, drain fuel tank and remove tank. Remove recoil starter and ignition exciter coil. Use suitable puller to remove flywheel. Remove muffler guard and muffler. Unbolt and separate blower housing. Remove fan retaining nut and tap end of crankshaft with plastic mallet to loosen fan from crankshaft. Remove four engine mounting screws, separate engine from blower housing and disconnect throttle linkage. Remove carburetor, carburetor housing, ignition module, heat shield and cylinder cover. Unbolt and remove engine mounting bracket from engine.

To reinstall engine, reverse removal procedure. Tighten engine mounting bracket cap screws and engine to blower housing cap screws to 3.5-4.0 N·m (30-35 in.-lbs.).

Models 3E-5E

R&R ENGINE. To remove engine, remove recoil starter, engine cover, air cleaner, carburetor, air cleaner base, fuel tank, carburetor insulator, muffler and cylinder cover. Disconnect ignition switch wire. Remove backpack frame, handle, outer fan housing and blower fan. Unbolt and remove engine from fan housing.

To reinstall engine, reverse removal procedure. Tighten engine mounting cap screws to 3.5-4.0 N·m (30-35 in.-lbs.).

Model 4E

R&R ENGINE. To remove engine, drain fuel and remove fuel tank. Remove muffler, ignition coil and cylinder cover. Remove backpack frame, fan cover and fan. Remove engine mounting screws and separate engine from blower housing.

To reinstall engine, reverse removal procedure. Tighten engine mounting screws to 6.0-7.0 N·m (55-60 in.lbs.).

THROTTLE CABLE

Models 3E, 4E and 5E

The throttle cable should be adjusted so there is slight free play in throttle cable. To adjust, relocate nuts at carburetor end of throttle cable. Tighten nuts after adjustment.

FAN

Tighten fan nut or screws to 15-20 N·m (133-177 in.-lbs.) on Model 2E, 30 N·m (22 ft.-lbs.) on Models 3E and 5E and 3.5-4.0 N·m (31-35 in.-lbs.) on Model 4E. If equipped with a concave washer under retaining nut, install washer so concave side is next to fan.

ECHO
GASOLINE POWERED STRING TRIMMERS

Model	Engine Manufacturer	Engine Model	Displacement
SRM-140D, SRM-140DA, GT-140, GT-140A, GT-140B	Echo	. . . . .	13.8 cc
GT-160, GT-160A, GT-160AE	Echo	. . . . .	16.0 cc
SRM-200, SRM-200AE, SRM-200BE, SRM-200D, SRM-200DA, SRM-200DB, SRM-200E, SRM-201F, SRM-201FA, SRM-202D, SRM-202DA, SRM-202F, SRM-202FA, SRM-210E, SRM-210AE, GT-200, GT-200A, GT-200B, GT-200BE	Echo	. . . . .	21.2 cc
SRM-300, SRM-302ADX	Echo	. . . . .	30.1 cc
SRM-300E, SRM-300E/1, SRM-300AE, SRM-300AE/1	Echo	. . . . .	30.8 cc
SRM-400E, SRM-400AE, SRM-402DE	Echo	. . . . .	40.2 cc

ENGINE INFORMATION

All Echo trimmers and brush cutters are equipped with Echo two-stroke air-cooled gasoline engines. Refer to ECHO ENGINE SERVICE section of this manual.

FUEL MIXTURE

All Models

Manufacturer recommends mixing regular grade gasoline (unleaded is an acceptable substitute) with a good quality two-stroke air-cooled engine oil at a 25:1 ratio. Do not use fuel containing alcohol.

STRING TRIMMER

Refer to Figs. E1 through E17 for an exploded view of string trimmer heads used on Echo string trimmers. Not all heads will be covered in detail; however, the most widely used heads are covered. Service procedure for remaining heads is similar.

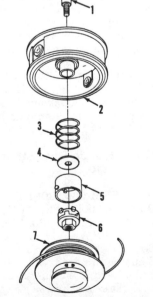

Fig. E1—Exploded view of dual strand semi-automatic trimmer head used on some SRM-200, SRM-201, SRM-202, SRM-300, SRM-302 and SRM-400 models.

1. Bolt
2. Drum
3. Spring
4. Washer
5. Outer drive
6. Inner cam
7. Spool

Semi-Automatic Dual Strand Trimmer Head

Models SRM-200, 200AE, 200BE, 200D, 200DA, 200DB, SRM-201F, 201FA, SRM-202D, 202DA, 202F, 202FA, SRM-300, 300AE, 300AE/1, 300E, 300E/1, SRM-302ADX, SRM-400AE, 400DE and 400E may be equipped with dual strand semi-automatic trimmer head as shown in Fig. E1. To manually advance line with engine stopped, push in on button (7) and pull on each line. Procedure may have to be repeated to obtain desired line length. To extend line with engine running, operate trimmer at full operating rpm and tap button (7) on the ground. Line will automatically advance a measured amount.

To renew trimmer line, hold drum firmly and turn spool in direction shown in Fig. E2 to remove slack. Twist with a hard snap until plastic peg is between holes. Pull spool out of drum. Remove old line from spool. Spool will hold approximately 20 feet (6 m) of monofilament line. Insert one end of new line through hole on

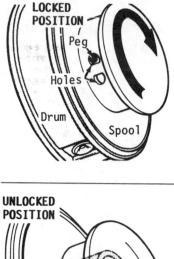

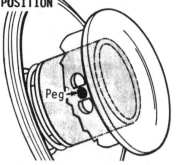

Fig. E2—To remove spool, hold drum firmly and turn spool in direction shown to take up slack, then twist with a sudden snap until plastic peg is between holes as shown in lower view.

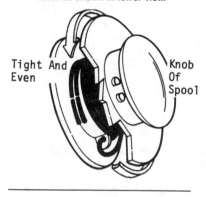

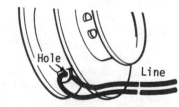

Fig. E3—End of line must be inserted through hole on spool as shown in lower view. Wind line tightly in direction indicated by arrow on spool.

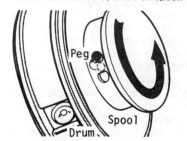

Fig. E4—Hold drum firmly and twist suddenly to lock spool in position.

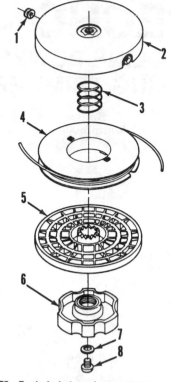

Fig. E5—Exploded view of manual trimmer head used on some SRM-200, SRM-201, SRM-202, SRM-300, SRM-302 and SRM-400 models. This head is no longer available.

1. Line guide
2. Hub
3. Spring
4. Spool
5. Cover
6. Ball lock
7. Washer
8. Screw

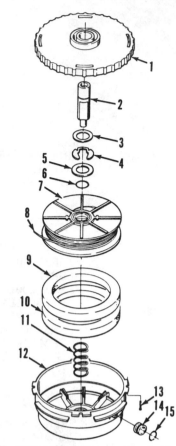

Fig. E6—Exploded view of semi-automatic trimmer head used on some GT-140, GT-160, GT-200 and GT-210 models.

1. Plate
2. Adapter
3. Washer
4. Retainer ring
5. Washer
6. Retainer ring
7. Spool
8. Line
9. Foam pad
10. Foam pad
11. Spring
12. Hub
13. Cotter pin
14. Line guide
15. Retainer

spool (Fig. E3) and pull line through until line is the same length on both sides of hole. Wind both ends of line at the same time in direction indicated by arrow marked "cc" on edge of spool. Wind tightly and evenly from side to side and do not twist line. Insert ends of line through line guide openings, align pegs on drum with slots in spool and push spool into drum. Hold drum firmly, twist spool suddenly in direction shown in Fig. E4 until peg enters hole with a click and locks spool in position. Trim extending lines to desired lengths.

Manual Advance Dual Strand Trimmer Head

Models SRM-200, 200AE, 200BE, 200D, 200DA, 200DB, SRM-201F, 201FA, SRM-202D, 202DA, 202F, 202FA, SRM-300, 300AE, 300AE/1, 300E, 300E/1, SRM-302ADX, SRM-400AE and 400E may be equipped with manual advance dual strand trimmer head shown in Fig. E5. To extend line, stop engine and wait until all head rotation has stopped. Loosen lock knob (6) approximately one turn. Pull out the line on each side until line lengths are 6 inches (152 mm).

To renew line, remove slotted screw (8) and washer (7). Unscrew ball lock (6),

remove cover (5) and spring (3). Remove spool (4). Cut two 12 foot (4 m) lengths of 0.095 inch (2.4 mm) monofilament line. Insert one end of each line through the slot and into the locating hole on bottom side of spool. Line ends should extend approximately ¼ inch (6.4 mm) through locating holes. Hold lines tight and wind in a counterclockwise direction using care not to cross the lines. Insert the end of each line into each slot leaving approximately 6 inches (152 mm) of line extending from spool. Place spool into drum and feed one line through each of the line guides. Install spring, cover, ball lock, washer and screw.

Semi-Automatic Single Strand Trimmer Head

Models GT-140B, GT-160, 160A, 160AE, GT-200A, 200B, 200BE, 200CE, SRM-210AE and 210E may be equipped with a semi-automatic single strand trimmer head shown in Fig. E6. Line may be manually advanced with engine stopped by depressing "bump" button and pulling line out as required.

Illustrations courtesy Echo Inc.

Fig. E7—Tape one end of line to center of spool.

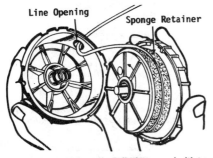

Fig. E9—Foam pads are installed on spool with trimmer line between them.

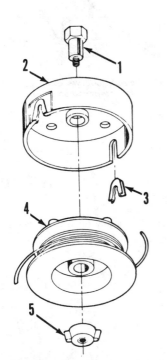

Fig. E10—Exploded view of manual trimmer head used on some GTL-140 and SRM-140 models. This head has also been used on light duty SRM-200, SRM-201 and SRM-202 models. Bolt (1) may be right or left hand thread according to model.

1. Bolt
2. Drum
3. Line guide
4. Spool
5. Wing nut

To renew line, remove cotter pin (13). Rotate housing (12) counterclockwise and remove housing and line spool (7). Remove foam pads (9 and 10) and any remaining old line. Clean spool and inner

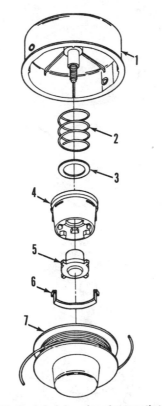

Fig. E11—Exploded view of semi-automatic trimmer head used on some SRM-140D and SRM-140DA models.

1. Hub
2. Spring
3. Washer
4. Outer drive
5. Inner cam
6. Clip
7. Spool

surface of outer housing (12). Check indexing teeth on spool and in housing. Cut off approximately 25 feet (7.6 mm) of 0.080 inch (2 mm) monofilament line and tape one end of line to spool (Fig. E7). Wind line on spool in direction indicated by arrow on spool (Fig. E9). Install foam pads (9 and 10—Fig. E6) with line between pads as shown in Fig. E9. Insert line end through line guide (14—Fig. E6) opening, then install spool and housing. Push housing in and rotate clockwise to lock in position. Install cotter pin (13).

Maxicut Trimmer Head

The "Maxicut" trimmer head (Fig. E17) is equipped with three plastic blades (2) attached to a plastic mounting disc (3) and is available as an after-market item. Note that nut (6) may be left or right-hand thread depending upon model being serviced.

BLADE

All Models So Equipped

An eight tooth weed and grass blade (A—Fig. E18) and an eighty tooth saw blade are available for some models. To install either blade, rotate the drive

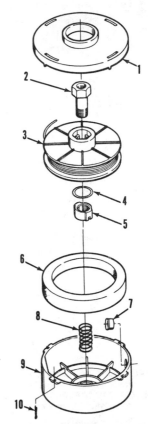

Fig. E12—Exploded view of semi-automatic trimmer head used on some GT-140B, GT-160, GT-160A, GT-200A, GT-200B and SRM-210E models. This head is no longer available.

1. Plate
2. Drive adapter
3. Spool
4. "O" ring
5. Drive adapter nut
6. Foam pad
7. Line guide
8. Spring
9. Hub
10. Cotter pin

shaft until the holes in upper adapter plate and the gear or bearing head are aligned. Insert a locking rod (Fig. E19) into holes. Install blade making certain it is centered correctly on the adapter plate. Install lower adapter plate and locking nut. Install cotter pin.

To sharpen the eight tooth weed and grass blade, round the tooth bottom 1-2 mm (0.04-0.08 in.) (Fig. E20) to prevent blade cracking. Length of cutting edge must be about 10 mm (0.4 in.) from the base of the tooth, but the rounded 2 mm part is not to be sharpened. Sharpen each blade equally to retain balance.

To sharpen the eighty tooth saw blade, setting can be done by using a circular saw setter. Sharpen blade as shown in Fig. E21.

BEARING HEAD

All Models So Equipped

Bearing heads (Fig. E22 or E23) are equipped with sealed bearings and require no periodic maintenance. To disassemble either bearing head, remove screw (1) and clamp screw (2). Remove adapter plate (10) and snap ring (8). Use

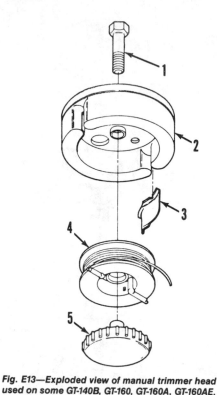

Fig. E13—Exploded view of manual trimmer head used on some GT-140B, GT-160, GT-160A, GT-160AE, GT-200A, GT-200B, GT-200CE, SRM-210E and SRM-210AE models.

1. Bolt
2. Drum
3. Line guide
4. Spool
5. Ball lock

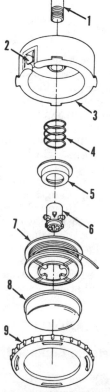

Fig. E14—Exploded view of semi-automatic trimmer head used on GT-200 model. This head is no longer available.

1. Bolt
2. Line guide
3. Drum
4. Spring
5. Spring adapter
6. Inner cam
7. Spool
8. Button
9. Cover

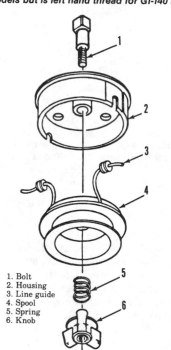

1. Body
2. Cover
3. Nut

Fig. E15—Exploded view of manual trimmer head used on some GT-140, GT-140A and GT-200 models. Nut (3) is right hand thread for GT-140A and GT-200 models but is left hand thread for GT-140 model.

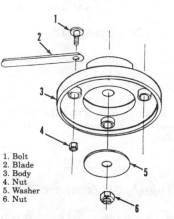

1. Bolt
2. Housing
3. Line guide
4. Spool
5. Spring
6. Knob

Fig. E16—Exploded view of heavy duty manual trimmer head used on some SRM-200, SRM-201, SRM-202, SRM-250, SRM-300, SRM-302 and SRM-400 models.

1. Bolt
2. Blade
3. Body
4. Nut
5. Washer
6. Nut

Fig. E17—Exploded view of "Maxicut" head which is available for all GT and SRM trimmers. Nut (6) may have left or right hand threads depending upon model.

Fig. E18—Weed and grass blade (A) and brush blade (B) are available for some models.

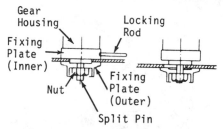

Fig. E19—Make certain blade is centered on adapter plate (fixing plate) during installation.

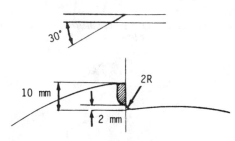

Fig. E20—The eight tooth weed and grass blade may be sharpened as shown.

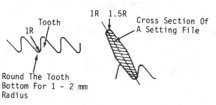

Fig. E21—The eighty tooth brush blade may be sharpened as shown.

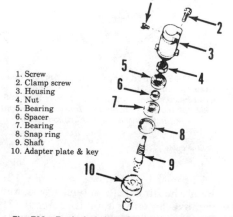

1. Screw
2. Clamp screw
3. Housing
4. Nut
5. Bearing
6. Spacer
7. Bearing
8. Snap ring
9. Shaft
10. Adapter plate & key

Fig. E22—Exploded view of bearing head used on some models.

suitable puller to remove bearing and arbor assemblies. Remove nut (4) and remove bearings and spacer as required.

GEAR HEAD

All Models So Equipped

Gear heads (Figs. E24, E25, E26 and E27) should have gear lubricant checked at 50 hour intervals. To check, remove check plug (15). Gear head housing should be ⅔ full of lithium base grease.

To disassemble gear heads shown in Figs. E24 and E25, remove trimmer head

or blade assembly. Remove screw (14) and clamp bolt (16). Remove seal (5) from housing (13) and remove snap ring (7). Remove bushing (6) as equipped. Remove snap ring (20). Use suitable puller to remove input shaft and gear (17). Use suitable puller to remove arbor shaft (9). Remove required snap rings and remove bearings and gears.

Gear heads shown in Figs. E26 and E27 are similarly constructed. Spacers (17 and 18—Fig. E27) may also be used in gear head shown in Fig. E26. Remove trimmer head or blade assembly. Remove screw (13—Figs. E26 or E27) and clamp bolt (14). Separate gear head from drive shaft housing tube. Remove snap ring (5), seal (6) and bushing (7). On gear head shown in Fig. E26, seal (6) must be removed to gain access to snap ring (5). Remove snap ring (21—Figs. E26 or E27). Use suitable pullers ro remove input shaft and arbor shaft assemblies. Remove required snap rings and remove bearings, gears and spacers.

To disassemble gear head shown in Fig. E28, separate gear head from drive shaft housing tube. Remove cotter pin (1), nut (2), adapter plate (3), blade and adapter plate (4). Remove snap ring (25) and use suitable puller to remove input shaft and bearing assembly (20). Remove plug (16). Remove seal (7) and snap ring (8). Remove

snap ring (14). Press arbor and bearing assembly from housing (19).

DRIVE SHAFT

All Models With Flexible Drive Shaft

Flexible drive shaft should be removed, cleaned and lubricated with lithium base grease at 18 hour intervals of use. To remove, separate drive shaft housing tube from engine assembly. Mark posi-

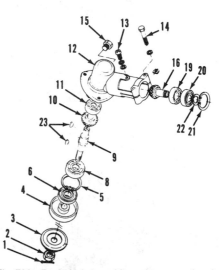

Fig. E26—Exploded view of flange type gear head with arbor shaft cut for keys (23). Refer to Fig. E27 for legend.

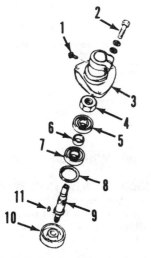

Fig. E23—Exploded view of bearing head used on some models.

1. Screw	5. Bearing	
2. Clamp screw	6. Spacer	9. Shaft
3. Housing	7. Bearing	10. Adapter
4. Nut	8. Snap ring	11. Key

Fig. E25—Exploded view of gear head assembly used on many models. Gear head shown is similar to gear head shown in Fig. E24 except arbor shaft has splines instead of keys.

1. Cotter pin
2. Nut
3. Adapter plate
4. Adapter plate
5. Seal
6. Bushing
7. Snap ring
8. Bearing
9. Arbor shaft
10. Snap ring
11. Gear
12. Bearing
13. Housing
14. Screw
15. Level check plug
16. Clamp bolt
17. Gear
18. Bearing
19. Bearing
20. Snap ring
21. Snap ring

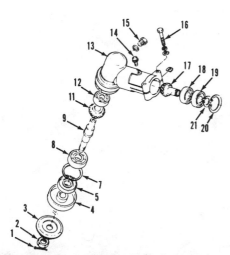

Fig. E24—Exploded view of gear head used on many models. Note arbor shaft (9) is cut for keys. Refer also to Fig. E25.

1. Cotter pin	9. Arbor shaft	
2. Nut	11. Gear	
3. Adapter plate	12. Bearing	17. Gear
4. Adapter plate	13. Housing	18. Bearing
5. Seal	14. Screw	19. Bearing
7. Snap ring	15. Level check plug	20. Snap ring
8. Bearing	16. Clamp bolt	21. Snap ring

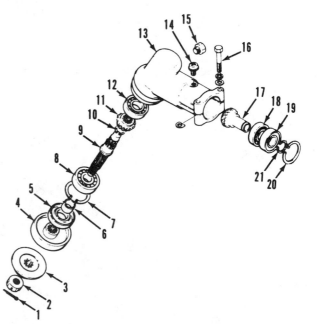

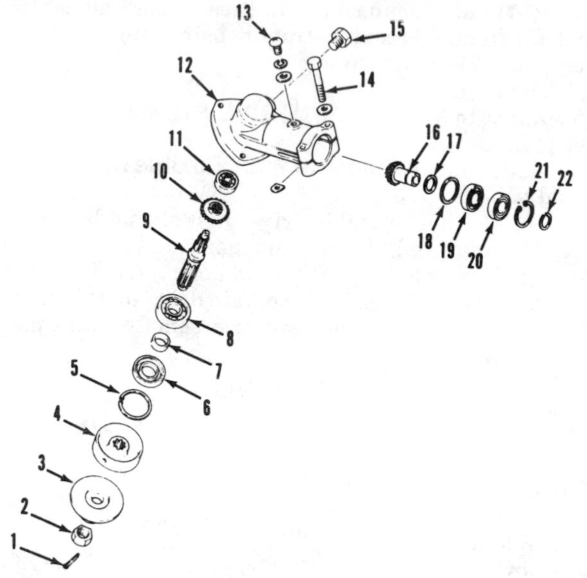

Fig. E27—Exploded view of gear head which is equipped with splined arbor shaft (9).

1. Cotter pin
2. Nut
3. Adapter plate
4. Adapter plate
5. Snap ring
6. Seal
7. Bushing
8. Bearing
9. Arbor shaft
10. Gear
11. Bearing
12. Housing
13. Screw
14. Clamp bolt
15. Level check plug
16. Gear
17. Spacer
18. Spacer
19. Bearing
20. Bearing
21. Snap ring
22. Snap ring

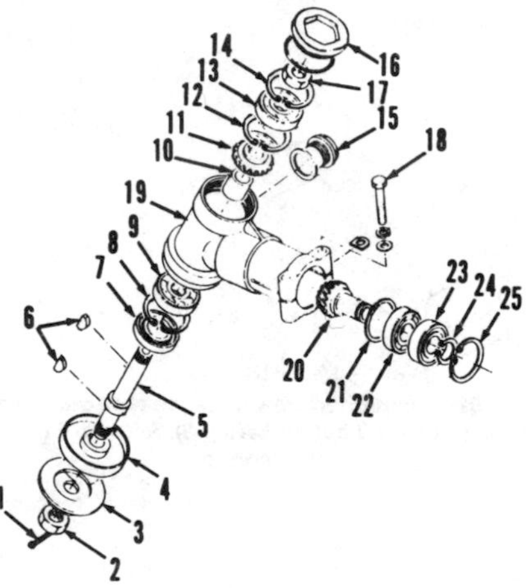

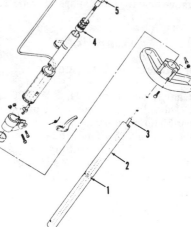

Fig. E29—Exploded view of housing and solid drive shaft.

1. Internal drive shaft bearing
2. Drive shaft housing
3. Solid steel drive shaft
4. Drive shaft bearing
5. Drive shaft adapter

Fig. E28—Exploded view of gear head used on SRM-302ADX models.

1. Cotter pin	10. Spacer	
2. Nut	11. Gear	
3. Adapter plate	12. Snap ring	19. Housing
4. Adapter plate	13. Bearing	20. Gear
5. Arbor shaft	14. Snap ring	21. Spacer
6. Keys	15. Level check plug	22. Bearing
7. Seal	16. Plug	23. Bearing
8. Snap ring	17. Nut	24. Snap ring
9. Bearing	18. Clamp bolt	25. Snap ring

tion of flexible drive shaft ends and remove drive shaft from housing. Reverse ends of drive shaft then reinstall shaft in housing. Reversing drive shaft each time it is serviced will greatly extend drive shaft life.

All Models With Solid Drive Shaft

A solid steel drive shaft is used on heavy duty models which may be equipped with grass and weed or saw blade. Drive shaft runs through housing and is supported in bushings in drive shaft housing tube (Fig. E29). No regular maintenance is required; however, if drive shaft is removed, lubricate with lithium base grease before reinstallation.

ELLIOT

GASOLINE POWERED STRING TRIMMERS

Model	Engine Manufacturer	Engine Model	Displacement
Tiger 4100	Kioritz	. . . . .	16.0 cc
Tiger 4200	Kioritz	. . . . .	21.2 cc

ENGINE INFORMATION

All Models

All Elliot trimmer models listed are equipped with Kioritz two-stroke air-cooled gasoline engines. Identify engine model by trimmer model or engine displacement. Refer to KIORITZ ENGINE SERVICE section of this manual.

FUEL MIXTURE

All Models

Manufacturer recommends mixing regular grade gasoline (unleaded is an acceptable substitute) with a good quality two-stroke air-cooled engine oil at a 25:1 ratio. Do not use fuel containing alcohol.

STRING TRIMMER

Tiger 4100 Model

Tiger 4100 model is equipped with a single strand semi-automatic trimmer head shown in Fig. EL10. Line may be manually advanced with engine stopped by pushing in on housing (9) while pulling on line. Procedure may have to be repeated to obtain desired line length. To advance line with engine running, operate engine at full rpm and tap housing (9) on the ground. Each time housing is tapped on the ground, a measured amount of trimmer line will be advanced.

To renew trimmer line, remove cotter key (10) and twist housing (9) counterclockwise to remove housing. Remove foam pad (6) and any remaining line on spool (3). Clean spool and inside of housing. Cut off approximately 25 feet (7.6 m) of 0.080 inch (2 mm) monofilament line and tape one end of line to spool (Fig. EL12). Wind line on spool in direction indicated by arrow on spool (Fig. EL13). Install foam pad with line end protruding from between foam pad and spool as shown in Fig. EL13. Insert line end through line guide and install housing and spring assembly on spool. Push in on housing and twist housing in a clockwise direction to lock into position. Install cotter key through hole in housing and cover.

Tiger 4200 Model

Tiger 4200 model is equipped with a single strand semi-automatic trimmer head shown in Fig. EL11. Line may be manually advanced with engine stopped

by pushing in on housing (12) while pulling on line. Procedure may have to be repeated until desired line length is obtained. To advance line with engine running, operate trimmer engine at full rpm and tap housing (12) on the ground. Each time housing is tapped on the ground, a measured amount of trimmer line is advanced.

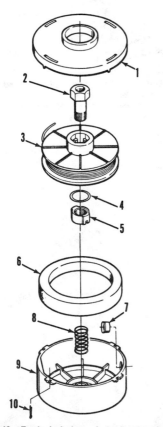

Fig. EL10—Exploded view of single strand semi-automatic trimmer head used on Tiger 4100 model.

1. Cover	6. Foam pad
2. Drive adapter	7. Line guide
3. Spool	8. Spring
4. "O" ring	9. Housing
5. Drive adapter nut	10. Cotter pin

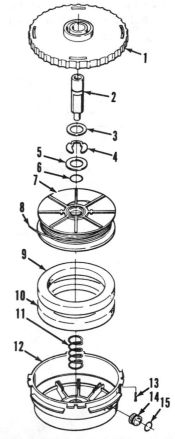

Fig. EL11—Exploded view of single strand semi-automatic trimmer head used on Tiger 4200 model.

1. Cover	6. Retainer ring	11. Spring
2. Drive adapter	7. Spool	12. Housing
3. Washer	8. Line	13. Cotter pin
4. Retainer	9. Foam pad	14. Line guide
5. Washer	10. Foam pad	15. Retainer

To renew trimmer line, remove cotter pin (13). Twist housing (12) counterclockwise and remove housing. Remove foam pads (9 and 10) and any remaining line from spool (7). Clean spool and inner area of housing. Cut off approximately 25 feet (7.6 m) of 0.080 inch (2 mm) monofilament line and tape one end of line to spool (Fig. EL12). Wind line on spool in direction indicated by arrow on spool (Fig. EL14). Install foam pads (9 and 10—Fig. EL11) so line is protruding from center of foam pads (Fig. EL 14). Insert end of line through line guide and install spool, housing and spring. Push in on housing and twist housing in a clockwise direction to lock in position and install cotter pin (13—Fig. EL11).

DRIVE SHAFT

All Models

All models are equipped with a flexible drive shaft enclosed in the drive shaft housing tube. Drive shaft has squared ends which engage adapters at each end. Drive shaft should be removed for maintenance at 50 hour intervals of use. Remove screw (4—Fig. EL15) and bolt (3) at bearing head housing and separate bearing head from drive shaft housing. Pull flexible drive shaft from housing.

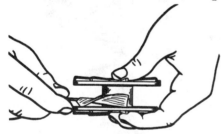

Fig. EL12—Tape one end of new line to center of spool as shown.

Lubricate drive shaft with lithium base grease and reinstall in housing with end that was previously at clutch end, at bearing head end. Reversing drive shaft ends extends drive shaft life. Make certain ends of drive shaft properly engage upper and lower square drive adapters when installing.

BEARING HEAD

All Models

All models are equipped with the bearing head shown in Fig. EL15. Bearing head is equipped with sealed bearings

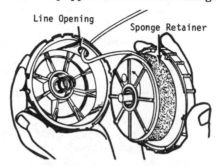

Fig. EL13—Install foam pad with line protruding between pad and spool as shown. Wind line in direction indicated by arrow on spool.

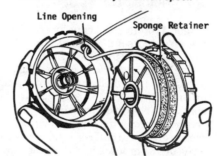

Fig. EL14—Install foam pads with line protruding from between pads. Wind line in direction indicated by arrow on spool.

and requires no regular maintenance. To disassemble bearing head, remove trimmer head assembly and cup washer (13). Remove screw (4) and bolt (3) and separate bearing head from drive shaft housing tube. Remove trimmer head assembly and cup washer (13). Remove snap ring (10) and use a suitable puller to remove arbor shaft (11) and bearing assembly. Remove nut (6) and press bearings (7 and 9) and spacer (8) from arbor shaft as required.

Fig. EL15—Exploded view of bearing head used on all models. Bearings (7 and 9) are sealed bearings and require no regular maintenance.

1. Drive shaft housing	8. Spacer
2. Shield	9. Bearing
3. Bolt	10. Snap ring
4. Screw	11. Arbor (output) shaft
5. Housing	12. Pin
6. Nut	13. Cup washer
7. Bearing	

GREEN MACHINE

GASOLINE POWERED
STRING TRIMMERS

Model	Engine Manufacturer	Engine Model	Displacement
1600	PPP	99D	31.0 cc
1730	Komatsu	G2E	25.4 cc
1800	PPP	99D	31.0 cc
1930	McCulloch	...	21.2 cc
1940	McCulloch	...	21.2 cc
2130	McCulloch	...	21.2 cc
2200	Komatsu	G2E	25.4 cc
2230	PPP	99E	31.0 cc
2340	Komatsu	G2E	25.4 cc
2500LP	Komatsu	G2D	22.5 cc
2510LP	Komatsu	G2D	22.5 cc
2540LP	Komatsu	G2D	22.5 cc
2800	Mitsubishi	T140	24.1 cc
2840	Mitsubishi	T140	24.1 cc
3000LP	Komatsu	G2K	25.4 cc
3000M	Mitsubishi	T140	24.1 cc
3000SS	Shindaiwa	...	24.1 cc
3010M	Mitsubishi	T140	24.1 cc
3040M	Mitsubishi	T140	24.1 cc
3540	Shindaiwa	...	24.1 cc
4000LP	Komatsu	G4K	41.5 cc
4000M	Mitsubishi	T200	40.6 cc
4500LP	Komatsu	G4K	41.5 cc

ENGINE INFORMATION

The models in this section are equipped with Komatsu, McCulloch, Mitsubishi, Piston Powered Products (PPP) or Shindaiwa engines. Refer to appropriate engine service section for engine service information.

FUEL MIXTURE

Manufacturer recommends mixing regular-grade gasoline, leaded or unleaded, with HMC One-Mix two-stroke engine oil mixed as indicated on container. Fuel:oil ratio should be 25:1 (5.12 ounces of oil to one U.S. gallon of gasoline) when using any other two-stroke oil, regardless of recommended ratio on oil container. Gasohol or other alcohol blended fuels are not approved by manufacturer.

STRING TRIMMER

All Models except 2200 and 3000SS

All models except 2200 and 3000SS may be equipped with the dual strand,

semi-automatic trimmer head (Tap-For-Cord) shown in Figs. GM10 or GM11. To extend line with trimmer engine stopped, push in on spool button and pull line ends out to desired length. To extend line with trimmer engine running, run engine at full rpm and tap spool button against the ground. Each time button is tapped a measured amount of line is advanced.

To renew trimmer line, refer to Fig. GM10. Push in on the two lock tabs on cap (10) and remove cap and spool. Remove any remaining line on spool. Clean spool, cap and inner cavity of housing. Refer to following table for line length and diameter:

	Line Length	Line Diameter
1600, 1730, 1800, 1930, 1940, 2130, 2230	15 ft. (4.6 m)	0.080 in. (2 mm)
2340, 2500LP, 2510LP, 2540LP, 2800, 2840, 3540 .	30 ft. (9.2 m)	0.080 in. (2 mm)

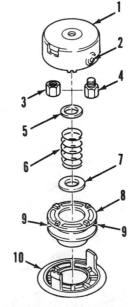

Fig. GM10—Exploded view of dual strand, semi-automatic (Tap-For-Cord) trimmer head used on most models except 2200 and 3000SS. Refer also to Fig. GM11. Note that only one adapter (3 or 4) is used according to model.

1. Housing	6. Spring
2. Line guides	7. Washer
3. Adapter	8. Spool
4. Adapter	9. Line notch
5. Washer	10. Cap

3000LP,		
3000M,		
3010M,		
3040M	50 ft.	0.095 in.
	(15.2 m)	(2.4 mm)
4000LP,		
4000M,		
4500LP	40 ft.	0.105 in.
	(12.2 m)	(2.6 mm)

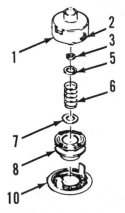

Fig. GM11—Exploded view of trimmer head used on some models that is similar to head shown in Fig. GM10. Note difference in housing and lack of adapter (3 or 4—Fig. GM10).

1. Housing		6. Spring
2. Line guides		7. Washer
3. Pal nut		8. Spool
5. Washer		10. Cap

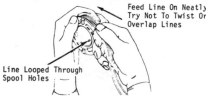

Fig. GM12—Rotate spool to wind line in direction indicated by arrow on spool.

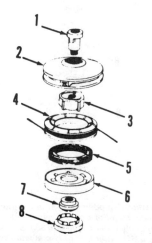

Fig. GM13—Exploded view of dual strand, semi-automatic trimmer head used on Model 2200.

1. Adapter	5. Foam pad
2. Upper housing	6. Lower housing
3. Cam	7. Screw (L.H.)
4. Spool	8. Button

Loop one end of new line through the two holes in spool (Fig. GM12) and rotate spool so line is wound tightly and neatly in direction indicated by arrow on spool. Slip lines into notches in spool (8—Fig. GM10 or GM11), insert line ends through line guides (2) and install spool in housing. Align locking tabs of trimmer head cap (10) with notches in housing (1) and snap cap onto housing. Advance line manually to make certain line is free.

Model 2200

Model 2200 is equipped with a dual strand, semi-automatic trimmer head shown in Fig. GM13. To extend line with trimmer engine stopped, pull on lines while pushing in on button (8). To extend line with engine running, operate trimmer engine at full rpm and tap button on the ground. Each time button is

Fig. GM14—Rotate spool to wind line in direction indicated by arrow on spool.

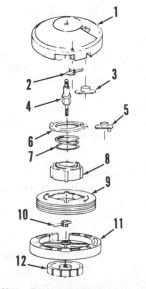

Fig. GM15—Exploded view of trimmer head used on Model 3000SS. Trimmer head may be manual line feed or semi-automatic line feed according to parts installed. Note parts designated (TFC) are for semi-automatic line feed heads and parts designated (M) are for manual line feed heads.

1. Upper housing	7. Spring
2. Line saver	8. Cam
3. Button (M)	9. Spool
4. Arbor	10. Line saver
5. Button (TFC)	11. Lower housing
6. Lock ring (M)	12. Lock knob

tapped a measured amount of new line will be advanced.

To renew line, unsnap button (8) from screw (7). Note that screw has left-hand threads. Remove screw (7), cover (6) and spool (4). Remove any remaining line from spool. Clean spool, cover and housing (2). Cut two 10-ft. (3.9 m) lengths of 0.080-in. (2 mm) diameter monofilament line. Insert one end of each line into each of the two holes in spool. Rotate spool to wind line evenly in direction indicated by arrow on spool (Fig. GM14). Install foam pad (5—Fig. GM13). Insert line ends through line guides and reinstall spool into housing. Spool is installed so side of spool with arrow will be towards the ground. Install cover, screw and snap button onto screw.

Model 3000SS

Model 3000SS may be equipped with trimmer head shown in Fig. GM15. Trimmer head may be a manual line feed or a semi-automatic (Tap-For-Cord) line feed according to model.

To extend line on manual models, stop trimmer engine. Loosen lock knob (12) and pull line ends out of housing until desired line length is obtained.

To extend line on semi-automatic trimmer head with engine stopped, push in on lock knob (12) while pulling lines from housing. Procedure may have to be repeated until desired line length has been obtained. To extend line with engine running, operate trimmer engine at full rpm and tap lock knob on the ground. Each time lock knob is tapped on the ground a measured amount of new line will be advanced.

To renew line on either model, remove lock knob (12—Fig. GM15) (note that lock knob has left-hand threads), cover (11) and spool (9). Remove any remaining line from spool. Clean spool, cover and inner cavity of housing (1). Cut two 20-ft. (6.1 m) lengths of 0.095-in. (2.4 mm) diameter monofilament line. Insert one end of each line into each of the two holes in inside wall of spool. Rotate spool to wind lines in direction indicated by arrow on spool (Fig. GM16). Insert line ends through line guides and install spool into upper housing with notched

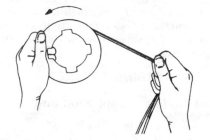

Fig. GM16—Rotate spool to wind line in direction indicated by arrow on spool.

SERVICE

side towards housing. Install cover and lock knob.

BLADE

All Models So Equipped

Some models may be equipped with one of the blades shown in Fig. GM17. To install blade, assemble parts in sequence shown in Fig. GM18. Note that screw (7) has left-hand threads. Make certain splines in cup washers (2 and 4) are aligned with splines on arbor and cup washer (4) is seated squarely.

DRIVE SHAFT

Curved Shaft Models

Models with a curved drive shaft housing tube are equipped with a flexible drive shaft. The drive shaft should be removed, cleaned and lubricated with lithium-base grease after every 10 hours of operation. Mark ends of drive shaft during removal so drive shaft can be reinstalled with ends in original position. The drive shaft cable may be wound for rotation in one direction only.

Straight Shaft Models

Models with a straight drive shaft housing tube may be equipped with a wire-wound shaft or a solid shaft. Peri-

odic maintenance is not required. If shaft is removed, lubricate with lithium-based grease before installation.

On some models the bushings (5—Fig. GM20) in the drive shaft housing (6) are renewable. A bushing removal and installation tool is available that is marked for correct locations of bushings. If tool is not available, mark locations of old bushings before removal so new bushings can be installed in correct location.

BEARING HEAD

Models 1600, 1730 and 1930

Models 1600, 1730 and 1930 are equipped with the bearing head shown in Fig. GM21. Bearing head requires no regular maintenance. A bearing kit (part 160305) is available for bearing head repair.

BEARING HEAD/LOWER CLUTCH

Model 1800

Model 1800 is equipped with a bearing head incorporated in the lower clutch unit (Fig. GM22). Bearing head is

equipped with sealed bearings and requires no regular maintenance.

To renew bearings or remove clutch assembly, remove trimmer head and cup washer (15). Remove the three bolts retaining bearing plate (11) to housing (4). Separate housing from bearing plate. Remove clutch shoe assembly (6) as required. Remove clutch drum (7) and shield (5). Press arbor shaft (8) from bearings. Remove snap rings (9 and 14). Remove bearings (10 and 13) and spacer (12).

GEAR HEAD

Split Gear Housing

Some models are equipped with a gear head that has a split housing (2 and 18—Fig. GM23). Lubricate gear head after every 10 hours of operation. To lubricate gear head, remove trimmer head or blade assembly. Pump a lithium-based grease through fitting on side of head until old grease is forced out. Failure to remove trimmer head or blade prior to lubrication will result in bearing/gear housing damage.

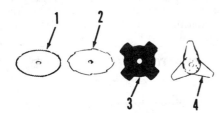

Fig. GM17—A variety of blades are offered for some models.

1. Saw blade
2. Eight-edge blade
3. Four-edge blade
4. Three-edge blade

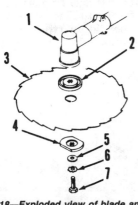

Fig. GM18—Exploded view of blade and attaching parts. Refer to text.

1. Gear head
2. Upper cup washer
3. Blade
4. Lower cup washer
5. Flat washer
6. Lockwasher
7. Screw (L.H.)

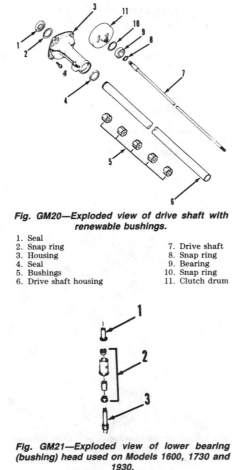

Fig. GM20—Exploded view of drive shaft with renewable bushings.

1. Seal
2. Snap ring
3. Housing
4. Seal
5. Bushings
6. Drive shaft housing
7. Drive shaft
8. Snap ring
9. Bearing
10. Snap ring
11. Clutch drum

Fig. GM21—Exploded view of lower bearing (bushing) head used on Models 1600, 1730 and 1930.

1. Arbor
2. Bushing kit
3. Arbor

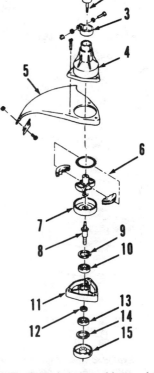

Fig. GM22—Exploded view of lower clutch and bearing head unit used on Model 1800.

1. Drive shaft housing
2. Drive shaft
3. Clamp
4. Housing
5. Shield
6. Clutch assy.
7. Clutch drum
8. Arbor
9. Snap ring
10. Bearing
11. Bearing plate
12. Spacer
13. Bearing
14. Snap ring
15. Upper cup washer

To disassemble gear head, remove trimmer head or blade assembly and separate gear head from drive shaft housing. Remove all bolts (19) and sep- arate gear housing halves (2 and 18). Remove shaft, bearing and gear assemblies. Press bearings and gears from input shaft (14) and arbor (5). Lubricate

parts during reassembly and pack housing with lithium-base grease prior to reassembly.

One-Piece Gear Housing

Some models are equipped with the one-piece gear housing shown in Fig. GM24. Lubricate gear head after every 30 hours of operation. To lubricate gear head, remove trimmer head or blade assembly. Pump lithium-base grease into grease fitting (1) until grease appears at seal (13) and pushes spacer (15) out. Make certain spacer (15) is pushed back into position and reinstall trimmer head or blade assembly. Failure to remove trimmer head or blade assembly prior to lubrication may result in bearing or housing damage.

To disassemble gear head, remove trimmer head or blade assembly. Separate gear head from drive shaft housing. Remove snap ring (7). Insert a screwdriver or suitable wedge into gear head housing split and carefully expand housing. Remove input shaft (3) and bearings as an assembly. Remove snap ring (6) and press bearings (4 and 5) from input shaft. Remove spacer (15) and snap ring (14). Use a suitable puller (Fig. GM25) to remove arbor (11—Fig. GM24) and bearing assembly. If bearing (9) stays in housing (8), heat housing to 140° F (60° C) and tap housing on a wooden block to remove bearing (9). Press bearing (12) and gear (10) from arbor. Lubricate all parts during reassembly. Pack housing with lithium-base grease prior to installing shaft and bearing assemblies.

THROTTLE TRIGGER AND CABLE

The inner throttle cable should be lubricated with engine oil after every 20 hours of operation.

The throttle cable should be adjusted so there is approximately 0.040-in. (1 mm) throttle trigger free play. To adjust free play, refer to Figs. GM26, GM27 or GM28, depending on type of carburetor, and reposition adjuster as needed.

Fig. GM23—Exploded view of a typical gear housing with a split housing.

1. Check plug
2. Housing
3. Bearing
4. Gear
5. Arbor
6. Bearing
7. Seal
8. Spacer
9. Upper cup washer
10. Lower cup washer
11. Flat washer
12. Lockwasher
13. Screw (L.H.)
14. Input shaft
15. Bearing
16. Bearing
17. Snap ring
18. Housing
19. Bolts

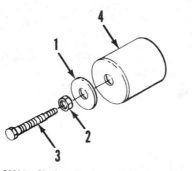

Fig. GM25—Shaft puller is available from Green Machine to pull arbor and input shaft.

1. Washer
2. Nut
3. Bolt
4. Puller body

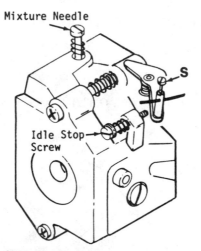

Fig. GM26—Loosen set screw (S) and move throttle cable to obtain throttle trigger free play of approximately 0.040 inch (1 mm).

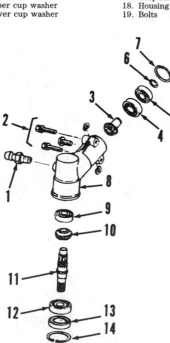
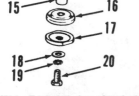

Fig. GM24—Exploded view of typical gear housing with a one-piece housing.

1. Grease fitting
2. Bolts
3. Input shaft
4. Bearing
5. Bearing
6. Snap ring
7. Snap ring
8. Housing
9. Bearing
10. Gear
11. Arbor
12. Bearing
13. Seal
14. Snap ring
15. Spacer
16. Upper cup washer
17. Lower cup washer
18. Flat washer
19. Lockwasher
20. Bolt (L.H.)

Fig. GM27—Loosen jam nut (3) and rotate adjuster nut (4) to obtain throttle trigger free play of approximately 0.040 inch (1 mm). Inner cable (1) slides in outer cable (2).

1. Inner throttle cable
2. Throttle cable housing
3. Jam nut
4. Adjustment nut

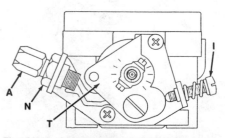

Fig. GM28—Loosen jam nut (N) and rotate adjuster nut (A) to obtain throttle trigger free play of approximately 0.040 inch (1 mm).

A. Cable adjuster nut
I. Idle speed adjustment screw
N. Jam nut
T. Throttle lever

Illustrations courtesy The Green Machine

GREEN MACHINE

GASOLINE POWERED BLOWERS

Model	Engine Manufacturer	Engine Model	Displacement
2600	Komatsu	G2D	22.5 cc
4600LP	Komatsu	...	41.5 cc

ENGINE INFORMATION

The models in this section are equipped with a Komatsu engine. Refer to Komatsu engine service section for engine service information.

FUEL MIXTURE

Manufacturer recommends mixing regular grade gasoline, leaded or unleaded, with HMC One-Mix two-stroke engine oil mixed as indicated on con-tainer. Fuel:oil ratio should be 25:1 (5.12 ounces oil mixed with one U.S. gallon of gasoline) when using any other two-stroke oil, regardless of recommended ratio on oil container. Gasohol or other alcohol blended fuels are not approved.

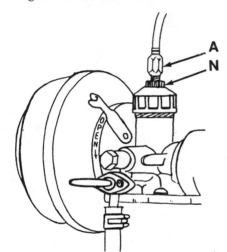

Fig. GM51—Loosen nut (N) and rotate adjuster (A) to adjust idle speed on Model 2600.

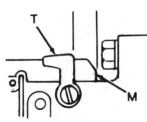

Fig. GM52—At wide-open throttle the carburetor throttle stop arm (T) should be parallel with carburetor mounting face (M).

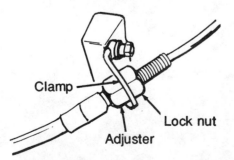

Fig. GM53—Turn cable adjusting nuts so carburetor throttle stop arm (T—Fig. GM52) is parallel with carburetor mounting face (M).

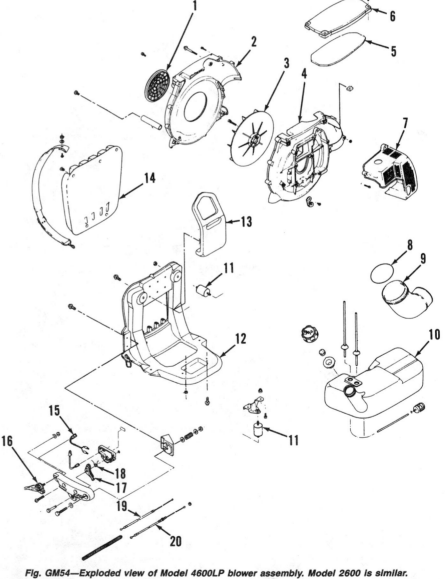

Fig. GM54—Exploded view of Model 4600LP blower assembly. Model 2600 is similar.

1. Intake guard	6. Cover	11. Rubber mounts	16. Throttle lever
2. Blower housing half	7. Engine cover	12. Backpack frame	17. Lever
3. Blower fan	8. "O" ring	13. Hanger bracket	18. Spring
4. Blower housing half	9. Elbow	14. Backpad	19. Choke cable
5. Gasket	10. Fuel tank	15. Stop switch	20. Throttle cable

THROTTLE CABLE

Model 2600

There is no free play in the throttle cable. Idle speed is adjusted by loosening lock ring (N—Fig. GM51) and rotating adjuster (A). Turn adjuster counterclockwise to increase idle speed. Recommended idle speed is 2800-3100 rpm.

Model 4600LP

The throttle cable should be adjusted so the throttle trigger and carburetor throttle plate are synchronized. With throttle trigger in wide-open position, the throttle stop arm (T—Fig. GM52) should be parallel with the carburetor mounting face (M). To adjust, relocate nuts (Fig. GM53) at throttle cable end. Tighten nuts after adjustment.

BLOWER FAN

To remove engine from blower housing, remove fuel tank (10—Fig. GM54) and engine cover (7). Remove screw retaining crankcase to backpack frame (12). Remove backpad (14) and pry off intake guard (1). Remove screws attaching blower fan (3) to flywheel. Remove four engine mounting screws and remove engine from blower housing.

To remove blower fan (3), remove cover (6) from blower housing. Remove screws holding blower housing halves (2 and 4) together. Separate blower housing and remove fan.

HOFFCO

GASOLINE POWERED STRING TRIMMERS

Model	Engine Manufacturer	Engine Model	Displacement
CRITTER, GT210, GT211, JP260	Kioritz	SI410	21.2 cc
GT14-B-T, LIL WHIZ 600, WT14H	Kioritz	G1-AH	13.8 cc
GT22, GT22A, GT225, GT225SPL, GT160B, GT160T, GT160TL, LIL WHIZ 1600, WT160H, WT160HT	Fuji	ECO1-R	15.4 cc
GT215B-H-T, JP215, JP270, WT215HB, WC215H-T	Kioritz	H1-AH	21.2 cc
GTX, GTX-R, HOFFIE 22, JP225, JP320, JP660, PC22, PC22A, PC225, PC380, WC22, WT230HT	Fuji	ECO2-R	22.5 cc
GT256SPL, JP300, WT250HT	Fuji	ECO2-F	25.6 cc
GT320, JP420, JP420D, WT320H	Tecumseh	TC200	32.8 cc
JP390, JP390XL	Fuji	ECO3-F	30.5 cc
P9, P10, P10A, P85, P850, WW76, WW77, WW85, WW88, WW850	Tecumseh	AV520-670	85 cc

ENGINE INFORMATION

All Models

Hoffco gasoline powered string trimmers and brush cutters may be equipped with two-stroke engines manufactured by Tecumseh, Fuji, or Kioritz. Refer to appropriate engine service section for engine service information.

FUEL MIXTURE

All Models

Hoffco recommends a fuel:oil mixture of 24:1. Mix regular grade gasoline with a high-quality oil recommended for air-cooled, two-stroke engines. Gasohol or other alcohol blended fuels are not approved by manufacturer.

STRING TRIMMER

Single Strand Trimmer Head

EARLY MODELS. Refer to Fig. HF10 for an exploded view of the semi-automatic, single strand trimmer head used on early models. To manually advance line with engine stopped, push hub assembly towards drive tube while pulling out line. Procedure may require repeating to provide adequate line length. To advance line with engine running, tap hub assembly on the ground with engine running at full throttle. Line will automatically advance a measured amount.

To disassemble trimmer head, remove cotter pin (13—Fig. HF10) and twist hub (12) counterclockwise. Remove hub and spool (7). Remove foam pads (9 and 10) and remaining old line. Clean parts.

New line length should be 25-ft. (7.6 m) long and with a diameter of 0.080 inch (2 mm). Tape one end to center of spool (Fig. HF11) and carefully wind line in direction indicated by arrow on spool (Fig. HF12). Leave a short length of line extending from spool and install foam pads (9 and 10—Fig. HF10) so line is between pads after installation (Fig. HF12). One side of spool is marked ''motor'' and the other side is marked ''top.''

Fig. HF10—Exploded view of early-type semi-automatic, single strand trimmer head.

1. Plate
2. Adapter
3. Washer
4. Retainer ring
5. Washer
6. Retainer ring
7. Spool
8. Line
9. Foam pad
10. Foam pad
11. Spring
12. Hub
13. Cotter pin
14. Line guide
15. Retainer

Side marked "motor" is installed towards cover (1—Fig. HF10). Side marked "top" is towards hub (12). Slip extended line end through line guide (14) in hub (12) and install spool in hub. Install hub and spool assembly on cover (1). Push in on hub against spring tension and rotate in a clockwise direction to engage lock tabs. Install cotter pin (13).

LATE MODELS. Refer to Figs. HF13 or HF14 for an exploded view of single strand semi-automatic trimmer head

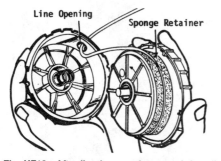

Fig. HF11—Tape line to spool center when installing new line.

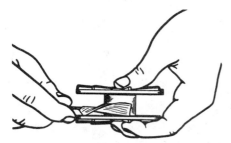

Fig. HF12—After line is wound on spool, install foam pads with line protruding as shown.

used on later models. To manually advance line with engine stopped, push button (7) and pull out line. Procedure may have to be repeated to obtain desired line length. To extend line with engine running, operate trimmer at full rpm and tap button (7) on the ground. Line will advance each time button is tapped.

To renew line on Critter and GT211 models, remove cover (5—Fig. HF13) by pushing in tabs that engage side of drum (1). Unscrew spool (4). Clean parts and remove any old line from spool. Insert end of 0.080-in. (2 mm) diameter monofilament line through hole in spool and wind line onto spool in direction indicated by arrow on spool. Insert outer end of line through line guide opening in drum (1) and install spool, button and cover.

To renew line on other late models, remove cover (8—Fig. HF14), button (7) and spool (5). Clean all parts thoroughly and remove any remaining old line from spool. Wind approximately 30 feet (9 m) of 0.080-in. (2 mm) diameter monofilament line onto spool in direction indicated by arrow on spool. Insert line end through line guide opening in drum (1) and install spool, button and cover.

Dual Strand Trimmer Head

Refer to Fig. HF15 for an exploded view of dual strand trimmer head used on some models. To manually advance line with engine stopped, push in on button (7) and pull on each line. Procedure may have to be repeated to obtain desired line length. To extend line with engine running, operate trimmer at full throttle and tap button (7) on the ground. Line will automatically advance a measured amount.

To install new trimmer line, hold drum firmly and turn spool in direction shown in Fig. HF16 to remove slack. Twist with a hard snap until plastic peg is between holes. Pull spool out of drum. Remove old line from spool. Spool will hold approximately 20 feet (6 m) of 0.095-in. (2.4 mm) diameter monofilament line. Insert end of new line through hole on spool (Fig. HF17) and pull line through until line is the same length on both sides of hole. Wind both ends of line at the same time in direction indicated by arrow on end of spool. Wind tightly and evenly from side to side and do not twist line. Insert ends of line through line openings, align pegs on drum with slots in spool and push spool into drum. Hold drum firmly, twist spool suddenly in direction shown in Fig. HF18 until peg enters hole with a click and locks spool in position.

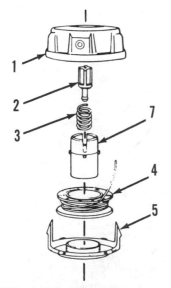

Fig. HF13—Exploded view of single strand semi-automatic trimmer head used on Critter and GT211 models.

1. Drum
2. Adapter
3. Spring
4. Spool
5. Cover
7. Button

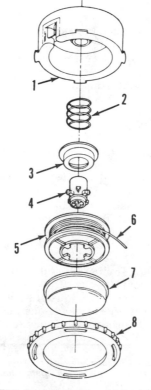

Fig. HF14—Exploded view of late-style semi-automatic, single line trimmer head.

1. Drum
2. Spring
3. Spring adapter
4. Inner cam
5. Spool
6. Line
7. Button
8. Cover

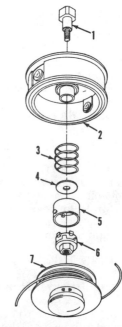

Fig. HF15—Exploded view of semi-automatic, dual line trimmer head.

1. Adapter
2. Drum
3. Spring
4. Washer
5. Outer cam
6. Inner cam
7. Spool

Illustrations courtesy Hoffco Inc.

Triple Strand Trimmer Head

Refer to Fig. HF19 for an exploded view of triple strand trimmer head used on some models.

To install new trimmer line, align hole in cup washer with hole in bearing head or gear housing. Insert a $^{5}/_{32}$-in. Allen wrench or similar tool into holes in cup washer and head to prevent drive shaft from turning. Turn tri-line head counterclockwise to remove head. Unscrew bolt (6) and remove cover (5). Clean inside of rotary head. Wind new line on spools as shown in Fig. HF20. Place spools (3—Fig. HF19) back in upper body (1), install springs (4) and cover (5).

TRI-KUT BLADE

The following Hoffco models may be equipped with a "TRI-KUT" blade (Fig. HF24) for cutting heavier weeds and grasses: GT210, GT211, JP215, JP225, JP260, JP270, JP300, JP320, JP390XL, JP420, JP660, P10, P85, P850, PC22, PC225, PC380, WT14, WT160, WT215, WT320, WW76, WW77, WW85, WW88 and WW850.

Models GT210, GT211, JP215, JP225, JP260, JP270, JP300, JP320, JP390XL, JP420, WT14, WT160, WT215 and WT320 may be equipped with an 8-in. "TRI-KUT" blade that fits a 20-mm arbor. Blade part number is 208559.

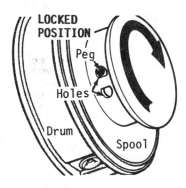

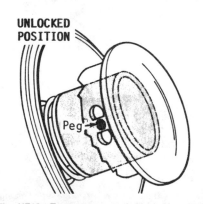

Fig. HF16—To remove spool, hold drum firmly and turn spool in direction shown to take up slack, then twist with a sudden snap until plastic peg is between holes as shown in lower view.

Models PC22, PC225 and PC380 may be equipped with an 8-in. "TRI-KUT" blade that fits a $^{5}/_{8}$-in. arbor. Blade part number is 205706.

Models P10, P85, P850, WW76, WW77, WW85, WW88, WW850 and JP660 may be equipped with an 11-in. "TRI-KUT" blade that fits a $^{5}/_{8}$-in. arbor. Blade part number is 10625.

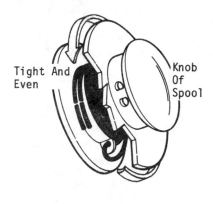

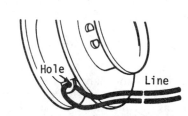

Fig. HF17—End of line must be inserted through hole on spool as shown in lower view. Wind line tightly in direction indicated by arrow on spool.

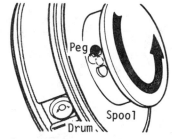

Fig. HF18—Hold drum firmly and twist suddenly to lock spool in position.

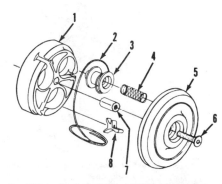

Fig. HF19—Exploded view of "Tri-Line" trimmer head used on some models.

1. Body
2. Line
3. Spool (3)
4. Spring
5. Cover
6. Screw
7. Retainer
8. Line retainer

To install a "TRI-KUT" blade, note rotation is clockwise as viewed from the engine end looking down the shaft toward the lower head. Make certain blade is centered on arbor and seated against the face of cup washer (3—Fig. HF25). Assemble the blade, arbor washer and anti-vibration lock nut in sequence shown in Fig. HF25. Insert a screwdriver tip (or similar tool) into the aligned notches of the lower head casting and cup washer, and hold them together. Make certain cup washer re-

Fig. HF20—Line is wound on spools and routed as shown.

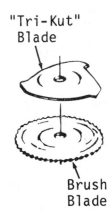

Fig. HF24—A "TRI-KUT" weed and grass blade and a brush blade are available for some models.

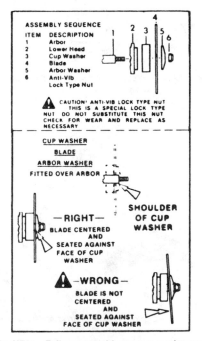

Fig. HF25—Follow assembly sequence shown to install blade.

mains in place flush against the lower head casting. This will allow nut, washer and blade to be tightened into position.

BRUSH BLADE

Models P10, P85, P850, WW76, WW77, WW85, WW88, WW850 and JP660 may be equipped with a 10-in. brush blade (Fig. HF24). Blade part number is 10624.

Models PC22, PC225 and PC380 may be equipped with a 9-in. brush blade (Fig. HF24). Blade part number is 205707.

Brush blade installation is similar to installation procedure outlined for "TRI-KUT" blade.

To sharpen brush blade, refer to Fig. HF26. Hoffco file template 208984 is available. Teeth angled toward the rear provide poor self-feed and saw feels dull. Forward angled teeth increase binding and kick-back.

If the blade has hit a stone or solid object, the entire damaged section must be filed off as shown in Fig. HF26. Make certain all teeth are the same length.

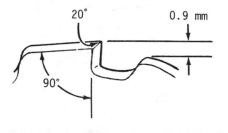

Fig. HF26—Sharpen brush blade to dimensions shown. Refer to text.

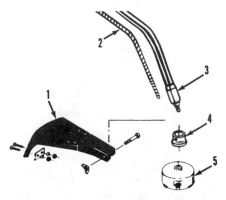

Fig. HF27—Exploded view of drive shaft housing and trimmer head.

1. Shield
2. Flexible drive shaft
3. Housing
4. Adapter
5. Trimmer head

Template provides correct filing height for front edge angle (90 degrees), side angle (20 degrees) and correct clearance depth of 0.9 mm (0.040 in.).

DRIVE SHAFT

All Models

All models are equipped with a flexible drive shaft. Some models are equipped with a grease fitting at upper end of drive shaft housing. Drive shaft should be removed, cleaned and inspected after every 20 hours of operation. To remove drive shaft, separate engine assembly from drive shaft tube. Mark drive shaft end locations and remove drive shaft. Clean and inspect drive shaft. Drive shaft is available as a unit assembly with drive shaft housing tube. Lubricate drive shaft with a high-quality, high-temperature wheel bearing grease. Exchange drive shaft ends before installation to extend drive shaft life. Be sure drive shaft properly engages clutch and trimmer head.

BEARING HEAD

Integrated Drive Shaft Housing/Bearing Head. Light-duty models are equipped with an integrated drive shaft housing/bearing head assembly (Fig.

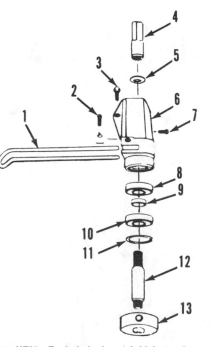

Fig. HF28—Exploded view of kick-stand-type bearing head.

1. Kick stand
2. Screw
3. Screw
4. Adapter
5. Washer
6. Housing
7. Screw
8. Bearing
9. Spacer
10. Bearing
11. Snap ring
12. Arbor
13. Cup washer

HF27). Bearings consist of two powder-metal-type bushings at upper end of housing and two prelubricated, precision ball bearings located between double seals. If bearing failure occurs, entire housing assembly must be renewed.

Kick-Stand-Type Bearing Head. Refer to Fig. HF28 for an exploded view of kick-stand-type bearing head. To service, remove clamping screw (3) and set screw (7). Slip head off trimmer tube. Remove trimmer head or blade assembly. Remove snap ring (11). Secure head assembly in a vise. Place a 1³/₈-in. wooden dowel with a ³/₄-in. hole drilled through center over arbor, against the square coupling end. Tap wooden dowel with a mallet. Bearings and arbor assembly will slip from lower head. Disassemble bearings, coupling and arbor assembly as necessary.

To reassemble, place coupling (4) and washer (5) on arbor (12). Press one bearing onto arbor. Install assembly into housing. Install spacer (9) and press remaining bearing onto arbor and into housing. Install snap ring.

Flange-Type Bearing Head. Refer to Fig. HF29 for an exploded view of flange-type bearing head used on some models. To service, remove shield (5). Remove clamp and screw securing head to drive shaft tube. Separate head from drive shaft housing tube. Remove trimmer head and cup washer (6). Remove snap ring (4) and press bearing and arbor assembly (3) from housing (1). Remove washer (2). Arbor and bearings (3) are renewed as an assembly.

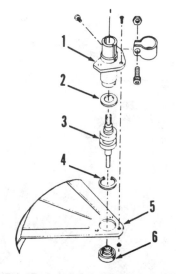

Fig. HF29—Exploded view of flange-type bearing head used on some models.

1. Housing
2. Washer
3. Arbor & bearing assy.
4. Snap ring
5. Shield
6. Cup washer

GEAR HEAD ASSEMBLY

All Models So Equipped

Refer to Fig. HF30 for an exploded view of gear head assembly. Gear head is equipped with sealed ball bearings, and periodic maintenance is not required.

To service gear head, remove trimmer head or blade assembly. Separate gear head from drive shaft housing tube. Remove retaining screws and separate housing halves. Lift input shaft (2) and bearing assembly from housing. Lift output shaft (7) and bearing assembly from housing. Renew bearings if required.

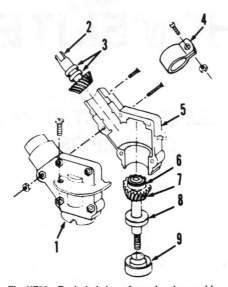

Fig. HF30—Exploded view of gear head assembly. Housing style may vary slightly.

1. Housing (left)
2. Input gear
3. Bearings
4. Clamp
5. Housing (right)
6. Bearing
7. Output gear & arbor
8. Bearing
9. Cup washer

HOMELITE

ELECTRIC STRING TRIMMERS

Model	Volts	Amps	Cutting Swath	Line Diameter
ST-20	120	2.2	10 in.	0.065 in.
ST-40	120	3.3	14 in.	0.065 in.
ST-60	120	4.0	16 in.	0.065 in.

ELECTRICAL REQUIREMENTS

Model ST-20, ST-40 and ST-60 string trimmers are designed to be used on electrical circuits with 120-volt alternating current. All models are double-insulated and do not require a ground wire. A two-wire extension cord is recommended and wire gage should be matched to cord length to prevent power loss. Use no more than 100 feet (30.5 m) of #18 wire or no more than 150 feet (45.7 m) of #16 wire.

All models are equipped with an automatic string advance system. The string trimmer will automatically feed out string by cycling the trimmer motor from on to off. The string spool must stop completely to advance the string, and if sufficiently short, it may be necessary to cycle the trimmer on and off several times. Operation is similar to that described in **OPERATING SAFETY** section in this manual.

If string will not advance on ST-40 or ST-60 models, it may be necessary to remove the high speed slider spring (the larger of the two springs) and compress the spring several times. This will reduce spring tension and allow the high speed slider to cock at a lower rpm. If a new high speed slider spring is being installed, it should also be compressed a couple of times before installation.

NOTE
All wiring must be routed exactly as shown in wiring diagram.

NOTE
All wiring must be routed exactly as shown in wiring diagram.
CAUTION
Make sure that the wire terminals do not touch after assembly of the motor housing

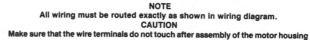

Fig. HL27-1—Wiring diagram showing correct routing of wire on Model ST-20.

Fig. HL27-2—Wiring diagram showing correct routing of wire on Models ST-40 and ST-60.

Illustrations courtesy Homelite Div. of Textron, Inc.

HOMELITE

ELECTRIC STRING TRIMMERS

Model	Volts	Amps	Cutting Swath	Line Diameter
ST-10, ST-10A	120	2.0	10 in.	0.065 in.
ST-30, ST-30C	120	3.3	12 in.	0.065 in.
ST-70	120	5.0	16 in.	0.065 in.

ELECTRICAL REQUIREMENTS

Models ST-10, ST-10A, ST-30, ST-30C and ST-70 string trimmers are designed to be used on electrical circuits with 120-volt alternating current. All models are double-insulated and do not require a ground wire. A two-wire extension cord is recommended and wire gage should be matched to cord length to prevent power loss. Use no more than 100 feet (30.5 m) of #16 wire or no more than 150 feet (45.7 m) of #14 wire.

STRING TRIMMER

Model ST-10

Model ST-10 is equipped with a single strand, manual advance trimmer head. To extend line, pull string down and around head until string extends from next slot in head.

To install new string, unscrew spool retaining nut and remove spool. New string length should be 15 feet (4.6 m). Attach string to hole in spool and wind string around spool in direction of arrow on spool. Reassemble trimmer head.

Models ST-10A, ST-30 And ST-30C

Models ST-10A, ST-30 and ST-30C are equipped with a single strand, automatic advance trimmer head. The string is advanced by a slider and spring mechanism when the trimmer motor is accelerated or decelerated.

Fig. HL28-1—Exploded view of trimmer. Trimmer head components (19 through 25) are used on later ST-70 models.

1. Motor housing
2. Switch
3. Trigger
4. Drive shaft housing
5. Liner
6. Drive shaft
7. Bearing
8. Gears
9. Gears
10. Spacer
11. Gear head housing
12. Deflector
13. Gear head housing
14. Housing
15. Spool
16. Spring
17. Slider
18. Cover
19. Cupped washer
20. Housing
21. Spool
22. Foam ring
23. Spring
24. Slider
25. Cover

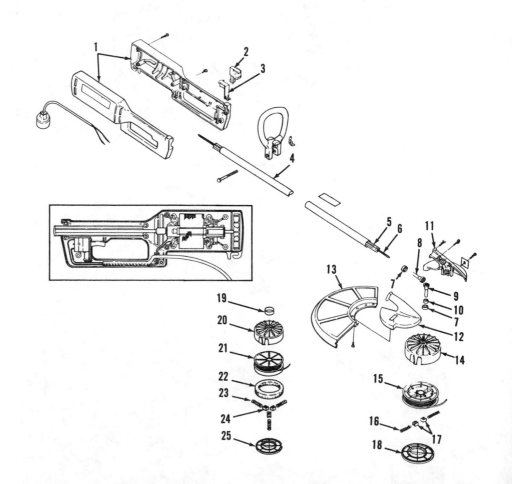

To install new string, twist and detach cover (18—Fig. HL28-1) and remove spool. New line length is 26 feet (7.9 m). Insert new line through hole in spool and tie end around post as shown in Fig. HL28-2. Wrap line around spool in direction indicated on spool. Install spool with 3 inches (7.6 cm) of line extended past eyelet and install cover.

Model ST-70

Model ST-70 may be equipped with an automatic advance trimmer head with single or dual strings. The string is advanced by a slider and spring mechanism when the trimmer motor is accelerated or decelerated. Refer to previous section covering ST-30 models for string installation on single string head.

To install string on dual strand trimmer head, twist and detach cover (25—

Fig. HL28-1). New line length should be 30 feet (9.1 m). Insert string through holes in the spool (Fig. HL28-3) and center the spool between the string ends. Pull loop tight and wind both lengths of string around the spool in direction indicated on spool. Position foam ring (22—Fig. HL28-1) around spool so string ends extend from top and bottom of foam ring. Place string ends in slots on spool as shown in Fig. HL28-3 (one string end will bend over outside of foam ring). Pass string ends through

Fig. HL28-2—When installing new line, attach string end to post. If line is proper diameter, the line will fit snugly in gage slot.

housing eyelets and reassemble trimmer head.

DRIVE SHAFT

The drive shaft does not require periodic maintenance. Lubricate drive shaft with molybdenum disulfide grease if removed. The drive shaft liner (5—Fig. HL28-1) is available separately.

GEAR HEAD

Models ST-30, ST-30C And ST-70

Models ST-30, ST-30C and ST-70 are equipped with a gear head. Periodic maintenance is not required. Individual gears and bearings are available. Gears should be lubricated with molybdenum disulfide grease if unit is disassembled.

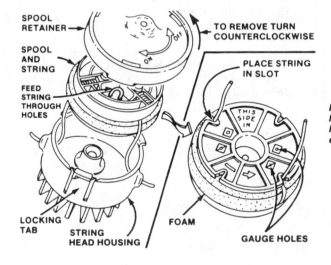

Fig. HL28-3—View of properly assembled trimmer head on Model ST-70 with dual strings. Note gage holes in spool to determine if line is proper diameter. Line will pass through one hole but not "no go" hole.

Illustrations courtesy Homelite Div. of Textron, Inc.

HOMELITE

GASOLINE POWERED STRING TRIMMERS

Model	Engine Make	Displ.
ST-80	Homelite	26.2 cc
ST-100	Homelite	26.2 cc
ST-120	Homelite	26.2 cc
ST-160	Homelite	26.2 cc
ST-160A	Homelite	26.2 cc
ST-165	Homelite	26.2 cc
ST-180	Homelite	26.2 cc
ST-200	Homelite	31.2 cc
ST-210	Homelite	31.2 cc
ST-260	Homelite	26.2 cc
ST-310	Homelite	31.2 cc

ENGINE INFORMATION

All models are equipped with a Homelite engine. Refer to appropriate HOMELITE ENGINE SERVICE section of this manual.

STRING TRIMMER

All Models Except ST-160A, ST-165, ST-260 And ST-310.

These models are equipped with an automatic string advance system (Model ST-210 is a brushcutter in a standard configuration but may be optionally equipped as a string trimmer). The string trimmer will automatically feed out string by cycling the engine throttle from full speed to idle speed. String head (17—Fig. HL29-1, HL29-3 and HL29-4) encases two slider and spring pairs for high speed and low speed engagements of string spool (18). Heavy spring (13) is used with high speed slider (14) and light spring (16) is used with low speed slider (15). Note position of lugs in Fig. HL29-2 to identify sliders. When string length is at desired cutting length engine speed is approximately 6500 rpm and high speed slider lug drives the string spool. As the string is shortened, engine speed will increase so that centrifugal force disengages the high speed slider lug from the string spool lug. The low speed slider lug picks up a string spool lug which allows the high speed slider to cock behind a string spool lug.

When the engine is slowed to idle speed, the low speed slider will disengage and the high speed slider will engage the next string spool lug thereby allowing the string spool to rotate 1/6 turn and feed out string. The amount of string ad-

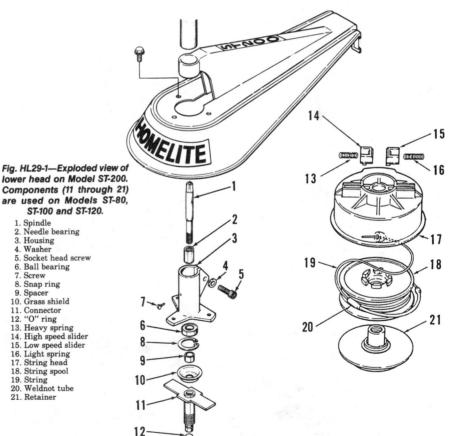

Fig. HL29-1—Exploded view of lower head on Model ST-200. Components (11 through 21) are used on Models ST-80, ST-100 and ST-120.

1. Spindle
2. Needle bearing
3. Housing
4. Washer
5. Socket head screw
6. Ball bearing
7. Screw
8. Snap ring
9. Spacer
10. Grass shield
11. Connector
12. "O" ring
13. Heavy spring
14. High speed slider
15. Low speed slider
16. Light spring
17. String head
18. String spool
19. String
20. Weldnot tube
21. Retainer

vanced automatically is determined by the amount of string on the spool. Approximately 2¼ inches (57 mm) of string will be advanced from a full spool, and about ¾ inch (19 mm) from a nearly empty spool.

If automatic string advance malfunctions, be sure proper string is used, string advance components move freely and engine is properly tuned and will run at

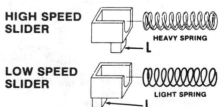

Fig. HL29-2—Note position of lug (L) when identifying high and low speed sliders. Be sure correct spring is installed in slider.

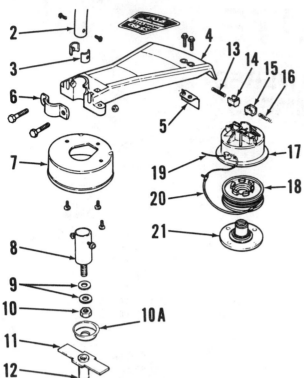

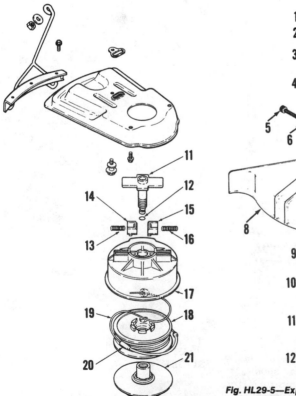

Fig. HL29-3—Exploded view of lower head on Models ST-160 and ST-180.

2. Drive tube
3. Inner clamp
4. Deflector
5. Cut-off blade
6. Clamp
7. Grass shield
8. Housing
9. Washer
10. Nut
10A. Shield
11. Connector
12. "O" Ring
13. Heavy spring
14. High speed slider
15. Low speed slider
16. Light spring
17. String head
18. String spool
19. String
20. Weldnot tube
21. Retainer

Fig. HL29-4—Exploded view of lower head on Model ST-80. Models ST-100 and ST-120 are similar.

11. Connector
12. "O" ring
13. Heavy spring
14. High speed slider
15. Low speed slider
16. Light spring
17. String head
18. String spool
19. String
20. Weldnot tube
21. Retainer

Fig. HL29-5—Exploded view of bruschcutter head which is standard on Model ST-210 and optional on Model ST-200.

1. Snap ring
2. Ball bearing
3. Pinion shaft
4. Needle bearing
5. Clamp screw
6. Washer
7. Socket head screw
8. Head
9. Ring gear
10. Ball bearing
11. Spindle
12. Snap ring
13. Cup washer
14. Shield
15. Nut

full speed of at least 7500 rpm. Engine must idle below 4200 rpm (refer to engine service section for carburetor adjustment).

Insufficient string length (less than 2 inches) will not allow automatic string advance. If string is less than 2 inches, remove string head and manually extract string until string length is 5 inches. Install Weldnot tube so large end is towards outer string end.

Spool retainer (21—Figs. HL29-1, HL29-3 and HL29-4) has left-hand threads and must be turned clockwise for removal. Connector (11) has left-hand threads.

Models ST-200 and ST-210, remove snap ring (8—Fig. HL29-1) and press bearings out of housing. When installing bearings, install needle bearing (2) with lettered end up and ball bearing (6) with sealed end out. Install snap ring (8) with square edge to outside.

Be sure connector (11—Figs. HL29-1, HL29-3 and HL29-4) is fully seated in recess of string head (17) to prevent slider ejection. Apply a light coat of multipurpose grease to bore of spool before installation.

Models ST-160A, ST-165, ST-260 And ST-310

Refer to Fig. HL29-6 for an exploded view of the string trimmer head assembly.

To remove string trimmer spool (13), unscrew retainer (14)—retainer has left-hand threads. When installing string, insert string end through holes in spool as shown in Fig. HL29-7. Wrap string around spool in direction of arrow on spool. Do not wrap more than 25 feet (7.6 m) of string onto spool. Position string between lugs on spool before passing string through outlet of string head. To check string advance operation, alternately press down and release retainer (14) while pulling on string.

To separate lower drive shaft assembly (8) from string head (10), retaining ring (11) must be cut and removed. To gain access to the retaining ring press drive shaft assembly down into string head approximately ¼ inch (6.4 mm). Cut retaining ring, then remove and discard ring. DO NOT attempt to reuse retaining ring. Separate drive shaft assembly from string head. When installing drive shaft assembly and string head, install retaining ring so inner points are towards end of drive shaft.

BRUSHCUTTER

A brushcutter head is standard on Model ST-210 and optional on Model ST-200. Refer to Fig. HL29-5 for an exploded view. Blade retaining nut (15) has

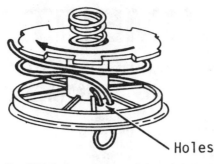

Fig. HL29-7—Insert string end through holes in spool as shown on Models ST-160A, ST-165, ST-260 and ST-310.

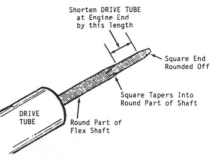

Fig. HL29-8—Shorten drive shaft as shown to prevent rounding off cable end.

Fig. HL29-6—Exploded view of lower head on Models ST-160A, ST-165, ST-260 and ST-310.

2. Drive tube
3. Inner clamp
4. Deflector
5. Cut-off blade
6. Clamp
7. Grass shield
8. Lower drive shaft assy.
9. Screw
10. String head
11. Retaining ring
12. Spring
13. String spool
14. Retainer

left-hand threads and must be turned clockwise for removal. Head (8) is aligned with drive tube by screw (7) which aligns holes in head and drive tube. Loosen clamp screw (5) to remove head from drive tube. When assembling head, install bearing (2) with sealed side up.

Note that the brushcutter kit for early Model ST-200 uses ball bearing (2) and needle bearing (4) to support pinion shaft (3). Two ball bearings (2) are used to support the pinion shaft on later models.

DRIVE SHAFT

Models ST-160 and ST-180 are equipped with a flexible drive shaft which should be inspected and greased annually. Detach drive tube from engine housing and pull drive shaft from drive tube. Clean drive shaft. Swap drive shaft end-to-end before inserting in drive tube to prolong shaft service life. While inserting drive shaft into drive tube, apply molybdenum disulfide grease to shaft; do not apply excess grease. Reconnect drive tube to engine housing while being sure drive shaft is properly connected.

Models ST-200 and ST-210 are equipped with a flexible drive shaft between the engine and drive head. The flexible drive shaft should be removed, inspected and lubricated after every 25 hours of operation. To remove drive shaft, remove screw (7—Fig. HL29-1 or HL29-5) and loosen clamp screw (5). Slide head off drive tube and pull flexible shaft from tube. Clean and inspect shaft, then lubricate shaft with lithium grease. Insert shaft into drive tube (shaft ends are identical and shaft ends may be reversed to extend shaft life). Install head while turning head to engage shaft ends in engine and head. Align holes in front side of head and drive tube and install screw (7). Tighten clamp screw (5) so head will not turn.

For early Models ST-200 and ST-210, bushing kit number A-96064 is available to install a bushing in the lower end of the drive tube. There must be at least 1¼ inches from bottom of drive tube to bottom of flex shaft. New drive tubes are equipped with bushings.

Early production ST-200 and ST-210 models were produced with a drive shaft housing having a bump on the end which was designed to index with a notch in the engine housing. Service parts will supply a drive shaft housing, part number A-96205-1, without a bump which is designed to fit all early and late models.

Some ST-160 and ST-180 models may have a drive shaft housing that is too long to allow full engagement of the flexible drive shaft. When a failure occurs, the drive shaft will be rounded off at the end as shown in Fig. HL29-8. Measure the length of the square tapers on the drive shaft and shorten the drive shaft housing at the engine end the same amount.

HOMELITE
GASOLINE POWERED
STRING TRIMMERS

Model	Cutting Swath	Line Diameter	Engine Make	Displacement
HBC-18	18 in.	0.095 in.	Homelite	30 cc
HBC-30, HBC-30B	18 in.	0.095 in.	Homelite	30 cc
HLT-16	16 in.	0.095 in.	Homelite	30 cc
HLT-17C	17 in.	0.095 in.	Homelite	30 cc
HLT-18	18 in.	0.095 in.	Homelite	30 cc
ST-145	15 in.	0.080 in.	Homelite	25 cc
ST-155	15 in.	0.080 in.	Homelite	25 cc
ST-175, ST-175C, ST-175BC	17 in.	0.080 in.	Homelite	25 cc
ST-185, ST-185C	17 in.	0.080 in.	Homelite	25 cc
ST-285, ST-285BC	17 in.	0.080 in.	Homelite	25 cc
ST-385, ST-385C	17 in.	0.105 in.	Homelite	25 cc
ST-485	17 in.	0.105 in.	Homelite	25 cc

ENGINE INFORMATION

All models are equipped with a Homelite engine. Refer to appropriate Homelite engine section for service information.

STRING TRIMMER

E-Z Line Advance. All models except Models ST-385, ST-385C and ST-485 are equipped with the Homelite E-Z Line Advance system as standard equipment. Models ST-385, ST-385C and ST-485 may be equipped with the Homelite E-Z Line Advance system as optional equipment. Models ST-145 and ST-155 use a single line system while other models use a dual line system. String is advanced by tapping the spool retainer on the ground while the engine is running. Each time

the retainer is tapped, the spring-loaded spool rotates $\frac{1}{6}$ turn and feeds out the string.

To replace or rewind the spool, remove spool retainer by turning counterclockwise. Lift spool with compression spring from stringhead. Inspect spool lugs and shaft bore for wear. Replace as required. Replacement spools are available prewound with 25 feet (7.6 m) of string.

To rewind string on spool for a single line system, insert one end of a 25-ft. length of premium quality 0.080-in. (2 mm) diameter string through one of the two holes in the outer spool flange and then back through the other hole forming a small loop. Pull loop tight. For a dual line system, center the spool in the 25-ft. (7.6 m) length of string (see table for line diameter) before pulling the loop tight. See Fig. HL30-1.

Wind string clockwise (when viewed from the bottom spool flange) in an even pattern (Fig. HL30-2). Be careful not to twist the strings when winding the spool on a dual line system.

To install the spool and string into the stringhead (Fig. HL30-3), capture the string(s) in the slotted lug(s) on the spool. Feed the string through the eyelet(s). Slide the spool onto the shaft. Push the spool into the string head until the string(s) are released from the lugs. Press down on the spool while installing the retainer by turning clockwise.

To test the operation of the string advance, pull on the string while alternately pressing down on end releasing the retainer.

Manual Advance. Models ST-385, ST-385C and ST-485 may be equipped with a manual advance trimmer head. Ad-

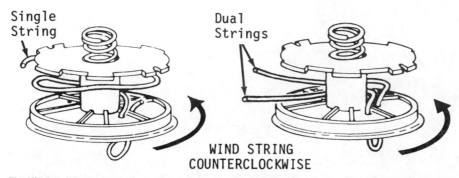

Single String

Dual Strings

WIND STRING
COUNTERCLOCKWISE

Fig. HL30-1—Wind string around spool in direction shown. Left view shows proper attachment of string to spool for single line models. Drawing on right shows correct attachment for dual string models.

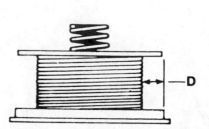

Fig. HL30-2—Line should be wound around spool until about $\frac{1}{4}$ inch (6.4 mm) from top (D).

Illustrations courtesy Homelite Div. of Textron, Inc.

vancing the string is accomplished by loosening the retainer nut by turning clockwise (L.H. thread). Loosen retainer enough so string can be pulled out about ¼ inch (6.4 mm) from string head. Pull down on spool and rotate to advance string. Each string should measure approximately 6½ inches (16.5 cm).

After advancing the string, rotate spool slightly in either direction to line up locating lugs on spool with locating holes in string head. Tighten retainer by turning counterclockwise (L.H. thread).

To replace or rewind the spool, remove retainer by turning clockwise (L.H. thread). Pull spool from string head. To rewind string on spool, insert one end of an 18-ft. (5.5 m) length of premium quality 0.105-in. (2.7 mm) diameter string through one of the two holes in the spool and then back through the other hole. Center the spool in the 18-ft. (5.5 m) length of string. Pull loop tight and wind both lengths of string in the same (either) direction around the spool taking care not to twist the string (Fig. HL30-4).

Install spool and string into string head (Fig. HL30-5). Feed 6½ inches (16.5 cm) of string through each eyelet. Tilt spool and place into string head taking care that the string does not slip under the spool flange. Rotate spool slightly in either direction to engage locating lugs on spool with locating holes in string head. Install retainer by turning counterclockwise (L.H. thread).

BLADE

All models except HLT-16, HLT-18, ST-145, ST-155 and ST-175 may be equipped with blades (3—Fig. HL30-6). The blade can be installed after removing the string head adapter shaft. Prevent lower head shaft or gear head shaft rotation by inserting a ⅛-in. (3.2 mm) diameter rod through hole or slot in upper flange

washer. Unscrew adapter shaft by turning clockwise on Models HBC-30, HBC-30B, ST-385, ST-385C and ST-485 or counterclockwise on all other models.

DRIVE SHAFT

All models with a curved drive shaft tube (12—Figs. HL30-7 and HL30-8) are equipped with a flexible drive shaft (21) that should be inspected and lubricated annually. Detach drive tube from engine housing or tube adapter and pull drive shaft from drive tube. Clean drive shaft. Swap drive shaft end-to-end before inserting in drive tube to prolong shaft service life. While inserting drive shaft into drive tube, apply molybdenum disulfide grease to shaft.

Reconnect drive tube to engine housing or tube adapter making sure drive shaft is properly connected.

Models HBC-30, HBC-30B, ST-285, ST-285BC, ST-385, ST-385C and ST-485 are equipped with a solid drive shaft (21—Figs. HL30-9 and HL30-10) that does not require periodic maintenance. Lubricate shaft if removed.

CLUTCH DRUM and TUBE ADAPTER

The clutch drum is supported in the tube adapter by a ball bearing. The bearing is pressed into the tube adapter and retained by an internal snap ring. The square adapter end of the clutch drum is pressed through the ball bearing and retained by an external snap ring.

LOWER BEARING HEAD

Models HBC-18, ST-185 and ST-185C

Removal of the lower bearing head assembly from the drive shaft housing is accomplished by loosening the clamp

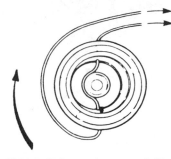

Fig. HL30-4—String can be wrapped either direction on manual advance models, but line should be routed through spool as shown.

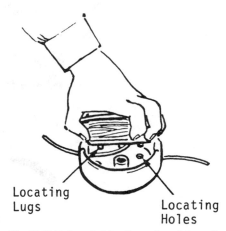

Locating Lugs

Locating Holes

Fig. HL30-5—Insert string through eyelets and insert spool as shown. Be sure lugs on spool engage holes.

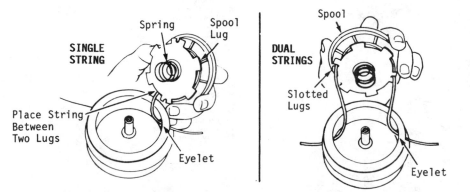

SINGLE STRING

Spring   Spool Lug

Place String Between Two Lugs

Eyelet

DUAL STRINGS

Spool

Slotted Lugs

Eyelet

Fig. HL30-3—Automatic feed models with a single string should position the string between lugs as shown at left. Models with dual strings should have strings located in slotted lugs as shown at right.

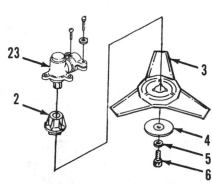

Fig. HL30-6—Model ST-285BC may be equipped with blade assembly shown above. Blade assembly on Models HLT-17C and ST-175BC is similar.

1. Gear head
2. Adapter
3. Blade
4. Cupped washer
5. Lockwasher
6. Screw

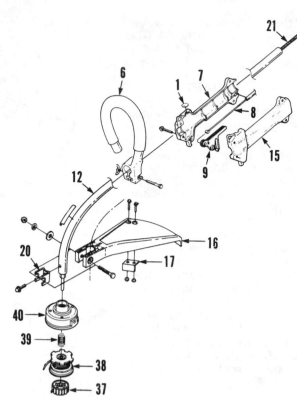

Fig. HL30-7—Exploded view of string trimmer assembly used on Models HLT-16, HLT-18, ST-145, ST-155 and ST-175. Model HLT-17C is similar but is equipped with throttle assembly shown in Fig. HL30-8. Refer to Fig. HL30-8 for parts identification except for:

6. Front handle
20. Clamp.

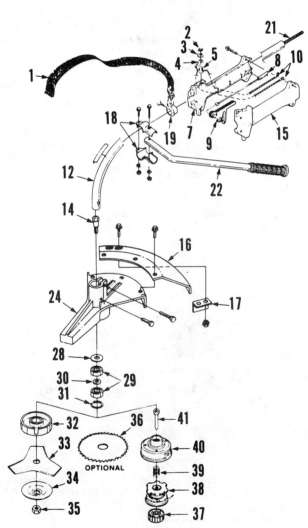

Fig. HL30-8—Exploded view of Model HBC-18 and ST-185 string trimmer assembly, saw and Tri-Arc blade. "Machete" blade (25—Fig. HL30-10) may be used.

1. Harness
2. Nut
3. Switch plate
4. Grounding washer
5. Stop switch
7. Grip half
8. Throttle cable
9. Throttle trigger
10. Stop switch lead wires
12. Drive shaft housing
14. Spindle shaft
15. Grip half
16. Grass deflector
17. Cut-off blade
18. Handle bar clamp
19. Hanger bracket
21. Flexible shaft
22. Handle bar
24. Lower bearing housing
28. Thrust washer
29. Ball bearings
30. Bearing spacer
31. Snap ring
32. Flange washer
33. Tri-Arc blade
34. Cupped washer
35. Locknut
36. Saw blade
37. Spool retainer
38. Spool & line
39. Compression spring
40. Housing & eyelet
41. Drive connector

screw and removing the locating screw on the side of the head. Remove the string head adapter shaft or the blade. Unscrew the flanged washer from the spindle shaft and remove the spindle shaft. Remove snap ring (31—Fig. HL30-8) from the bottom of the lower bearing head. Press the two ball bearings, spacer and thrust washer from the lower head, Inspect bearing and renew if necessary.

GEAR HEAD

Models HBC-30, HBC-30B, ST-285, ST-285BC, ST-385, ST-385C and ST-485

To remove gear head (23—Figs. HL30-9 and HL30-10), loosen the two clamp screws and locating screw. Slide gear head from drive shaft housing. Gear head must be serviced as a unit assembly; individual components are not available.

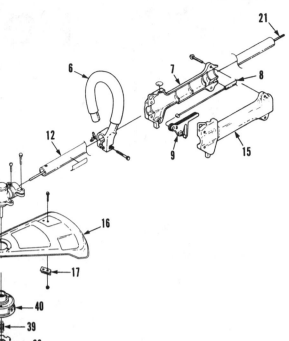

Fig. HL30-9—Exploded view of Model ST-285 string trimmer assembly. Refer to Fig. HL30-8 for legend except for:
6. Front handle
23. Gear head.

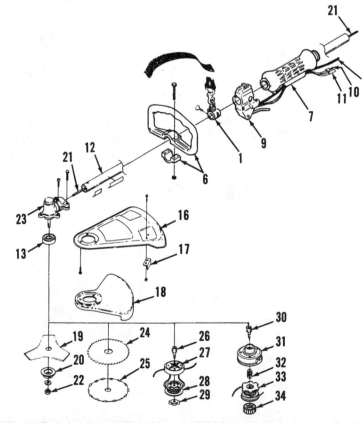

Fig. HL30-10—Exploded view of string trimmer and brush cutter components used on later Model ST-385 and Models HBC-30 and HBC-30B. Model ST-485 is similar, but with a different handle bar configuration. Early Model ST-385 is equipped with a handle bar throttle assembly similar to Fig. HL30-8.

1. Harness & hanger bracket	12. Drive shaft housing	23. Gear head
6. Handle assy.	13. Flange washer	24. Saw blade
7. Grip	16. Grass deflector	25. "Machete" blade
8. Throttle cable	17. Cut-off blade	26. Drive connector (L.H. thread)
9. Throttle trigger & ignition switch	18. Saw guard	27. Housing & eyelet
10. Ignition lead	19. Tri-Arc blade	28. Spool & line
11. Ground lead	20. Flange washer	29. Spool retainer (L.H. thread)
	21. Drive shaft	30. Drive connector (L.H. thread)
	22. Nut (L.H. thread)	31. Housing
		32. Compression spring
		33. Spool & line
		34. Retainer (L.H. thread)

HOMELITE

BRUSHCUTTER

Model	Engine Make	Displ.
ST-400	Homelite	54 cc

ENGINE INFORMATION

Model ST-400 brushcutter is powered by a Homelite engine. Refer to appropriate HOMELITE ENGINE SERVICE section of this manual.

SAW BLADE

The saw blade may be removed after unscrewing retaining nut. Prevent shaft rotation by inserting a suitable pin through the grass shield. Note when in-stalling a toothed saw blade that shaft rotation is clockwise as viewed from underside.

DRIVE SHAFT

The flexible drive shaft should be removed, inspected and lubricated after every 25 hours of operation. To remove drive shaft, loosen clamp screw and remove screw in front side of lower head (26—Fig. HL32-1). Slide head off drive tube (23) and pull flexible shaft (15) from tube. Clean and inspect shaft, then lubricate shaft with Homelite Multi-Purpose Grease 17237 or a suitable lithium grease. Insert shaft into drive tube (shaft ends are identical and shaft ends may be reversed to extend shaft life). With 3-5 inches (7.6-12.7 cm) of shaft extending from drive tube engage shaft in lower head. Then while turning lower head so upper end of shaft engages clutch drum, install lower head on drive tube. Align holes in front side of lower head and drive tube and install screw. Tighten clamp screw so lower head will not turn.

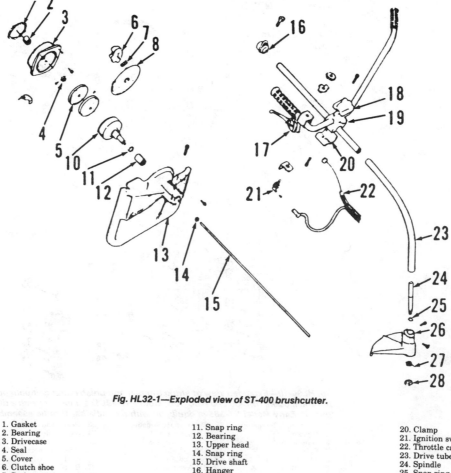

Fig. HL32-1—Exploded view of ST-400 brushcutter.

1. Gasket	11. Snap ring
2. Bearing	12. Bearing
3. Drivecase	13. Upper head
4. Seal	14. Snap ring
5. Cover	15. Drive shaft
6. Clutch shoe	16. Hanger
7. Spring	17. Throttle lever
8. Clutch hub	18. Clamp
10. Clutch drum	19. Block

20. Clamp
21. Ignition switch
22. Throttle cable
23. Drive tube
24. Spindle
25. Snap ring
26. Lower head
27. Bearing
28. Snap ring

Homelite

TRIMMER/BRUSHCUTTER

Model	Cutting Swath	Engine Make	Displacement
HK-18	14 in.	Homelite	18.4 cc
HK-24	16 in.	Homelite	24.1 cc
HK-33	18 in.	Homelite	33.3 cc

ENGINE INFORMATION

All models are equipped with a Homelite engine. Refer to appropriate HOMELITE ENGINE SERVICE section of this manual.

STRING TRIMMER

Model HK-18 is equipped with a string trimmer head while Models HK-24 and HK-33 may be equipped with a string trimmer head or brushcutting blade.

The string trimmer head may be removed after unscrewing retaining nut (L.H. threads). The string is advanced manually by unscrewing retaining nut, then pulling out spool so lugs disengage while rotating spool. String will be expelled from outlet holes if spool is rotated in proper direction. Push spool back into head while engaging lugs in holes of head. Reinstall retainer nut.

To install string on an empty spool, a length of string 15 feet should be inserted through the holes in the spool as shown in Fig. HL33-3. The spool should be centered between both ends of the string. Wrap both ends of string around spool in the same direction; wrapping may be done in either direction as long as both ends are wrapped in the same direction. Install the spool in the head while inserting string ends through the outlet holes in the head. Do not trap string between underside of spool and head. Complete assembly of trimmer head.

SAW BLADE

The saw blade may be removed after unscrewing retaining screw or nut. Note that screw or nut has left-hand threads. Prevent blade rotation by inserting shaft holder tool into lower flange (1—Fig. HL33-1 or 28—Fig. HL33-2). Install saw blade so blade cuts when turning clockwise as viewed from underside.

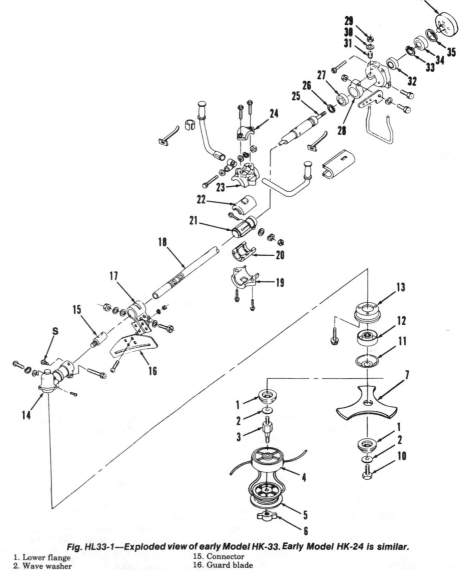

Fig. HL33-1—Exploded view of early Model HK-33. Early Model HK-24 is similar.

1. Lower flange	15. Connector	
2. Wave washer	16. Guard blade	
3. Shaft bolt	17. Bracket	27. Collar
4. Head	18. Drive shaft housing	28. Clutch housing
5. Spool	19. Bracket	29. Locknut
6. Nut (L.H.)	20. Isolator	30. Washer
7. Blade	21. Handle hoop	31. Screw
10. Screw (L.H.)	22. Isolator	32. Collar
11. Cup	23. Bracket	33. Snap ring
12. Upper flange	24. Bracket	34. Bearing
13. Cover	25. Drive shaft	35. Snap ring
14. Gear head	26. Snap ring	36. Clutch drum

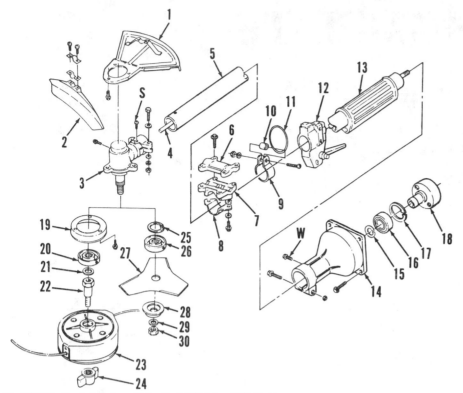

Fig. HL33-2—Exploded view of later Model HK-24 and HK-33. Model HK-18 is similar. Washer (21) is not used on Model HK-18.

1. Shield	11. Ring	21. Special washer
2. Shield	12. Throttle assy.	22. Shaft bolt
3. Gear head	13. Grip	23. Trimmer assy.
4. Drive shaft	14. Clutch housing	24. Nut (L.H.)
5. Drive shaft housing	15. Snap ring	25. Snap ring
6. Bracket	16. Bearing	26. Upper flange
7. Bracket	17. Snap ring	27. Blade
8. Bracket	18. Clutch drum	28. Lower flange
9. Hanger	19. Cover	29. Special washer
10. Spacer	20. Upper flange	30. Nut (L.H.)

Fig. HL33-5—Loosen nut and cap and withdraw throttle valve assembly from carburetor on Models HK-24 and HK-33.

Fig. HL33-6—Snap ring is accessible through slot in clutch drum.

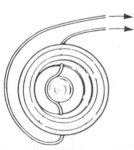

Fig. HL33-3—Install string on spool as shown and as outlined in text. Ends may be wrapped around spool in either direction as long as both ends are in the same direction.

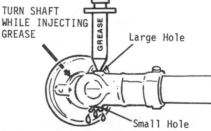

Fig. HL33-4—Lubricate gear head by injecting grease into gear head as shown.

Fig. HL33-7—Throttle trigger end play should be 1/16 inch (1.6 mm) measured at end of lever.

GEAR HEAD

Gear head (14—Fig. HL33-1 or 3—Fig. HL33-2) is lubricated using Multi-purpose All-Temp Grease (part 17193). The gear head should be lubricated after every 50 hours of operation.

To lubricate gear head, remove large slotted screw and small Phillips head screw on sides of gear head. While rotating gear head shaft, inject grease in-to large screw hole as shown in Fig. HL33-4 until grease is expelled from small screw hole. Reinstall screws and clean off excess grease.

To remove shaft bolt (3—Fig. HL33-1) on early models, secure lower flange (1) using shaft holder tool and turn bolt clockwise (L.H. threads). To remove shaft bolt (22—Fig. HL33-2) on later models, prevent shaft rotation by inserting a 3/16 inch (4 mm) rod through cover (19) and into upper flange (20). Turn shaft bolt clockwise (L.H. threads) to remove.

To remove gear head, back out alignment screw (S—Fig. HL33-1 or HL33-2) approximately 1/8 inch (3.2 mm). Loosen clamp screw(s) and separate gear head from drive shaft housing. On early models, use a suitable tool to engage shaft connector (15—Fig. HL33-1) and unscrew connector from gear head shaft.

The gear head on all models must be serviced as a unit assembly. Individual components are not available.

Illustrations courtesy Homelite Div. of Textron, Inc.

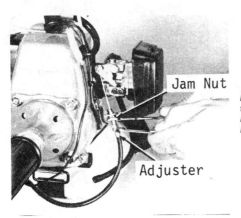

Fig. HL33-8—Adjust throttle trigger end play on Model HK-18 by loosening locknut and turning cable adjuster.

Fig. HL33-9—Adjust throttle trigger end play on Models HK-24 and HK-33 by loosening locknut and turning cable adjuster.

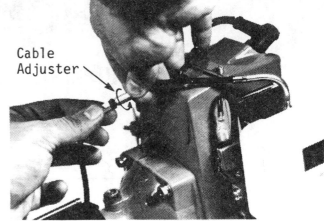

DRIVE SHAFT

The drive shaft does not normally require lubrication. If a new drive shaft is installed or the old drive shaft is removed, the drive shaft should be lubricated. Apply Homelite Multipurpose Grease 17237 or a suitable lithium base grease to the drive shaft. Do not apply an excessive amount of grease.

To remove drive shaft assembly, refer to preceding section and remove gear head. On Model HK-18, detach throttle cable bracket from engine fan housing, disconnect throttle cable and disconnect stop switch wire at connector adjacent to throttle cable bracket. On Models HK-24 and HK-33, loosen throttle cable guidenut (Fig. HL33-5), unscrew carburetor cap and lift out throttle valve assembly (cover carburetor opening and be careful not to damage throttle valve components). Remove four screws securing clutch housing (28—Fig. HL33-1 or 14—Fig. HL33-2) to engine and detach clutch housing with drive shaft housing. On early Model HK-33, loosen locknuts (29—Fig. HL33-1) and back out locating screws (31). On later models, back out housing alignment screw (W—Fig. HL33-2). On all models, loosen clamp screw and withdraw drive shaft housing from clutch housing. Drive shaft will remain

attached to clutch.

To detach the drive shaft from the clutch drum, proceed as follows: On early models, insert a suitable rod through the clutch housing and the holes in the clutch drum so the drum cannot rotate. Grasp the opposite end of the drive shaft with a wrench and unscrew the drive shaft from the clutch drum. On later models, grasp the drive shaft in a soft-jawed vise then use a suitable tool inserted in the two-holes in the clutch drum and unscrew the drum off the drive shaft.

Reassemble by reversing the disassembly procedure. Be sure throttle valve assembly is properly installed on Model HK-18.

CLUTCH

The clutch assembly is accessible after removing the clutch housing as outlined in the preceding DRIVE SHAFT section. Inspect components and renew any which are damaged or excessively worn.

To remove the clutch drum on early Model HK-33, remove the drive shaft as previously outlined. Working through the elongated slot in the clutch drum, detach snap ring (35—Fig. HL33-1) as shown in Fig. HL33-6. Using Homelite tool 94455 or a suitable equivalent, press clutch drum and bearing (34—Fig.

HL33-1) out of clutch housing. Remove snap ring (33) and press clutch drum out of bearing. If necessary, remove rear collar (32), snap ring (26) and front collar (27).

To remove the clutch drum on Models HK-18, HK-24 and later Model HK-33, remove snap ring (33—Fig. HL33-1 or 15—Fig. HL33-2). Press clutch drum out of bearing. Remove snap ring (35—Fig. HL33-1 or 17—Fig. HL33-2). Using Homelite tool 94455 or a suitable equivalent, press bearing out of clutch housing.

Reassemble by reversing disassembly procedure.

THROTTLE TRIGGER

Throttle trigger end play must be properly adjusted to obtain desired engine operation and to allow clutch to disengage. Throttle trigger end play should be 1/16 inch (1.6 mm) measured at end of trigger lever. See Fig. HL33-7. Loosen locknut and rotate cable adjuster shown in Fig. HL33-8 or HL33-9 to adjust end play. Tighten locknut against adjuster after performing adjustment.

NOTE: Insufficient throttle trigger end play may not allow engine to reach idle speed and clutch may not disengage.

HOMELITE

TRIMMERS/BRUSHCUTTERS

Model	Cutting Swath	Line Diameter	Engine Make	Displacement
HBC-38	18 in.	0.105 in.	Homelite	40 cc
HBC-40	20 in.	0.105 in.	Homelite	40 cc

ENGINE INFORMATION

All models are equipped with a Homelite engine. Refer to appropriate Homelite engine section for service information.

STRING TRIMMER

The brushcutter may be equipped with a dual string, manual advance string trimmer head. Advancing the trimmer line is accomplished by loosening retainer nut (12—Fig. HL34-1) by turning clockwise (L.H. thread). Loosen retainer enough so line can be pulled out about ¼ inch (6.4 mm) from string head. Pull down on spool (10) and rotate to advance line. Each line should measure approximately 6¾ inches (17 cm) on Model HBC-38 or 7¾ inches (19.7 cm) on Model HBC-40.

After advancing the line, rotate spool slightly in either direction to line up locating lugs on spool with locating holes in string head. Tighten retainer by turning counterclockwise (L.H. thread).

To replace or rewind the spool, remove retainer (12) by turning clockwise (L.H. thread). Pull spool from string head. To rewind new line on spool, insert one end of an 18-ft. (5.5 m) length of premium quality 0.105-in. (2.7 mm) diameter monofilament line through hole in the spool (Fig. HL34-2). Center the spool in the 18-ft. (5.5 m) length of line. Pull loop tight and wind both lengths of line around the spool in clockwise direction as viewed from top of spool, taking care not to twist the line.

Install spool and line into string head. Feed 6½ inches (16.5 cm) of line through each eyelet. Tilt spool and place into string head taking care that the line does not slip under the spool flange. Rotate spool slightly in either direction to engage locating lugs on spool with locating holes in string head. Install retainer by turning counterclockwise (L.H. thread).

BLADE

The brushcutter may be equipped with either a Tri-Arc or "machete" blade. Refer to Fig. HL34-1 for configuration of blade components. Note that nut (7) has left-hand threads.

DRIVE SHAFT

Models HBC-38 and HBC-40 are equipped with a solid drive shaft (2—Fig. HL34-1) that does not require periodic maintenance. Lubricate shaft if removed.

GEAR HEAD

The gear head (3—Fig. HL34-1) should be lubricated after every 100 hours of operation. Recommended lubricant is Homelite All-Temp Multi-Purpose Grease or equivalent. Remove plug (P) in side of gear head and inject grease into gear head.

To remove gear head, loosen the two clamp screws and locating screw. Slide gear head from drive shaft housing. Gear head must be serviced as a unit assembly; individual components are not available.

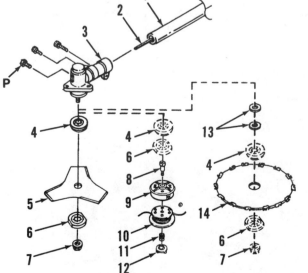

Fig. HL34-1—Exploded view of trimmer and brushcutter components.

1. Drive shaft housing
2. Drive shaft
3. Gear head
4. Washer
5. Tri-Arc blade
6. Washer
7. Nut (L.H. threads)
8. Drive connector
9. Housing & eyelet
10. Spool
11. Spring
12. Retainer nut (L.H. threads)
13. Washers
14. "Machete" blade

Fig. HL34-2—End of trimmer line must be routed through hole on spool.

Illustrations courtesy Homelite Div. of Textron, Inc.

HOMELITE

GASOLINE POWERED BLOWERS

Model	Engine Manufacturer	Engine Model	Displacement
BP-250	Homelite	...	1.53 cu. in.
HB-100	Homelite	...	1.53 cu. in.
HB-180	Homelite	...	1.53 cu. in.
HB-280	Homelite	...	1.6 cu. in.
HB-380	Homelite	...	1.6 cu. in.
HB-480	Homelite	...	1.9 cu. in.
HB-680	Homelite	...	1.9 cu. in.

ENGINE INFORMATION

The models included in this section are powered by a Homelite engine. Refer to appropriate Homelite engine service section for service procedures and specifications.

R&R ENGINE

All Models

To remove engine, first unbolt and remove back rest pad and back rest on models so equipped. On all models, remove engine cover (1—Fig. HL37-1). Remove screws holding blower volute halves (4 and 7) together and separate volute halves. Disconnect throttle cable and ignition wires from engine. Remove blower fan (6) from flywheel (5). Unbolt and remove engine from blower volute half (4).

REWIND STARTER

Models BP-250, HB-100 And HB-180

The rewind starter is located in the blower volute half adjacent to the engine. The engine must be removed to service the starter.

To disassemble starter, remove rope handle (4—Fig. HL37-2) and allow rope to wind into starter. Remove pulley retainer (7) and remove starter components as needed. Wear appropriate safety eyewear and gloves when working with or around rewind spring (5) as spring may uncoil uncontrolled.

Before assembling starter, lubricate center post of housing and side of spring with light grease. Install rewind spring (4) in a clockwise direction from outer end. Rope length should be 46 inches (117 cm). Assemble starter while pass-

ing rope through housing rope outlet and attach rope handle to rope. To place tension on starter rope, rotate pulley clockwise so notch in pulley is aligned with rope outlet, then hold pulley to prevent pulley rotation. Pull rope back into housing while positioning rope in pulley notch. Turn rope pulley clockwise until spring is tight. Allow pulley to turn counterclockwise until notch aligns with rope outlet. Disengage rope from notch then release pulley and al-

low rope to wind on pulley. Check starter operation. Rope handle should be held against housing by spring tension, but it must be possible to rotate pulley at least $1/4$ turn clockwise when rope is pulled out fully.

Models HB-280, HB-380, HB-480 And HB-680

The backrest pad and backrest must be removed on Models HB-480 and HB-

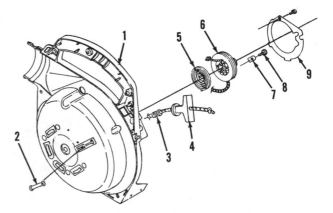

Fig. HL37-1—Exploded view of Model HB280 blower assembly. Other models are similar.

1. Cover
2. Engine
3. Backplate
4. Blower volute
5. Flywheel
6. Blower fan
7. Blower volute

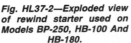

Fig. HL37-2—Exploded view of rewind starter used on Models BP-250, HB-100 And HB-180.

1. Volute half
2. Rope guide
3. Rope guide
4. Rope handle
5. Rewind spring
6. Pulley
7. Retainer
8. Screw
9. Plate

680 for access to starter. On all models, unscrew mounting screws and remove starter. remove rope handle and allow rope to wind into starer. Unscrew retaining screw (3—Fig. HL37-3) and remove ratchet (5) and pulley while being careful not to dislodge rewind spring in housing. Wear appropriate safety eyewear and gloves when working with or around rewind spring as spring may uncoil uncontrolled.

When assembling starter, wind rope around rope pulley in a clockwise direction as viewed with pulley in housing. To place tension on rewind spring, pass

rope through rope outlet in housing and install rope handle. Pull rope out and hold rope pulley so notch in pulley is adjacent to rope outlet. Pull rope back through outlet between notch in pulley and housing. Turn rope pulley clockwise to place tension on spring. Release pulley and check starter action. Do not place more tension on rewind spring than is necessary to draw rope handle up against housing. Install ratchet (5) with hooked end of ratchet lever wire (6) up and between posts of starter housing. Install screw (3) and washer (4) then install starter housing.

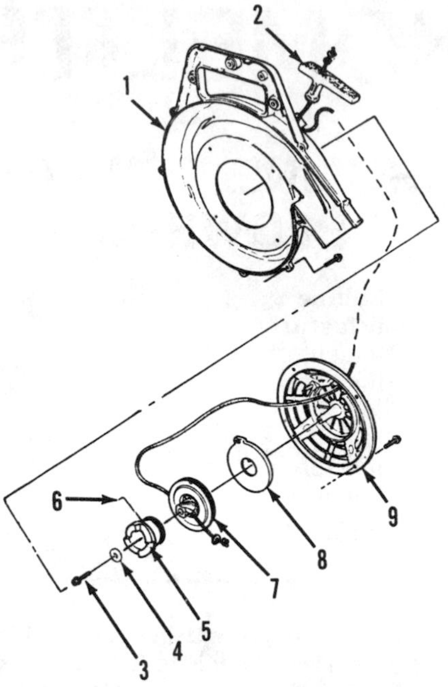

Fig. HL37-3—Exploded view of rewind starter used on Models HB-280, HB-380, HB-480 and HB-680.

1. Volute half
2. Rope handle
3. Screw
4. Washer
5. Ratchet
6. Ratchet lever wire
7. Pulley
8. Rewind spring
9. Starter housing

HUSQVARNA

GASOLINE POWERED STRING TRIMMERS

Model	Engine Manufacturer	Engine Model	Displacement
18RL	Husqvarna	18	18.5 cc
22LD	Husqvarna	22	21.2 cc
22R, 22RL	Husqvarna	22	21.2 cc
25BL, 25BT	Husqvarna	25	24.1 cc
25R, 25RD, 25RL	Husqvarna	25	24.1 cc
26LC	Husqvarna	26	26 cc
26RLC	Husqvarna	26	26 cc
32LC	Husqvarna	32	32 cc
32R, 32RL, 32RLC	Husqvarna	32	32 cc
36R	Husqvarna	36	36 cc
39R	Husqvarna	39	40 cc
125L, 125LD	Husqvarna	125	25.4 cc
125R, 125RD	Husqvarna	125	25.4 cc
132L, 132LD	Husqvarna	132	31.8 cc
132R, 132RD	Husqvarna	132	31.8 cc
140R	Husqvarna	140	40 cc
165R, 165RX	Husqvarna	165	65 cc
240R	Husqvarna	240	40 cc
244R, 244RX	Husqvarna	244	44 cc
245R, 245RX	Husqvarna	245	44 cc
250RX	Husqvarna	250	49 cc

ENGINE INFORMATION

The models in this section are equipped with a Husqvarna engine. Refer to appropriate engine service section for engine service information.

FUEL MIXTURE

Manufacturer recommends mixing regular unleaded grade gasoline with a high-quality, two-stroke engine oil designed for air-cooled engines. Recommended oil is Husqvarna oil mixed at fuel:oil ratio indicated on oil container. Fuel:oil ratio should be 16:1 when using any other two-stroke oil.

STRING TRIMMER

The unit may be equipped with a manual advance or semi-automatic advance string trimmer head. The trimmer head may be equipped with right- or left-hand threads. Observe arrow on trimmer head when removing head.

Refer to Fig. HQ10 for an exploded view of a typical manual advance trimmer head. Refer to Fig. HQ11 for an exploded view of one version of the semi-automatic trimmer head used on some models. When installing string on this type, route string around pin (P—Fig. HQ12), otherwise string will feed continuously. On some semi-automatic trimmer heads, new string can be fed into head as shown in Fig. HQ13 and wound on spool by turning lower plate.

BLADE

Some models may be equipped with a blade, which may be a three- or four-edge blade, or a saw blade. To remove blade, carefully rotate blade until hole in upper driving disc is aligned with hole in gear housing as shown in Fig. HQ14. Insert a 4.5 mm (0.16 in.) round rod into holes to prevent blade rotation. Blade retaining nut has left-hand threads. Remove nut and blade assembly. When installing blade, tighten nut to 35-50 N·m (26-30 ft.-lbs.).

Fig. HQ11—Exploded view of semi-automatic trimmer head used on some models.

1. Housing
2. Spring
3. Button
4. Spool
5. Cover

Fig. HQ10—Exploded view of manual trimmer head used on some models.

1. Housing
2. Spool
3. Cover

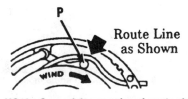

Fig. HQ12—On models so equipped, route string around pin (P) as shown.

Route Line as Shown

WIND

Husqvarna

To sharpen saw blade, use a 5.5 mm (7.32 in.) round file in file holder 501 58 02-01 and follow sharpening procedure depicted in Figs. HQ15 through HQ21. Three-edge and four-edge blades may be sharpened using a single-cut flat file.

DRIVE SHAFT

The flexible drive shaft on models with a curved drive shaft tube should be removed and lubricated after every 10 hours of operation. Recommended lubricant is Husqvarna lubricant 530-030102 or equivalent.

The drive shaft on models with a straight drive shaft tube does not require periodic lubrication. If removed, lubricate drive shaft with Husqvarna lubricant 530-030102 or equivalent before reinstalling drive shaft.

GEAR HEAD

Series 22, 25, 125 And 132

These models are equipped with the gear head shown in Fig. HQ22. Gear

Fig. HQ13—To extend line on trimmer head shown, follow procedure in top two views. To install line, insert line then turn lower plate as shown in bottom three views.

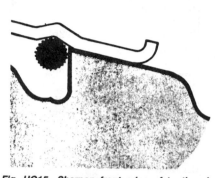

Fig. HQ15—Sharpen front edge of tooth only. Make certain file holder is held firmly against edge of tooth.

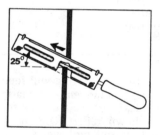

Fig. HQ16—Alternate filing one tooth to the right and the next tooth to the left. File at a 25-degree angle.

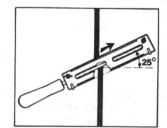

Fig. HQ17—Sharpen outer edge of tooth at a 5-degree angle.

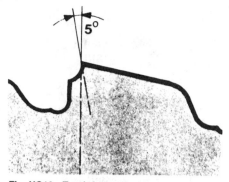

Fig. HQ18—Tooth front edge angle should be 5-degree. Hard wood and large trees may require a smaller angle.

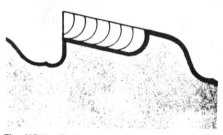

Fig. HQ19—Reduce tooth height evenly during repeated sharpening.

Fig. HQ20—Use set gage (501 31 77-01) to adjust tooth set when teeth have been filed down approximately 50 percent.

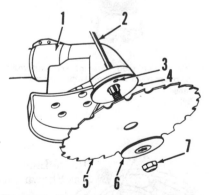

Fig. HQ14—View showing location of blade assembly components on some models.

1. Gear head
2. Tool
3. Hole
4. Drive disc
5. Blade
6. Washer
7. Nut (L.H.)

Fig. HQ21—Tooth set should provide 1 mm (0.04 in.) distance between tooth tips.

head lubricant level should be checked after every 50 hours of operation. Remove plug (9) to check lubricant level and inject grease. Gear head should be ³/₄ full. Recommended lubricant is a lithium-base grease.

To disassemble gear head, remove trimmer head or blade assembly. Detach gear head from drive shaft housing tube. Remove snap ring (14) and pull arbor shaft (12) from gear head (8). Remove snap ring (1) and pull input shaft (7) and bearings from gear head. If necessary, heat housing to ease removal of bearings.

To reassemble, reverse disassembly procedure.

Models 36R, 140R, 244R And 244RX

Models 36R, 140R, 244R and 244RX are equipped with the gear head shown in Fig. HQ23. Gear head lubricant level should be checked after every 50 hours of operation. Remove plug (11) to check lubricant level and inject grease. Gear head should be ³/₄ full. Recommended lubricant is a lithium-base grease.

To disassemble gear head, remove trimmer head or blade assembly. Remove four screws (3) retaining cover (5) and use puller 502 50 09-11 to separate cover from housing. Separate gear head from drive shaft housing tube. Remove sleeve (19) using remover 502 51 11-01. Heat housing to 140° F (60° C) and remove input shaft (16) and bearing assembly, and arbor (9) and bearing assembly. If bearing (10) remains in housing, tap housing against a wooden block while housing is still hot to remove bearing. Remove snap ring (21) and press bearings (17 and 18) from input shaft as required. Remove bearing (7) and spacer (8) if required.

To reassemble, reverse disassembly procedure.

Model 165R

Model 165 is equipped with the gear head shown in Fig. HQ24. Gear head lubricant level should be checked after every 50 hours of operation. Remove plug (9) to check lubricant level and inject grease. Gear head should be ³/₄ full. Recommended lubricant is a lithium-base grease.

To disassemble gear head, remove trimmer head or blade assembly. Remove five screws (4) from the blade guard and remove guard. Separate gear head from drive shaft housing tube. Heat housing to 140° F (60° C) and use puller 502 50 65-01 to remove arbor (7) and bearing assembly. Remove locking screw (16) and use puller 502 50 63-01 to remove input shaft (13) and bearing assembly. Press bearings and spacer (12) from input shaft if required.

To reassemble, reverse disassembly procedure.

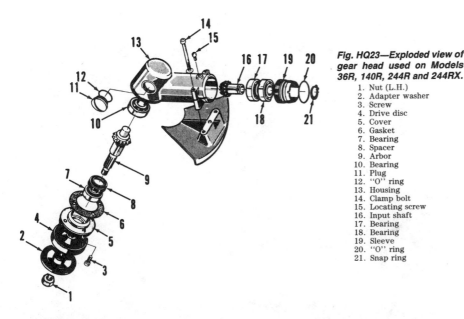

Fig. HQ22—Exploded view of gear head used on Series 22, 25, 125 and 132 models. Spacers (2 and 5) are not used on later models.

1. Snap ring
2. Spacer
3. Snap ring
4. Bearing
5. Spacer
6. Bearing
7. Input shaft
8. Housing
9. Plug
10. Bearing
11. Gear
12. Arbor
13. Bearing
14. Snap ring

Fig. HQ23—Exploded view of gear head used on Models 36R, 140R, 244R and 244RX.

1. Nut (L.H.)
2. Adapter washer
3. Screw
4. Drive disc
5. Cover
6. Gasket
7. Bearing
8. Spacer
9. Arbor
10. Bearing
11. Plug
12. "O" ring
13. Housing
14. Clamp bolt
15. Locating screw
16. Input shaft
17. Bearing
18. Bearing
19. Sleeve
20. "O" ring
21. Snap ring

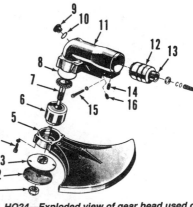

Fig. HQ24—Exploded view of gear head used on Model 165R.

1. Nut (L.H.)
2. Adapter washer
3. Drive disc
4. Screw
5. Shield & cover assy.
6. Bearing
7. Arbor
8. "O" ring
9. Plug
10. "O" ring
11. Housing
12. Bearing & spacer assy.
13. Input shaft
14. Locating screw
15. Clamp bolt
16. Locking screw

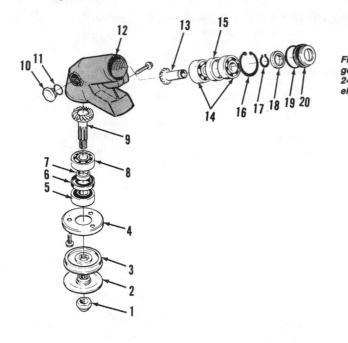

Models 165RX, 240R, 245R And 245RX

Fig. HQ25—Exploded view of gear head used on Models 240R, 245R and 245RX. Model 165RX is similar but snap ring (16) is not used.

1. Nut (L.H.)
2. Adapter washer
3. Drive disc
4. Cover
5. Bearing
6. Seal
7. Spacer
8. Bearing
9. Arbor
10. Plug
11. "O" ring
12. Housing
13. Input shaft
14. Bearing
15. Spacer
16. Snap ring
17. Snap ring
18. Seal
19. "O" ring
20. Sleeve

Models 165RX, 240R, 245R and 245RX are equipped with the gear head shown in Fig. HQ25. Gear head lubricant level should be checked after every 50 hours of operation. Remove plug (10) to check lubricant level and inject grease. Gear head should be ³/₄ full. Recommended lubricant is a lithium-base grease.

To disassemble gear head, remove trimmer head or blade assembly. Separate gear head from drive shaft housing tube. Unscrew and remove cover (4). Remove sleeve (20) and detach snap ring (16). Remove components as needed. Heat housing to ease removal of bearings.

To reassemble, reverse disassembly procedure.

Illustrations courtesy Husqvarna Forest & Garden

IDC

GASOLINE POWERED STRING TRIMMERS

Model	Engine Manufacturer	Engine Model	Displacement
364	IDC	...	31.0 cc
500	IDC	...	28.5 cc
520	IDC	...	28.5 cc
540	IDC	...	31.0 cc
580	IDC	...	31.0 cc

ENGINE INFORMATION

The models in this section are equipped with an Inertia Dynamics Corporation (IDC) engine. Refer to IDC engine service section for engine service information.

FUEL MIXTURE

Manufacturer recommends mixing regular grade gasoline, leaded or unleaded, with a high-quality, two-stroke engine oil. Recommended fuel:oil ratio is 32:1 when using IDC Two-Cycle Engine Oil. When using any other two-stroke oil, mix 6 ounces (0.177 mL) of oil with 1 gallon (3.8 L) of gasoline, regardless of recommended ratio on oil container. The use of gasohol or other alcohol blended fuels are not approved by manufacturer.

STRING TRIMMER

Model 364

Model 364 is equipped with a single line, semi-automatic trimmer head (Fig. ID10). To extend line with engine stopped, push in on bump button (20) and pull on line until desired length is obtained. To extend line with engine running, operate trimmer engine at full rpm and tap bump button (20) on the ground. Line will automatically advance a measured amount.

To renew trimmer line, hold drum (15) and unscrew bump button (20). Remove spool (19). Clean inner surface of drum and spool. Check indexing teeth on spool and drum for wear. Insert one end of a 25-ft. (7.6 m) length of 0.080-in. (2 mm) diameter monofilament line into one of the holes in spool from the inside out, and back through the second hole to the inside. Wind line in direction in-

dicated by arrow on spool until all but about 3 inches (76.2 mm) of line is wrapped, then clip line temporarily in one of the line lock slots (LS) on spool.

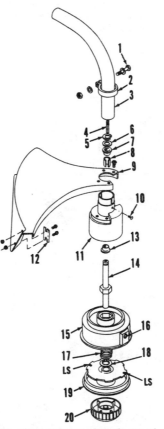

Fig. ID10—Exploded view of single strand, semi-automatic trimmer head used on Model 364.

1. Bolt
2. Clamp
3. Drive shaft housing
4. Drive shaft
5. Retaining ring
6. Washer
7. Bushing
8. Bushing
9. Shield
10. Locating screw
11. Bushing housing
12. Line length trimmer
13. Bushing
14. Shaft
15. Drum
16. Line guide
17. Spring
18. Retainer
19. Spool
20. Bump button
LS. Line slot

Insert line end through line guide (16) in drum and install spool and bump button. Pull line to release from line lock slot on spool after assembly is complete.

Models 500, 520, 540 And 580

These models are equipped with a dual strand, semi-automatic trimmer head (Fig. ID11). To extend line with engine off, push bump button (8) in and pull lines out. Procedure may have to be repeated until desired line length has been obtained. To extend line with engine running, operate trimmer engine at full operating rpm and tap bump button

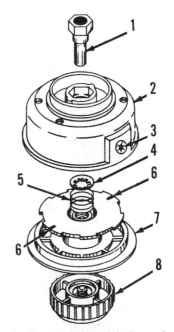

Fig. ID11—Exploded view of dual strand, semi-automatic trimmer head used on Models 500, 520 and 540. Model 580 is similar.

1. Adapter
2. Drum
3. Line guide
4. Retainer
5. Spring
6. Line slot
7. Spool
8. Bump button

on the ground. Each time bump button is tapped on the ground, approximately 1 inch (25 mm) of new line will be advanced.

To renew line, hold drum (2) and unscrew bump button (8). Note that screw in bump button on Model 580 has left-hand threads. Remove spool (7) and remove any remaining old line. Clean spool and inner surface of drum. Check indexing teeth in drum and on spool. On Models 500, 520 and 540, loop a 25-ft. (7.6 cm) length of 0.080-in. (2 mm) diameter monofilament line into two equal lengths. On Model 580, loop a 50-ft. (15.2 m) length of 0.095-in. (2.4 mm) diameter line into two equal lengths. Insert the two line ends into the two holes in spool from the bottom and pull line out until end of loop is against spool. Wind both strands of line around spool in direction indicated by arrow on spool. Wind in tight even layers. Clip lines into line slots (6) in spool. Insert line ends through line guides (3) in drum and install spool and bump button. Bump button screw on Model 580 has left-hand threads. Pull line ends to free from line slots.

On Model 580, note that trimmer housing (2) has left-hand threads.

BLADE

Models 540 And 580

Models 540 and 580 may be equipped with a four-edge cutting blade (9—Figs. ID12 and ID13). To install blade, refer to Figs. ID12 or ID13 for assembly sequence. Note that nut (11) on Model 580 has left-hand threads. Tighten nut (11) to 225-250 in.-lbs. (26-28 N·m).

DRIVE SHAFT

All Models Except 580

All models except Model 580 are equipped with a flexible drive shaft enclosed in the drive shaft housing. The drive shaft has squared ends that engage adapters at each end. The drive shaft should be removed for maintenance after every 10 hours of operation.

To remove drive shaft, loosen clamp (2—Fig. ID10 or 6—Fig. ID12) and remove set screw attaching drive shaft tube to trimmer bearing housing. Remove and clean drive shaft, then inspect shaft for damage. Coat with a

high-quality, high-temperature wheel bearing grease and install drive shaft. Make certain ends of shaft are properly located in upper and lower drive adapters.

Model 580

Model 580 is equipped with a solid steel drive shaft (2—Fig. ID13) that rides in bushings in the drive shaft housing (1). The drive shaft requires no maintenance. If shaft is removed, it should be lubricated with high-temperature wheel bearing grease before installation.

BEARING HOUSING

Models 364, 500, And 520

Refer to Fig. ID10 for an exploded view of the bearing housing used on Models 364, 500, and 520. Bushings are available only with housing (11), not separately.

Model 540

The bearing head (7—Fig. ID12) on Model 540 is equipped with a sealed bearing and must be serviced as a unit assembly.

GEAR HEAD

Model 580

Model 580 is equipped with a gear head assembly (4—Fig. ID13). Plug (3) in side of gear head should be removed and lubricant level checked after every 50 hours of operation. Housing should be ²/₃ full of lithium-base grease. Service parts are not available. Gear head must be renewed as a complete unit.

THROTTLE TRIGGER AND CABLE

All Models

The throttle trigger assembly is attached to the drive shaft housing (Fig. ID14) on all models. The throttle cable inner wire (2) should be lubricated after every 20 hours of operation. Apply SAE 30 oil to each end of wire. The throttle cable should be adjusted to provide 0.02-0.04-in. (0.5-1.0 mm) throttle trigger movement before the carburetor throttle lever begins to move. Adjust by

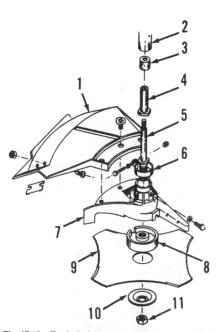

Fig. ID12—Exploded view of weed, grass and light brush blade assembly used on Model 540.

1. Shield
2. Drive shaft housing
3. Retainer & bushing
4. Drive shaft adapter
5. Head drive shaft
6. Clamp assy.
7. Bearing housing assy.
8. Blade adapter
9. Blade
10. Lower blade adapter
11. Nut

Fig. ID13—Exploded view of weed, grass and light brush blade assembly used on Model 580. Nut (11) has left-hand threads.

1. Drive shaft housing
2. Drive shaft
3. Lubricant check plug
4. Gear head
5. Guard mount
6. Guard
7. Line length trimmer blade
8. Blade adapter
9. Blade
10. Retaining washer
11. Nut

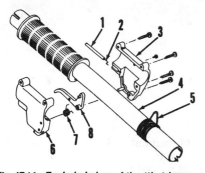

Fig. ID14—Exploded view of throttle trigger and cable assembly used on all models.

1. Throttle cable
   housing
2. Inner throttle cable
3. Throttle trigger
   housing
4. Drive shaft housing

5. Strap bracket
6. Throttle trigger
   housing
7. Spring
8. Throttle trigger

loosening set screw (S—Fig. ID15) and moving cable housing and inner wire to provide specified free play. Tighten set screw (S).

Fig. ID15—Loosen screw (S) and move throttle cable and housing to provide correct throttle trigger free play. Refer to text.

IDC
GASOLINE POWERED BLOWERS

Model	Engine Manufacturer	Engine Model	Displacement
200	IDC	...	31.0 cc
300BV	IDC	...	31.0 cc

ENGINE INFORMATION

The models in this section are equipped with an Inertia Dynamics Corporation (IDC) engine. Refer to IDC engine service section for engine service information.

FUEL MIXTURE

Manufacturer recommends mixing regular grade gasoline, leaded or unleaded, with a high-quality, two-stroke engine oil. Recommended fuel:oil ratio is 32:1 when using IDC Two-Cycle Engine Oil. When using any other two-stroke oil, mix 6 ounces (0.177 mL) of oil with 1 gallon (3.8 L) of gasoline, regardless of recommended ratio on oil container. Gasohol or other alcohol blended fuels are not approved by manufacturer.

BLOWER ASSEMBLY

Model 200

Refer to Fig. ID75 for exploded view of blower assembly. To remove blower impeller (4), remove mounting screws from starter housing (1) and blower housing (3). Separate blower housing halves (3 and 6). Remove mounting screws from blower impeller (4) and separate impeller from flywheel.

To separate engine from blower housing, remove impeller as outlined above. Remove engine cover (10). Disconnect fuel line, throttle cable and ignition wires from engine. Remove engine mounting screws and withdraw engine from blower housing half (6).

Model 300BV

Refer to Fig. ID76 for exploded view of blower assembly. To remove blower impeller (8), remove blower tube (12). Remove screws attaching blower lower housing (10) to upper housing (7) and separate housing. Remove impeller mounting screw and separate impeller (8) from flywheel.

To separate engine from blower housing, remove impeller as outlined above. Remove screws securing engine covers (1 and 4). Separate covers and disconnect throttle cable, fuel line and ignition wires from engine. Remove engine mounting screws and withdraw engine from blower upper housing (7).

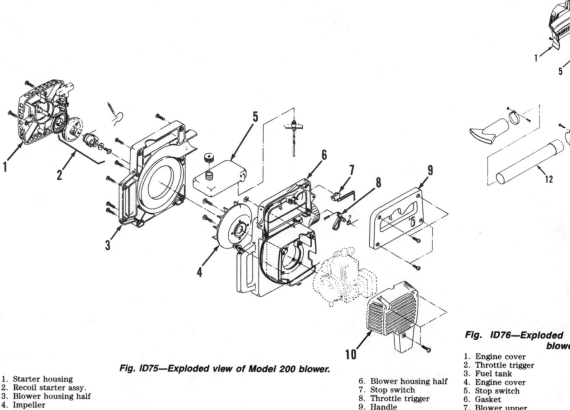

Fig. ID75—Exploded view of Model 200 blower.

1. Starter housing
2. Recoil starter assy.
3. Blower housing half
4. Impeller
5. Fuel tank
6. Blower housing half
7. Stop switch
8. Throttle trigger
9. Handle
10. Engine cover

Fig. ID76—Exploded view of Model 300BV blower/vac.

1. Engine cover
2. Throttle trigger
3. Fuel tank
4. Engine cover
5. Stop switch
6. Gasket
7. Blower upper housing
8. Impeller
9. Shield
10. Blower lower housing
11. Intake cover
12. Blower tube

JONSERED

GASOLINE POWERED STRING TRIMMERS

Engine Model	Engine Manufacturer	Model	Displacement
J200B	EFCO	200	22.5 cc
J200L	EFCO	200	22.5 cc
J220B	EFCO	220	22.5 cc
J220L	EFCO	220	22.5 cc
J260B	EFCO	260	25.4 cc
J260L	EFCO	260	25.4 cc
J300B	EFCO	300	30.5 cc
J320B	EFCO	300	30.5 cc
J400B	EFCO	400	37.7 cc
J420B	EFCO	400	37.7 cc
J450B	EFCO	450	37.7 cc
J460B	EFCO	450	37.7 cc

ENGINE INFORMATION

The models in this section are equipped with an EFCO engine. Refer to EFCO engine service section for engine service information.

FUEL MIXTURE

Manufacturer recommends mixing regular grade gasoline, preferably leaded, with a high-quality, two-stroke engine oil. Recommended fuel:oil ratio is 40:1.

STRING TRIMMER

All models are equipped with a manual advance, dual strand trimmer head. To pull out line, stop engine and push up against spool (against spring pressure). While pushing spool up, turn spool counterclockwise (as viewed from bottom) to eject new line. Release spool.

To install new line, unscrew retaining screw (5—Fig. J11)—screw has left-hand threads. Remove housing (4), spool (3) and spring (2). Remove old string and clean components. Specified string diameter on Models J300B, J320B, J400B, J420B, J450B and J460B is 0.095 inch (2.4 mm). Specified string diameter for all other models is 0.080 inch (2.0 mm). Spool capacity is 36 feet (11 m) for Models J300B, J320B, J400B, J420B, J450B and J460B and 42 feet (13 m) for all other models. Insert line (6) through holes in spool as shown in Fig. J11 and pull line through holes until ends are even. Wrap line around spool in direction indicated by arrows on spool. Do not twist lines. Reassemble trimmer

head. Tighten retaining screw (5—Fig. J11) to 25 N·m (18 ft.-lbs.).

BLADE

All straight-shaft models may be equipped with a blade. Refer to Figs. J13, J14 or J15 for configuration of blade assembly. Blade retaining screw has left-hand threads. Note that direction of blade rotation is usually indicated by an arrow on the gear head. Tighten retaining screw to 25 N·m (18 ft.-lbs.).

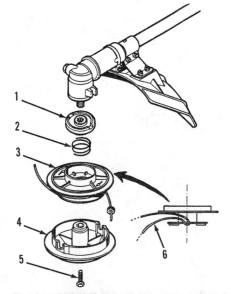

Fig. J11—Exploded view of dual strand, manual advance trimmer used on Models J200B, J200L, J220B, J220L, J260B and J260L. All other models are similar. Insert new trimmer line (6) through spool holes as shown.

1. Flange
2. Spring
3. Spool
4. Cup washer
5. Lockwasher
6. Screw (L.H.)

DRIVE SHAFT

Models J200B and J200L

Models J200B and J200L are equipped with a flexible drive shaft. Periodically remove drive shaft and lubricate with a lithium-base grease. To remove drive shaft, remove bearing head and extract drive shaft. When installing drive shaft, be sure drive shaft end is properly seated at drive end.

All Other Models

All models except Models J200B and J200L are equipped with a solid drive

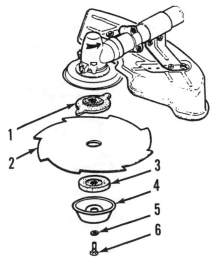

Fig. J13—Blade assembly used on some models.

1. Flange
2. Blade
3. Washer
4. Housing
5. Screw (L.H.)
6. Trimmer line

shaft that does not require periodic lubrication. If drive shaft is removed, apply a lithium-base grease to drive shaft. The drive shaft rides in bushings that are renewable. If bushings are to be renewed, mark position of old bushings before removal so new bushings can be installed in original positions.

BEARING HEAD

Models J200B and J200L

The bearing head does not require periodic lubrication.

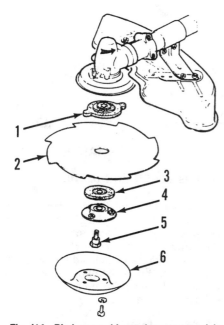

Fig. J14—Blade assembly used on some models.
1. Flange
2. Blade
3. Washer
4. Shield flange
5. Screw (L.H.)
6. Shield

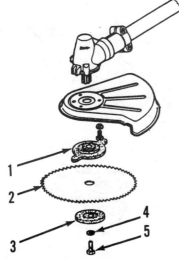

Fig. J15—Blade assembly used on some models.
1. Flange
2. Blade
3. Washer
4. Lockwasher
5. Screw (L.H.)

To disassemble bearing head, remove trimmer assembly (trimmer head retaining screw has left-hand threads). Separate bearing head from drive shaft tube. Detach snap ring (5—Fig. J16). Use a suitable puller and extract arbor (3) with bearings (4) from housing (1). Press or pull bearings off arbor. Reassemble by reversing disassembly procedure.

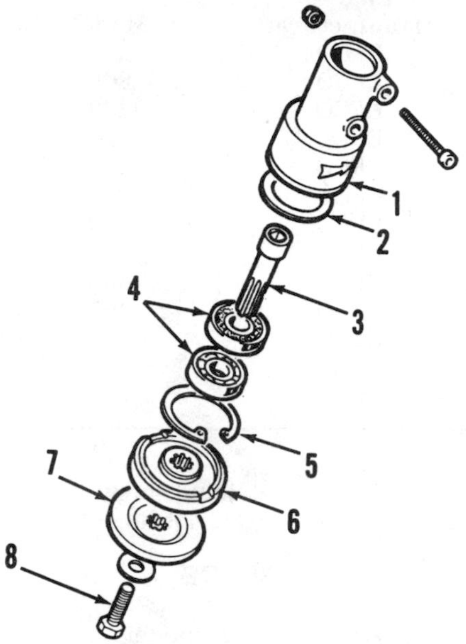

Fig. J16—Exploded view of bearing head used on Models J200B and J200L.
1. Housing
2. Washer
3. Arbor
4. Bearings
5. Snap ring
6. Flange
7. Flange
8. Screw (L.H.)

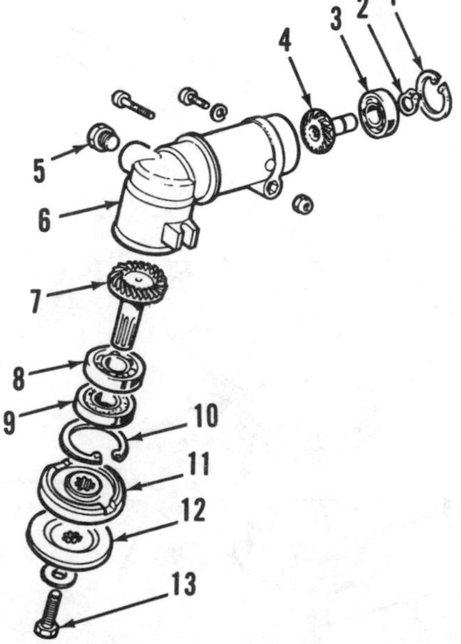

Fig. J17—Exploded view of gear head used on Models J220B, J220L, J260B and J260L.
1. Snap ring
2. Snap ring
3. Bearing
4. Input gear
5. Plug
6. Housing
7. Output gear
8. Bearing
9. Bearing
10. Snap ring
11. Flange
12. Flange
13. Screw (L.H.)

GEAR HEAD

Models J220B, J220L, J260B and J260L

Models J220B, J220L, J260B and J260L are equipped with the gear head shown in Fig. J17. Lubricant level should be checked after every 80 hours of operation. Remove fill plug (5) in side of housing and add lubricant so housing is $\frac{1}{2}$ full. Maximum amount that should be added if housing is dry is 9 mL (0.3 oz.). Recommended lubricant is molybdenum disulfide grease.

To disassemble gear head, remove trimmer or blade assembly (retaining screw has left-hand threads). Separate gear head from drive shaft tube. Remove flange (11) and detach snap ring (10). Use a suitable puller and extract gear (7) and bearings. Press or pull bearings off gear shaft. Detach snap ring (1). Reach through output opening of housing and drive out input shaft (4) and bearing (3). Remove snap ring (2) and separate bearing from shaft.

Reassemble by reversing disassembly procedure. Note that lower bearing (9) is a sealed bearing.

Models J300B, J320B, J400B, J420B, J450B and J460B

Models J300B, J320B, J400B, J420B, J450B and J460B are equipped with the bearing head shown in Fig. J18. Lubricant level should be checked after eve-

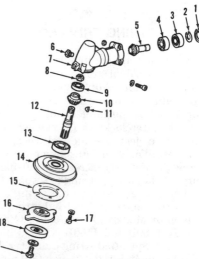

Fig. J18—Exploded view of gear head used on Models J300B, J320B, J400B, J420B, J450B and J460B.
1. Snap ring
2. Snap ring
3. Bearing
4. Bearing
5. Input gear
6. Plug
7. Housing
8. Nut
9. Bearing
10. Output gear
11. Key
12. Arbor
13. Bearing
14. Shield
15. Retainer
16. Flange
17. Screw
18. Flange
19. Screw (L.H.)

ry 80 hours of operation. Remove fill plug (6) in side of housing and add lubricant so housing is ½ full. Maximum amount that should be added if housing is dry is 11 mL (0.37 oz.). Recommended lubricant is molybdenum disulfide grease.

To disassemble gear head, remove blade or trimmer head. Detach gear head from drive shaft tube. Remove snap ring (1—Fig. J18) and using a suitable puller, extract pinion gear (5) and bearings as an assembly from housing. Detach snap ring (2) and press or pull bearings (3 and 4) off pinion gear (5). Remove flange (16), retainer (15) and shield (14). Using a suitable puller, extract arbor (12) assembly. Pull bearing (13) off of arbor (12). Unscrew nut (8) and remove gear (10) and bearing (9) from arbor.

Clean and inspect components. Reassemble by reversing disassembly procedure. Tighten pinion gear retaining nut (8) to 30 N·m (22 ft.-lbs.). Align slot in retainer (15) with hole (H—Fig. J19) in

shield (14). Before tightening screws (17), position flange (16—Fig. J18) on arbor shaft to center the retainer (15). Then, remove flange and tighten screws (17).

Fig. J19—Align slot on retainer (15) with hole (H) in shield (14). Center retainer before tightening screws (17). Refer to text.

THROTTLE FREE PLAY

To adjust throttle free play, loosen locknut (N—Fig. J20) and turn adjuster (A) so cable free play at carburetor is 1 mm (0.04 in.). Tighten locknut. The carburetor throttle plate should be fully open when throttle trigger is in full throttle position.

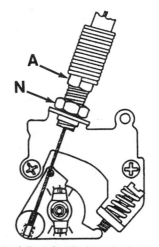

Fig. J20—Adjust throttle free play by loosening nut (N) and turning adjuster (A).

KAAZ

GASOLINE POWERED BRUSH CUTTERS

Model	Engine Manufacturer	Engine Model	Displacement
V20	Mitsubishi	T110PD	21.2 cc
V20	Kawasaki	TD18	18.4 cc
V25	Mitsubishi	T140PD	24.1 cc
V25	Kawasaki	TD24	24.1 cc
V35	Mitsubishi	T180PD	32.5 cc
V35	Kawasaki	TD33	33.3 cc
V40	Mitsubishi	T200PD	40.6 cc

ENGINE INFORMATION

All Models

Kaaz brush cutters are available in each model with Kawasaki or Mitsubishi two-stroke air-cooled gasoline engines. Engines may be identified by engine model number and engine displacement. Refer to KAWASAKI ENGINE SERVICE or MITSUBISHI ENGINE SERVICE sections of this manual.

FUEL MIXTURE

All Models

Manufacturer recommends mixing regular grade gasoline (unleaded is an acceptable substitute) with a good quality two-stroke air-cooled engine oil at a 25:1 ratio. Do not use fuel containing alcohol.

BLADE

All Models

All models may be equipped with a four cutting edge brush blade, an eight cutting edge blade or a sixty tooth saw blade. Make certain upper cup washer and lower adapter washer are centered and squarely seated on blade.

DRIVE SHAFT

All Models

All models are equipped with a solid steel drive shaft supported in bushings located in drive shaft housing tube. Drive shaft requires no regular mainte-nance; however, if drive shaft has been removed, lubricate drive shaft with lithium base grease before reinstallation. Bushings (2-Fig. KZ10) in drive shaft housing tube (1) may be renewed. Mark locations of old bushings in drive shaft housing before removing bushings. Install new bushings at old bushing locations.

GEAR HEAD

All Models

Refer to Fig. KZ11 for an exploded view of the gear head used on all models. Gear head lubricant level should be checked at 30 hour intervals of use. To check, remove check plug (8). Gear head housing should be 2/3 full of lithium base grease.

To disassemble gear head, remove blade assembly. Remove clamp bolts (10) and locating screw (9) and separate gear head from drive shaft housing. Remove snap ring (16) and use a suitable puller to remove input shaft (12) and bearing assembly. Remove snap ring (1) and use a suitable puller to remove arbor shaft (4) and bearing assembly. If bearing (6) stays in housing (7), heat housing to 140° F (60° C) and tap housing on wooden block to remove bearing. Note spacers (11) are installed at gear head housing clamp split to prevent housing damage from overtightening clamp bolts.

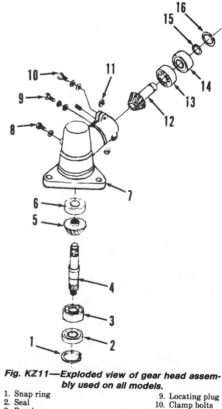

Fig. KZ11—Exploded view of gear head assembly used on all models.

1. Snap ring	9. Locating plug
2. Seal	10. Clamp bolts
3. Bearing	11. Shim (spacer)
4. Arbor shaft	12. Input shaft
5. Gear	13. Bearing
6. Bearing	14. Bearing
7. Housing	15. Snap ring
8. Check plug	16. Snap ring

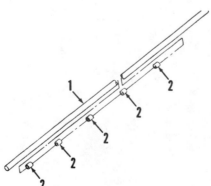

Fig. KZ10—Exploded view of drive shaft housing (1) and bushings (2) used on most models.

LAWN BOY
GASOLINE POWERED
STRING TRIMMER

Model	Engine Manufacturer	Engine Model	Displacement
SSI	PPP	....	31.0 cc
SSII	PPP	....	31.0 cc
1100	PPP	....	31.0 cc
1150	PPP	....	31.0 cc
1400	PPP	....	31.0 cc
1480	PPP	....	31.0 cc

ENGINE INFORMATION

All Models

All models are equipped with a two-stroke engine manufactured by Piston Powered Products. Refer to PISTON POWERED PRODUCTS ENGINE SERVICE section of this manual. Trimmer model number decal is located on engine cover.

FUEL MIXTURE

All Models

Manufacturer recommends mixing 8 ounces (236.6 mL) of Lawn Boy 2 cycle oil with 2 gallons (7.5 L) of regular grade gasoline of at least 87 octane rating. Unleaded regular gasoline is an acceptable substitute.

STRING TRIMMER

Trimmer may be equipped with a single strand semi-automatic trimmer head or a dual strand semi-automatic trimmer head. Refer to appropriate paragraph for model being serviced.

Single Strand Trimmer Head

To extend line on single strand trimmer head (Fig. LB10) with engine off, push in on bump button (20) and pull on line until desired length is obtained. To extend line with engine running, operate trimmer engine at full rpm and bump the button (20) on the ground. Line will automatically advance a measured amount.

To renew trimmer line, hold drum (15) and unscrew bump button (20).

Remove spool (19). Clean inner surface of drum and spool. Check indexing teeth on spool and drum for wear. Insert one end of a 25 foot (7.6 m) length of 0.080 inch (2 mm) monofilament line into one of the holes in spool

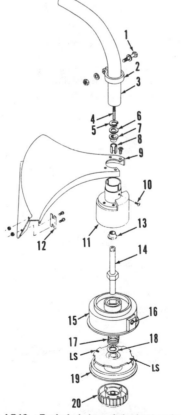

Fig. LB10—Exploded view of single strand semi-automatic trimmer head used on some models.

1. Bolt	
2. Clamp	12. Line cutter
3. Drive shaft housing	13. Bushing
4. Drive shaft	14. Drive shaft adapter
5. Retainer	15. Housing
6. Washer	16. Line guide
7. Bushing	17. Spring
8. Bushing	18. Retainer
9. Shield	19. Spool
10. Locating screw	20. Lock knob & bump button
11. Bushing housing	LS. Line slot

from the inside out, and back through the second hole to the inside. Wind line in direction indicated by arrow on spool until all but about 3 inches (76.2 mm) of line is wrapped on spool, then clip line temporarily into one of the line lock slots (LS) on spool. Insert line end through line guide in drum and install spool and bump button. Pull line to release from line lock slot on spool after assembly is complete.

Dual Strand Trimmer Head

To extend line on the dual strand semi-automatic trimmer head (Fig. LB11) with engine off, push in on bump button (8) while pulling lines out. Procedure may have to be repeated until desired line length has been obtained. To extend line with engine running, operate trimmer engine at full operating rpm and bump the button (8) on the ground. Each time bump button is tapped on the ground, approximately 1 inch (25 mm) of new line will be advanced.

To renew line, hold drum (2) and unscrew bump button (8). Remove spool (7) and remove any remaining old line. Clean spool and inner surface of drum. Check indexing teeth in drum and on spool. Loop a 25 foot (7.6 m) length of 0.080 inch (2 mm) monofilament line into two equal lengths. Insert the two line ends into the two holes in spool from the bottom and pull line out until loop is against spool. Wind both strands of line around spool at the same time and in the direction indicated by arrow on spool. Wind in tight even layers until almost all line is wrapped around spool, then temporarily clip each line into one of the two line slots (6). Insert line ends through line guides (3) in housing (2), install spool and tighten lock knob and bump button (8). Pull line ends to free from line slots after assembly is complete.

BLADE

Model 1480

Model 1480 may be equipped with the optional four-point brush blade (Fig. LB13). To install blade, refer to Fig. LB13 for assembly sequence. Tighten nut (11) to 225-250 in.-lbs. (26-28 N·m).

DRIVE SHAFT

Models SSI, SSII, 1100, 1150 And 1400

Models SSI, SSII, 1100, 1150 and 1400 are equipped with a flexible drive shaft enclosed in the drive shaft housing tube. Models 1100 and 1150 are direct drive models with no clutch. All other models are equipped with a centrifugal clutch. Drive shaft has squared ends which engage clutch adapter at engine end and head adapter at trimmer head end. Drive shaft should be removed for maintenance at 10 hour intervals of continuous use. Remove drive shaft, mark end positions, then clean shaft and inspect for damage. Lubricate drive shaft with a good quality high temperature wheel bearing grease and make certain shaft is installed with ends in

opposite locations. Alternating drive shaft squared ends between clutch and trimmer head ends will extend life of the shaft.

Model 1480

Model 1480 is equipped with a solid steel drive shaft mounted in bushings in the drive shaft housing. Drive shaft requires no regular maintenance; however, if drive shaft has been removed, lubricate with lithium base grease before reinstallation.

LOWER DRIVE SHAFT BUSHINGS

Models SSI, 1100, 1150 And 1400

Models SSI, 1100, 1150 and 1400 are equipped with drive shaft support bushings located in bushing head as shown in Fig. LB14. Bushing head requires no regular maintenance. A bushing kit (2) is available for service.

BEARING HEAD/LOWER CLUTCH

Model SSII

Model SSII is equipped with a bearing head incorporated in the lower clutch unit (Fig. LB15). Bearing head is equipped with sealed bearings and requires no regular maintenance.

To renew bearings or remove clutch assembly, remove trimmer head and cup washer (15). Remove the three bolts retaining bearing plate (11) to housing (4). Separate housing from bearing plate. Remove clutch shoe assembly (6) as required. Remove clutch drum (7) and shield (5). Press arbor shaft (8) from bearings. Remove snap rings (9 and 14). Remove bearings (10 and 13) and spacer (12).

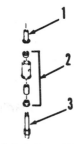

Fig. LB14—Exploded view of lower drive shaft support bushing assembly.

1. Adapter
2. Bushing kit
3. Drive shaft (head)

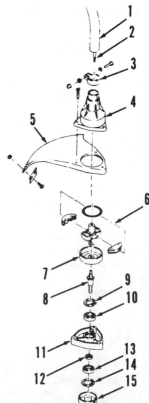

Fig. LB15—Exploded view of lower clutch and bearing head assembly used on Model SSII.

1. Drive shaft housing
2. Drive shaft
3. Clamp
4. Housing
5. Shield
6. Clutch assy.
7. Clutch drum
8. Shaft
9. Snap ring
10. Bearing
11. Bearing plate
12. Spacer
13. Bearing
14. Snap ring
15. Cup washer

Fig. LB11—Exploded view of dual strand semi-automatic trimmer head used on most models.

1. Drive shaft adapter
2. Housing
3. Line guide
4. Retainer
5. Spring
6. Line slot
7. Spool
8. Lock knob & bump button

Fig. LB13—Exploded view of blade assembly.

1. Shield
2. Drive shaft housing
3. Sleeve
4. Drive shaft adapter
5. Drive shaft (head)
6. Clamp
7. Bearing housing
8. Cup washer
9. Blade
10. Adapter plate
11. Nut

GEAR HEAD

Model 1480

Model 1480 is equipped with a gear head assembly. Check plug in gear head should be removed and lubricant level checked at 50 hour intervals of use. Gear head housing should be 2/3 full of lithium base grease. Service parts are not available from Lawn Boy. Gear head must be renewed as a complete unit.

ENGINE COVER

Models SSI And SSII

Models SSI and SSII are equipped with a full engine cover (Fig. LB17). To remove cover, remove all Phillips screws around outer cover. Remove head adjustment screw (12). Remove

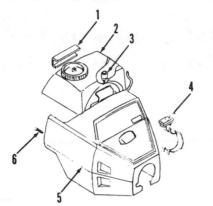

Fig. LB18—Exploded view of partial engine cover used on Models 1150, 1400 and 1480.

1. Fuel tank mount	4. Switch
2. Fuel tank	5. Engine cover
3. Fuel line assy.	6. Screw

the side of housing (7) opposite fuel tank filler cap (11). Covers are mounted in rubber grommets (1) also and may be slightly difficult to remove. Note locations of starter rope guide (2), throttle trigger (5), spring (6), switch (3) and fuel tank mounting before removing cover side (10). Fuel tank cap (11) must be removed to separate cover from fuel tank.

Models 1150, 1400 And 1480

Models 1150, 1400, and 1480 are equipped with a partial engine cover (Fig. LB18). To remove cover, disconnect spark plug lead and remove screw retaining cover extension stand (8— Fig. LB19). Remove cover extension stand. Disconnect the two wire leads at the ignition module. Remove the two inner engine cover retaining screws located just under fuel tank at each side (6— Fig. LB18). A long screwdriver is required to reach inner screws. Slide cover forward on tube as starter handle is worked through opening in engine cover.

Before reinstalling engine cover make certain the two ignition module wire leads are secured in retainer slot.

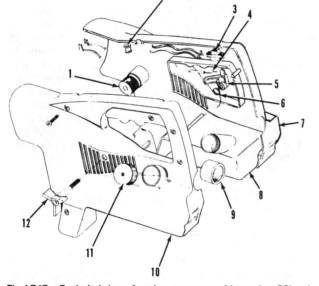

Fig. LB17—Exploded view of engine cover assembly used on SSI and SSII models.

1. Rubber grommet	7. Cover half
2. Rope guide	8. Fuel tank
3. Switch	9. Rubber sleeve
4. Throttle cable	10. Cover half
5. Throttle trigger	11. Fuel tank cap
6. Throttle spring	12. Tube clamp screw

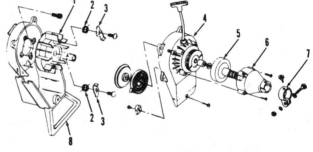

Fig. LB19—Exploded view of engine inner cover assembly.

1. Flywheel	5. Clutch drum
2. Spring	6. Clutch cover
3. Pawl	7. Clamp
4. Recoil housing	8. Stand

MARUYAMA

GASOLINE POWERED
STRING TRIMMERS

Model	Engine Manufacturer	Engine Model	Displacement
BC184	Kawasaki	KE18	18.4 cc
BC184C	Kawasaki	KE18	18.4 cc

ENGINE INFORMATION

All Models

Maruyama line trimmers and brush cutters are equipped with Kawasaki two-stroke air-cooled gasoline engines. Engines may be identified by manufacturer, engine model number and engine displacement. Refer to KAWASAKI ENGINE SERVICE section of this manual.

FUEL MIXTURE

All Models

Manufacturer recommends mixing regular grade gasoline (unleaded is an acceptable substitute) with a good quality two-stroke air-cooled engine oil at a 25:1 ratio. Do not use fuel containing alcohol.

STRING TRIMMER

All Models

Refer to Fig. MA10 for an exploded view of the dual strand manual trimmer head used on most models. To extend line, stop trimmer engine and wait until all head rotation has stopped. Loosen lock knob (6) (left-hand thread) until line ends may be pulled from housing. Pull lines until desired length has been obtained. Correct line length is 3.4-4.7 inches (10-12 cm).

To renew line, remove lock knob (6) and housing (5). Remove any remaining line on spool (2) and clean spool and housing. Install new line on spool. Wind line in direction indicated by arrow on spool. Diameter when new line is wound on spool must not exceed spool flange diameter. Insert line ends through line guides (4) then reinstall housing and lock knob.

BLADE

Model BC184

Model BC184 may be equipped with a 9 inch blade. Blade may be a four cutting edge blade, an eight cutting edge blade or a saw blade. To remove blade, rotate anti-wrap guard (1-Fig. MA11) until hole (H) in guard is aligned with hole (H) in cup washer (2). Insert a round tool into aligned holes to prevent blade rotation. Remove bolt (7) (left-hand thread), washer (6), cover (5) and adapter (4). Remove blade (3). When installing blade, tighten bolt (7) to 250 in.-lbs. (28 N·m).

DRIVE SHAFT

Model BC184

Model BC184 is equipped with a solid steel drive shaft supported in drive shaft housing tube. Drive shaft requires no regular maintenance; however, if drive shaft has been removed, lubricate drive shaft with lithium base grease before reinstallation.

Model BC184C

Model BC184C is equipped with a flexible drive shaft enclosed in the drive shaft housing tube. Drive shaft has squared ends which engage adapters at each end. Drive shaft should be removed for maintenance at 20 hour intervals of use. To remove, separate drive shaft housing from engine. Mark locations of drive shaft ends and pull drive shaft out of housing. Clean drive shaft and lubricate with lithium base grease. Reinstall drive shaft in housing. Make certain drive shaft ends are installed at original location.

BEARING HEAD

Model BC184C

Model BC184C is equipped with sealed bearing housing (3-Fig. MA12). No regular maintenance is required and no service parts are available.

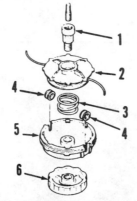

Fig. MA10—Exploded view of the dual strand manual trimmer head standard on most models.

1. Drive shaft adapter
2. Spool
3. Spring
4. Line guides
5. Housing
6. Lock knob

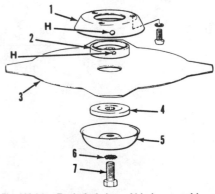

Fig. MA11—Exploded view of blade assembly on Model BC184.

1. Anti-wrap guard
2. Cup washer
3. Blade
4. Adapter plate
5. Cover
6. Washer
7. Bolt (LH)

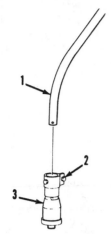

Fig. MA12—Bearing head assembly (3) is attached to drive shaft housing tube (1) by clamp (2). No service parts are available for bearing head.

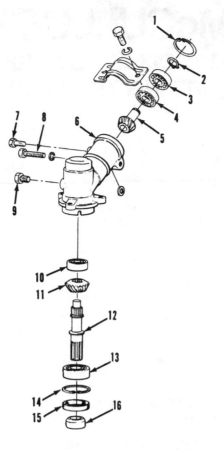

Fig. MA13—Exploded view of gear head used on Model BC184.

1. Snap ring	9. Check plug
2. Snap ring	10. Bearing
3. Bearing	11. Gear
4. Bearing	12. Arbor (output)
5. Input shaft	shaft
6. Housing	13. Bearing
7. Locating screw	14. Snap ring
8. Clamp bolt	15. Seal
	16. Spacer

GEAR HEAD

Model BC184

Model BC184 is equipped with the gear head shown in Fig. MA13. Gear head lubricant level should be checked at 50 hour intervals of use by removing check plug (9). Gear head housing should be 2/3 full of lithium base grease. Do not use a pressure grease gun to install grease as bearing seal and housing damage will occur.

To disassemble gear head, remove trimmer head or blade assembly. Remove locating screw (7) and clamp bolt (8) then separate gear head from drive shaft housing. Remove snap ring (1). Insert a screwdriver into clamp split in gear head housing and carefully expand housing. Remove input shaft (5) and bearing assembly. Remove snap ring (2) and press bearings (3 and 4) as required. Remove spacer (16) and seal (15). Remove snap ring (14) and use a suitable puller to remove arbor shaft (12) and bearing assembly. If bearing (10) stays in housing, heat housing to 140° F (60° C) and tap housing on wooden block to remove bearing. Remove gear (11) from arbor shaft. Press bearing (13) from arbor shaft as required.

McCULLOCH
GASOLINE POWERED
STRING TRIMMERS

Model	Engine Manufacturer	Engine Model	Displacement
MAC 60, 70	Kioritz	...	13.8 cc
MAC 80, 95	Kioritz	...	21.2 cc
MAC 60A, 80A, 85A	McCulloch	...	21.2 cc
MAC 90A, 95A, 100A, 100A-HD	McCulloch	...	21.2 cc
PRO SCAPER I, II, II-HD	McCulloch	...	21.2 cc
SUPER MAC 90A, 95A	McCulloch	...	21.2 cc
SUPER EAGER BEAVER IV	McCulloch	...	21.2 cc

ENGINE INFORMATION

All Models

Early model trimmers and brush cutters are equipped with engines manfactured by Kioritz. Late model trimmers and brush cutters are equipped with engine manufactured by McCulloch. Service procedure and specifications are similar. Identify engine by manufacturer and engine displacement. Refer to appropriate McCULLOCH ENGINE SERVICE or KIORITZ ENGINE SERVICE section of this manual.

FUEL MIXTURE

All Models

Manufacturer recommends mixing regular or unleaded gasoline with a high-quality, two-stroke engine oil designed for air-cooled engines. Recommended fuel:oil ratio is 40:1 when using McCulloch Custom Lubricant. Fuel:oil ratio should be 20:1 when using any other two-stroke oil, regardless of recommended ratio on oil container. Manufacturer recommends addition of Sta-Bil to fuel to prevent fuel degradation. Manufacturer does not recommend using fuel blended with any type of alcohol (gasohol).

STRING TRIMMER

All Models

Trimmer may be equipped with a single strand semi-automatic trimmer head or dual strand trimmer head. Two basic single strand trimmer heads have

been used. An early model head (Fig. MC10) and a late model head (Fig. MC14). The dual strand semi-automatic trimmer head is shown in Fig. MC16.

Early Style Single Strand Trimmer Head

Early style single strand semi-automatic trimmer head is shown in Fig. MC10. Line may be manually advanced with engine stopped by pushing in on housing (9) while pulling on line. Procedure may have to be repeated to obtain desired line length. To advance line with engine running, operate engine at full rpm and tap housing (9) on the ground. Each time housing is tapped on the ground, a measured amount of trimmer line will be advanced.

To renew trimmer line, remove cotter pin (10) and twist housing (9) counterclockwise to remove housing. Remove foam pad (6) and any remaining line on spool (3). Clean spool and inside of housing. Cut off approximately 25 feet (7.6 m) of 0.080 inch (2 mm) monofilament line and tape one end of line to spool (Fig. MC11). Wind line on spool in direction indicated by arrow on spool (Fig. MC12). Install foam pad with line end protruding from between foam pad and spool as shown in Fig. MC12. Insert end of line through line guide and install spool, housing and spring. Push housing in and twist in clockwise direction to lock in position, then install cotter pin (10—Fig. MC10).

Late Style Single Strand Trimmer Head

Late style single strand semi-automatic trimmer head is shown in Fig.

MC14. Line may be manually advanced with engine stopped by pushing in on housing (12) while pulling on line. Procedure may have to be repeated until desired line length is obtained. To advance line with engine running, operate

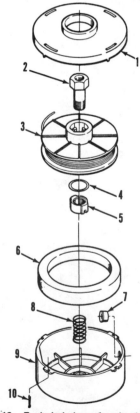

Fig. MC10—Exploded view of early style single strand semi-automatic trimmer head used on some models.

1. Cover	6. Foam pad
2. Drive shaft adapter	7. Line guide
3. Spool	8. Spring
4. "O" ring	9. Housing
5. Drive adapter nut	10. Cotter pin

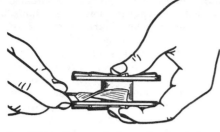

Fig. MC11—Tape end of new line to center of spool as shown.

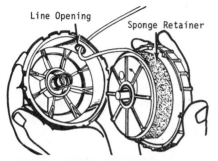

Fig. MC12—Install foam pad with line protruding from between pad and spool. Wind line in direction indicated on spool.

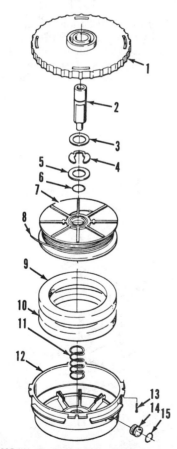

Fig. MC14—Exploded view of the single strand semi-automatic trimmer head used on some late models.

1. Cover
2. Drive shaft adapter
3. Washer
4. Retainer
5. Washer
6. Retainer
7. Spool
8. Line
9. Foam pad
10. Foam pad
11. Spring
12. Housing
13. Cotter pin
14. Line guide
15. Retainer

trimmer engine at full rpm and tap housing (12) on the ground. Each time housing is tapped on the ground, a measured amount of trimmer line is advanced.

To renew trimmer line, remove cotter pin (13). Twist housing (12) counterclockwise and remove housing. Remove foam pads (9 and 10) and any remaining line from spool (7). Clean spool and inner area of housing. Cut off approximately 25 feet (7.6 m) of 0.080 inch (2 mm) diameter monofilament line and tape one end of line to spool (Fig. MC11). Wind line on spool in direction indicated by arrow on spool (Fig. MC15). Install foam pads so line is protruding from center of pads (Fig. MC15). Insert end of line through line guide and install

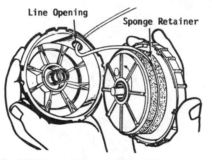

Fig. MC15—Install foam pads with line protruding from between pads. Wind line in direction indicated by arrow on spool.

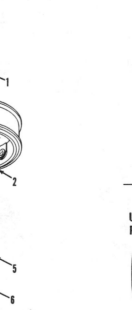

Fig. MC16—Exploded view of the dual strand semi-automatic trimmer head used on some models.

1. Drive shaft adapter
2. Housing
3. Spring
4. Washer
5. Outer cam
6. Inner cam
7. Spool & button

spool, housing and spring. Push housing and twist in clockwise direction to lock in position, then install cotter pin (13—Fig. MC14).

Dual Strand Trimmer Head

Heavy duty dual strand trimmer head is shown in Fig. MC16. To manually advance line with engine stopped, push in on button (7) and pull on each line. Procedure may have to be repeated to obtain desired line length. To extend line with engine running, operate trimmer at full operating rpm and tap button (7) on the ground. Line will automatically advance a measured amount.

To renew trimmer line, hold drum firmly and turn spool in direction shown in Fig. MC17 to remove slack. Twist with a hard snap until plastic peg is between holes. Pull spool out of drum. Remove old line from spool. Spool will hold approximately 20 feet (6 m) of monofilament line. Insert one end of new line through hole on spool (Fig. MC18) and pull line through until line is the same length on both sides of hole. Wind both ends of line at the same time in direction indicated by arrow on spool. Wind line tightly and evenly from side to side and do not twist line.

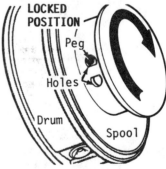

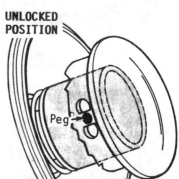

Fig. MC17—To remove spool, hold drum firmly and turn spool in direction shown to take up slack, then twist with a sudden snap until plastic peg is between holes as shown in lower view.

Illustrations courtesy McCulloch Corp.

McCulloch

Insert ends of line through line guide openings, align pegs on drum with slots in spool and push spool into drum. Hold drum firmly, twist spool suddenly in direction shown in Fig. MC19 until peg enters hole with a click and locks spool in position. Trim extending lines to desired length.

BLADE

All Models So Equipped

Some models may be equipped with a four cutting edge blade (Fig. MC20) or a saw blade (Fig. MC21). To remove blade, rotate cup washer (2—Figs. MC20 or MC21) and align hole in cup washer with hole in gear head housing. Insert a suitable tool into hole to prevent drive shaft from turning. Remove cotter pin (6—Figs. MC20 or MC21). Nut (5—Figs. MC20 or MC21) has left-hand threads. Remove nut (5), adapter and blade. Tighten nut (5) to 260 in.-lbs. (30 N·m) and install a new cotter pin.

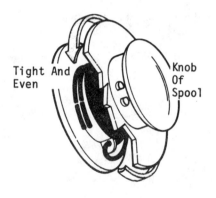

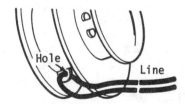

Fig. MC18—End of line must be inserted through hole on spool as shown in lower view. Wind line tightly in direction indicated by arrow on spool.

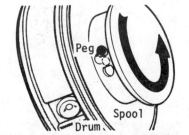

Fig. MC19—Hold drum firmly and twist suddenly to lock spool in position.

DRIVE SHAFT

Models With Curved Drive Shaft Housing

All models with a curved drive shaft housing are equipped with a flexible drive shaft enclosed in the drive shaft housing tube. Drive shaft has squared ends which engage adapters at each end. Drive shaft should be removed for

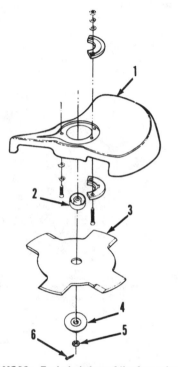

Fig. MC20—Exploded view of the four edge cutting blade used on some models.
1. Shield
2. Cup washer
3. Blade
4. Adapter washer
5. Nut
6. Cotter pin

Fig. MC21—Exploded view of saw blade used on some models.
1. Shield
2. Cup washer
3. Saw blade
4. Adapter washer
5. Nut
6. Cotter pin

TRIMMER

maintenance at 20 hour intervals of use. To remove, separate drive shaft housing from engine. Mark locations of drive shaft ends and pull drive shaft out of housing. Clean drive shaft and lubricate with lithium base grease. Reinstall drive shaft in housing with the drive shaft end previously at engine now at trimmer head end. Reversing drive shaft in this manner will extend drive shaft life.

Models With Straight Drive Shaft Housing

Models with straight drive shaft housings are equipped with a solid steel drive shaft supported in drive shaft housing tube. Drive shaft requires no regular maintenance; however, if drive shaft has been removed, lubricate drive shaft with lithium base grease before reinstallation.

BEARING HEAD

All Models So Equipped

Refer to Fig. MC24 and MC25 for an exploded view of the two different bearing heads used on some models. Bearing heads are equipped with sealed bearings and require no regular maintenance.

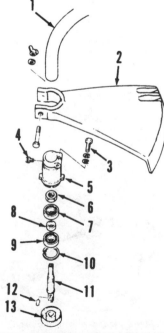

Fig. MC24—Exploded view of bearing head used on some models.
1. Drive shaft housing
2. Shield
3. Clamp bolt
4. Locating screw
5. Housing
6. Nut
7. Bearing
8. Spacer
9. Bearing
10. Snap ring
11. Arbor (output) shaft
12. Pin
13. Cup washer

Illustrations courtesy McCulloch Corp.

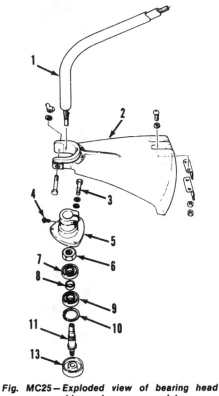

Fig. MC25—Exploded view of bearing head assembly used on some models.

1. Drive shaft housing	7. Bearing
2. Shield	8. Spacer
3. Clamp bolt	9. Bearing
4. Locating screw	10. Snap ring
5. Housing	11. Arbor (output) shaft
6. Nut	13. Cup washer

To disassemble either bearing head, remove clamp bolt (3—Figs. MC24 or MC25) and locating screw (4). Separate bearing head from drive shaft housing. Remove trimmer head or blade assembly and cup washer (13). Remove snap ring (10) and use a suitable puller to remove arbor shaft and bearing assembly. Remove nut (6) and press bearings from arbor shaft as required.

GEAR HEAD

All Models So Equipped

Refer to Fig. MC26 for an exploded view of the gear head used on heavy duty string trimmers and brush cutters. Check plug (15) should be removed and gear head housing lubricant level checked at 30 hour intervals of use. Gear head should be 2/3 full of lithium base grease. Do not use a pressure grease gun to install grease as bearing seal and housing damage will occur.

To disassemble gear head, remove trimmer head or blade assembly. Remove clamp bolts (14) and locating screw (13) and separate gear head from drive shaft housing tube. Remove snap ring (21). Insert screwdriver or other suitable wedge into clamp splits in housing and carefully expand housing. Remove input shaft (16) and bearing assembly. Remove snap ring (22) and press bearings from input shaft as required. Remove snap ring (5) and seal (6). Use a suitable puller to remove arbor shaft and bearing assembly. If bearing (11) stays in housing, heat housing to 140° F (60° C) and tap housing on wooden block to remove bearing. Press bearings and gear from arbor shaft as required.

Fig. MC26—Exploded view of gear head used on heavy duty trimmers and brush cutters.

1. Cotter pin	
2. Nut	
3. Adapter plate	
4. Cup washer	
5. Snap ring	
6. Seal	
7. Spacer	
8. Bearing	
9. Arbor shaft	
10. Gear	
11. Bearing	
12. Housing	
13. Locating screw	
14. Clamp bolt	
15. Check plug	
16. Input shaft	
17. Spacer	
18. Spacer	
19. Bearing	
20. Bearing	
21. Snap ring	
22. Snap ring	

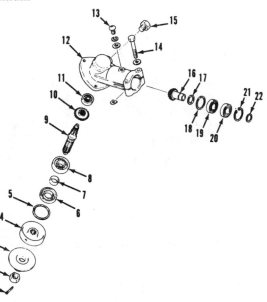

McCULLOCH

GASOLINE POWERED
STRING TRIMMERS

Model	Engine Manufacturer	Engine Model	Displacement
EAGER BEAVER I-SX, II-SX	McCulloch	...	21.2 cc
EAGER BEAVER III-SL, III-SX, IV-SL	McCulloch	...	21.2 cc
EAGER BEAVER SUPER, SUPER-SL	McCulloch	...	21.2 cc
MAC 60-SX, 65, 65-SL	McCulloch	...	21.2 cc
MAC 80-SX, 85-SL, 85-SX, 99-SL	McCulloch	...	21.2 cc
PRO SCAPER I-SX	McCulloch	...	21.2 cc
PRO SCAPER III, IV	McCulloch	...	30.0 cc
PRO SCAPER V	McCulloch	...	38.0 cc
ROADRUNNER	McCulloch	...	21.2 cc
SUPER EAGER BEAVER I-SX SPECIAL	McCulloch	...	21.2 cc

ENGINE INFORMATION

The models included in this section are powered by a McCulloch engine. Refer to appropriate McCulloch engine service section for service procedures and specifications.

FUEL MIXTURE

Manufacturer recommends mixing regular or unleaded grade gasoline with a high-quality two-stroke engine oil designed for air-cooled engines. Recommended fuel:oil ratio is 40:1 when using McCulloch Custom Lubricant. Fuel:oil ratio should be 20:1 when using any other two-stroke oil, regardless of recommended ratio on oil container. Manufacturer recommends addition of Sta-Bil to fuel to prevent fuel degradation. Manufacturer does not recommend using fuel blended with any type of alcohol (gasohol).

STRING TRIMMER

Models EAGER BEAVER III-SL, III-SX, IV-SL; MAC 85-SL, 85-SX, 99-SL; PRO SCAPER I-SX

These models are equipped with the semi-automatic string trimmer head shown in Fig. MC30. Models EAGER BEAVER III-SX, MAC 85-SX and PRO SCAPER I-SX are equipped with a single strand head; other models are equipped with a dual strand head.

To advance line with engine stopped, push in on button (2—Fig. MC30) and pull on line. Procedure may have to be repeated to obtain desired line length. To extend line with engine running, operate trimmer at full operating rpm and tap button (2) on ground. Line will automatically advance a measured amount.

To install new line on single strand head, press against tab marked "PUSH" and remove cover (1—Fig. MC30), button (2) and spool (3). Clean and inspect all parts. New line should be 0.095 inch (2.4 mm) diameter and 12 feet (3.7 m) long. Insert end of line through eye of spool as shown in Fig. MC31 so approximately 1 inch (25 mm) extends past eye. Wrap line on spool in direction indicated by arrow on spool. Install spool while directing line end through eye of drum (6—Fig. MC30). Install button and cover. Cover should snap into place after locking tabs of cover engage tabs on drum next to eye hole. Trim line so approximately 3 inches (75 mm) of line extends from drum.

To install new line on dual strand head, press against tab marked "PUSH" and remove cover (1—Fig. MC30), button (2) and spool (3). Clean and inspect all parts. New line should be 0.095 inch (2.4 mm) diameter and 15 feet (4.6 m) long. Insert line through eye in spool and pull line through eye until ends of line are even. Wrap line on spool in direction indicated by arrow on spool as shown in Fig. MC31A. Install spool while directing line end through each eye (7—Fig. MC30) of drum. Install button and cov-

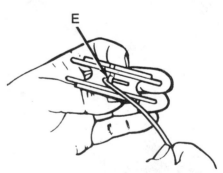

Fig. MC31—Insert trimmer line end through eye (E) on spool as shown so approximately 1 inch (25 mm) extends past eye.

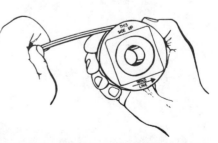

Fig. MC31A—Wind line onto trimmer spool in direction indicated by arrow on spool. Dual line spool is shown; single line spool is similar.

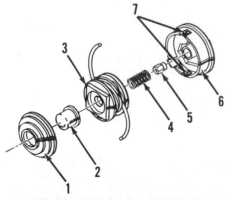

Fig. MC30—Exploded view of string trimmer head used on EAGER BEAVER III-SL, III-SX, IV-SL; MAC 85-SL, 85-SX, 99-SL; PRO SCAPER I-SX.

1. Cover
2. Button
3. Spool
4. Spring
5. Nut
6. Drum
7. Eyelets

Illustrations courtesy McCulloch Corp.

er. Cover should snap into place after locking tabs of cover engage tabs on drum next to eye hole. Trim line so approximately 4 inches (102 mm) of line extends from drum.

If trimmer head retaining nut (5—Fig. MC30) must be unscrewed, prevent shaft rotation by inserting a pin through hole provided in bearing head to lock shaft.

Models EAGER BEAVER SUPER, SUPER SL; MAC 65, 65-SL; ROAD RUNNER

These models are equipped with the semi-automatic string trimmer head shown in Fig. MC32. Models EAGER BEAVER SUPER, MAC 65 and early ROAD RUNNER are equipped with a single strand head; Models EAGER BEAVER SUPER SL, MAC 65-SL and later ROAD RUNNER are equipped with a dual strand head.

To advance line with engine stopped, push in on button (B—Fig. MC32) and pull on line. Procedure may have to be repeated to obtain desired line length. To extend line with engine running, operate trimmer at full operating rpm and tap button on ground. Line will automatically advance a measured amount.

To install new line on Models EAGER BEAVER SUPER, MAC 65 and early ROAD RUNNER, press against tab marked "PUSH" and twist cover (8—Fig. MC32) counterclockwise. Remove cover and spool (7) assembly. Clean and inspect all parts. New line should be 0.095 inch (2.4 mm) diameter and 12 feet (3.7 m) long. Insert end of line through eye of spool as shown in Fig. MC33 so approximately ¾ inch (19 mm) extends past eye. Wrap line on spool in clockwise direction (note arrow on spool). Install spool while directing line end through eye (2—Fig. MC32) of drum (3). Install cover (8) so lug aligns with tab of drum and twist clockwise so cover snaps into place. Trim line so approximately 3 inches (75 mm) extend from drum.

To install new line on Models EAGER BEAVER SUPER SL, MAC 65-SL and later ROAD RUNNER, press against tab marked "PUSH" and twist cover (8—Fig. MC32) counterclockwise. Remove cover and spool (7) assembly. Clean and inspect all parts. New line should be 0.095 inch (2.4 mm) diameter and 12 feet (3.7 m) long. Insert line through eye and pull line through eye until ends of line are even. Wrap line on spool in clockwise direction (note arrow on spool). Install spool while directing line ends through eyes (2—Fig. MC32) of drum. Install cover by twisting clockwise so cover snaps into place. Trim line

so approximately 3 inches (75 mm) extend from drum.

Models EAGER BEAVER I-SX, II-SX; MAC 60-SX, 80-SX; SUPER EAGER BEAVER I-SX SPECIAL

These models are equipped with the semi-automatic single strand string trimmer head shown in Fig. MC34.

To advance line with engine stopped, push in on button and pull on line. Procedure may have to be repeated to obtain desired line length. To extend line with engine running, operate trimmer at full operating rpm and tap button on ground. Line will automatically advance a measured amount.

To install new line, remove screw (1—Fig. MC34) and separate trimmer spool assembly (2) from head. Clean and inspect all parts. New line on EAGER BEAVER I-SX, MAC 60-SX and SUPER EAGER BEAVER I-SX SPECIAL should be 0.080 inch (2 mm) diameter and 17 feet (5.2 m) long. New line on EAGER BEAVER II-SX and MAC 80-SX should be 0.095 inch (2.4 mm) diameter and 14 feet (4.3 m) long. Using a 2 inch (50 mm) piece of tape, wrap tape around 1 inch (25 mm) of line end and attach remainder of tape to spool as shown in Fig. MC35. Wind line around spool in direction indicated by arrow on spool. Install spool while directing line end through eye of drum (6—Fig. MC34). Install retaining screw (1). Trim line so approximately 3 inches (75 mm) extend from drum.

Models PRO SCAPER III, IV, V

Models PRO SCAPER III, PRO SCAPER IV and PRO SCAPER V are equipped with the manual advance, dual strand string trimmer head shown in Fig. MC36. To extend line, loosen lock knob (8) approximately two turns by turning knob clockwise (note that knob has left-hand threads). Pull out 6 inches (152 mm) of line from each side.

To install new line, remove screw (9) and washer. Unscrew lock knob (8) by turning clockwise (note that knob has left-hand threads). Remove cover (6), spring (5) and spool (4); do not lose eyelets (3). New line should be 0.095 inch (2.4 mm) diameter and 17½ feet (5.3 m) long. Loop the line through two holes in spool and pull both ends so each strand is equal length. Then, wrap both strands at the same time onto spool in clockwise direction as viewed from unnotched side of spool shown in Fig. MC37. Place eyelets (3—Fig. MC36) on line ends and install spool (4) into drum (2) with notched side out. Snap eyelets into drum. Install spring (5), cover (6), knob

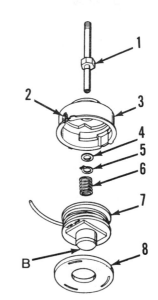

Fig. MC32—Exploded view of string trimmer head used on EAGER BEAVER SUPER, SUPER SL; MAC 65, 65-SL; ROAD RUNNER.

1. Arbor	5. Snap ring
2. Eyelet	6. Spring
3. Drum	7. Spool
4. Washer	8. Cover

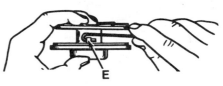

Fig. MC33—Insert trimmer line end through eye (E) on spool as shown so approximately ¾ inch (19 mm) extends past eye.

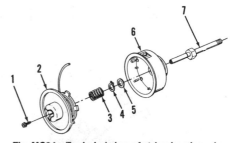

Fig. MC34—Exploded view of string head used on EAGER BEAVER I-SX, II-SX; MAC 60-SX, 80-SX; SUPER EAGER BEAVER I-SX SPECIAL.

1. Screw	
2. Spool	5. Washer
3. Spring	6. Drum
4. Snap ring	7. Arbor

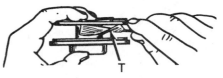

Fig. MC35—Using a 2-in. (50 mm) piece of tape (T), wrap tape around 1 inch (25 mm) of line end and attach remainder of tape to spool.

(8), washer and screw (9). Trim line on each side so line length is 6 inches (152 mm).

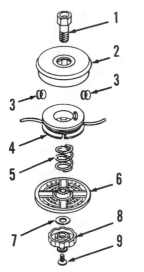

Fig. MC36—Exploded view of string head used on PRO SCAPER III, IV, V.

1. Adapter
2. Drum
3. Eyelets
4. Spool
5. Spring
6. Cover
7. Washer
8. Knob
9. Screw

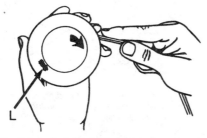

Fig. MC37—Pull line (L) through holes in spool so each line is of equal length, then wrap both strands of line around spool as shown.

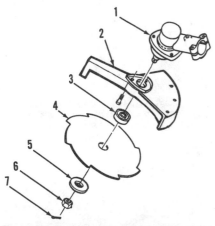

Fig. MC38—Exploded view of typical blade installation on EAGER BEAVER III-SL, III-SX, IV-SL; MAC 85-SL, 85-SX, 99-SL. Nut (6) has left-hand threads on EAGER BEAVER III-SX, EAGER BEAVER IV-SL, MAC 85-SX and MAC 99-SL.

1. Gear head
2. Shield
3. Cup washer
4. Blade
5. Washer
6. Nut
7. Cotter pin

BLADE

Models EAGER BEAVER III-SL, III-SX, IV-SL; MAC 85-SL, 85-SX, 99-SL; PRO SCAPER IV, V

These models may be equipped with a blade. Refer to Figs. MC38 or MC39. To remove blade (4), rotate cup (3) so hole in cup aligns with hole in head (1). Insert a suitable pin through holes and unscrew blade retaining nut or screw. Note that nut or screw on Models EAGER BEAVER III-SX, EAGER BEAVER IV-SL, MAC 85-SX, MAC 99-SL, PRO SCAPER IV and PRO SCAPER V has left-hand threads. Blade nut on Models MAC 85-SL and EAGER BEAVER III-SL has right-hand threads.

Install blade on Models EAGER BEAVER III-SX, EAGER BEAVER IV-SL, MAC 85-SX, MAC 99-SL, PRO SCAPER IV and PRO SCAPER V so teeth point in clockwise direction as viewed from ground side of blade. Install blade on Models MAC 85-SL and EAGER BEAVER III-SL so teeth point in counterclockwise direction as viewed from ground side of blade. On models shown in Fig. MC39, install washer (5) with concave side against blade. Tighten blade nut or screw to 176-265 in.-lbs. (20-30 N·m).

DRIVE SHAFT

All Models

The drive shaft should be removed, cleaned and lubricated after every 50

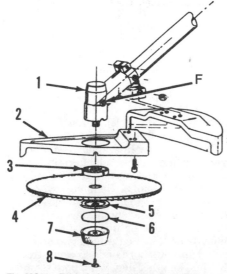

Fig. MC39—Exploded view of blade installation on PRO SCAPER IV and PRO SCAPER V. Install step washer (5) with concave side towards blade. Screw (8) has left-hand threads. Gear head is lubricated by injecting grease through fitting (F).

1. Gear head
2. Shield
3. Collar
4. Blade
5. Step washer
6. Washer
7. Scuff plate
8. Screw (L.H.)

hours of operation. Separate drive shaft housing (tube) from engine for access to shaft. Apply a high-quality, lithium-base grease to drive shaft.

BEARING HEAD

All Models So Equipped

The bearing head is sealed and does not require maintenance.

Bearing head must be serviced as a unit assembly; no components are available.

GEAR HEAD

All Models So Equipped

The gear head on Models PRO SCAPER III, PRO SCAPER IV and PRO SCAPER V should be lubricated after every 50 hours of operation by injecting a high-quality lithium-base grease through grease fitting (F—Fig. MC39) located on side of gear head.

On other models with a gear head, periodically check grease level by removing screw (S—Fig. MC40). Gear head should be ⅔ full of lithium-base grease. Rotate shaft to be sure grease is distributed throughout. Do not install grease with a pressure grease gun.

Gear head must be serviced as a unit assembly; no components are available.

THROTTLE TRIGGER AND CABLE

Adjusting nuts are located at carburetor end of throttle cable. Turn nuts as needed so carburetor throttle plate opens fully when throttle trigger is at full-speed position, and so there is slight free play at throttle trigger when released.

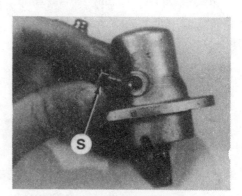

Fig. MC40—Periodically check gear head lubricant level by removing screw (S). Gear head should be ⅔ full of lithium-base grease.

McCULLOCH

GASOLINE POWERED
STRING TRIMMERS

Model	Engine Manufacturer	Engine Model	Displacement
TITAN 2100, 2200	McCulloch	…	21.2 cc
TITAN 2300, 2300AV	McCulloch	…	21.2 cc
TITAN 2500, 2500AV	McCulloch	…	25 cc

ENGINE INFORMATION

The models included in this section are powered by a McCulloch engine. Refer to appropriate McCulloch engine service section for service procedures and specifications.

FUEL MIXTURE

Manufacturer recommends mixing regular or unleaded gasoline with a high-quality two-stroke engine oil designed for air-cooled engines. Recommended fuel:oil ratio is 40:1 when using McCulloch Custom Lubricant. Fuel:oil ratio should be 20:1 when using any other two-stroke oil, regardless of recommended ratio on oil container. Manufacturer recommends addition of Sta-Bil to fuel to prevent fuel degradation. Manufacturer does not recommend using fuel blended with any type of alcohol (gasohol).

STRING TRIMMER

All models are equipped with the dual strand, semi-automatic string trimmer head shown in Fig. MC50.

To advance line with engine stopped, push in on button (2) and pull on line. Procedure may have to be repeated to obtain desired line length. To extend line with engine running, operate trimmer at full operating rpm and tap button (2) on ground. Line will automatically advance a measured amount.

To install new line, press against tab marked "PUSH" and remove cover (1—Fig. MC50), button (2) and spool (3). Clean and inspect all parts. New line should be 0.095-in. (2.4 mm) diameter and 20-ft. (6.1 m) long on Titan 2100 and Titan 2200 or 30-ft. long (9 m) on Titan 2300 and Titan 2500. Insert line through eye of spool (Fig. MC51) and pull line through eye until ends of line are even. Wrap both strands of line evenly on spool in direction indicated by arrow on

spool. Install spool while directing line end through eyes (7—Fig. MC50) of drum (6). Install button (2) and cover (1). Cover should snap into place after locking tabs of cover engage tabs on drum next to eye hole. Trim line so approximately 4 inches (102 mm) extend from drum.

If trimmer head retaining nut (5—Fig. MC50) must be unscrewed, prevent shaft rotation by inserting a pin through hole provided in bearing head to lock shaft. Note that nut (5) on Models 2300, 2300AV, 2500 and 2500AV has left-hand threads and nut or trimmer head must be rotated clockwise for removal.

BEARING HEAD

Models 2100 And 2200

The spindle bearing head is sealed and does not require maintenance.

Bearing head must be serviced as a unit assembly; no components are available.

GEAR HEAD

Models 2300, 2300AV, 2500 And 2500AV

Periodically check grease level by removing screw (S—Fig. MC52). Gear head should be ²/₃ full of lithium-base grease. Do not install grease with a pressure grease gun.

Gear head must be serviced as a unit assembly; no components are available.

THROTTLE TRIGGER AND CABLE

Adjusting nuts are located at carburetor end of throttle cable. Turn nuts as needed so carburetor throttle plate opens fully when throttle trigger is at full-speed position, and so there is slight free play at throttle trigger when released.

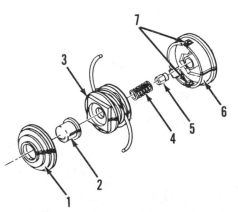

Fig. MC50—Exploded view of dual strand, semi-automatic string trimmer head used on all models.

1. Cover	5. Nut
2. Button	6. Drum
3. Spool	7. Eyelets
4. Spring	

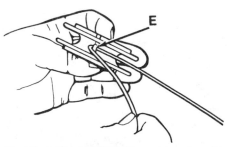

Fig. MC51—Thread new line through spool eye (E) so both ends are equal length.

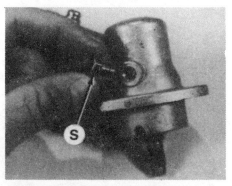

Fig. MC52—Periodically check gear head lubricant level by removing screw (S). Gear head should be ²/₃ full of lithium-base grease.

McCULLOCH

GASOLINE POWERED BLOWERS

Engine Model	Engine Manufacturer	Model	Displacement
EAGER BEAVER	McCulloch	...	21.2 cc
EAGER BEAVER III, IV	McCulloch	...	21.2 cc
PRO STREAM	McCulloch	...	21.2 cc
SUPER AIR STREAM III, IV, V	McCulloch	...	21.2 cc

ENGINE INFORMATION

The models included in this section are powered by a McCulloch engine. Refer to appropriate McCulloch engine service section for service procedures and specifications.

FUEL MIXTURE

Manufacturer recommends mixing regular or unleaded gasoline with a high-quality, two-stroke engine oil designed for air-cooled engines. Recommended fuel:oil ratio is 40:1 when using McCulloch Custom Lubricant. Fuel:oil ratio should be 20:1 when using any other two-stroke oil, regardless of recommended ratio on oil container. Manufacturer recommends addition of Sta-Bil to fuel to prevent fuel degradation. The use of any fuel blended with any type of alcohol (gasohol) is not recommended by the manufacturer.

ENGINE AIR FILTER

Engine air filter element should be removed, inspected and cleaned (if necessary) after each use of blower. Tap the filter element to remove loose dirt. Filter may be washed in warm, soapy water. Rinse in clean water and allow to dry completely before installing.

If filter is damaged, install a new filter. Engine will be damaged if operated with a faulty filter. Do not operate engine without the air filter.

MUFFLER

Muffler and exhaust ports should be inspected periodically for carbon build-up. Rotate crankshaft until piston skirt covers the exhaust ports, then use a wooden scraper to clean carbon from ports. Use scraper or wire brush to clean carbon from muffler and spark arrestor screen as necessary.

BLOWER ASSEMBLY

To disassemble blower, remove blower tube and adapter (5—Fig. MCB1) from impeller housing. Remove screws holding impeller housing halves (4 and 10) together. Remove spark plug and insert end of a rope into cylinder to lock the piston and crankshaft. Remove blower impeller retaining nut (6) and remove impeller (8) from engine crankshaft.

To reassemble, reverse disassembly procedure. Tighten impeller nut (6) to 90-100 in.-lbs. (10.2-11.3 N·m). Tighten impeller housing screws to 20-25 in.-lbs. (2.3-2.8 N·m).

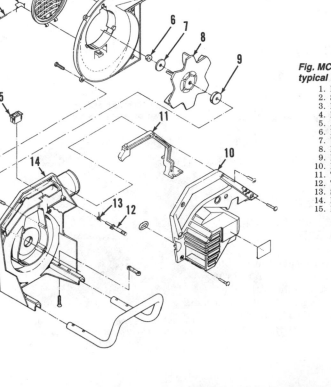

Fig. MCB1—Exploded view of typical blower/vac assembly.

1. Pin
2. Spring
3. Inlet cover
4. Impeller housing, outer
5. Adapter tube
6. Nut
7. Washer
8. Impeller
9. Drive disc
10. Engine shroud
11. Throttle trigger
12. Throttle lock
13. Spring
14. Impeller housing, inner
15. Ignition switch

OLYMPYK

GASOLINE POWERED STRING TRIMMERS

Model	Engine Manufacturer	Engine Model	Displacement
OL200B	EFCO	200	22.5 cc
OL200L	EFCO	200	22.5 cc
OL220B	EFCO	220	22.5 cc
OL220L	EFCO	220	22.5 cc
OL260B	EFCO	260	25.4 cc
OL260L	EFCO	260	25.4 cc
OL300B	EFCO	300	30.5 cc
OL320B	EFCO	300	30.5 cc
OL400B	EFCO	400	37.7 cc
OL420B	EFCO	400	37.7 cc
OL450B	EFCO	450	37.7 cc
OL460B	EFCO	450	37.7 cc

ENGINE INFORMATION

The models in this section are equipped with an EFCO engine. Refer to EFCO engine service section for engine service information.

FUEL MIXTURE

Manufacturer recommends mixing regular grade gasoline, preferably leaded, with a high-quality, two-stroke engine oil. Recommended fuel:oil ratio is 40:1

STRING TRIMMER

All models are equipped with a manual advance, dual strand trimmer head. To pull out line, stop engine and push up against spool (against spring pressure). While pushing spool up, turn spool counterclockwise (as viewed from bottom) to eject new line. Release spool. To install new line, unscrew retaining screw (5—Fig. OL11). Screw has left-hand threads. Remove housing (4), spool (3) and spring (2). Remove old string and clean components. Specified string diameter on Models OL300B, OL320B, OL400B, OL420B, OL450B and OL460B is 0.095 inch (2.4 mm). Specified string diameter for all other models is 0.080 inch (2.0 mm). Spool capacity is 36 feet (11 m) for Models OL300B, OL320B, OL400B, OL420B, OL450B and OL460B and 42 feet (13 m) for all other models. Insert line (6) through holes in spool as shown in Fig. OL11 and pull line through holes until ends are even. Wrap line around spool in direction indicated by arrows on spool. Do not twist lines.

Reassemble trimmer head. Tighten retaining screw (5—Fig. OL11) to 25 N·m (18 ft.-lbs.).

BLADE

All straight-shaft models may be equipped with a blade. Refer to Figs. OL13, OL14 or OL15 for configuration of blade assembly. Blade retaining screw has left-hand threads. Note that direction of blade rotation is usually indicated by an arrow on the gear head. Tighten retaining screw to 25 N·m (18 ft.-lbs.).

DRIVE SHAFT

Models OL200B And OL200L

Models OL200B and OL200L are equipped with a flexible drive shaft. Periodically remove drive shaft and lubricate with a lithium-base grease. To remove drive shaft, remove bearing head and extract drive shaft. When installing drive shaft, be sure drive shaft end is properly seated at drive end.

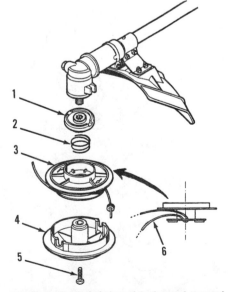

Fig. OL11—Exploded view of dual strand, manual advance trimmer used on Models OL200B, OL200L, OL220B, OL220L, OL260B and OL260L. All other models are similar. Insert trimmer line through spool holes as shown.

1. Flange
2. Spring
3. Spool
4. Housing
5. Screw (L.H.)
6. Line

Fig. OL13—Blade assembly used on some models.

1. Flange
2. Blade
3. Washer
4. Cup washer
5. Lockwasher
6. Screw (L.H.)

All Other Models

All models except Models OL200B and OL200L are equipped with a solid drive shaft that does not require periodic lubrication. If drive shaft is removed, apply a lithium-base grease to drive shaft. The drive shaft rides in bushings that are renewable. If bushings are to be renewed, mark position of old bushings before removal so new bushings can be installed in original positions.

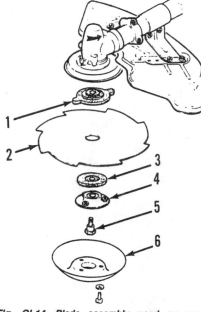

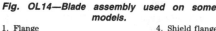

Fig. OL14—Blade assembly used on some models.

1. Flange
2. Blade
3. Washer
4. Shield flange
5. Screw (L.H.)
6. Shield

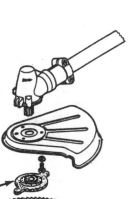

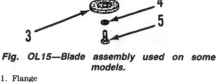

Fig. OL15—Blade assembly used on some models.

1. Flange
2. Blade
3. Washer
4. Lockwasher
5. Screw (L.H.)

BEARING HEAD

Models OL200B And OL200L

The bearing head does not require periodic lubrication.

To disassemble bearing head, remove trimmer assembly (trimmer head retaining screw has left-hand threads). Separate bearing head from drive shaft tube. Detach snap ring (5—Fig. OL16). Use a suitable puller and extract arbor (3) with bearings (4) from housing (1). Press or pull bearings off arbor. Reassemble by reversing disassembly procedure.

GEAR HEAD

Models OL220B, OL220L, OL260B And OL260L

Models OL220B, OL220L, OL260B and OL260L are equipped with the gear head shown in Fig. OL17. Lubricant level should be checked after every 80 hours of operation. Remove fill plug (5) in side of housing and add lubricant so housing is 1/2 full. Maximum amount that should be added if housing is dry is 9 mL (0.3 oz.). Recommended lubricant is molybdenum disulfide grease.

To disassemble gear head, remove trimmer or blade assembly (retaining screw has left-hand threads). Separate gear head from drive shaft tube. Remove flange (11) and detach snap ring (10). Use a suitable puller and extract gear (7) and bearings as an assembly.

Fig. OL16—Exploded view of bearing head used on Models OL200B and OL200L.

1. Housing
2. Washer
3. Arbor
4. Bearings
5. Snap ring
6. Flange
7. Flange
8. Screw (L.H.)

Press or pull bearings (8 and 9) off gear shaft. Detach snap ring (1). Reach through output opening of housing and drive out input shaft (4) and bearing (3). Remove snap ring (2) and separate bearing from shaft.

Reassemble by reversing disassembly procedure. Note that lower bearing (9) is a sealed bearing.

Models OL300B, OL320B, OL400B, OL420B, OL450B And OL460B

Models OL300B, OL320B, OL400B, OL420B, OL450B and OL460B are equipped with the gear head shown in Fig. OL18. Lubricant level should be checked after every 80 hours of operation. Remove fill plug (6) in side of housing and add lubricant so housing is 1/2 full. Maximum amount that should be added if housing is dry is 11 mL (0.37 oz.). Recommended lubricant is molybdenum disulfide grease.

To disassemble gear head, remove blade or trimmer head. Detach gear head from drive shaft tube. Remove snap ring (1—Fig. OL18) and, using a suitable puller, extract pinion gear (5) and bearings as an assembly from housing. Detach snap ring (2) and press or pull bearings (3 and 4) off pinion gear (5). Remove flange (16), retainer (15) and shield (14). Using a suitable puller, extract arbor (12) assembly. Pull bearing (13) off arbor (12). Unscrew nut (8) and

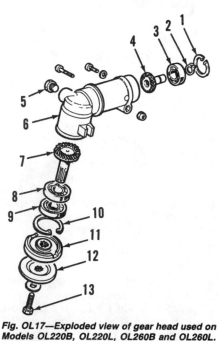

Fig. OL17—Exploded view of gear head used on Models OL220B, OL220L, OL260B and OL260L.

1. Snap ring
2. Snap ring
3. Bearing
4. Input gear
5. Plug
6. Housing
7. Output gear
8. Bearing
9. Bearing
10. Snap ring
11. Flange
12. Flange
13. Screw (L.H.)

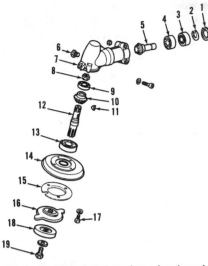

Fig. OL18—Exploded view of gear head used on Models OL300B, OL320B, OL400B, OL420B, OL450B and OL460B.

1. Snap ring	11. Key
2. Snap ring	12. Arbor
3. Bearing	13. Bearing
4. Bearing	14. Shield
5. Input gear	15. Retainer
6. Plug	16. Flange
7. Housing	17. Screw
8. Nut	18. Flange
9. Bearing	19. Screw
10. Output gear	

remove gear (10) and bearing (9) from arbor.

Clean and inspect components. Reassemble by reversing disassembly procedure. Tighten nut (8) to 30 N·m (22 ft.-lbs.). Align slot in retainer (15) with hole (H—Fig. OL19) in shield (14). Before tightening screws (17), position flange (16—Fig. OL18) on arbor shaft to center the retainer (15). Then, remove flange and tighten screws (17).

Fig. OL19—Align slot on retainer (15) with hole (H) in shield (14). Center retainer before tightening screws (17).

THROTTLE FREE PLAY

To adjust throttle free play, loosen locknut (N—Fig. OL20) and turn adjuster (A) so cable free play at carburetor is 1 mm (0.04 in.). Tighten locknut. The carburetor throttle plate should be fully open when throttle trigger is in full throttle position.

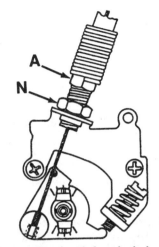

Fig. OL20—Adjust throttle free play by loosening nut (N) and turning adjuster (A).

Illustrations courtesy Olympyk/Oleo-Mac

PIONEER/PARTNER
GASOLINE POWERED STRING TRIMMERS

Model	Engine Manufacturer	Engine Model	Displacement
B180	Kawasaki	KE18	18.4 cc
B250	Kawasaki	KE24	24.1 cc
B370	Husqvarna	....	44.0 cc
B440	Husqvarna	....	44.0 cc

ENGINE INFORMATION

All Models

Pioneer/Partner line trimmers and brush cutters are equipped with a Kawasaki or Husqvarna two-stroke air-cooled gasoline engines. Engines may be identified by engine manufacturer, trimmer model number or engine displacement. Refer to KAWASAKI ENGINE SERVICE or HUSQVARNA ENGINE SERVICE sections of this manual.

FUEL MIXTURE

All Models

Manufacturer recommends mixing regular grade gasoline (unleaded is an acceptable substitute) with a good quality two-stroke air cooled engine oil at a 25:1 ratio. Do not use fuel containing alcohol.

STRING TRIMMER

Models B180 And B250

Refer to Fig. PR10 for an exploded view of the dual strand manual trimmer head used on Models B180 and B250. To extend line, stop trimmer engine and wait until all head rotation has stopped. Loosen lock knob (6) (left-hand thread) until line ends may be pulled from housing. Pull lines until desired length has been obtained. Correct line length is 3.4-4.7 inches (10-12 cm).

To renew line, remove lock knob (6) and housing (5). Remove any remaining line on spool (2) and clean spool and housing. Install new line on spool. Wind line in direction indicated by arrow on spool. Diameter when new line is wound on spool must not exceed spool flange

diameter. Insert line ends through line guides (4) then reinstall housing and lock knob.

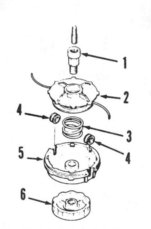

Fig. PR10—Exploded view of dual strand manual trimmer head used on Models B180 and B250.

1. Drive shaft adapter
2. Spool
3. Spring
4. Line guides
5. Lower housing
6. Lock knob

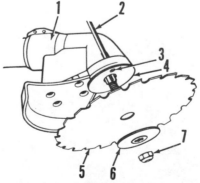

Fig. PR11—View showing parts assembly sequence to install blade on Models B370 and B440.

1. Gear head
2. Locking tool
3. Hole
4. Drive disc
5. Blade
6. Adapter washer
7. Nut (LH)

Models B370 And B440

Models B370 and B440 may be equipped with a trimmer head as an option. To install trimmer head, insert a locking rod (2—Fig. PR 11) in hole in gear head and hole in drive disc (4). Some models have a slot at front of gear head housing instead of hole. Remove left-hand threaded nut (7), adapter washer (6) and blade (5). Some models may have a cover between nut (7) and adapter washer (6). Install trimmer head as shown in Fig. PR12. Tighten trimmer head to 20 N·m (15 ft.-lbs.).

To renew line in trimmer head, align hole in trimmer housing and line guide opening and feed new line onto spool while winding lower plate (Fig. PR13).

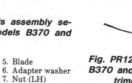

Fig. PR12—Trimmer head available for Models B370 and B440 has left-hand threads. Tighten trimmer head to 20 N·m (15 ft.-lbs.).

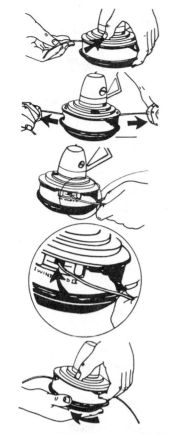

Fig. PR13—To renew line on Models B370 and B440 trimmer head, refer to text and follow sequence in illustration.

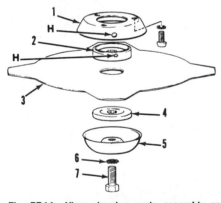

Fig. PR14—View showing parts assembly sequence to install blade on Model B250.

1. Anti-wrap guard
2. Cup washer
3. Blade
4. Adapter plate
5. Cover
6. Washer
7. Bolt (LH)

Fig. PR15—Sharpen front edge of tooth only. Make certain file holder is held firmly against the edge of tooth.

BLADE

Model B250

Model B250 may be equipped with a four cutting edge blade (Fig. PR14). To remove blade, rotate anti-wrap guard (1) until hole (H) in guard is aligned with hole (H) in cup washer (2). Insert a round tool into aligned holes to prevent blade rotation. Remove bolt (7) (left-hand thread), washer (6), cover (5) and adapter (4). Remove blade (3). When installing blade, tighten bolt (7) to 28 N·m (250 in.-lbs.).

Models B370 And B440

Models B370 and B440 may be equipped with a saw blade, a four cutting edge blade or a three cutting edge blade. To remove blade, carefully rotate blade until hole in upper driving disc is aligned with hole or slot in gear head housing. Insert a 4.5 mm (0.16 in.) round rod into holes to prevent blade rotation. Note nut retaining blade has left-hand threads and remove nut, cover, drive disc and blade. When installing blade, tighten left-hand thread nut to 35-50 N·m (26-30 ft.-lbs.).

To sharpen saw blade, use a 5.5 mm (7.32 in.) round file in file holder (part number 501 58 02-01). File front edge of tooth only with file holder firmly against the rear edge of tooth (Fig. PR15). Alternate filing one tooth to the right and the next tooth to the left at a 25° angle (Fig. PR16). Sharpen outer edge of tooth at a 5° angle (Fig. PR17). Use tooth set gage (part number 501 31 77-01) to adjust tooth set when teeth have been filed down 50 percent (Fig. PR18). Correct tooth set should provide 1 mm (0.04 in.) distance between tooth tips (Fig. PR19).

DRIVE SHAFT

Model B180

Model B180 is equipped with a flexible drive shaft enclosed in the drive shaft housing tube. Drive shaft has squared ends which engage adapters at each end. Drive shaft should be removed for maintenance at 20 hour in-tervals of use. To remove, separate drive shaft housing from engine. Clean drive shaft and lubricate with lithium base grease. Reinstall drive shaft in housing.

Models B250, B370 And B440

Models B250, B370 and B440 are equipped with a solid steel drive shaft supported in drive shaft housing tube. Drive shaft requires no regular maintenance; however, if drive shaft has been removed, lubricate drive shaft with lithium base grease before reinstallation.

BEARING HEAD

Model B180

Model B180 is equipped with sealed bearing housing (3—Fig. PR20). No regular maintenance is required and no service parts are available.

GEAR HEAD

Model B250

Model B250 is equipped with the gear head shown in Fig. PR21. Gear head lubricant level should be checked at 50 hour intervals of use by removing check plug (9). Gear head housing should be 2/3 full of lithium base grease. Do not use a pressure grease gun to install grease as bearing seal and housing damage will occur.

To disassemble gear head, remove trimmer head or blade assembly. Remove locating screw (7) and clamp bolt (8) then separate gear head from drive shaft housing. Remove spacer (16) and seal (15). Remove snap ring (14) and use a suitable puller to remove arbor shaft (12) and bearing assembly. If bearing (10) stays in housing, heat housing to 140° F (60° C) and tap housing on wooden block to remove bearing. Remove gear (11) from arbor shaft. Press bearing (13) from arbor shaft as required. Remove snap ring (1). Insert a screwdriver into clamp split in gear head housing and carefully expand housing. Remove input shaft (5) and bearing

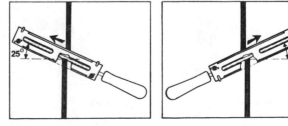

Fig. PR16—Alternate filing one tooth to the right and the next tooth to the left. File at a 25° angle.

assembly. Remove snap ring (2) and press bearings (3 and 4) as required.

Models B370 And B440

Models B370 and B440 are equipped with gear head shown in Fig. PR22. Gear head lubricant level should be checked at 50 hour intervals of use. To check, remove check plug (11). Gear head housing should be kept 3/4 full of lithium base grease.

To disassemble gear head, remove trimmer head or blade assembly. Remove the four screws (3) retaining cover (5) to housing and use puller (part number 502 50 09-01) to remove cover. Remove clamp bolts (14) and locating screw (15). Separate gear head assembly from drive shaft housing tube. Remove sleeve (19) using remover (part number 502 51 09-01). Heat housing (13) to 140° F (60° C) and remove input shaft (16) and bearing assembly and arbor shaft (9) and bearing assembly. If bearing (10) remains in housing, tap housing against a wooden block while housing is still hot to remove bearing. Remove snap ring (21) and press bearings (17 and 18) from input shaft as required. Remove bearing (7) and spacer (8) as required.

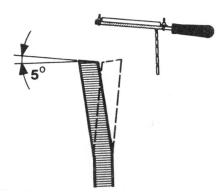

Fig. PR17—Sharpen outer edge of tooth at a 5° angle.

Fig. PR18—Use set gage (part number 501 31 77-01) to adjust tooth set when teeth have been filed down approximately 50 percent.

Fig. PR19—Tooth set should provide 1 mm (0.04 in.) distance between tooth tips.

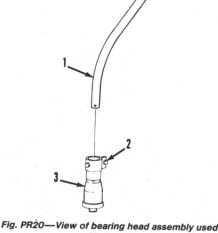

Fig. PR20—View of bearing head assembly used on Model B180.
1. Drive shaft housing
2. Clamp bolt
3. Bearing head

Fig. PR21—Exploded view of gear head used on Model B250.

1. Snap ring	9. Check plug
2. Snap ring	10. Bearing
3. Bearing	11. Gear
4. Bearing	12. Arbor shaft
5. Input gear	13. Bearing
6. Housing	14. Snap ring
7. Bolt	15. Seal
8. Clamp bolt	16. Spacer

Fig. PR22—Exploded view of gear head used on Models B370 and B440.
1. Nut (LH)
2. Adapter plate
3. Screw
4. Drive disc
5. Cover
6. Gasket
7. Bearing
8. Spacer
9. Arbor shaft
10. Bearing
11. Check plug
12. Sealing ring
13. Housing
14. Clamp bolts
15. Locating screw
16. Input gear
17. Bearing
18. Bearing
19. Sleeve
20. "O" ring
21. Snap ring

POULAN

GASOLINE POWERED STRING TRIMMERS

Model	Engine Manufacturer	Engine Model	Displacement
111	Poulan	...	22 cc
114	Poulan	...	30 cc
117	Poulan	...	30 cc
175	Poulan	...	30 cc
185	Poulan	...	30 cc
195	Poulan	...	30 cc
2600	Poulan	...	26.2 cc
2610	Poulan	...	26.2 cc
2620	Poulan	...	26.2 cc

ENGINE INFORMATION

The models in this section are equipped with a Poulan engine. Refer to appropriate engine service section for engine service information.

FUEL MIXTURE

Manufacturer recommends mixing regular grade gasoline with Poulan/Weed Eater two-stroke engine oil mixed as indicated on container. Gasohol or other alcohol blended fuels are not approved by manufacturer.

STRING TRIMMER

Models 2600 And 2610

Models 2600 and 2610 are equipped with the single strand, semi-automatic trimmer head shown in Figs. PN10 or PN11. Early type trimmer head (Fig. PN10) is identified by the adapter (1) that drives the trimmer head. Service procedure for both heads is similar.

To extend line with trimmer engine stopped, push in on button (7) while pulling on line end. Repeat procedure as needed to obtain desired line length. To extend line with trimmer engine running and head rotating, tap button (7) on ground. Each time button is tapped on ground a measured amount of line is advanced.

To install new line, remove cover (8), button (7) and spool (6). Clean all parts thoroughly and remove any remaining old line from spool. Wind approximately 30 feet (9 m) of 0.080 inch (2 mm) diameter monofilament line on spool in direction indicated by arrow on spool. Insert line end through line guide open-ing in housing (2) and install spool, button and cover.

Model 2620

Model 2620 is equipped with the dual strand, manual trimmer head shown in Fig. PN12. To extend line, stop trimmer engine and push in on plate (8) while pulling each line out of housing (2).

To install new trimmer line, remove screw (9), plate (8), spring (6) and spool (7). Remove any remaining line from each side of spool. Clean spool, housing and plate. Insert ends of two new 0.095 inch (2.4 mm) diameter lines in holes located within spool and wind lines in direction indicated by arrow on spool.

Fig. PN10—Exploded view of early-style, single strand, semi-automatic trimmer head used on early Models 2600 and 2610.

1. Drive shaft adapter	5. Drive cam
2. Housing	6. Spool
3. Spring	7. Button
4. Spring adapter	8. Cover

Fig. PN11—Exploded view of later-style, single strand, semi-automatic trimmer head used on Models 2600 and 2610.

1. Line guide	5. Drive cam
2. Housing	6. Spool
3. Spring	7. Button
4. Spring adapter	8. Cover

Fig. PN12—Exploded view of dual strand, manual trimmer head used on Model 2620.

1. Lock ring cap	
2. Housing	6. Spring
3. Line guide	7. Spool
4. Drive shaft adapter	8. Cover
5. Lock ring	9. Screw

Total amount of installed line should not exceed spool diameter. Make certain line savers (3) are in position and install spool in housing with the "THIS SIDE IN" instructions on spool toward inside

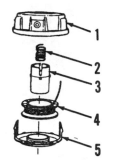

Fig. PN13—Exploded view of single strand, semi-automatic trimmer head used on some Models 111, 114 and 117.

1. Housing
2. Spring
3. Button
4. Spool
5. Cover

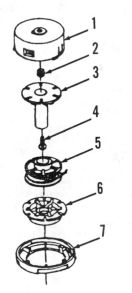

Fig. PN14—Exploded view of single strand, semi-automatic trimmer head used on some Models 111, 114, 117, 175, 185 and 195.

1. Housing
2. Spring
3. Spool post
4. Screw
5. Spool
6. Button
7. Cover

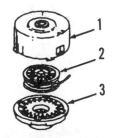

Fig. PN15—Exploded view of single strand, semi-automatic trimmer head used on some Models 111, 114, 117, 175 and 195.

1. Housing
2. Spool
3. Cover & button assy.

of trimmer head. Install spring (6), cover (8) and screw (9).

Models 111, 114 And 117

Models 111, 114 and 117 may be equipped with the single strand, semi-automatic trimmer head shown in Fig. PN13.

To extend line with trimmer engine stopped, push in on button (3) while pulling on line end. Repeat procedure as needed to obtain desired line length. To extend line with trimmer engine running and head rotating, tap button (3) on ground. Each time button is tapped on ground a measured amount of line is advanced.

To install new line, disengage tabs on cover (5) from housing (1). Remove old line and clean parts. Recommended line diameter is 0.080 inch (2 mm). Wind line around spool in direction indicated by arrow on spool.

Models 111, 114, 117, 175, 185 And 195

Models 111, 114, 117, 175, 185 and 195 may be equipped with the single strand, semi-automatic trimmer head shown in Fig. PN14.

To extend line with trimmer engine stopped, push in on button (6) while pulling on line end. Repeat procedure as needed to obtain desired line length. To extend line with trimmer engine running and head rotating, tap button (6) on ground. Each time button is tapped on ground a measured amount of line is advanced.

To install new line, remove cover (7), button (6) and spool (5). Clean all parts thoroughly and remove any remaining old line from spool. Wind 0.080 inch (2 mm) diameter monofilament line on spool in direction indicated by arrow on spool. Insert line end through line guide opening in housing (1) and install spool, button and cover.

Models 111, 114, 117, 175 And 195

Models 111, 114, 117, 175 and 195 may be equipped with the single strand, semi-automatic trimmer head shown in Fig. PN15.

To extend line with trimmer engine stopped, push in on button while pulling on line end. Repeat procedure as needed to obtain desired line length. To extend line with trimmer engine running and head rotating, tap button on ground. Each time button is tapped on ground a measured amount of line is advanced.

To install new line, detach cover (3) from housing (1). Remove old line and

clean parts. Recommended line diameter is 0.080 inch (2 mm). Wind line around spool in direction indicated by arrow on spool.

BLADE

Some models may be equipped with a blade. When installing blade, be sure all adapter plates are centered and seated squarely against blade. Blade nut has left-hand threads.

DRIVE SHAFT

Curved Shaft Models

Models with a curved drive shaft housing are equipped with a flexible drive shaft. The drive shaft should be removed, cleaned and lubricated after every 20 hours of operation. Detach head assembly from drive shaft housing and remove shaft. Apply lithium-based grease to shaft.

Straight Shaft Models

Periodic maintenance is not required for the drive shaft on models with a straight drive shaft housing. If removed, apply lithium-based grease to shaft.

BEARING HEAD

Models 111, 114 And 117

These models are equipped with a bearing head that is an integral part of the drive shaft housing tube. Regular maintenance is not required. Service parts are not available.

Early Models 2600 And 2610

Early Models 2600 And 2610 are equipped with the bearing head shown in Fig. PN16. To disassemble bearing head, remove trimmer head assembly. Remove locating screw (2) and slip bearing head off drive shaft housing tube. Remove dust cover (6), spacer (5) and arbor shaft (4). Lubricate arbor with lithium-base grease before installation.

Late Models 2600 And 2610

Late Models 2600 And 2610 are equipped with the bearing head shown in Fig. PN17. The bearing head is equipped with sealed bearings; regular maintenance is not required.

To disassemble bearing head, remove trimmer head or blade assembly. Remove clamp bolt (2) and locating screw (3). Separate bearing head assembly from drive shaft housing. Remove shield (6) and bracket (5), if so equipped. Remove cup washer (13) and washer (12). Carefully press drive shaft adapter (1) out of bearings. Remove snap rings (7 and 11). Press bearings (8 and 10) and spacer (9) out of housing.

GEAR HEAD

Models 175, 185, 195 And 2620

The gear head should be lubricated after every 10 hours of operation by injecting lithium-based grease through screw hole in side of gear head. Fill housing so it is approximately two-thirds full of grease.

The gear head on Models 175, 185 and 195 must be serviced as a unit assembly; individual components are not available.

Model 2620 is equipped with the gear head shown in Fig. PN18. To disassemble gear, remove trimmer head or blade assembly. Remove clamp bolt and head locating screw and separate gear head from drive shaft housing tube. Remove cup washer (17) and spacer (14). Remove snap ring (2) and use a suitable puller to remove input shaft (5) and bearing assembly. Remove snap ring (1) and press bearings (3 and 4) from input shaft as required. Remove seal (16) and snap ring (15). Use a suitable puller to remove arbor (12) and bearing assembly. Press bearing (13) and gear (11) from shaft as required. If bearing (10) remains in housing (6), heat housing to 140° F (60° C) and tap housing on wooden block to remove bearing.

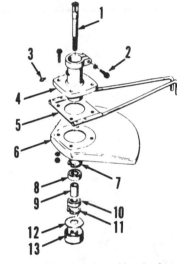

Fig. PN17—Exploded view of bearing head used on late Models 2600 and 2610.

1. Drive shaft adapter	7. Snap ring
2. Clamp bolt	8. Bearing
3. Locating screw	9. Spacer
4. Housing	10. Bearing
5. Bracket (if equipped)	11. Snap ring
	12. Washer
6. Shield	13. Drive disc

ENGINE COVER

All Models So Equipped

Some models are equipped with the full engine cover shown in Fig. PN19. Note that two styles (9 or 10) have been used. Style (9) is secured to drive shaft housing by a clamp bolt (8). Style (10) has a threaded collar on drive shaft tube that connects to threads on housing. To remove engine cover, separate engine assembly from drive shaft housing. Remove the four 10-24 screws and separate housings (5) and (9 or 10) slightly. Disconnect ignition wire from module and separate fuel line so junction fitting stays with crankcase side of fuel line. Separate housings completely. Remove

the three 8-24 screws from inner side of housing (5) and remove the air baffle. Remove the five 10-24 screws located under air baffle and separate housing (4) from housing (5). Remove fuel tank cap and remove fuel tank. Remove the four screws securing carburetor cover plate and remove carburetor cover. Disconnect spark plug, remove the four 10-24 screws at drive shaft housing side of cover (9 or 10), then remove cover.

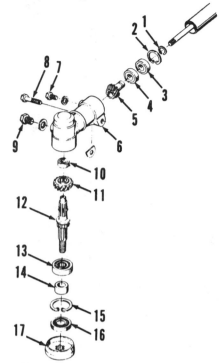

Fig. PN18—Exploded view of gear head used on Model 2620.

1. Snap ring	10. Bearing
2. Snap ring	11. Gear
3. Bearing	12. Arbor shaft
4. Bearing	13. Bearing
5. Input shaft	14. Spacer
6. Housing	15. Snap ring
7. Clamp bolt	16. Seal
8. Bolt	17. Cup washer
9. Check plug	

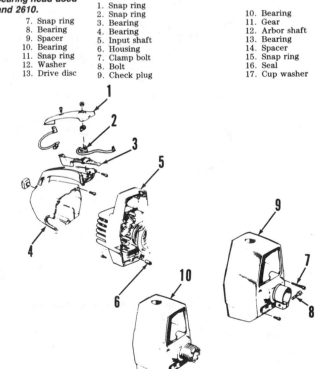

Fig. PN19—Exploded view of engine cover assembly used on some models.

1. Throttle housing cover
2. Ignition switch
3. Throttle trigger
4. Handle
5. Fan housing
6. Spacer
7. Screw
8. Clamp bolt
9. Cover (clamp style)
10. Cover (threaded style)

Fig. PN16—Exploded view of drive shaft and bearing head used on early Models 2600 and 2610.

1. Drive shaft housing	
2. Locating screw	5. Spacer
3. Bearing housing	6. Dust cover
4. Arbor	7. Nut

POULAN

GASOLINE POWERED BLOWERS

Model	Engine Manufacturer	Engine Model	Displacement
420	Poulan	...	26.2 cc
422	Poulan	...	22 cc
432	Poulan	...	30 cc

ENGINE INFORMATION

The models in this section are equipped with a Poulan engine. Refer to appropriate engine service section for engine service information.

FUEL MIXTURE

Manufacturer recommends mixing regular grade gasoline with Poulan/Weed Eater two-stroke engine oil mixed as indicated on container. Gasohol or other alcohol blended fuels are not approved by manufacturer.

FAN

To remove blower fan (11—Fig. PN40) on Model 420, remove tube clamp (9) from blower housing. Remove blower housing screws and separate blower housing halves (6 and 13). Remove fan mounting nut (12) and withdraw fan from drive shaft (4). When installing fan, tighten fan retaining nut to 19-20 N·m (14-15 ft.-lbs.).

To remove blower fan (3—Fig. PN41) on Model 422, remove screws from blower housing and separate outer

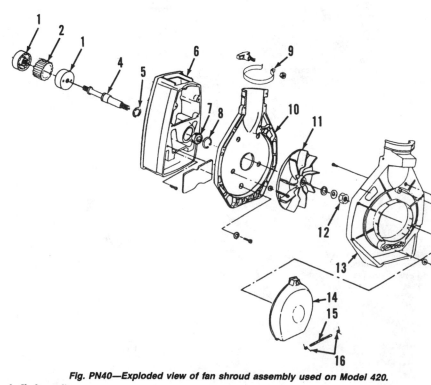

Fig. PN40—Exploded view of fan shroud assembly used on Model 420.

1. Shaft coupling
2. Coupling hub
4. Fan shaft
5. Washer
6. Shroud
7. Bearing
8. Snap ring
9. Clamp
10. Blower housing
11. Fan
12. Nut
13. Blower housing
14. Inlet door
15. Pivot pin
16. Springs

blower housing (4) and recoil starter assembly from inner blower housing (2). Remove screws mounting fan (3) to flywheel (1) and remove fan.

To remove blower fan (7—Fig. PN42) on Model 432, remove retaining screws from blower housing and separate blower housing halves (5 and 12). Remove fan retaining nut (11) and withdraw fan from end of crankshaft.

SHROUD BEARING

The fan shaft (4—Fig. PN40) on Model 420 is supported by a bearing (7) in the fan shroud (6). To remove bearing and drive shaft, first remove blower housing (10 and 13) and fan (11). Unbolt and remove fan shroud from engine. Detach snap ring (8), then heat shroud to 300° F (149° C) and remove bearing and shaft.

The fan end of crankshaft on Model 432 is supported by bearing (3—Fig. PN42) in starter housing (1). To remove bearing, first separate blower housing (5 and 12), fan (7) and starter housing (1) from engine. Press bearing out of starter housing.

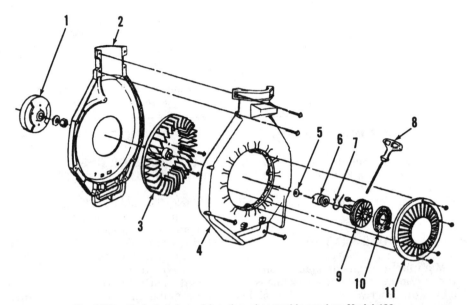

Fig. PN41—Exploded view of fan shroud assembly used on Model 422.

1. Flywheel
2. Blower housing
3. Fan
4. Blower housing
5. Screw
6. Starter pinion
7. Spring
8. Rope handle
9. Starter pulley
10. Recoil spring
11. Pulley housing

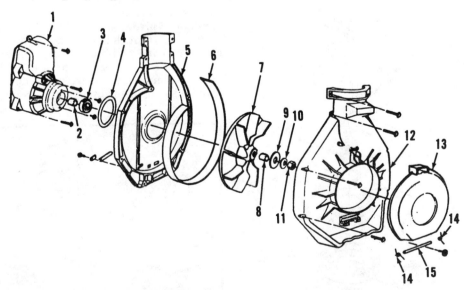

Fig. PN42—Exploded view of fan shroud assembly used on Model 432.

1. Starter housing
2. Spacer
3. Bearing
4. "O" ring
5. Housing
6. Band
7. Fan
8. Spacer
9. Washer
10. Washer
11. Nut
12. Housing
13. Inlet door
14. Springs
15. Pivot pin

REDMAX

GASOLINE POWERED STRING TRIMMERS

Model	Engine Manufacturer	Engine Model	Displacement
BC220DL	Komatsu	G2KC-4	22.5 cc
BC260DL	Komatsu	G2K33-D	25.4 cc
BC340DL	Komatsu	G3K27-D	33.6 cc
BC440DWM	Komatsu	G4K60-D	41.5 cc
BT17	Komatsu	G1E	17.2 cc
BT220	Komatsu	G2KC-8	22.5 cc
SGC220DL	Komatsu	G2KC-45	22.5 cc

ENGINE INFORMATION

The models included in this section are powered by a Komatsu engine. Refer to appropriate Komatsu engine service section for service procedures and specifications.

FUEL MIXTURE

Manufacturer recommends mixing regular or unleaded grade gasoline with a high-quality two-stroke engine oil designed for air-cooled engines. Recommended fuel:oil ratio is 32:1 when using RedMax oil or any other high-quality two-stroke oil. Manufacturer does not recommend using gasohol or other fuels that include alcohol.

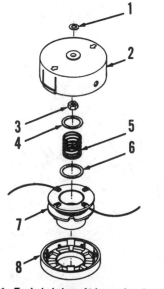

Fig. RM11—Exploded view of trimmer head assembly used on Models BT17, BT220 and (if so equipped) Model BC220DL. Some units are not equipped with nut (3).

1. Washer
2. Drum
3. Nut
4. Washer
5. Spring
6. Washer
7. Spool
8. Cover

STRING TRIMMER

Models BC220DL (If So Equipped), BT17 And BT220

Models BT17 and BT220, and BC220DL if so equipped, are equipped with the dual strand, semi-automatic trimmer head assembly shown in Fig. RM11. To extend line with engine stopped, push in on spool button and pull out line to desired length. To extend line with engine running, tap spool button against ground with engine running at full speed. Each time button is tapped a measured amount of line will be advanced.

To install new line, push in tabs on cover (8) and remove cover, spool (7), washers (4 and 6) and spring (5). Clean components and inside of drum (2). Remove any remaining old line and note direction of arrow on spool. Insert ends of new line through holes of spool (A—Fig. RM12) and pull line through until line is the same length at both ends. Wind both ends of line at the same time in direction indicated by arrow on spool

(B). Line on Models BT17 and BT220 should be 20-ft. (6.1 m) long with a diameter of 0.080 inch (2 mm). Line on Model BC220DL may be 20-ft. (6.1 m) long with a diameter of 0.080 inch (2 mm), or 15-ft. (4.6 m) long with a diameter of 0.095 inch (2.4 mm). Reassemble trimmer head while routing string ends through eyelets in drum (C). Be sure locking tabs on drum (2—Fig. RM11) properly engage slits in cover (8). Manually extend lines, or cut lines, so each line is approximately 6 inches (15 cm) long.

Models BC220DL (If So Equipped), BC260DL, BC340DL And BC440DWM

These models are equipped with the dual strand, semi-automatic trimmer head shown in Fig. RM13. To manually extend line with the engine stopped, loosen knob (10) and pull out line to desire length. To extend line with engine running, allow engine to run at idle speed, then rapidly accelerate engine to

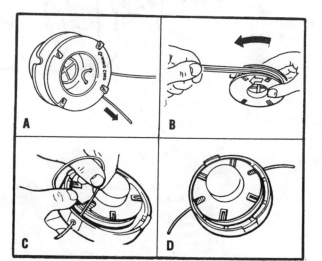

Fig. RM12—To install new trimmer line on Models BT17 and BT220, insert ends of new line through holes in spool and pull line through until line is the same length at both ends. Refer to text for remainder of procedure.

full speed. Return to idle speed. Line should extend when a rapid change in engine speed occurs.

BLADE

Model BT220

Model BT220 may be equipped with an eight-tooth blade (Fig. RM16). When installing blade make certain all adapter washers are centered and square with blade surface. Concave side of flange (3) must be against blade. Install blade so cutting surfaces will cut when blade rotates counterclockwise as viewed from ground side of blade. Tighten blade retaining nut to 14.7-19.7 N·m (130-174 in.-lbs.).

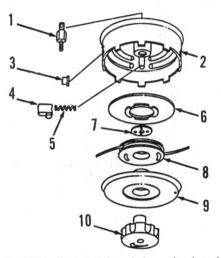

Fig. RM13—Exploded view of trimmer head used on Models BC260DL, BC340DL, BC440DWM and (if so equipped) Model BC220DL.

1. Adapter
2. Drum
3. Eyelet
4. Slider
5. Spring
6. Cam disc
7. Retainer
8. Spool
9. Cover
10. Knob

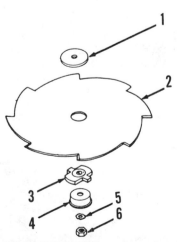

Fig. RM16—Model BT220 may be equipped with the eight-tooth blade shown above.

1. Washer
2. Blade
3. Flange
4. Cup
5. Washer
6. Nut

Models BC220DL, BC260DL, BC340DL And BC440DWM

These models may be equipped with an eight-tooth blade (1—Fig. RM17). Models BC220DL and BC260DL may be equipped with a four-tooth blade (2), while Models BC340DL and BC440DWM

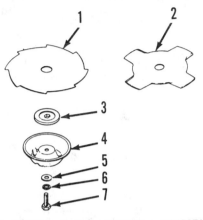

Fig. RM17—Models BC220DL, BC260DL, BC340DL and BC440DWM may be equipped with the eight-tooth blade (1) shown above. Some models may be equipped with a four-tooth blade (2) or a saw blade.

1. Blade
2. Blade
3. Washer
4. Cup
5. Washer
6. Lockwasher
7. Screw (L.H.)

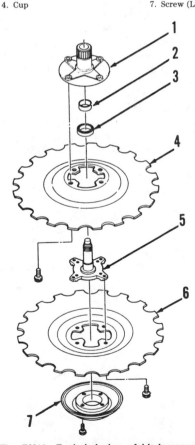

Fig. RM18—Exploded view of blade assembly used on Model SGC220DL.

1. Outer shaft
2. Bushing
3. Seal
4. Blade
5. Inner shaft
6. Blade
7. Stabilizer

may be equipped with a saw blade. Note that screw (7) has left-hand threads. Concave side of washer (3) must be against blade. Install blade so cutting surfaces will cut when blade rotates clockwise as viewed from ground side of blade. Tighten blade retaining screw (7) to 14.7-19.7 N·m (130-174 in.-lbs.).

Model SGC220DL

Two reciprocating blades are used on the Model SGC220DL to cut grass and brush. An articulated mechanism in the gear head transmits reciprocating motion to the blades. The blades move in opposite directions resulting in a cutting action when the blade edges pass by each other. See Fig. RM18 for an exploded view of blade assembly.

Blades may be sharpened to restore cutting efficiency. To sharpen blades, insert a hex wrench in hex screw on top of gear head and turn wrench so blades are offset 3.1 mm ($^1/_8$ in.) as shown in Fig. RM19. Note desired blade shape in Fig. RM20. Grind cutting surfaces light-

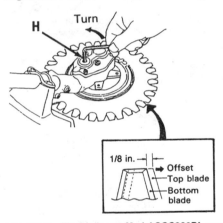

Fig. RM19—The blades on Model SGC220DL can be rotated with engine stopped by inserting a hex wrench in hex screw (H) on top of gear head and turning wrench. To sharpen blades, position blades so they are offset as shown in inset.

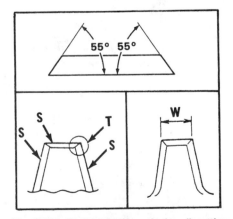

Fig. RM20—Desired blade angle for all cutting edges on Model SGC220DL is 55 degrees. Sharpen three surfaces (S), making sure blade tip corners (T) are sharp, not rounded. Renew blade when tip width (W) is less than 8 mm ($^5/_{16}$ in.).

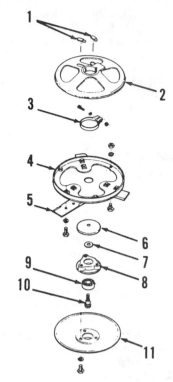

Fig. RM21—Exploded view of mower unit that may be used on Models BC340DL and BC440DWM.

1. Plugs
2. Cover
3. Clamp
4. Ring
5. Blade
6. Cover
7. Spacer
8. Bearing holder
9. Bearing
10. Shaft
11. Stabilizer

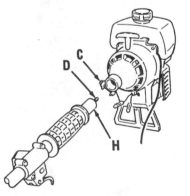

Fig. RM22—Loosen clamp (C) to detach drive shaft housing (H) from power unit on Model BT17.

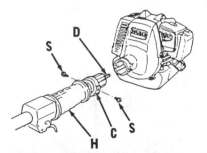

Fig. RM23—Remove two retaining screws (S) from collar (C) to separate power unit from drive shaft housing (H) on Model BT220.

ly and quickly to avoid overheating blade, which can soften the temper of the blade. Corners of blade tip (T) should be sharp, not rounded. Desired blade angle for all cutting edges is 55 degrees. Renew blade when tip width (W) is less than 8 mm ($^5/_{16}$ in.).

The blades may be removed after unscrewing the mounting screws. The blades are identical when new. Minimum blade thickness is 6.65 mm (0.262 in.). Tighten blade mounting screws to 11.8-14.7 N·m (104-130 in.-lbs.). Tighten stabilizer (7—Fig. RM18) mounting screws to 2.0-2.9 N·m (18-26 in.-lbs.).

MOWER

Models BC340DL And BC440DWM

Models BC340DL and BC440DWM may be equipped with the mower assembly shown in Fig. RM21. The blades (5) are renewable.

DRIVE SHAFT

Models BT17 And BT220

These models are equipped with a flexible cable drive shaft that runs inside the lined drive shaft housing. Periodic maintenance is not required. If removed, lubricate shaft with lithium grease.

To gain access to the drive shaft, the power unit and drive shaft housing must be separated as follows. Disconnect ignition wire(s) between engine and trigger assembly. Disconnect throttle cable

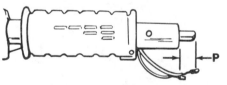

Fig. RM24—When properly installed, the drive shaft on Model BT17 should extend (P) 18 mm (0.7 in.) from end of housing.

at trigger. On Model BT17, loosen clamp (C—Fig. RM22) and separate power unit from drive shaft housing (H). On Model BT220, remove retaining screws (S—Fig. RM23) and separate power unit from drive shaft housing (H). Withdraw drive shaft (D) from housing. Clean, inspect and lubricate drive shaft.

When reinstalling drive shaft, end of shaft must protrude 18 mm (0.7 in.) as shown in Fig. RM24. Be sure drive shaft end properly mates with engine clutch shaft when joining drive shaft housing and power unit.

Models BC220DL, BC260DL, BC340DL And BC440DWM

These models are equipped with a solid drive shaft that rides in bushings in the drive shaft housing. Periodic maintenance is not required.

To remove drive shaft (4—Fig. RM25), unscrew gear head locating screw (3) and clamp screw (2) and detach gear head (5) from drive shaft housing (6). Extract drive shaft. Bushings (7) are available separately. Mark location of bushings before removal and install new bushings in same location. A bushing installation tool is available from manufacturer. If necessary, separate drive shaft housing from power unit after disconnecting throttle cable, wiring and loosening clamp screws. Tighten gear head locating screw to 2.0-2.9 N·m (18-26 in.-lbs.) and clamp screw to 5.0-8.8 N·m (44-78 in.-lbs.).

Model SGC220DL

Model SGC220DL is equipped with a solid drive shaft that rides in bushings in the drive shaft housing. Periodic maintenance is not required.

To remove drive shaft (2—Fig. RM26), unscrew gear head locating screw (L) and clamp screw (C) and detach gear head (3) from drive shaft housing (1). Extract drive shaft. Five renewable bushings (3—Fig. RM27) are located in drive shaft housing. Mark location of

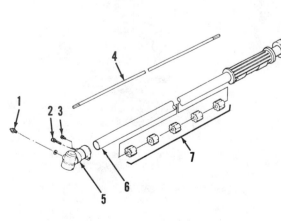

Fig. RM25—Exploded view of solid drive shaft used on some models.

1. Grease fitting
2. Clamp screw
3. Locating screw
4. Drive shaft
5. Gear head
6. Housing
7. Bushings

bushings before removal and install new bushings in same location. If necessary, separate drive shaft housing from power unit after removing plastic cover, disconnecting throttle cable and wiring, and loosening locating screws (5) on both sides of collar (4). If drive shaft housing (1) is stuck in gear reduction housing (6), apply heat to gear reduction housing.

BEARING HEAD

Models BT17 And BT220

Refer to Fig. RM28 for an exploded view of bearing head assembly. Periodic maintenance is not required. To disassemble, remove trimmer head or blade (insert a suitable tool in hole of bearing head to prevent shaft rotation). If so equipped, unscrew nut (8). Remove cover (7) and snap ring (4). Attach RedMax puller 3238-99100 (or other suitable tool) to arbor (2) and pull arbor and bearing assembly out of housing. Clean and inspect components. Reverse disassembly procedure to assemble unit.

GEAR HEAD

Models BC220DL, BC260DL, BC340DL And BC440DWM

The gear head on Models BC220DL, BC260DL, BC340DL and BC440DWM should be lubricated after every 30 hours of operation. Remove trimmer head or blade and using a hand-operated grease gun, inject lithium grease through fitting (F—Fig. RM29) until old grease is expelled around arbor.

To disassemble gear head, remove blade or trimmer head. Detach gear head from drive shaft housing. Remove snap ring (6—Fig. RM30) and extract pinion gear (2) and bearings as an assembly from housing. If bearings are tight in housing, carefully widen gap in housing at clamp screw.

CAUTION: Excessive force or widening gap too far will break housing.

Detach snap ring (5) and press bearings (3 and 4) off pinion gear (2). Remove cover (13). Depending on model, snap ring (12) or seal (11) may be lowermost in housing. Remove seal and snap ring, then use a suitable puller and remove bearing (10), arbor (9) and gear (8). Warm housing (1), then tap to dislodge bearing (7).

Clean and inspect components. Reassemble by reversing disassembly procedure. Tighten gear head locating screw (L) to 2.0-2.9 N·m (18-26 in.-lbs.) and clamp screw (C) to 5.0-8.8 N·m (44-78 in.-lbs.).

Fig. RM26—To remove drive shaft on Model SGC220DL, unscrew gear head locating screw (L) and clamp screw (C) and detach gear head (3) from drive shaft housing (1).

Fig. RM27—Exploded view of solid drive shaft used on Model SGC220DL. Loosen locating screws (5) on both sides of collar (4) to separate drive shaft housing (1) from gear reduction case.

1. Drive shaft housing
2. Drive shaft
3. Bushings
4. Collar
5. Locating screw (2)
6. Gear reduction case

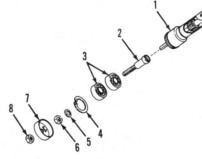

Fig. RM28—Exploded view of bearing head assembly used on Models BT17 and BT220.

1. Drive shaft housing	5. Washer
2. Arbor	6. Nut
3. Bearings	7. Cover
4. Snap ring	8. Nut

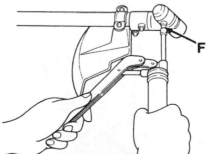

Fig. RM29—Apply lithium-base grease at gear head fitting (F) until old grease is forced out opening around arbor shaft.

Fig. RM30—Exploded view of gear head assembly used on Models BC220DL, BC260DL, BC340DL and BC440DWM. Note that seal (11) is below snap ring (12) on some models.

1. Housing
2. Pinion gear
3. Bearing
4. Bearing
5. Snap ring
6. Snap ring
7. Bearing
8. Gear
9. Arbor
10. Bearing
11. Seal
12. Snap ring
13. Cover
14. Washer
15. Washer
16. Lockwasher
17. Screw (L.H.)

Model SGC220DL

Two reciprocating blades are used on the Model SGC220DL to cut grass and brush. An articulated mechanism in the gear head transmits reciprocating motion to the blades.

LUBRICATION. After every 50 hours of operation, remove screw (S—Fig. RM31) and check and refill the gear head with lithium grease. Fluid capacity is 40 grams (1.4 oz.).

BLADE BASE GAP. To obtain desired contact between the blades, the distance between the flanges of the blade drive shafts must be maintained. Remove blades and measure distance (D—Fig. RM32) between flanges. Distance should be 11.8-12.0 mm (0.465-0.472 in.). The distance is adjusted by varying thickness of shim (8—Fig. RM33). Refer to OVERHAUL section and remove or install shim as needed to obtain correct blade base gap.

OVERHAUL. To overhaul gear head, remove blades and separate unit from drive shaft housing as previously outlined. Lock blade flanges (22 and 26—Fig. RM33) so they cannot turn and unscrew hex screw (1). Remove top cover (2) while being careful not to lose spacer (13), which may be stuck to bearing (4A). Use a suitable puller and remove bearing (4) from shaft. Unscrew nut (7).

If adjusting blade gap, remove or add shims (8) as needed. Shims are available in thicknesses of 0.1, 0.2 and 0.3 mm. Tighten inner shaft nut (7) to 29.4-39.2 N·m (22-29 ft.-lbs.) and cover screws to 4.9-6.8 N·m (44-61 in.-lbs.) and assemble components. Apply Loctite to hex screw (1).

To disassemble remainder of gear housing, remove shim (8) and tap inner shaft (26) out. Remove links, crankshaft (16) and bevel gear (17). Remove snap ring (11) and tap out outer shaft (22). Remove bearings (12) and oil seal (21). It may be necessary to heat housing to

free bearings. Use a hook shaped tool to pull sleeve (34) and packing (33) from housing. Remove snap ring (32) and pull pinion gear (29) and bearings (30) from housing. It may be necessary to heat housing to free bearings. Remove snap ring (31) and press bearings off pinion shaft. Remove bearing (18) from housing.

Inspect components for excessive wear and damage. Note that two types of links have been used. Early links (35 and 36) are equipped with roller bearings and link ends are inseparable. Roller bearing in early link is not available separately. Later links (9, 10, 14 and 15) do not have a bearing in crankshaft end, but may be separated. The crankshafts

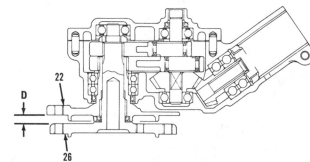

Fig. RM32—On Model SGC220DL, the distance (D) between blade mounting flanges (22 and 26) should be 11.8-12.0 mm (0.465-0.472 in.). See text.

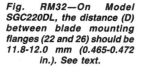

Fig. RM33—Exploded view of gear head assembly used on Model SGC220DL. Links (35 and 36) are used on early production units.

1. Hex screw
2. Cover
3. Seal
4. & 4A. Bearing
5. Gasket
6. Spacer
7. Nut
8. Shim
9. Splined link end
10. Link end
11. Snap ring
12. Bearings
13. Washer
14. Splined link end
15. Link end
16. Crankshaft
17. Bevel gear
18. Bearing
19. Dowel pin
20. Housing
21. Seal
22. Outer shaft
23. Bushing
24. Seal
25. Upper blade
26. Inner shaft
27. Lower blade
28. Stabilizer
29. Pinion gear
30. Bearings
31. Snap ring
32. Snap ring
33. Packing
34. Sleeve
35. Link assy.
36. Link assy.

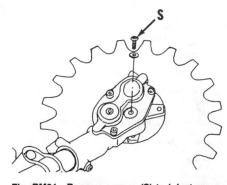

Fig. RM31—Remove screws (S) to inject grease into gear reduction case on Model SGC220DL.

used with early or later links are not interchangeable.

To reassemble unit, reverse disassembly procedure while noting the following: Apply grease to links and bearings and contact surface of crankshaft (16). Punch marks on links must be visible and align with punch marks on ends of shafts (22 and 26) as shown in Fig. RM34. Install oil seal (3—Fig. RM33) so open side is toward top of cover (2). Install oil seals (21 and 24) with open side in. Install packing (33) so tapered side is toward sleeve (34). Install sleeve (34) so hole in side aligns with locating screw hole in housing. Before installing top cover (2), check blade base gap as previously outlined. Tighten inner shaft nut (7) to 29.4-39.2 N·m (22-29 ft.-lbs.) and cover screws to 4.9-6.8 N·m (44-61 in.-lbs.). Apply Loctite to hex screw (1).

With unit assembled and filled with grease, operate assembly by turning hex screw (1). If screw is difficult to turn, tap housing to seat gears. If binding occurs, inspect unit.

GEAR REDUCTION

Model SGC220DL

Model SGC220DL is equipped with a gear reduction unit that is attached to the front of the engine. The clutch drum shaft transmits power to the gear unit from the engine. The bore of the output gear of the gear reduction accepts the upper end of the cutter drive shaft.

LUBRICATION. After every 50 hours of operation, remove screws (S—Fig. RM35) on both sides of gearcase. Check and refill the gearcase with lithium grease.

OVERHAUL. To disassemble gear reduction unit, remove plastic covers (17—Fig. RM36) and disconnect throttle cable and wiring. Loosen locating screws (4) on both sides of collar (2) and detach drive shaft housing (1) from gear reduction case. If drive shaft housing is stuck in gear reduction case, apply heat to gear reduction case. Unscrew four mounting screws and separate gear reduction case (25) from engine. Unscrew and separate front case (5) from rear case (25). Detach snap ring (3) and press output gear (13) out of bearings (11 and 12). Detach snap ring (20) and press clutch drum (26) out of bearings (23 and 24). Remove snap ring (22) and press bearings out of housing (25).

Two different idler gear assemblies have been used. Idler gear components (14, 15 and 16) were used on early models; idler gear components (7, 8 and 9) are used on later models. Cases (5 and 25) are machined to accept either early

or late idler gear. Early and late components cannot be interchanged.

Reassemble gear reduction unit by reversing disassembly procedure. Note that bearings (11 and 24) are sealed. On early models, fill bushings (14 and 16) and case holes with grease before installing idler gear (15). Tighten case screws in a crossing pattern to 6.9 N·m (61 in.-lbs.). Install gear reduction unit on engine and attach drive shaft housing. Remove screws (S—Fig. RM35) and fill gearcase with lithium grease.

THROTTLE FREE PLAY

Models BC220DL, BC260DL, BT220 And SGC220DL

To adjust throttle free play, remove the air cleaner for access to the carbu-

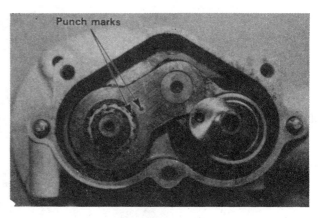
Fig. RM34—Punch marks on links and end of inner and outer shafts must align.

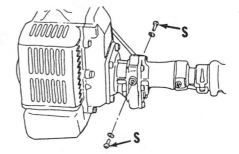
Fig. RM35—To lubricate reduction gears on Model SGC220DL, remove both screws (S) and inject lithium-base grease through one of the screw openings.

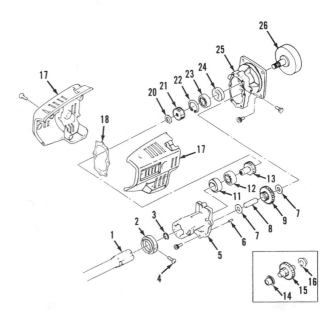
Fig. RM36—Exploded view of gear reduction unit used on Model SGC220DL. Idler gear (15) is used on early production units.

1. Drive shaft housing
2. Collar
3. Snap ring
4. Locating screw
5. Front case
6. Dowel pin
7. Thrust washer
8. Shaft
9. Idler gear
11. Bearing (sealed)
12. Bearing
13. Output gear
14. Bushing
15. Idler gear
16. Bushing
17. Cover
18. Gasket
20. Snap ring
21. Input gear
22. Snap ring
23. Bearing
24. Bearing (sealed)
25. Rear case
26. Clutch drum

retor. Loosen locknut (N—Fig. RM37) and turn adjuster (A) so cable free play (P) at carburetor is 1-2 mm (0.04-0.08 in.). Tighten locknut.

Model BC340DL

To adjust throttle free play, pull back sleeve (S—Fig. RM38). Loosen locknut (N) and turn adjuster (A) so throttle cable (C) free play is 1-2 mm (0.4-0.8 in.). Tighten locknut.

Model BC440DWM

To adjust throttle free play, detach the air cleaner cover for access to the carburetor. Loosen locknut (N—Fig. RM39) and turn adjuster (A) so cable free play at carburetor is 1-2 mm (0.04-0.08 in.). Tighten locknut.

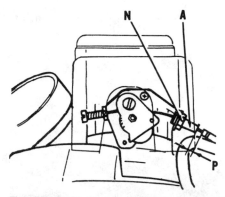

Fig. RM37—On Models BC220DL, BC260DL, BT220 and SGC220DL, loosen locknut (N) and turn adjuster (A) so cable free play (P) is 1-2 mm (0.04-0.08 in.).

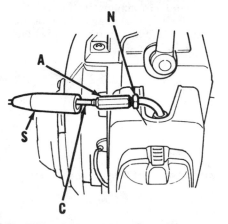

Fig. RM38—On Model BC340DL, loosen locknut (N) and turn adjuster (A) so cable (C) free play is 1-2 mm (0.04-0.08 in.).

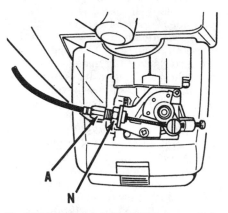

Fig. RM39—On Model BC440DWM, loosen locknut (N) and turn adjuster (A) so cable free play is 1-2 mm (0.04-0.08 in.).

REDMAX

GASOLINE POWERED BLOWERS

Model	Engine Manufacturer	Engine Model	Displacement
EB430, EBA430	Komatsu	...	41.5 cc
EB440, EBA440	Komatsu	...	41.5 cc
HB260	Komatsu	...	25.4 cc

ENGINE INFORMATION

The models included in this section are powered by a Komatsu engine. Refer to appropriate Komatsu engine service section for service procedures and specifications.

FUEL MIXTURE

Manufacturer recommends mixing regular or unleaded gasoline with a high-quality, two-stroke engine oil designed for air-cooled engines. Recommended fuel:oil ratio is 32:1 when using RedMax oil or any other high-quality two-stroke oil. Manufacturer does not recommend using gasohol or other fuels that include alcohol.

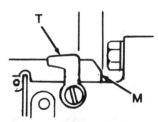

Fig. RM101—At wide-open throttle, the carburetor throttle stop arm (T) should be parallel with carburetor mounting face (M).

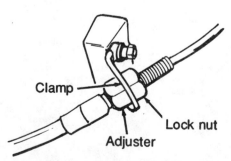

Fig. RM102—Turn cable adjusting nuts so carburetor throttle stop arm (T—Fig. RM101) is parallel with carburetor mounting face (M).

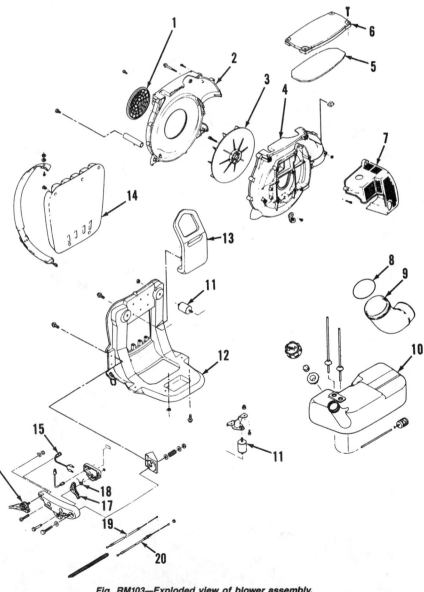

Fig. RM103—Exploded view of blower assembly.

1. Intake guard	6. Cover	11. Rubber mounts	16. Throttle lever
2. Blower housing half	7. Engine cover	12. Backpack frame	17. Lever
3. Blower fan	8. "O" ring	13. Hanger bracket	18. Spring
4. Blower housing half	9. Elbow	14. Backpad	19. Choke cable
5. Gasket	10. Fuel tank	15. Stop switch	20. Throttle cable

THROTTLE CABLE

Models EB430, EB440, EBA430 And EBA440

The throttle cable should be adjusted so the throttle trigger and carburetor throttle plate are synchronized. With throttle trigger in wide-open position, the throttle stop arm (T—Fig. RM101) should be parallel with the carburetor mounting face (M). To adjust, loosen locknut (RM102) at throttle cable end and reposition adjusting nut as necessary. Tighten nuts after adjustment.

Blower Fan

To remove engine from blower housing, remove fuel tank (10—Fig. RM103) and engine cover (7). Remove screw retaining crankcase to backpack frame (12). Remove backpad (14) and pry off intake guard (1). Remove screws attaching blower fan (3) to flywheel. Remove four engine mounting screws and remove engine from blower housing.

To remove blower fan (3), remove cover (6) from blower housing. Remove screws holding blower housing halves (2 and 4) together. Separate blower housing and remove fan.

ROBIN

GASOLINE POWERED
STRING TRIMMERS

Model	Engine Manufacturer	Engine Model	Displacement
NB02, NB02-3A, NB02-3B, NB02T*	Fuji	EC02	22.2 cc
NB04	Fuji	EC04	37.7 cc
NB16, NB16F, NB16S, NB16T†	Fuji	EC01	15.4 cc
NB23, NB23F, NB23S, NB23T‡	Fuji	EC02	22.2 cc
NB26	Fuji	EC02	25.6 cc
NB30	Fuji	EC03	30.5 cc
NB50L	Fuji	EC05	51.7 cc
NB211, NB211C, NB211T§	Fuji	EC02	20.3 cc
NB231	Fuji	EC02	22.2 cc
NB351	Fuji	EC03	34.4 cc
NB411	Fuji	EC04	40.2 cc
NBF171	Fuji	EC01	15.4 cc
PT	Fuji	EC01	15.4 cc

*May be designated Series NB02 in text.
†May be designated Series NB16 in text.
‡May be designated Series NB23 in text.
§May be designated Series NB211 in text.

ENGINE INFORMATION

All models are equipped with Fuji two-stroke, air-cooled gasoline engines. Refer to Fuji engine section in this manual for engine service information.

FUEL MIXTURE

Manufacturer recommends mixing regular grade gasoline (unleaded gasoline is acceptable) and a high-quality oil designed for use in a two-stroke, air-cooled engine. Recommended fuel:oil ratio is 24:1. Do not use gasoline containing alcohol.

STRING TRIMMER

Models NB231, NBF171 And Series NB02, NB16, NB23, And NB211 With Semi-Automatic Head

These models may be equipped with the dual strand, semi-automatic trimmer head shown in Fig. RB10. To extend line with trimmer engine stopped, push in on spool button (7) while pulling on each line. Procedure may have to be repeated until desired line length is obtained. To extend line with trimmer engine running, operate trimmer at full rpm and tap button on the ground. Each time button is tapped on the ground, a measured amount of line will be advanced.

To install new trimmer line, hold drum firmly and turn spool in direction shown in Fig. RB11 to remove slack. Twist with a hard snap until plastic peg is between holes. Pull spool out of drum. Remove old line from spool. Spool will hold approximately 20 feet (6 m) of monofilament line. Insert one end of new line through hole on spool (Fig. RB12) and pull line through until line is the same length on both sides of hole. Wind both ends of line at the same time in direction indicated by arrow on spool. Wind tightly and evenly from side to side and do not twist line. Insert ends of line through line guide openings, align pegs on drum with slots in spool and push spool into drum. Hold drum firmly, twist spool suddenly in direction shown in Fig. RB13 until peg enters hole with a click and locks spool in position.

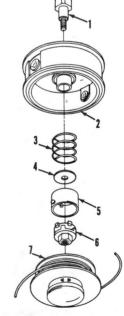

Fig. RB10—Exploded view of the dual strand, semi-automatic trimmer head used on Models NB231, NBF171 and Series NB02, NB16, NB23 and NB211.

1. Drive shaft adapter
2. Housing
3. Spring
4. Washer
5. Outer cam
6. Inner cam
7. Spool

Models NB231, NBF171 And Series NB02, NB16, NB23, And NB211 With Low Profile Manual Head

These models may be equipped with the Low Profile manual trimmer head

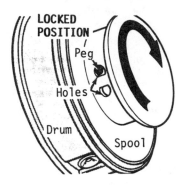

Fig. RB11—To remove spool, hold drum firmly and turn spool in direction shown to take up slack, then twist with a sudden snap until plastic peg is between holes as shown in lower view.

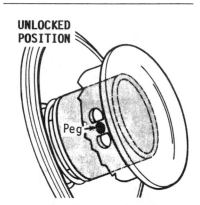

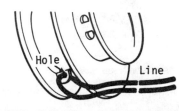

Fig. RB12—End of line must be inserted through hole on spool as shown in lower view. Wind line tightly in direction indicated by arrow on spool.

shown in Fig. RB14. To extend line, stop trimmer engine and wait until head rotation has stopped. Loosen knob (6) until spool (4) may be turned to advance line. Tighten knob when desired line length has been obtained.

To install new line, remove lock knob (6), spring (5) and spool (4). Remove any remaining old line. Wind new line in direction indicated by arrow on spool. Do not exceed spool diameter with line. Insert line ends through line guides (3) of housing (2) and install spool, spring and lock knob.

Models NB04, NB30 And NB50L

Models NB04, NB30 and NB50L may be equipped with the four strand, manual head shown in Fig. RB15. To extend line, loosen lock knob (8) and pull each of the four lines out until desired line length is obtained. Tighten lock knob (8).

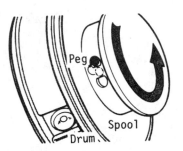

Fig. RB13—Hold drum firmly and twist suddenly to lock spool in position.

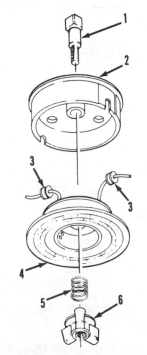

Fig. RB14—Exploded view of low profile manual trimmer head used on Models NB231, NBF171 and Series NB02, NB16, NB23 and NB211.

1. Drive shaft adapter	4. Spool
2. Housing	5. Spring
3. Line guides	6. Lock knob

To install new line, remove lock knob (8), cover (7), spools (5 and 3) and spring (4). Remove any remaining old line. Wind new line on spools in direction indicated by arrow on spool. Do not wrap line to greater diameter than diameter of spool. Insert line ends through line guides (6), then install spools, spring cover (7) and lock knob (8).

Models NB04, NB30 And NB50L

Models NB04, NB30 and NB50L may be equipped with a manual trimmer head (Fig. RB16) that is similar to Low Profile head (Fig. RB14). Refer to preceding paragraph for service information.

BLADE

Some models may be equipped with a blade. Refer to Fig. RB17 for a typical arrangement of parts. Note that some models use a lockwasher (7) and nut (8), while other models use two nuts.

To sharpen the four-cutting-edge blade, refer to Fig. RB18. Blade edge should have a length of 1.18-1.58 inch (30-40 mm). Do not grind the chamfered section of the blade root. Make certain the root of cutting blade remains chamfered to prevent breakage. Sharpen all teeth equally to maintain blade balance.

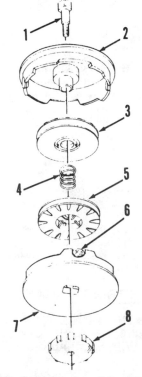

Fig. RB15—Exploded view of the four strand, manual trimmer head used on Models NB04, NB30 and NB50L.

1. Drive shaft adapter	5. Spool
2. Upper housing	6. Line guides
3. Spool	7. Lower housing
4. Spring	8. Lock knob

Illustrations courtesy Robin

To sharpen the eight cutting edge blade, refer to Fig. RB19. Sharpened section must not be closer than 0.08 inch (2 mm) to the root. Root chamfer should have a 0.08 inch (2 mm) radius. Sharpen all teeth equally to maintain blade balance.

To sharpen the saw blade, refer to Fig. RB20. Maintain a 0.04-0.08 inch (1-2 mm) radius at the tooth root. Maintain a 0.08-0.09 inch (2-2.5 mm) tooth set. Sharpen all teeth equally to maintain blade balance.

DRIVE SHAFT

Series NB16 And NB23

Series NB16 and NB23 are equipped with a flexible drive shaft supported in a drive shaft housing tube (Fig. RB21). The drive shaft should be removed, cleaned and lubricated with lithium-base grease after every 30 hours of operation.

Model NB26 And Series NB02

These trimmers are equipped with a solid steel drive shaft (14—Fig. RB22) supported in renewable bushings (13) located in the drive shaft housing tube (12). Drive shaft requires no maintenance; however, if removed, the drive shaft should be lubricated with lithium-base grease before reinstalling. Drive shaft bushings (13) may be renewed.

Mark locations of old bushings in drive shaft housing before removing so new bushings can be installed at the same locations.

Models NB04, NB30, NB351 And NB411

Models NB04, NB30, NB351 and NB411 are equipped with a solid steel drive shaft supported in renewable bushings located in drive shaft housing tube (Fig. RB23 or RB24). Drive shaft requires no maintenance; however, if removed, the drive shaft should be lubricated with lithium-base grease before reinstalling. Drive shaft bushings may be renewed. Mark locations of old bushings in drive shaft housing before removing so new bushings can be installed at the same locations. On some models, bushings may be held in position by pins through drive shaft housing and bushing.

Model NB231 And Series NB211

Model NB231 and Series NB211 trimmers are equipped with a solid steel drive shaft (8—Fig. RB25) supported in renewable bushings (7) located in drive shaft housing tube (6). Drive shaft requires no maintenance; however, if removed, the drive shaft should be lubricated with lithium-base grease before reinstalling. Drive shaft bushings (7) may be renewed. Mark locations of old bushings in drive shaft housing before removing so new bushings can be installed at the same locations.

BEARING HEAD

Model PT

The drive shaft rides in a bushing at drive end of drive shaft housing. Parts

are not available and service is not possible.

Model NBF and Series NB16 And NB23

Series NB16 and NB23 trimmers are equipped with sealed bearings in the

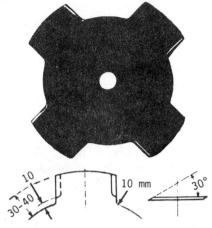

Fig. RB18—View of the four-cutting-edge blade available for some models. Sharpen to dimensions shown and outlined in text.

Fig. RB19—View of the eight-cutting-edge blade available for some models. Sharpen to dimensions shown and outlined in text.

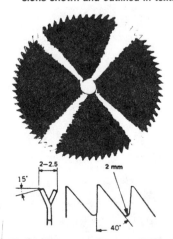

Fig. RB20—View of saw blade available for some models. Sharpen to dimensions shown and outlined in text.

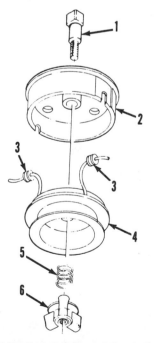

Fig. RB16—Exploded view of the dual strand, manual trimmer head used on NB04, NB30 and NB50L.

1. Drive shaft adapter
2. Housing
3. Line guides
4. Spool
5. Spring
6. Lock knob

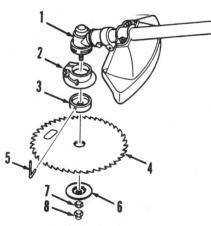

Fig. RB17—Exploded view of typical blade assembly.

1. Gear head
2. Grass guard
3. Cup washer
4. Blade
5. Tool
6. Adapter plate
7. Washer
8. Nut

bearing head (Fig. RB26). Bearing head requires no maintenance. To renew bearings (3 and 4), remove trimmer head or blade assembly and separate bearing head from drive shaft housing tube. Remove snap ring (5) and use a suitable puller to remove arbor (2) and bearing assembly. Press bearings from arbor.

Model NB26 And Series NB02

These models are equipped with the gear head shown in Fig. RB27. Remove check plug (8) after every 30 hours of operation and make certain that gear head housing is $^2/_3$ full of lithium-base grease. Do not force grease into housing with a pressure-type gun as seal may be damaged.

To disassemble gear head, separate gear head from drive shaft housing. Remove blade, adapters (16 and 17) and

spacer (13). Pry out seal (1) and remove snap ring (2). Insert a screwdriver or other suitable wedge into gear head housing clamp splits and carefully expand housing. Remove input shaft (6) and bearings as an assembly. Remove snap ring (5) and press bearings (3 and 4) off input shaft. Remove snap ring (14) and use a suitable puller to remove arbor (11) and bearing assembly. If bearing (9) stays in housing, heat housing to 140° F (60° C) and tap housing on a wood block to dislodge bearing.

Models NB04, NB30, NB50L, NB351 And NB411

Models NB04, NB30, NB50L, NB351 and NB411 are equipped with the gear head shown in Fig. RB28. Remove check plug (8) after every 30 hours of operation and make certain that gear head housing is $^2/_3$ full of lithium-base grease.

Do not force grease into housing with a pressure-type gun as seal may be damaged.

To disassemble gear head, separate gear head from drive shaft housing. Remove trimmer head or blade assembly. Remove snap ring (2). Insert a screwdriver or other suitable wedge into gear head housing clamp split and carefully expand housing. Remove input shaft (4) and bearing assembly. Remove snap ring (1) and press bearing (3) from input shaft. Remove snap ring (13) and use a suitable puller to remove arbor shaft (9) and bearing assembly. If bearing (6) stays in housing, heat housing to 140° F (60° C) and tap housing on a wood block to dislodge bearing. Remove bearing (11) and gear (7) from arbor.

Model NB231 And Series NB211

These models are equipped with the gear head shown in Fig. RB29. Remove check plug (6) after every 30 hours of operation and make certain that gear head housing is $^2/_3$ full of lithium-base grease. Do not force grease into housing with a pressure-type gun as seal may be damaged.

To disassemble gear head, separate gear head from drive shaft housing. Remove trimmer head or blade assembly. Remove snap ring (1). Extract input shaft (4) and bearing assembly. Remove snap ring (2) and press bearing (3) off input shaft. Detach snap ring (10) and pry out seal (11). Remove arbor (8) and bearing assembly. Remove bearing (9) from shaft.

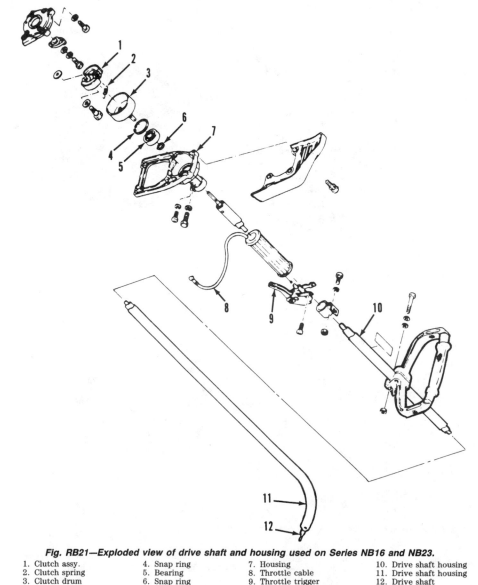

Fig. RB21—Exploded view of drive shaft and housing used on Series NB16 and NB23.

1. Clutch assy.	4. Snap ring	7. Housing	10. Drive shaft housing
2. Clutch spring	5. Bearing	8. Throttle cable	11. Drive shaft housing
3. Clutch drum	6. Snap ring	9. Throttle trigger	12. Drive shaft

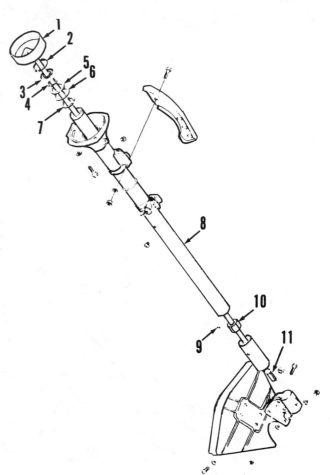

Fig. RB23—Exploded view of drive shaft and housing assembly used on Model NB04.

1. Clutch drum
2. Snap ring
3. Bearing
4. Snap ring
5. Washer
6. Spacer
7. Snap ring
8. Drive shaft housing
9. Pin
10. Bushing
11. Drive shaft

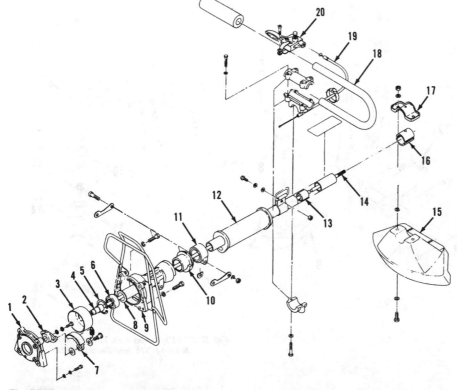

Fig. RB22—Exploded view of drive shaft and housing used on Series NB02. Model NB26 is similar.

1. Locating plate	6. Bearing	11. Clamp	16. Spacer
2. Clutch hub	7. Clutch shoe	12. Hand grip	17. Clamp
3. Clutch drum	8. Drive tube	13. Bushing	18. Handle
4. Adapter	9. Drive housing	14. Drive shaft	19. Throttle cable
5. Snap ring	10. Insulator	15. Safety cover	20. Throttle trigger

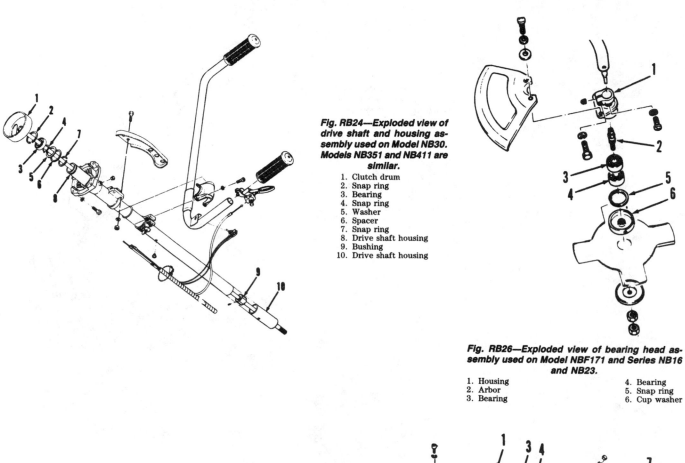

Fig. RB24—Exploded view of drive shaft and housing assembly used on Model NB30. Models NB351 and NB411 are similar.

1. Clutch drum
2. Snap ring
3. Bearing
4. Snap ring
5. Washer
6. Spacer
7. Snap ring
8. Drive shaft housing
9. Bushing
10. Drive shaft housing

Fig. RB26—Exploded view of bearing head assembly used on Model NBF171 and Series NB16 and NB23.

1. Housing
2. Arbor
3. Bearing
4. Bearing
5. Snap ring
6. Cup washer

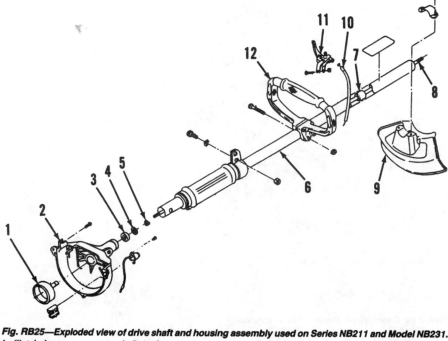

Fig. RB25—Exploded view of drive shaft and housing assembly used on Series NB211 and Model NB231.

1. Clutch drum
2. Clutch housing
3. Bearing
4. Snap ring
5. Snap ring
6. Drive shaft housing
7. Bushing
8. Drive shaft
9. Safety shield
10. Throttle cable
11. Throttle trigger
12. Handle

Fig. RB27—Exploded view of gear head used on Model NB26 and Series NB02.

1. Seal
2. Snap ring
3. Bearing
4. Bearing
5. Snap ring
6. Input shaft
7. Housing
8. Check plug
9. Bearing
10. Gear
11. Arbor
12. Bearing
13. Spacer
14. Snap ring
15. Seal
16. Cup washer
17. Adapter plate
18. Nut
19. Jam nut

Illustrations courtesy Robin

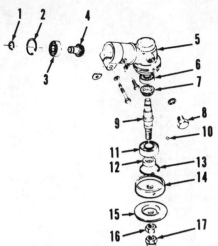

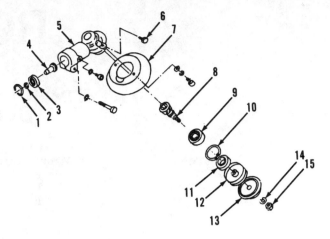

Fig. RB29—Exploded view of gear head used on Model NB231 and Series NB211.

1. Snap ring
2. Snap ring
3. Bearing
4. Input shaft
5. Gear head
6. Check plug
7. Safety guard
8. Arbor & gear
9. Bearing
10. Snap ring
11. Seal
12. Cup washer
13. Adapter plate
14. Lockwasher
15. Nut

Fig. RB28—Exploded view of gear head used on Models NB04, NB30, NB50L, NB351 and NB411.

1. Snap ring
2. Snap ring
3. Bearing
4. Input shaft
5. Housing
6. Bearing
7. Gear
8. Check plug
9. Arbor
10. Pin
11. Bearing
12. Spacer
13. Snap ring
14. Cup washer
15. Adapter plate
16. Nut
17. Jam nut

ROBIN

GASOLINE POWERED BLOWERS

Model	Engine Manufacturer	Engine Model	Displacement
FL21	Fuji	EC02	20.3 cc
FL40, FL40A	Fuji	EC04	37.7 cc
FL411	Fuji	EC04	37.7 cc
NF40	Fuji	EC04	37.7 cc

ENGINE INFORMATION

The models included in this section are powered by a Fuji engine. Refer to appropriate Fuji engine service section for service procedures and specifications.

FUEL MIXTURE

Manufacturer recommends mixing regular grade gasoline (unleaded gasoline is acceptable) and a good quality oil designed for use in a two-stroke, air-cooled engine. Recommended fuel:oil ratio is 24:1. Do not use gasoline containing alcohol.

IMPELLER

The blower impeller (5—Fig. RB51) is attached to the flywheel. The impeller and flywheel on some models are marked to insure proper balance. To remove impeller, first separate engine and blower housing from back pack frame (13) if so equipped. Remove blower tube elbow (16). Remove screws securing blower case halves (3 and 7) and separate case halves. Remove impeller mounting screws or nut and withdraw impeller (5) from flywheel.

When installing impeller, align marks (if used) on impeller and flywheel as shown in Fig. RB52. Tighten fan nut or screws to following torque:

FL21 . . . . .3.9-4.9 N·m
(35-43 in.-lbs.)
FL40, FL40A & NF40. . .27.4-37.2 N·m
(20-27 ft.-lbs.)
FL411 . . . . .8.8-9.8 N·m
(78-87 in.-lbs.)

ENGINE

To remove engine from blower, first remove impeller as outlined above. Remove engine cover. Disconnect throttle cable, fuel line and stop switch wire from engine. Remove engine mounting screws and separate engine from blower case.

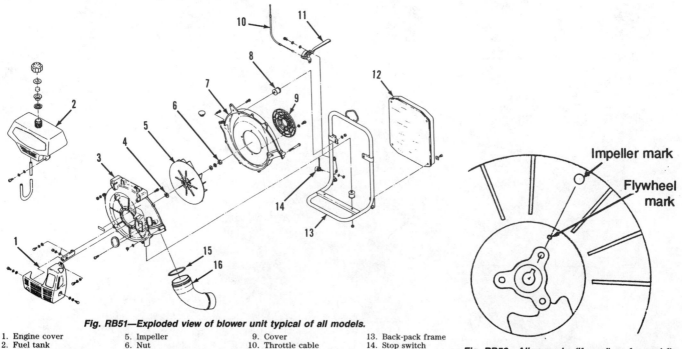

Fig. RB51—Exploded view of blower unit typical of all models.

1. Engine cover	5. Impeller	9. Cover	13. Back-pack frame
2. Fuel tank	6. Nut	10. Throttle cable	14. Stop switch
3. Blower case (rear)	7. Blower case (front)	11. Throttle trigger	15. "O" ring
4. Spacer	8. Vibration insulator	12. Shoulder pad	16. Blower pipe

Fig. RB52—Align marks (if used) on fan and flywheel during assembly.

Illustrations courtesy Robin

ROPER/RALLY

GASOLINE POWERED STRING TRIMMERS

Model	Engine Manufacturer	Engine Model	Displacement
FE32	PPP	99E	31.0 cc
FE33	PPP	99E	31.0 cc

ENGINE INFORMATION

All Models

All models are equipped with a two-stroke air-cooled gasoline engine manufactured by Piston Powered Products (PPP). Refer to PISTON POWERED

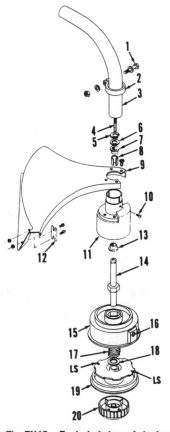

Fig. RY10—Exploded view of single strand semi-automatic trimmer head used on all models.

1. Bolt
2. Clamp
3. Drive shaft housing
4. Drive shaft
5. Retaining ring
6. Washer
7. Bushing
8. Bushing
9. Shield
10. Locating screw
11. Bushing housing
12. Line length trimmer
13. Bushing
14. Shaft
15. Drum
16. Line guide
17. Spring
18. Retainer
19. Spool
20. Bump button
LS. Line slot

PRODUCTS ENGINE SERVICE section of this manual.

FUEL MIXTURE

All Models

Manufacturer recommends mixing 6 ounces (177 mL) of a good quality two-stroke air-cooled engine oil with 1 gallon (3.8 L) of regular grade (unleaded grade is an acceptable substitute) gasoline.

STRING TRIMMER

All Models

All models are equipped with a single line semi-automatic trimmer head (Fig. RY10). To extend line with engine stopped, push in on bump button (20) and pull on line until desired length is obtained. To extend line with engine running, operate trimmer engine at full rpm and tap bump button (20) on the ground. Line will automatically advance a measured amount.

To renew trimmer line, hold drum (15) and unscrew bump button (20). Remove spool (19). Clean inner surface

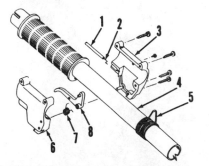

Fig. RY12—Exploded view of throttle trigger and cable assembly used on all models.

1. Throttle cable housing
2. Inner throttle cable
3. Throttle trigger housing
4. Drive shaft housing
5. Strap bracket
6. Throttle trigger housing
7. Spring
8. Throttle trigger

of drum and spool. Check indexing teeth on spool and drum for wear. Insert one end of a 25 foot (7.6 m) length of 0.080 inch (2 mm) monofilament line into one of the holes in spool from the inside out, and back through the second hole to the inside. Wind line in direction indicated by arrow on spool and clip line in one of the line lock slots (LS) on spool. Insert line end through line guide in drum and install spool and bump button. Pull line to release from line lock slot on spool.

DRIVE SHAFT

All Models

All models are equipped with a flexible drive shaft enclosed in the tube housing. Drive shaft has squared ends which engage adapters at each end. Drive shaft should be removed for maintenance at 10 hour intervals of use. Remove and clean drive shaft. Inspect for damage. Coat with a good quality high temperature wheel bearing grease and install drive shaft. Make certain

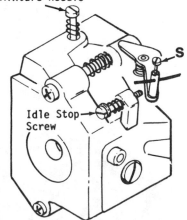

Fig. RY15—Loosen screw (S) and move throttle cable and housing to provide correct throttle trigger free play. Refer to text.

ends of drive shaft are properly located into upper and lower square drive adapters when installing.

LOWER DRIVE SHAFT BUSHINGS

All Models

All models are equipped with drive shaft support bushings (7 and 13-Fig. RY10) located in bushing housing (11). Assemble in sequence shown.

THROTTLE TRIGGER AND CABLE

All Models

Throttle trigger assembly is located on drive shaft housing tube (Fig. RY12) on all models. Throttle cable inner wire (2) should be lubricated at each end at 20 hour intervals of use with SAE 30 oil. Throttle cable should be adjusted to provide 0.02-0.04 inch (0.5-1.0 mm) throttle trigger movement before carburetor throttle lever begins to move. Adjust by loosening set screw (S-Fig. RY15) and moving cable housing and inner wire to provide specified free play. Tighten set screw (S) to maintain adjustment.

RYAN

GASOLINE POWERED
STRING TRIMMERS

Model	Engine Manufacturer	Engine Model	Displacement
261	PPP	99E	31.0 cc
264	IDC	…	31.0 cc
265	PPP	99E	31.0 cc
275	PPP	99E	31.0 cc
284	IDC	…	31.0 cc
285	PPP	99E	31.0 cc

ENGINE INFORMATION

The models in this section are equipped with an Inertia Dynamics Corporation (IDC) or Piston Powered Products (PPP) engine. Refer to appropriate engine service section for engine service information.

FUEL MIXTURE

Manufacturer recommends mixing regular gasoline, leaded or unleaded, with a high-quality two-stroke engine oil. Recommended fuel:oil ratio is 32:1 when using IDC Two-Cycle Engine Oil. When using any other two-stroke oil, mix 6 oz. (0.177 mL) of oil with 1 gal. (3.8 L) of gasoline, regardless of recommended ratio on oil container. Gasohol or other alcohol blended fuels are not approved by manufacturer.

STRING TRIMMER

Models 261, 264, 265 And 275

These models are equipped with a single line, semi-automatic trimmer head (Fig. RN10). To extend line with engine stopped, push in on bump button (20) and pull on line until desired length is obtained. To extend line with engine running, operate trimmer engine at full rpm and tap bump button (20) on the ground. Line will automatically advance a measured amount.

To renew trimmer line, hold drum (15) and unscrew bump button (20). Remove spool (19). Clean inner surface of drum and spool. Check indexing teeth on spool and drum for wear. Insert one end of a 25-ft. (7.6 m) length of 0.080 in. (2 mm) diameter monofilament line into one of the holes in spool from the inside out, then back through the second hole to the inside. Wind line in direction indicated by arrow on spool until all but

about 3 inches (76.2 mm) of line is wrapped, then clip line temporarily in one of the line lock slots (LS) on spool. Insert line end through line guide (16)

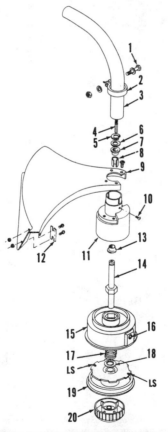

Fig. RN10—Exploded view of single strand, semi-automatic trimmer head used on Models 261, 264, 265 and 275.

1. Bolt
2. Clamp
3. Drive shaft housing
4. Drive shaft
5. Retaining ring
6. Washer
7. Bushing
8. Bushing
9. Shield
10. Locating screw
11. Bushing housing
12. Line length trimmer
13. Bushing
14. Shaft
15. Drum
16. Line guide
17. Spring
18. Retainer
19. Spool
20. Bump button
LS. Line slot

in drum and install spool and bump button. Pull line to release from line lock slot on spool after assembly is complete.

Models 274, 284 And 285

These models are equipped with a dual strand, semi-automatic trimmer head (Fig. RN11). To extend line with engine off, push bump button (8) in and pull lines out. Procedure may have to be repeated until desired line length has been obtained. To extend line with engine running, operate trimmer engine at full operating rpm and tap bump button on the ground. Each time bump button

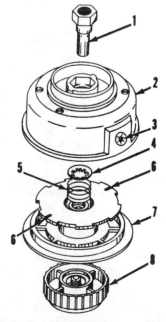

Fig. RN11—Exploded view of dual strand, semi-automatic trimmer head used on Models 284 and 285.

1. Adapter
2. Drum
3. Line guide
4. Retainer
5. Spring
6. Line shot
7. Spool
8. Bump button

is tapped on the ground, approximately 1 inch (25 mm) of new line will be advanced.

To renew line, hold drum (2) and unscrew bump button (8). Remove spool (7) and remove any remaining old line. Clean spool and inner surface of drum. Check indexing teeth in drum and on spool. Loop a 25-ft. (7.6 m) length of 0.080 in. (2 mm) diameter monofilament line into two equal lengths. Insert the two line ends into the two holes in spool from the bottom and pull line out until loop is against spool. Wind both strands of line around spool in direction indicated by arrow on spool. Wind in tight even layers. Clip lines into line slots (6). Insert line ends through line guides (3) in drum and install spool and bump button. Pull line ends to free from line slots.

BLADE

Models 284 And 285

Models 284 and 285 may be equipped with a four-edge cutting blade (Fig. RN12). To install blade, refer to Fig.

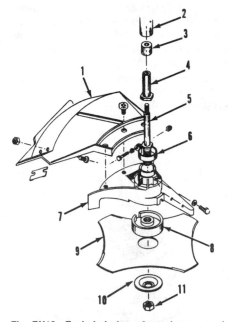

Fig. RN12—Exploded view of weed, grass and light brush blade assembly used on Models 284 and 285.

1. Shield
2. Drive shaft housing
3. Retainer & bushing
4. Drive shaft adapter
5. Head drive shaft
6. Clamp assy.
7. Bearing housing assy.
8. Blade adapter
9. Blade
10. Lower blade adapter
11. Nut

RN12 for assembly sequence. Tighten nut (11) to 225-250 in.-lbs. (26-28 N·m).

DRIVE SHAFT

All Models

All models are equipped with a flexible drive shaft enclosed in the drive shaft housing. The drive shaft has squared ends that engage adapters at each end. The drive shaft should be removed for maintenance after every 10 hours of operation. Remove and clean drive shaft, then inspect shaft for damage. Coat with a high-quality, high-temperature wheel bearing grease and install drive shaft. Make certain ends of

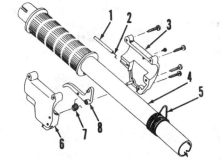

Fig. RN13—Exploded view of throttle trigger and cable assembly used on all models.

1. Throttle cable housing
2. Inner throttle cable
3. Throttle trigger housing
4. Drive shaft housing
5. Strap bracket
6. Throttle trigger housing
7. Spring
8. Throttle trigger

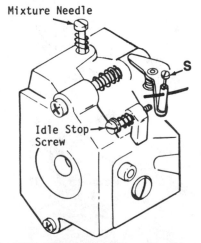

Fig. RN14—Loosen screw (S) and move throttle cable and housing to provide correct throttle trigger free play. Refer to text.

shaft are properly located in upper and lower drive adapters.

BEARING HOUSING

Models 261, 264, 265 And 275

Refer to Fig. RN10 for an exploded view of the bearing housing used on Models 261, 264, 265 and 275. Bushings are not available separately, only with housing (11).

Models 284 And 285

The bearing housing (7—Fig. RN12) on Models 284 and 285 is equipped with a sealed bearing and must be serviced as a unit assembly.

THROTTLE TRIGGER AND CABLE

All Models

The throttle trigger assembly is attached to the drive shaft housing (Fig. RN13) on all models. The throttle cable inner wire (2) should be lubricated after every 20 hours of operation. Apply SAE 30 oil to each end of wire. The throttle cable should be adjusted to provide 0.02-0.04 inch (0.5-1.0 mm) throttle trigger movement before the carburetor throttle lever begins to move. Adjust by loosening set screw (S—Fig. RN14) and moving cable housing and inner wire to provide specified free play. Tighten set screw (S).

RYAN

GASOLINE POWERED BLOWERS

Model	Engine Manufacturer	Engine Model	Displacement
200	IDC	...	31.0 cc
300BV	IDC	...	31.0 cc

ENGINE INFORMATION

The models in this section are equipped with an Inertia Dynamics Corporation (IDC) engine. Refer to IDC engine service section for engine service information.

FUEL MIXTURE

Manufacturer recommends mixing regular gasoline, leaded or unleaded, with a high-quality, two-stroke engine oil. Recommended fuel:oil ratio is 32:1 when using IDC Two-Cycle Engine Oil. When using any other two-stroke oil, mix 6 oz. (0.177 mL) of oil with 1 gal. (3.8 L) of gasoline, regardless of recommended ratio on oil container. Gasohol or other alcohol blended fuels are not approved by manufacturer.

BLOWER ASSEMBLY

Model 200

Refer to Fig. RN50 for exploded view of blower assembly. To remove blower impeller (4), remove mounting screws from starter housing (1) and blower housing (3). Separate blower housing halves (3 and 6). Remove mounting screws from blower impeller (4) and separate impeller from flywheel.

To separate engine from blower housing, remove impeller as outlined above. Remove engine cover (10). Disconnect fuel line, throttle cable and ignition wires from engine. Remove engine mounting screws and withdraw engine from blower housing half (6).

Model 300BV

Refer to Fig. RN51 for exploded view of blower assembly. To remove blower impeller (8), remove blower tube (12). Remove screws attaching blower lower housing (10) to upper housing (7) and separate housing. Remove impeller mounting screw and separate impeller (8) from flywheel.

To separate engine from blower housing, remove impeller as outlined above. Remove screws securing engine covers (1 and 4). Separate covers and disconnect throttle cable, fuel line and ignition wires from engine. Remove engine mounting screws and withdraw engine from blower upper housing (7).

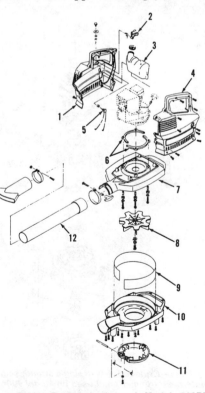

Fig. RN51—Exploded view of Model 300BV blower/vac.

1. Engine cover
2. Throttle trigger
3. Fuel tank
4. Engine cover
5. Stop switch
6. Gasket
7. Blower upper housing
8. Impeller
9. Shield
10. Blower lower housing
11. Intake cover
12. Blower tube

Fig. RN50—Exploded view of Model 200 blower.

1. Starter housing
2. Recoil starter assy.
3. Blower housing half
4. Impeller
5. Fuel tank
6. Blower housing half
7. Stop switch
8. Throttle trigger
9. Handle
10. Engine cover

RYOBI

GASOLINE POWERED STRING TRIMMERS

Model	Engine Manufacturer	Engine Model	Displacement
700r	IDC	...	28.5 cc
720r	IDC	...	31.0 cc
740r	IDC	...	31.0 cc
780r	IDC	...	31.0 cc

ENGINE INFORMATION

The models in this section are equipped with an Inertia Dynamics Corporation (IDC) engine. Refer to IDC engine service section for engine service information.

FUEL MIXTURE

Manufacturer recommends mixing regular gasoline, leaded or unleaded, with a high-quality, two-stroke engine oil. Recommended fuel:oil ratio is 32:1 when using IDC Two-Cycle Engine Oil. When using any other two-stroke oil, mix 6 oz. (0.177 mL) of oil with 1 gal. (3.8 L) of gasoline, regardless of recommended ratio on oil container. Gasohol or other alcohol blended fuels are not approved by manufacturer.

STRING TRIMMER

Model 700r

Model 700r is equipped with a single line, semi-automatic trimmer head (Fig. RY10). To extend line with engine stopped, push in on bump button (20) and pull on line until desired length is obtained. To extend line with engine running, operate trimmer engine at full rpm and tap bump button (20) on the ground. Line will automatically advance a measured amount.

To renew trimmer line, hold drum (15) and unscrew bump button (20). Remove spool (19). Clean inner surface of drum

and spool. Check indexing teeth on spool and drum for wear. Insert one end of a 25-ft. (7.6 m) length of 0.080 in. (2 mm) diameter monofilament line into one of the holes in spool from the inside out, then back through the second hole to the inside. Wind line in direction indicated by arrow on spool until all but about 3 inches (76.2 mm) of line is wrapped, then clip line temporarily in one of the line lock slots (LS) on spool. Insert line end through line guide (16) in drum and install spool and bump button. Pull line to release from line lock slot on spool after assembly is complete.

Models 720r, 740r And 780r

These models are equipped with a dual strand, semi-automatic trimmer head (Fig. RY11). To extend line with engine off, push bump button (8) in and pull lines out. Procedure may have to be repeated until desired line length has been obtained. To extend line with engine running, operate trimmer engine at full operating rpm and tap bump button on the ground. Each time bump button is tapped on the ground, approximately 1 inch (25 mm) of new line will be advanced.

To renew line, hold drum (2) and unscrew bump button (8). Note that screw in bump button on Model 780r has left-hand threads. Remove spool (7) and remove any remaining old line. Clean spool and inner surface of drum. Check indexing teeth in drum and on spool. On Models 720r and 740r, loop a 25-ft. (7.6 m) length of 0.080-in. (2 mm) diameter

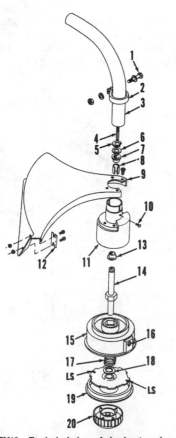

Fig. RY10—Exploded view of single strand, semi-automatic trimmer head used on Model 700r.

1. Bolt			
2. Clamp		12. Line length trimmer	
3. Drive shaft housing		13. Bushing	
4. Drive shaft		14. Shaft	
5. Retaining ring		15. Drum	
6. Washer		16. Line guide	
7. Bushing		17. Spring	
8. Bushing		18. Retainer	
9. Shield		19. Spool	
10. Locating screw		20. Bump button	
11. Bushing housing		LS. Line slot	

Illustrations courtesy Ryobi Outdoor Products

monofilament line into two equal lengths. On Model 780r, loop a 50-ft. (15.2 m) length of 0.095-in. (2.4 mm) diameter line into two equal lengths. Insert the two line ends into the two holes in spool from the bottom and pull line out until loop is against spool. Wind both strands of line around spool in direction indicated by arrow on spool. Wind in tight even layers. Clip lines into line slots (6). Insert line ends through line guides (3) in drum and install spool and bump button. Bump button screw on Model 780r has left-hand threads. Pull line ends to free from line slots.

On Model 780r, note that trimmer housing (2) has left-hand threads.

BLADE

Models 740r And 780r

Models 740r and 780r may be equipped with a four-edge cutting blade (9—Figs. RY12 or RY13). To install blade, refer to Figs. RY12 or RY13 for assembly sequence. Note that nut (11) on Model 780r has left-hand threads. Tighten nut (11) to 225-250 in.-lbs. (26-28 N·m).

DRIVE SHAFT

All Models Except 780r

All models except Model 780r are equipped with a flexible drive shaft enclosed in the drive shaft housing. The drive shaft has squared ends that engage adapters at each end. The drive shaft should be removed for maintenance after every 10 hours of operation.

To remove drive shaft, loosen clamp (2—Fig. RY10 or 6—Fig. RY12) and remove set screw attaching drive shaft tube to trimmer bearing housing. Remove and clean drive shaft, then inspect shaft for damage. Coat with a high-quality, high-temperature wheel bearing grease and install drive shaft. Make certain ends of shaft are properly located in upper and lower drive adapters.

Model 780r

Model 780r is equipped with a solid steel drive shaft (2—Fig. RY13) that rides in bushings in the drive shaft housing (1). The drive shaft requires no maintenance. If shaft is removed, it should be lubricated with high-temperature wheel bearing grease before installation.

BEARING HOUSING

Models 700r And 720r

Refer to Fig. RY10 for an exploded view of the bearing housing used on Models 700r and 720r. Bushings are not available separately, only with housing (11).

Model 740r

The bearing head (7—Fig. RY12) on Model 740r is equipped with a sealed bearing and must be serviced as a unit assembly.

GEAR HEAD

Model 780r

Model 780r is equipped with a gear head assembly (4—Fig. RY13). Plug (3) in side of gear head should be removed and lubricant level checked after every 50 hours of operation. Housing should be 2/3 full of high-temperature wheel bearing grease. Service parts are not available. Gear head must be renewed as a complete unit.

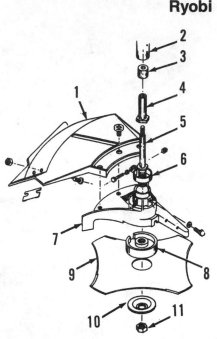

Fig. RY12—Exploded view of weed, grass and light brush blade assembly used on Model 740r.

1. Shield
2. Drive shaft housing
3. Retainer & bushing
4. Drive shaft adapter
5. Head drive shaft
6. Clamp assy.
7. Bearing housing assy.
8. Blade adapter
9. Blade
10. Lower blade adapter
11. Nut

Fig. RY11—Exploded view of dual strand, semiautomatic trimmer head used on Models 720r and 740r. Model 780r is similar.

1. Adapter
2. Drum
3. Line guide
4. Retainer
5. Spring
6. Line slot
7. Spool
8. Bump button

Fig. RY13—Exploded view of weed, grass and light brush blade assembly used on Model 780r. Nut (11) has left-hand threads.

1. Drive shaft housing
2. Drive shaft
3. Check plug
4. Gear head
5. Guard mount
6. Guard
7. Line length trimmer blade
8. Blade adapter
9. Blade
10. Retaining washer
11. Nut

133

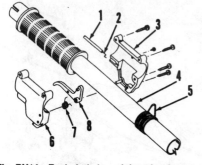

Fig. RY14—Exploded view of throttle trigger and cable assembly used on all models.

1. Throttle cable
   housing
2. Inner throttle cable
3. Throttle trigger
   housing
4. Drive shaft housing

5. Strap bracket
6. Throttle trigger
   housing
7. Spring
8. Throttle trigger

THROTTLE TRIGGER AND CABLE

All Models

The throttle trigger assembly is attached to the drive shaft housing (Fig. RY14) on all models. The throttle cable inner wire (2) should be lubricated after every 20 hours of operation. Apply SAE 30 oil to each end of wire. The throttle cable should be adjusted to provide 0.02-0.04 inch (0.5-1.0 mm) throttle trigger movement before the carburetor throttle lever begins to move. Adjust by loosening set screw (S—Fig. RY15) and moving cable housing and inner wire to provide specified free play. Tighten set screw (S).

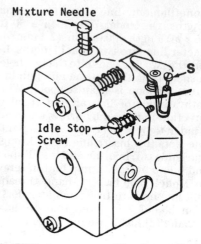

Fig. RY15—Loosen screw (S) and move throttle cable and housing to provide correct throttle trigger free play. Refer to text.

RYOBI

GASOLINE POWERED BLOWERS

Model	Engine Manufacturer	Engine Model	Displacement
210r	IDC	...	31.0 cc
310BVR	IDC	...	31.0 cc

ENGINE INFORMATION

The models in this section are equipped with an Inertia Dynamics Corporation (IDC) engine. Refer to IDC engine service section for engine service information.

FUEL MIXTURE

Manufacturer recommends mixing regular grade gasoline, leaded or unleaded, with a high-quality, two-stroke engine oil. Recommended fuel:oil ratio is 32:1 when using IDC Two-Cycle Engine Oil. When using any other two-stroke oil, mix 6 oz. (0.177 mL) of oil with 1 gal. (3.8 L) of gasoline, regardless of recommended ratio on oil container. Gasohol or other alcohol blended fuels are not approved by manufacturer.

BLOWER ASSEMBLY

Model 210r

Refer to Fig. RY50 for exploded view of blower assembly. To remove blower impeller (4), remove mounting screws from starter housing (1) and blower housing (3). Separate blower housing halves (3 and 6). Remove mounting screws from blower impeller (4) and separate impeller from flywheel.

To separate engine from blower housing, remove impeller as outlined above. Remove engine cover (10). Disconnect fuel line, throttle cable and ignition wires from engine. Remove engine mounting screws and withdraw engine from blower housing half (6).

Model 310BVR

Refer to Fig. RY51 for exploded view of blower assembly. To remove blower impeller (8), remove blower tube (12). Remove screws attaching blower lower housing (10) to upper housing (7) and separate housing. Remove impeller mounting screws and separate impeller (8) from flywheel.

To separate engine from blower housing, remove impeller as outlined above. Remove screws securing engine covers (1 and 4). Separate covers and disconnect throttle cable, fuel line and ignition wires from engine. Remove engine mounting screws and withdraw engine from blower upper housing (7).

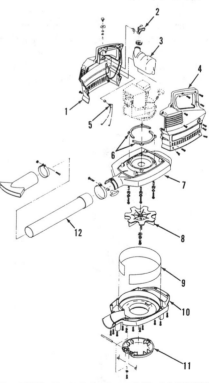

Fig. RY51—Exploded view of Model 310BVR blower/vac.

1. Engine cover
2. Throttle trigger
3. Fuel tank
4. Engine cover
5. Stop switch
6. Gasket
7. Blower upper housing
8. Impeller
9. Shield
10. Blower lower housing
11. Intake cover
12. Blower tube

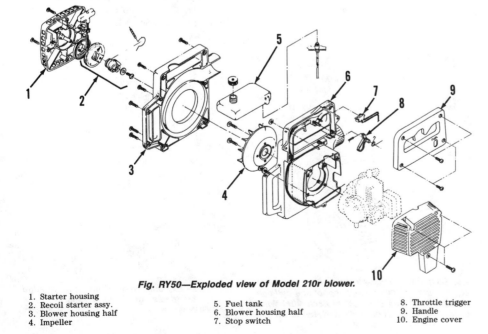

Fig. RY50—Exploded view of Model 210r blower.

1. Starter housing
2. Recoil starter assy.
3. Blower housing half
4. Impeller
5. Fuel tank
6. Blower housing half
7. Stop switch
8. Throttle trigger
9. Handle
10. Engine cover

SACHS-DOLMAR

GASOLINE POWERED STRING TRIMMERS

Model	Engine Manufacturer	Engine Model	Displacement
LT-16	Fuji	EC01	15.4 cc
LT-250	Sachs	....	33.0 cc
BC-250	Sachs	....	33.0 cc
BC-330	Sachs	....	33.0 cc
BC-400	Sachs	....	40.0 cc

ENGINE INFORMATION

Model LT-16 is equipped with an engine manufactured by Fuji. All other models are equipped with Sachs-Dolmar engine. Refer to appropriate FUJI or SACHS-DOLMAR ENGINE SERVICE sections of this manual.

FUEL MIXTURE

Model LT-16

Manufacturer recommends mixing regular grade gasoline with an octane rating of at least 87, with a good quality two-stroke air-cooled engine oil at a ratio of 24:1. Do not use fuel containing alcohol.

All Other Models

Sachs-Dolmar recommends mixing SACHS-DOLMAR two-stroke engine oil with regular grade gasoline at a ratio of 40:1. When using regular two-stroke engine oil, mix at a ratio of 25:1. Do not use fuel containing alcohol.

STRING TRIMMER

Model LT-16

Refer to Fig. SD10 for an exploded view of the semi-automatic trimmer head used on Model LT-16. To extend line with engine stopped, push button (9) and pull line out of line guide to desired length. Button may have to be pushed several times. To extend line with engine running, operate engine at full rpm and tap button (9) on the ground. A measured amount of line will automatically be advanced each time button is tapped on the ground. Line will be cut off by the cutter attached to the shield.

To renew line, unsnap cover (10) and remove cover, button and line spool. Clean and inspect all parts. Wind 25

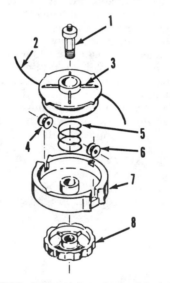

Fig. SD11—Exploded view of manual dual strand trimmer head used on Models LT-250, BC-250, BC-330 and BC-400.

1. Bolt
2. Line
3. Spool
4. Line guide
5. Spring
6. Line guide
7. Hub
8. Knob

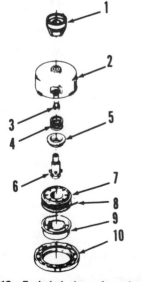

Fig. SD10—Exploded view of semi-automatic trimmer head used on Model LT-16.

1. Adapter
2. Hub
3. Line guide
4. Spring
5. Spring adapter
6. Drive post
7. Spool
8. Line
9. Button
10. Cover

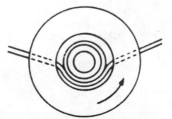

Fig. SD12—When installing new line, insert line end through the two holes in spool and pull line through until equal in length at each side. Wind lines in the direction indicated by arrow on spool.

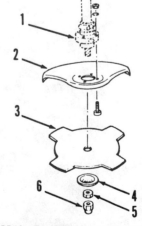

Fig. SD13—Exploded view of four cutting edge blade used on Model BC-250.

1. Bearing head
2. Shield
3. Blade
4. Adapter
5. Nut
6. Jam nut

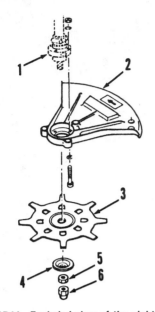

Fig. SD14—Exploded view of the eight cutting edge blade used on Model BC-250.

1. Bearing head
2. Shield
3. Blade
4. Adapter
5. Nut
6. Jam nut

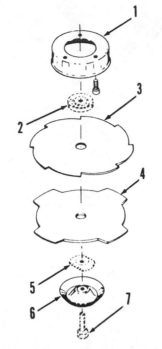

Fig. SD16—Exploded view of four and eight cutting edge blades available for Models LT-250, BC-250, BC-330 and BC-400.

1. Anti-Wind plate
2. Adapter
3. Eight edge blade
4. Four edge blade
5. Adapter
6. Cap
7. Bolt

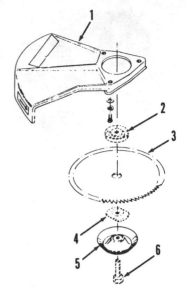

Fig. SD17—Exploded view of saw blade available for Models BC-330 and BC-400.

1. Shield
2. Adapter
3. Blade
4. Adapter
5. Cap
6. Bolt

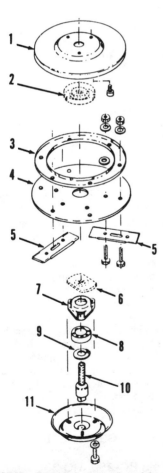

Fig. SD15—Exploded view of mulch cutting blade available for Models BC-330 and BC-400.

1. Anti-Wind plate
2. Adapter
3. Spacer
4. Blade plate
5. Blades
6. Adapter
7. Support bearing housing
8. Bearing
9. Washer
10. Arbor
11. Sliding cup

feet (7.6 m) of 0.080 inch (2 mm) monofilament line on spool in direction indicated by arrow on spool. Insert end of line through line guide (3) and install spool (7) in drum (2). Install button (9) and cover (10).

Models LT-250, BC-250, BC-330 And BC-400

Refer to Fig. SD11 for an exploded view of the manual dual strand trimmer head used. To advance trimmer line, shut off engine and wait until all head rotation has stopped. Loosen knob (8) (left-hand threads) until locating teeth between spool (3) and body (7) are disengaged. Carefully pull out each line to a length of 4 inches (101 mm). Make certain locating teeth are engaged and tighten knob (8).

To renew line, remove knob (8) (left-hand threads), body (7), spring (5), spool (3) and bolt (1). Remove any remaining line. Spool will hold approximately 25 feet (7.6 m) of monofilament line. Insert one end of line through the two holes in the spool (Fig. SD12). Pull line through holes until line is equal length at each side. Wind both ends of line in direction indicated by arrow on spool. Insert line ends through line guides in body and install bolt, spool, spring, body and knob.

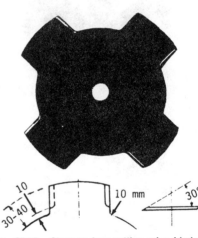

Fig. SD18—Sharpen four cutting edge blade to dimensions shown on all models except Model BC-250. Refer to text.

BLADE

Model BC-250 may be equipped with a four cutting edge blade (Fig. SD13) or an eight cutting edge blade (Fig. SD14). Model BC-330 and BC-400 may be equipped with a mulch cutting blade (Fig. SD15), a four cutting edge blade (4—Fig. SD16), an eight cutting edge blade (3—Fig. SD16) or a multi-tooth saw blade (Fig. SD17). Refer to appropriate illustration for installation sequence.

The mulch cutting blade should be sharpened using the same procedure as used for the four cutting edge blade.

To sharpen the four cutting edge blade, refer to Fig. SD18. Blade edge should have a length of 1.18-1.58 inch (30-40 mm) for all models except Model

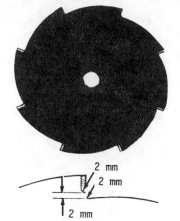

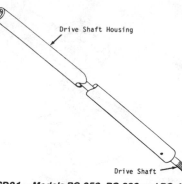

Fig. SD21—Models BC-250, BC-330 and BC-400 are equipped with a solid drive shaft.

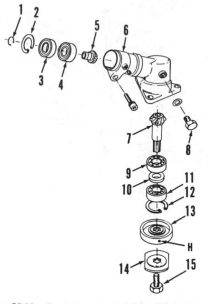

Fig. SD19—Sharpen the eight cutting edge blade to dimensions shown. Refer to text.

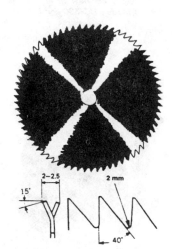

Fig. SD20—Set and sharpen saw blade teeth to dimensions shown. Refer to text.

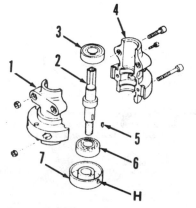

Fig. SD22—Exploded view of bearing head used on Model LT-250.

1. Housing
2. Arbor
3. Bearing
4. Housing
5. Key
6. Bearing
7. Cup washer
H. Hole

Fig. SD23—Exploded view of gear head used on some models. Refer also to Fig. SD24. Note hole (H) in cup washer can be aligned with hole in drive shaft housing to insert a 5/32 inch Allen wrench or similar tool to prevent drive shaft rotation when removing or installing cutting head or blade.

1. Snap ring
2. Snap ring
3. Bearing
4. Bearing
5. Input shaft
6. Housing
7. Arbor (output) shaft
8. Check plug
9. Bearing
10. Spacer
11. Bearing
12. Snap ring
13. Cup washer
14. Adapter
15. Bolt
H. Hole

BC-250. Model BC-250 should be sharpened to a length of 0.59-0.79 inch (15-20 mm). Do not grind the chamfered section of the blade root. Make certain the root of cutting blade remains chamfered to prevent breakage. Sharpen all teeth equally to maintain blade balance.

To sharpen the eight cutting edge blade, refer to Fig. SD19. Sharpened section must be kept 0.08 inch (2 mm) from the root. Root chamfer should have a 0.08 inch (2 mm) radius. Sharpen all teeth equally to maintain blade balance.

To sharpen the saw blade, refer to Fig. SD20. Maintain a 0.04-0.08 inch (1-2 mm) radius at the tooth root. Maintain a 0.08-0.09 inch (2-2.5 mm) tooth set. Sharpen all teeth equally to maintain blade balance.

DRIVE SHAFT

Models LT-16 And LT-250

Both models are equipped with a flexible drive shaft. Drive shaft should be removed, cleaned and lubricated at 20 hour intervals of use. Use a good quality lithium base grease. Drive shaft may be removed by separating drive shaft housing (tube) and engine.

Models BC-250, BC-330 And BC-400

Models BC-250, BC-330 and BC-400 are equipped with a solid steel drive shaft (Fig. SD21) supported in bushings in drive shaft housing. No regular maintenance is required.

BEARING HEAD

Model LT-16

Model LT-16 bearing head is an integral part of the drive shaft housing. If

bearing head becomes worn or damaged, entire housing assembly must be renewed.

Model LT-250

Refer to Fig. SD22 for an exploded view of bearing head used on LT-250 models. Bearings (3 and 6) are sealed and require no regular maintenance. To disassemble bearing head, remove bolts and separate gear head housing (1 and 4). Remove arbor and bearing assembly. Press cup washer (7) from arbor. Remove key (5) and press bearings from arbor as necessary. Note hole (H) in cup washer is an aid to tighten or remove cutting head or blade assemblies. Align hole in cup washer with hole in drive shaft housing tube and insert a 5/32 inch Allen wrench or similar tool into hole to prevent drive shaft turning while removing cutting head or blade.

GEAR HEAD

Models BC-250, BC-330 And BC-400

Models BC-250, BC-330 and BC-400 may be equipped with the gear head assembly shown in Fig. SD23 or

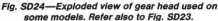

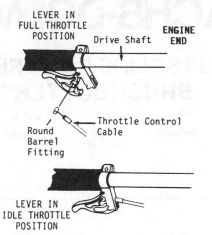

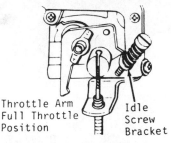

Fig. SD26—Threaded end of throttle cable should be adjusted as outlined in text.

Fig. SD24—Exploded view of gear head used on some models. Refer also to Fig. SD23.

1. Snap ring	10. Bearing
2. Snap ring	11. Bearing
3. Bearing	12. Snap ring
4. Spacer	13. Spacer
5. Bearing	14. Bearing
6. Input shaft	15. Snap ring
7. Housing	16. Cup washer
8. Check plug	17. Adapter
9. Arbor (output) shaft	18. Bolt

Fig. SD25—Engine speed is controlled by throttle trigger located on drive shaft housing tube. Inner wire of cable should be lubricated with SAE 30 oil at 20 hour intervals of use.

SD24. Gear head should be lubricated at 30-hour intervals of use. Remove check plug (8—Figs. SD23 or SD24) and fill gear head housing approximately ²/₃ full with a good quality lithium-base grease. Do not use a pressure grease gun to fill gear head as damage to bearing seals and housing will occur.

To disassemble gear head shown in Fig. SD23, separate gear head from drive shaft housing and drive shaft. Remove cutting head or blade. Pull cup washer (13) from arbor shaft. Remove snap ring (12). Heat gear head housing to approximately 212° F (100° C) and remove arbor shaft and bearing assembly. Press bearings (11) from arbor

shaft (7). Remove spacer (10). Press bearing (9) from arbor shaft. Remove snap ring (2). Insert screwdriver or suitable wedge in clamp split in housing and carefully expand housing. Remove input shaft and bearing assembly. Remove snap ring (1) and press bearings (3 and 4) from input shaft. After reassembly, fill gear head approximately 2/3 full with lithium base grease. Do not use a pressure grease gun to fill gear head.

To disassemble gear head shown in Fig. SD24, separate gear head from drive shaft housing and drive shaft. Remove cutting head or blade. Remove cup washer (16). Remove snap ring (15) and heat gear head housing to 212° F (100° C). Remove arbor shaft and bearing assembly. Remove snap ring (2) and insert a screwdriver or similar wedge into housing clamp splits and carefully expand housing. Remove input shaft and bearing assembly. Remove snap ring (1). Press bearing (3), spacer (4) and bearing (5) from input shaft. After reassembly, fill gear head approxi-

mately 2/3 full with a good quality lithium base grease. Do not use a pressure grease gun to fill gear head.

THROTTLE TRIGGER AND CABLE

Model LT-16

Throttle trigger located on drive shaft housing tube controls engine rpm. Throttle cable should be lubricated at each end by applying SAE 30 oil to inner throttle wire (Fig. SD25 and SD26). Lubricate throttle cable at 20 hour intervals of use. Cable should be threaded in or out of cable bracket at carburetor so that throttle arm contacts idle screw bracket at full throttle and return to idle screw when throttle trigger is released (Fig. SD26).

Models LT-250, BC-250, BC-330 And BC-400

Throttle trigger located on drive shaft housing tube controls engine rpm. Throttle cable should be lubricated at each end by applying SAE 30 oil to inner throttle wire. Throttle cable should be adjusted at knurled nut at throttle cable junction at engine. Loosen jam nut and adjust knurled nut to provide 0.08-0.10 inch (2-3 mm) cable movement before carburetor actuation begins. Tighten jam nut.

SACHS-DOLMAR

GASOLINE POWERED
BRUSHCUTTERS

Model	Engine Manufacturer	Engine Model	Displacement
BC-225-E	Fuji	....	22.5 cc
BC-377	Fuji	....	37.7 cc
BC-377-EES	Fuji	....	37.7 cc

ENGINE INFORMATION

Models BC-225-E, BC-377 and BC-377-EES brushcutters are equipped with Fuji two-stroke air-cooled gasoline engines. Identify engine by engine displacement or trimmer model number and refer to appropriate FUJI ENGINE SERVICE section of this manual.

FUEL MIXTURE

Manufacturer recommends mixing regular grade gasoline with an octane rating of at least 87, with a good quality two-stroke air-cooled engine oil at a ratio of 24:1. Do not use fuel containing alcohol.

BLADE

Model BC-225-E is equipped with a four cutting edge blade and Models BC-377 and BC-377-EES are equipped with a saw type blade (Fig. SD30). To remove blade from all models, align hole in cup washer with hole in gear head. Insert suitable tool (5—Fig. SD30) to prevent turning of arbor in gear head and remove jam nut (8) and nut (7). Remove adapter (6) and blade. When reassembling, tighten nut (7) to 130-215 in.-lbs. (15-24 N·m).

DRIVE SHAFT

All models are equipped with a solid steel drive shaft supported in sealed ball bearings and bushings in drive shaft housing tube (Figs. SD31 and SD32). Drive shaft requires no regular maintenance; however, if removed, lightly oil with SAE 30 oil before reinstalling drive shaft.

GEAR HEAD

Model BC-225-E

Refer to Fig. SD33 for an exploded view of the gear head used on Model BC-225-E. At 30-hour intervals of use,

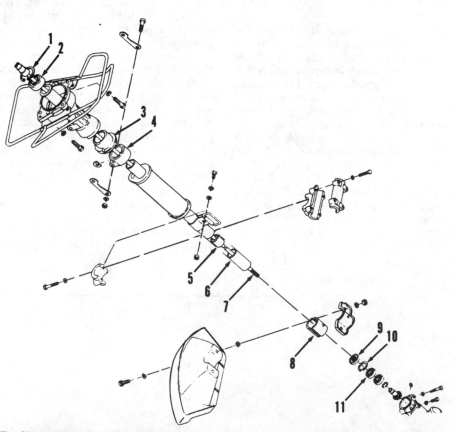

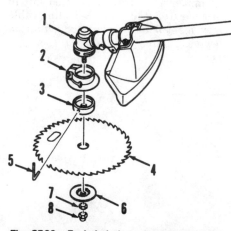

Fig. SD30—Exploded view of saw blade available for Models BC-377 and BC-377-EES.

1. Gear head
2. Anti-wrap plate
3. Cup washer
4. Saw blade
5. Tool
6. Adapter
7. Nut
8. Jam nut

Fig. SD31—Exploded view of drive shaft and housing used on Model BC-225-E. Solid drive shaft is supported at each end in ball bearings and along drive shaft housing by bushings (5).

1. Snap ring
2. Bearing
3. Rubber vibration dampner
4. Locating collar
5. Bushing
6. Drive shaft housing
7. Drive shaft
8. Split spacer
9. Seal
10. Snap ring
11. Bearing

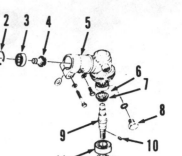

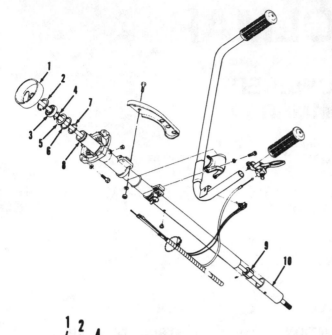

Fig. SD32—Exploded view of drive shaft and housing assembly used on Models BC-377 and BC-377-EES. Solid drive shaft is supported at each end by ball bearings and along drive shaft housing by bushings (9).

1. Drum & drive shaft assy.
2. Snap ring
3. Bearing
4. Snap ring
5. Spacer
6. Washer
7. Snap ring
8. Housing holder
9. Bushings
10. Housing

Fig. SD34—Exploded view of gear head used on Models BC-377 and BC-377-EES.

1. Snap ring		10. Key
2. Snap ring		11. Bearing
3. Bearing		12. Spacer
4. Input shaft & gear		13. Snap ring
5. Housing		14. Cup washer
6. Bearing		15. Adapter
7. Gear		16. Nut
8. Check plug		17. Jam nut
9. Arbor (output) shaft		

Fig. SD33—Exploded view of gear head assembly used on Models BC-225-E.

1. Seal	11. Arbor (output) shaft
2. Snap ring	12. Bearing
3. Bearing	13. Spacer
4. Bearing	14. Snap ring
5. Snap ring	15. Seal
6. Input shaft	16. Cup washer
7. Housing	17. Adapter
8. Check plug	18. Nut
9. Bearing	19. Jam nut
10. Gear	

remove check plug (8) and pump a good-quality lithium-base grease into gear head housing until grease appears at lower seal (15).

To disassemble gear head, separate gear head from drive shaft housing. Remove blade. Remove seal (15) and snap ring (14). Use a suitable puller to remove arbor shaft (11) and bearing assembly. If bearing (9) stays in housing, heat housing to 140° F (60° C) and tap housing on wooden block to remove bearing. Remove seal (1) and snap ring (2). Insert screwdriver or suitable wedge into housing clamp split and carefully expand housing to remove input shaft (6) and bearing assembly. Remove snap ring (5) and press bearings (3 and 4) from input shaft.

Models BC-377 And BC-377-EES

Models BC-377 and BC-377-EES are equipped with gear housing shown in Fig. SD34. Remove check plug (8) at 30 hour intervals of use and make certain gear head housing is 2/3 full of a good quality lithium base grease. Do not use a pressure type grease gun to pump grease into housing as bearing seal damage will occur.

To disassemble gear head, separate gear head from drive shaft housing. Remove blade, adapters and spacer. Remove snap ring (13) and use a suitable puller to remove arbor (9) and bearing assembly. If bearing (6) stays in housing, heat housing to 140° F (60° C) and tap housing on wooden block to remove bearing. Remove snap ring (2). Insert screwdriver or suitable wedge into gear head housing clamp split and carefully expand housing to remove input shaft (4) and bearing assembly. Remove necessary snap rings to remove bearings and gears from shafts.

THROTTLE TRIGGER AND CABLE

Throttle trigger located on drive shaft housing tube controls engine rpm by a cable and housing assembly running from trigger to carburetor. Inner wire of throttle cable should be lubricated at each end with SAE 30 oil at 20 hour intervals of use. Adjusting nuts are installed on throttle cable housing at carburetor end to provide throttle cable adjustment. Cable should be adjusted so that carburetor throttle plate will be fully opened at high speed position of throttle trigger; however, throttle trigger should have 0.08-0.10 inch (2-3 mm) movement before beginning to operate throttle lever on carburetor.

SACHS-DOLMAR

GASOLINE POWERED
STRING TRIMMERS

Model	Engine Manufacturer	Engine Model	Displacement
LT-210	Fuji	…	21.2 cc
BC-210	Fuji	…	21.2 cc
BC-212	Fuji	…	21.2 cc

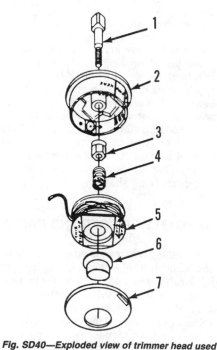

Fig. SD40—Exploded view of trimmer head used on Model LT-210.

1. Adapter
2. Drum
3. Nut (L.H.)
4. Spring
5. Spool
6. Button
7. Cover

Fig. SD41—Insert trimmer line end through eye (E) on spool as shown so approximately 1 inch (25 mm) extends past eye.

ENGINE INFORMATION

The models in this section are equipped with a Fuji engine. Refer to Fuji engine service section for engine service information.

FUEL MIXTURE

Oil must be mixed with the fuel. Unleaded fuel may be used. Recommended fuel:oil ratio when using Sachs-Dolmar two-stroke oil is 40:1. When using other two-stroke oils, ratio should be 25:1.

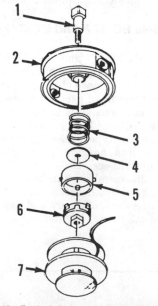

Fig. SD42—Exploded view of trimmer head used on Models BC-210 and BC-212. Unscrew cam (6) by turning clockwise.

1. Adapter
2. Drum
3. Spring
4. Washer
5. Outer drive cam
6. Inner drive cam
7. Spool

STRING TRIMMER

LT-210

Model LT-210 is equipped with a dual-strand, semi-automatic trimmer head. To manually advance line with engine stopped, push in button at bottom of head and pull on each line. To extend line with engine running, operate trimmer at full operating rpm and tap button on ground. Line will automatically advance a given amount.

To install new line, press against tab marked "PUSH" and remove cover (7—Fig. SD40), button (6) and spool (5). Clean and inspect all parts. New line should be 0.080-in. (2 mm) diameter and 12 feet (366 cm) long. Insert end of line through eye of spool as shown in Fig. SD41 so approximately 1 inch (25 mm) extends past eye. Wrap line on spool in clockwise direction as viewed from top side of spool (note arrow on spool). Install spool while directing line end through eye of drum (2—Fig. SD40). Install button and cover. Cover should snap into place after locking tabs of cover engage tabs on drum next to eye hole. Trim line so approximately 3 inches (75 mm) extend from drum.

If trimmer head retaining nut (3) must be unscrewed, prevent shaft rotation by inserting a pin through hole provided in bearing head to lock shaft.

Models BC-210 And BC-212

Models BC-210 and BC-212 are equipped with a dual-strand, semi-automatic trimmer head shown in Fig. SD42. To manually advance line with engine stopped, push in button at bottom of head and pull on each line. Procedure may have to be repeated to

Illustrations courtesy Dolmar USA, Inc.

obtain desired line length. To extend line with engine running, operate trimmer at full operating rpm and tap button on ground. Line will automatically advance a given amount.

To install new line, hold drum (2) firmly and turn spool (7) in direction shown in Fig. SD43 to remove slack. Twist with a hard snap until plastic peg is behind ridge and separate spool from drum. Remove old line from spool. Spool will hold approximately 20 feet (6 m) of 0.095 inch (2.4 mm) diameter line. Insert one end of new line through eye on spool (E—Fig. SD44) and pull line through until line is the same length on both sides of hole. Wind both ends of line at the same time in direction indicated by arrow on spool (Fig. SD44). Wind tightly and evenly from side-to-side and do not twist line. Position each line in notches (N—Fig. SD45) in spool and insert ends of line through line guide openings (O) in drum. Align pegs (P) on drum with slots in spool and push spool into drum. Hold drum firmly, twist spool quickly in direction shown in Fig. SD46 so peg enters hole with a click and locks spool in position. Cut off lines to approximately 4 inches (10 cm).

If trimmer head inner drive cam (6—Fig. SD42) must be unscrewed, prevent shaft rotation by inserting a pin through hole located in bearing head. Cam has left-hand threads.

BLADE

Models BC-210 and BC-212 may be equipped with an eight-edge cutting blade. Note that blade retaining nut has left-hand threads. When sharpening cutting edges, refer to Fig. SD47. Sharpened section must be kept 0.08 inch (2 mm) from the blade root. Root chamfer should have a 0.08 mm (2 mm) radius. Sharpen all teeth equally to maintain blade balance.

DRIVE SHAFT

Model LT-210

Model LT-210 is equipped with a flexible drive shaft. The drive shaft should be removed, cleaned and lubricated after every 20 hours of operation. Disconnect throttle cable and separate drive shaft housing (tube) from engine for access to shaft. Apply a high-quality lithium-base grease to drive shaft.

Models BC-210 And BC-212

Models BC-210 And BC-212 are equipped with a solid drive shaft supported in bushings. No maintenance is required. Drive shaft and tube are available separately.

BEARING HEAD

Model LT-210

The bearing head (2—Fig. SD48) may be separated from the drive tube (4) after loosening clamp bolt (6). Bearing head is available only as a unit assembly.

GEAR HEAD

Models BC-210 And BC-212

The amount of grease in the gear head should be checked after every 30 hours of operation. Remove screw (S—Fig. SD49) and fill unit with multipurpose grease as needed.

The gear head is available only as a unit assembly.

THROTTLE TRIGGER AND CABLE

The inner throttle cable (C—Fig. SD50) should be lubricated with engine oil after every 20 hours of operation.

Adjusting nuts (N) are located at carburetor end of throttle cable. Turn nuts as needed so carburetor throttle plate opens fully when throttle trigger is at full-speed position, and so there is 0.08-0.10 inch (2-3 mm) free play at throttle trigger when released.

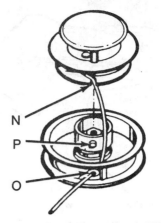

Fig. SD45—Position each line in notch (N) in spool and through opening (O) in drum. Align peg (P) with slot in spool and push spool into drum.

Fig. SD46—Hold drum firmly and twist quickly in direction indicated to lock spool in position.

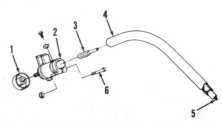

Fig. SD47—Sharpen blade edges to dimensions shown. Refer to text.

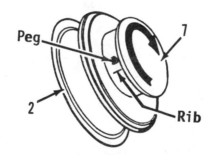

Fig. SD43—To remove spool (7), hold drum (2) firmly and turn spool in direction shown to take up slack, then twist with a sudden snap until plastic peg is behind rib.

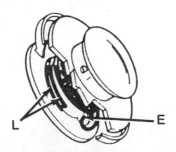

Fig. SD44—End of line on Models BC-210 and BC-212 must be inserted through eye on spool. Wind both strands of line at the same time in direction indicated on spool.

Fig. SD48—Trimmer bearing head (2), used on Model LT-210, is serviced as an assembly.

1. Mounting disc
2. Bearing head
3. Adapter
4. Drive shaft tube
5. Drive shaft
6. Clamp bolt

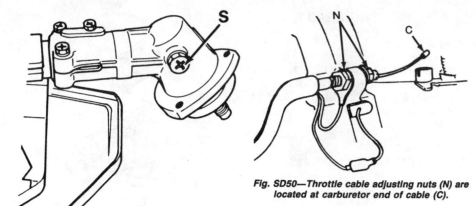

Fig. SD50—Throttle cable adjusting nuts (N) are located at carburetor end of cable (C).

Fig. SD49—Fill gear head on Models BC-210 and BC-212 with grease through hole for screw (S).

Illustrations courtesy Dolmar USA, Inc.

SEARS
GASOLINE POWERED
STRING TRIMMERS

Model	Engine Manufacturer	Engine Model	Displacement
28151	Kioritz	....	21.2 cc
281510	Kioritz	....	21.2 cc
281511	Kioritz	....	21.2 cc
281512	Kioritz	....	21.2 cc
28161	Kioritz	....	30.1 cc
281610	Kioritz	....	30.1 cc
281611	Kioritz	....	30.1 cc
28171	Kioritz	....	13.8 cc
281711	Kioritz	....	13.8 cc
79545	Fuji	....	37.7 cc
79555	Poulan	....	26.2 cc
79556	Fuji	....	28.0 cc
79558	Poulan	....	26.2 cc
79559	Fuji	....	28.0 cc
79623	Fuji	....	37.7 cc
79812	Poulan	....	26.2 cc
79813	Poulan	....	26.2 cc
79814	Fuji	....	28.0 cc
79821	Fuji	....	28.0 cc
79822	Fuji	....	28.0 cc

ENGINE INFORMATION

All Models

Sears and Sears "Brushwacker" line trimmers and brush cutters are equipped with Kioritz, Fuji or Poulan two-stroke air-cooled gasoline engines. Identify engine manufacturer by trimmer model number or engine displacement and refer to appropriate POULAN, KIORITZ or FUJI ENGINE SERVICE section in this manual.

FUEL MIXTURE

All Models

Manufacturer recommends mixing regular grade gasoline (unleaded is an acceptable substitute) with a good quality two-stroke air-cooled engine oil at a 25:1 ratio. Do not use fuel containing alcohol.

STRING TRIMMER

All Models

Single Strand Semi-Automatic Head. All models may be equipped with a single strand semi-automatic line trimmer head shown in Figs. SR10 and SR11. Fig. SR10 shows an exploded view of early style trimmer head which may be identified by the rough portion of upper housing (2). Fig. SR11 shows an exploded view of late style trimmer head which may be identified by the smooth portion of upper housing (2). Service procedure for both heads is similar.

To extend line with trimmer engine stopped, push in on button (7) while pulling on line end. Procedure may have to be repeated to obtain desired line length. To extend line with trimmer engine running, operate trimmer engine at full rpm and tap button (7) on the ground. Each time button (7) is tapped on the ground a measured amount of new line will be advanced.

To renew line, remove cover (8), button (7) and spool (6). Clean all parts thoroughly and remove any remaining old line from spool. Wind approximately 30 feet (9 m) of 0.080 inch (2 mm) monofilament line on spool in

Fig. SR10—Exploded view of old style single strand semi-automatic trimmer head used on some early models.

1. Drive shaft adapter
2. Housing
3. Spring
4. Spring adapter
5. Drive cam
6. Spool
7. Button
8. Cover

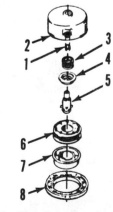

Fig. SR11—Exploded view of late style single strand semi-automatic trimmer head used on some models.

1. Line guide
2. Housing
3. Spring
4. Spring adapter
5. Drive cam
6. Spool
7. Button
8. Cover

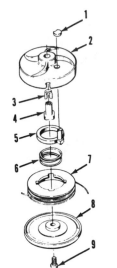

Fig. SR12—Exploded view of dual strand manual trimmer head used on some models.

1. Lock ring cap
2. Housing
3. Line guide
4. Drive shaft adapter
5. Lock ring
6. Spring
7. Spool
8. Cover
9. Screw

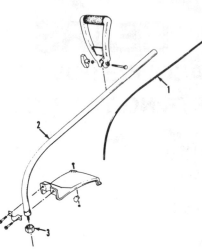

Fig. SR13—Exploded view of typical flexible drive shaft (1), drive shaft housing tube (2) and dust cover (3) used on some models. Note this style drive shaft and housing are also used with heavy duty bearing head models.

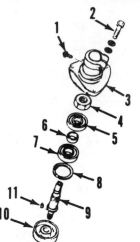

Fig. SR14—Exploded view of bearing head used on Models 281512, 28171 and 281711.

1. Locating screw
2. Clamp bolt
3. Bearing housing
4. Nut
5. Bearing
6. Spacer
7. Bearing
8. Snap ring
9. Arbor shaft
10. Cup washer
11. Pin

direction indicated by arrow on spool. Insert line end through line guide opening in housing (2) and install spool, button and cover.

Dual Strand Manual Head. Some models may be equipped with a dual strand manual trimmer head shown in Fig. SR12. To extend line, stop trimmer engine and wait until all trimmer head rotation has stopped. Push in on plate (8) while pulling each line out of housing (2).

To renew trimmer line, remove screw (9), plate (8), spring (6) and spool (7). Remove any remaining line from each side of spool. Clean spool, housing and plate. Insert ends of two new 0.095 inch (2.4 mm) lines in holes located within spool and wind lines in direction indicated by arrow on spool. Diameter of line wound on spool should not exceed diameter of spool sides. Make certain line savers (3) are in position and install spool in housing with the "THIS SIDE IN" instructions on spool toward inside of trimmer head. Install spring (6), cover (8) and screw (9).

BLADE

All Models So Equipped

Some models may be equipped with a four cutting edge grass and weed blade or a saw blade. When installing blade, make certain all adapter plates are centered and seated squarely against blade and tighten nut (left-hand thread) securely.

DRIVE SHAFT

Flexible Drive Shaft Models

Most models equipped with a flexible drive shaft (1—Fig. SR13) have a curved drive shaft housing tube (2). Drive shaft has squared ends which engage adapters at each end. Drive shaft should be removed for maintenance at 20 hour intervals of use. To remove, separate drive shaft housing from engine. Mark locations of drive shaft ends and pull drive shaft out of housing. Clean drive shaft and lubricate with lithium base grease. Reinstall drive shaft in housing making certain ends are not reversed.

Solid Drive Shaft

Models equipped with a solid steel drive shaft have a straight drive shaft housing tube. Drive shaft requires no regular maintenance; however, if drive shaft has been removed, lubricate drive shaft with lithium base grease before reinstallation.

BEARING HEAD

Models 79812 And 79813

Models 79812 and 79813 are equipped with a bearing head which is an integral part of drive shaft housing (Fig. SR13). Bearing head requires no regular maintenance and service parts are not available.

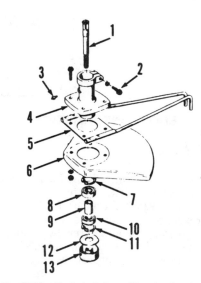

Fig. SR15—Exploded view of bearing head used on Models 79814 and 79821.

1. Drive shaft adapter
2. Clamp bolt
3. Locating screw
4. Housing
5. Bracket (as equipped)
6. Shield
7. Snap ring
8. Bearing
9. Spacer
10. Bearing
11. Snap ring
12. Washer
13. Drive disc

Models 281512, 28171 And 281711

Models 281512, 28171 and 281711 are equipped with the bearing head shown in Fig. SR14. Bearing head is equipped with sealed bearings and requires no regular maintenance.

To disassemble bearing head, remove trimmer head assembly and cup washer (10). Remove clamp bolt (2) and locating screw (1). Separate bearing head from drive shaft housing tube. Remove snap ring (8) and use a suitable puller to remove arbor shaft (9) and bearing assembly. Remove nut (4), bearing (5), spacer (6) and bearing (7) as required.

Models 79814 And 79821

Models 79814 and 79821 are equipped with the bearing head shown in Fig. SR15. Bearing head is equipped with sealed bearings and requires no regular maintenance.

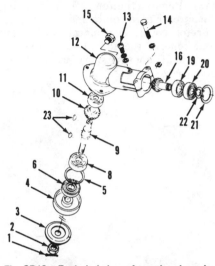

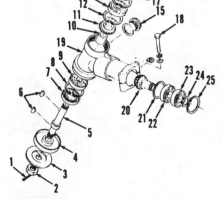

Fig. SR16—Exploded view of gear head used on Models 28151, 281510 and 281511.

1. Cotter pin	12. Housing
2. Nut	13. Screw
3. Adapter plate	14. Clamp bolt
4. Adapter plate	15. Level check plug
5. Snap ring	16. Gear
6. Seal	19. Bearing
8. Bearing	20. Bearing
9. Arbor shaft	21. Snap ring
10. Gear	22. Snap ring
11. Bearing	23. Keys

Fig. SR17—Exploded view of gear head used on Models 28161, 281610 and 281611.

1. Cotter pin	
2. Nut	14. Snap ring
3. Adapter plate	15. Level check plug
4. Adapter plate	16. Plug
5. Arbor shaft	17. Nut
6. Keys	18. Clamp bolt
7. Seal	19. Housing
8. Snap ring	20. Gear
9. Bearing	21. Spacer
10. Spacer	22. Bearing
11. Gear	23. Bearing
12. Snap ring	24. Snap ring
13. Bearing	25. Snap ring

To disassemble bearing head, remove trimmer head or blade assembly. Remove clamp bolt (2) and locating screw (3). Separate bearing head assembly from drive shaft housing. Remove shield (6) and bracket (5) (as equipped). Remove cup washer (13) and washer (12). Carefully press drive shaft adapter (1) out of bearings. Remove snap

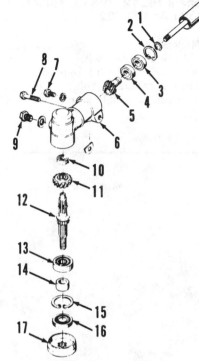

Fig. SR18—Exploded view of gear head used on Model 79822.

1. Snap ring	
2. Snap ring	10. Bearing
3. Bearing	11. Gear
4. Bearing	12. Arbor shaft
5. Input shaft	13. Bearing
6. Housing	14. Spacer
7. Clamp bolt	15. Snap ring
8. Bolt	16. Seal
9. Check plug	17. Cup washer

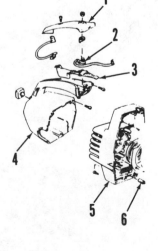

rings (7 and 11). Press bearings (8 and 10) and spacer (9) out of housing.

GEAR HEAD

Models 28151, 281510 And 281511

Models 28151, 281510 and 281511 are equipped with the gear head shown in Fig. SR16. Remove check plug (15) and check lubricant level at 50 hour intervals of use. Gear head housing should be kept 2/3 full of lithium base grease.

To disassemble gear head, remove trimmer head or blade assembly. Separate gear head from drive shaft housing tube. Remove snap ring (21) and use suitable puller to remove input shaft (16) and bearing assembly. Remove snap ring (22) and press bearings (19 and 20) from input shaft as required. Remove seal (6) and snap ring (5). Use suitable puller to remove arbor shaft (9) and bearing assembly. Press bearings from arbor shaft as required. Remove gear (10). If bearing (11) stays in housing (12), heat housing to 140° F (60° C) and tap housing on wooden block to remove bearing.

Models 28161, 281610 And 281611

Models 28161, 281610 and 281611 are equipped with the gear head shown in Fig. SR17. Remove check plug (15) and check lubricant level at 50 hour intervals of use. Gear head housing should be kept 2/3 full of lithium base grease.

To disassemble gear head, remove trimmer head or blade assembly. Separate gear head from drive shaft housing tube. Remove snap ring (25) and use suitable puller to remove input shaft and bearing assembly (20). Remove plug (16). Remove seal (7) and snap ring (8). Remove snap ring (14). Press arbor (5) and bearing assembly from housing (19).

Model 79822

Model 79822 is equipped with the gear head shown in Fig. SR18. Check plug (9) should be removed and gear

Fig. SR19—Exploded view of engine cover used on some models.

1. Throttle housing cover
2. Ignition switch
3. Throttle trigger
4. Handle
5. Fan housing
6. Spacer
7. Screw
8. Clamp bolt
9. Cover

head lubricant checked at 10 hour intervals of use. Gear head housing should be kept 2/3 full of lithium base grease.

To disassemble gear head, remove trimmer head or blade assembly. Remove clamp bolt and head locating screw and separate gear head from drive shaft housing. Remove cup washer (17) and spacer (14). Remove snap ring (2) and use a suitable puller to remove input shaft (5) and bearing assembly. Remove snap ring (1) and press bearings (3 and 4) from input shaft as required. Remove seal (16) and snap ring (15). Use suitable puller to remove arbor shaft (12) and bearing assembly. Press bearing (13) and gear (11) from shaft as required. If bearing

(10) remains in housing (6), heat housing to 140° F (60° C) and tap housing on wooden block to remove bearing.

ENGINE COVER

Models 79812, 79813, 79814, 79821 And 79822

Models 79812, 79813, 79814, 79821 and 79822 are equipped with a full engine cover (Fig. SR19). To remove engine cover, remove clamp bolt (8) and separate engine assembly from drive shaft

housing. Remove the four 10-24 screws and separate housings (5) and (9) slightly. Disconnect ignition wire from module and separate fuel line so junction fitting stays with crankcase side of fuel line. Separate housings completely. Remove the three 8-24 inch screws from inner side of housing (5) and remove the air baffle. Remove the five 10-24 screws located under air baffle and separate housing (4) from housing (5). Remove fuel tank cap and remove fuel tank. Remove the four screws securing carburetor cover plate and remove carburetor cover. Disconnect spark plug and remove the four 10-24 screws at drive shaft housing side of cover (9) and remove cover (9).

SHINDAIWA

GASOLINE POWERED STRING TRIMMERS

Model	Engine Manufacturer	Engine Model	Displacement
F20	Shindaiwa	....	19.8 cc
T20	Shindaiwa	....	21.1 cc
T25	Shindaiwa	....	24.1 cc
C25	Shindaiwa	....	24.1 cc
C35	Shindaiwa	....	33.6 cc
BP35	Shindaiwa	....	33.6 cc
B40	Shindaiwa	....	39.4 cc

ENGINE INFORMATION

All Models

All models are equipped with a two-stroke air-cooled gasoline engine manufactured for Shindaiwa. Engine may be identified by trimmer model or by engine displacement. Refer to appropriate SHINDAIWA ENGINE SERVICE section of this manual.

FUEL MIXTURE

All Models

Shindaiwa recommends mixing regular grade gasoline (unleaded regular gasoline is an acceptable substitute) with an octane rating of at least 87 with a good quality two-stroke, air-cooled engine oil at a ratio of 25:1.

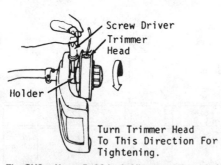

Fig. SH9—Use a 5/32 inch Allen wrench or similar tool inserted into hole in cup washer and drive shaft housing to prevent drive shaft from turning when removing trimmer head.

STRING TRIMMER

All Models

Refer to Figs. SH10 and SH11 for an exploded view of trimmer heads. To remove either head from drive shaft tube (housing), insert a tool into cup washer and bearing head (Fig. SH9) to lock head in position. Turn head counterclockwise to remove.

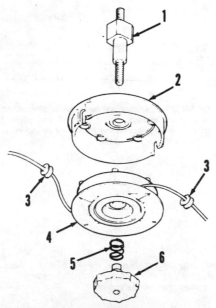

Fig. SH10—Exploded view of trimmer head used on some models. Use only 0.095 inch (2.4 mm) diameter trimmer line.

1. Adapter
2. Drum
3. Line guides
4. Spool
5. Spring
6. Knob

To renew line on head shown in Fig. SH10, unscrew knob (6) and release. Remove spool housing (2), spring (5) and spool (4). Wind new 0.095 inch (2.4 mm) monofilament line on spool evenly. Insert line ends through line guides and reinstall spool, spring and housing. To adjust line length, loosen knob (6) and turn trimmer head base counterclockwise. Pull both lines to 4 inch (102 mm) lengths. Tighten knob.

To renew line on trimmer head shown in Fig. SH11, unscrew knob (6) and remove. Remove spool housing (5) and spool (2). Wind new monofilament line onto spool evenly. Models F20 and T20 use 0.080 inch (2 mm) line, Models T25 and C25 use 0.095 inch (2.4 mm) line and Model C35 uses 0.105 inch (2.7 mm) line. Insert line ends through line guides (3) in housing. Reinstall spool, housing and knob.

BLADE

All models except Model F20 may be equipped with a steel brush blade. To install or remove blade, insert tool (5-Fig. SH12) into hole in upper adapter (1) and gear head to prevent drive shaft turning. Remove bolt (4), lower adapter (3) and blade.

DRIVE SHAFT

Model F20

Model F20 is equipped with a flexible steel drive shaft. Drive shaft should be removed and lubricated at 20 hour intervals of use. Use a good quality lithium base grease.

All Other Models

Models T20, T25, C25, C35 and B40 are equipped with a solid high carbon steel drive shaft splined at each end. Model BP35 is equipped with both a flexible drive shaft portion and a solid high carbon steel drive shaft. Solid drive shaft is supported in bushings located in drive shaft housing. Any discoloration or wear on steel drive shaft indicates bushing wear in housing. On Model T20, refer to Fig. SH13 and install bushings at equal distances with dimension (D) as 9.84 inches (250 mm). On Models T25 and C25, bushings are installed as shown in Fig. SH14. On Model BP35, refer to Fig. SH13 and install bushings at equal distances with dimension (D) as 11.02 inches (280 mm). On Model B40, refer to Fig. SH13 and install bushings at equal distances with

dimension (D) as 9.17 inches (233 mm). On all models, lubricate inside of housing and all bushings with oil for easier installation. Lubricate drive shaft with lithium base grease and install in housing and bushings.

BEARING HEAD

Model F20

Model F20 is equipped with a flange type bearing head equipped with sealed type bearings. Bearing head requires no regular maintenance except external cleaning.

To disassemble bearing head, refer to Fig. SH15. Remove trimmer head. Remove clamp bolt (2) and locating screw (1). Separate bearing head from drive shaft housing. Remove snap ring (8) and use suitable puller to remove arbor and bearing assembly. Remove bearings from arbor shaft as required.

GEAR HEAD

Models T20, T25, C25, C35, BP35 And B40

Refer to Fig. SH17 for cut-away view of gear head used on all models. Gear head should be lubricated at 50 hour intervals. Remove trimmer head or blade assembly. Remove grease plug from side of gear head housing. Pump a

good quality lithium base grease into housing through plug opening until grease appears at bearing seal (Fig. SH18). Failure to remove trimmer head

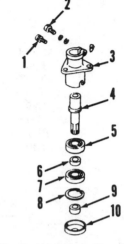

Fig. SH15—Exploded view of bearing head used on Model F20.

1. Locating screw	6. Spacer
2. Clamp bolt	7. Bearing
3. Housing	8. Snap ring
4. Arbor	9. Spacer
5. Bearing	10. Adapter plate

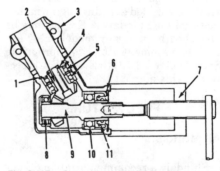

Fig. SH17—Cut-away view of gear head used on all models so equipped.

1. Snap ring	
2. Input shaft & gear	
3. Housing	7. Puller
4. Snap ring	8. Bearing
5. Bearings	9. Arbor shaft & gear
6. Snap ring	10. Bearing
	11. Seal

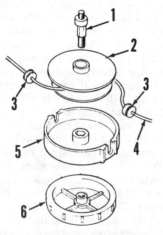

Fig. SH11—Exploded view of trimmer head used on some models.

1. Adapter	4. Line
2. Spool	5. Drum
3. Line guides	6. Knob

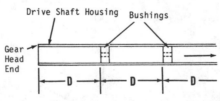

Fig. SH13—Bushings are installed in drive shaft housing as shown. Refer to text for correct dimension (D) according to model being serviced.

Fig. SH12—Use a 5/32 inch Allen wrench or similar tool to lock drive shaft when installing brush blade.

1. Upper adapter plate	
2. Blade	4. Screw
3. Lower adapter plate	5. Tool

Fig. SH14—Bushings for Models T25 and C25 are installed at locations shown.

or blade before lubricating gear head may result in bearing, seal or housing damage.

To disassemble gear head, remove clamp bolts and head locating screw (Fig. SH19). Separate gear head from drive shaft housing. Remove snap ring (6—Fig. SH17). Install suitable puller (7) as illustrated in Fig. SH17 and remove

arbor shaft (9) with bearing (10) and seal (11). To remove bearing (8), heat gear head housing to 212° F (100° C) and tap housing against a flat wooden surface. Remove seal (11) and press bearing (10) off shaft. Remove snap ring (1—Fig. SH17). Insert suitable puller bolt through input shaft and thread a nut on puller bolt against input gear as shown

in Fig. SH20. Remove input shaft and bearings as an assembly from housing. Remove snap ring (4—Fig. SH17) and press bearings (5) from input shaft.

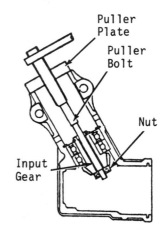

Fig. SH20—To remove input shaft, gear and bearing assembly, install puller as shown.

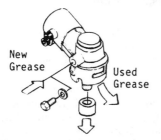

Fig. SH18—A good quality lithium base grease should be pumped into gear head through filler opening until grease appears at arbor shaft seal. Refer to text.

Fig. SH19—To separate gear head from drive shaft housing, remove clamp bolts and locking (head locating) bolt.

SMC
GASOLINE POWERED STRING TRIMMERS

Model	Engine Manufacturer	Engine Model	Displacement
GT-140	Kioritz	....	13.8 cc
GT-200	Kioritz	....	21.2 cc

ENGINE INFORMATION

All Models

All models are equipped with Kioritz two-stroke air-cooled engines. Identify engine model by trimmer model or engine displacement. Refer to KIORITZ ENGINE SERVICE section of this manual.

FUEL MIXTURE

All Models

Manufacturer recommends mixing regular grade gasoline (unleaded is an acceptable substitute) with a good quality two-stroke air-cooled engine oil at a 25:1 ratio. Do not use fuel containing alcohol.

STRING TRIMMER

Model GT-140

Model GT-140 is equipped with a single strand semi-automatic trimmer head shown in Fig. SC10. Line may be manually advanced with engine stopped by pushing in on housing (9) while pulling on line. Procedure may have to be repeated to obtain desired line length. To advance line with engine running, operate engine at full rpm and tap housing (9) on the ground. Each time housing is tapped on the ground, a measured amount of trimmer line will be advanced.

To renew trimmer line, remove cotter key (10) and twist housing (9) counterclockwise to remove housing. Remove foam pad (6) and any remaining line on spool (3). Clean spool and inside of housing. Cut off approximately 25 feet (7.6 m) of 0.080 inch (2 mm) monofilament line and tape one end of line to spool (Fig. SC12). Wind line on spool in direction indicated by arrow on spool (Fig. SC13). Install foam pad with line end protruding from between foam pad

and spool as shown in Fig. SC13. Insert line end through line guide and install housing and spring assembly on spool. Push in on housing and twist housing to lock into position. Install cotter key through hole in housing and cover.

Model GT-200

Model GT-200 is equipped with a single strand semi-automatic trimmer head shown in Fig. SC11. Line may be manually advanced with engine stopped by pushing in on housing (12) while pulling on line. Procedure may have to be repeated until desired line length is obtained. To advance line with engine running, operate trimmer engine at full rpm and tap housing (12) on the ground. Each time housing is tapped on the ground, a measured amount of trimmer line is advanced.

To renew trimmer line, remove cotter pin (13). Twist housing (12) counterclockwise and remove housing. Remove

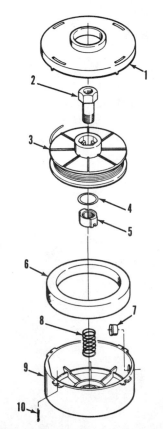

Fig. SC10—Exploded view of single strand semi-automatic trimmer head used on Model GT-140.

1. Cover	6. Foam pad
2. Drive adapter	7. Line guide
3. Spool	8. Spring
4. "O" ring	9. Housing
5. Drive adapter nut	10. Cotter pin

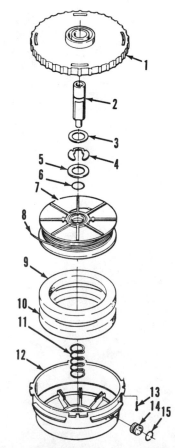

Fig. SC11—Exploded view of single strand semi-automatic trimmer head used on Model GT-200.

1. Cover	
2. Drive adapter	9. Foam pad
3. Washer	10. Foam pad
4. Retainer	11. Spring
5. Washer	12. Housing
6. Retainer ring	13. Cotter pin
7. Spool	14. Line guide
8. Line	15. Retainer

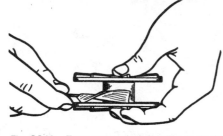

Fig. SC12—Tape one end of new line to center of spool as shown.

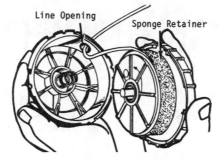

Fig. SC-13—Install foam pad with line protruding between pad and spool as shown. Wind line in direction indicated by arrow on spool.

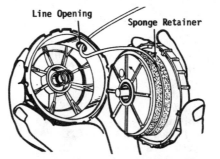

Fig. SC-14—Install foam pads with line protruding from between pads. Wind line in direction indicated by arrow on spool.

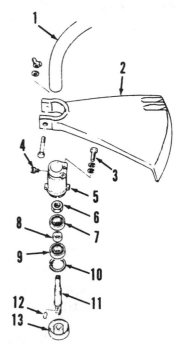

Fig. SC15—Exploded view of bearing head used on all models. Bearings (7 and 9) are sealed bearings and require no regular maintenance.

1. Drive shaft housing	
2. Shield	8. Spacer
3. Bolt	9. Bearing
4. Screw	10. Snap ring
5. Housing	11. Arbor (output) shaft
6. Nut	12. Pin
7. Bearing	13. Cup washer

foam pads (9 and 10) and any remaining line from spool (7). Clean spool and inner area of housing. Cut off approximately 25 feet (7.6 mm) of 0.080 inch (2 mm) monofilament line and tape one end of line to spool (Fig. SC12). Wind line on spool in direction indicated by arrow on spool (Fig. SC14). Install foam pads (9 and 10—Fig. SC11) so line is protruding from center of foam pads (Fig. SC14). Insert end of line through line guide and install spool, housing and spring. Push in on housing and twist housing to lock in position and install cotter pin (13—Fig. SC11).

DRIVE SHAFT

All Models

All models are equipped with a flexible drive shaft enclosed in the drive shaft housing tube. Drive shaft has squared ends which engage adapters at each end. Drive shaft should be removed for maintenance at 50-hour intervals of use. Remove screw (4—Fig. SC15) and bolt (3) at bearing head housing and separate bearing head from drive shaft housing. Pull flexible drive shaft from housing. Lubricate drive shaft with lithium base grease

and reinstall in drive shaft housing with end which was previously at clutch end bearing head end. Reversing drive shaft ends extends drive shaft life. Make certain ends of drive shaft are properly located into upper and lower square drive adapters when installing.

BEARING HEAD

All Models

All models are equipped with the bearing head shown in Fig. SC15. Bear-

ing head is equipped with sealed bearings and requires no regular maintenance. To disassemble bearing head, remove screw (4) and bolt (3) and separate bearing head from drive shaft housing tube. Remove trimmer head assembly and cup washer (13). Remove snap ring (10) and use a suitable puller to remove arbor shaft (11) and bearing assembly. Remove nut (6) and press bearings (7 and 9) and spacer (8) from arbor shaft as required.

SNAPPER

GASOLINE POWERED STRING TRIMMERS

Model	Engine Manufacturer	Engine Model	Displacement
210SS	Mitsubishi	T110	21.2 cc
211SST	Mitsubishi	T110	21.2 cc
212CST	McCulloch	...	21.2 cc
213CST	McCulloch	...	21.2 cc
214DCST	McCulloch	...	21.2 cc
215SST	McCulloch	...	21.2 cc
240SS	Mitsubishi	T140	24.1 cc
240SST	Mitsubishi	T140	24.1 cc
311	PPP	99E	31.0 cc
410	Mitsubishi	T200-PD	40.6 cc
2111SST	Mitsubishi	TMX-21	21.2 cc
2401SST	Mitsubishi	TM-24	24.1 cc
4111SST	Mitsubishi	T200	40.6 cc
P212CST	McCulloch	...	21.2 cc

ENGINE INFORMATION

The models in this section are equipped with a McCulloch, Mitsubishi or Piston Powered Products (PPP) engine. Refer to appropriate engine service section for engine service information.

FUEL MIXTURE

Manufacturer recommends mixing leaded or unleaded gasoline with a high-quality two-stroke engine oil designed

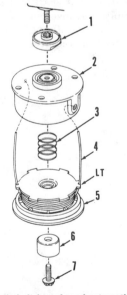

Fig. SP10—Exploded view of semi-automatic trimmer head used on Models 210SS, 211SST and 311, and as an option on some other models.

1. Washer
2. Hub
3. Spring
4. Line
5. Spool
6. Button
7. Screw
LT. Lock tab (line)

for air-cooled engines. Recommended fuel:oil ratio is 32:1 when using Snapper two-stroke oil. Use of 50:1 oils is not recommended. Manufacturer recommends addition of a fuel stabilizer, such as Sta-Bil, to fuel to prevent fuel degradation.

STRING TRIMMER

Models 210SS, 211SST And 311

Models 210SS, 211SST and 311 are equipped with a dual strand, semi-automatic trimmer head (Fig. SP10). To extend line with engine stopped, push up on bump button (6) and pull out each line. Repeat procedure if needed to reach desired length.

To extend line with engine running, operate trimmer at full rpm and tap button (6) on the ground. Each time button is tapped a measured amount of line is automatically advanced.

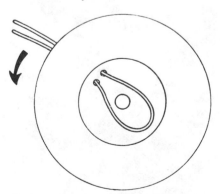

Fig. SP11—Insert line ends through holes in spool and pull line out in two equal lengths. Wind line in direction indicated by arrow on spool.

To install new trimmer line, hold hub (2) and push spool (5) upward against hub. Twist spool to the left until tabs lock the spool to the hub. Tabs can be viewed through the four holes in the hub. Remove screw (7) and bump button (6). Twist spool to the right to unlock tabs and pull spool downward to remove. Loop 40 feet (12 m) of 0.095-in. (2.4 mm) diameter monofilament line into two equal lengths. Insert line ends through the two holes in spool as shown in Fig. SP11. Wind both lines in direction indicated by arrow on spool. Snap lines into lock tabs (LT—Fig. SP10) of spool and insert line ends through the line guide holes in hub. Install spool and bump button. Install screw. Pull lines to free them from lock tabs.

Models 240SS, 240SST And 410

Models 240SS, 240SST and 410 are equipped with a heavy-duty manual, dual strand trimmer head (Fig. SP12). To extend line, stop trimmer engine. Loosen knob (9) and pull each line until desired length is obtained. Tighten knob.

To install new line, cut 15 feet (4.6 m) of 0.095-in. (2.4 mm) diameter monofilament line. Remove lock knob (9) and remove lower housing (8) and spool (5). Remove any remaining old line. Clean all parts of trimmer head with a wet, soapy cloth. Pull line guides (3) down (do not remove) and clean outside surfaces. Apply a few drops of oil into cavities after cleaning. Loop new line into two equal lengths and insert line ends through holes at center of spool. Pull line ends out until stopped by spool. Wind both lines in direction indicated by arrow on spool. Insert line ends in line guides and reinstall spool, lower housing and lock knob.

Models 212CST, 213CST, 214DCST, 215SST, 2111SST And P212CST

Models 212CST, 213CST, 214DCST, 215SST, 2111SST and P212CST are equipped with the dual strand, semi-automatic trimmer head shown in Fig. SP13. To extend line with engine stopped, push up on bump button (9) and pull out each line. Repeat procedure if needed to reach desired length.

To extend line with engine running, operate trimmer at full rpm and tap button (9) on the ground. Each time button is tapped a measured amount of line is automatically advanced.

To install new line, unscrew cover (7) by rotating clockwise (L.H. threads). Remove spool and remaining old line. Clean parts. Loop 20 feet (6 m) of 0.080-in. (2 mm) diameter monofilament line into two equal lengths. Insert loop in slot (S—Fig. SP14) on spool and wind both lines in clockwise direction as viewed from ground side of spool. Leave 6 inches (152 mm) extending at each end. While positioning string ends in line guides, reassemble trimmer head.

Models 2401SST And 4111SST

Models 2401SST and 4111SST are equipped with a multiple strand, fixed trimmer head. Trimmer string is routed between two flanges. To install new string, insert new string in passages between two flanges.

BLADE

Some models may be equipped with the blades shown in Fig. SP15. Install

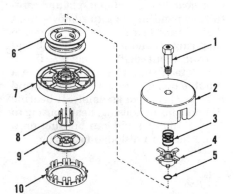

Fig. SP13—Exploded view of dual strand, semi-automatic trimmer head used on Models 212CST, 213CST, 214DCST, 215SST, 2111SST and P212CST.

1. Adapter	6. Spool
2. Housing	7. Cover
3. Spring	8. Actuator
4. Indexer	9. Button
5. Retainer	10. Retainer

blade as shown in Fig. SP16.

To sharpen saw blade, refer to Fig. SP17. Check blade for nicks and cracks and discard blade if damaged. Sharpen blade cutting edges as shown in Fig. SP17. Maintain radius at base of tooth to prevent blade cracking. Note also that idle speed of engine must be lowered when blade is installed.

DRIVE SHAFT

Models 212CST, 213CST, 214DCST, 311 And P212CST

Models 212CST, 213CST, 214DCST, 311 and P212CST are equipped with a flexible drive shaft. The drive shaft should be removed, cleaned and lubricated with lithium-base grease after every 20 hours of operation. Mark shaft ends before removal, then reverse ends during installation to extend life of drive shaft. Be sure drive shaft is properly seated at engine end.

All Other Models

These models are equipped with a straight, steel drive shaft. Bushings on Model 215SST are not renewable. Bushings on all other models are renewable. Periodic maintenance is not required. If

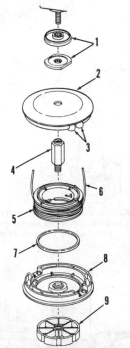

Fig. SP12—Exploded view of manual advance, dual strand trimmer head used on Models 240SS, 240SST and 410, and as an option on some other models.

1. Washers	
2. Upper housing	6. Line
3. Line guides	7. "O" ring
4. Adapter	8. Lower housing
5. Spool	9. Lock knob

Fig. SP14—When installing new line, insert looped end of line into slot (S) in spool.

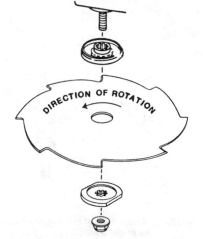

Fig. SP16—Install blade with cutting edges located as shown.

Fig. SP15—Some models may be equipped with a four-edge cutting blade, eight-edge cutting blade or saw blade.

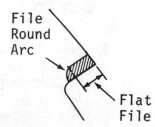

Fig. SP17—To prevent blade cracking, the blade teeth must be sharpened as shown so the arc in the cutting edge is maintained.

drive shaft is removed, lubricate shaft with lithium-base grease before installation.

To renew bushings, except on Model 215SST, mark location of old bushings so new bushings can be installed in original position. Use a suitable puller or driver to dislodge bushings.

BEARING HEAD

Models 212CST, 213CST, 214DCST, 311 And P212CST

The bearing head on Models 212CST, 213CST, 214DCST, 311 and P212CST has sealed bearings so periodic maintenance is not required. Bearing and arbor assembly (2—Fig. SP18) on Model 214DCST is available separately from housing. The bearing head on all other models so equipped is available only as a unit assembly.

GEAR HEAD

All Models So Equipped

The gear head, on models so equipped, should be lubricated after every 50 hours of operation. Remove trimmer head or blade assembly and inject lithium-base grease through grease fitting in side of housing (see Fig. SP19) until grease appears at lower seal. Failure to remove trimmer head or blade assembly before injecting grease may damage bearing, seal or housing.

To disassemble gear, remove trimmer head or blade, adapters and spacer. Separate gear head from drive shaft housing. Remove snap ring (1—Fig. SP20). Insert a screwdriver or suitable wedge into gear head housing clamp split and carefully expand housing to remove input shaft (7) and bearing assembly. Remove snap ring (2) and press bearings (3 and 4) from input shaft. Remove seal (16) and detach snap ring (15), then use a suitable puller to remove arbor (13) and bearing (14) as an assembly. If bearing (11) remains in housing, heat housing to 140° F (60° C) and tap housing on a wood block to dislodge bearing.

THROTTLE TRIGGER AND CABLE

The inner throttle cable should be lubricated with engine oil after every 20 hours of operation.

The throttle cable should be adjusted so there is approximately 0.04 inch (1 mm) throttle trigger free play. To adjust free play, refer to Figs. SP21, SP22 or SP23, depending on type of carburetor, and reposition adjuster or cable as needed.

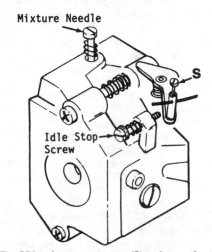

Fig. SP21—Loosen set screw (S) and move throttle cable to obtain throttle trigger free play of approximately 0.4 inch (1 mm).

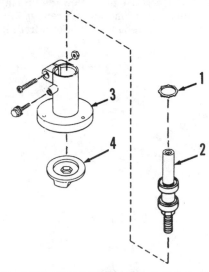

Fig. SP18—Exploded view of bearing head used on Model 214DCST.

1. Retainer
2. Arbor & bearing assy.
3. Housing
4. Washer

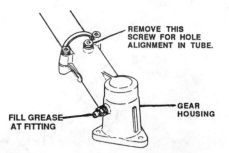

Fig. SP19—To lubricate gear head, inject grease through grease fitting until grease appears at lower seal.

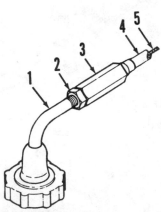

Fig. SP20—Exploded view of gear head used on models with straight drive shaft tube.

1. Snap ring
2. Snap ring
3. Bearing
4. Bearing
5. Snap ring
6. Washer
7. Input shaft
8. Spacer
9. Housing
10. Grease fitting
11. Bearing
12. Gear
13. Arbor
14. Bearing
15. Snap ring
16. Seal
17. Spacer

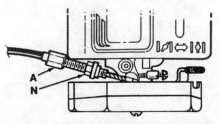

Fig. SP22—Loosen jam nut (2) and rotate adjuster nut (3) to obtain throttle trigger free play of approximately 0.4 inch (1 mm).

1. Cable housing
2. Jam nut
3. Adjuster nut
4. Housing
5. Inner cable

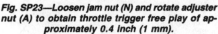

Fig. SP23—Loosen jam nut (N) and rotate adjuster nut (A) to obtain throttle trigger free play of approximately 0.4 inch (1 mm).

STIHL
GASOLINE POWERED STRING TRIMMERS

Model	Engine Manufacturer	Engine Model	Displacement
FR106, FS106	Stihl	...	34.4 cc
FS36, FS40, FS44	Stihl	...	30.2 cc
FS48, FS52	Stihl	...	17.1 cc
FS50, FS51	Stihl	...	16.0 cc
FS56, FS60, FS62, FS62AVE, FS62AVRE, FS65, FS66, FS66AVE, FS66AVRE	Stihl	...	19.6 cc
FS80, FS81, FS81AVE, FS81AVRE	Stihl	...	22.5 cc
FS86AVE, FS86AVRE	Stihl	...	25.4 cc
FS90, FS96, FS150, FS151	Stihl	O15	32.0 cc
FS160	Stihl	...	29.8 cc
FS180, FS220	Stihl	...	35.2 cc
FS200	Stihl	O20	32.0 cc
FS202	Stihl	O20	35.0 cc
FS280	Stihl	...	39.0 cc
FS353	Stihl	O8S	56.0 cc
FS360	Stihl	...	51.7 cc
FS410	Stihl	O41	61.0 cc
FS420	Stihl	...	56.5 cc

ENGINE INFORMATION

The trimmer or brush cutter may be equipped with a two-stroke, air-cooled engine manufactured by Stihl. Refer to appropriate engine section in this manual for engine service information.

FUEL MIXTURE

Manufacturer recommends mixing regular or unleaded gasoline with a high-quality, two-stroke engine oil designed for air-cooled engines. Recommended fuel:oil ratio is 50:1 when using Stihl oil. Fuel:oil ratio should be 25:1 when using any other two-stroke oil.

STRING TRIMMER

Several types of string trimmer heads have been used. Some trimmers may be equipped with more than one type of trimmer head. Refer to Figs. SL10 through SL16 for an exploded view of trimmer head.

To extend trimmer line on manual trimmer heads (Figs. SL11 and SL12), stop engine and loosen lock knob (6) until lines may be pulled from spool. Pull lines out to desired length, then tighten knob.

To extend trimmer line on semi-automatic advance trimmer heads (Figs. SL10, SL13 and SL14), stop engine and push in on spool button and pull lines out to desired length. To advance trimmer line with engine running, operate engine at full rpm with trimmer head

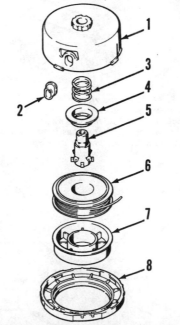

Fig. SL10—Exploded view of single-strand, semi-automatic advance trimmer head used on some models. Refill with 33 feet (10 m) of 0.080-in. (2.0 mm) diameter monofilament line.

1. Drum	5. Cam
2. Eyelet	6. Spool
3. Spring	7. Button
4. Sleeve	8. Cover

horizontal above the ground and tap trimmer head lightly against the ground. Each time head is tapped, a measured amount of line is advanced.

The trimmer heads shown in Figs. SL15 and SL16 automatically dispense line while engine is running without tapping trimmer head on ground.

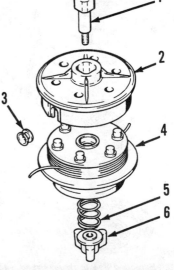

Fig. SL11—Exploded view of dual-strand, manual advance trimmer head used on some models. Refill with 17 feet (5.2 m) of 0.095-in. (2.4 mm) diameter line.

1. Adapter	4. Spool
2. Drum	5. Spring
3. Eyelet	6. Nut (L.H.)

To remove trimmer head, observe arrow on head when unscrewing head. Trimmer head, or head mounting nut if so equipped, has left-hand threads (turn clockwise to remove). Insert stop pin in bore at top of gear head to lock drive shaft when removing and installing trimmer head.

To install new line, remove trimmer head screw cap or push in on locking tabs and separate spool from trimmer drum. Remove any remaining old line from spool and clean all components. On most models, install new line by inserting end of line into hole in spool hub as far as possible. Note arrow on spool when winding new string on spool. On trimmer head shown in Fig. SL14, insert line in slots (T—Fig. SL14A) before installing spool.

When installing new line in trimmer head shown in Fig. SL15, route line around wire guide (2—Fig. SL15A). Extended line length should be 10-14 cm (4-5½ in.).

BLADE

A "Polycut" blade is available for some models. To install, refer to Fig. SL17. Note that "Polycut" head has left-hand threads and is self-tightening as trimmer is used. Base of trimmer head is marked to indicate minimum blade length. If blade length is less than indicated, renew blades.

A "Rotocut 200" (Fig. SL18) is available for some models. To install, place blade (3) on thrust plate (1). Install thrust washer (4) over shaft (2) and install cover (5). Install nut (6) (left-hand threads). A round pin may be inserted through hole in side of gear head to prevent head rotation during tightening.

Models with a gear head may be equipped with a variety of weed and grass blades (Fig. SL19). Heavy-duty

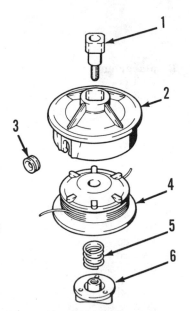

Fig. SL12—Exploded view of dual-strand, manual advance trimmer head used on some models. Refill with 33 feet (10 m) of 0.080-in. (2.0 mm) diameter line.

1. Adapter
2. Drum
3. Eyelet
4. Spool
5. Spring
6. Nut

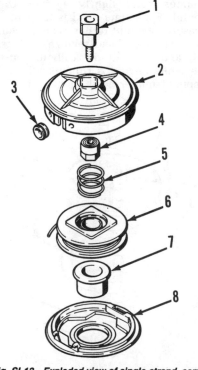

Fig. SL13—Exploded view of single-strand, semi-automatic advance trimmer head used on some models. Refill with 33 feet (10 m) of 0.080-in. (2.0 mm) diameter line.

1. Adapter
2. Drum
3. Eyelet
4. Nut
5. Spring
6. Spool
7. Button
8. Cover

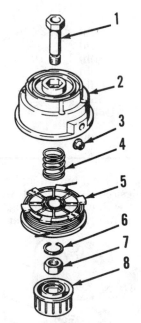

Fig. SL14—Exploded view of dual-strand, semi-automatic advance trimmer head used on some models. Refill with 25 feet (7.6 m) of 0.080-in. (2.0 mm) diameter line. Nut (7) has left-hand threads on some models. Adapter (1) is not used on some models.

1. Adapter
2. Drum
3. Eyelet
4. Spring
5. Spool
6. Snap ring
7. Nut
8. Button

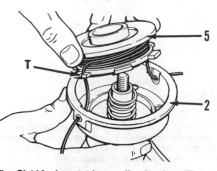

Fig. SL14A—Insert trimmer line in slots (T) on spool before installing spool (5) in drum (2) of trimmer head shown in Fig. SL14.

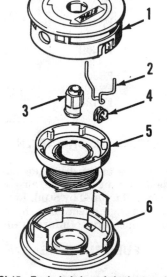

Fig. SL15—Exploded view of single-strand, automatic advance trimmer head used on some models. Refill with 25 feet (7.6 m) of 0.080-in. (2.0 mm) diameter line. Nut (3) has left-hand threads on some models.

1. Drum
2. Wire guide
3. Nut
4. Eyelet
5. Spool
6. Cover

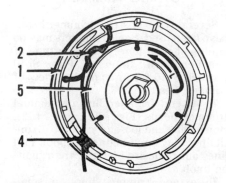

Fig. SL15A—Place trimmer line around wire guide (2) before passing line through eyelet (4) on trimmer head shown in Fig. SL15.

Illustrations courtesy Stihl Inc.

units may be equipped with a brush or saw blade (Fig. SL20). Blades are installed using procedure outlined for installation of "Rotocut 200" blade.

DRIVE SHAFT

Flexible Drive Shaft Models

The flexible drive shaft on models so equipped should be removed and cleaned after every 20 hours of operation. Lubricate shaft with lithium-based grease.

Solid Drive Shaft Models

Regular maintenance is not required for the solid drive shaft. If shaft is removed, lubricate shaft with lithium-based grease before installation.

The bushings in the drive shaft housing may be removed on some models. Check parts availability before attempting removal. Mark location of old bushings before removal. A recommended tool that may be used to pull out the bushings is a suitably sized tap that is threaded into the bushing. Early FS410 models were equipped with two bushings; later models are equipped with three bushings. Three bushings may be installed on early models by referring to Fig. SL21 for new bushing location. A 4.1 mm (0.016 in.) hole must be drilled in the housing at location shown for spring clip that retains bushing.

BEARING HEAD

All Models So Equipped

Model FS36 is equipped with flanged bushings (3—Fig. SL22) to support the

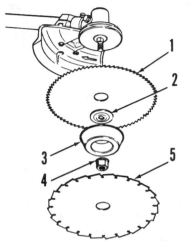

Fig. SL20—Exploded view of saw blades available for some models.

1. Saw blade
2. Washer
3. Cover
4. Nut (L.H.)
5. Chisel tooth saw blade

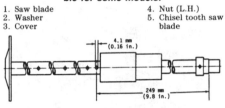

Fig. SL21—On Model FS410, install a third bushing in the drive shaft housing at the location shown. Refer to text.

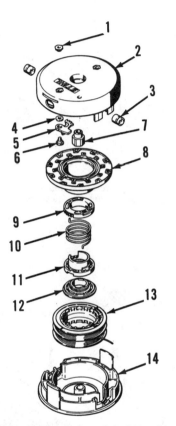

Fig. SL16—Exploded view of dual-strand, automatic advance trimmer head used on some models. Refill with 25 feet (7.6 m) of 0.095-in. (2.4 mm) diameter line.

1. Nut
2. Drum
3. Eyelet
4. Washer
5. Pawl
6. Screw
7. Nut
8. Index plate
9. Synchronizer
10. Spring
11. Adjuster
12. Ratchet
13. Spool
14. Cover

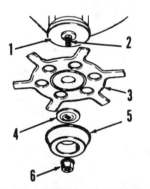

Fig. SL18—View of "Rotocut 200" blade available for some models.

1. Thrust plate
2. Shaft (L.H. threads)
3. Blade
4. Washer
5. Cover
6. Nut (L.H.)

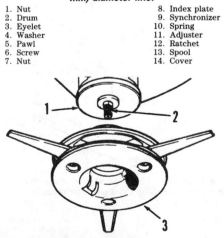

Fig. SL17—View of "Polycut" trimmer head available for some models.

1. Thrust plate
2. Shaft (L.H. threads)
3. Trimmer head

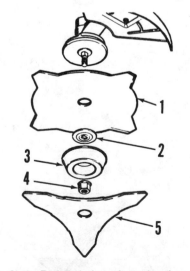

Fig. SL19—Exploded view of weed and grass blades available for some models.

1. Four-cutting-edge blade
2. Washer
3. Cover
4. Nut (L.H.)
5. Three-cutting-edge blade

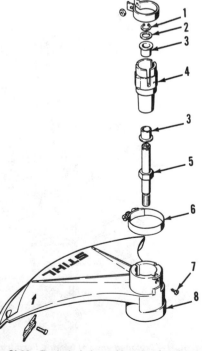

Fig. SL22—Exploded view of bearing head used on Model FS36.

1. Snap ring
2. Washer
3. Flanged bushing
4. Bearing housing
5. Arbor
6. Clamp
7. Locating screw
8. Deflector

arbor (5). Model FS40 is equipped with needle bearings (2—Fig. SL23) to support the arbor (5). All other models with a bearing head use ball bearings (5 and 7—Figs. SL24 or SL25) to support the arbor (4).

To disassemble, remove trimmer head and trimmer deflector from bearing head. Remove clamp screw and set screw from bearing housing and separate housing from drive tube. Remove

snap ring from arbor shaft and pull shaft out of housing. Drive bearings from housing.

When reassembling, press new bearings into housing until they bottom against shoulder of housing. Align holes (H—Fig. SL26) on bearing housing and drive shaft housing. Align rib (R—Fig. SL27) on bearing housing with notch (N) in deflector.

GEAR HEAD

All Models So Equipped

Trimmer or brush cutter may be equipped with a one- or two-piece gear head housing. Refer to appropriate following service section.

ONE-PIECE HOUSING. Lubricant level should be checked after every 20 hours of operation. Remove fill plug in side of housing and add lubricant so

housing is ²/₃ full. Recommended lubricant is lithium-based grease.

Refer to Figs. SL28 through SL31 for an exploded view of gear heads with a one-piece housing. To disassemble gear head, remove trimmer head or blade assembly. Remove clamp bolt (7) and

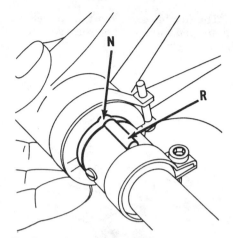

Fig. SL27—On Models FS36 and FS40, rib (R) on bearing housing must align with notch (N) in deflector shield.

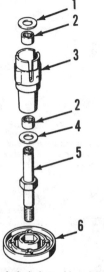

Fig. SL23—Exploded view of bearing head used on Model FS40.

1. Washer	4. Washer
2. Needle bearing	5. Arbor
3. Bearing housing	6. Thrust plate

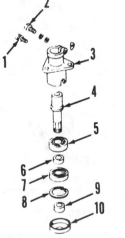

Fig. SL25—Exploded view of bearing head used on some models.

1. Locating screw	6. Spacer
2. Clamp bolt	7. Bearing
3. Housing	8. Snap ring
4. Arbor	9. Spacer
5. Bearing	10. Thrust plate

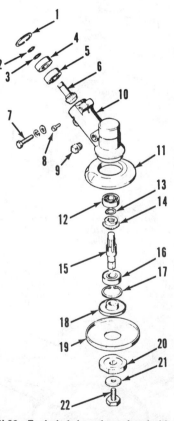

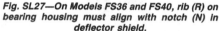

Fig. SL28—Exploded view of gear head with one-piece housing used on some models.

1. Snap ring	12. Bearing
2. Snap ring	13. Shim
3. Shim	14. Output gear
4. Bearing	15. Arbor
5. Bearing	16. Bearing
6. Input shaft	17. Snap ring
7. Clamp bolt	18. Adapter
8. Locating screw	19. Thrust plate
9. Check plug	20. Washer
10. Housing	21. Washer
11. Anti-wrap guard	22. Bolt

Fig. SL24—Exploded view of bearing head used on some models.

1. Locating screw	6. Washer
2. Clamp bolt	7. Bearing
3. Housing	8. Snap ring
4. Arbor	9. Deflector
5. Bearing	10. Thrust plate

Fig. SL26—When attaching drive shaft housing and bearing housing, align holes (H) then install locating screw.

Illustrations courtesy Stihl Inc.

locating screw (8) if used. Separate gear head from drive shaft housing tube. Remove snap ring (1) and use a suitable puller to remove input shaft (6) and bearings as an assembly from housing (10). Remove snap ring (2) and press input shaft out of bearings as required. Remove snap ring (17) and use a suitable puller to remove arbor shaft (15) and bearing assembly. Press bearings from arbor shaft as necessary. It may be necessary to heat housing to approximately 140° C (280° F) to ease removal and installation of bearings. Some units are equipped with shims that allow adjustment of gear mesh and backlash.

TWO-PIECE HOUSING. Lubricant level should be checked after every 20 hours of operation. Remove fill plug (1—Fig. SL32) to check lubricant. Gear head should contain 40 cc (1.35 oz.) of SAE 90 gear lubricant.

To disassemble gear head, remove trimmer head or blade assembly. Remove clamp bolt and separate gear head from drive shaft housing tube. Remove screws and separate lower gear head housing (21) from upper gear head housing (2). Press arbor (14) and gear assembly out of the thrust plate and ball bearing. Remove snap ring (16). Heat housing to 280° F (140° C) and press bearing (18) out of housing. Remove seal (23). Press gear (15) off arbor. Remove the two

locating screws (3). Heat housing to 280° F (140° C) and press input shaft (11) and bearing assembly out of housing. Remove snap rings and press bearings from input shaft as required. Remove needle bearing (13) only if bearing is to be renewed.

During gear head assembly, shims should be installed to provide a slight amount of gear backlash. Shafts should turn freely with no binding.

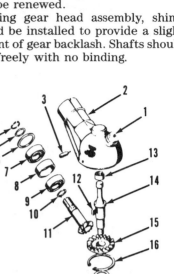

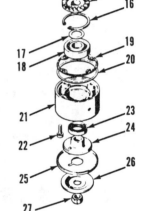

Fig. SL32—Exploded view of gear head with two-piece housing used on some models.

1. Fill plug	
2. Housing	
3. Locating screws	15. Gear
4. Snap ring	16. Snap ring
5. Shim	17. Shim
6. Shim	18. Bearing
7. Bearing	19. Gasket
8. Spacer	20. Shim
9. Bearing	21. Housing
10. Shim	22. Bolt
11. Input shaft	23. Seal
12. Key	24. Adapter
13. Needle bearing	25. Thrust plate
14. Arbor	26. Washer
	27. Nut (L.H.)

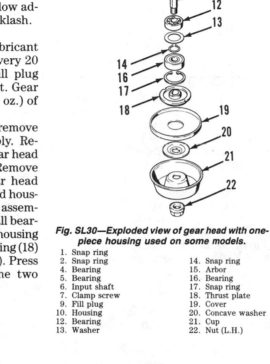

Fig. SL30—Exploded view of gear head with one-piece housing used on some models.

1. Snap ring	
2. Snap ring	14. Snap ring
4. Bearing	15. Arbor
5. Bearing	16. Bearing
6. Input shaft	17. Snap ring
7. Clamp screw	18. Thrust plate
9. Fill plug	19. Cover
10. Housing	20. Concave washer
12. Bearing	21. Cup
13. Washer	22. Nut (L.H.)

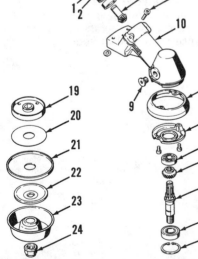

Fig. SL29—Exploded view of gear head with one-piece housing used on some models.

1. Snap ring	
2. Snap ring	15. Arbor
4. Bearing	16. Bearing
5. Bearing	17. Snap ring
6. Input shaft	18. Cover plate
7. Clamp screw	19. Thrust plate
9. Fill plug	20. Washer
10. Housing	21. Cover
11. Anti-wrap guard	22. Concave washer
12. Bearing	23. Cup
14. Gear	24. Nut (L.H.)

Fig. SL31—Exploded view of gear head with one-piece housing used on some models. Unscrew set screw (8) before removing bearing.

1. Snap ring	13. Shims
2. Washer	15. Arbor
4. Bearing	16. Bearing
6. Input shaft	17. Snap ring
7. Clamp screw	18. Cover
8. Locating screw	19. Washer
9. Fill plug	20. Concave washer
10. Housing	21. Cup
12. Bearing	22. Nut (L.H.)

STIHL

GASOLINE POWERED BLOWERS

Model	Engine Manufacturer	Engine Model	Displacement
BG17, SG17	Stihl	...	56.5 cc
BR320, SR320	Stihl	...	56.5 cc
BR400, SR400	Stihl	...	56.5 cc

ENGINE INFORMATION

These blowers are equipped with a two-stroke, air-cooled engine manufactured by Stihl. Refer to appropriate engine section in this manual for engine service information.

FUEL MIXTURE

Manufacturer recommends mixing regular or unleaded gasoline with a high-quality, two-stroke engine oil designed for air-cooled engines. Recommended fuel:oil ratio is 50:1 when using Stihl oil. Fuel:oil ratio should be 25:1 when using any other two-stroke oil.

FAN

The blower fan (3—Fig. SL1) is attached to the engine flywheel and is accessible after separating engine and blower assembly from back plate. Remove blower tube elbow from blower housing. Remove mounting screws from outer half of fan housing (5). Remove cap (1) on blower models or bellows on sprayer models. Separate blower housing halves (2 and 5). Remove fan mounting screws and remove fan.

To install fan, reverse removal procedure. Tighten fan retaining screws to 8 N·m (71 in.-lbs.).

SPRAYER PUMP

Models So Equipped

The sprayer pressure pump is mounted on blower housing outer case (5—Fig. SL1) and is driven by a coupling (1—Fig. SL2) on flywheel retaining nut. To remove pump, first remove engine and blower assembly from back plate. Disconnect hoses from pump housing base (11), remove mounting screws and remove pump assembly.

To disassemble, remove pump mounting screws and separate pump housing (7) from housing base (11). Remove retaining nut (9) and pull impeller (8) off pump shaft (2). Remove bearing retaining screws (3), then press shaft (2) and bearing (4) out of pump housing. Remove snap ring (5) and press shaft out of bearing. Drive seal (6) from housing.

When reassembling, install seal (6) with open side facing outward. Press into housing until bottomed against shoulder of housing. Heat bearing (4) to approximately 50° C (120° F) before pressing onto pump shaft. Press shaft and bearing assembly into pump housing until bottomed in housing.

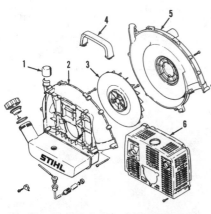

Fig. SL1—Exploded view of blower housing.

1. Cap	4. Handle
2. Blower inner case	5. Blower outer case
3. Fan	6. Engine shroud

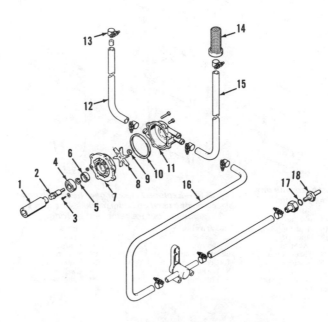

Fig. SL2—Exploded view of pressure pump used on mist/blower models.

1. Drive coupling
2. Pump shaft
3. Screw
4. Bearing
5. Snap ring
6. Seal
7. Pump housing
8. Impeller
9. Nut
10. Seal ring
11. Pump housing base
12. Return line
13. Restrictor
14. Strainer
15. Suction line
16. Pressure line
17. "O" ring
18. Metering jet

TANAKA

GASOLINE POWERED STRING TRIMMERS

Model	Engine Manufacturer	Engine Model	Displacement
AST-5000	Tanaka	…	20 cc
AST-7000	Tanaka	…	21 cc
SUM-321	Tanaka	…	31 cc
TBC-160, TBC-162	Tanaka	…	16 cc
TBC-202, TBC-205, TBC-215	Tanaka	…	20 cc
TBC-210, TBC-220	Tanaka	…	21 cc
TBC-220SS	Tanaka	…	22.6 cc
TBC-232, TBC-240	Tanaka	…	22.6 cc
TBC-265	Tanaka	…	26 cc
TBC-322, TBC-325	Tanaka	…	31 cc
TBC-355	Tanaka	…	34 cc
TBC-373	Tanaka	…	37.4 cc
TBC-425	Tanaka	…	40 cc
TBC-501	Tanaka	…	50.2 cc
TBC-4000, TBC-4500, TBC-5000	Tanaka	…	20 cc
TST-218	Tanaka	…	20 cc

ENGINE INFORMATION

Tanaka (TAS) two-stroke, air-cooled gasoline engines are used on all Tanaka trimmers and brush cutters. Identify engine by displacement and refer to Tanaka engine service section in this manual.

FUEL MIXTURE

Oil must be mixed with the fuel. Recommended fuel is regular or unleaded gasoline. Do not use gasoline containing alcohol. Recommended oil is Tanaka or another high-quality oil designed for use in air-cooled, two-stroke engines. Mix oil with gasoline at ratio recommended on oil container, otherwise, fuel:oil ratio should be 25:1.

STRING TRIMMER

The trimmer may be equipped with a manual advance or automatic advance trimmer head. Refer to following paragraphs.

Manual Advance Head

Refer to Fig. TA10 for view of dual strand, manual advance trimmer head used on some models. To extend line, loosen lock knob (6) until line can be pulled from housing. Pull line to desired length and tighten lock knob (6).

To install new line, remove lock knob (6), spring (5) and spool (4). remove any remaining old line and install new line on spool. Wind line in direction indicated by arrow on spool and insert line ends through line guides (3). Install spool, spring and lock knob.

Automatic Advance Head

Some models may be equipped with a dual strand, automatic advance trimmer head. The line is extended when the engine is accelerated or decelerated. Line will advance approximately 14 mm (1/2 in.) each time.

To install new line, press against tabs of drum (1—Fig. TA11) and separate cover (12) from drum. Disassemble, remove old line and clean components. Note letter (L) on top of drum. All trimmers can use line with diameter of 0.095 inch (2.4 mm) or 0.105 inch (2.7 mm). Trimmer heads with letter L or LS on head also can use line with diameter of 0.130 inch (3.3 mm). Line length should be 39 feet (11.9 m) if using 0.095-in. or 0.105-in. line on trimmer heads marked with letter L or LS. Line length for 0.130-in. line is 19 feet (5.8 m). On trimmer heads marked with letter R, S, M or X, line

length should be 20 feet (6.1 m). Hold ends of line together and insert looped end in notch (N—Fig. TA12). Wrap each line around spool in direction indicated

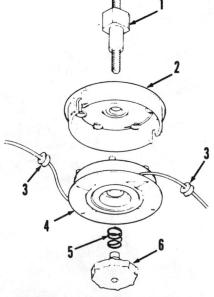

Fig. TA10—Exploded view of dual strand, manual advance trimmer head used on some models.

1. Drive shaft adapter
2. Drum
3. Eyelet
4. Spool
5. Spring
6. Lock knob

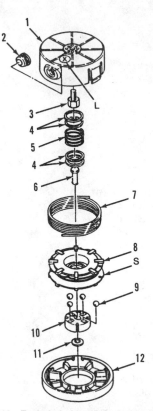

Fig. TA11—Exploded view of dual strand, automatic advance trimmer head used on some models. Note location of identifying letter (L).

1. Drum
2. Eyelet
3. Adapter
4. Washers
5. Spring
6. Hook
7. Line
8. Spool
9. Balls (4)
10. Slider
11. Washer
12. Cover

by the arrow on spool, then insert each line into each slot (S) on opposite sides of spool. There must be at least 4 inches (101 mm) of line extending from spool. Reassemble trimmer head while passing line through eyelets (2—Fig. TA11). Be sure line is not trapped by lugs on spool. After assembly, pull out lines so they disengage from slots in spool. Trim lines to equal lengths of 2-4 inches (50-100 mm).

CAUTION. If line length is less than 2 inches (50 mm), trimmer will not adjust line length properly and engine may overspeed.

Note that to remove trimmer head from shaft, head must be rotated counterclockwise on curved shaft models or clockwise (L.H. threads) on straight shaft models.

BLADE

All Models So Equipped

Some models may be equipped with a four-edge cutting blade or a saw blade. Note that blade retaining screw on straight shaft models has left-hand threads. Be sure that all components fit properly and are centered.

DRIVE SHAFT

Curved Shaft Models

Models with a curved drive shaft housing are equipped with a flexible drive shaft. The drive shaft should be removed, cleaned and lubricated after every 30 hours of operation. Detach head assembly from drive shaft housing and remove shaft. Apply lithium-based grease to shaft. The drive shaft liner is available separately on some models.

Straight Shaft Models

Periodic maintenance is not required for the drive shaft on models with a straight drive shaft housing. If removed, apply lithium-based grease to shaft. The drive shaft rides in bushings that are renewable on some models.

Model TST-218 is equipped with a telescoping drive shaft. See Fig. TA13. The upper drive shaft (6) rides in ball bearings (8) and lower drive shaft (15) rides in renewable bushings (14).

BEARING HEAD

Curved Shaft Models

The bearing head is equipped with sealed bearings and does not require

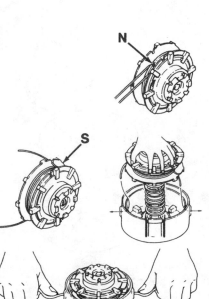

Fig. TA12—When installing new trimmer line, insert line in notch (N) on spool divider and wind in direction indicated by arrow on spool. Refer to text.

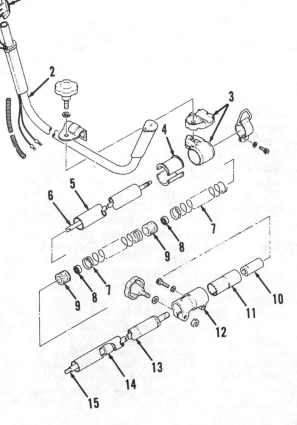

Fig. TA13—Exploded view of drive shaft housing used on Model TST-218.

1. Throttle trigger
2. Handle
3. Handle bracket
4. Spacer
5. Drive shaft housing
6. Upper drive shaft
7. Springs
8. Bearing
9. Bearing holder
10. Drive shaft connector
11. Sleeve
12. Coupler
13. Housing
14. Bushing
15. Lower drive shaft

periodic maintenance. Two types of bearing heads have been used. Early models are equipped with a snap ring (7—Fig. TA14). No snap ring is used on later models (Fig. TA15).

To disassemble bearing head on early models, remove trimmer head. Remove clamp bolt (1—Fig. TA14) and locating screw (2) and separate bearing head from drive shaft housing tube. Remove snap ring (7), then use a suitable puller to extract arbor (5) and bearing (6). Use a suitable puller and remove bearing (4). If required, press bearing (6) off arbor (5). To reassemble, install bearing (4) in housing, then install arbor (5) in bearing and housing. Press bearing (6) onto arbor shaft and into housing until snap ring (7) can be installed.

To disassemble later-style bearing head, remove trimmer head (13—Fig. TA15), cup washer (12), covers (10) and sleeve (9). Unscrew locating screw (5) and clamp screw (6) and separate bearing head (4) from drive shaft housing tube. Remove washers (7 and 8) and press or pull arbor (1) and bearings (2) from housing. Reassemble by reversing disassembly sequence.

GEAR HEAD

Straight Shaft Models

The gear head should be lubricated after every 50 hours of operation. Remove trimmer head or blade and unscrew plug (7—Fig. TA16) in side of gear head. Inject lithium-based grease until housing is approximately $2/3$ full.

To disassemble gear head, first remove blade. Remove clamp bolt (Fig. TA17) and head lock bolt. Separate head from drive shaft and housing. Detach snap ring (14—Fig. TA16). Install Tanaka puller 015-29339-000 shown in Fig. TA18, or other suitable puller, and withdraw arbor assembly. Remove gear (11—Fig. TA16). Detach snap ring (1). Install Tanaka puller 016-29373-000 shown in Fig. TA19, or other suitable puller, and withdraw input shaft and bearings as an assembly. Detach snap ring (2—Fig. TA16) and press shaft out of bear-

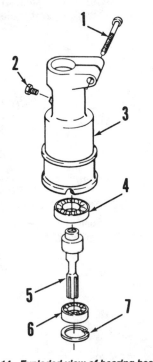

Fig. TA14—Exploded view of bearing head used on early models.

1. Clamp bolt
2. Locating screw
3. Housing
4. Bearing
5. Arbor
6. Bearing
7. Snap ring

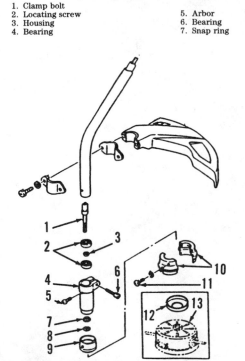

Fig. TA15—Exploded view of bearing head used on later models.

1. Arbor
2. Bearings
3. Spacer
4. Housing
5. Locating screw
6. Clamp bolt
7. Special washer
8. Special washer
9. Sleeve
10. Covers
11. Screw
12. Cup washer
13. Trimmer head

Fig. TA16—Exploded view of gear head. Early models may have a seal between snap ring (14) and bearing (13).

1. Snap ring
2. Snap ring
3. Bearing
4. Bearing
5. Input shaft
6. Locating screw
7. Fill plug
8. Clamp bolt
9. Housing
10. Bearing
11. Gear
12. Arbor
13. Bearing
14. Snap ring
15. Blade holder
16. Blade holder
17. Cup washer
18. Cap screw

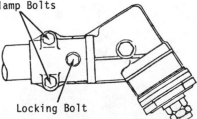

Fig. TA17—To separate gear head from drive shaft housing, remove clamp bolts and locking (head locating) bolt. Later models are equipped with only one clamp bolt.

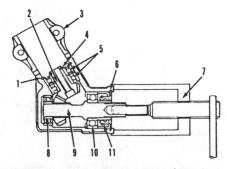

Fig. TA18—Install puller tool (7) as shown to remove arbor shaft (9) and bearing (10).

Illustrations courtesy Tanaka Ltd.

ings. If necessary, heat housing and tap housing against a wood block to dislodge bearing (10).

Reassemble gear head by reversing disassembly procedure. Tanaka tool 031-

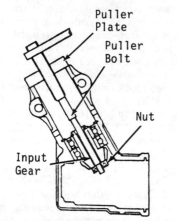

Fig. TA19—To remove input shaft and bearing assembly, install puller as shown.

29373-000 can be used to install bearing (10). Tanaka tool 032-29373-000 can be used to install input shaft and bearing assembly.

BATTERY

Models AST-5000 And AST-7000

Models AST-5000 and AST-7000 are equipped with an electric starter. A battery pack of ni-cad batteries provides power to drive the starter. The battery pack should fully recharge using charger within 15 hours. To check battery pack, recharge battery pack, then disconnect four-wire connector leading to handlebar. With engine stopped, con-

nect negative lead of a voltmeter to terminal (1—Fig. TA20) of female connector and positive tester lead to terminal (2). Battery voltage reading should be at least 4.8 volts on Model AST-5000 or 7.0 volts on Model AST-7000.

Refer to engine service section for information on remainder of electrical system.

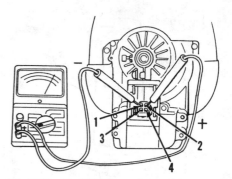

Fig. TA20—Check battery voltage by attaching tester to connector terminals as outlined in text.

TANAKA
GASOLINE POWERED BLOWERS

Model	Engine Manufacturer	Engine Model	Displacement
THB-300	Tanaka	...	31 cc
TBL-455	Tanaka	...	43 cc
TBL-500	Tanaka	...	43 cc

ENGINE INFORMATION

Tanaka (TAS) two-stroke, air-cooled gasoline engines are used on Tanaka blowers. Identify engine by displacement and refer to Tanaka engine service section in this manual.

FUEL MIXTURE

Oil must be mixed with the fuel. Recommended fuel is regular or unleaded gasoline. Do not use gasoline containing alcohol. Recommended oil is Tanaka or another high-quality oil designed for use in air-cooled, two-stroke engines. Mix oil with gasoline at ratio recommended on oil container. Otherwise, fuel:oil ratio should be 25:1.

BLOWER ASSEMBLY

To remove blower impeller (4—Figs. TA50 or TA51), first remove engine and blower assembly from frame on backpack models. On all models, remove tube clamps and remove blower tube (10) from blower case. On Models TBL-455 and TBL-500, remove air cleaner body (13—Fig. TA51) and air guide plate (15). On all models, remove blower case mounting screws and separate blower case halves (2 and 5). On Model THB-300, remove nut (3—Fig. TA50) and pull impeller and flywheel assembly (4) off crankshaft. On Models TBL-455 and TBL-500, remove screws (3—Fig. TA51) attaching impeller (4) to engine flywheel and remove impeller.

To remove engine from blower, first remove impeller as outlined above. Disconnect fuel line, throttle cable and stop switch wires. Remove engine cover and fuel tank. On Models TBL-455 and TBL-500, remove flywheel mounting nut and pull flywheel off crankshaft. On all models, remove engine mounting screws and separate engine from blower case.

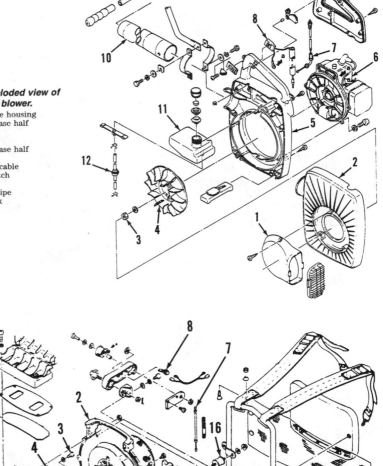

Fig. TA50—Exploded view of THB-300 blower.

1. Air intake housing
2. Blower case half
3. Nut
4. Impeller
5. Blower case half
6. Engine
7. Throttle cable
8. Stop switch
9. Handle
10. Blower pipe
11. Fuel tank
12. Fuel line

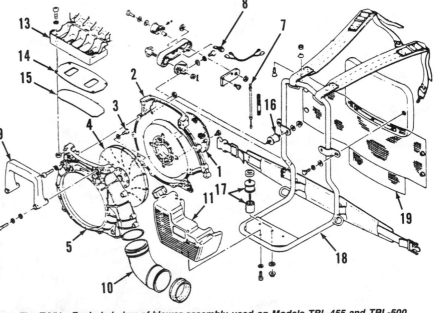

Fig. TA51—Exploded view of blower assembly used on Models TBL-455 and TBL-500.

1. Screen
2. Blower case half
3. Cap screw
4. Impeller
5. Blower case half
7. Throttle cable
8. Stop switch
9. Handle
10. Blower pipe
11. Fuel tank
13. Air cleaner body
14. Gasket
15. Air guide plate
16. Rubber cushion
17. Vibration damper
18. Back-pack frame
19. Cushion

Illustrations courtesy Tanaka Ltd.

TORO

GASOLINE POWERED STRING TRIMMERS

Model	Engine Manufacturer	Engine Model	Displacement
30900	Kioritz	....	21.2 cc
30910	Kioritz	....	21.2 cc
30920	Kioritz	....	30.1 cc
51600	Kioritz	....	13.8 cc
51625	Kioritz	....	13.8 cc
51700	Kioritz	....	21.2 cc
TC-3000	Mitsubishi	T140	24.1 cc
TC-4000	Mitsubishi	T140	24.1 cc
TC-5000	Mitsubishi	T180	32.5 cc

ENGINE INFORMATION

Early model Toro trimmers are equipped with Kioritz engines and later models are equipped with Mitsubishi engines. Identify engine by manufacturer and engine displacement and refer to appropriate KIORITZ ENGINE SERVICE or MITSUBISHI ENGINE SERVICE sections of this manual.

FUEL MIXTURE

All Models

Manufacturer recommends mixing regular grade gasoline with an octane rating of at least 87, with a good quality two-stroke engine oil at a ratio of 32:1. Do not use fuel containing alcohol.

STRING TRIMMER

Models 30900, 30910 And 30920

Models 30900, 30910 and 30920 are equipped with a dual strand semi-automatic trimmer head shown in Fig. TO10. To manually advance line with engine stopped, push in on button (7) and pull on each line. Procedure may have to be repeated to obtain desired line length. To extend line with engine running, operate trimmer at full operating rpm and tap button (7) on the ground. Line will automatically advance a measured amount.

To renew trimmer line, hold drum firmly and turn spool in direction shown in Fig. TO11 to remove slack. Twist with a hard snap until plastic peg is between holes. Pull spool out of drum. Remove old line from spool. Spool will

hold approximately 20 feet (6 mm) of monofilament line. Insert one end of new line through hole on spool (Fig. TO12) and pull line through until line is the same length on both sides of hole. Wind both ends of line at the same time in direction indicated by arrow on spool. Wind tightly and evenly from side to side and do not twist line. Insert ends of line through line guide openings, align pegs on drum with slots in spool and push spool into drum. Hold drum firmly, twist spool suddenly in direction shown in Fig. TO13 until peg

enters hole with a click and locks spool in position. Trim extended lines to desired lengths.

Models 51600 And 51625

Models 51600 and 51625 are equipped with the dual strand semi-automatic trimmer head shown in Fig. TO14. To extend line with trimmer engine stopped, push in on spool button (8) while pulling on line ends. Procedure may have to be repeated until desired

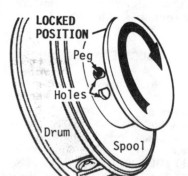

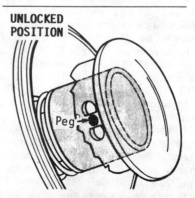

Fig. TO11—To remove spool, hold drum firmly and turn spool in direction shown to take up slack, then twist with a sudden snap until plastic peg is between holes as shown in lower view.

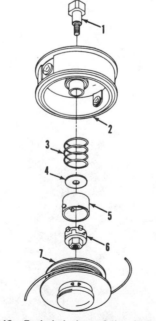

Fig. TO10—Exploded view of the dual strand semi-automatic line trimmer head used on Models 30900, 30910 and 30920.

1. Drive shaft adapter
2. Housing
3. Spring
4. Washer
5. Outer drive cam
6. Inner drive cam
7. Spool

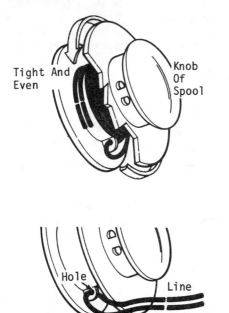

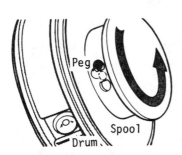

Fig. TO12—End of line must be inserted through hole on spool as shown in lower view. Wind line tightly in direction indicated by arrow on spool.

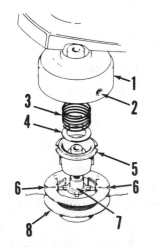

Fig. TO13—Hold drum firmly and twist suddenly in direction indicated to lock spool in position.

Fig. TO14—Exploded view of dual strand semi-automatic trimmer head used on Models 51600 and 51625.

1. Housing	5. Outer drive cam
2. Line guide	6. Line slots
3. Spring	7. Inner drive cam
4. Washer	8. Spool

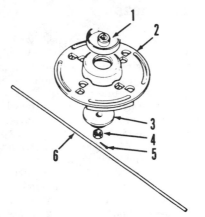

Fig. TO15—Exploded view of four strand fixed line trimmer head used on Model 51700 with 0.130 inch (3.3 mm) line. Dual strand fixed line trimmer head with 0.105 inch (2.7 mm) line used on Model TC-3000 is similar.

1. Cup washer	
2. Plate	4. Nut (LH)
3. Plate	5. Cotter pin

Fig. TO16—Exploded view of drive shaft housing and gear head assembly used on Model 51625.

1. Drive shaft	6. Bearing
2. Drive shaft housing	7. Arbor shaft
3. Clamp bolt	8. Bearing
4. Locating screw	9. Spacer
5. Bearing housing	10. Snap ring

line length is obtained. To extend line with trimmer engine running, operate trimmer at full rpm and tap trimmer head on the ground. Each time trimmer head is tapped on the ground, a measured amount of line will be advanced.

To renew line, insert widest possible screwdriver into slot in spool cap and twist to "pop" off spool assembly (8). Remove any remaining old line and install new line on spool. Wind line in direction indicated by arrow on spool and clip the two ends in line slots (6). Insert line ends in line guides (2) and install spool in housing (1). Pull on line ends to release from line slots (6).

Model 51700

Model 51700 is equipped with a four strand fixed line trimmer head shown in Fig. TO15. Trimmer head is equipped with two 14 inch (35.6 cm) lengths of 0.130 inch (3.3 mm) monofilament line (6) secured to trimmer head plate (2) by plate (3), left-hand thread nut (4) and cotter pin (5). Lines clip in locking slots in trimmer head plate (2) also.

Model TC-3000

Model TC-3000 is equipped with a dual strand fixed line trimmer head similar to trimmer head used on Model 51700. Trimmer head is equipped with a single 16 inch (40.6 cm) length of 0.105 inch (2.7 mm) line.

Models TC-4000 And TC-5000

Models TC-4000 and TC-5000 are equipped with a dual strand manual trimmer head similar to the dual strand semi-automatic trimmer head used on Models 51600 and 51625. To extend line, pull out on cutting head and rotate it counterclockwise to advance line. Model TC-4000 trimmer head is equipped with 0.080 inch (2 mm) line and Model TC-5000 trimmer head is equipped with 0.105 inch (2.7 mm) line.

BLADE

Models 30920, 51700, TC-3000, TC-4000 And TC-5000

Models 30920, 51700, TC-3000, TC-4000 and TC-5000 may be equipped with an eight cutting edge grass, weed and brush blade or a saw blade. Units equipped with a blade should be equipped with shoulder harness.

DRIVE SHAFT

Models 30900, 30910, 51600 And 51625

Models 30900, 30910, 51600 and 51625 are equipped with a flexible drive shaft mounted in the drive shaft housing tube. Drive shaft should be removed, cleaned and lubricated with lithium base grease at 50 hour intervals of use. To remove drive shaft, remove clamp bolt (3–Fig. TO16) and locating screw (4). Separate bearing head assembly (5) from drive shaft housing (2). Pull drive shaft (1) out of lower end of drive shaft housing. When reinstalling drive shaft, make certain drive shaft ends fully

169

engage adapters at engine and bearing head ends.

Models 30920, 51700, TC-3000, TC-4000 And TC-5000

Models 30920, 51700, TC-3000, TC-4000 and TC-5000 are equipped with a solid drive shaft supported in drive shaft housing in five renewable bushings. Toro recommends removing, cleaning and lubricating drive shaft at 50 hour intervals of use. To renew any or all of the five drive shaft bushings, mark bushing locations in drive shaft housing. Use a wooden dowel to remove old bushings and to install new bushings at the same locations from which old bushings were removed.

BEARING HEAD

Models 30900, 30910 And 51600

Models 30900, 30910 and 51600 are equipped with the bearing head shown in Fig. TO17. Bearing head is equipped with sealed bearings (5 and 7) and requires no regular maintenance.

To disassemble bearing head, remove trimmer head assembly and cup washer (10). Remove clamp bolt (2) and locating screw (1). Separate bearing head from drive shaft housing tube. Remove snap ring (8) and use a suitable puller (part number 897603-05330) to remove arbor shaft (9) and bearing assembly. Remove nut (4), bearing (5), spacer (6) and bearing (7) as required.

Model 51625

Model 51625 is equipped with the bearing head shown in Fig. TO16. Bearing head is equipped with sealed bearings (6 and 8) and requires no regular maintenance. To disassemble bearing head, remove trimmer head assembly and cup washer. Remove snap ring (10) and use a suitable puller (part number 897603-05330) to remove arbor shaft (7) and bearing assembly. Press bearings from shaft as required. If bearing (6) remains in housing (5), it may be necessary to slightly heat bearing housing and tap housing on wooden block to remove bearing.

GEAR HEAD

Model 30920

Model 30920 is equipped with the gear head shown in Fig. TO18. Gear head lubricant should be checked at 50 hour intervals of use. To check lubricant, remove check plug (15). Gear head should be kept 2/3 full of lithium base grease.

To disassemble gear head, remove trimmer head or blade assembly. Separate gear head from drive shaft housing tube. Remove snap ring (25) and use a suitable puller to remove input shaft and bearing assembly (20). Remove

plug (16), seal (7), snap ring (8), and snap ring (14). Press arbor and bearing assembly from housing (19). Remove required snap rings to remove gears and bearings.

Models 51700, TC-3000, TC-4000 And TC-5000

Refer to Fig. TO19 for an exploded view of gear head used on Model 51700. Models TC-3000, TC-4000 and TC-5000 use a similar gear head. On all models, gear head lubricant should be checked at 50 hour intervals of use. To check, remove check plug (12). Gear head housing should be kept 2/3 full of lithium base grease.

To disassemble gear head, remove trimmer head or blade assembly. Remove cup washer (21) and key (17). Remove snap ring (2). Use suitable puller (part number 897603-05330) to remove input shaft (8) and bearing assembly. Remove seal (20) and snap ring (19). Use suitable puller (part number 897703-04130) to remove arbor shaft (16) and bearing assembly. If bearing

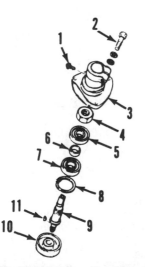

Fig. TO17—Exploded view of bearing head used on Models 30900, 30910 and 51600.

1. Locating screw
2. Clamp bolt
3. Bearing housing
4. Nut
5. Bearing
6. Spacer
7. Bearing
8. Snap ring
9. Arbor shaft
10. Cup washer
11. Pin

Fig. TO18—Exploded view of gear head used on Model 30920.

1. Cotter pin
2. Nut
3. Adapter plate
4. Cup washer
5. Arbor shaft
6. Keys
7. Seal
8. Snap ring
9. Bearing
10. Spacer
11. Gear
12. Snap ring
13. Bearing
14. Snap ring
15. Level check plug
16. Plug
17. Nut
18. Clamp bolt
19. Housing
20. Gear
21. Spacer
22. Bearing
23. Bearing
24. Snap ring
25. Snap ring

Fig. TO19—Exploded view of gear head used on Models 51700, TC-3000, TC-4000 and TC-5000.

1. Drive shaft housing
2. Snap ring
3. Snap ring
4. Bearing
5. Bearing
6. Spacer washer
7. Spacer washer
8. Input gear
9. Clamp bolt
10. Locating screw
11. Housing
12. Check plug
13. Bearing
14. Gear
15. Key
16. Arbor shaft
17. Key
18. Bearing
19. Snap ring
20. Seal
21. Cup washer

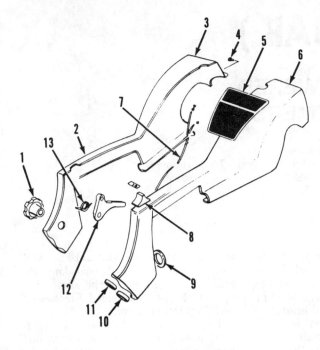

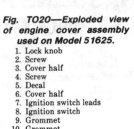

Fig. TO20—Exploded view of engine cover assembly used on Model 51625.

1. Lock knob
2. Screw
3. Cover half
4. Screw
5. Decal
6. Cover half
7. Ignition switch leads
8. Ignition switch
9. Grommet
10. Grommet
11. Grommet
12. Throttle trigger
13. Throttle trigger spring

(13) stays in gear head housing (11), heat housing slightly and tap housing on wooden block to remove bearing. Press bearings from shafts as required.

ENGINE COVER

Model 51625

Model 51625 is equipped with a partial engine cover (Fig. TO20). To remove engine cover, carefully remove decal (5) or cut down housing seam. Remove the eight screws and lock knob (1) securing engine cover halves together and carefully separate the cover. Note positions of internal parts. Lift out the stop switch (8). Disconnect throttle cable at throttle trigger (12). Remove throttle trigger and spring (13).

TML (TRAIL)

GASOLINE POWERED STRING TRIMMERS

Model	Engine Manufacturer	Engine Model	Displacement
BC-35	TML	150528	35.0 cc
LT-35	TML	150528	35.0 cc

ENGINE INFORMATION

All Models

All models are equipped with a two-stroke air-cooled gasoline engine manufactured by TML (Trail). Refer to TML (TRAIL) ENGINE SERVICE section of this manual.

FUEL MIXTURE

All Models

Manufacturer recommends mixing regular grade (unleaded is an acceptable substitute) gasoline with a good quality two-stroke air-cooled engine oil at a ratio of 20:1. Do not use fuel containing alcohol.

STRING TRIMMER

All Models

Trimmer may be equipped with a single strand (Fig. TL10) or a dual strand (Fig. TL16) manual trimmer head. Refer to appropriate paragraph for model being serviced.

Single Strand Trimmer Head. Refer to Fig. TL10 for an exploded view of the single strand trimmer head used on some models. To extend line, stop trimmer engine and wait until all head rotation has stopped. Pull down on spool cover (Fig. TL11) and rotate top in direction of arrow (Fig. TL12) while pulling line out of head. Procedure may have to be repeated until line end reaches mark on trimmer head (Fig. TL13) provided to gage correct line length.

To renew line, push in on spool cover (5-Fig. TL10) and unscrew knob (8). Refer to Fig. TL14. Remove knob (8-Fig. TL10), spring (7), spool cover (5) and spool (3). Remove any remaining line and clean spool and inside of spool cover. Insert the end of the new line into "V" shaped slot in spool (Fig. TL15). Wind line in direction indicated by arrow on spool. Insert line through line guide in spool cover and reinstall spool, spool cover, spring and knob.

Dual Strand Trimmer Head. Refer to Fig. TL16 for exploded view of the dual strand manual trimmer head used on some models. To extend line, stop trimmer engine and wait until all head rotation has stopped. Loosen knob (6). Pull each line end at the same time until each line is extended 6 inches (15 cm). Tighten knob (6).

To renew line, cut 15 feet (4.6 m) of 0.095 inch (2.4 mm) monofilament line. Remove lock knob (6) and remove lower housing (5) and spool (4). Remove any remaining old line. Clean all parts of trimmer head. Pull line guides (2) down (do not remove) and clean outside surfaces with a wet soapy cloth. Apply a few drops of oil into cavities after cleaning. Loop new line into two equal lengths and insert line ends through holes at center of spool. Pull line ends out until stopped by spool. Wind both ends onto spool in direction indicated

Fig. TL13—Spool is marked to indicate correct line length.

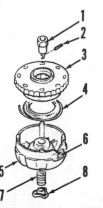

Fig. TL10—Exploded view of single strand manual trimmer head used on some models.

1. Adapter
2. Pin
3. Spool
4. Line
5. Spool cover
6. Line guide
7. Spring
8. Lock knob

Fig. TL11—To extend line, pull down on spool cover and rotate. Refer to Fig. TL12.

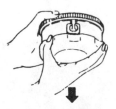

Fig. TL12—Pull out line as cover is rotated. Refer to text.

Fig. TL14—To remove spool, push up on cover and remove lock knob. Refer to text.

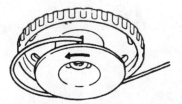

Fig. TL15—Wind new line on spool in direction indicated by arrow on spool.

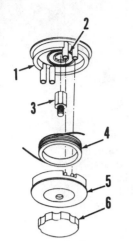

Fig. TL16—Exploded view of dual strand manual trimmer head used on some models.

1. Upper cover
2. Line guides
3. Adapter
4. Spool
5. Lower cover
6. Lock knob

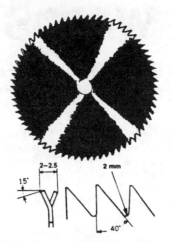

Fig. TL18—Some models may be equipped with an eighty tooth saw blade. Refer to illustration and text for sharpening procedure.

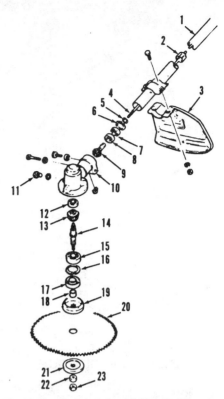

Fig. TL19—Exploded view of drive shaft housing and gear head assembly.

1. Drive shaft housing
2. Bushings
3. Shield
4. Drive shaft
5. Snap ring
6. Snap ring
7. Bearing
8. Bearing
9. Input shaft
10. Housing
11. Check plug
12. Bearing
13. Output gear
14. Arbor (output) shaft
15. Bearing
16. Snap ring
17. Seal
18. Spacer
19. Adapter
20. Blade
21. Adapter
22. Nut
23. Jam nut

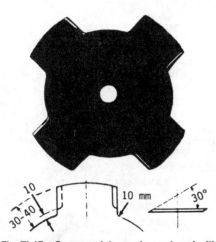

Fig. TL17—Some models may be equipped with a four cutting edge blade. Refer to illustration and text for sharpening procedure.

by arrow on spool. Insert line ends through line guides in upper cover and install spool, lower cover and lock knob.

BLADE

All Models

Trimmer may be equipped with a four cutting edge blade (Fig. TL17) or an eighty tooth saw blade (Fig. TL18). Blade should be installed with parts assembled in sequence shown in Fig. TL19.

To sharpen the four cutting edge blade, refer to Fig. TL17. Blade edge

should have a length of 1.18-1.58 inch (30-40 mm). Do not grind the chamfered section of the blade root. Make certain the root of cutting blade remains chamfered to prevent cracking or breakage. Sharpen all teeth equally to maintain blade balance.

To sharpen the eighty tooth saw blade, refer to Fig. TL18. Maintain a 0.04-0.08 inch (1-2 mm) radius at the tooth root. Maintain a 0.08-0.09 inch (2-2.5 mm) tooth set. Sharpen all teeth equally to maintain blade balance.

DRIVE SHAFT

All Models

All models are equipped with a solid steel drive shaft (4-Fig. TL19) which is supported in drive shaft housing (1) in four renewable bushings (2). Drive shaft and bushings require no regular maintenance; however, before removing bushings (2), mark bushing locations in drive shaft housing. Install new bushings at old bushing locations. When installing drive shaft, lightly lubricate with SAE 30 oil prior to installation.

GEAR HEAD

All Models

All models are equipped with gear head shown in Fig. TL19. At 30 hour intervals of use, lubricate gear head by removing trimmer head or blade as-

sembly and check plug (11). Pump lithium base grease into gear head housing until grease appears at lower seal (17).

To disassemble gear head, separate gear head from drive shaft housing. Remove trimmer head or blade. Remove snap ring (6). Insert screwdriver or suitable wedge in gear head housing clamp split. Carefully expand housing and remove input shaft (9) and bearing assembly. Remove snap ring (5) and press bearings (8 and 7) from input shaft as necessary. Remove spacer (18) and seal (17). Remove snap ring (16). Use suitable puller to remove arbor shaft (14) and bearing assembly. Remove bearing (15) and gear (13) from arbor shaft as necessary. If bearing (12) stays in housing, heat housing to 140° F (60° C) and tap housing on wooden block to remove bearing.

WARDS

GASOLINE POWERED STRING TRIMMERS

Model	Engine Manufacturer	Engine Model	Displacement
2049	Tecumseh	AV520	85.0 cc
24206	Kioritz	....	16.0 cc
24207	Kioritz	....	21.2 cc
24369	Tecumseh	AV520	85.0 cc
XEC-24300	Kioritz	....	13.8 cc
XEC-24340	Kioritz	....	13.8 cc
XEC-24341	Kioritz	....	16.0 cc
XEC-24342	Kioritz	....	21.2 cc
XEC-24358	Kioritz	....	13.8 cc
XEC-24359	Kioritz	....	21.2 cc
XEC-24361	Kioritz	....	30.8 cc

ENGINE INFORMATION

All Models

Wards line trimmers and brush cutters may be equipped with Kioritz or Tecumseh two-stroke air-cooled gasoline engines. Identify engine model by engine manufacturer, trimmer model number or engine displacement. Refer to KIORITZ ENGINE SERVICE or TECUMSEH ENGINE SERVICE section of this manual.

FUEL MIXTURE

All Models

Manufacturer recommends mixing regular grade gasoline (unleaded is an acceptable substitute) with a good quality two-stroke air-cooled engine oil at a 25:1 ratio. Do not use fuel containing alcohol.

STRING TRIMMER

Models XEC-24359 And XEC-24361

Semi-Automatic Dual Strand Trimmer Head. Models XEC-24359 and XEC-24361 may be equipped with dual strand trimmer head as shown in Fig. WD10. To manually advance line with engine stopped, push in on button (7) and pull on each line. Procedure may have to be repeated to obtain desired line length. To extend line with engine running, operate trimmer at full operating rpm and tap button (7) on the ground. Line will automatically extend a measured amount.

To renew trimmer line, hold drum firmly and turn spool in direction shown in Fig. WD11 to remove slack. Twist with a hard snap until plastic peg is between holes. Pull spool out of drum. Remove old line from spool. Spool will hold aproximately 20 feet (6 m) of monofilament line. Insert one end of new line through hole on spool (Fig. WD12) and pull line through until line is the same length on both sides of hole. Wind both ends of line at the same time in direction indicated by arrow on spool. Wind tightly and evenly from side to side and do not twist line. Insert ends of line through line guide openings, align pegs on drum with slots in spool and push spool into drum. Hold drum firmly, twist spool suddenly in direction shown in Fig. WD13 until peg enters hole with a click and locks spool in posi-

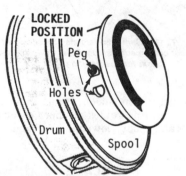

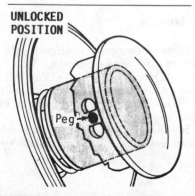

Fig. WD10—Exploded view of dual strand semi-automatic trimmer head used on some models.

1. Bolt
2. Drum
3. Spring
4. Washer
5. Outer drive
6. Inner cam
7. Spool

Fig. WD11—To remove spool, hold housing firmly and turn spool in direction shown to take up slack, then twist with a sudden snap until plastic peg is between holes as shown in lower view.

tion. Trim extending lines to correct lengths.

Manual Advance Dual Strand Trimmer Head. Models XEC-24359 and XEC-24361 may be equipped with manual advance dual strand trimmer head shown in Fig. WD14. To extend line, loosen lock knob (6) approximately one turn. Pull out the line on each side until line lengths are 6 inches (152 mm).

To renew line, remove slotted screw (8) and washer (7). Unscrew ball lock (6). Remove cover (5) and spring (3). Remove spool (4). Cut two 12 foot (4 m) lengths of 0.095 inch (2.4 mm) monofilament line. Insert one end of each line through the slot and into the locating hole on bottom side of spool. Line ends should extend approximately 1/4 inch (6.4 mm) through locating holes. Hold lines tight and wind in a counterclockwise direction using care not to cross the lines. Insert the end of each line into each slot leaving approximately 6 inches (152 mm) of line extending from

spool. Place spool into drum and feed one line through each of the line guides. Install spring, cover, ball lock, washer and screw.

Models XEC-24300, XEC-24340, XEC-24341, XEC-24342, XEC-24358, 24206 And 24207

Models XEC-24300, XEC-24340, XEC-24341, XEC-24342, XEC-24358, 24206 and 24207 may be equipped with a semi-automatic single strand trimmer head shown in Fig. WD15. Line may be manually advanced with engine stopped by pushing in on housing (12) and pulling line out as required.

To renew line, remove cotter pin (13-Fig. WD15). Rotate housing (12) counterclockwise and remove housing and line spool (7). Remove foam pads (9 and 10) and any remaining old line. Clean spool and inner surface of outer housing (12). Check indexing teeth on spool and in housing. Cut off approximately 25 feet (7.6 mm) of 0.080 inch (2 mm) monofilament line and tape one end of line to spool (Fig. WD16). Wind line on spool in direction indicated by arrow on spool (Fig. WD17). Install foam pads (9 and 10) with line between them as shown in Fig. WD17. Insert line end through line guide (14-Fig.

WD15) opening and install spool and housing. Push in on housing and rotate housing clockwise to lock in position, then install cotter pin (13).

Models 2049 And 24369

Models 2049 and 24369 may be equipped with a four strand trimmer head shown in Fig. WD18.

To renew trimmer line, remove bolt (8) and cover (7). Remove spools (6) and remove any remaining old line. Clean inside of upper body. Wind new monofilament line on the four spools (6). Place spools (6) back in upper body (1), install springs (5) and install cover (7). Install bolt (8) and tighten securely.

BLADE

Models XEC-24359, XEC-24361, 2049 And 24369

Models XEC-24359, XEC-24361, 2049 and 24369 may be equipped with a 10

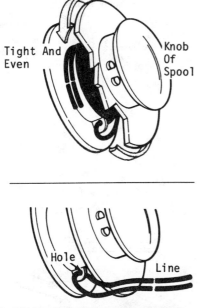

Fig. WD12—End of line must be inserted through hole on spool as shown in lower view. Wind line tightly in direction indicated by arrow on spool.

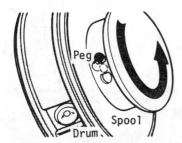

Fig. WD13—Hold drum firmly and twist suddenly to lock spool in position.

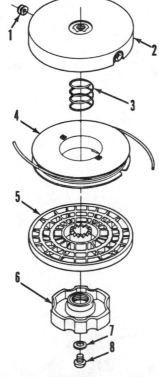

Fig. WD14—Exploded view of manual trimmer head used on some models. This head is no longer available.

1. Line guide	5. Cover
2. Hub	6. Ball lock
3. Spring	7. Washer
4. Spool	8. Screw

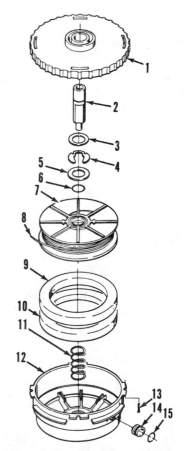

Fig. WD15—Exploded view of semi-automatic trimmer head used on some models.

1. Plate	
2. Adapter	
3. Washer	9. Foam pad
4. Retainer ring	10. Foam pad
5. Washer	11. Spring
6. Retainer ring	12. Hub
7. Spool	13. Cotter pin
8. Line	14. Line guide
	15. Retainer

inch saw blade. When installing blade, make certain all adapter plates are centered and seated squarely against blade and tighten nut (left-hand thread) securely.

DRIVE SHAFT

Models 24206, 24207, XEC-24300, XEC-24340, XEC-24341, XEC-24342 And XEC-24358

Models 24206, 24207, XEC-24300, XEC-24340, XEC-24341, XEC-24342 and XEC-24358 are equipped with flexible drive shafts supported in a curved drive shaft housing. Drive shaft should be removed at 18 hour intervals of use, cleaned and lubricated with lithium base grease. Reverse positions of drive shaft ends (engine end now at trimmer head end) and install drive shaft in housing. Reversing drive shaft ends each time it is lubricated will extend drive shaft life.

Models 2049, 24369, XEC-24358 And XEC-24361

Models 2049, 24369, XEC-24358 and XEC-24361 are equipped with a solid drive shaft supported in a straight drive shaft housing tube. No regular maintenance is required; however, if drive shaft is removed, lubricate drive shaft with lithium base grease before reinstallation.

Fig. WD16—Tape one end of line to center of spool as shown.

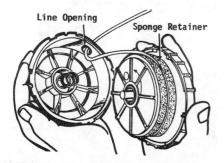

Fig. WD17—Foam pads are installed on spool with trimmer line between them.

BEARING HEAD

All Models So Equipped

Bearing heads used on all models except Models 2049 and 24369 are shown in Fig. WD19 or WD20. Bearing heads are equipped with sealed bearings and require no regular maintenance. To disassemble either bearing head, remove screw (1) and clamp screw (2). Remove adapter plate (10) and snap ring (8). Use suitable puller to remove bearing and arbor assemblies. Remove nut (4) and remove bearings and spacer as required.

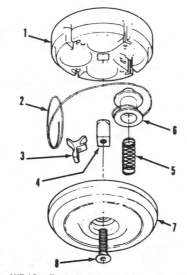

Fig. WD18—Exploded view of four strand trimmer head used on Models 2049 and 24369.

1. Upper housing	5. Spring
2. Line	6. Spools
3. Line retainer	7. Cover
4. Arbor post	8. Screw

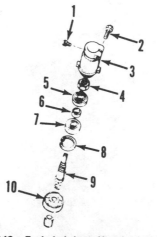

Fig. WD19—Exploded view of bearing head used on some models.

1. Screw	6. Spacer
2. Clamp screw	7. Bearing
3. Housing	8. Snap ring
4. Nut	9. Shaft
5. Bearing	10. Adapter plate & key

Bearing head used on Models 2049 and 24369 is shown in Fig. WD21. Bearing head is equipped with sealed bearings and requires no regular maintenance.

To disassemble bearing head, remove trimmer head or blade assembly. Re-

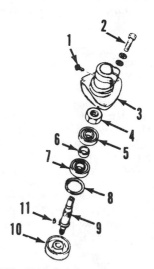

Fig. WD20—Exploded view of bearing head used on some models.

1. Screw	
2. Clamp screw	7. Bearing
3. Housing	8. Snap ring
4. Nut	9. Shaft
5. Bearing	10. Adapter
6. Spacer	11. Key

Fig. WD21—Exploded view of bearing head used on Models 2049 and 24369.

1. Wire bracket	
2. Bolt	8. Bearing
3. Bolt	9. Spacer
4. Drive shaft adapter	10. Bearing
5. Washer	11. Snap ring
6. Housing	12. Arbor shaft
7. Locating screw	13. Cup washer

move clamp bolt (3) and locating screw (7). Separate gear head from drive shaft housing tube. Remove snap ring (11). Secure head assembly in a vise. Place a 1-3/8 inch wooden dowel with a 3/4 inch hole drilled through center over arbor shaft, against the square coupling end. Tap wooden dowel with a mallet to remove arbor shaft and bearing assembly. Disassemble bearings, coupling and arbor assembly as required.

To reassemble, place coupling (4) and washer (5) on arbor (12). Press one bearing onto arbor. Install assembly into housing. Install spacer (9) and press remaining bearing onto arbor and into housing. Install snap ring.

WEED EATER

ELECTRIC POWERED STRING TRIMMERS

Model	Volts	Amps	Cutting Swath	Line Diameter	Rpm
1208	120	2.0	8 in.	0.065 in.	N/A
1210	120	2.8	10 in.	0.065 in.	N/A
1214	120	3.5	14 in.	0.065 in.	N/A
1216	120	4.5	16 in.	0.080 in.	N/A

N/A—Rpm specifications not available.

ELECTRICAL REQUIREMENTS

All models require electrical circuits with 120-volt alternating current. Extension cord length should not exceed 100 feet (30.5 m). Make certain all circuits and connections are properly grounded at all times.

STRING TRIMMER

All Models

All models are equipped with a single strand semi-automatic trimmer head shown in Fig. WE1. Models 1208 and 1210 are equipped with 35 feet (10.7 m) of 0.065 inch (1.6 mm) line, Model 1214 is equipped with 50 feet (15.2 m) of 0.065 inch (1.6 m) line and Model 1216 is

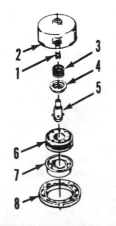

Fig. WE1—Exploded view of single strand semi-automatic trimmer head used on all models.

1. Line guide
2. Housing
3. Spring
4. Spring adapter
5. Drive cam
6. Spool
7. Button
8. Cover

equipped with 40 feet (12.2 m) of 0.080 inch (2.0 mm) line.

To extend line with trimmer engine stopped, push in on button (7) while pulling on line end. Procedure may have to be repeated to obtain desired line length. To extend line with trimmer engine running, operate trimmer engine at full rpm and tap button (7) on the ground. Each time button (7) is tapped on the ground a measured amount of new line will be advanced.

To renew line, remove cover (8), button (7) and spool (6). Clean all parts thoroughly and remove any remaining old line from spool. Wind correct length and diameter line on spool in direction indicated by arrow on spool. Insert line end through line guide opening in housing (2) and install spool, button and cover.

WEED EATER

GASOLINE POWERED
STRING TRIMMERS

Model	Engine Manufacturer	Engine Model	Displacement
650, 657, 670	Tecumseh	AV520	85 cc
1000	Fuji	…	37.7 cc
1400, 1400T	Poulan	…	22.2 cc
1500	Poulan	…	26.2 cc
1600, 1600T	Poulan	…	26.2 cc
1700, 1700A	Poulan	…	26.2 cc
1740	Poulan	…	26.2 cc
1900	Poulan	…	26.2 cc
GTI-15, GTI-15T	Poulan	…	22 cc
GTI-16	Poulan	…	30 cc
GTI-16 Super	Poulan	…	30 cc
GTI-17	Poulan	…	26 cc
GTI-17XP	Poulan	…	30 cc
GTI-18, GTI-18K	Poulan	…	30 cc
GTI-19	Poulan	…	30 cc
HP-30	Poulan	…	30 cc
XR-20, XR-20T	Poulan	…	22.2 cc
XR-30	Poulan	…	26.2 cc
XR-50, XR-50A	Poulan	…	26.2 cc
XR-70	Poulan	…	26.2 cc
XR-75	Poulan	…	26.2 cc
XR-80, XR-80A	Poulan	…	28 cc
XR-85	Poulan	…	28 cc
XR-90	Poulan	…	28 cc
XR-95	Poulan	…	28 cc
XR-100	Poulan	…	26.2 cc
XR-105	Poulan	…	22.2 cc
XR-125	Poulan	…	22.2 cc
XT-20, XT-20T	Poulan	…	22 cc
XT-50	Poulan	…	30 cc
XT-85	Poulan	…	30 cc
XT-100	Poulan	…	30 cc
XT-125	Poulan	…	30 cc

ENGINE INFORMATION

The models in this section are equipped with a Fuji, Poulan or Tecumseh engine. Refer to appropriate engine service section for engine service information.

FUEL MIXTURE

Manufacturer recommends combining regular gasoline with Poulan/Weed Eater two-stroke engine oil mixed as indicated on container. Gasohol or other alcohol blended fuels are not approved by manufacturer.

STRING TRIMMER

Models 1400, 1500, 1600, 1700, 1740, XR-20, XR-30, XR-50, XR-70, XR-75, XR-80, XR-85 And XR-105

These models are equipped with the single strand, semi-automatic trimmer head shown in Figs. WE10 or WE11. Early type trimmer head (Fig. WE10) is identified by the adapter (1) that drives the trimmer head. Service procedure for both heads is similar.

To extend line with trimmer engine stopped, push in on button (7) while pulling on line end. Repeat procedure as needed to obtain desired line length. To extend line with trimmer engine running and head rotating, tap button (7) on ground. Each time button is tapped on ground, a measured amount of line is advanced.

To install new line, remove cover (8), button (7) and spool (6). Clean all parts thoroughly and remove any remaining old line from spool. Wind approximately 30 feet (9 m) of 0.080-in. (2 mm) diameter monofilament line on spool in direction indicated by arrow on spool. Insert line end through line guide opening in housing (2) and install spool, button and cover.

Models XR-90, XR-95, XR-100 And 1000

Models XR-90, XR-95, XR-100 and 1000 are equipped with the dual strand, manual trimmer head shown in Fig. WE12. To extend line, stop trimmer engine and push in on plate (8) while pulling each line out of housing (2).

To install new trimmer line, remove screw (9), plate (8), spring (6) and spool (7). Remove any remaining line from

Illustrations courtesy Poulan/Weed Eater

each side of spool. Clean spool, housing and plate. Insert ends of two new 0.095-in. (2.4 mm) diameter lines in holes located within spool and wind lines in direction indicated by arrow on spool. Total amount of installed line should not exceed spool diameter. Make certain line savers (3) are in position and install spool in housing with the "THIS SIDE IN" instructions on spool toward inside of trimmer head. Install spring (6), cover (8) and screw (9).

Models 650, 657 And 670

Models 650, 657 and 670 are equipped with the four strand trimmer head shown in Fig. WE13.

To install new line, remove screw (8) and cover (7). Remove spools (6) and remove any old line. Clean inside of head.

Wind new monofilament line on the four spools (6). Reassemble trimmer head.

Models GTI-15T, GTI-17XP, XT-20T And Some GTI-16, GTI-16 Super Models

Models GTI-15T, GTI-17XP, XT-20T and some GTI-16 and GTI-16 Super Models are equipped with the single strand, semi-automatic trimmer head shown in Fig. WE14.

To extend line with trimmer engine stopped, push in on button (4) while pulling on line end. Repeat procedure as needed to obtain desired line length. To extend line with trimmer engine running and head rotating, tap button (4) on ground. Each time button is tapped on ground, a measured amount of line is advanced.

To install new line, disengage tabs on cover (6) from housing (1). Remove old line and clean parts. Recommended line diameter is 0.080 inch (2 mm). Wind line around spool in direction indicated by arrow on spool.

Models 1400T, 1600T, GTI-15, GTI-17, XR-20, XR-20T And Some HP-30 Models

Models 1400T, 1600T, GTI-15, GTI-17, XR-20, XR-20T and some HP-30 models are equipped with the single strand, semi-automatic trimmer head shown in Fig. WE15.

To extend line with trimmer engine stopped, push in on button (6) while pulling on line end. Repeat procedure as needed to obtain desired line length. To extend line with trimmer engine running and head rotating, tap button (6) on ground. Each time button is tapped on ground a measured amount of line is advanced.

To install new line, remove cover (7), button (6) and spool (5). Clean all parts thoroughly and remove any remaining old line from spool. Wind 0.080 inch (2 mm) diameter monofilament line on spool in direction indicated by arrow on spool. Insert line end through line guide opening in housing (1) and install spool, button and cover.

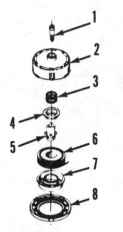

Fig. WE10—Exploded view of old style single strand, semi-automatic trimmer head used on early Models 1500, 1700, XR-30, XR-50, XR-70, XR-75, XR-80 and XR-85.

1. Drive shaft adapter
2. Housing
3. Spring
4. Spring adapter
5. Drive cam
6. Spool
7. Button
8. Cover

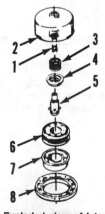

Fig. WE11—Exploded view of later style single strand, semi-automatic trimmer head used on Models 1400, 1600, 1740 and XR-20, and later Models 1500, 1700, XR-30, XR-50, XR-70, XR-75, XR-80 and XR-85.

1. Line guide
2. Housing
3. Spring
4. Spring adapter
5. Drive cam
6. Spool
7. Button
8. Cover

Fig. WE12—Exploded view of dual strand, manual trimmer head used on Models XR-90, XR-95, XR-100 and 1000.

1. Lock ring cap
2. Housing
3. Line guide
4. Drive shaft adapter
5. Lock ring
6. Spring
7. Spool
8. Cover
9. Screw

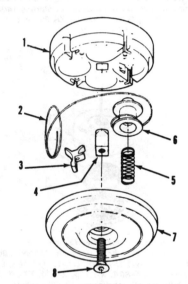

Fig. WE13—Exploded view of the four strand trimmer head used on Models 650, 657 and 670.

1. Upper housing
2. Line
3. Line retainer
4. Arbor post
5. Spring
6. Spool
7. Cover
8. Screw

Fig. WE14—Exploded view of single strand, semi-automatic trimmer head used on Models GTI-15T, GTI-17XP and XT-20T, and some GTI-16 and GTI-16 Super models.

1. Housing
2. Adapter
3. Spring
4. Button
5. Spool
6. Cover

Illustrations courtesy Poulan/Weed Eater

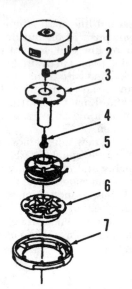

Fig. WE15—Exploded view of single strand, semi-automatic trimmer head used on Models 1400T, 1600T, GTI-15, GTI-17, XR-20, XR-20T and some HP-30 models.

1. Housing
2. Spring
3. Spool post
4. Screw
5. Spool
6. Button
7. Cover

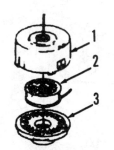

Fig. WE16—Exploded view of single strand, semi-automatic trimmer head used on Models 1700A, 1900, GTI-16, GTI-16 Super, GTI-18, GTI-18K, GTI-19, XR-50A, XR-80A, XR-125, XT-50, XT-85, XT-100, XT-125 and some HP-30 models.

1. Housing
2. Spool
3. Cover & button assy.

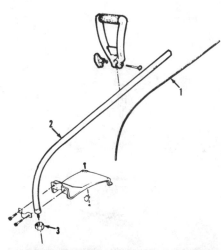

Fig. WE17—Exploded view of flexible drive shaft (1), drive shaft housing tube (2) and dust cover (3) used on Models 1400, 1400T, 1500, 1600, 1600T, 1740, GTI-15, GTI-15T, GTI-16, GTI-16 Super, GTI-17, GTI-17XP, HP-30, XR-20, XR-20T, XR-30, XR-50A, XT-20, XT-20T and XT-50.

Models 1700A, 1900, GTI-16, GTI-16 Super, GTI-18, GTI-18K, GTI-19, XR-50A, XR-80A, XR-125, XT-50, XT-85, XT-100, XT-125 And Some HP-30 Models

These models are equipped with the single strand, semi-automatic trimmer head shown in Fig. WE16.

To extend line with trimmer engine stopped, push in on button while pulling on line end. Repeat procedure as needed to obtain desired line length. To extend line with trimmer engine running and head rotating, tap button on ground. Each time button is tapped on ground, a measured amount of line is advanced.

To install new line, detach cover (3) from housing (1). Remove old line and clean parts. Recommended line diameter is 0.080 inch (2 mm). Wind line around spool in direction indicated by arrow on spool.

BLADE

Some models may be equipped with a blade. When installing blade, be sure all adapter plates are centered and seated squarely against blade. Blade nut has left-hand threads.

DRIVE SHAFT

Curved Shaft Models

Models with a curved drive shaft housing (2—Fig. WE17) are equipped with a flexible drive shaft (1). The drive shaft should be removed, cleaned and

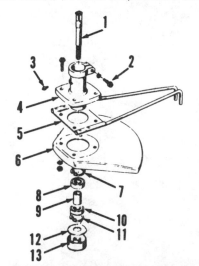

Fig. WE18—Exploded view of bearing head used on Models 1700, 1700A, 2600, 2610, GTI-18, GTI-18K, XR-50, XR-70, XR-75, XR-80, XR-80A, XR-85 and XT-85.

1. Drive shaft adapter
2. Clamp bolt
3. Locating screw
4. Housing
5. Bracket (if equipped)
6. Shield
7. Snap ring
8. Bearing
9. Spacer
10. Bearing
11. Snap ring
12. Washer
13. Drive disc

lubricated after every 20 hours of operation. Detach head assembly from drive shaft housing and remove shaft. Apply lithium-based grease to shaft.

Straight Shaft Models

Periodic maintenance is not required for the drive shaft on models with a straight drive shaft housing. If removed, apply lithium-based grease to shaft.

BEARING HEAD

Models 1400, 1400T, 1500, 1600, 1600T, 1740, GTI-15, GTI-15T, GTI-16, GTI-16 Super, GTI-17, GTI-17XP, HP-30, XR-20, XR-20T, XR-30, XR-50A, XT-20, XT-20T And XT-50

These models are equipped with a bearing head that is an integral part of the drive shaft housing tube (Fig. WE17). Regular maintenance is not required. Service parts are not available.

Models 1700, 1700A, 2600, 2610, GTI-18, GTI-18K, XR-50, XR-70, XR-75, XR-80, XR-80A, XR-85 And XT-85

These models are equipped with the bearing head shown in Fig. WE18. The bearing head is equipped with sealed bearings; regular maintenance is not required.

To disassemble bearing head, remove trimmer head or blade assembly. Remove clamp bolt (2) and locating screw (3). Separate bearing head assembly from drive shaft housing. Remove shield (6) and bracket (5), if so equipped. Remove cup washer (13) and washer (12). Carefully press drive shaft adapter (1) out of bearings. Remove snap rings (7 and 11). Press bearings (8 and 10) and spacer (9) out of housing.

Models 650, 657 And 670

Models 650, 657 and 670 are equipped with the bearing head shown in Fig. WE19. The bearing head is equipped with sealed bearings; regular maintenance is not required.

To disassemble bearing head, remove trimmer head or blade assembly. Remove clamp bolt (3) and locating screw (7). Separate gear head from drive shaft housing tube. Remove snap ring (11). Secure head assembly in a vise. Place a 1 3/8-in. wood dowel with a 3/4-in. hole drilled through center over arbor (12), against the square coupling end. Tap wood dowel with a mallet to remove arbor and bearing assembly. Disassemble bearings, coupling and arbor assembly as required.

To reassemble, place coupling (4) and washer (5) on arbor (12). Press one bearing onto arbor. Install assembly into housing. Install spacer (9) and press remaining bearing onto arbor and into housing. Install snap ring (11).

GEAR HEAD

All Models So Equipped

The gear head should be lubricated after every 10 hours of operation by injecting lithium-based grease through screw hole in side of gear head. Fill housing so it is approximately two-thirds full of grease.

The gear head on Models 1000, 1900, XR-105, XR-125, XT-100, XT-125 and XT-200 must be serviced as a unit assembly; individual components are not available.

Models XR-90, XR-95 and XR-100 are equipped with the gear head shown in Fig. WE20. To disassemble gear head, remove trimmer head or blade assembly. Remove clamp bolt and head locating screw and separate gear head from drive shaft housing tube. Remove cup washer (17) and spacer (14). Remove snap ring (2) and use a suitable puller to remove input shaft (5) and bearings as an assembly. Remove snap ring (1) and press bearings (3 and 4) from input shaft as required. Remove seal (16) and snap ring (15). Use a suitable puller to remove arbor (12) and bearing assembly. Press bearing (13) and gear (11) from shaft as required. If bearing (10) remains in housing (6), heat housing to 140° F (60° C) and tap housing on wood block to remove bearing.

ENGINE COVER

All Models So Equipped

Some models are equipped with the full engine cover shown in Fig. WE21. To remove engine cover, remove clamp bolt (8) and separate engine assembly from drive shaft housing. Remove the four 10-24 screws and separate housings (5) and (9) slightly. Disconnect ignition wire from module and separate fuel line so junction fitting stays with crankcase side of fuel line. Separate housings completely. Remove the three 8-24 screws from inner side of housing (5) and remove the air baffle. Remove the five 10-24 screws located under air baffle and

separate housing (4) from housing (5). Remove fuel tank cap and remove fuel tank. Remove the four screws securing carburetor cover plate and remove carburetor cover. Disconnect spark plug, re-

move the four 10-24 screws at drive shaft housing side of cover (9), then remove cover.

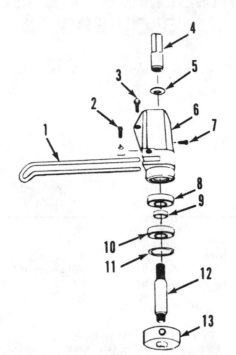

Fig. WE19—Exploded view of bearing head used on Models 650, 657 and 670.

1. Wire bracket
2. Screw
3. Bolt
4. Drive shaft adapter
5. Washer
6. Housing
7. Locating screw
8. Bearing
9. Spacer
10. Bearing
11. Snap ring
12. Arbor
13. Cup washer

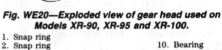

Fig. WE20—Exploded view of gear head used on Models XR-90, XR-95 and XR-100.

1. Snap ring
2. Snap ring
3. Bearing
4. Bearing
5. Input shaft
6. Housing
7. Locating bolt
8. Clamp bolt
9. Check plug
10. Bearing
11. Gear
12. Arbor shaft
13. Bearing
14. Spacer
15. Snap ring
16. Seal
17. Cup washer

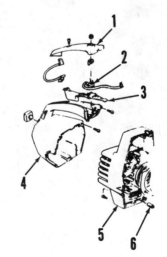

Fig. WE21—Exploded view of engine cover assembly used on some models.

1. Throttle housing cover
2. Ignition switch
3. Throttle trigger
4. Handle
5. Fan housing
6. Spacer
7. Screw
8. Clamp bolt
9. Cover

WEED EATER

GASOLINE POWERED BLOWERS

Model	Engine Manufacturer	Engine Model	Displacement
920	Poulan	…	26.2 cc
925	Poulan	…	26.2 cc
940	Poulan	…	26.2 cc
960	Poulan	…	26.2 cc
1925	Poulan	…	26.2 cc
1960	Poulan	…	26.2 cc
GBI-20	Poulan	…	22 cc
GBI-22, GBI-22V	Poulan	…	22 cc
GBI-30V	Poulan	…	30 cc

ENGINE INFORMATION

The models in this section are equipped with a Poulan engine. Refer to appropriate engine service section for engine service information.

FUEL MIXTURE

Manufacturer recommends mixing regular gasoline with Poulan/Weed Eater two-stroke engine oil mixed as indicated on container. Gasohol or other alcohol-blended fuels are not approved by manufacturer.

FAN

To remove blower fan (11—Fig. WE40) on Models 920, 925, 940, 960, 1925 and 1960, remove tube clamp (9) from blower housing. Remove blower housing screws and separate blower housing halves (6 and 13). Remove fan mounting nut (12) and withdraw fan from drive shaft (4). When installing fan, tighten fan retaining nut to 19-20 N·m (14-15 ft.-lbs.).

To remove blower fan (7—Fig. WE41) on Models GBI-22, GBI-22V and GBI-30V, remove retaining screws from blower housing and separate blower housing halves (5 and 12). Remove fan retaining nut (11) and withdraw fan from end of crankshaft.

To remove blower fan (3—Fig. WE42) on Model GBI-20, remove screws from blower housing and separate outer blower housing (4) and recoil starter assembly from inner blower housing (2). Remove screws mounting fan (3) to flywheel (1) and remove fan.

SHROUD BEARING

The fan shaft (4—Fig. WE40) on Models 920, 925, 940, 960, 1925 and 1960 is supported by a bearing (7) in the fan shroud (6). To remove bearing and drive shaft, first remove blower housing (10 and 13) and fan (11). Unbolt and remove fan shroud from engine. Detach snap ring (8), then heat shroud to 300° F (149° C) and remove bearing and shaft.

The fan end of crankshaft on Models GBI-22, GBI-22V and GBI-30V is supported by bearing (3—Fig. WE41) in starter housing (1). To remove bearing, first separate blower housing (5 and 12), fan (7) and starter housing (1) from engine. Press bearing out of starter housing.

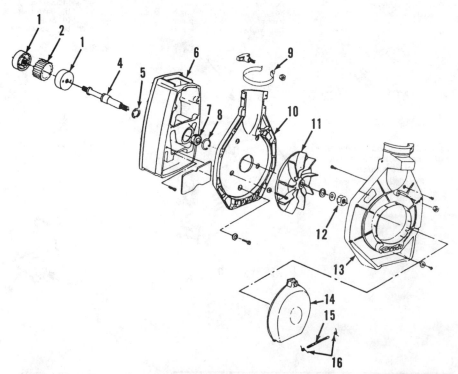

Fig. WE40—Exploded view of fan shroud assembly used on Models 920, 925, 940, 960, 1925 and 1960.

1. Shaft coupling	7. Bearing	12. Nut
2. Coupling hub	8. Snap ring	13. Blower housing
4. Fan shaft	9. Clamp	14. Inlet door
5. Washer	10. Blower housing	15. Pivot pin
6. Shroud	11. Fan	16. Springs

Illustrations courtesy Poulan/Weed Eater

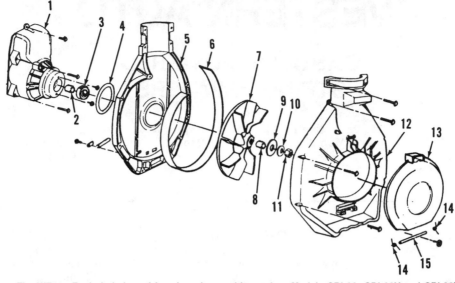

Fig. WE41—Exploded view of fan shroud assembly used on Models GBI-22, GBI-22V and GBI-30V.

1. Starter housing	6. Band	11. Nut
2. Spacer	7. Fan	12. Housing
3. Bearing	8. Spacer	13. Inlet door
4. "O" ring	9. Washer	14. Springs
5. Housing	10. Washer	15. Pivot pin

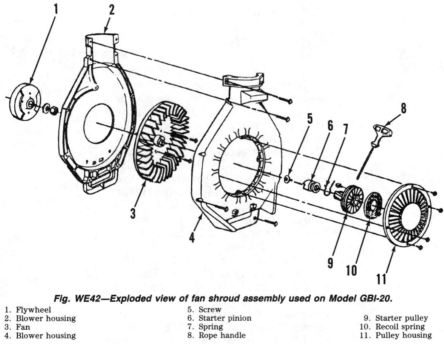

Fig. WE42—Exploded view of fan shroud assembly used on Model GBI-20.

1. Flywheel	5. Screw	9. Starter pulley
2. Blower housing	6. Starter pinion	10. Recoil spring
3. Fan	7. Spring	11. Pulley housing
4. Blower housing	8. Rope handle	

WESTERN AUTO

GASOLINE POWERED STRING TRIMMERS

Model	Engine Manufacturer	Engine Model	Displacement
95-2027-1	Kioritz	G2	16.0 cc
95-2028-9	Kioritz	H-1A	21.2 cc

ENGINE INFORMATION

All Models

All models are equipped with Kioritz two-stroke air-cooled engines. Identify engine model by trimmer model or engine displacement. Refer to KIORITZ ENGINE SERVICE section of this manual.

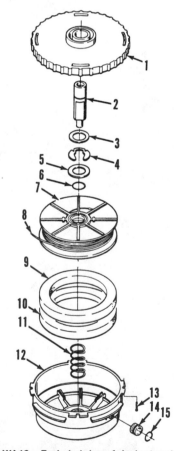

Fig. WA10—Exploded view of single strand semi-automatic trimmer head for Model 95-2027-1.

1. Cover
2. Drive shaft adapter
3. Washer
4. Retainer ring
5. Washer
6. Retainer ring
7. Spool
8. Line
9. Foam pad
10. Foam pad
11. Spring
12. Housing
13. Cotter pin
14. Line guide
15. Retainer

FUEL MIXTURE

All Models

Manufacturer recommends mixing regular grade gasoline (unleaded is an acceptable substitute) with a good quality two-stroke air-cooled engine oil at a 25:1 ratio. Do not use fuel containing alcohol.

STRING TRIMMER

Model 95-2027-1

Model 95-2027-1 is equipped with a single strand semi-automatic trimmer head shown in Fig. WA10. Line may be manually advanced with engine stopped by pushing in on housing (12) while pulling on line. Procedure may have to be repeated until desired line length is obtained. To advance line with engine running, operate trimmer engine at full rpm and tap housing (12) on the ground. Each time housing is tapped on the ground, a measured amount of trimmer line is advanced.

To renew trimmer line, remove cotter pin (13). Twist housing (12) counterclockwise and remove housing. Remove foam pads (9 and 10) and any remaining line from spool (7). Clean spool and inner area of housing. Cut off approximately 25 feet (7.6 m) of 0.080 inch (2 mm) monofilament line and tape one end of line to spool (Fig. WA11). Wind

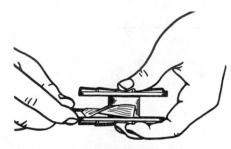

Fig. WA11—Tape new trimmer line end to center of spool as shown.

line on spool in direction indicated by arrow on spool (Fig. WA12). Install foam pads (9 and 10) so line is protruding from center of foam pads (Fig. WA12). Insert end of line through line guide and install spool, housing and spring. Push in on housing and twist housing to lock in position and install cotter pin (13—Fig. WA10).

Model 95-2028-9

Model 95-2028-9 is equipped with a single strand semi-automatic trimmer head shown in Fig. WA13. Line may be manually advanced with engine stopped by pushing in on housing (9) while pulling on line. Procedure may have to be repeated to obtain desired line length. To advance line with engine running, operate engine at full rpm and tap housing (9) on the ground. Each time housing is tapped on the ground, a measured amount of trimmer line will be advanced.

To renew trimmer line, remove cotter pin (10) and twist housing (9) counterclockwise to remove housing. Remove foam pad (6) and any remaining line on spool (3). Clean spool and inside of housing. Cut off approximately 25 feet (7.6 m) of 0.080 inch (2 mm) monofilament line and tape one end of line to spool (Fig. WA11). Wind line on spool in direction indicated by arrow on spool

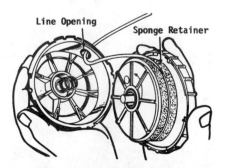

Line Opening

Sponge Retainer

Fig. WA12—Install foam pads with line protruding from center of pads as shown. Wind line in direction indicated by arrow on spool.

(Fig. WA14). Install foam pad with line end protruding from between foam pad and spool as shown in Fig. WA14. Insert line end through line guide and install housing and spring assembly on spool. Push in on housing and twist housing to lock into position. Install cotter pin through hole in housing and cover.

BLADE

Model 95-2028-9

Model 95-2028-9 may be equipped with a 60 tooth saw blade or an eight tooth weed and grass blade. To install blade with trimmer head removed, rotate cup washer (13–Fig. WA16) until hole in cup washer aligns with hole in gear head housing. Install a round tool into hole to prevent drive shaft turning. Install blade and lower adapter plate. Install and tighten nut. Install a new split pin in arbor to prevent nut loosening.

DRIVE SHAFT

All Models

All models are equipped with a flexible drive shaft enclosed in the drive shaft housing tube. Drive shaft has squared ends which engage adapters at each end. Drive shaft should be removed for maintenance at 50 hour intervals of use. Remove screw (4—Fig. WA15 or Fig. WA16) and bolt (3) at bearing head housing, then separate bearing head from drive shaft housing. Pull flexible drive shaft from housing. Lubricate drive shaft with lithium base grease and reinstall in drive shaft housing with end which was previously at clutch end at bearing head end. Reversing drive shaft ends extends drive shaft life. Make certain ends of drive shaft engage upper and lower square drive adapters when installing.

BEARING HEAD

Model 95-2027-1

Model 95-2027-1 is equipped with the bearing head shown in Fig. WA15. Bearing head is equipped with sealed bearings (7 and 9) and requires no regular maintenance. To disassemble bearing head, remove bolt (3) and screw (4) and separate bearing head from drive shaft housing tube. Remove trimmer head or blade assembly. Remove cup washer (13) and snap ring (10). Use a suitable puller to remove arbor shaft (11) and bearing assembly. Remove nut (6) and press bearings from arbor shaft as required.

Model 95-2028-9

Model 95-2028-9 is equipped with the bearing head shown in Fig. WA16. Bearing head is equipped with sealed bearings (7 and 9) and requires no regular maintenance. To disassemble bearing head, remove bolt (3) and screw (4) and separate bearing head from drive shaft housing tube. Remove trimmer head or blade assembly. Remove cup washer (13) and snap ring (10). Use suitable puller to remove arbor shaft (11) and bearing assembly. Remove nut (6) and press bearings from arbor shaft as required.

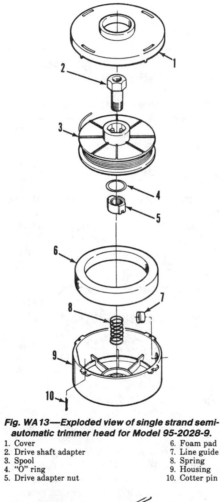

Fig. WA13—Exploded view of single strand semi-automatic trimmer head for Model 95-2028-9.

1. Cover	6. Foam pad
2. Drive shaft adapter	7. Line guide
3. Spool	8. Spring
4. "O" ring	9. Housing
5. Drive adapter nut	10. Cotter pin

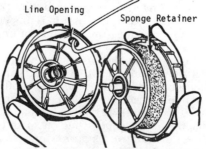

Fig. WA14—Install foam pad with line protruding from between pad and spool as shown. Wind line in direction indicated by arrow on spool.

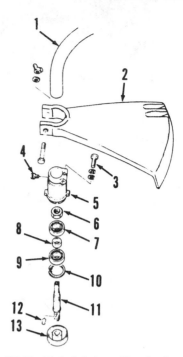

Fig. WA15—Exploded view of bearing head assembly used on Model 95-2027-1.

1. Drive shaft housing tube	7. Bearing
2. Shield	8. Spacer
3. Bolt	9. Bearing
4. Screw	10. Snap ring
5. Housing	11. Arbor (output) shaft
6. Nut	12. Pin
	13. Cup washer

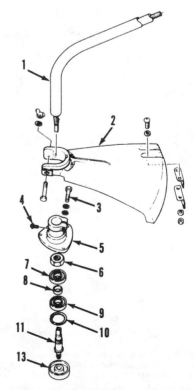

Fig. WA16—Exploded view of gear head assembly used on Model 95-2028-9. Refer to Fig. WA15 for legend.

YARD PRO

GASOLINE POWERED STRING TRIMMERS

Model	Engine Manufacturer	Engine Model	Displacement
110	Poulan	...	26.2 cc
116	Poulan	...	28 cc
120, 120A	Poulan	...	26.2 cc
130, 130A	Poulan	...	28 cc
140	Poulan	...	26.2 cc
145	Poulan	...	28 cc
150	Poulan	...	28 cc
160	Poulan	...	28 cc

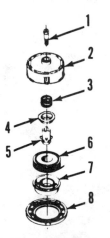

Fig. YP10—Exploded view of early style single strand, semi-automatic trimmer head used on early Models 110, 120, 130 and 140.

1. Drive shaft adapter
2. Housing
3. Spring
4. Spring adapter
5. Drive cam
6. Spool
7. Button
8. Cover

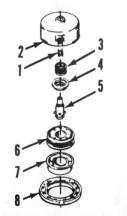

Fig. YP11—Exploded view of later style single strand, semi-automatic trimmer head used on Models 110, 120, 130 and 140.

1. Line guide
2. Housing
3. Spring
4. Spring adapter
5. Drive cam
6. Spool
7. Button
8. Cover

ENGINE INFORMATION

The models in this section are equipped with a Poulan engine. Refer to appropriate engine service section for engine service information.

FUEL MIXTURE

Manufacturer recommends mixing regular gasoline with Poulan/Weed Eater two-stroke engine oil mixed as indicated on container. Gasohol or other alcohol blended fuels are not approved by manufacturer.

STRING TRIMMER

Models 110, 120, 130 And 140

Models 110, 120, 130 and 140 are equipped with the single strand, semi-automatic trimmer head shown in Figs. YP10 or YP11. Early type trimmer head (Fig. YP10) is identified by the adapter (1) that drives the trimmer head. Service procedure for both heads is similar.

To extend line with trimmer engine stopped, push in on button (7) while pulling on line end. Repeat procedure as needed to obtain desired line length. To extend line with trimmer engine running and head rotating, tap button (7) on ground. Each time button is tapped on ground, a measured amount of line is advanced.

To install new line, remove cover (8), button (7) and spool (6). Clean all parts thoroughly and remove any remaining old line from spool. Wind approximately 30 feet (9 m) of 0.080-in. (2 mm) diameter monofilament line on spool in direction indicated by arrow on spool. Insert line end through line guide opening in housing (2) and install spool, button and cover.

Models 150 And 160

Models 150 And 160 are equipped with the dual strand, manual trimmer head shown in Fig. YP12. To extend line, stop trimmer engine and push in on plate (8) while pulling each line out of housing (2).

To install new trimmer line, remove screw (9), plate (8), spring (6) and spool (7). Remove any remaining line from each side of spool. Clean spool, housing and plate. Insert ends of two new 0.095-in. (2.4 mm) diameter lines in holes located within spool and wind lines in direction indicated by arrow on spool. Total amount of installed line should not exceed spool diameter. Make certain line

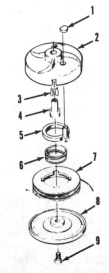

Fig. YP12—Exploded view of dual strand, manual trimmer head used on Models 150 and 160.

1. Lock ring cap
2. Housing
3. Line guide
4. Drive shaft adapter
5. Lock ring
6. Spring
7. Spool
8. Cover
9. Screw

savers (3) are in position and install spool in housing with the "THIS SIDE IN" instructions on spool toward inside of trimmer head. Install spring (6), cover (8) and screw (9).

Model 116

Model 116 is equipped with the single strand, semi-automatic trimmer head shown in Fig. YP13.

To extend line with trimmer engine stopped, push in on button (6) while pulling on line end. Repeat procedure as needed to obtain desired line length. To extend line with trimmer engine running and head rotating, tap button (6) on ground. Each time button is tapped on ground, a measured amount of line is advanced.

To install new line, remove cover (7), button (6) and spool (5). Clean all parts thoroughly and remove any remaining old line from spool. Wind 0.080-in. (2 mm) diameter monofilament line on spool in direction indicated by arrow on spool. Insert line end through line guide opening in housing (1) and install spool, button and cover.

Models 120A, 130A And 145

Models 120A, 130A and 145 are equipped with the single strand, semi-automatic trimmer head shown in Fig. YP14.

To extend line with trimmer engine stopped, push in on button while pulling on line end. Repeat procedure as needed to obtain desired line length. To extend line with trimmer engine running and head rotating, tap button on ground. Each time button is tapped on ground, a measured amount of line is advanced.

To install new line, detach cover (3) from housing (1). Remove old line and clean parts. Recommended line diameter is 0.080 inch (2 mm). Wind line around spool in direction indicated by arrow on spool.

BLADE

Some models may be equipped with a blade. When installing blade, be sure all adapter plates are centered and seated squarely against blade. Blade mounting nut has left-hand threads.

DRIVE SHAFT

Curved Shaft Models

Models with a curved drive shaft housing (2—Fig. YP15) are equipped with a flexible drive shaft (1). The drive shaft should be removed, cleaned and lubricated after every 20 hours of operation. Detach head assembly from drive shaft housing and remove shaft. Apply lithium-based grease to shaft.

Straight Shaft Models

Periodic maintenance is not required for the drive shaft on models with a straight drive shaft housing. If removed, apply lithium-based grease to shaft.

BEARING HEAD

Models 110, 116, 120 And 120A

Models 110, 116, 120 and 120A are equipped with a bearing head that is an integral part of the drive shaft housing tube (Fig. YP15). Regular maintenance is not required. Service parts are not available.

Models 130 And 130A

Models 130 and 130A are equipped with the bearing head shown in Fig. YP16. The bearing head is equipped with sealed bearings; regular maintenance is not required.

To disassemble bearing head, remove trimmer head or blade assembly. Remove clamp bolt (2) and locating screw (3). Separate bearing head assembly from drive shaft housing. Remove shield (6) and bracket (5), if so equipped. Remove cup washer (13) and washer (12). Carefully press drive shaft adapter (1) out of bearings. Remove snap rings (7 and 11). Press bearings (8 and 10) and spacer (9) out of housing.

To reassemble, reverse disassembly procedure.

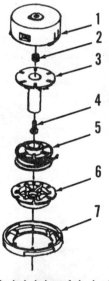

Fig. YP13—Exploded view of single strand, semi-automatic trimmer head used on Model 116.

1. Housing
2. Spring
3. Spool post
4. Screw
5. Spool
6. Button
7. Cover

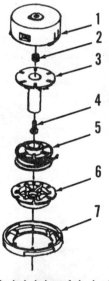

Fig. YP14—The single strand, semi-automatic trimmer head used on Models 120A, 130A and 145 consists of housing (1), spool (2) and cover (3). Line release button is located in cover.

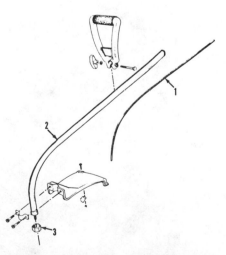

Fig. YP15—Exploded view of flexible drive shaft (1), drive shaft housing tube (2) and dust cover (3) used on Models 110, 116, 120 and 120A.

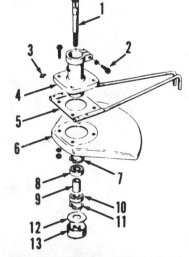

Fig. YP16—Exploded view of bearing head used on Models 130 and 130A.

1. Drive shaft adapter
2. Clamp bolt
3. Locating screw
4. Housing
5. Bracket (if equipped)
6. Shield
7. Snap ring
8. Bearing
9. Spacer
10. Bearing
11. Snap ring
12. Washer
13. Drive disc

GEAR HEAD

All Models So Equipped

The gear head should be lubricated after every 10 hours of operation by injecting lithium-based grease through screw hole in side of gear head. Fill housing so it is approximately two-thirds full of grease.

The gear head must be serviced as a unit assembly; individual components are not available.

ENGINE COVER

All Models So Equipped

Some models are equipped with the full engine cover shown in Fig. YP17. To remove engine cover, remove clamp bolt (8) and separate engine assembly from drive shaft housing. Remove the four 10-24 screws and separate housings (5) and (9) slightly. Disconnect ignition wire from module and separate fuel line so junction fitting stays with crankcase side of fuel line. Separate housings completely. Remove the three 8-24 screws from inner side of housing (5) and remove the air baffle. Remove the five 10-24 screws located under air baffle and separate housing (4) from housing (5). Remove fuel tank cap and remove fuel tank. Remove the four screws securing carburetor cover plate and remove carburetor cover. Disconnect spark plug, remove the four 10-24 screws at drive shaft housing side of cover (9), then remove cover.

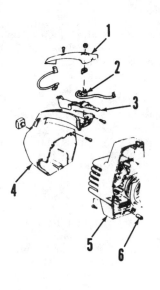

Fig. YP17—Exploded view of engine cover assembly used on some models.
1. Throttle housing cover
2. Ignition switch
3. Throttle trigger
4. Handle
5. Fan housing
6. Spacer
7. Screw
8. Clamp bolt
9. Cover

YAZOO
GASOLINE POWERED STRING TRIMMERS

Model	Engine Manufacturer	Engine Model	Displacement
YBC-16	Tanaka	....	16.0 cc
YBC-23	Tanaka	....	22.6 cc
YBC-31	Tanaka	....	30.5 cc

ENGINE INFORMATION

All Models

Yazoo line trimmers and brush cutters are equipped with Tanaka (TAS) two-stroke air-cooled engines. Engines may be identified by engine displacement. Refer to TANAKA (TAS) ENGINE SERVICE sections of this manual.

FUEL MIXTURE

All Models

Manufacturer recommends mixing regular grade gasoline (unleaded is an acceptable substitute) with a good quality two-stroke air-cooled engine oil at a 25:1 ratio. Do not use fuel containing alcohol.

STRING TRIMMER

All Models

Model YBC-16 is equipped with an eight blade plastic flexible blade with

line trimmer head offered as an option. The dual strand manual trimmer head is standard on Models YBC-23 and YBC-31.

Refer to Fig. YA10 for an exploded view of the dual strand manual trimmer head available for most models. To extend line, stop trimmer engine and wait until all head rotation has stopped. Loosen lock knob (6) (left-hand thread) until line ends can be pulled from housing. Pull lines until desired length has been obtained. Correct line length is 3.4-4.7 inches (10-12 cm).

To renew line, remove lock knob (6) and housing (5). Remove any remaining line on spool (2) and clean spool and housing. Install new line on spool. Wind line in direction indicated by arrow on spool. New line diameter when wound on spool must not exceed spool diameter. Insert line ends through line guides (4) and reinstall housing and lock knob.

BLADE

Models YBC-23 And YBC-31

Models YBC-23 and YBC-31 may be equipped with a four cutting edge blade or a saw blade. To remove blade, rotate blade until hole (H-Fig. YA11) in guard is aligned with hole (H) in cup washer (2). Insert a round tool into aligned holes to prevent blade rotation. Remove bolt (7) (left-hand thread), washer (6), cover (5) and adapter (4). Remove blade (3). When installing blade, tighten bolt (7) to 250 in.-lbs. (28 N·m).

DRIVE SHAFT

Model YBC-16

Model YBC-16 is equipped with a flexible drive shaft enclosed in the drive shaft housing tube. Drive shaft has squared ends which engage adapters at each end. Drive shaft should be removed for maintenance at 20 hour

intervals of use. To remove, separate drive shaft housing from engine, then pull drive shaft from housing. Clean drive shaft and lubricate with lithium base grease. Reinstall drive shaft in housing.

Models YBC-23 And YBC-31

Models YBC-23 and YBC-31 are equipped with a solid steel drive shaft supported in five renewable bushing assemblies located in drive shaft housing tube (Fig. YA12). Drive shaft requires no regular maintenance; however, if drive shaft has been removed, lubricate drive shaft with lithium base gease before reinstallation. To renew bushing assemblies, mark locations of old bushings on drive shaft housing, then remove all old bushings. Install new bushings with suitable driver at old bushing locations.

BEARING HEAD

Model YBC-16

Model YBC-16 is equipped with sealed bearing housing (3-Fig. YA13).

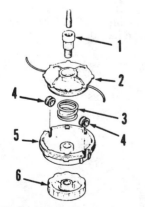

Fig. YA10—Exploded view of the dual strand manual trimmer head standard on most models.

1. Drive shaft adapter
2. Spool
3. Spring
4. Line guides
5. Housing
6. Lock knob

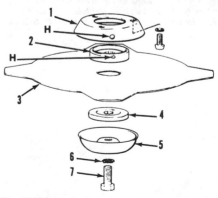

Fig. YA11—Exploded view of blade assembly available for Models YBC-23 and YBC-31.

1. Anti-wrap guard
2. Cup washer
3. Blade
4. Adapter plate
5. Cover
6. Washer
7. Bolt (LH)
H. Hole

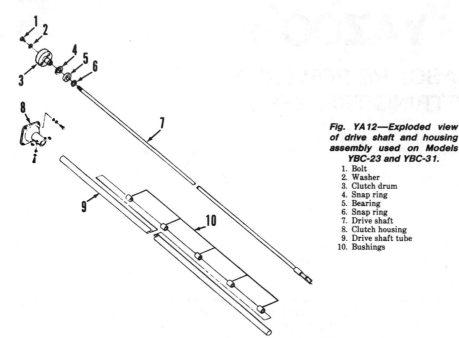

Fig. YA12—Exploded view
of drive shaft and housing
assembly used on Models
YBC-23 and YBC-31.
1. Bolt
2. Washer
3. Clutch drum
4. Snap ring
5. Bearing
6. Snap ring
7. Drive shaft
8. Clutch housing
9. Drive shaft tube
10. Bushings

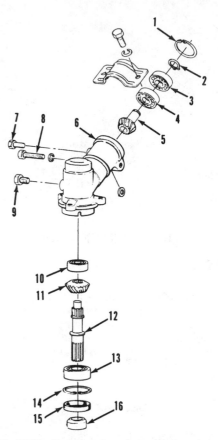

No regular maintenance is required and
no service parts are available.

GEAR HEAD

Models YBC-23 And YBC-31

Models YBC-23 and YBC-31 are
equipped with the gear head shown in
Fig. YA 14. Gear head lubricant level
should be checked at 50 hour intervals
of use by removing check plug (9). Gear
head housing should be 2/3 full of lithium base grease. Do not use a pressure
grease gun to install grease as bearing
seal and housing damage will occur.

To disassemble gear head, remove
trimmer head or blade assembly. Remove locating screw (7) and clamp bolt
(8) and separate gear head from drive
shaft housing. Remove spacer (16) and
seal (15). Remove snap ring (14) and use
a suitable puller to remove arbor shaft
(12) and bearing assembly. If bearing
(10) stays in housing, heat housing to
140° F (60° C) and tap housing on wood-

Fig. YA14—Exploded view of gear head used on
Models YBC-23 and YBC-31.

1. Snap ring		9. Check plug
2. Snap ring		10. Bearing
3. Bearing		11. Gear
4. Bearing		12. Arbor (output) shaft
5. Input shaft		13. Bearing
6. Housing		14. Snap ring
7. Locating screw		15. Seal
8. Clamp bolt		16. Spacer

en block to remove bearing. Remove
gear (11) from arbor shaft. Press bearing (13) from arbor shaft as required.
Remove snap ring (1). Insert a screwdriver into clamp split in gear head
housing and carefully expand housing.
Remove input shaft (5) and bearing
assembly. Remove snap ring (2) and
press bearings (3 and 4) from input
shaft as required.

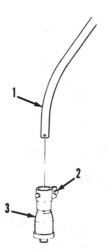

Fig. YA13—Bearing head assembly (3) is attached to drive shaft housing tube (1) by clamp
(2). No service parts are available for bearing
head.

DEERE

ENGINE SERVICE

Model	Bore	Stroke	Displacement
110	32 mm (1.26 in.)	26 mm (1.02 in.)	21.2 cc (1.29 cu. in.)
210	32 mm (1.26 in.)	26 mm (1.02 in.)	21.2 cc (1.29 cu. in.)
220	32 mm (1.26 in.)	26 mm (1.02 in.)	21.2 cc (1.29 cu. in.)
240	32 mm (1.26 in.)	26 mm (1.02 in.)	21.2 cc (1.29 cu. in.)
250	32 mm (1.26 in.)	26 mm (1.02 in.)	21.2 cc (1.29 cu. in.)
260	32 mm (1.26 in.)	26 mm (1.02 in.)	21.2 cc (1.29 cu. in.)
300	32.2 mm (1.27 in.)	30 mm (1.18 in.)	24.4 cc (1.49 cu. in.)
350	35 mm (1.38 in.)	32 mm (1.26 in.)	30.8 cc (1.88 cu. in.)
450	40 mm (1.57 in.)	32 mm (1.26 in.)	40.2 cc (2.45 cu. in.)

ENGINE INFORMATION

These two-stroke, air-cooled engines are used on Deere trimmers and brush cutters. Refer to Deere equipment sections for a list of engines used on other Deere models.

MAINTENANCE

LUBRICATION. Engine lubrication is obtained by mixing gasoline with an oil designed for two-stroke, air-cooled engines. Refer to trimmer or brush cutter service section for manufacturer's recommended fuel:oil mixture ratio.

SPARK PLUG. Recommended spark plug for Model 350 engine is Champion CJ8 or equivalent. Recommended spark plug for all other models is Champion CJ7Y, or equivalent. Specified electrode gap is 0.6-0.7 mm (0.024-0.028 in.). Tighten spark plug to 16 N·m (142 in.-lbs.).

CARBURETOR. Various types of carburetors have been used. Refer to the appropriate following section for carburetor service.

Walbro WA. Some engines are equipped with a Walbro WA diaphragm-type carburetor. Initial adjustment of idle mixture screw (18—Fig. JD101) is one turn out from a lightly seated position. Initial adjustment of high-speed mixture screw (17) is 1¼ turns out. Final adjustments are performed with trimmer line at recommended length or blade installed. Engine must be at operating temperature and running. Adjust idle speed screw to approximately 3000 rpm (trimmer head or blade should not rotate on models with a clutch). Adjust idle mixture screw so engine runs at maximum idle speed and accelerates without hesitation. Readjust idle speed. Operate unit at full throttle (no-load) and adjust high-speed mixture screw to obtain maximum engine rpm, then turn counterclockwise until engine just starts to four-cycle.

When overhauling carburetor, refer to exploded view in Fig. JD101. Examine fuel inlet valve (7) and seat. Inlet valve is renewable, but carburetor body must be renewed if seat is excessively worn or damaged. Inspect mixture screws and seats. Renew carburetor body if seats are excessively worn or damaged. Clean fuel screen (24). Inspect diaphragms (2 and 26) for tears and other damage.

Check metering lever height as shown in Fig. JD102 using Walbro tool 500-13. Metering lever should just touch leg on tool. Bend lever to obtain correct lever height.

Walbro WY and WYL. Some engines may be equipped with a Walbro WY or WYL carburetor. This is a diaphragm-type carburetor that uses a barrel-type throttle rather than a throttle plate.

Idle fuel for the carburetor flows up into the throttle barrel where it is fed into the air stream. On some models, the idle fuel flow can be adjusted by turning an idle limiter plate (P—Fig. JD103). Initial setting is in center notch. Rotating the plate clockwise will lean the idle mixture.

Inside the idle limiter plate is an idle mixture needle (N—Fig. JD104) that is preset at the factory. If removed, use the following procedure to determine correct position. Back out needle (N) until unscrewed, then screw in needle five turns on Model WY or 15 turns on Model WYL. Rotate idle mixture plate (P—Fig. JD103) to center notch. Run engine until normal operating temperature is attained. Adjust idle speed screw (I) to approximately 3000 rpm (trimmer head or blade should not rotate on models with a clutch). Rotate idle mixture needle (N—Fig. JD104) and obtain highest rpm (turning needle clockwise leans the mixture), then turn needle ⅛ turn counterclockwise. Readjust idle speed screw. Note that idle mixture screw and needle are available only as an assembly with throttle barrel.

The high-speed mixture is controlled by a removable fixed jet (11—Fig. JD105).

To overhaul carburetor, refer to exploded view in Fig. JD105 and note the following: On models with a plastic body, clean only with solvents approved for use with plastic. Do not use wires or drills to clean orifices. Do not disassemble throttle barrel assembly. Examine fuel inlet valve and seat. Inlet valve (18) is renewable, but fuel pump body (17) must be renewed if seat is excessively worn or damaged. Clean fuel screen. Inspect diaphragms for tears and other damage.

When installing plates and gaskets (12 through 15) note that tabs (T) on ends

will "stair step" when correctly installed. Metering lever (Fig. JD106) should be 1.5 mm (0.059 in.) below carburetor body gasket surface. To ad-

just metering lever height (H), bend the metering lever while taking care not to force inlet valve against its seat.

Zama C1U. Refer to Fig. JD107 for an exploded view of the Zama C1U carburetor used on some engines.

Initial setting of idle mixture screw (14) and high-speed mixture screw (12) is $1\frac{1}{8}$ turns out from a lightly seated position. Final adjustment is performed with engine at normal operating temperature. Before final adjustment, trimmer line should be at desired length or blade installed. Adjust idle speed screw to approximately 3000 rpm (trimmer head or blade should not rotate on

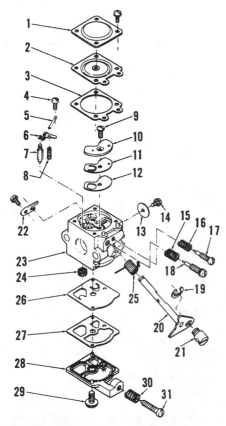

Fig. JD101—Exploded view of Walbro WA carburetor.

1. Cover
2. Metering diaphragm
3. Gasket
4. Metering lever screw
5. Metering lever pin
6. Metering lever
7. Fuel inlet valve
8. Metering lever spring
9. Circuit plate screw
10. Circuit plate
11. Check valve
12. Gasket
13. Throttle valve
14. Shutter screw
15. Spring
16. Spring
17. High-speed mixture needle
18. Idle mixture needle
19. "E" clip
20. Throttle shaft
21. Swivel
22. Throttle shaft clip
23. Body
24. Inlet screen
25. Return spring
26. Fuel pump diaphragm
27. Gasket
28. Cover
29. Cover screw
30. Spring
31. Idle speed screw

Fig. JD102—Metering lever should just touch leg of Walbro tool 500-13. Bend lever to obtain correct lever height.

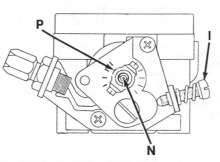

Fig. JD103—On Walbro WY or WYL carburetor, idle speed screw is located at (I), idle limiter plate is located at (P) and idle mixture needle is located at (N). A plug covers the idle mixture needle.

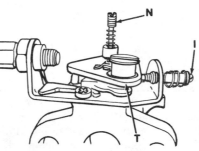

Fig. JD104—View of idle mixture needle (N) used on Walbro WY and WYL carburetor.

Fig. JD105—Exploded view of Walbro WY carburetor. Model WYL is similar.

1. Bracket
2. Spring
3. Idle speed screw
4. Swivel
5. Washer
6. Throttle barrel assy.
7. "E" ring
8. Sleeve
9. "O" ring
10. "O" ring
11. Main jet
12. Gasket
13. Fuel pump diaphragm
14. Fuel pump plate
15. Gasket
16. Fuel screen
17. Fuel pump body
18. Fuel inlet valve
19. Spring
20. Pin
21. Metering lever
22. Gasket
23. Metering diaphragm
24. Plate
25. Primer bulb
26. Cover

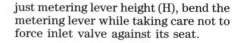

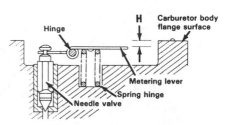

Fig. JD106—Metering lever height (H) must be set on diaphragm-type carburetors. Refer to text for specified height.

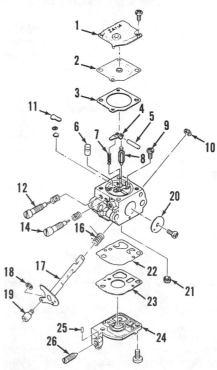

Fig. JD107—Exploded view of Zama C1U carburetor.

1. Cover
2. Metering diaphragm
3. Gasket
4. Metering lever
5. Pin
6. Nozzle
7. Spring
8. Fuel inlet valve
9. Screw
10. "E" ring
11. Welch plug
12. High-speed mixture screw
13. (not listed)
14. Idle mixture screw
16. Spring
17. Throttle shaft
18. "E" ring
19. Swivel
20. Throttle plate
21. Fuel inlet screen
22. Fuel pump diaphragm
23. Gasket
24. Cover
25. Pin
26. Idle speed screw

Illustrations for Fig. JD101, Fig. JD102, Fig. JD103, Fig. JD104, Fig. JD105, Fig. JD106 and Fig. JD107 reproduced by permission of Deere & Company. Copyright Deere & Company.

models with a clutch). Adjust idle mixture screw (14) so engine idles smoothly and accelerates cleanly without hesitation. Operate unit at full throttle (no-load) and adjust high-speed mixture screw (12) to obtain maximum engine rpm, then turn counterclockwise until engine just starts to four-cycle.

Carburetor disassembly and reassembly is evident after inspection of carburetor and referral to Fig. JD107. Clean and inspect all components. Clean fuel channels using compressed air; do not use wires or drills to clean orifices. Exercise care when removing Welch plug (11). To remove plug, pierce toward the end of the "tail" portion with a suitable punch, but do not insert punch deeply as underlying body metal may be damaged. Apply sealant to new plug. Inspect diaphragms (2 and 22) for defects that may affect operation. Examine fuel inlet valve (8) and seat. Inlet valve is renewable, but carburetor body must be renewed if seat is damaged or excessively worn. Discard carburetor body if mixture screw seats are damaged or excessively worn. Clean fuel screen.

To reassemble carburetor, reverse disassembly procedure. Clearance (C—Fig. JD108) between metering lever and a straightedge placed across gasket surface of carburetor body should be 0-0.3 mm (0-0.012 in.). Bend metering lever as needed, being careful not to force inlet needle onto the seat.

IGNITION SYSTEM. The engine is equipped with an electronic ignition system. On Model 450 and early Model 250 and 350 engines, the ignition module and ignition coil are separate. On all other engines, the ignition module and coil are one piece.

Ignition system performance is considered satisfactory if a spark will jump across a 3 mm (1/8 in.) electrode gap on a test spark plug. If no spark is produced, check on/off switch, wiring and

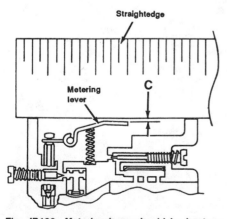

Fig. JD108—Metering lever should be bent so height (C) is 0-0.3 mm (0.000-0.012 in.) on Zama CU1 carburetor.

Illustration for Fig. JD108 reproduced by permission of Deere & Company. Copyright Deere & Company.

ignition module air gap. Ignition module air gap should be 0.2-0.3 mm (0.008-0.012 in.) on Models 250 and 350 and 0.3-0.4 mm (0.012-0.016 in.) on all other models. If switch, wiring and module air gap are satisfactory but spark is not present, refer to REPAIRS section and check service specifications.

REPAIRS

COMPRESSION PRESSURE. For optimum performance, cylinder compression pressure should be 586 kPa (85 psi) on Model 250 prior to serial number 030101, 689 kPa (100 psi) on Models 350 and 450, or 540 kPa (78 psi) on all other models.

TIGHTENING TORQUES. Recommended tightening torques are as follows:

Carburetor . . . . 4 N·m
(35 in.-lbs.)
Clutch hub:
210, 240 & 260 . . . . 19 N·m
(168 in.-lbs.)
250 before
ser. no. 030101 . . . . 13.6-15.8 N·m
(121-140 in.-lbs.)
450 . . . . 3.4-4.5 N·m
(30-40 in.-lbs.)
Clutch flange
450 . . . . 40-44 N·m
(30-32 ft.-lbs.)
Clutch shoes:
220 . . . . 7.8-9.7 N·m
(69-86 in.-lbs.)
250 after
ser. no. 030100 . . . . 7.8-9.7 N·m
(69-86 in.-lbs.)
300 . . . . 4.9-5.8 N·m
(43-51 in.-lbs.)
Crankcase . . . . 3.6 N·m
(32 in.-lbs.)
Cylinder:
110, 220,
250 & 300 . . . . 5.9 N·m
(52 in.-lbs.)
210, 240,
260 & 350 . . . . 3.9 N·m
(35 in.-lbs.)
450 . . . . 7.4-8.5 N·m
(65-75 in.-lbs.)
Flywheel:
110 & 220 . . . . 18 N·m
(160 in.-lbs.)
250 after
ser. no. 030100 . . . . 18 N·m
(160 in.-lbs.)
300 . . . . 10.7-12.7 N·m
(95-112 in.-lbs.)
Ignition module:
110, 210,
240 & 260 . . . . 2 N·m
(18 in.-lbs.)
220 & 300 . . . . 3.6 N·m
(32 in.-lbs.)

250 before
ser. no. 030101 . . . . 2.2 N·m
(19 in.-lbs.)
250 after
ser. no. 030100 . . . . 3.6 N·m
(32 in.-lbs.)
350 & 450 . . . . 2.2 N·m
(19 in.-lbs.)
Spark plug . . . . 16 N·m
(142 in.-lbs.)

IGNITION. When checking for faulty ignition components, the ignition module on Model 450 must be replaced with a module known to be good. The ignition module on other models can be tested by connecting an ohmmeter to the stop switch lead and ground. Module is good if ohmmeter reading is within 10 percent of following specification:

110 . . . . 1.0-1.5 ohms
210 . . . . 1.0-2.0 ohms
240 & 260 . . . . 1.5-2.5 ohms
220 & 300 . . . . 160-240 ohms
250 . . . . 110-220 ohms
350 . . . . 70-132 ohms

To check the ignition coil on models so equipped, refer to following resistance specifications (values are in ohms):

	Primary	Secondary
250	0.0-0.2	1500-3000
350	0.0-0.2	500-1500
450	0.0-0.22	1350-3300

PISTON, PIN AND RINGS. To remove piston (4—Fig. JD109, JD110, JD111 or JD112), remove cooling shroud and recoil starter. Remove gear case or drive shaft assembly. Remove spark plug and insert a piece of rope into spark plug hole to stop crankshaft from turning. Remove clutch assembly and flywheel nut. Use a suitable puller to remove flywheel. Remove carburetor, muffler and ignition coil. Remove cylinder mounting screws and pull cylinder off piston. Remove piston pin retaining rings, push out piston pin and separate piston from connecting rod. When separating piston from connecting rod on Models 110, 210, 240 and 260 (Fig. JD109), and Model 250 before serial number 030101 (Fig. JD111), note that thrust washers (8) will be loose when pin is removed.

Maximum allowable piston ring end gap is 0.5 mm (0.020 in.). Maximum allowable piston ring side clearance is 0.1 mm (0.004 in.). Piston and rings are available in standard size only.

Standard piston pin diameter is 8 mm (.0315 in.) on Models 220, 250 and 300, and 10 mm (0.394 in.) on Models 350 and 450. Maximum allowable pin-to-piston bore clearance is 0.03 mm (0.0012 in.) on all models.

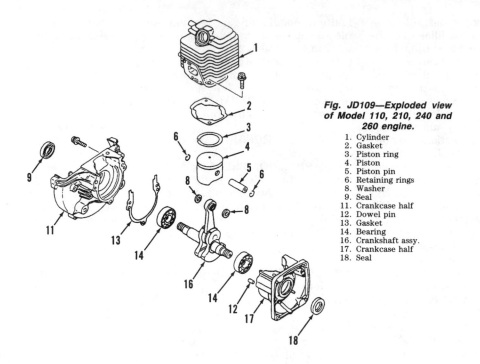

Fig. JD109—Exploded view of Model 110, 210, 240 and 260 engine.

1. Cylinder
2. Gasket
3. Piston ring
4. Piston
5. Piston pin
6. Retaining rings
8. Washer
9. Seal
11. Crankcase half
12. Dowel pin
13. Gasket
14. Bearing
16. Crankshaft assy.
17. Crankcase half
18. Seal

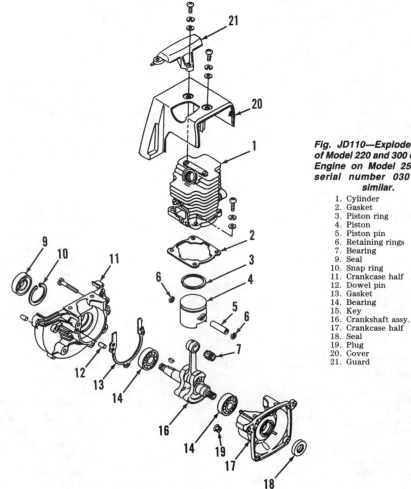

Fig. JD110—Exploded view of Model 220 and 300 engine. Engine on Model 250 after serial number 030100 is similar.

1. Cylinder
2. Gasket
3. Piston ring
4. Piston
5. Piston pin
6. Retaining rings
7. Bearing
9. Seal
10. Snap ring
11. Crankcase half
12. Dowel pin
13. Gasket
14. Bearing
15. Key
16. Crankshaft assy.
17. Crankcase half
18. Seal
19. Plug
20. Cover
21. Guard

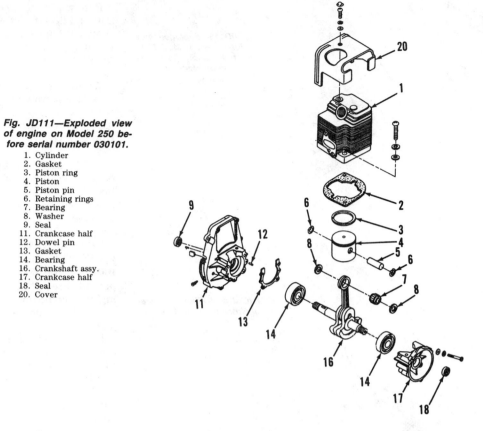

Fig. JD111—Exploded view of engine on Model 250 before serial number 030101.

1. Cylinder
2. Gasket
3. Piston ring
4. Piston
5. Piston pin
6. Retaining rings
7. Bearing
8. Washer
9. Seal
11. Crankcase half
12. Dowel pin
13. Gasket
14. Bearing
16. Crankshaft assy.
17. Crankcase half
18. Seal
20. Cover

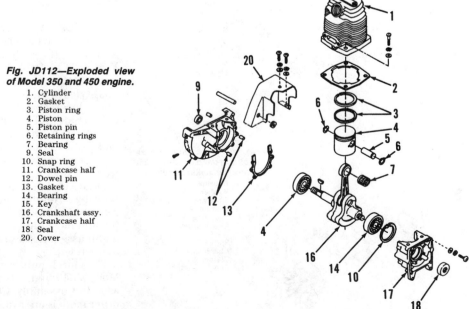

Fig. JD112—Exploded view of Model 350 and 450 engine.

1. Cylinder
2. Gasket
3. Piston ring
4. Piston
5. Piston pin
6. Retaining rings
7. Bearing
9. Seal
10. Snap ring
11. Crankcase half
12. Dowel pin
13. Gasket
14. Bearing
15. Key
16. Crankshaft assy.
17. Crankcase half
18. Seal
20. Cover

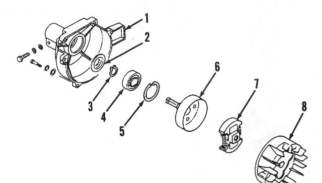

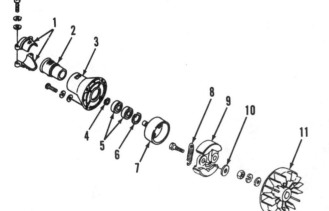

Renew piston pin on Models 110, 210, 240 and 260 if piston pin is worn more than 0.013 mm (0.0005 in.). Maximum allowable piston pin clearance in piston on Models 110, 210, 240 and 260 is 0.03 mm (0.0012 in.).

When installing piston, position piston on rod so arrow on piston crown is toward exhaust port. Be sure piston ring gap properly surrounds locating pin in ring groove.

CYLINDER. The cylinder is available only in standard size and cannot be bored. The cylinder bore is plated. Inspect cylinder for excessive wear and damage.

CRANKSHAFT, ROD AND CRANKCASE. The crankshaft and connecting rod are a unit assembly; individual components are not available. The connecting rod small end is equipped with a renewable needle bearing on some models.

To remove crankshaft and connecting rod assembly, remove cylinder and piston as previously outlined. Remove crankcase screws and separate crankcase halves. Some models are equipped with a snap ring next to one of the main bearings. If main bearings remain in crankcase, warm crankcase to ease bearing removal. If main bearings remain on crankshaft, use a suitable puller or press to remove main bearings. Warm crankcase before installing bearing.

Renew crankshaft assembly if rod big end side clearance exceeds 0.45 mm (0.018 in.) on Model 300 or 0.4 mm (0.016 in.) on all other models. Maximum allowable crankshaft runout is 0.05 mm (0.002 in.) measured at crankshaft ends with crankshaft supported at main bearings.

CLUTCH. Most engines used on trimmers or brush cutters are equipped with a two- or three-shoe clutch. Refer to Figs. JD113, JD114, JD115, JD116, JD117 and JD118 for exploded views of various styles of clutches. The shoe assembly is located at the drive end of the crankshaft and mounted on a flange or on the back side of the flywheel. The clutch drum rides in the drive housing.

To remove the clutch drum, reach through slot and detach snap ring, then separate clutch drum and bearing from housing. Heating housing will ease removal. On Model 210, the drum assembly and its shroud are available only as a unit assembly; disassembly is not recommended.

The clutch hub, springs and shoes on Models 240 and 260 are available only as a unit assembly. Clutch shoes on all other models are available only as a set.

Fig. JD113—Exploded view of clutch used on Model 240. Clutch assembly (7) is also used on Model 210.

1. Housing
2. Washer
3. Snap ring
4. Bearing
5. Snap ring
6. Clutch drum
7. Clutch assy.
8. Flywheel

Fig. JD114—Exploded view of clutch used on Model 260.

1. Collar
2. Vibration isolator
3. Housing
4. Snap ring
5. Bearings
6. Snap ring
7. Clutch drum
8. Clutch assy.
9. Flywheel

Fig. JD115—Exploded view of clutch used on Model 250 after serial number 030100 and Model 300. Model 220 is similar but is equipped with one bearing (5).

1. Collar
2. Vibration isolator
3. Housing
4. Snap ring
5. Bearings
6. Snap ring
7. Clutch drum
8. Clutch spring
9. Clutch shoe
10. Washer
11. Flywheel

Fig. JD116—Exploded view of clutch used on Model 250 before serial number 030101.

1. Housing
2. Washer
3. Snap ring
4. Bearing
5. Snap ring
6. Clutch drum
7. Hub
8. Spring
9. Clutch shoe
10. Washer
11. Flywheel

Maximum allowable clutch drum inside diameter is 51.5 mm (2.028 in.) for Models 210, 240, 250 and 260, 55.5 mm (2.185 in.) for Models 220 and 300, 63.5 mm (2.500 in.) for Model 350, and 73.5 mm (2.894 in.) for Model 450.

On Model 450, tighten clutch flange (10—Fig. JD118) to 40-44 N·m (30-32 ft.-lbs.). Install clutch so recessed portion of bore in hub (9) is toward flange (10). Tighten screws securing clutch hub and shoe assembly to flange to 3.4-4.5 N·m (30-40 in.-lbs.).

On Model 260 and early Model 250, install washer (2—Fig. JD113 or JD116) so concave side is toward bearing.

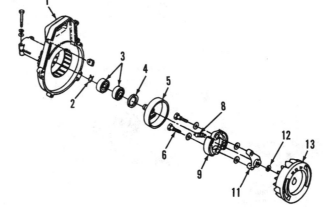

Fig. JD117—Exploded view of clutch used on Model 350.

1. Housing
2. Snap ring
3. Bearings
4. Snap ring
5. Clutch drum
6. Pivot screw
7. Washer
8. Spring
9. Clutch shoe
10. Washer
11. Hub
12. Lockwasher
13. Flywheel

Fig. JD118—Exploded view of clutch used on Model 450.

1. Housing
2. Snap ring
3. Bearings
4. Snap ring
5. Clutch drum
6. Plate
7. Spring
8. Clutch shoe
9. Hub
10. Flange
11. Washer
12. Flywheel

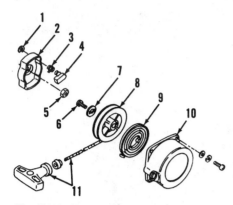

Fig. JD119—Exploded view of rewind starter used on Models 110, 220, 240, 260, 300 and Model 250 after serial number 030100.

1. "E" ring
2. Pawl carrier
3. Spring
4. Pawl
5. Nut
6. Screw
7. Washer
8. Pulley
9. Rewind spring
10. Starter housing
11. Rope & handle

REWIND STARTER. Refer to Figs. JD119, JD120 and JD121 for exploded views of typical starters. To disassemble starter, detach starter housing from engine. Remove rope handle and allow rope to wind into starter. Unscrew center screw and remove rope pulley. Wear appropriate safety eyewear and gloves before detaching rewind spring from housing as spring may uncoil uncontrolled.

On models with removable pawl (4—Fig. JD119), install pawl in hole of pawl carrier (2). When installing pawl carrier assembly on crankshaft, apply Loctite to threads of pawl carrier. Tighten pawl carrier to 18 N·m (160 in.-lbs.) on Models 350 and 450, or tighten to 9 N·m (80 in.-lbs.) on all other models. On all models except 350 and 450, tighten pawl carrier retaining nut to 18 N·m (160 in.-lbs.).

To assemble starter, lubricate center post of housing and spring side with light grease. Rewind spring is installed with coils wrapped in a counterclockwise direction from outer end. Rope length is 850 mm (33.5 in.). Assemble starter while passing rope through housing rope outlet and attach rope handle to rope. Apply Loctite to center retaining screw. To place tension on starter rope, pull rope out of housing. Engage rope in notch on pulley and turn pulley counterclockwise three turns. Hold pulley and disengage rope from pulley notch. Release pulley and allow rope to wind on pulley. Check starter operation. Rope handle should be held against housing by spring tension, but it must be possible to rotate pulley at least ½ turn against spring tension when rope is pulled out fully.

Fig. JD120—Exploded view of rewind starter used on Model 250 before serial number 030101.

1. Gasket
2. Pawl carrier
3. Nut
4. Screw
5. Lockwasher
6. Washer
7. Pulley
8. Rewind spring
9. Starter housing
10. Rope & handle

Fig. JD121—Exploded view of rewind starter used on Model 450.

1. Pawl carrier
2. Screw
3. Lockwasher
4. Washer
5. Flange
6. Retainer
7. Pulley
8. Plate
9. Rewind spring
10. Plate
11. Bushing
12. Starter housing
13. Rope & handle

DEERE

ENGINE SERVICE

Model	Bore	Stroke	Displacement
2E	30 mm	30 mm	21.2 cc
	(1.18 in.)	(1.18 in.)	(1.29 cu. in.)
3E	35 mm	32 mm	30.8 cc
	(1.38 in.)	(1.26 in.)	(1.88 cu. in.)
4E	38 mm	35 mm	39.7 cc
	(1.50 in.)	(1.38 in.)	(2.42 cu. in.)
5E	40 mm	35 mm	44 cc
	(1.57 in.)	(1.38 in.)	(2.68 cu. in.)

ENGINE INFORMATION

These two-stroke, air-cooled engines are used on Deere blowers. Refer to Deere equipment sections for a list of engines used on other Deere models.

MAINTENANCE

LUBRICATION. Engine lubrication is obtained by mixing gasoline with an oil designed for two-stroke, air-cooled engines. Refer to BLOWER service section for manufacturer's recommended fuel:oil mixture ratio.

SPARK PLUG. Recommended spark plug for Model 4E engine is Champion CJ8 or equivalent. Recommended spark plug for all other models is Champion CJ7Y, or equivalent. Specified electrode gap is 0.6-0.7 mm (0.024-0.028 in.). Tighten spark plug to 16 N·m (142 in.-lbs.).

CARBURETOR. All models are equipped with a variation of the Walbro WA diaphragm-type carburetor. Refer to Figs. JD201 and JD202.

Initial adjustment of idle mixture screw (18—Figs. JD201 or JD202) is ⅞ turn out from a lightly seated position on Model 5E or 1¼ turns out on all other models. Initial adjustment of high-speed mixture screw (17) is 1¼ turns out on all models. Final adjustments are performed with engine at operating temperature and running. Adjust idle speed screw to approximately 2600 rpm. Adjust idle mixture screw so engine runs

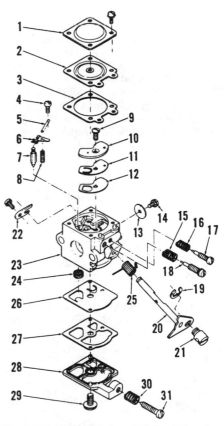

Fig. JD202—Exploded view of Walbro WA carburetor used on Model 4E.

1. Cover		
2. Metering diaphragm		
3. Gasket		
4. Screw	18. Idle mixture needle
5. Pin	19. "E" ring
6. Metering lever	20. Throttle shaft
7. Fuel inlet valve	21. Swivel
8. Spring	22. Throttle shaft clip
9. Screw	23. Carburetor body
10. Circuit plate	24. Screen
11. Check valve	25. Spring
12. Gasket	26. Fuel pump
13. Throttle plate	diaphragm
14. Screw	27. Gasket
15. Spring	28. Cover
16. Spring	29. Screw
17. High-speed mixture	30. Spring
needle	31. Idle speed screw

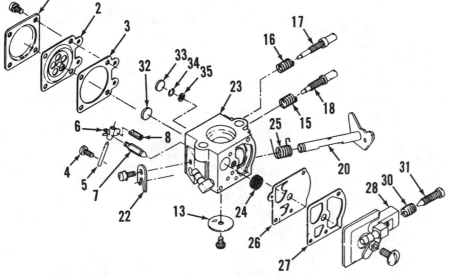

Fig. JD201—Exploded view of Walbro WA carburetor used on Models 2E, 3E and 5E.

1. Cover		
2. Metering diaphragm		
3. Gasket	13. Throttle valve	22. Retainer clip
4. Screw	15. Spring	24. Inlet screen
5. Pin	16. Spring	25. Spring
6. Metering lever	17. High-speed mixture	26. Fuel pump
7. Fuel inlet valve	needle	diaphragm
8. Metering lever	18. Idle mixture needle	27. Gasket
spring	20. Throttle shaft	28. Cover
		30. Spring
		31. Idle speed screw
		32. Plug
		33. Plug
		34. Snap ring
		35. Screen

at maximum idle speed and accelerates without hesitation. Readjust idle speed. Operate unit at full throttle (no-load) and adjust high-speed mixture screw to obtain maximum engine rpm, then turn counterclockwise until engine just starts to four-cycle.

When overhauling carburetor, refer to exploded view in Figs. JD201 or JD202. Clean carburetor using suitable solvent and compressed air. Do not use drills or wires to clean orifices. Examine fuel inlet valve and seat. Inlet valve is renewable, but carburetor body must be renewed if seat is excessively worn or damaged. Inspect mixture screws and seats. Renew carburetor body if seats are excessively worn or damaged. Clean fuel screen. Inspect diaphragms for tears and other damage.

Check metering lever height as shown in Fig. JD203 using Walbro tool 500-13. Metering lever should just touch leg on tool. Bend lever to obtain correct lever height.

IGNITION SYSTEM. The engine is equipped with an electronic ignition system that uses a separate ignition module and ignition coil. Ignition system performance is considered satisfactory if a spark will jump across a 3 mm (1/8 in.) electrode gap on a test spark plug. If no spark is produced, check on/off switch, wiring and ignition module air gap. Ignition module air gap should be 0.3-0.4 mm (0.012-0.016 in.). If switch, wiring and module air gap are satisfactory, but spark is not present, refer to REPAIRS section and check service specifications.

REPAIRS

COMPRESSION PRESSURE. For optimum performance, cylinder compression pressure should be 689 kPa (100 psi) on Models 2E and 5E, 640 kPa (93 psi) on Model 3E, or 586 kPa (85 psi) on Model 4E.

TIGHTENING TORQUES. Recommended tightening torques are as follows:

Carburetor . . . . .4 N·m
(35 in.-lbs.)
Crankcase
4E .9-11 N·m
(80-97 in.-lbs.)
All other models . . . . .3.6 N·m
(32 in.-lbs.)
Cylinder:
4E .9-11 N·m
(80-97 in.-lbs.)
All other models . . . . .7.9 N·m
(70 in.-lbs.)
Fan:
2E .15-20 N·m
(133-177 in.-lbs.)
3E & 5E . . . . .30 N·m
(22 ft.-lbs.)
4E .3.5-4.0 N·m
(31-35 in.-lbs.)
Flywheel:
2E .12-14 N·m
(106-124 in.-lbs.)
4E .39.5-44 N·m
(29-32 ft.-lbs.)
Ignition module:
2E, 3E & 5E . . . . .2 N·m
(18 in.-lbs.)
4E .3.5-4.0 N·m
(31-35 in.-lbs.)
Spark plug . . . . .16 N·m
(142 in.-lbs.)
Starter pawl plate:
3E & 5E . . . . .18 N·m
(159 in.-lbs.)
4E .20-24 N·m
(177-212 in.-lbs.)

IGNITION. When checking for faulty ignition components, the ignition module must be replaced with a module known to be good. To check the ignition coil, refer to following resistance specifications (values are in ohms). Primary resistance is not measured on Model 2E, substitute a known good coil if faulty ignition coil is suspected.

	Primary	Secondary
2E	. . . .	1500-3000
3E & 5E	0.0-0.5	1500-3000
4E	0.0-0.2	500-1500

PISTON, PIN AND RINGS. Refer to Fig. JD204, Fig. JD205 or Fig. JD206 for exploded view of engine assembly. Piston and rings are available in standard size only. To remove and install piston, refer to CRANKSHAFT, CONNECTING ROD AND CRANKCASE section.

Use a feeler gage to measure piston ring side clearance with new ring installed in piston ring groove. Maximum allowable piston ring side clearance is 0.1 mm (0.004 in.). Renew piston if clearance is excessive.

Renew piston pin if piston pin is worn more than 0.013 mm (0.0005 in.). Maximum allowable piston pin clearance is 0.03 mm (0.001 in.).

When installing piston, position piston on rod so arrow on piston crown is toward exhaust port. Be sure piston ring gap properly surrounds locating pin in ring groove.

CYLINDER. The cylinder is available only in standard size and cannot be bored. The cylinder bore is plated. Inspect cylinder for excessive wear and damage.

CRANKSHAFT, CONNECTING ROD AND CRANKCASE. Refer to Fig. JD204, Fig. JD205 or Fig. JD206 for exploded view of engine assembly. The crankshaft and connecting rod are a unit assembly; individual components are not available. The connecting rod small end is equipped with a renewable needle bearing on some models.

To remove crankshaft and connecting rod, unbolt and remove recoil starter, engine cover (if used), fuel tank, air cleaner, carburetor, muffler and ignition coil. Remove cylinder cover and backpack frame. Remove spark plug and

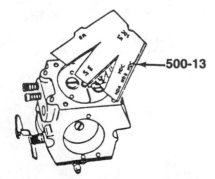

Fig. JD203—Metering lever should just touch leg of Walbro tool 500-13. Bend lever to obtain correct lever height.

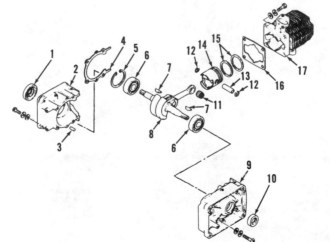

Fig. JD204—Exploded view of Model 2E engine.

1. Seal
2. Crankcase half
3. Dowel pin
4. Gasket
5. Snap ring
6. Bearing
7. Key
8. Crankshaft & connecting rod assy.
9. Crankcase half
10. Seal
11. Bearing
12. Snap ring
13. Piston pin
14. Piston
15. Piston rings
16. Gasket
17. Cylinder

place the end of a rope into cylinder to prevent crankshaft from turning. Remove nuts retaining fan and flywheel and remove both from crankshaft. Unbolt and separate crankcase from blower housing. Scribe a line on the cylinder base and one of the crankcase halves to ensure correct reassembly, then unbolt and remove cylinder from crankcase. Remove piston pin retaining rings, then push piston pin out of piston and connecting rod. If piston pin cannot be removed by hand, use JDZ-23 piston pin tool, or similar tool, to push pin out of piston. Remove crankcase screws and separate crankcase halves by tapping end of crankshaft with a rubber mallet.

Some models are equipped with a snap ring next to one of the main bearings. The main bearings usually stay in the crankcase halves. If main bearings remain on crankshaft, use a suitable puller or press to remove main bearings.

Renew crankshaft assembly if rod big end side clearance exceeds 0.4 mm (0.016 in.). Maximum allowable crankshaft runout is 0.05 mm (0.002 in.) measured at crankshaft ends with crankshaft supported at main bearings.

When installing new main bearings, do not use any type of sealant between outer race of bearing and crankcase bore. Lubricate all parts with 2-cycle oil during assembly. Be sure that crankshaft rotates freely after crankcase screws are tightened. Piston must be installed with arrow on crown pointing toward exhaust side of engine. Be sure that piston ring end gaps are positioned around pins in piston ring groove. Compress piston rings with fingertips and slide cylinder over piston. Do not rotate cylinder when placing it over piston as ring gap may become disengaged from locating pin and damage cylinder. Adjust air gap between ignition module laminations and flywheel magnets to 0.3-0.4 mm (0.012-0.016 in.). Complete reassembly by reversing disassembly procedure.

REWIND STARTER. Model 2E. Refer to Fig. JD207 for an exploded view of starter. To disassemble starter, detach starter housing from engine. Remove rope handle and allow rope to wind into starter. Unscrew center screw (6) and remove rope pulley (10). Wear appropriate safety eyewear and gloves before detaching rewind spring from housing as spring may uncoil uncontrolled.

Install pawl assemblies as shown in Fig. JD208. Apply Loctite to threads of pawl screws and tighten to 3.4-4.5 N·m (30-40 in.-lbs.).

To assemble starter, lubricate center post of housing and spring side with light grease. Rewind spring is installed with coils wrapped in a counterclock-

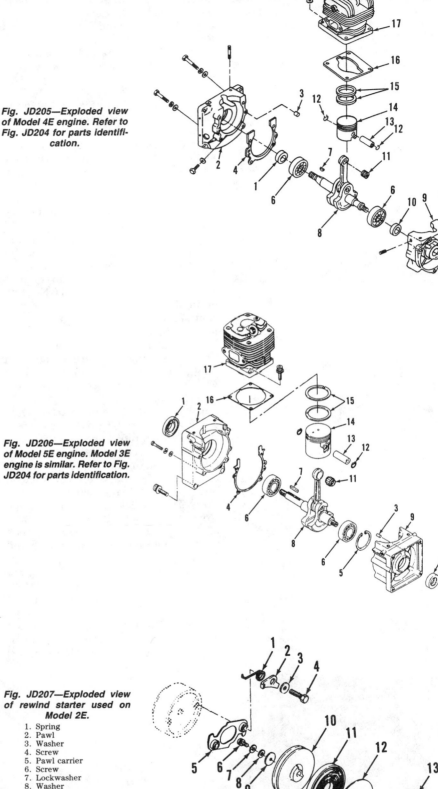

Fig. JD205—Exploded view of Model 4E engine. Refer to Fig. JD204 for parts identification.

Fig. JD206—Exploded view of Model 5E engine. Model 3E engine is similar. Refer to Fig. JD204 for parts identification.

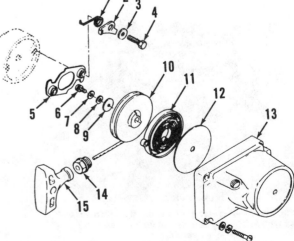

Fig. JD207—Exploded view of rewind starter used on Model 2E.

1. Spring
2. Pawl
3. Washer
4. Screw
5. Pawl carrier
6. Screw
7. Lockwasher
8. Washer
9. Washer
10. Pulley
11. Rewind spring
12. Plate
13. Starter housing
14. Rope guide
15. Rope handle

wise direction from outer end. Rope length is 850 mm (33.5 in.). Assemble starter while passing rope through housing rope outlet and attach rope handle to rope. Apply Loctite to center retaining screw. To place tension on starter rope, pull rope out of housing. Engage rope in notch on pulley and turn pulley counterclockwise three turns. Hold pul-

Fig. JD208—Assemble pawls (P) on Model 2E as shown.

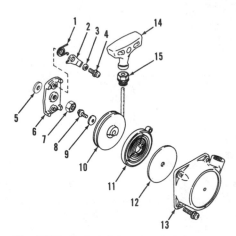

Fig. JD209—Exploded view of rewind starter used on Model 3E.

1. Spring
2. Pawl
3. Spacer
4. Screw
5. Washer
6. Pawl carrier
7. Nut
8. Screw
9. Washer
10. Pulley
11. Rewind spring
12. Plate
13. Starter housing
14. Rope guide
15. Rope handle

Fig. JD210—Assemble pawls on Model 3E as shown. Nut (7) and pawl carrier (6) have left-hand threads.

ley and disengage rope from pulley notch. Release pulley and allow rope to wind on pulley. Check starter operation. Rope handle should be held against housing by spring tension, but it must be possible to rotate pulley at least ½ turn against spring tension when rope is pulled out fully.

Model 3E. Refer to Fig. JD209 for an exploded view of starter. To disassemble starter, detach starter housing (13) from engine. Remove rope handle and allow rope to wind into starter. Unscrew center screw (8) and remove rope pulley (10). Wear appropriate safety eyewear and gloves before detaching rewind spring from housing as spring may uncoil uncontrolled.

Pawl plate (6—Fig. JD209) and retaining nut (7) have left-hand threads. Install pawl assemblies (2) as shown in Fig. JD210. Apply Loctite to threads of pawl screws (4) and tighten to 3.5-4.5 N·m (30-40 in.-lbs.). Tighten pawl plate to 8-10 N·m (71-88 in.-lbs.). Tighten retaining nut to 16-20 N·m (142-177 in.-lbs.).

To assemble starter, lubricate center post of housing and spring side with light grease. Rewind spring is installed with coils wrapped in a clockwise direction from outer end. Rope length is 850 mm (33.5 in.). Assemble starter while passing rope through housing rope outlet and attach rope handle to rope. Apply Loctite to center retaining screw. To place tension on starter rope, pull rope out of housing. Engage rope in notch on pulley and turn pulley clockwise three turns. Hold pulley and disengage rope from pulley notch. Release pulley and allow rope to wind on pulley. Check starter operation. Rope handle should be held against housing by spring tension, but it must be possible to rotate pulley at least ½ turn against spring tension when rope is pulled out fully.

Model 4E. Refer to Fig. JD211 for an exploded view of starter. To disassemble starter, detach starter housing (12)

from engine. Remove rope handle and allow rope to wind into starter. Unscrew center screw (4) and remove rope pulley (9). Wear appropriate safety eyewear and gloves before detaching rewind spring from housing as spring may uncoil uncontrolled.

To assemble starter, lubricate center post of housing and side of spring with light grease. Rewind spring is installed with coils wrapped in a counterclockwise direction from outer end. Rope length is 950 mm (37.5 in.). Install pawl spring (7—Fig. JD212) on friction plate (5) so short end of spring engages tab (T) on plate. Install pawls (6) in pulley as shown in Fig. JD212. Tighten pawl plate to 8-10 N·m (71-88 in.-lbs.). Position spring (8) over center post of starter housing. Be sure rope is located in notch (N). Install friction plate (5), placing long end of spring (7) into hole (H) in pulley. Apply Loctite to center retaining screw. Turn friction plate to align pawls with openings in friction plate, then install acorn nut (13—Fig. JD211). To place tension on starter rope, pull rope out of housing. Engage rope in notch on pulley and turn pulley counterclockwise three turns. Hold pulley and disengage rope from pulley notch. Release pulley and allow rope to wind on pulley. Check starter operation. Rope handle should be held against housing by spring tension, but it must be possible to rotate pulley at least ½ turn against spring tension when rope is pulled out fully.

Model 5E. Refer to Fig. JD213 for an exploded view of starter. To disassemble starter, detach starter housing from engine. Remove rope handle and allow rope to wind into starter. Unscrew center screw and remove rope pulley. Wear appropriate safety eyewear and gloves before detaching rewind spring from housing as spring may uncoil uncontrolled.

Tighten pawl carrier to 18 N·m (160 in.-lbs.).

To assemble starter, lubricate center post of housing and spring side with

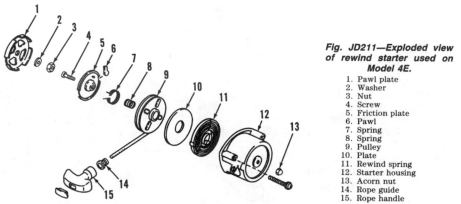

Fig. JD211—Exploded view of rewind starter used on Model 4E.

1. Pawl plate
2. Washer
3. Nut
4. Screw
5. Friction plate
6. Pawl
7. Spring
8. Spring
9. Pulley
10. Plate
11. Rewind spring
12. Starter housing
13. Acorn nut
14. Rope guide
15. Rope handle

light grease. Rewind spring is installed with coils wrapped in a clockwise direction from outer end. Rope length is 850 mm (33.5 in.). Assemble starter while passing rope through housing rope outlet and attach rope handle to rope. Apply Loctite to center retaining screw. To place tension on starter rope, pull rope out of housing. Engage rope in notch on pulley and turn pulley clockwise three turns. Hold pulley and disengage rope from pulley notch. Release pulley and allow rope to wind on pulley. Check starter operation. Rope handle should be held against housing by spring tension, but it must be possible to rotate pulley at least $1/2$ turn against spring tension when rope is pulled out fully.

Fig. JD212—On Model 4E, insert short end of spring (7) in tab (T) on friction plate (5). Note installation of pawls (6) on pulley.

Fig. JD213—Exploded view of rewind starter used on Model 5E.

1. Pawl carrier
2. Screw
3. Lockwasher
4. Washer
5. Washer
6. Flange
7. Retainer
8. Pulley
9. Bushing
10. Plate
11. Rewind spring
12. Plate
13. Starter housing
14. Rope guide
15. Rope handle

ECHO

ENGINE SERVICE

Model	Bore	Stroke	Displacement
SRM-140D, SRM-140DA, GT-140, GT-140A, GT-140B	26 mm (1.024 in.)	26 mm (1.024 in.)	13.8 cc (0.842 cu. in.)
GT-160, GT-160A, GT-160AE	28 mm (1.102 in.)	26 mm (1.024 in.)	16.0 cc (0.976 cu. in.)
SRM-200, SRM-200AE, SRM-200BE, SRM200D, SRM-200DA, SRM-200DB, SRM-200E, SRM-201F, SRM-201FA, SRM-202D, SRM-202DA, SRM-202F, SRM-202FA, SRM-210E, SRM-210AE, GT-200, GT-200A, GT-200B, GT-200BE	32.2 mm (1.268 in.)	26 mm (1.024 in.)	21.2 cc (1.294 cu. in.)
SRM-300, SRM-302ADX	28 mm (1.102 in.)	37 mm (1.457 in.)	30.1 cc (1.837 cu. in.)
SRM-300E, SRM-300E/1, SRM-300AE, SRM-300AE/1	35 mm (1.378 in.)	32 mm (1.260 in.)	30.8 cc (1.880 cu. in.)
SRM-400E, SRM-400AE, SRM-402DE	40 mm (1.575 in.)	32 mm (1.260 in.)	40.2 cc (2.452 cu. in.)

ENGINE INFORMATION

These two-cycle engines are used on Echo grass trimmers, weed trimmers and brush cutters. Engine has a detachable cylinder and two-piece crankcase. Crankshaft and connecting rod are considered an assembly and are not serviced separately. On all models, crankshaft/connecting rod assembly is supported by two ball bearing mains. All modles except Model SRM-202FA use a diaphragm type carburetor which allows engine to be operated in any position. Model SRM-202FA uses a float type carburetor.

MAINTENANCE

SPARK PLUG. Recommended spark plug for all models is a Champion CJ8, or equivalent. Electrode gap is 0.6-0.7 mm (0.024-0.028 in.). Tighten spark plug to specified torque.

CARBURETOR. All engines are equipped with Walbro diaphragm type carburetors except Model SRM-202FA which is equipped with a Keihin float type carburetor. Refer to Fig. EC1 or EC2 for exploded view of carburetors. Refer to appropriate paragraphs for model being serviced.

Walbro Carburetor. Refer to Fig. EC-1 for identification and exploded view of Walbro carburetor.

Initial adjustment of idle mixture (18) and high speed mixture (17) needles from a lightly seated position is 1 turn open for each needle.

Final adjustments are made with trimmer line at recommended length. Engine should be at operating temperature and running. Turn idle speed adjusting screw (31) until engine runs smoothly at 2500-3000 rpm. Adjust low speed needle (18) to obtain consistent idling and smooth acceleration. Readjust idle speed adjusting screw (31) as necessary. Open throttle fully and adjust high speed needle (17) about 1/8 turn counterclockwise from maximum high speed position.

Fig. EC1—Exploded view of Walbro carburetor.
1. Cover
2. Metering diaphragm
3. Gasket
4. Metering lever screw
5. Meter lever pin
6. Metering lever
7. Fuel inlet valve
8. Meter lever spring
9. Circuit plate screw
10. Circuit plate
11. Check valve
12. Gasket
13. Throttle valve
14. Shutter screw
15. Spring
16. Spring
17. High speed mixture needle
18. Idle mixture needle
19. "E" clip
20. Throttle shaft
21. Swivel
22. Throttle shaft clip
23. Body
24. Inlet screen
25. Return spring
26. Fuel pump diaphragm
27. Gasket
28. Cover
29. Cover screw
30. Spring
31. Idle speed screw

Illustrations courtesy Echo Inc.

CAUTION: Do not go any leaner with high speed needle adjustment as it could result in improper lubrication and engine seizure could result.

Fuel inlet lever (6) should be flush with top of circuit plate (Fig. EC4). Carefully bend fuel inlet lever to obtain correct setting.

Keihin Carburetor. Refer to Fig. EC2 for identification and exploded view of Keihin float type carburetor.

To adjust idle speed, engine must be at operating temperature and running. Turn idle speed screw (1) to obtain 2500-3000 rpm idle. Counterclockwise rotation lowers idle speed and clockwise rotation increases idle speed. Screw rotation raises or lowers throttle valve (29).

Standard height of metering lever is 3.05 mm (0.120 in.) measured from top of rim of float chamber as shown in Fig. EC3.

Full load adjustment is obtained by changing position of "E" clip (27—Fig. EC2) on jet needle (28). To increase fuel volume, install clip at lower groove on jet needle. To reduce fuel volume, install "E" clip at higher groove on jet needle. Refer to Fig. EC5.

IGNITION SYSTEM. Engines may be equipped with a magneto type ignition with breaker points and condenser or a CDI (capacitor-discharge) ignition system which requires no regular maintenance and has no breaker points or condensers. Ignition module (CDI) is located outside of flywheel. Refer to appropriate paragraph for model being serviced.

Breaker Point Ignition System. Breaker points may be located behind recoil starter or behind flywheel. Note location of breaker points and refer to following paragraphs for service.

To inspect or service magneto ignition with breaker points and condenser located behind recoil starter and cover, first remove fan cover. Refer to Fig. EC6 and check pole gap between flywheel and ignition coil laminations. Gap should be 0.35-0.40 mm (0.014-0.016 in.). To adjust pole gap, loosen two retaining screws in coil (threads or retaining screws must be treated with Loctite or equivalent), place correct gage between flywheel and coil laminations. Pull coil to flywheel by hand as shown, then tighten screws and remove feeler gage.

Breaker points are accessible after removal of starter case, nut and pawl carrier.

NOTE: Nut and pawl carrier are both left-hand thread.

To adjust point gap and ignition timing, disconnect stop switch wire from stop switch. Connect one lead from a timing tester (Echo 990510-00031) or equivalent to stop switch wire. Ground remaining timing tester lead to engine body. Position flywheel timing mark as shown in Fig. EC7 and set breaker point gap to 0.3-0.4 mm (0.012-0.016 in.). Rotate flywheel and check timing with timing tester. Readjust as necessary.

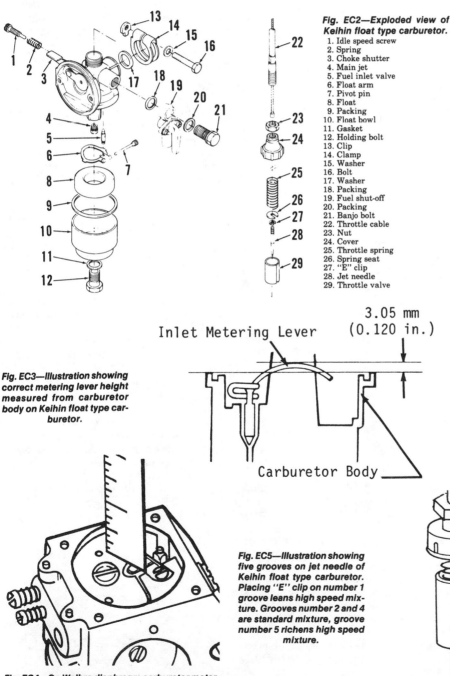

Fig. EC2—Exploded view of Keihin float type carburetor.

1. Idle speed screw
2. Spring
3. Choke shutter
4. Main jet
5. Fuel inlet valve
6. Float arm
7. Pivot pin
8. Float
9. Packing
10. Float bowl
11. Gasket
12. Holding bolt
13. Clip
14. Clamp
15. Washer
16. Bolt
17. Washer
18. Packing
19. Fuel shut-off
20. Packing
21. Banjo bolt
22. Throttle cable
23. Nut
24. Cover
25. Throttle spring
26. Spring seat
27. "E" clip
28. Jet needle
29. Throttle valve

Fig. EC3—Illustration showing correct metering lever height measured from carburetor body on Keihin float type carburetor.

Inlet Metering Lever

3.05 mm (0.120 in.)

Carburetor Body

Fig. EC4—On Walbro diaphragm carburetor metering lever is correctly adjusted when its upper surface is flush with circuit plate.

Fig. EC5—Illustration showing five grooves on jet needle of Keihin float type carburetor. Placing "E" clip on number 1 groove leans high speed mixture. Grooves number 2 and 4 are standard mixture, groove number 5 richens high speed mixture.

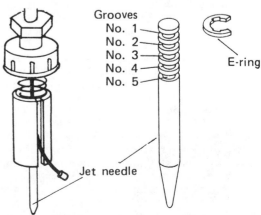

Grooves
No. 1
No. 2
No. 3
No. 4
No. 5

E-ring

Jet needle

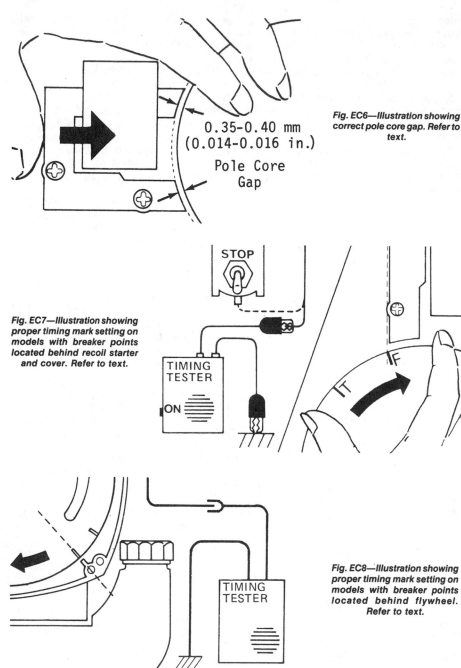

Fig. EC6—Illustration showing correct pole core gap. Refer to text.

0.35-0.40 mm (0.014-0.016 in.)

Pole Core Gap

Fig. EC7—Illustration showing proper timing mark setting on models with breaker points located behind recoil starter and cover. Refer to text.

STOP

TIMING TESTER

ON

IT

F

Fig. EC8—Illustration showing proper timing mark setting on models with breaker points located behind flywheel. Refer to text.

TIMING TESTER

NOTE: Be accurate when setting breaker point gap. A gap greater than 0.4 mm (0.016 in.) will advance timing; a gap less than 0.3 mm (0.012 in.) will retard timing.

With point gap and flywheel correctly set, timing will be 30° BTDC. Tighten flywheel nut to specified torque.

Primary and secondary ignition coil resistance may be checked with an ohmmeter without removing coil.

To check primary coil resistance, connect ohmmeter to disconnected ignition coil primary lead and ground remaining lead to engine. Primary coil resistance should register 0.5-0.8 ohms for Models GT-140A, GT-140B, GT-160 and GT-160A; 0.5-0.6 ohms for Models SRM-200D, SRM-200DA, SRM-200DB, SRM-202DA and SRM-202FA; 0.6-0.8 ohms for Models SRM-140D, SRM-140DA, GTL-140 and GT-200 or 0.5-0.7 ohms for Models SRM-200, SRM-302ADX, GT-200A and GT-200B.

To check secondary coil resistance connect one lead of ohmmeter to spark plug cable and remaining lead to ground on engine. Secondary coil resistance should register 6-9 ohms for Models SRM-200, 7-10 ohms for Models GTL-140 and GT-140A, GT-140B, GT-160 and GT160A; 5-6 ohms for Models SRM-200D, SRM-200DA, SRM-200DB, SRM-202DB, SRM-202DA, SRM-202FA and GT200; 8-10 ohms for Models SRM-140D and SRM-140DA or 8-9.5 for Models SRM-302ADX, GT-200A and GT200B.

CD Ignition System. CD ignition system requires no regular maintenance and has no moving parts except for magnets cast in flywheel.

Ignition timing is fixed at 30° BTDC and clearance between CDI module laminations and flywheel should be 0.3 mm (0.012 in.). To check ignition timing refer to Fig. EC9. If timing is not correct, CDI module must be renewed.

Ignition coil may be checked by connecting one ohmmeter lead to spark plug cable and remaining lead to coil primary

NOTE: Be accurate when setting breaker point gap. A gap greater than 0.4 mm (0.016 in.) will advance timing; a gap less than 0.3 mm (0.012 in.) will retard timing.

With point gap and flywheel correctly set, timing will be 23° BTDC.

To inspect or service magneto and breaker points on models with breaker points and condenser located behind flywheel, first remove starter case. Disconnect wire from stop switch and connect to timing tester (Echo 990510-0031) or equivalent. Ground remaining lead from timing tester to engine body. Position flywheel timing mark as shown in Fig. EC8. If timing is not correct, loosen retaining screw on breaker points

through flywheel slot openings. Squeeze screwdriver in crankcase groove to adjust point gap. Breaker point gap should be 0.3-0.4 mm (0.012-0.016 in.) with flywheel at TDC.

If breaker points require renewal, flywheel must be removed. When installing breaker points note that stop lead (black) from condenser must pass under coil. White wire from coil must pass between condenser bracket and oiler felt. Push wire down to avoid contact with flywheel.

If ignition coil is loosened or removed, install coil by pushing coil towards crankshaft while tightening retaining screws which have been treated with Loctite or equivalent.

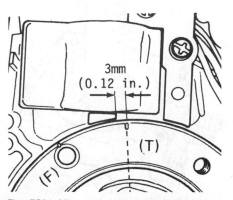

3mm (0.12 in.)

(T)

(F)

Fig. EC9—Align top dead center mark (T) on flywheel with laminations as shown to check timing on models with CD ignition. Refer to text.

lead; ohmmeter should register 0.0-0.2 ohms for all models. Connect ohmmeter lead to coil primary lead (red) wire and remaining ohmmeter lead to either the coil exciter lead (grounded wire), if so equipped, or to coil laminations. Ohmmeter should register 0.5-1.5k ohms for models with exciter lead or 1.5-3.0k ohms for remaining models. On models so equipped, connect one ohmmeter lead to exciter lead and remaining lead to coil laminations; ohmmeter should register 120-200 ohms.

CARBON. Muffler and cylinder exhaust ports should be cleaned periodically to prevent loss of power due to carbon build-up. Remove muffler cover and baffle plate and scrape muffler free of carbon. With muffler cover removed, position engine so piston is at top dead center and carefully remove carbon from exhaust ports with wooden scraper. Be careful not to damage the edges of exhaust ports or to scratch piston. Do not attempt to run engine without muffler baffle plate or cover.

LUBRICATION. Engine is lubricated by mixing oil with the fuel. Thoroughly mix two-cycle air-cooled engine oil at 20:1 ratio for Models SRM-200D, SRM-200DA, SRM-200DB, SRM-202DA, SRM-202FA, SRM-140D, SRM-140DA, SRM-302ADX and GTL-140. Thoroughly mix Echo special two-cycle engine oil at a 32:1 ratio for all other models. Do not use premium gasoline.

TIGHTENING TORQUES. Recommended tightening torque specifications are as follows:

Spark plug . . . . .17 N·m
(150 in.-lbs.)

Cylinder cover
(as equipped) . . . . .1.5-1.9 N·m
(13-17 in.-lbs.)

Cylinder:
SRM-200D, SRM-200DA,
SRM-200DB, SRM-202D,
SRM-202DA, SRM-202FA . .3-4 N·m
(30-35 in.-lbs.)
SRM-140D, SRM-140DA,
SRM-200, SRM-200E,
SRM-200AE, SRM-200BE,
SRM-200F, SRM-200FA,
SRM-210E, SRM-210AE,
GT160, GT-160A, GT-160AE,
GT-200, GT-200BE,
GTL-140 . . . . .5.7-6 N·m
(50-55 in.-lbs.)
SRM-400, SRM-300,
SRM-300E, SRM-300E/1,
SRM-300AE, SRM-300AE/1,
SRM-400E, SRM-400AE,
SRM-402DE . . . . .7-8 N·m
(65-75 in.-lbs.)
SRM-302ADX . . . . .8-9 N·m
(13-17 in.-lbs.)

Crankcase:
SRM-140D, SRM-140DA,
SRM-302ADX, GTL-140 4.5-5.7 N·m
(40-50 in.-lbs.)
All others . . . . .4-5 N·m
(35-45 in.-lbs.)

Flywheel nut:
SRM-302ADX, GT-140, GT-160,

GT-200 . . . . .8-10 N·m
(70-90 in.-lbs.)
SRM-200, SRM-200AE,
SRM-200BE, SRM-210E,
SRM-210AE, GT-160AE,
GT-200BE . . . . .14-16 N·m
(120 to 140 in.-lbs.)
SRM-140D, SRM-140DA,
SRM-200D, SRM-200DA,
SRM-200DB, SRM-202DA,
SRM-202FA, SRM-300,
SRM-300E, SRM-300E/1,
SRM-300AE, SRM-300AE/1,
GTL-140 . . . . .20-24 N·m
(175-210 in.-lbs.)

PISTON, PIN AND RINGS. Rings are pinned to prevent ring rotation on all models. Piston may be equipped with one or two compression rings according to model and application.

Cylinder is removed and pulled off piston. On models with needle bearings in connecting rod small end, make certain needle bearings are not lost when separating piston from connecting rod.

Standard ring end gap for all models is 0.3 mm (0.012 in.). If ring end gap is 0.5 mm (0.020 in.) or more, renew rings and/or cylinder bore.

Standard ring side clearance in piston groove for all models is 0.06 mm (0.0024 in.). If ring side clearance is 0.10 mm (0.004 in.) or more, renew ring and/or piston.

Standard piston pin bore diameter in piston is 6.0 mm (0.2362 in.) for

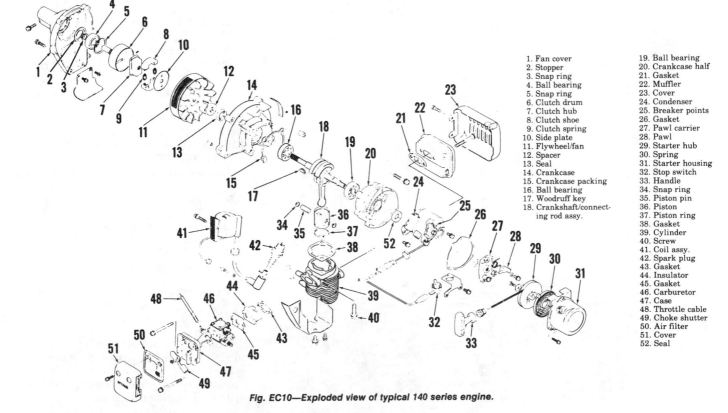

1. Fan cover
2. Stopper
3. Snap ring
4. Ball bearing
5. Snap ring
6. Clutch drum
7. Clutch hub
8. Clutch shoe
9. Clutch spring
10. Side plate
11. Flywheel/fan
12. Spacer
13. Seal
14. Crankcase
15. Crankcase packing
16. Ball bearing
17. Woodruff key
18. Crankshaft/connecting rod assy.
19. Ball bearing
20. Crankcase half
21. Gasket
22. Muffler
23. Cover
24. Condenser
25. Breaker points
26. Gasket
27. Pawl carrier
28. Pawl
29. Starter hub
30. Spring
31. Starter housing
32. Stop switch
33. Handle
34. Snap ring
35. Piston pin
36. Piston
37. Piston ring
38. Gasket
39. Cylinder
40. Screw
41. Coil assy.
42. Spark plug
43. Gasket
44. Insulator
45. Gasket
46. Carburetor
47. Case
48. Throttle cable
49. Choke shutter
50. Air filter
51. Cover
52. Seal

Fig. EC10—Exploded view of typical 140 series engine.

SRM-140D model, 9.0 mm (0.3543 in.) for SRM-302ADX model, 10.0 mm (0.3937 in.) for SRM-300, SRM-300E, SRM-300AE, SRM-400E, SRM-400AE and SRM-402DE models, and 8.0 mm (0.3150 in.) for all other models. If piston pin bore diameter is 6.3 mm (0.2374 in.) or more for SRM-140D model, 9.027 mm (0.3554 in.) or more for SRM-302ADX model, 10.03 mm (0.3949 in.) for SRM-300, SRM-300E, SRM-300AE, SRM-400E, SRM-400AE and SRM-402DE models, or 8.03 mm (0.3161 in.) or more for all other models, renew piston.

Standard piston pin diameter is 6.0 mm (0.2362 in.) for SRM-140D model, 9.0 mm (0.3543 in.) for SRM-302ADX model, 10.0 mm (0.3957 in.) for SRM-300, SRM-300E, SRM-300AE, SRM-400E, SRM-400AE and SRM-402DE models, and 8.0 mm (0.3150 in.) for all other models. If piston pin diameter is 5.98 mm (0.2354 in.) or less for SRM-140 model, 8.98 mm (0.3535 in.) or less for SRM-302ADX model, 9.98 mm (0.3929 in.) or less for SRM-300, SRM-300E, SRM-300AE, SRM-400E, SRM-400AE and SRM-402DE models, and 7.98 mm (0.3142 in.) or less for all other models, renew pin.

Standard piston skirt diameter is 25.90 mm (1.020 in.) for models with 26 mm bore, 27.90 mm (1.101 in.) for models with 28 mm (1.102 in.) bore, 32.1 mm (1.264 in.) for models with 32.2 mm (1.268 in.) bore, 34.90 mm (1.374 in.) for models with 35 mm (1.378 in.) bore and 39.90 mm (1.571 in.) for models with 40 mm (1.575 in.) bore. If piston diameter is 0.10 mm (0.004 in.) or less than standard, renew piston.

When installing piston, ring end gaps must be correctly positioned over pins in ring grooves. Install piston on connecting rod with arrow on top of piston toward exhaust side of engine. Make certain piston pin retaining rings are correctly seated in piston pin bore of piston. Use care when slipping piston into cylinder that cylinder does not rotate.

CYLINDER. Cylinder bores of all models are chrome plated and should be renewed at the first sign of aluminum showing through plated surface or if surface is scored or flaking.

CRANKSHAFT AND CONNECTING ROD ASSEMBLY. The crankshaft and connecting rod are serviced as an assembly only and crankshaft and connecting rod are not available separately.

To remove crankshaft and connecting rod assembly on all models, remove fan housing and clutch assembly. Remove carburetor, muffler and fuel tank. Remove starter assembly, flywheel, magneto, points and condenser or igni-tion module (as equipped). Carefully remove cylinder, separate piston from connecting rod and remove piston. Separate crankcase halves and remove crankshaft and connecting rod assembly.

Ball bearing type main bearings are used on all models. Bearings may be removed and installed using a suitable puller.

Standard connecting rod side clearance on crankpin journal is 0.55-0.60 mm (0.022-0.026 in.) for Models SRM-140D, SRM-140DA, GT-140, GT-140A, GT-140B, GTL-140, GT-160, GT-160A, GT-160AE, GT-200, GT-200A, GT-200B and GT-200BE. If side clearance is 0.7 mm (0.028 in.) or more for any of these models, crankshaft and connecting rod assembly must be renewed. Standard connecting rod side clearance for all other models is 0.25-0.30 mm (0.010-0.012 in.), and if side clearance is 0.40 mm (0.016 in.) or more, connecting rod and crankshaft assembly must be renewed.

Connecting rod piston pin bearing bore standard and maximum diameters are as follows:

Models

SRM-140D
Standard diameter	6.0 mm (0.2362 in.)
Maximum diameter	6.06 mm (0.2386 in.)

SRM-140D, GT-140, GT-160, GTL-140
Standard diameter	8.0 mm (0.3150 in.)
Maximum diameter	8.06 mm (0.3173 in.)

SRM-200D, SRM-200DA, SRM-200DB, SRM-202DA, SRM-202FA
Standard diameter	11.0 mm (0.4336 in.)
Maximum diameter	11.03 mm (0.4341 in.)

SRM-200, SRM-S00AE, SRM-200BE, SRM-210E, SRM-210AE, SRM-302ADX, GT-200, GT-200BE
Standard diameter	12.0 mm (0.4729 in.)
Maximum diameter	12.03 mm (0.4734 in.)

SRM-300, SRM-300E, SRM-300AE, SRM-400E, SRM-400AE, SRM-402DE
Standard diameter	14.0 mm (0.5517 in.)
Maximum diameter	14.03 mm (0.5522 in.)

When reassembling crankcase on all models, use a light coat of sealer on crankcase halves as sealing crankcase against pressure and vacuum leaks is critical to engine operation.

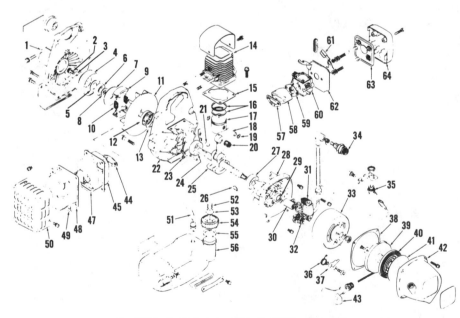

Fig. EC11—Exploded view of typical 200 series engine.

1. Fan cover	14. Cylinder	26. Woodruff key	39. Starter drum
2. Bolt	15. Gasket	27. Ball bearing	40. Spring
3. Washer	16. Piston rings	28. Crankcase half	41. Plate
4. Clutch drum	17. Piston	29. Seal	42. Starter housing
5. Spacer	18. Piston pin	30. Sleeve	43. Handle
6. Ball bearing	19. Snap ring	31. Coil assy.	44. Gasket
7. Plate	20. Needle bearing	32. Breaker points	45. Case
8. Spacer	21. Woodruff key	33. Flywheel	47. Baffle
9. Clutch shoe	22. Crankcase half	34. Spark plug	48. Gasket
10. Clutch spring	23. Packing	35. Stop switch	49. Case
11. Fan	24. Ball bearing	36. Spring	50. Cover
12. Seal	25. Crankshaft/connect-	37. Pawl	51. Fuel line
13. Snap ring	ing rod assy.	38. Gasket	52. Vent

53. Check valve	
54. Cap	
55. Gasket	
56. Fuel tank	
57. Gasket	
58. Insulator	
59. Gasket	
60. Carburetor	
61. Choke shutter	
62. Case	
63. Air filter	
64. Cover	

Illustrations courtesy Echo Inc.

Always install new crankcase seals and packing when reassembling crankcase. Seal lips must face inward. Use caution during assembly so seal lips are not damaged during crankcase installation over ends of crankshaft. Packing excess must be trimmed from cylinder surface to avoid crankcase leaks. Tighten crankcase bolts to specified torque.

KIORITZ-ECHO SPECIAL TOOLS

The following special tools are available from Echo Central Service Distributors.

FLYWHEEL HOLDER
897712-06030...   SRM-140, SRM-140DA
897712-07930...   GTL-140
897501-03932...   SRM-200D, SRM-200DA, SRM200DB, SRM-202DA, SRM-202FA, SRM-302ADX

895115-00330...   GT-160AE, GT-200BE, SRM-200, SRM-200E, SRM-200AE, SRM-200BE, SRM-201F, SRM-201FA, SRM-210E, SRM-210AE, SRM-300E, SRM-300AE, SRM-400E, SRM-400AE, SRM-402DD

MAGNETO SPANNER AND GAGE
895115-00330...   All models

BEARING WEDGE SET
897701-06030...   SRM140D, SRM-140DA, GT-140A, GTL-140, GT-160, GT-160AE, GT-200, GT-200A, GT-200B, GT-200BE, SRM-200, SRM-200AE, SRM-200BE, SRM-200E, SRM-201F, SRM-201FA, SRM-202DA, SRM202-FA, SRM-210E, SRM-210AE, SRM-300E, SRM-300AE, SRM-400E, SRM-400AE

897701-02830...   SRM-200D, SRM-200DA, SRM-200DB, SRM-202DA, SRM-202FA, SRM-300

DRIVERS
897718-06030...   SRM-140D, SRM-140DA, SRM-200, SRM-200AE, SRM-200BE, SRM-200E, GT-140A, GT140-B, GT-160, GT-160A, GTL-140, GT-200, SRM-302ADX
897718-02830...   SRM-300E, SRM-300AE, SRM-400E, SRM-400AE, SRM-402DD

PISTON PIN TOOL
097702-06030...   All models

PRESSURE TESTER
990510-0020...   All models

TIMING TESTER
990510-00031...   All models

EFCO

ENGINE SERVICE

Model	Bore	Stroke	Displacement
200	32 mm	28 mm	22.5 cc
	(1.26 in.)	(1.10 in.)	(1.37 cu. in.)
220	32 mm	28 mm	22.5 cc
	(1.26 in.)	(1.10 in.)	(1.37 cu. in.)
260	34 mm	28 mm	25.4 cc
	(1.34 in.)	(1.10 in.)	(1.55 cu. in.)

ENGINE INFORMATION

The EFCO Model 200, 220 and 260 two-stroke, air-cooled gasoline engines are used on Jonsered and Olympyk string trimmers and brush cutters. The engine is equipped with a cantilever-type crankshaft that is supported in two ball bearings at the flywheel end. Refer to following section for other EFCO engine models.

MAINTENANCE

LUBRICATION. Engine lubrication is obtained by mixing gasoline with an oil designed for two-stroke, air-cooled engines. Refer to trimmer service section for manufacturer's recommended fuel:oil mixture ratio.

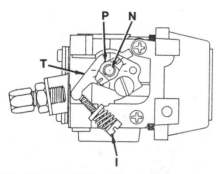

Fig. EF101—On Walbro WZ carburetor idle speed screw is located at (I), idle mixture limiter plate is located at (P) and idle mixture needle is located at (N). A plug covers the idle mixture needle.

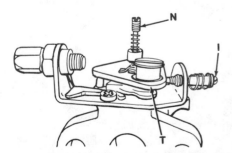

Fig. EF102—View of idle mixture needle (N). Refer to text for adjustment procedure.

SPARK PLUG. Recommended spark plug is a Champion CJ7Y or equivalent. Specified electrode gap for all models is 0.6-0.7 mm (0.024-0.028 in.).

CARBURETOR. The engine is equipped with a Walbro WZ carburetor. This is a diaphragm-type carburetor that uses a barrel-type throttle rather than a throttle plate.

Idle fuel for the carburetor flows up into the throttle barrel where it is fed into the air stream. Idle fuel flow can be adjusted by turning idle limiter plate (P—Fig. EF101). Initial setting is in center notch. Rotating the plate clockwise will lean the idle mixture. Inside the limiter plate is an idle mixture needle (N—Fig. EF102) that is preset at the factory (a plug covers the needle). If idle mixture needle is removed, use the following procedure to determine correct position. Back out needle (N) until unscrewed, then screw in needle six turns. Rotate idle mixture limiter plate (P—Fig. EF101) to center notch. Run engine until normal operating temperature is attained. Adjust idle speed screw (I) so trimmer head or blade does not rotate. Rotate idle mixture needle (N—Fig. EF102) and obtain highest rpm (turning needle clockwise leans the mixture), then turn needle counterclockwise until rpm decreases 200-500 rpm. Readjust idle speed screw. Note that idle mixture limiter and needle are available only as an assembly with throttle barrel.

Initial setting of high-speed mixture screw (23—Fig. EF103) is 1½ turns out from a lightly seated position. Adjust high-speed mixture screw to obtain highest engine speed. On Model 200 engine, turn high-speed screw counterclockwise so engine rpm is 7400-7500 on a new engine or 7900-8000 on an engine that has run over 50 hours. On Model 220 and 260 engines, turn high-speed screw counterclockwise so engine rpm is 9000-9200 on a new engine or 9400-9500 on an engine that has run over 50 hours. Do not adjust mixture too lean as engine may be damaged.

To overhaul carburetor, refer to exploded view in Fig. EF103 and note the following: Clean only with solvents approved for use with plastic. Do not disassemble throttle barrel assembly. Examine fuel inlet valve and seat. Inlet valve is renewable, but carburetor body must be renewed if seat is excessively worn or damaged. Inspect high-speed mixture screw and seat. Renew carburetor body if seat is excessively worn or damaged. Clean fuel screen. Inspect diaphragms for tears and other damage. When installing plates and gaskets (13, 14 and 15), note that tabs on edges will "stairstep" when correctly installed. Adjust metering lever height to obtain 1.5 mm (0.059 in.) between carburetor body surface and lever as shown in Fig. EF104.

IGNITION SYSTEM. The engine is equipped with an electronic ignition system. Ignition system performance is considered satisfactory if a spark will jump across a 3 mm (⅛ in.) electrode gap on a test spark plug. If no spark is produced, check on/off switch, wiring and ignition module air gap. Ignition module air gap should be 0.3 mm (0.012 in.). If switch, wiring and module air gap are satisfactory, but spark is not present, renew ignition module.

REPAIRS

TIGHTENING TORQUES. Recommended tightening torque specifications are as follows:
Clutch hub . . . . 18 N·m
(160 in.-lbs.)
Crankcase . . . . 6 N·m
(53 in.-lbs.)
Crankpin . . . . 30 N·m
(22 ft.-lbs.)

PISTON, CONNECTING ROD, RINGS AND CYLINDER. The cylinder and crankcase are one piece. To remove piston, the crankshaft must be removed. Disconnect ignition wires and throttle cable from engine. Unbolt and remove drive shaft assembly from engine. Remove spark plug and install a suitable tool or insert end of rope into spark plug hole to prevent crankshaft from turning. Remove clutch assembly from crankshaft. Remove muffler cover and flywheel shroud. Remove recoil starter assembly. Remove flywheel retaining nut and tap flywheel with a plastic mallet to loosen flywheel from crankshaft taper. Remove gas tank and tank bracket. Detach crankcase cover (17—Fig. EF105). Unscrew crankpin (11) on early models or detach snap ring (20) on later models. Remove bearing (10A) on later models. Position big end of rod so it is clear of crankshaft as shown in Fig. EF106, then press crankshaft out of crankcase. Withdraw rod and piston assembly from crankcase.

Inspect components for excessive wear and damage. Specified piston ring end gap is 0.15-0.35 mm (0.006-0.014 in.). Piston and cylinder are stamped with letter "A," "B" or "F" according to size. Install new piston or cylinder with same letter grade as discarded part.

Connecting rod bearings are available only with rod. Do not attempt to remove bearings from rod on early models. On later models, big end bearing is removable, but small end bearing is not removable.

During assembly, note the following: Assemble piston on rod so closed end of piston pin is on same side as arrow on piston crown. Install piston and rod so arrow on piston crown points toward exhaust port. Be sure piston ring end gap properly surrounds locating pin in piston ring groove. Lubricate piston, cylinder and connecting rod bearing with oil. Apply Loctite to threads of crankpin (11—Fig. EF105) on early models and tighten to 30 N·m (22 ft.-lbs.). On late models, install thrust washer (19) and snap ring (20). On all models, tighten crankcase cover screws to 6 N·m (53 in.-lbs.). Complete reassembly by reversing disassembly procedure.

CRANKSHAFT AND CRANKCASE. The crankshaft is a cantilever-type that is supported by two bearings in the crankcase. To remove the crankshaft, remove flywheel and detach crankcase cover (17—Fig. EF105). Unscrew crankpin (11) on early models or detach snap ring (20) on later models. Remove bearing (10A) on later models. Position big

end of rod so it is clear of crankshaft as shown in Fig. EF106. Press crankshaft out of crankcase. Drive or press bearings (2 and 5—Fig. EF105) and seal (4) out of crankcase while removing snap rings (3). Note depth of seal before removal as reference for installation of new seal, or use EFCO seal installation tool 4138347.

During assembly, note the following: Outer bearing (2) is sealed. Position bearings against snap rings. Apply Loctite to threads of crankpin (11—Fig. EF105) on early models and tighten to 30 N·m (22 ft.-lbs.). On late models, install thrust washer (19) and snap ring (20). On all models, tighten crankcase cover screws to 6 N·m (53 in.-lbs.).

CLUTCH. All models are equipped with the two-shoe clutch shown in Fig. EF107. Note that clutch hub (3) has left-hand threads. Minimum allowable thickness of clutch shoe lining is 0.8 mm (0.032 in.). Clutch shoes (2) are available only as a pair. Tighten clutch hub (3) to 18 N·m (160 in.-lbs.).

To disassemble clutch drum assembly, separate housing (2—Fig. EF108) from engine and drive shaft tube. On Models 220 and 260, the drive shaft must be unscrewed from the clutch drum. Detach snap ring (1) and press or drive clutch drum out of housing. Detach snap ring (5) and remove bearing (4). Reassemble by reversing disassembly procedure.

REWIND STARTER. The engine may be equipped with the starter shown in Fig. EF107 or EF109. To disassemble starter, remove clutch hub (3—Fig. EF107) and shroud (4). Note that clutch hub has left-hand threads. Remove starter housing. Detach rope handle and allow rope to wind into starter. On models so equipped, remove snap ring (5—Fig. EF109). Disassemble starter. Wear appropriate safety eyewear and gloves when working with or around rewind spring as spring may uncoil uncontrolled.

Before assembling starter, lubricate center post of housing and spring side of pulley with light grease. Install rewind spring in a counterclockwise direction from outer end. Assemble starter

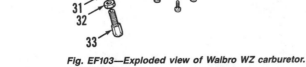

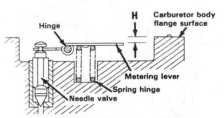

Fig. EF103—Exploded view of Walbro WZ carburetor.

1. Cover	11. Gasket	20. Retainer	29. Metering diaphragm
2. Air cleaner element	12. Screen	21. Spring	30. Cover
3. Plate	13. Gasket	22. Washer	31. Bracket
4. Plate	14. Fuel pump	23. High-speed mixture	32. Nut
5. Throttle barrel assy.	diaphragm	screw	33. Cable adjuster
6. Spring	15. Plate	24. Fuel inlet valve	34. Support
7. Idle speed screw	16. Gasket	25. Spring	35. Sleeve
8. Swivel	17. Fuel pump cover	26. Metering lever	36. Seal
9. Washer	18. Gasket	27. Pin	37. Cover
10. "E" ring	19. Primer bulb	28. Gasket	

Fig. EF104—Metering lever height (H) must be set on diaphragm-type carburetors. Refer to text for specified height.

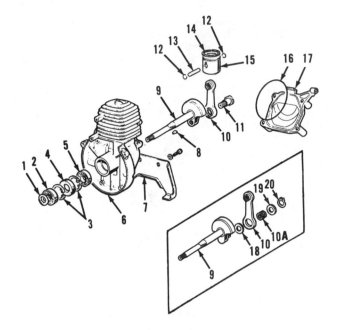

while passing rope through housing rope
outlet and attach rope handle to rope.
To place tension on starter rope, rotate
pulley counterclockwise so notch in pulley is aligned with rope outlet, then hold
pulley to prevent pulley rotation. Pull
rope back into housing while positioning rope in pulley notch. Turn rope pulley counterclockwise six turns. Allow
pulley to turn clockwise until notch
aligns with rope outlet. Disengage rope
from notch then release pulley and allow rope to wind on pulley. Check starter operation. Rope handle should be
held against housing by spring tension,
but it must be possible to rotate pulley
at least $1/4$ turn counterclockwise when
rope is pulled out fully.

**Fig. EF106—Connecting rod (10) must be posi-
tioned as shown so crankshaft (9) can be
removed.**

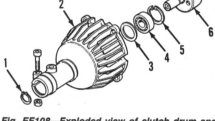

**Fig. EF108—Exploded view of clutch drum and
housing assembly. Washer (3) is absent on some
models.**

1. Snap ring	4. Bearing
2. Housing	5. Snap ring
3. Washer	6. Clutch drum

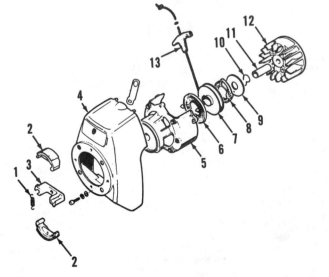

**Fig. EF107—Exploded view
of clutch and rewind starter.
Refer also to Fig. EF109 for
alternate-type rewind starter.**

1. Clutch spring
2. Clutch shoe
3. Clutch hub
4. Shroud
5. Starter housing
6. Rewind spring
7. Pulley
8. Pawl
9. Washer
10. Clip
11. Spacer
12. Flywheel
13. Rope handle

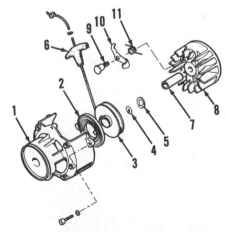

**Fig. EF109—Exploded view of rewind starter used
on some models.**

1. Starter housing	
2. Rewind spring	7. Spacer
3. Pulley	8. Flywheel
4. Washer	9. Stud
5. Snap ring	10. Pawl
6. Rope handle	11. Spring

EFCO

ENGINE SERVICE

Model	Bore	Stroke	Displacement
300, 320	36 mm (1.42 in.)	30 mm (1.18 in.)	30.5 cc (1.86 cu. in.)
400, 420	40 mm (1.50 in.)	30 mm (1.18 in.)	37.7 cc (2.30 cu. in.)
450, 460	40 mm (1.50 in.)	30 mm (1.18 in.)	37.7 cc (2.30 cu. in.)

ENGINE INFORMATION

The EFCO Model 300, 320, 400, 420, 450 and 460 two-stroke, air-cooled gasoline engines are used on Jonsered and Olympyk string trimmers and brush cutters. Refer to preceding section for other EFCO engine models.

MAINTENANCE

LUBRICATION. Engine lubrication is obtained by mixing gasoline with an oil designed for two-stroke, air-cooled engines. Refer to trimmer service section for manufacturer's recommended fuel:oil mixture ratio.

SPARK PLUG. Recommended spark plug is a Champion CJ7Y or equivalent. Specified electrode gap for all models is 0.6-0.7 mm (0.024-0.028 in.).

CARBURETOR. The engine may be equipped with a Walbro or Zama diaphragm-type carburetor. Refer to following section for service information.

Walbro WT. To adjust carburetor, turn idle mixture screw (15—Fig. EF201) and high-speed mixture screw (17) so each is one turn open. Final adjustment is performed with engine at normal operating temperature. Trimmer line should be extended fully or blade assembly installed during adjustment. Adjust idle mixture screw so engine accelerates cleanly without hesitation. Run engine at full throttle and adjust high-speed mixture screw so engine runs at highest speed. Turn high-speed screw counterclockwise so engine rpm is 9500-9600 on a new engine or 10,300-10,500 on an engine that has run over 50 hours. Do not adjust mixture too lean as engine may be damaged. Adjust idle speed screw so engine idles smoothly.

Some models are equipped with an accelerator pump that forces additional fuel into the carburetor bore when the throttle shaft is rotated. The pump piston (8—Fig. EF201) rests against a flat on the throttle shaft. Shaft rotation moves the piston against fuel in a passage.

Carburetor disassembly and reassembly is evident after inspection of carburetor and referral to Fig. EF201. Accelerator pump piston (8) is released when throttle shaft is withdrawn. Clean and inspect all components. Inspect diaphragms for defects that may affect operation. Examine fuel inlet valve and seat. Inlet valve is renewable, but carburetor body must be renewed if seat is damaged or excessively worn. Discard carburetor body if mixture screw seats are damaged or excessively worn. Clean fuel screen. Inspect diaphragms for tears and other damage. Inspect primer bulb and reject if cracked, hardened or otherwise damaged.

Check metering lever height as shown in Fig. EF202 using Walbro tool 500-13. Metering lever should just touch leg on tool. Bend lever to obtain correct lever height.

Walbro WZ. This is a diaphragm-type carburetor that uses a barrel-type throttle rather than a throttle plate.

Idle fuel for the carburetor flows up into the throttle barrel where it is fed into the air stream. Idle fuel flow can be adjusted by turning idle mixture limiter plate (P—Fig. EF203). Initial setting is in center notch. Rotating the plate clockwise will lean the idle mixture. Inside the limiter plate is an idle mixture needle (N—Fig. EF204) that is preset at the factory (a plug covers the needle). If idle mixture needle is removed, use the following procedure to determine correct position. Back out needle (N) until unscrewed, then screw in needle six turns. Rotate idle mixture plate (P—Fig. EF203) to center notch. Run engine until normal operating temperature is attained. Adjust idle speed screw so trimmer head or blade does not rotate. Rotate idle mixture needle (N—Fig. EF204) and obtain highest rpm

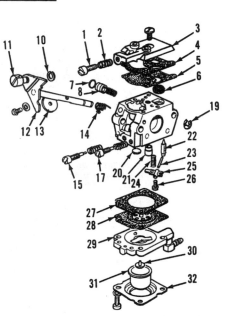

Fig. EF201—Exploded view of Walbro WT carburetor.

1. Idle speed screw	17. High-speed mixture screw
2. Spring	
3. Cover	19. "E" ring
4. Gasket	20. Welch plug
5. Fuel pump diaphragm	21. Nozzle
6. Screen	22. Fuel inlet valve
7. "O" ring	23. Pin
8. Accelerator pump piston	24. Spring
9. Clip	25. Metering lever
10. Clip	26. Screw
11. Swivel	27. Gasket
12. Throttle shaft	28. Metering diaphragm
13. Throttle plate	29. Cover
14. Spring	30. Check valve
15. Idle mixture screw	31. Primer bulb
	32. Bulb retainer

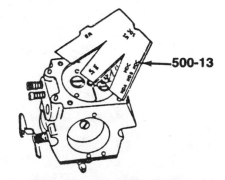

Fig. EF202—Metering lever should just touch leg of Walbro tool 500-13. Bend lever to obtain correct lever height.

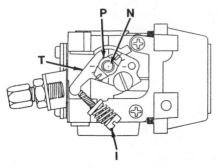

Fig. EF203—On Walbro WZ carburetor, idle speed screw is located at (I), idle mixture limiter plate is located at (S) and idle mixture needle is located at (N). A plug covers the idle mixture needle.

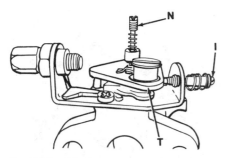

Fig. EF204—View of idle mixture needle (N). Refer to text for adjustment procedure.

(turning needle clockwise leans the mixture), then turn needle counterclockwise until rpm decreases 200-500 rpm. Readjust idle speed screw. Note that idle mixture plate and needle are available only as an assembly with throttle barrel.

Initial setting of high-speed mixture screw (23—Fig. EF205) is 1½ turns out from a lightly seated position. Adjust high-speed mixture screw to obtain highest engine speed. Turn high-speed screw counterclockwise so engine rpm is 9500-9600 on a new engine or 10,300-10,500 on an engine that has run over 50 hours. Do not adjust mixture too lean as engine may be damaged.

To overhaul carburetor, refer to exploded view in Fig. EF205 and note the following: Clean only with solvents approved for use with plastic. Do not disassemble throttle barrel assembly. Examine fuel inlet valve and seat. Inlet valve is renewable, but carburetor body must be renewed if seat is excessively worn or damaged. Inspect high-speed mixture screw and seat. Renew carburetor body if seat is excessively worn or damaged. Clean fuel screen. Inspect diaphragms for tears and other damage. When installing plates and gaskets (13,

14 and 15), note that tabs on edges will "stairstep" when correctly installed. Adjust metering lever height to obtain 1.5 mm (0.059 in.) between carburetor body surface and lever as shown in Fig. EF206.

Zama C1S. Refer to Fig. EF207 for an exploded view of carburetor. Initial adjustment of idle mixture screw (14) and high-speed mixture screw (16) is one turn out from a lightly seated position.

Final adjustment is performed with engine at normal operating temperature. Trimmer line should be extended fully or blade assembly installed during adjustment. Adjust idle mixture screw so engine accelerates cleanly without hesitation. Run engine at full throttle and adjust high-speed mixture screw so engine runs at highest speed. Turn high-speed screw counterclockwise so engine rpm is 9500-9600 on a new engine or 10,300-10,500 on an engine that has run over 50 hours. Do not adjust mixture too

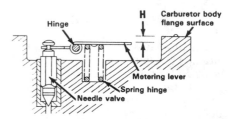

Fig. EF206—Metering lever height (H) must be set on diaphragm-type carburetors. Refer to text for specified height.

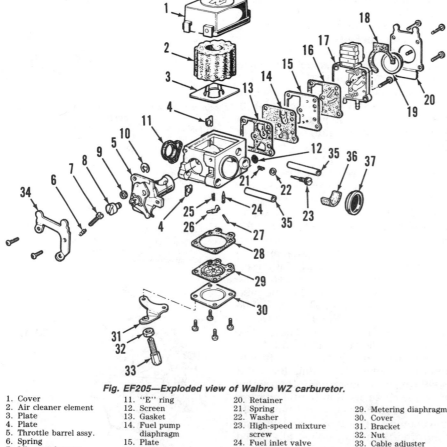

Fig. EF205—Exploded view of Walbro WZ carburetor.

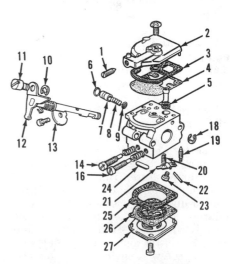

Fig. EF207—Exploded view of Zama C1S carburetor.

1. Cover	11. "E" ring
2. Air cleaner element	12. Screen
3. Plate	13. Gasket
4. Plate	14. Fuel pump diaphragm
5. Throttle barrel assy.	15. Plate
6. Spring	16. Gasket
7. Idle speed screw	17. Fuel pump cover
8. Swivel	18. Gasket
9. Washer	19. Primer bulb
10. Gasket	20. Retainer

21. Spring	29. Metering diaphragm
22. Washer	30. Cover
23. High-speed mixture screw	31. Bracket
24. Fuel inlet valve	32. Nut
25. Spring	33. Cable adjuster
26. Metering lever	34. Support
27. Pin	35. Sleeve
28. Gasket	36. Seal
	37. Cover

1. Idle speed screw	13. Throttle plate
2. Cover	14. Idle mixture screw
3. Gasket	16. High-speed mixture screw
4. Fuel pump diaphragm	18. "E" ring
5. Screen	19. Fuel inlet valve
6. "O" ring	20. Spring
7. Accelerator pump piston	21. Metering lever
8. Spring	22. Pin
9. Screen	23. Screw
10. Clip	24. Welch plug
11. Swivel	25. Gasket
12. Throttle shaft	26. Metering diaphragm
	27. Cover

lean as engine may be damaged. Adjust idle speed screw so engine idles smoothly.

Some models are equipped with an accelerator pump that forces additional fuel into the carburetor bore when the throttle shaft is rotated. The pump piston (7—Fig. EF207) rests against a flat on the throttle shaft. Shaft rotation moves the piston against fuel in a passage.

Carburetor disassembly and reassembly is evident after inspection of carburetor and referral to Fig. EF207. Clean and inspect all components. Inspect diaphragms for defects that may affect operation. Examine fuel inlet valve and seat. Inlet valve is renewable, but carburetor body must be renewed if seat is damaged or excessively worn. Discard carburetor body if mixture screw seats are damaged or excessively worn. Clean fuel screen. Inspect diaphragms for tears and other damage.

To reassemble carburetor, reverse disassembly procedure. Note the two types of metering levers in Fig. EF208. Adjust clearance "A" to 0-0.03 mm (0-0.012 inch). Bend metering lever as needed.

IGNITION SYSTEM. The engine is equipped with an electronic ignition system. Ignition system performance is considered satisfactory if a spark will jump across a 3 mm (1/8 in.) electrode gap on a test spark plug. If no spark is produced, check on/off switch, wiring and ignition module air gap. Ignition module air gap should be 0.3 mm (0.012 in.). If switch, wiring and module air gap are satisfactory but spark is not present, renew ignition module.

REPAIRS

TIGHTENING TORQUES. Recommended tightening torque specifications are as follows:

Clutch hub . . . . 25 N·m
(220 in.-lbs.)
Crankcase . . . . 6 N·m
(53 in.-lbs.)
Flywheel . . . . 15 N·m
(132 in.-lbs.)

CYLINDER, PISTON, PIN AND RINGS. Crankcase and cylinder halves (1 and 12—Fig. EF209) must be split to

remove piston (10). Refer to CONNECTING ROD, CRANKSHAFT AND CRANKCASE section for procedure. The piston may be equipped with one or two piston rings. Ring rotation is prevented by a locating pin in each piston ring groove.

Specified piston ring end gap is 0.15-0.35 mm (0.006-0.014 in.).

Piston and cylinder on Models 300 and 320 are stamped with letter "A," "B" or "F," according to size. Piston and cylinder on Models 400, 420, 450 and 460 are stamped with letter "B," "C" or "D," according to size. Install new piston or cylinder with same letter grade as discarded part.

Install piston so arrow on piston crown points toward exhaust port (Fig. EF210). Be sure piston ring gaps are correctly indexed with locating pins in piston ring grooves when installing cylinder.

CONNECTING ROD, CRANKSHAFT AND CRANKCASE. Crankcase and cylinder halves (1 and 12—Fig. EF209) must be split for access to crankshaft. Disconnect ignition wires and throttle cable from engine. Unbolt and remove clutch housing and drive shaft assembly. Remove engine from frame. Remove spark plug and install piston locking tool or insert end of a rope into cylinder to prevent crankshaft from rotating. Unscrew clutch assembly from crankshaft. Remove recoil starter, fan cover and flywheel. Remove carburetor, gas tank, tank bracket, muffler cover and muffler. Remove screws from crankcase and separate crankcase and cylinder halves. Do not damage crankcase and cylinder mating surfaces. Lift crankshaft, connecting rod and piston assembly from cylinder. Remove snap rings (8), push out piston pin (9) and separate piston (10) from connecting rod. Use a puller to remove bearings (5) from crankshaft.

Connecting rod, crankpin and crankshaft are a pressed-together assembly and available only as a unit. Connecting rod big end rides on a roller bearing and should be inspected for excessive wear and damage. If rod, bearing or crankshaft is damaged, complete crankshaft and connecting rod assembly must be renewed.

There is no gasket between crankcase and cylinder halves. Apply a suitable

gasket sealer to crankcase and cylinder mating surfaces when reassembling.

On early models, be sure snap rings (4—Fig. EF209) properly fit into grooves in cylinder half (12). On all models, seals (S) should not obstruct oil holes (H—Fig. EF211). On later models, seal (2—Fig. EF209) replaces seal (3) and snap ring (4). Edge of seal (2) must fit in groove in cylinder half. Tighten crankcase screws to 6 N·m (53 in.-lbs.).

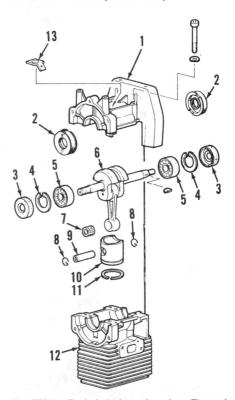

Fig. EF209—Exploded view of engine. Flanged seal (2) replaces seal (3) and snap ring (4) on later models.

1. Crankcase half
2. Flanged seal
3. Seal
4. Snap ring
5. Bearing
6. Crankshaft assy.
7. Bearing
8. Retaining rings
9. Piston pin
10. Piston
11. Piston ring
12. Cylinder

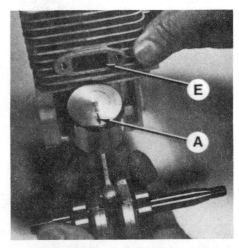

Fig. EF210—Piston must be installed with arrow (A) facing exhaust port (E) side of cylinder.

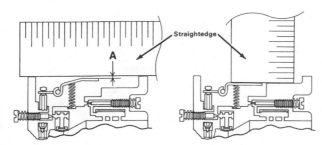

Fig. EF208—Note shape of metering lever and refer to drawing for correct metering lever height. Stepped type metering lever should be bent so height (A) is 0-0.3 mm (0.000-0.012 in.). Straight type metering lever should be flush with chamber floor as shown.

Fig. EF211—Seal (S) should not obstruct lubricating oil hole (H).

CLUTCH. All models are equipped with the two-shoe clutch shown in Fig. EF212. Minimum allowable thickness of clutch shoe lining is 0.8 mm (0.032 in.). Clutch shoes are available only as a pair.

To disassemble clutch drum assembly, separate housing (6—Fig. EF212 or EF213) from engine and drive shaft tube. On later models, separate support (2) from housing. Detach snap ring (5) and press or drive clutch drum (9) out of housing. Detach snap ring (8) and remove bearing(s) (7). Reassemble by reversing disassembly procedure.

REWIND STARTER. The engine is equipped with the starter shown in Fig.

EF214. To disassemble starter, detach rope handle and allow rope to wind into starter. Remove starter housing (10). Remove screw (6) and disassemble starter. Wear appropriate safety eyewear and gloves when working with or around rewind spring as spring may uncoil uncontrolled.

Before assembling starter, lubricate center post of housing and spring side of pulley with light grease. Install rewind spring in a counterclockwise direction from outer end. Assemble starter while passing rope through housing rope outlet and attach rope handle to rope. To place tension on starter rope, rotate pulley counterclockwise so notch in pulley is aligned with rope outlet, then hold pulley to prevent pulley rotation. Pull rope back into housing while positioning rope in pulley notch. Turn rope pulley counterclockwise six turns. Allow pulley to turn clockwise until notch aligns with rope outlet. Disengage rope from notch then release pulley and allow rope to wind on pulley. Check starter operation. Rope handle should be held against housing by spring tension, but it must be possible to rotate pulley at least $1/4$ turn counterclockwise when rope is pulled out fully.

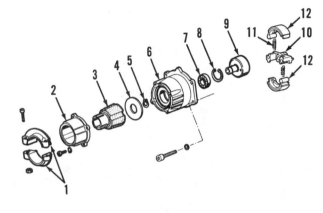

Fig. EF212—Exploded view of clutch assembly used on later models.

1. Collar
2. Support
3. Vibration isolator
4. Washer
5. Snap ring
6. Housing
7. Bearing
8. Snap ring
9. Clutch drum
10. Clutch hub
11. Spring
12. Clutch shoe

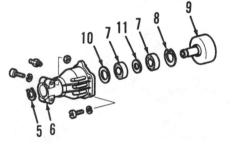

Fig. EF213—Exploded view of clutch drive assembly used on some early models.

5. Snap ring
6. Housing
7. Bearing
8. Snap ring

9. Clutch drum
10. Washer
11. Washer

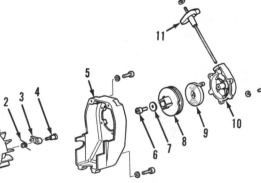

Fig. EF214—Exploded view of rewind starter.

1. Flywheel
2. Spring
3. Pawl
4. Stud
5. Shroud
6. Screw
7. Washer
8. Pulley
9. Rewind spring
10. Starter housing
11. Rope handle

FUJI

ENGINE SERVICE

Model	Bore	Stroke	Displacement
EC01A	28 mm (1.10 in.)	25 mm (0.98 in.)	15.4 cc (0.94 cu. in.)
EC02E	31.5 mm (1.24 in.)	26 mm (1.02 in.)	20.3 cc (1.24 cu. in.)
EC02EH	31.5 mm (1.24 in.)	28 mm (1.10 in.)	22.5 cc (1.37 cu. in.)
EC02F	33 mm (1.30 in.)	30 mm (1.18 in.)	25.6 cc (1.56 cu. in.)
EC02R	31.5 mm (1.24 in.)	28 mm (1.10 in.)	22.5 cc (1.37 cu. in.)
EC03-1R	36 mm (1.42 in.)	28 mm (1.10 in.)	28.0 cc (1.71 cu. in.)
EC03-2R	36 mm (1.42 in.)	30 mm (1.18 in.)	30.5 cc (1.86 cu. in.)
EC03E	37 mm (1.46 in.)	32 mm (1.26 in.)	34.4 cc (2.10 cu. in.)
EC04-3R	40 mm (1.58 in.)	30 mm (1.18 in.)	37.7 cc (2.30 cu. in.)
EC04E	40 mm (1.58 in.)	32 mm (1.26 in.)	40.2 cc (2.45 cu. in.)
EC05M	44 mm (1.73 in.)	34 mm (1.34 in.)	51.7 cc (3.15 cu. in.)

ENGINE INFORMATION

Fuji two-stroke, air-cooled gasoline engines are used by several manufacturers of string trimmers, brush cutters and blowers.

MAINTENANCE

LUBRICATION. Engine lubrication is obtained by mixing gasoline with an oil designed for two-stroke, air-cooled engines. Refer to service section for trimmer or blower for manufacturer's recommended fuel:oil mixture ratio.

SPARK PLUG. Recommended spark plug for Model EC03E and EC04E engines is NGK BPM7A or equivalent. Recommended spark plug for Model EC03-2R and EC04-3R engines is NGK B7HS or equivalent. Recommended spark plug for Model EC05M engine is NGK BM6A or equivalent. Recommended spark plug for all other models is NGK BM7A or equivalent. Specified electrode gap is 0.6-0.7 mm (0.024-0.028 in.) for all engines.

CARBURETOR. Various carburetors have been used. Refer to appropriate following section.

Walbro WA. Some engines are equipped with a Walbro WA diaphragm-type carburetor. Initial adjustment of idle and high-speed mixture screws is one turn out from a lightly seated position. Final adjustments are performed with trimmer line at recommended length or blade installed. Be sure engine air filter is clean before adjusting carburetor. Engine must be at operating temperature and running.

Adjust idle speed screw (1—Fig. FJ101) so trimmer head or blade does not rotate. Adjust idle mixture screw (14) to obtain maximum idle speed possible, then turn idle mixture screw $^1/_6$ turn counterclockwise. Readjust idle speed. Operate unit at full throttle and adjust high-speed mixture screw (16) to obtain maximum engine rpm, then turn high-speed mixture screw $^1/_6$ turn counterclockwise.

When overhauling carburetor, refer to exploded view in Fig. FJ101. Examine fuel inlet valve and seat. Inlet valve (21) is renewable, but carburetor body must be renewed if seat is excessively worn or damaged. Inspect mixture screws and

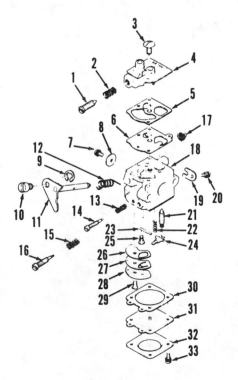

Fig. FJ101—Exploded view of Walbro WA carburetor used on some models.

1. Idle speed screw	17. Screen
2. Spring	18. Body
3. Screw	19. Clip
4. Pump cover	20. Screw
5. Gasket	21. Fuel inlet valve
6. Fuel pump diaphragm	22. Spring
7. Screw	23. Pin
8. Throttle plate	24. Metering lever
9. "E" ring	25. Screw
10. Cable clamp	26. Gasket
11. Throttle shaft	27. Gasket
12. Spring	28. Circuit plate
13. Spring	29. Screw
14. Idle mixture screw	30. Gasket
15. Spring	31. Metering diaphragm
16. High-speed mixture screw	32. Cover
	33. Screw

seats. Renew carburetor body if seats are excessively worn or damaged. Clean fuel screen (17). Inspect diaphragms (6 and 31) for tears and other damage.

Check metering lever height as shown in Fig. FJ102. Metering lever should be flush with body. Bend lever to obtain correct lever height.

Walbro WY, WYJ and WYL. Some engines may be equipped with a Walbro WY, WYJ or WYL carburetor. This is a diaphragm-type carburetor that uses a barrel-type throttle rather than a throttle plate.

Idle fuel for the carburetor flows up into the throttle barrel where it is fed into the air stream. On some models, the idle fuel flow can be adjusted by turn-

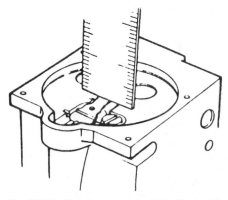

Fig. FJ102—Metering lever should be flush with carburetor body.

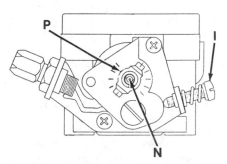

Fig. FJ103—On Walbro WY, WYJ and WYL carburetors, idle speed screw is located at (I), idle mixture plate is located at (P) and idle mixture needle is located at (N). A plug covers the idle mixture needle.

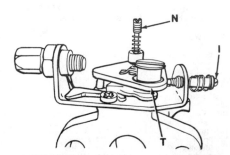

Fig. FJ104—View of idle mixture needle (N) used on Walbro WY, WYJ and WYL carburetors.

ing an idle mixture limiter plate (P—Fig. FJ103). Initial setting is in center notch. Rotating the plate clockwise will lean the idle mixture. Inside the mixture plate is an idle mixture needle (N) that is preset at the factory. If removed, use the following procedure to determine correct position. Back out needle (N—Fig. 104) until unscrewed. Screw in needle five turns on Model WY or 15 turns on Models WYJ and WYL. Rotate idle mixture plate (P—Fig. FJ103) to center notch. Run engine until normal operating temperature is attained. Adjust idle speed screw so trimmer head or blade does not rotate. Rotate idle mixture needle (N—Fig. FJ104) and obtain highest rpm (turning needle clockwise leans the mixture), then turn needle ¼ turn counterclockwise. Readjust idle speed screw. Note that idle mixture plate and needle are available only as an assembly with throttle barrel (19—Fig. FJ105).

The high-speed mixture is controlled by a removable fixed jet (16—Fig. FJ105).

To overhaul carburetor, refer to exploded view in Fig. FJ105 and note the following: On models with a plastic body, clean only with solvents approved for use with plastic. Do not use wire or drill bits to clean fuel passages as fuel flow could be affected if passages are enlarged. Do not disassemble throttle barrel assembly (19). Examine fuel inlet valve and seat. Inlet valve (9) is renewable, but fuel pump body (10) must be renewed if seat is excessively worn or damaged. Clean fuel screen (11). Inspect diaphragms for tears and other damage. When installing plates and gaskets (10 through 15), note that

tabs (T) on ends will "stairstep" when correctly installed. Adjust metering lever height dimension (D—Fig. FJ106) to obtain 1.5 mm (0.059 in.) between carburetor body surface and lever.

Walbro WZ. Some engines may be equipped with a Walbro WZ carburetor. This is a diaphragm-type carburetor that uses a barrel-type throttle rather than a throttle plate.

Idle fuel for the carburetor flows up into the throttle barrel where it is fed into the air stream. Idle fuel flow can be adjusted by turning idle mixture limiter plate (P—Fig. FJ107). Initial setting is in center notch. Rotating the plate clockwise will lean the idle mixture. Inside the mixture plate is an idle mixture needle (N—Fig. FJ104) that is preset at the factory (a plug covers the needle). If idle mixture needle is removed, use the following procedure to determine correct position. Back out needle (N) until unscrewed, then screw in needle six turns. Rotate idle mixture plate (P—Fig. FJ107) to center notch. Run engine until normal operating temperature is attained. Adjust idle speed screw so trimmer head or blade does not rotate. Rotate idle mixture needle (N—Fig. FJ104) and obtain highest rpm (turning needle clockwise leans the mixture), then turn needle counterclockwise until rpm decreases 200-500 rpm. Readjust idle speed screw. Note that idle mixture plate and needle are available only as an assembly with throttle barrel (24—Fig. FJ108).

Initial setting of high-speed mixture screw (42—Fig. FJ108) is 1½ turns out

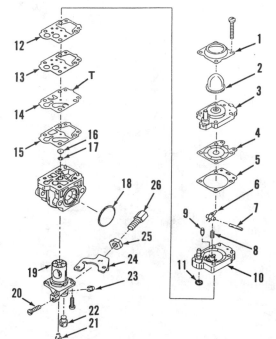

Fig. FJ105—Exploded view of Walbro WY carburetor. Models WYJ and WYL are similar.

1. Cover
2. Primer bulb
3. Plate
4. Metering diaphragm
5. Gasket
6. Metering lever
7. Pin
8. Spring
9. Fuel inlet valve
10. Fuel pump body
11. Fuel screen
12. Gasket
13. Fuel pump plate
14. Fuel pump diaphragm
15. Gasket
16. Main jet
17. "O" ring
18. "O" ring
19. Throttle barrel assy.
20. Idle speed screw
21. Plug
22. Swivel
23. "E" ring
24. Bracket
25. Nut
26. Adjuster

from a lightly seated position. Adjust high-speed mixture screw to obtain highest engine speed, then turn screw ¼ turn counterclockwise. Do not adjust mixture too lean as engine may be damaged.

To overhaul carburetor, refer to exploded view in Fig. FJ108 and note the following: Clean only with solvents approved for use with plastic. Do not use wire or drill bits to clean fuel passages as fuel delivery may be affected if passages are enlarged. Do not disassemble throttle barrel assembly (24). Examine fuel inlet valve and seat. Inlet valve (10) is renewable, but carburetor body must be renewed if seat is excessively worn or damaged. Inspect high-speed mixture screw and seat. Renew carburetor body if seat is excessively worn or damaged. Clean fuel screen. Inspect diaphragms for tears and other damage. When installing plates and gaskets (6 through 9) note that tabs on outer edges will "stair-step" when correctly installed. Adjust metering lever height dimension (D—Fig. FJ106) to obtain 1.5 mm (0.059 in.) between carburetor body surface and lever.

TK Series. Refer to Fig. FJ109 for an exploded view of the TK diaphragm-type carburetor used on some models. Initial setting for the idle mixture screw (18) is ¾ turn open from a lightly seated

position. Initial setting for the high-speed mixture screw (21) is two turns open from a lightly seated position. Be sure engine air filter is clean before adjusting carburetor.

Final adjustments are made with engine at normal operating temperature. Trimmer line must be fully extended or blade assembly installed on trimmer models. Adjust idle speed screw (17) so

engine rpm is 2500-3000. Trimmer head or blade should not rotate. Adjust idle mixture screw (18) so engine accelerates cleanly without hesitation. If necessary, readjust idle speed screw. Operate engine at full throttle and adjust high-speed mixture screw (21) to obtain maximum engine speed, then turn screw counterclockwise ⅙ turn to enrich fuel mixture slightly.

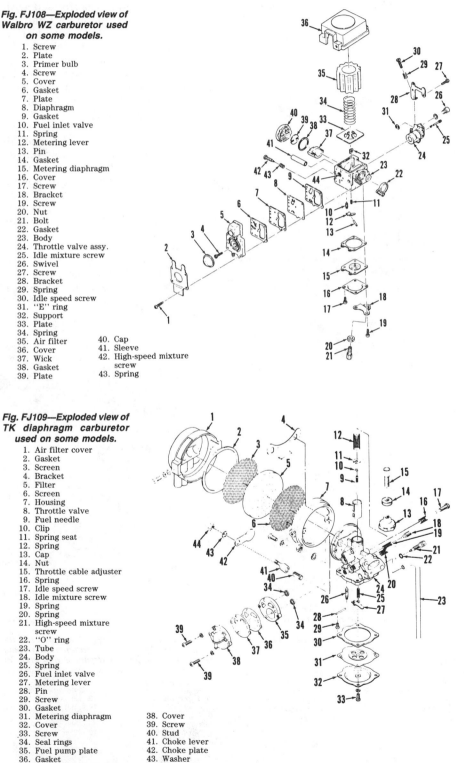

Fig. FJ108—Exploded view of Walbro WZ carburetor used on some models.

1. Screw
2. Plate
3. Primer bulb
4. Screw
5. Cover
6. Gasket
7. Plate
8. Diaphragm
9. Gasket
10. Fuel inlet valve
11. Spring
12. Metering lever
13. Pin
14. Gasket
15. Metering diaphragm
16. Cover
17. Screw
18. Bracket
19. Screw
20. Nut
21. Bolt
22. Gasket
23. Body
24. Throttle valve assy.
25. Idle mixture screw
26. Swivel
27. Screw
28. Bracket
29. Spring
30. Idle speed screw
31. "E" ring
32. Support
33. Plate
34. Spring
35. Air filter
36. Cover
37. Wick
38. Gasket
39. Plate
40. Cap
41. Sleeve
42. High-speed mixture screw
43. Spring

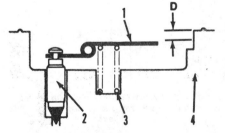

Fig. FJ106—Bend metering lever (1) as needed so height dimension (D) is as specified in text.

1. Metering lever
2. Fuel inlet valve
3. Spring
4. Body

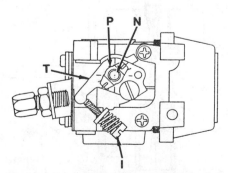

Fig. FJ107—On Walbro WZ carburetor, idle speed screw is located at (I), idle mixture plate is located at (P) and idle mixture needle is located at (N). A plug covers the idle mixture needle.

Fig. FJ109—Exploded view of TK diaphragm carburetor used on some models.

1. Air filter cover
2. Gasket
3. Screen
4. Bracket
5. Filter
6. Screen
7. Housing
8. Throttle valve
9. Fuel needle
10. Clip
11. Spring seat
12. Spring
13. Cap
14. Nut
15. Throttle cable adjuster
16. Spring
17. Idle speed screw
18. Idle mixture screw
19. Spring
20. Spring
21. High-speed mixture screw
22. "O" ring
23. Tube
24. Body
25. Spring
26. Fuel inlet valve
27. Metering lever
28. Pin
29. Screw
30. Gasket
31. Metering diaphragm
32. Cover
33. Screw
34. Seal rings
35. Fuel pump plate
36. Gasket
37. Fuel pump diaphragm
38. Cover
39. Screw
40. Stud
41. Choke lever
42. Choke plate
43. Washer
44. Nut

Midrange mixture is determined by the position of clip (10) on jet needle (9). There are three grooves in upper end of the jet needle and normal position of clip is in the middle groove. See Fig. FJ110. The mixture will be leaner if clip is installed in the top groove, or richer if clip is installed in the bottom groove.

Overhaul is evident after inspecting carburetor and referring to Fig. FJ109. Fuel inlet lever spring (25) free length should be 9.5 mm (0.35 in.). Metering lever height dimension (D—Fig. FJ106)

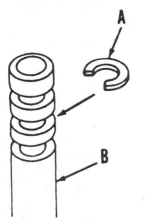

Fig. FJ110—Normal position for jet needle clip (A) is in the center groove of jet needle (B).

should be 2.0 mm (0.08 in.). Carefully bend lever to obtain dimension.

Teikei. Some models may be equipped with the Teikei diaphragm carburetor shown in Fig. FJ111. Initial setting of idle mixture screw (29) is 1¼ turns out from a lightly seated position. Initial setting of high-speed mixture screw (28) is ¾ turn out. Be sure engine air filter is clean before adjusting carburetor.

Final adjustment is performed with engine at normal operating temperature. Before final adjustment on trimmer models, cutter line should be desired length or blade assembly installed. Adjust idle mixture screw (29) so engine idles smoothly and accelerates cleanly without hesitation. Adjust idle speed screw (1) so engine idles just below clutch engagement speed. Open throttle to wide open position and adjust high-speed mixture screw (28) so engine speed is 9000 rpm. If an accurate tachometer is not available, do not adjust high-speed mixture needle beyond initial setting. Do not adjust high-speed mixture screw too lean as engine may be damaged.

Overhaul is evident after inspecting carburetor and referring to Fig. FJ111. Metering lever height dimension (D—Fig. FJ106) should be 2.0 mm (0.08 in.). Carefully bend lever to obtain dimension.

Float-Type Carburetor. Some models are equipped with the float-type carburetor shown in Fig. FJ112. If equipped with an idle mixture screw (8), initial setting is one turn out from a lightly seated position.

Jet needle clip (5) should be installed in second groove (B—Fig. FJ113) on EC02 models or in the third groove (C) on EC03 and EC04 models.

Float level (D—Fig. FJ114) should be 3.5 mm (0.138 in.) from gasket surface at fuel inlet needle side and 3 mm (0.118 in.) from gasket surface at opposite side of float.

DPK Series. Some models are equipped with the DPK diaphragm-type carburetor shown in Fig. FJ115. Initial setting of high-speed mixture screw (15) is 1½ turns out from a lightly seated position. Perform final adjustment with trimmer line fully extended or blade assembly installed and engine at normal operating temperature. Be sure engine air filter is clean before adjusting carburetor.

Operate engine at full throttle and turn high-speed mixture screw (15) so

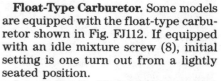

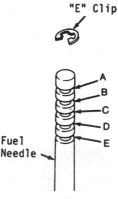

Fig. FJ113—Normal position of clip on jet needle is determined according to engine model. Refer to text.

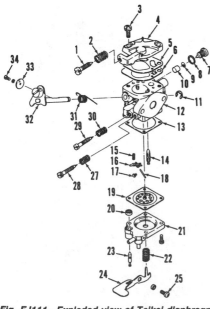

Fig. FJ111—Exploded view of Teikei diaphragm carburetor used on some models.

1.	Idle speed screw	18.	Pin
2.	Spring	19.	Diaphragm
3.	Screw	20.	Seat
4.	Fuel pump cover	21.	Cover
5.	Gasket	22.	Spring
6.	Diaphragm	23.	Plunger
7.	Plug	24.	Primer lever
8.	"O" ring	25.	Screw
9.	Screen	27.	Spring
10.	Felt	28.	High-speed mixture
11.	"E" ring		screw
12.	Body	29.	Idle mixture screw
13.	Gasket	30.	Spring
14.	Fuel inlet valve	31.	Spring
15.	Spring	32.	Throttle shaft
16.	Fuel inlet lever	33.	Throttle plate
17.	Screw	34.	Screw

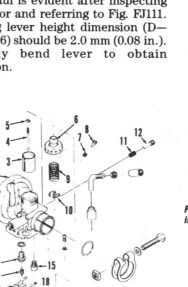

Fig. FJ112—Exploded view of float-type carburetor used on some models. Fitting (13) on some models may be equipped with a fuel shut-off valve.

1.	Choke lever		
2.	Body	12.	Idle speed screw
3.	Throttle valve	13.	Fitting
4.	Fuel inlet valve	14.	Fuel inlet valve seat
5.	Clip	15.	Main jet
6.	Cap	16.	Fuel inlet valve
7.	Spring	17.	Float lever
8.	Air screw	18.	Pin
9.	Spring	19.	Gasket
10.	Spring seat	20.	Float
11.	Spring	21.	Float bowl

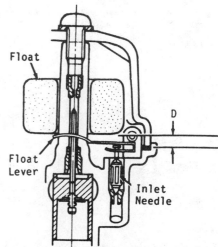

Fig. FJ114—Float level should be measured as shown. Refer to text for distance measurement (D).

engine runs smoothly at maximum speed, then back out screw ⅛ turn. Normal range of adjustment is 1-2 turns out. Adjust idle speed screw (12) so engine idles just below clutch engagement speed.

Midrange mixture is determined by the position of clip (7) on jet needle (8). There are three grooves in upper end of the jet needle and normal position of clip is in the middle groove. See Fig. FJ110. The mixture will be leaner if clip is installed in the top groove, or richer if clip is installed in the bottom groove.

Overhaul is evident after inspecting carburetor and referring to Fig. FJ115. Metering lever height dimension (D—Fig. FJ106) should be 2.0-2.4 mm (0.08-0.09 in.). Carefully bend lever to obtain dimension.

IGNITION SYSTEM. Fuji engines may be equipped with a breaker point ignition system or an electronic ignition system. Refer to appropriate following section for service information.

Breaker Point Ignition System. The ignition condenser and breaker point set are located behind the flywheel. To adjust breaker point setting, remove flywheel and rotate crankshaft so breaker point contacts are at widest gap. Adjust gap to 0.35 mm (0.014 in.).

Ignition timing should be set at 26 degrees BTDC on EC01 engine or 25 degrees BTDC on EC02 engine. To check timing, rotate flywheel until the "F" mark cast on flywheel surface aligns with setting mark on crankcase (Fig. FJ116). Carefully remove flywheel and make certain contact set is just beginning to open.

Air gap between flywheel and ignition coil should be 0.5 mm (0.020 in.) for EC01 and EC02 engines or 0.2 mm (0.008 in.) for EC03 and EC04 engines.

Electronic Ignition System. Some engines are equipped with an electronic ignition system. Ignition system performance is considered satisfactory if a spark will jump across a 3 mm (⅛ in.) electrode gap on a test spark plug. If no spark is produced, check on/off switch, wiring and ignition module air gap. Ignition module air gap should be 0.2 mm (0.008 in.). If switch, wiring and module air gap are satisfactory, but spark is not present, renew ignition module.

REPAIRS

TIGHTENING TORQUES. Recommended tightening torques are as follows:
Crankcase:
EC01A, EC02F
& EC02R ....4.1-4.7 N·m
(36-42 in.-lbs.)
EC02E & EC02EH .....3.9-4.9 N·m
(35-43 in.-lbs.)
EC03-1R, EC03-2R
& EC04-3R ....4-7 N·m
(35-62 in.-lbs.)
EC03E, EC04E
& EC05M ....6.4-7.8 N·m
(57-69 in.-lbs.)

Cylinder:
EC01A, EC02F
& EC02R ....4.1-4.7 N·m
(36-42 in.-lbs.)
EC02E, EC02EH
& EC05M ....6.4-7.8 N·m
(57-69 in.-lbs.)
EC03-1R, EC03-2R
& EC04-3R ....9-11 N·m
(78-95 in.-lbs.)
EC03E & EC04E .....10.8-12.7 N·m
(96-112 in.-lbs.)

Flywheel:
EC01A ....11.8-13.7 N·m
(104-121 in.-lbs.)
EC02E, EC02EH
& EC02F ....10.8-12.7 N·m
(96-112 in.-lbs.)
EC02R ....13.7-15.6 N·m
(121-138 in.-lbs.)
EC03-1R, EC03-2R
& EC04-3R ....14-18 N·m
(124-159 in.-lbs.)
EC03E & EC04E ......9.8-13.7 N·m
(87-121 in.-lbs.)
EC05M ....28.4-34.3 N·m
(21-25 ft.-lbs.)

Spark plug:
EC02R ....21.6-29.4 N·m
(191-260 in.-lbs.)
EC02F & EC05M .....14.7-24.5 N·m
(130-217 in.-lbs.)
All other models .....14.7-19.6 N·m
(130-173 in.-lbs.)

PISTON, PIN AND RINGS. To remove piston, first remove cooling shroud and recoil starter assembly. Remove carburetor and muffler. Remove all bolts retaining cylinder to crankcase and carefully pull cylinder off piston. Remove piston pin retaining rings and press pin out of piston pin bore. Piston and needle bearing may now be removed from connecting rod.

Piston and rings are available in standard size only. Refer to following service specifications.
Piston Diameter:
EC01A ....28.00 mm
(1.102 in.)

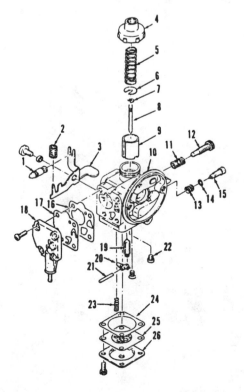

Fig. FJ115—Exploded view of DPK diaphragm-type carburetor used on some models.

1. Primer valve
2. Spring
3. Lever
4. Cap
5. Spring
6. Retainer
7. Clip
8. Jet needle
9. Throttle slide
10. Body
11. Spring
12. Idle speed screw
13. Spring
14. "O" ring
15. Main fuel mixture screw
16. Pump gasket
17. Pump diaphragm
18. Pump cover
19. Fuel inlet valve
20. Metering lever
21. Pin
22. Main jet
23. Spring
24. Gasket
25. Diaphragm
26. Cover

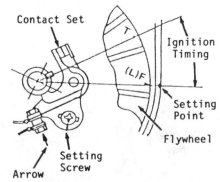

Fig. FJ116—View showing location of timing mark on flywheel and crankcase. Refer to text.

EC02E . . . . 31.47 mm
(1.239 in.)
EC02EH & EC02F . . . . . . 32.97 mm
(1.298 in.)
EC02R . . . . 31.99 mm
(1.260 in.)
EC03-1R & EC03-2R . . . . . 35.96 mm
(1.416 in.)
EC03E . . . . 36.98 mm
(1.456 in.)
EC04-3R . . . . 39.94 mm
(1.572 in.)
EC04E . . . . 39.98 mm
(1.574 in.)
EC05M . . . . 43.96 mm
(1.730 in.)

Renew piston if piston diameter is less than 0.05 mm (0.002 in.) of standard size.

Piston ring end gap should be 0.1-0.3 mm (0.004-0.012 in.). Maximum allowable ring end gap is 1.0 mm (0.040 in.). Maximum allowable piston ring side clearance in piston ring groove is 0.15 mm (0.006 in.) for all models.

Piston pin diameter and piston pin bore diameter for Models EC01A, EC02E, EC02EH and EC02R is 8.00 mm (0.315 in.). Minimum allowable pin diameter is 7.99 mm (0.3146 in.). Maximum allowable piston pin bore diameter is 8.02 mm (0.3157 in.).

Piston pin diameter and piston pin bore diameter for Models EC03-1R, EC03-2R and EC03E is 10.00 mm (0.3937 in.). Minimum allowable pin diameter is 9.983 mm (0.3930 in.). Maximum allowable piston pin bore diameter is 10.03 mm (0.3949 in.).

Piston pin diameter and piston pin bore diameter for Models EC04-3R and

EC05M is 12.00 mm (0.4724 in.). Minimum allowable pin diameter is 11.983 mm (0.4718 in.). Maximum piston pin bore diameter is 12.03 mm (0.4736 in.).

When installing piston, position piston on rod so "M" mark on piston crown is towards flywheel end of crankshaft.

CYLINDER. Inspect cylinder for excessive wear and damage. Renew cylinder if piston-to-cylinder clearance with a new piston installed exceeds 0.08 mm (0.003 in.) on Model EC01A, 0.1 mm (0.004 in.) on Models EC02E and EC02EH, 0.12 mm (0.0047 in.) on Model EC02R, or 0.18 mm (0.007 in.) on all other models.

CRANKSHAFT, ROD AND CRANKCASE. The crankshaft and connecting rod are a unit assembly; individual components are not available. The connecting rod small end is equipped with a renewable needle bearing on some models.

To remove crankshaft assembly, remove fuel tank, muffler cover, muffler and carburetor. Remove rewind starter and cooling shroud. Remove spark plug and install locking bolt or end of a rope in spark plug hole to lock piston and connecting rod. Remove flywheel and clutch. Separate cylinder from crankcase and piston. Remove piston from connecting rod. Remove bolts retaining crankcase halves and separate crankcase being careful not to damage crankcase mating surfaces. Press main bearings off crankshaft as necessary. If main bearings remain in crankcase halves, heat crankcase slightly to aid in removal

of bearings. Pry seals out of crankcase halves.

Renew crankshaft assembly if connecting rod side clearance on crankshaft exceeds 0.7 mm (0.028 in.). Maximum allowable crankshaft runout is 0.1 mm (0.004 in.) measured at main bearing journals with crankshaft supported at ends. Maximum allowable crankshaft end play is 0.8 mm (0.031 in.).

REED VALVE. Some models are equipped with a reed valve induction system. Inspect reed valve petals and seats on reed valve plate (33—Fig. FJ118). Renew reed valve assembly if petals or seats are damaged.

CLUTCH. Most engines used on trimmers or brush cutters are equipped with a two- or three-shoe clutch. The shoe assembly is located at the drive end of the crankshaft and mounted on a flange or on the back side of the flywheel. The clutch drum rides in the drive housing.

To remove the clutch drum (11—Figs. FJ119 or FJ120), unbolt and remove clutch housing and drive tube from engine. Separate drive tube from clutch housing. On models with slots in clutch face, reach through slot and detach snap ring (12), then separate clutch drum and bearing (13) from clutch housing. Note that on some models, clutch drum and drive shaft must be removed as a unit. Heating housing will ease removal. On engines without slotted clutch drum, detach snap ring (2—Fig. FJ122) and press clutch drum shaft (5) out of bearing (1). Detach snap ring (3), heat housing and remove bearing. Reverse

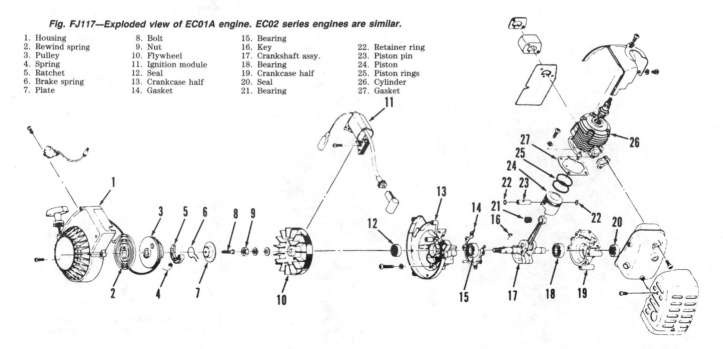

Fig. FJ117—Exploded view of EC01A engine. EC02 series engines are similar.

1. Housing
2. Rewind spring
3. Pulley
4. Spring
5. Ratchet
6. Brake spring
7. Plate
8. Bolt
9. Nut
10. Flywheel
11. Ignition module
12. Seal
13. Crankcase half
14. Gasket
15. Bearing
16. Key
17. Crankshaft assy.
18. Bearing
19. Crankcase half
20. Seal
21. Bearing
22. Retainer ring
23. Piston pin
24. Piston
25. Piston rings
26. Cylinder
27. Gasket

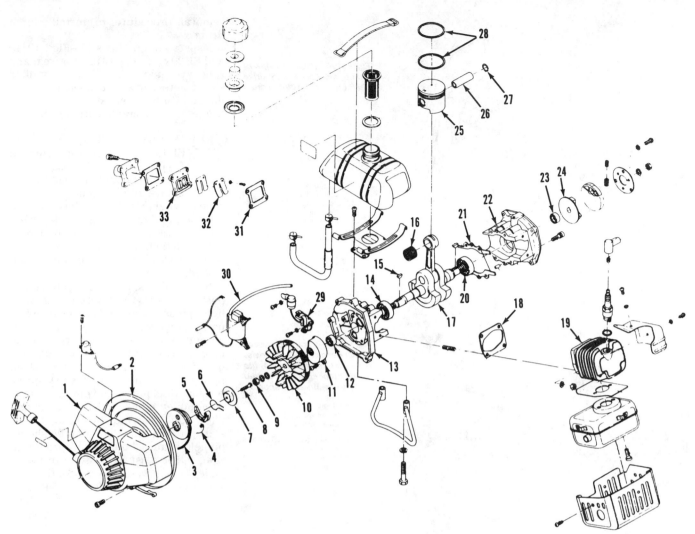

Fig. FJ118—Exploded view of EC04 series engine. EC03 engines are similar.

1. Housing	7. Plate	13. Crankcase half	19. Cylinder	25. Piston	
2. Rewind spring	8. Bolt	14. Bearing	20. Bearing	26. Piston pin	30. Ignition coil
3. Pulley	9. Nut	15. Key	21. Gasket	27. Retainer ring	31. Gasket
4. Spring	10. Flywheel	16. Bearing	22. Crankcase half	28. Piston rings	32. Reed backup plate
5. Ratchet	11. Cover	17. Crankshaft assy.	23. Seal	29. Breaker points	33. Reed plate
6. Brake spring	12. Seal	18. Gasket	24. Clutch retainer		

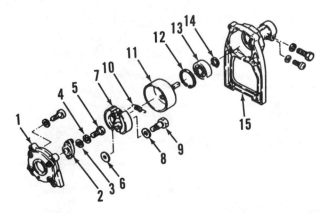

Fig. FJ119—Exploded view of clutch used on some models.

1. Plate
2. Flange
3. Washer
4. Lockwasher
5. Screw
6. Washer
7. Clutch shoes
8. Washer
9. Screw
10. Spring
11. Clutch drum
12. Snap ring
13. Bearing
14. Snap ring
15. Clutch housing

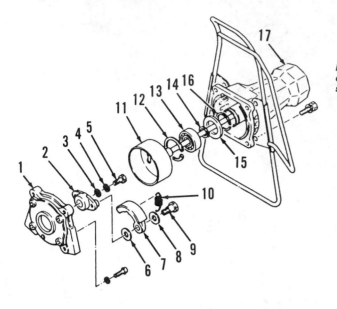

Fig. FJ120—Exploded view of clutch assembly with drive shaft attached to clutch drum (11).

1. Plate
2. Flange
3. Washer
4. Lockwasher
5. Screw
6. Washer
7. Clutch shoes
8. Washer
9. Screw
10. Spring
11. Clutch drum
12. Snap ring
13. Bearing
14. Snap ring
15. Washer
16. Snap ring
17. Clutch housing

removal procedure to install clutch drum.

Inspect clutch shoes (7—Figs. FJ119 and FJ120 or 2—Fig. FJ121) for wear and renew as necessary. When installing shoes, note arrows on shoes indicating direction of rotation. Arrows must point in direction of crankshaft rotation.

REWIND STARTER. Refer to Figs. FJ117, FJ118 and FJ123 for exploded views of typical starters. To disassemble starter, detach starter housing from engine. Remove rope handle and allow rope to wind into starter. Unscrew center screw and remove rope pulley. Wear appropriate safety eyewear and gloves before detaching rewind spring from housing as spring may uncoil uncontrolled.

To assemble starter, lubricate center post of housing and spring side with light grease. Assemble starter while passing rope through housing rope outlet and attach rope handle to rope. To place tension on starter rope, pull rope out of housing. Engage rope in notch on pulley and turn pulley against spring tension. Hold pulley and disengage rope from pulley notch. Release pulley and allow rope to wind on pulley. Check starter operation. Rope handle should be held against housing by spring tension, but it must be possible to rotate pulley at least $1/4$ turn against spring tension when rope is pulled out fully.

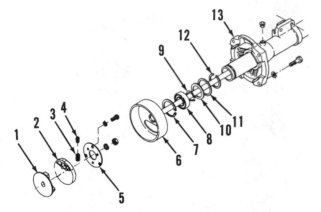

Fig. FJ121—Exploded view of clutch used on some models. Note that inner spring (4) fits inside outer spring (3) on hub (1) to retain each shoe.

1. Hub
2. Shoes
3. Outer spring
4. Inner spring
5. Plate
6. Clutch drum
7. Snap ring
8. Bearing
9. Snap ring
10. Spacer
11. Washer
12. Snap ring
13. Clutch housing

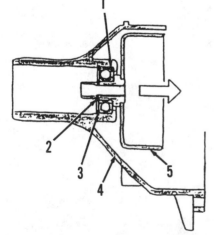

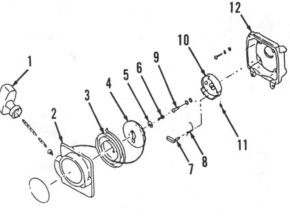

Fig. FJ123—Exploded view of rewind starter used on some models.

1. Rope handle
2. Starter housing
3. Rewind spring
4. Pulley
5. Washer
6. Screw
7. Pawl
8. Spring
9. Screw
10. Plate
11. "E" ring
12. Housing

Fig. FJ122—Some models are equipped with clutch drum assembly shown above.

1. Bearing
2. Snap ring
3. Snap ring
4. Clutch housing
5. Clutch drum

HOMELITE

ENGINE SERVICE

Model	Bore	Stroke	Displacement
HB-280, HB-380	$1^5/_{16}$ in. (33.3 mm)	$1^3/_{16}$ in. (30.2 mm)	1.6 cu. in. (26.2 cc)
HB-480*, HB-680*	$1^7/_{16}$ in. (36.5 mm)	$1^3/_{16}$ in. (30.2 mm)	1.9 cu. in. (31.2 cc)
ST-80, ST-100, ST-120, ST-160, ST-160A, ST-165 ST-180, ST-260	$1^5/_{16}$ in. (33.3 mm)	$1^3/_{16}$ in. (30.2 mm)	1.6 cu. in. (26.2 cc)
ST-200, ST-210 ST-310	$1^7/_{16}$ in. (36.5 mm)	$1^3/_{16}$ in. (30.2 mm)	1.9 cu. in. (31.2 cc)

*Early Models HB-480 and HB-680 are equipped with 1.6 cu. in. (26.2 cc) displacement engine.

ENGINE INFORMATION

The Homelite two-stroke, air-cooled engines covered in this section are used on Homelite string trimmers, brush cutters and blowers.

MAINTENANCE

LUBRICATION. The engine on all models is lubricated by mixing oil with gasoline. Homelite oil is recommended and should be mixed at ratio designated on container. If Homelite oil is not used, manufacturer specifies that only oils designed for two-stroke engines with a fuel:oil ratio of 32:1 or more should be used.

An antioxidant fuel stabilizer (such as Sta-Bil) should be added to fuel if Homelite oil is not used. Homelite oil contains an antioxidant fuel stabilizer.

SPARK PLUG. Recommended spark plug is Champion DJ7J for Models ST-80, ST-100, ST-120, ST-200 and ST-210. Recommended spark plug for all other models is Champion DJ7Y. Spark plug electrode gap should be 0.025 inch (0.6 mm).

CARBURETOR. Various carburetors are used depending on equipment model. Refer to appropriate carburetor section below for service information.

Keihin. A Keihin float-type carburetor is used on some blower engines. Adjust idle speed so engine idles at 3350-3500 rpm. Idle mixture is not adjustable. High-speed mixture is controlled by

removable fixed jet (14—Fig. HL40-1). Midrange mixture is determined by the position of clip (7) on jet needle (6). There are three grooves in upper end of the jet needle and normal position of clip is in the middle groove. The mixture will be leaner if clip is installed in the top groove, or richer if clip is installed in the bottom groove.

Overhaul of carburetor is evident after inspection and referral to Fig. HL40-1. Before removing carburetor from engine, unscrew cap (3) and withdraw throttle slide (8) assembly. When overhauling carburetor, refer to Fig. HL40-1 and note the following: Examine fuel inlet valve and seat. Inlet valve (13) is renewable. The inlet seat is not renewable and carburetor body (12) must be renewed if seat is excessively worn or damaged. When installing throttle slide, be sure groove in side of throttle slide indexes with pin in bore of carburetor body.

Walbro HDC. Initial setting of low speed mixture screw (10—Fig. HL40-2) is $1^1/_2$ turns out from a lightly seated po-

sition. Initial setting of high-speed mixture screw (11), on models so equipped, is $^3/_4$ turn out. Final adjustment is performed with engine running at normal operating temperature. Adjust idle speed screw (9) so engine idles at 2800-

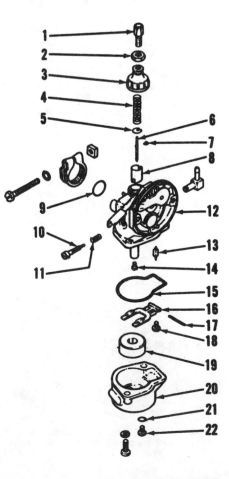

Fig. HL40-1—Exploded view of Keihin carburetor used on later Models HB-280, HB-380, HB-480 and HB-680.

1. Cable adjusting nut	12. Body
2. Nut	13. Fuel inlet valve
3. Cap	14. Main jet
4. Spring	15. Gasket
5. Retainer	16. Float arm
6. Jet needle	17. Float pin
7. Clip	18. Screw
8. Throttle slide	19. Float
9. "O" ring	20. Fuel bowl
10. Idle speed screw	21. Gasket
11. Spring	22. Drain screw

3200 rpm on Models ST-160, ST-160A, ST-165, ST-180 and ST-260, or just below clutch engagement speed on other models. Adjust idle mixture screw so engine runs at highest idle speed and will accelerate cleanly, then readjust idle speed screw. Adjust high-speed mixture screw, if so equipped, so at full throttle, engine fluctuates between two-stroke and four-stroke operation. Recheck idle adjustment.

Carburetor disassembly and reassembly is evident after inspection of carburetor and referral to Fig. HL40-2. Some carburetors are equipped with an accelerator pump that uses a bladder to eject additional fuel through the main fuel orifice when needed. Clean and inspect all components. Inspect diaphragms (3 and 21) for defects that may affect operation. Examine fuel inlet valve and seat. Inlet valve (16) is renewable, but carburetor body must be renewed if seat is damaged or excessively worn. Wires or drill bits should not be used to clean passages as fuel flow may be altered. Discard carburetor body if mixture screw seats are damaged or excessively worn. Screens should be clean. Be sure choke and throttle plates fit shafts and carburetor bore properly. Apply Loctite to retaining screws. Adjust metering lever height so metering lever tip is flush with body as shown in Fig. HL40-3.

Walbro WA. Some engines are equipped with a Walbro WA diaphragm-type carburetor.

To adjust carburetor on trimmers, proceed as follows: Initial adjustment of idle mixture screw (12—Fig. HL40-4) is $1\frac{1}{4}$ turns out from a lightly seated position. Final adjustments are performed with trimmer line at recommended length or blade installed. Engine must be at operating temperature and running. Adjust idle speed screw so engine idles at 2800-3200 rpm on Models ST-80, ST-100 and ST-120. Adjust idle mixture screw so engine runs at highest idle speed and will accelerate cleanly, then readjust idle speed screw. High-speed mixture is not adjustable.

To adjust carburetor on blowers, proceed as follows: Initial adjustment of idle and high-speed mixture screws is one turn out. Adjust idle speed so engine idles at 3350-3500 rpm. Adjust idle mixture screw (12—Fig. HL40-4) so engine will accelerate cleanly. Adjust high-speed mixture screw (9) so maximum engine rpm is 7200-7800 for HB-280, 7800-8600 for HB-480 and 7600-8400 for HB-680.

When overhauling carburetor, refer to exploded view in Fig. HL40-4. Examine fuel inlet valve and seat. Inlet valve (7) is renewable, but carburetor body must be renewed if seat is excessively worn or damaged. Inspect mixture screws and seats. Renew carburetor body if seats are excessively worn or damaged. Clean fuel screen. Inspect diaphragms for tears and other damage.

Check metering lever height as shown in Fig. HL40-5 using Walbro tool 500-13. Metering lever should just touch leg on tool. Bend lever to obtain correct lever height.

Zama C1S or C2S. Some engines are equipped with a Zama C1S or C2S diaphragm-type carburetor.

To adjust carburetor, proceed as follows: Initial adjustment of idle mixture

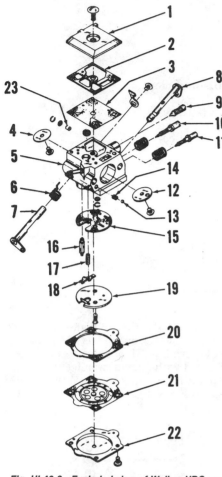

Fig. HL40-2—Exploded view of Walbro HDC carburetor. High-speed mixture screw (11) is absent on some models.

1. Cover
2. Gasket
3. Fuel pump diaphragm
4. Throttle plate
5. Body
6. Return spring
7. Throttle shaft
8. Choke shaft
9. Idle speed screw
10. Idle mixture screw
11. High-speed mixture screw
12. Choke plate
13. Detent ball
14. Spring
15. Gasket
16. Fuel inlet valve
17. Spring
18. Metering lever
19. Circuit plate
20. Gasket
21. Metering diaphragm
22. Cover
23. Limiting jet

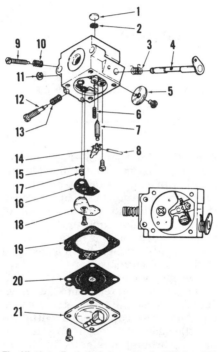

Fig. HL40-4—Exploded view of typical Walbro WA carburetor.

1. Welch plug
2. Screen
3. Spring
4. Throttle shaft
5. Throttle plate
6. Spring
7. Fuel inlet valve
8. Lever pin
9. High-speed mixture screw
10. Spring
11. Clip
12. Idle mixture screw
13. Spring
14. Metering lever
15. Screen
16. Gasket
17. Check valve
18. Circuit plate
19. Gasket
20. Metering diaphragm
21. Fuel inlet cover

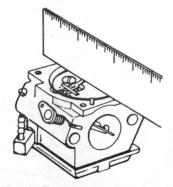

Fig. HL40-3—Tip of metering lever should be flush with body on Walbro HDC carburetor. Bend metering lever as needed.

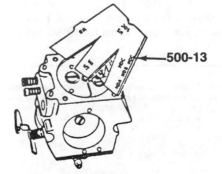

500-13

Fig. HL40-5—On Walbro WA carburetor, metering lever should just touch leg of Walbro tool 500-13. Bend lever to obtain correct lever height.

screw (13—Fig. HL40-6) is 1¼ turns out from a lightly seated position. Final adjustments are performed with trimmer line at recommended length or blade installed. Engine must be at operating temperature and running. Adjust idle speed screw so engine idles at 2800-3200 rpm. Adjust idle mixture screw so engine runs at highest idle speed and will accelerate cleanly, then readjust idle speed screw. High-speed mixture is not adjustable.

Carburetor disassembly and reassembly is evident after inspection of carburetor and referral to Fig. HL40-6. On Model C2S, do not lose detent ball when withdrawing choke shaft. Clean and inspect all components. Inspect diaphragms (5 and 27) for defects that may affect operation. Examine fuel inlet valve and seat. Inlet valve (22) is renewable, but carburetor body must be renewed if seat is damaged or excessively worn. Discard carburetor body if mix-

ture screw seat is damaged or excessively worn. Clean fuel screen.

To reassemble carburetor, reverse disassembly procedure. Metering lever should be level with chamber floor as shown in Fig. HL40-7. Bend metering lever as needed.

IGNITION. Early Model ST-100 is equipped with a conventional breaker-point, flywheel magneto. Breaker point gap should be 0.015 inch (0.38 mm). Ignition timing is not adjustable. However, an incorrect breaker point gap setting will affect ignition timing.

A solid state ignition is used on all models except early ST-100 models. The ignition module is attached to the side of the engine cylinder. Ignition service is accomplished by replacing ignition components until the faulty component is located. Air gap between ignition module and flywheel is adjustable and should be 0.015 inch (0.38 mm). Loosen ignition module mounting screws and adjust module position to set air gap.

REPAIRS

TIGHTENING TORQUE VALUES. Tightening torque values are listed in following table:

Flywheel............100-150 in.-lbs. (11.3-16.9 N·m)
Spark plug..........120-180 in.-lbs. (13.6-20.3 N·m)
Crankcase screws—
socket head.........45-55 in.-lbs. (5.1-6.2 N·m)

COMPRESSION PRESSURE. For optimum performance of all models, cylinder compression pressure should be 115-145 psi (792-1000 kPa) with engine at normal operating temperature. Engine should be inspected and repaired when compression pressure is 90 psi (621 kPa) or below.

CYLINDER, PISTON, PIN AND RINGS. The cylinder (6—Figs. HL40-8, HL40-9 or HL40-10) may be removed after unscrewing four screws in bottom of crankcase (19). Be careful when removing cylinder as crankshaft assembly will be loose in crankcase. Care should be

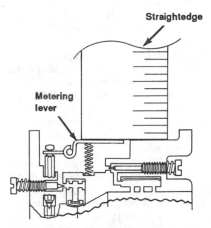

Fig. HL40-7—On Zama C1S and C2S carburetors, metering lever should be flush with metering chamber floor. Bend metering lever as needed.

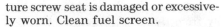

Fig. HL40-6—Exploded view of typical Zama C1S carburetor. Model C2S is similar. Model C2S is equipped with a choke shaft and plate.

2. Fuel pump cover
3. Gasket
4. Plate
5. Fuel pump diaphragm
6. Screen
7. Body
8. Throttle plate
9. Throttle shaft
10. Spring
11. "E" ring
13. Idle mixture screw
15. Spring
16. Plug
20. Check valve
21. Spring
22. Fuel inlet valve
23. Metering lever
24. Pin
25. Metering disc
26. Gasket
27. Metering diaphragm
28. Cover

Fig. HL40-8—Exploded view of engine used on Models ST-80, ST-100 and ST-120. Early Model ST-100 trimmers are equipped with breaker point ignition shown in inset.

1. Coil core
2. Ignition coil
3. Breaker point assy.
4. Ignition module
5. Spark plug
6. Cylinder
7. Piston ring
8. Retaining rings
9. Piston pin
10. Piston
11. Seal
12. Seal spacer
13. Needle bearing
14. Thrust washer
15. Crankshaft
16. Flywheel
17. Air cover
18. Seal
19. Crankcase
20. Gasket
21. Reed valve petal
22. Throttle cable
23. Cable clamp
24. Carburetor housing
25. Gasket
26. Carburetor
27. "O" ring
28. Filter
29. Gasket
30. Fuel inlet
31. Choke
32. Filter support
33. Air filter
34. Cover
35. Ground wire (early ST-100)
36. Ground wire (solid state ign.)
37. Key

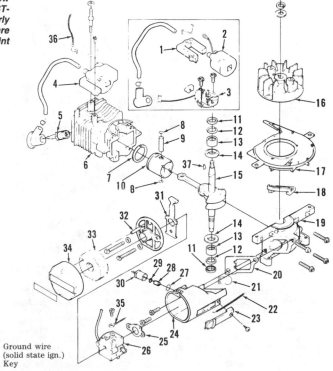

taken not to damage mating surfaces of cylinder and crankcase. Pry out piston pin retaining ring (8) and push piston pin (9) out of piston to separate piston from connecting rod.

Inspect piston and cylinder for wear, scoring or other damage and renew as necessary. Use a wooden scraper to remove carbon from cylinder ports. Cylinder and crankcase mating surfaces should be flat and free of nicks and scratches. Mating surfaces should be cleaned then coated with room temperature vulcanizing (RTV) silicone sealer before assembly.

Piston must be assembled to connecting rod so that piston ring end gap is located opposite exhaust port side of cylinder. Some pistons have a locating pin in piston ring groove, and piston ring end gap must index with the locating pin. Some pistons do not have a pin in the ring groove. On these models, piston and ring must be assembled to connecting rod so ring gap and notch in piston are located opposite exhaust port side of cylinder. Lubricate piston and cylinder with engine oil before installing piston in cylinder.

CRANKSHAFT AND CONNECTING ROD. The crankshaft and connecting rod are serviced as an assembly. To disassemble, first separate engine from string trimmer or blower unit. Remove carburetor and muffler. Remove spark plug and place end of a starter rope into cylinder to lock the piston and crankshaft. Remove flywheel retaining nut and pull flywheel off crankshaft. On

trimmer models, remove clutch assembly from flywheel. On all models, remove screws attaching crankcase (19—Figs. HL40-8, HL40-9 or HL40-10) to cylinder (6). Tap crankcase with plastic mallet to break seal between mating surfaces, then separate crankcase from cylinder and remove crankshaft and connecting rod assembly. Pry out piston pin retaining ring, push piston pin out of piston and separate piston from connecting rod. Note that main bearing rollers are loose in their cages and may fall out when removed. To aid in their removal, wrap a piece of paper around crankshaft and slide bearings out over the paper. Remove the bearing and paper sleeve together to hold needle bearings in place.

Inspect crankshaft bearings (13) and renew if scored or worn. Crankshaft and connecting rod must be renewed as an assembly if worn or damaged.

Thrust washers (14) should be installed with shoulder to outside. Bearings are installed with lettered side facing outward. Lubricate seals (11) with oil and install onto crankshaft with lip to inside. Thoroughly clean crankcase and cylinder mating surfaces, then apply light coat of silastic sealant to mating surfaces. Assemble crankshaft, cylinder and crankcase, but do not tighten crankcase screws at this time. When properly assembled, outer surface of seals should be flush with cylinder and crankcase. Gently tap each end of crankshaft with a plastic hammer to establish end play in crankshaft. Tighten crankcase screws evenly to 50 in.-lbs. (5.6 N·m).

Make certain that crankshaft does not bind when rotated.

REED VALVE. All models are equipped with a reed valve induction system. Reed petal (21—Figs. HL40-8, HL40-9 or HL40-10) is accessible after removing carburetor and manifold spacer from crankcase. Renew reed petal if cracked, bent or otherwise damaged. Do not attempt to straighten a bent reed petal. Seating surface for reed petal should be flat, clean and smooth. When reassembling, apply a light coat of silastic sealant to mating surface of manifold. Use grease to hold reed petal in place when manifold is assembled to crankcase.

CLUTCH. Models ST-200 and ST-210 are equipped with centrifugal clutches (29—Fig. HL40-9), which are accessible after removing engine housing. Clutch hub (29) has left-hand threads. Inspect bushing (31) and renew if excessively worn. Install clutch hub (29) while noting "OUTSIDE" marked on side of hub.

REWIND STARTER. Refer to blower section for service of rewind starters used on blowers.

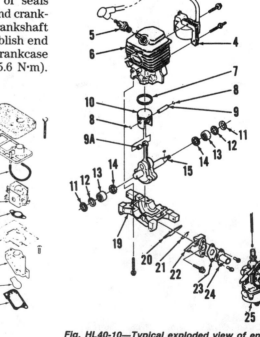

Fig. HL40-10—Typical exploded view of engine used on Model HB-280, HB-480 and HB-680 blowers. Bearing (9A) is only used on later Model HB-480 and HB-680.

4. Ignition module	14. Thrust washer
5. Spark plug	15. Crankshaft
6. Cylinder	19. Crankcase
7. Piston ring	20. Gasket
8. Retaining ring	21. Reed valve petal
9. Piston pin	22. Carburetor spacer
10. Piston	23. Gasket
11. Seal	24. Intake manifold
12. Seal spacer	25. Carburetor
13. Needle bearing	

Fig. HL40-9—Exploded view of engine used on Models ST-160, ST-180, ST-200 and ST-210. Adapter (34) is used in place of clutch components (29, 30 and 31) on Models ST-160 and ST-180.

4. Ignition modul	11. Seal	17. Key	23. Air baffle	29. Clutch hub
5. Spark plug	12. Seal spacer	18. Shroud	24. Gasket	30. Clutch drum
6. Cylinder	13. Needle bearing	19. Crankcase	25. Carburetor	31. Bushing
7. Piston ring	14. Thrust washer	20. Gasket	26. Tubing	32. Drive shaft
8. Retaining ring	15. Crankshaft	21. Reed valve petal	27. Filter support	33. Drive tube
9. Piston pin	16. Flywheel	22. Carburetor spacer	28. Air filter	34. Adapter
10. Piston				

To service rewind starters on trimmers, remove starter housing (10—Figs. HL40-11 or HL40-12). Pull starter rope and hold rope pulley with notch in pulley adjacent to rope outlet. Pull rope back through outlet so that it engages notch in pulley and allow pulley to completely unwind. Unscrew pulley retaining screw (5) and remove rope pulley, being careful not to dislodge rewind spring in housing. Wear appropriate safety eyewear and gloves before detaching rewind spring from housing as spring may uncoil uncontrolled.

Rewind spring is wound in clockwise direction in starter housing. Rope is wound on rope pulley in clockwise direction as viewed with pulley in housing. To place tension on rewind spring, pass rope through rope outlet in housing and install rope handle. Pull rope out and hold rope pulley so notch on pulley is adjacent to rope outlet. Pull rope back through outlet between notch in pulley and housing. Turn rope pulley clockwise to place tension on spring. Pull rope out of notch, release pulley and allow rope to wind onto pulley. Check starter action. Do not place more tension on rewind spring than is necessary to draw rope handle up against housing.

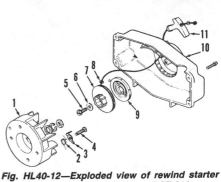

Fig. HL40-12—Exploded view of rewind starter used on Models ST-200 and ST-210.

1. Flywheel
2. Spring
3. Pawl
4. Pawl pin
5. Screw
6. Washer
7. Rope pulley
8. Nylon washer
9. Rewind spring
10. Housing
11. Rope handle

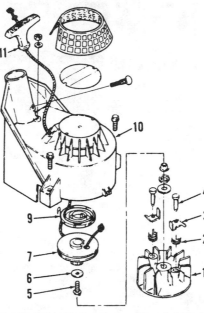

Fig. HL40-11—Exploded view of rewind starter used on Models ST-80, ST-100 and ST-120.

1. Flywheel
2. Spring
3. Pawl
4. Pawl pin
5. Screw
6. Washer
7. Rope pulley
8. Rewind spring
9. Rewind spring
10. Housing
11. Rope handle

HOMELITE
ENGINE SERVICE

Model	Bore	Stroke	Displacement
ST-400	1¾ in. (44 mm)	1-1/8 in. (35 mm)	3.3 cu. in. (54 cc)

ENGINE INFORMATION

The 3.3 cu. in. (54 cc) displacement engine is used to power the ST-400 brushcutter.

MAINTENANCE

SPARK PLUG. Recommended spark plug is a Champion CJ6. Spark plug electrode gap should be 0.025 inch (0.6 mm).

CARBURETOR. Model ST-400 brushcutter is equipped with a Tillotson HS-207A carburetor.

To adjust carburetor, turn idle speed stop screw in until it just contacts throttle lever tab, then turn screw in ½-turn further. Turn idle and main fuel adjustment needles in gently until they just contact seats, then back each needle out one turn. With engine warm and running, adjust idle fuel needle so that engine runs smoothly, then adjust idle stop screw so that engine runs at 2600 rpm, or just below clutch engagement speed. Check engine acceleration and open idle fuel needle slightly if engine will not accelerate properly. Adjust main fuel needle under load so engine will neither slow down nor smoke excessively.

GOVERNOR. The engine is equipped with an air-vane type governor; refer to Fig. HL43-1.

To adjust governor using vibrating reed or electronic tachometer, proceed as follows: With engine warm and running and throttle trigger released, adjust position of cable nuts (see Fig. HL43-1A) on remote control cable so that engine slow idle speed is 2500 rpm, or just below clutch engagement speed. Then when throttle trigger is fully depressed, engine no-load speed should be 6300 rpm. To adjust maximum governed no-load speed, loosen screw (14—Fig. HL43-1) and move speed adjusting plate (13) as required to obtain no-load speed of 6300 rpm. When adjusting maximum no-load speed, be sure that governor link (26) is reconnected at hole "A" in carburetor throttle shaft lever. Governor spring (12) is connected to third hole away from hole "A" (two open holes between link and spring). Be sure that governor linkage moves smoothly throughout range of travel.

MAGNETO AND TIMING. All engines are equipped with a solid-state ignition (Fig. HL43-4). Ignition service is accomplished by replacing ignition components until faulty part is located. Air gap between ignition module (3) and flywheel is adjustable and should be 0.015 inch (0.4 mm). Loosen ignition module mounting screws and adjust module position to set air gap.

LUBRICATION. The engine is lubricated by mixing oil with regular gasoline. Recommended oil is Homelite

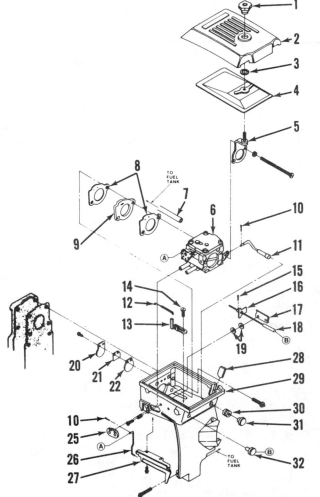

Fig. HL43-1—Exploded view of air box assembly on Model XL-12 engine.

1. Nut
2. Air filter cover
3. Retaining ring
4. Air filter element
5. Mounting bracket
6. Carburetor
7. Fuel line
8. Gasket
9. Spacer
10. Cotter pin
11. Choke rod
12. Governor spring
13. Adjusting plate
14. Screw
15. Cotter pin
16. Collar
17. Clamp
18. Throttle cable
19. Washers
20. Reed stop
21. Reed backup
22. Reed valve
25. Grommet
26. Governor link
27. Governor air vane
28. Felt plug
29. Air box
30. Grommet
31. Choke button
32. Throttle button

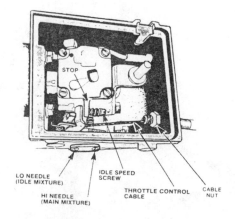

Fig. HL43-1A—View of brushcutter air box. Outside throttle cable nut is not shown.

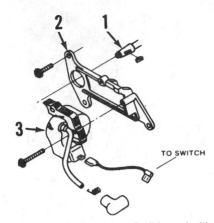

Fig. HL43-4—Exploded view of solid-state ignition.
1. Crankshaft
2. Stator plate
3. Ignition module

TO SWITCH

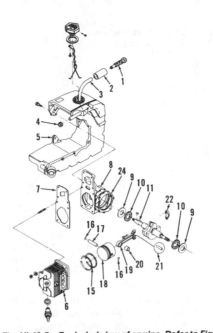

Fig. HL43-5—Exploded view of engine. Refer to Fig. HL43-5A for brushcutter drivecase.

1. Fuel pickup
2. Fuel filter
3. Fuel line
4. Grommet
5. Fuel tank
6. Cylinder
7. Gasket
8. Crankcase
9. Thrust washer
10. Thrust bearing
11. Crankshaft
15. Piston rings
16. Retaining ring
17. Retaining ring
18. Piston
19. Connecting rod
20. Needle bearing
21. Crankpin rollers (31)
22. Rod cap
24. Gasket

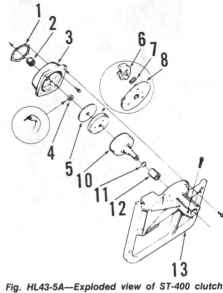

Fig. HL43-5A—Exploded view of ST-400 clutch assembly.

1. Gasket
2. Bearing
3. Drivecase
4. Seal
5. Cover
6. Clutch shoe
7. Spring
8. Clutch hub
10. Clutch drum
11. Snap ring
12. Bearing
13. Frame

two-stroke oil mixed at ratio as designated on oil container. If Homelite oil is not available, a good quality oil designed for two-stroke engines may be used when mixed at a 16:1 ratio, however, an anti-oxidant fuel stabilizer (such as Sta-Bil) should be added to fuel mix. Anti-oxidant fuel stabilizer is not required with Homelite® oils as they contain fuel stabilizer so the fuel mix will stay fresh up to one year.

CARBON. Muffler, manifold and cylinder exhaust ports should be cleaned periodically to prevent loss of power through carbon build up. Remove muffler and scrape free of carbon. With muffler or manifold removed, turn engine so that piston is at top dead center and carefully remove carbon from exhaust ports with a wooden scraper. Be careful not to damage chamfered edges of exhaust ports or to scratch piston. Do not run engine with muffler removed.

REPAIRS

COMPRESSION PRESSURE. For optimum performance, cylinder compression pressure should be 130-155 psi (896-1069 kPa) with engine at normal operating temperature. Engine should be inspected and repaired when compression is 90 psi (621 kPa) or below.

CONNECTING ROD. Connecting rod and piston assembly can be removed after removing cylinder from crankcase. Refer to Fig. HL43-5. Be careful not to lose any of the 31 needle rollers when detaching rod from crankpin.

Renew connecting rod if bent or twisted, or if crankpin bearing surface is scored, burned or excessively worn. The caged needle roller piston pin bearing can be renewed by pressing old bearing out and pressing new bearing in with Homelite tool No. 23756. Press on lettered end of bearing cage only.

It is recommended that the crankpin needle rollers be renewed as a set whenever engine is disassembled for service. When assembling connecting rod on crankshaft, stick 16 rollers in rod and 15 rollers in rod cap. Assemble rod to cap with match marks aligned, and with open end of piston pin towards flywheel side of engine. Wiggle the rod as cap retaining screws are being tightened to align the fractured mating surfaces of rod and cap.

PISTON, PIN AND RINGS. The piston is fitted with two pinned compression rings. Renew piston if scored, cracked or excessively worn, or if ring side clearance in top ring groove exceeds 0.0035 inch (0.09 mm).

Recommended piston ring end gap is 0.070-0.080 inch (1.8-2.0 mm); maximum allowable ring end gap is 0.085 inch (2.2 mm). Desired ring side clearance of groove is 0.002-0.003 inch (0.05-0.08 mm).

Piston, pin and rings are available in standard size only. Piston and pin are available in a matched set, and are not available separately.

Piston pin has one open and one closed end and may be retained in piston with snap rings or a Spirol pin. A wire retaining ring is used on exhaust side of piston on some models and should not be removed.

To remove piston pin remove the snap ring at intake side of piston. On piston with Spirol pin at exhaust side, drive pin from piston and rod with slotted driver (Homelite tool No. A-23949). On all other models, insert a 3/16-inch pin through snap ring at exhaust side and drive piston pin out.

When reassembling, be sure closed end of piston pin is to exhaust side of piston (away from piston pin ring locating pin). Install Truarc snap ring with sharp edge out.

The cylinder bore is chrome plated. Renew the cylinder if chrome plating is worn away exposing the softer base metal.

CRANKCASE, BEARING HOUSING AND SEALS. CAUTION: Do not lose crankcase screws. New screws of the same length must be installed in place of old screws. Refer to parts book if correct screw length is unknown.

The crankshaft is supported in two caged needle roller bearings and crankshaft end play is controlled by a roller bearing and hardened steel thrust washer at each end of the shaft. Refer to Fig. HL43-5.

The needle roller main bearings and crankshaft seals in crankcase and drivecase can be renewed using Homelite tools Nos. 23757 and 23758. Press bearings and seals from crankcase or bearing housing with large stepped end of tool No. 23757, pressing towards outside of either case.

To install new needle bearings, use the shouldered short end of tool No. 23757 and press bearings into bores from inner

Fig. HL43-6—When installing flat reed valve, reed backup and reed stop, be sure reed is centered between two points indicated by black arrows.

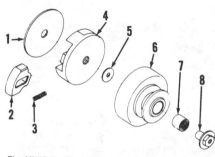

Fig. HL43-7—Exploded view of clutch used on saw engines.

1. Cover
2. Clutch shoe
3. Spring
4. Plate
5. Thrust washer
6. Clutch drum
7. Needle bearing
8. Nut

side of either case. Press on lettered end of bearing cage only.

To install new seals, first lubricate the seal and place seal on long end of tool No. 23758 so that lip of seal will be towards needle bearing as it is pressed into place.

To install crankshaft, lubricate thrust bearings (10) and place on shaft as shown. Place a hardened steel thrust washer to the outside of each thrust bearing. Insert

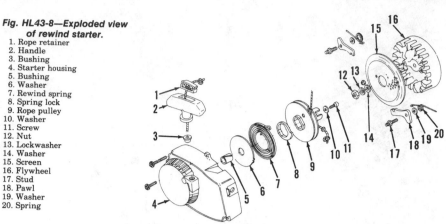

Fig. HL43-8—Exploded view of rewind starter.

1. Rope retainer
2. Handle
3. Bushing
4. Starter housing
5. Bushing
6. Washer
7. Rewind spring
8. Spring lock
9. Rope pulley
10. Washer
11. Screw
12. Nut
13. Lockwasher
14. Washer
15. Screen
16. Flywheel
17. Stud
18. Pawl
19. Washer
20. Spring

crankshaft into crankcase being careful not to damage seal in crankcase. Place a seal protector sleeve (Homelite tool No. 23759) on crankshaft and gasket on shoulder of drivecase or pump housing. Lubricate seal protector sleeve, seal and needle bearing and mate drivecase or pump housing to crankshaft and crankcase. Use **NEW** retaining screws. Clean the screw threads and apply Loctite to threads before installing screws. Be sure the screws are correct length; screw length is critical. Tighten the screws alternately and remove seal protector sleeve from crankshaft.

CLUTCH. To service clutch on ST-400 models, unscrew cap screws securing frame (13—Fig. HL43-5A) to drivecase (3) and separate brushcutting unit from engine. Remove snap ring (11) and clutch drum (10). Rotate clutch hub in counterclockwise direction to remove clutch assembly. Inspect clutch components and renew any which are damaged or excessively worn.

REWIND STARTER. To disassemble starter, refer to exploded view in Fig. HL43-8 and proceed as follows: Pull starter rope out fully, hold pulley (9) and place rope in notch of pulley. Let pulley rewind slowly. Hold pulley while removing screw (11) and washer (10). Turn pulley counterclockwise until disengaged from spring, then carefully lift pulley off starter post. Turn open side of housing down and rap housing sharply against top of work bench to remove spring. CAUTION: Be careful not to dislodge spring when removing pulley as spring could cause injury if it should uncoil rapidly.

Install new spring with loop in outer end over pin in blower housing and be sure spring is coiled in direction shown in Fig. HL43-8. Install pulley (9), turning pulley clockwise until it engages spring and secure with washer and screw. Insert new rope through handle and hole in blower housing. Knot both ends of the rope and harden the knots with cement. Turn pulley clockwise eight turns and slide knot in rope into slot and keyhole in pulley. Let starter pulley rewind slowly.

Starter pawl spring outer ends are hooked behind air vanes on flywheel in line with starter pawls when pawls are resting against flywheel nut. Pull starter rope slowly when installing blower housing so that starter cup will engage pawls.

HOMELITE

ENGINE SERVICE

Model	Bore	Stroke	Displacement
HK-18	1.14 in.	1.10 in.	1.12 cu. in.
	(28.9 mm)	(27.9 mm)	(18.4 cc)
HK-24	1.26 in.	1.18 in.	1.47 cu. in.
	(32.0 mm)	(30.0 mm)	(24.1 cc)
HK-33	1.45 in.	1.22 in.	2.03 cu. in.
	(36.8 mm)	(30.9 mm)	(33.3 cc)

ENGINE INFORMATION

These engines are used as the power units for the Model HK-18, HK-24 and HK-33 Trimmer/Brushcutter.

MAINTENANCE

SPARK PLUG. Recommended spark plug is a Champion CJ8. Specified electrode gap is 0.025 inch (0.6 mm).

CARBURETOR. Initial setting for both mixture needles on Model HK-18 is one turn out from a lightly seated position. Initial setting of the high speed mixture needle on Models HK-24 and HK-33 is 1½ turns out from a lightly seated position. On all later models, the setting of the high speed mixture needle may be out as much as 2½ turns to obtain best performance.

After running engine so normal operating temperature is reached, run engine at wide open throttle (string must be at normal cutting length). Turn high speed mixture needle in so engine begins to run smoothly, then back out screw 1/8 turn. On Model HK-18, adjust idle mixture needle so engine idles smoothly and will accelerate without hesitation. Adjust idle speed screw on all models so engine idles just below clutch engagement speed (string head does not rotate).

On Models HK-24 and HK-33, midrange mixture is determined by the position of clip (7—Fig. HL45-1) on jet needle (8). There are three grooves located at the upper end of the jet needle (see Fig. HL45-2) and the normal position of clip (7) is in the middle groove. The mixture will be leaner if clip is installed in the top groove or richer if clip is installed in the bottom groove.

Model HK-18 is equipped with a Walbro WA series carburetor.

Models HK-24 and HK-33 are equipped with the slide-valve, diaphragm type carburetor shown in Fig. HL45-1. Carburetor is equipped with an integral fuel pump (16, 17 and 18). During servicing inspect fuel pump and metering diaphragms for pin holes, tears and other damage. Diaphragms should be flexible. Metal button must be tight on metering diaphragm. When assembling the carburetor note that the metering diaphragm lever should be flush with the

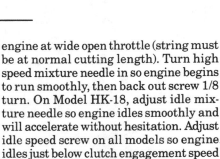

Fig. HL45-1—Exploded view of carburetor used on Models HK-24 and HK-33.

1. Tickler valve
2. Spring
3. Lever
4. Cap
5. Spring
6. Retainer
7. Clip
8. Jet needle
9. Throttle slide
10. Body
11. Spring
12. Idle speed screw
13. Spring
14. "O" ring
15. Main fuel mixture screw
16. Pump gasket
17. Pump diaphragm
18. Pump cover
19. Inlet needle valve
20. Metering lever
21. Pin
22. Jet
23. Spring
24. Gasket
25. Diaphragm
26. Cover

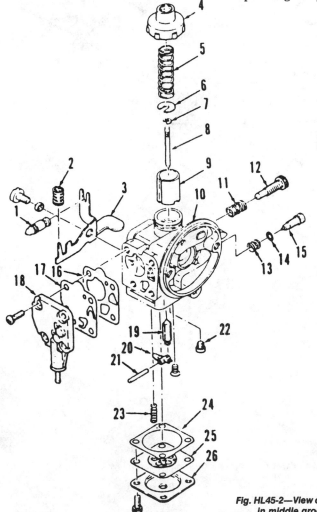

Fig. HL45-2—View of jet needle and clip. Install clip in middle groove for normal operation.

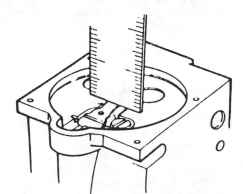

Fig. HL45-3—Adjust metering lever so lever just touches straightedge.

Illustrations courtesy Homelite Div. of Textron, Inc.

floor of cavity as shown in Fig. HL45-3. If necessary, adjust lever. Be sure retainer (6—Fig. HL45-1) is properly installed and secures jet needle and clip in throttle slide (9). Groove in side of throttle slide must engage pin in carburetor body when installing slide assembly.

IGNITION SYSTEM. All models use a transistorized ignition system consisting of a coil and an igniter. The flywheel-to-coil air gap is not adjustable.

The ignition system is operating satisfactorily if spark will jump across the 1/8 inch (3 mm) gap of a test spark plug (Homelite part JA-31316-4). If no spark is produced, check on/off switch and wiring.

The igniter may be tested with an ohmmeter as follows: Set ohmmeter to the R X 10K scale and connect the black ohmmeter lead to the igniter case and connect the red ohmmeter lead to the igniter lead tab. Ohmmeter needle should deflect from infinity to slightly more than zero ohms. Reverse the ohmmeter leads and the ohmmeter needle should again deflect from infinity to slightly more than zero ohms. The ohmmeter needle should not return all the way back to zero ohms after deflecting to infinity. Replace igniter if any faults are noted.

The coil may be tested wth an ohmmeter as follows: Set ohmmeter to the R X 1 scale and connect the red ohmmeter lead to the primary lead wire. Connect the black ohmmeter lead wire to the coil core. Specified resistance of the primary winding is 0.5 ohms for Model HK-18 and 0.6-0.7 ohms for Models HK-24 and HK-33. Connect the red ohmmeter lead to the spark plug wire and connect the black ohmmeter lead to the coil core. Specified resistance of the secondary coil winding is 0.97 ohms for Model HK-18 and 0.7-0.8 ohms for Models HK-24 and HK-33. Replace coil assembly if other test results are obtained.

REPAIRS

HOMELITE SPECIAL TOOLS. Special tools which will aid in servicing are as follows:

Tool No. and Description.
22828—Snap ring pliers.
JA-31316-4—Test spark plug.
94194—Compression gage.
94197—Carburetor tester.
17789—Carburetor repair tool kit.
94455—Alignment tool (for clutch drum removal).
A-98059—Flywheel puller.
98061-42—Tool kit (early models).
PR-24A—External snap ring pliers (Snap-On).
TM-30—Clutch head driver (Snap-On).

COMPRESSION PRESSURE. For optimum performance, compression pressure should be as follows with a hot engine and throttle and choke open. Crank engine until maximum pressure is observed on compression gage.
HK-18:
  Low .115 psi
                              (793 kPa)
  High . . . . .145 psi
                             (1000 kPa)
HK-24:
  Low .140 psi
                              (965 kPa)
  High . . . . .170 psi
                             (1172 kPa)
HK-33:
  Low .160 psi
                             (1103 kPa)
  High . . . . .190 psi
                             (1310 kPa)
A compression reading of 90 psi (620 kPa) or lower indicates a need for repairs.

TIGHTENING TORQUES. Engine tightening torques are listed below. All values are in inch-pounds (in.-lbs. x 0.113=N · m).
Air cleaner:
  HK-24 & HK-33 . . . . .14.5-17 in.-lbs.
Clutch pin to flywheel:
  HK-18 & HK-24 . . . . . .69-85 in.-lbs.
  HK-33 . . . . .120-137 in.-lbs.
Crankcase . . . . .30-34 in.-lbs.
Cylinder to crankcase:
  HK-24 & HK-33 . . . . . .30-34 in.-lbs.
Flywheel:
  HK-18 & HK-24 . . . . . .69-85 in.-lbs.
  HK-33 . . . . .120-137 in.-lbs.
Muffler . . . . .34-39 in.-lbs.
Rope pulley . . . . .120-137 in.-lbs.
Spark plug . . . . .103-146 in.-lbs.

CRANKSHAFT AND CONNECTING ROD. Refer to Figs. HL45-5 and HL45-6 for exploded views. Crankshaft is pressed together at connecting rod journal, therefore crankshaft and

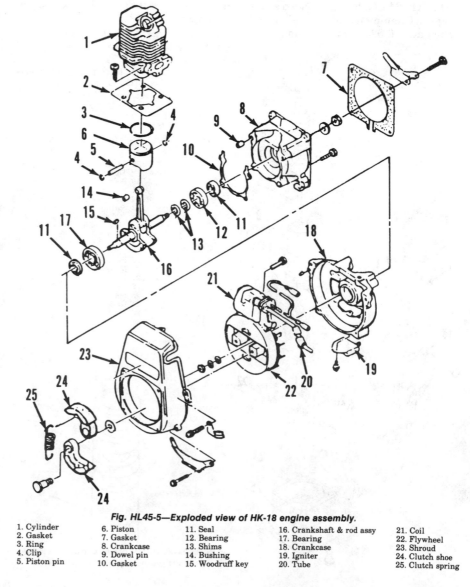

Fig. HL45-5—Exploded view of HK-18 engine assembly.

1. Cylinder	6. Piston	11. Seal	16. Crankshaft & rod assy	21. Coil
2. Gasket	7. Gasket	12. Bearing	17. Bearing	22. Flywheel
3. Ring	8. Crankcase	13. Shims	18. Crankcase	23. Shroud
4. Clip	9. Dowel pin	14. Bushing	19. Igniter	24. Clutch shoe
5. Piston pin	10. Gasket	15. Woodruff key	20. Tube	25. Clutch spring

Illustrations courtesy Homelite Div. of Textron, Inc.

connecting rod must be replaced as an assembly. Crankshaft is supported by ball bearings at both ends.

To remove crankshaft assembly, remove shroud and starter. On Model HK-18, unscrew starter pulley retaining nut and pry starter pulley off of crankshaft. On Models HK-24 and HK-33, the starter pulley is threaded onto crankshaft and is removed by unscrewing. On all models, remove flywheel, carburetor, muffler and cylinder. Split crankcase and remove crankshaft. Remove piston. Renew crankshaft assembly.

Inspect crankshaft assembly for damage and excessive wear. Be sure to inspect main bearings and roller bearing in small end of connecting rod.

Check crankshaft end play during reassembly. Crankshaft end play should be 0.002-0.010 inch (0.05-0.27 mm). Shims (13—Fig. HL45-5 or 21—Fig.

HL45-6) are available in thicknesses of 0.004 inch (0.1 mm), 0.008 inch (0.2 mm), 0.016 inch (0.4 mm) and 0.024 inch (0.06 mm). To determine the correct shim pack thickness the following measurements must be taken: Magneto side of crankshaft half (dimension "A"); starter side of crankshaft half (dimension "B"); distance between outside edges of crankshaft counterweights (dimension "C"). Place a straightedge across gasket surface of magneto side of crankcase half. Measure the distance from the face of the outside bearing race to the bottom of the

straightedge. This measurement is dimension "A". Place a straightedge across gasket surface of starter side of crankcase half. Measure the distance from the face of the outside bearing race to the bottom of the straightedge. This measurement is dimension "B". Using a vernier caliper, measure the distance between the machined surfaces of the crankshaft counterweights as shown in Fig. HL45-7. This measurement is dimension "C". Add dimensions "A" and "B", then deduct dimension "C". This will give the total thickness of the shim pack that will be needed. Refer to Table 1 for correct shim pack thickness. Shims must be installed on the starter side of crankshaft.

PISTON AND RINGS. Model HK-18 is equipped with one piston ring and Models HK-24 and HK-33 are equipped with two piston rings. Piston pin is retained in bore with two retaining rings.

Renew piston if scored, cracked, excessively worn or if side clearance in ring groove exceeds 0.027 inch (0.7 mm).

CYLINDER. Cylinder may be unbolted and removed from crankcase after shroud, muffler, carburetor and starter housing are removed.

Replace cylinder if scored, cracked or otherwise damaged. Use a crossing "X" pattern when retorquing cylinder retaining screws.

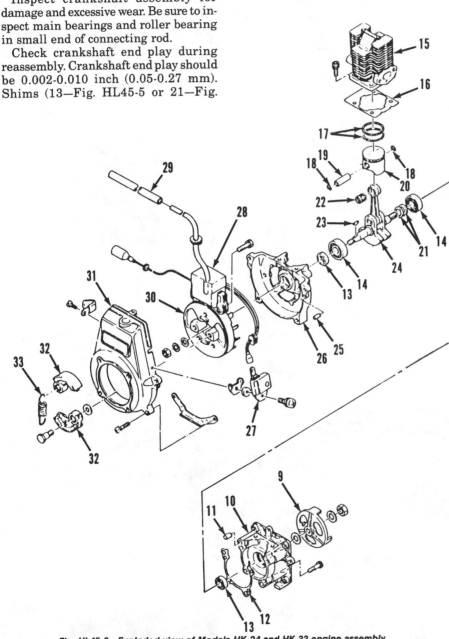

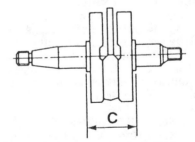

Fig. HL45-7—Measure distance (C) between machined surfaces of crankshaft counterweights to determine crankshaft end play.

Fig. HL45-6—Exploded view of Models HK-24 and HK-33 engine assembly.

9. Pulley	16. Gasket	23. Woodruff key	28. Coil
10. Crankcase	17. Rings	24. Crankshaft & rod assy.	29. Tube
11. Dowel pin	18. Clips		30. Flywheel
12. Gasket	19. Piston pin	25. Dowel pin	31. Shroud
13. Seal	20. Piston	26. Crankcase	32. Clutch shoe
14. Bearing	21. Shims	27. Igniter	33. Clutch spring
15. Cylinder	22. Bushing		

Fig. HL45-8—Lobes on clutch shoes should be in position shown when assembling clutch.

CLUTCH. Install clutch shoes onto flywheel with the lobes positioned as shown in Fig. HL45-8. Clutch will not engage if shoes are installed backwards. Shoes and clutch drum should be inspected for excessive wear or damage and replaced if necessary.

RECOIL STARTER. Model HK-18. Refer to Fig. HL45-9 for an exploded view of starter assembly. To disassemble starter, remove starter assembly from engine. Pull rope 6 inches (15.2 cm) out of housing (8). Align notch in pulley (5) with rope hole in housing. While holding pulley and rope hole in alignment, pull slack rope back through rope hole in side housing. Hold rope in notch while slowly allowing pulley to unwind relieving spring (6) tension.

Remove the center screw and washer, then slowly lift pulley off center post of housing. Do not dislodge rewind spring. Use care if spring must be removed. Do not allow spring to uncoil uncontrolled.

Inspect rope and spring. Lubricate center post of housing with light grease prior to reassembly. Reassembly is reverse of disassembly procedure. Wind all but 6 inches (15.2 cm) of rope onto pulley before installing pulley in starter housing. Wrap rope around pulley in a counterclockwise direction as viewed from pawl side of pulley. Press down on pulley while turning to engage pulley with spring hook. Install retaining screw and washer. Three prewinds counterclockwise are required on the rewind spring. After assembly, check for rewind spring bottoming out. With rope pulled all the way out of starter, pulley should still rotate, counterclockwise. If pulley will not rotate any further with rope pulled out, then release one prewind from spring and recheck.

Models HK-24 and HK-33. Refer to Fig. HL45-10 for an exploded view of starter assembly. To disassemble starter, first remove starter assembly from engine. Slide rope guide (8) out of starter housing (10) and slip rope (6) into slot on pulley. Hold rope in notch while slowly allowing pulley to unwind, relieving spring (7) tension.

Remove the center screw, retainer (1), pawl (2) and springs (3 and 4). Slowly lift pulley off starter housing post while using a small screwdriver to release pulley from spring hook. Use care if spring must be removed. Do not allow spring to uncoil uncontrolled.

Inspect rope, pawl and springs for breakage and excessive wear and replace as needed. Lubricate center post of housing with light grease prior to reassembly. Reassembly is reverse of disassembly procedure. Install spring in a counterclockwise direction from outer end. Wind

all but 6 inches (15.2 cm) of rope onto pulley before installing pulley in starter housing. Wrap rope around pulley in a counterclockwise direction as viewed from pawl side of pulley. Press down on pulley while turning to engage pulley with spring hook. Reinstall retaining

screw, retainer, pawl, pawl spring and loop spring. Make sure loop spring is installed properly as shown in Fig. HL45-11. Three prewinds counterclockwise are required on the rewind spring. Recheck to be sure pulley rewinds completely when released.

CLEARANCE "0" (Inch)	CLEARANCE "0" (mm)	SHIM NO.
−.004" to −.001"	−0.11 to +0.03	NONE
+.001" to +.005"	+0.03 to +0.13"	.004"
+.005" to +.009"	+0.13 to +0.23	.008"
+.009" to +.013"	+0.23 to +0.33	.012"
+.013" to +.017"	+0.33 to +0.43	.016"
+.017" to +.021"	+0.43 to +0.53	.020"
+.021" to +.025"	+0.53 to +0.63	.024"

TABLE 1—Select shim to obtain specified end play.

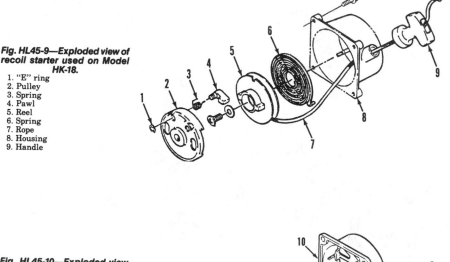

Fig. HL45-9—Exploded view of recoil starter used on Model HK-18.
1. "E" ring
2. Pulley
3. Spring
4. Pawl
5. Reel
6. Spring
7. Rope
8. Housing
9. Handle

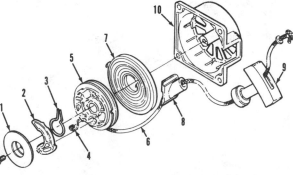

Fig. HL45-10—Exploded view of recoil starter used on Models HK-24 and HK-33.
1. Retainer
2. Pawl
3. Loop spring
4. Pawl spring
5. Pulley
6. Rope
7. Spring
8. Guide
9. Handle
10. Housing

Fig. HL45-11—Loop spring must be installed as shown.

Spring End

Illustrations courtesy Homelite Div. of Textron, Inc.

HOMELITE

ENGINE SERVICE

Model	Bore	Stroke	Displacement
BP-250	1⁵/₁₆ in. (33.3 mm)	1¹/₈ in. (28.8 mm)	1.53 cu. in. (25 cc)
HB-100, HB-180	1⁵/₁₆ in. (33.3 mm)	1¹/₈ in. (28.8 mm)	1.53 cu. in. (25 cc)
HBC-18, HBC-30, HBC-30B	1⁷/₁₆ in. (36.5 mm)	1¹/₈ in. (28.8 mm)	1.83 cu. in. (30 cc)
HLT-16, HLT-17C, HLT-18	1⁷/₁₆ in. (36.5 mm)	1¹/₈ in. (28.8 mm)	1.83 cu. in. (30 cc)
ST-145, ST-155	1⁵/₁₆ in. (33.3 mm)	1¹/₈ in. (28.8 mm)	1.53 cu. in. (25 cc)
ST-175, ST-175C, ST-175BC	1⁵/₁₆ in. (33.3 mm)	1¹/₈ in. (28.8 mm)	1.53 cu. in. (25 cc)
ST-185, ST-185C	1⁵/₁₆ in. (33.3 mm)	1¹/₈ in. (28.8 mm)	1.53 cu. in. (25 cc)
ST-285, ST-285BC	1⁵/₁₆ in. (33.3 mm)	1¹/₈ in. (28.8 mm)	1.53 cu. in. (25 cc)
ST-385, ST-385C	1⁵/₁₆ in. (33.3 mm)	1¹/₈ in. (28.8 mm)	1.53 cu. in. (25 cc)
ST-485	1⁵/₁₆ in. (33.3 mm)	1¹/₈ in. (28.8 mm)	1.53 cu. in. (25 cc)

ENGINE INFORMATION

The Homelite two-stroke, air-cooled engines covered in this section are used on Homelite string trimmers, brush cutters and blowers.

MAINTENANCE

LUBRICATION. The engine on all models is lubricated by mixing oil with gasoline. Homelite oil is recommended and should be mixed at ratio designated on container. If Homelite oil is not used, manufacturer specifies that only oils designed for two-stroke engines with a fuel:oil ratio of 32:1 or more should be used.

An antioxidant fuel stabilizer (such as Sta-Bil) should be added to fuel if Homelite oil is not used. Homelite oil contains an antioxidant fuel stabilizer.

SPARK PLUG. Recommended spark plug is Champion DJ7Y. Spark plug electrode gap should be 0.025 inch (0.6 mm).

CARBURETOR. Walbro and Zama carburetors are used depending on equipment model. Refer to appropriate carburetor section below for service information.

Walbro WT. To adjust carburetor on trimmer, proceed as follows: Turn idle mixture screw (12—Fig. HL46-1) and high-speed mixture screw (14) counterclockwise until stopped. Back out idle speed screw (28) until it doesn't contact throttle lever. Turn idle speed screw back in so it contacts throttle lever, then turn in four more turns. Run engine until normal operating temperature is reached. Turn idle mixture screw clockwise until highest engine idle speed is reached, then turn screw counterclockwise ⅛ turn. Run engine at full throttle under load (string must be fully extended). Turn high-speed mixture screw in until highest engine speed is attained. Set idle speed screw so engine idles smoothly.

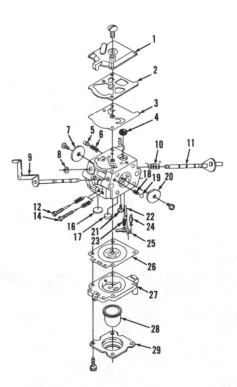

Fig. HL46-1—Exploded view of Walbro WT carburetor. Throttle shaft (11) is on opposite side shown on some models. Accelerator piston (5) and spring (6) are not used on all models.

1. Cover
2. Gasket
3. Fuel pump diaphragm
4. Screen
5. Accelerator piston
6. Spring
7. Throttle plate
8. "E" ring
9. Choke shaft
10. Spring
11. Throttle shaft
12. Idle mixture screw
14. High-speed mixture screw
16. Welch plug
17. Nozzle
18. Spring
19. Detent ball
20. Choke plate
21. Screw
22. Pin
23. Spring
24. Fuel inlet valve
25. Metering lever
26. Metering diaphragm
27. Cover
28. Primer bulb
29. Bulb retainer

To adjust carburetor on blower, turn idle mixture screw and (12) high-speed mixture screw (14) clockwise until lightly seated, then turn each mixture screw counterclockwise one turn open. Final

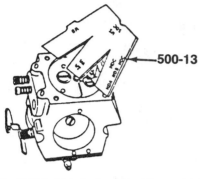

Fig. HL46-2—Metering lever should just touch leg of Walbro tool 500-13. Bend lever to obtain correct lever height.

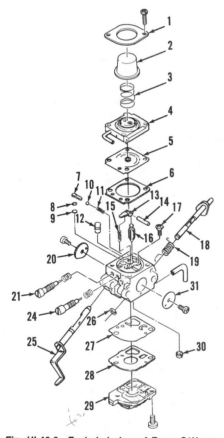

Fig. HL46-3—Exploded view of Zama C1U carburetor.

1. Cover
2. Primer bulb
3. Spring
4. Cover
5. Metering diaphragm
6. Gasket
7. Welch plug
8. Retainer
9. Screen
10. Detent ball
11. Spring
12. Nozzle
13. Metering lever
14. Pin
15. Spring
16. Fuel inlet valve
17. Screw
18. Throttle shaft
19. Spring
20. Choke plate
21. Idle mixture screw
24. High-speed mixture screw
25. Choke shaft
26. "E" ring
27. Fuel pump diaphragm
28. Gasket
29. Fuel inlet screen
30. Cover
31. Throttle plate

adjustment is performed with engine at normal operating temperature. Adjust idle mixture screw so engine accelerates cleanly without hesitation. Run engine at full throttle and adjust high-speed mixture screw so engine runs at highest speed, then turn screw counterclockwise until engine speed begins to decrease. Adjust idle speed screw so engine idles smoothly.

Some models are equipped with an accelerator pump that forces additional fuel into the carburetor bore when the throttle shaft is rotated. The pump piston (5—Fig. HL46-1) rests against a flat on the throttle shaft. Shaft rotation moves the piston against fuel in a passage.

Carburetor disassembly and reassembly is evident after inspection of carburetor and referral to Fig. HL46-1. Do not lose detent ball (19) when withdrawing choke shaft. Accelerator pump piston (5) is released when throttle shaft is withdrawn.

Clean and inspect all components. Do not use wire or drill bits to clean fuel passages as fuel flow may be altered. Inspect diaphragms (3 and 26) for defects that may affect operation. Examine fuel inlet valve and seat. Inlet valve (24) is renewable, but carburetor body must be renewed if seat is damaged or excessively worn. Discard carburetor body if mixture screw seats are damaged or excessively worn. Clean fuel screen (4). Inspect primer bulb (28) and reject if cracked, hardened or otherwise damaged.

Check metering lever height as shown in Fig. HL46-2 using Walbro tool 500-13. Metering lever should just touch leg on tool. Bend lever to obtain correct lever height.

Zama C1U. To adjust carburetor, turn idle mixture screw (21—Fig. HL46-3) and high-speed mixture screw (24) as necessary, following adjustment procedure outlined for Walbro WT carburetor.

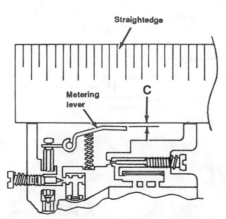

Fig. HL46-4—Metering lever on Zama should be bent so height (C) is 0-0.3 mm (0.000-0.012 in.).

Carburetor disassembly and reassembly is evident after inspection of carburetor and referral to Fig. HL46-3. Do not lose detent ball (10) when withdrawing choke shaft.

Clean and inspect all components. Exercise care when removing Welch plug (7). To remove plug, pierce the plug towards the end of the "tail" portion with a suitable punch, but do not insert punch deeply as underlying body metal may be damaged. Apply sealant to new plug. Inspect diaphragms (5 and 27) for defects that may affect operation. Examine fuel inlet valve and seat. Inlet valve (16) is renewable, but carburetor body must be renewed if seat is damaged or excessively worn. Discard carburetor body if mixture screw seats are damaged or excessively worn. Clean fuel screen (9). Do not use wire or drill bits to clean fuel passages as calibration of carburetor may be affected.

To reassemble carburetor, reverse disassembly procedure. Clearance (C—Fig. HL46-4) between metering lever and a straightedge placed across metering side of carburetor body should be 0-0.03 mm (0-0.012 inch). Bend metering lever as needed.

IGNITION. A solid state ignition is used on all models. The ignition module is attached to the side of the engine cylinder. Ignition service is accomplished by replacing ignition components until the faulty component is located. Air gap between ignition module and flywheel magnet is adjustable and should be 0.015 inch (0.4 mm). Loosen ignition module mounting screws and adjust module position to set air gap.

REPAIRS

TIGHTENING TORQUE VALUES. Tightening torque values are listed in following table:

Air box cover	20-30 in.-lbs. (2.3-3.3 N·m)
Carburetor and air box	30-40 in.-lbs. (3.3-4.5 N·m)
Clutch adapter shaft	100-150 in.-lbs. (11.3-16.9 N·m)
Clutch housing	40-50 in.-lbs. (4.5-5.6 N·m)
Clutch	80-100 in.-lbs. (9.0-11.3 N·m)
Crankcase cover	40-50 in.-lbs. (4.5-5.6 N·m)
Cylinder	55-65 in.-lbs. (6.2-7.3 N·m)
Drive connector	100-150 in.-lbs. (11.3-16.9 N·m)
Engine housing	40-50 in.-lbs. (4.5-5.6 N·m)

Heat dam . . . . 40-50 in.-lbs.
(4.5-5.6 N·m)
Ignition module . . . . 30-40 in.-lbs.
(3.3-4.5 N·m)
Muffler . . . . 40-50 in.-lbs.
(4.5-5.6 N·m)
Spark plug . . . . 120-180 in.-lbs.
(13.6-20.3 N·m)

COMPRESSION PRESSURE. For optimum performance of all models, cylinder compression pressure should be 95-105 psi (656-725 kPa) with engine at normal operating temperature. Cold compression pressure should be 100-110 psi (690-759 kPa).

CYLINDER, PISTON, PIN AND RINGS. Piston, bearings and connecting rod are serviced only as an assembly. Assembly is offered in standard size only. The connecting rod has a caged roller bearing at both ends. The piston is equipped with a single piston ring.

To remove cylinder (25—Fig. HL46-5) and piston and rod assembly (22), remove muffler (35), carburetor (30), fuel tank (33) and crankcase cover (27). Remove cylinder mounting screws. Lift and tilt cylinder to release connecting rod from crankpin, then remove cylinder, piston and rod as an assembly from crankcase. Withdraw piston and rod from cylinder.

The cylinder has a chrome bore and cannot be refinished. Inspect cylinder for scoring, scratches, excessive wear or other damage and renew if necessary. Piston, piston ring and cylinder are available in standard size only.

There is no piston ring locating pin in the piston ring groove. When installing cylinder onto piston assembly, locate piston ring end gap towards the center of the exhaust port.

CRANKSHAFT AND CRANKCASE. All models use a half-crankshaft sup-ported by two ball bearings. To remove crankshaft, first install end of a rope in spark plug hole to lock piston and crankshaft. Remove flywheel nut and tap flywheel on side opposite magnet with a plastic mallet to loosen flywheel from crankshaft. Remove cylinder and piston as previously outlined. Press crankshaft out of bearings in crankcase. To remove outer (small) ball bearing (16—Fig. HL46-5), insert a $^9/_{16}$-in. (14 mm) rod through the inner bearing and press on inner race of outer bearing. Remove snap ring (17) and press out seal (19) and bearing (20). New crankcases include bearings, seal and snap ring.

Install seal (19) so face is $^5/_8$ inch (16 mm) from outer end (flywheel end) of bearing bore in crankcase. Press bearing (16) against snap ring (17) with shielded side out (towards flywheel). Press bearing (20) against shoulder in crankcase. Press crankshaft into bearings until seated against inner bearing (20).

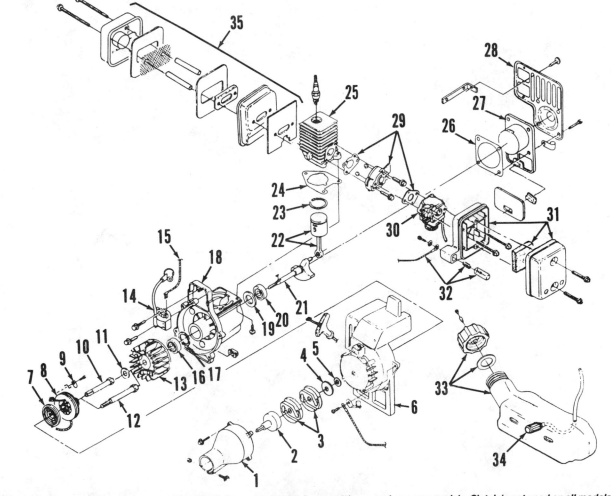

Fig. HL46-5—Exploded view of typical engine used on trimmers. Three clutch rotors (3) are used on some models. Clutch is not used on all models. Blower engine is similar.

1. Tube adapter	13. Flywheel	19. Seal	25. Cylinder	31. Air filter & housing
2. Clutch drum	14. Ignition module	20. Ball bearing	26. Gasket	32. Stop switch
3. Clutch rotors	15. Wire to stop switch	21. Crankshaft	27. Crankcase cover	33. Fuel tank
4. Washer	16. Ball bearing	22. Piston & rod assy.	28. Shield	34. Fuel filter
5. Washer	17. Snap ring	23. Piston ring	29. Heat dam & gasket	35. Muffler assy.
6. Engine housing	18. Crankcase	24. Gasket	30. Carburetor	
7. Rewind spring				
8. Rope pulley				
9. Retainer				
10. Drive adapter				
11. Washer				
12. Clutch adapter				

Illustrations courtesy Homelite Div. of Textron, Inc.

CLUTCH. Some trimmers are equipped with a double S-clutch. The clutch rotors (3—Fig. HL46-5) must be unscrewed singly. DO NOT attempt to remove both rotors at once or threads on adapter shaft may be damaged. Homelite tool A-93791 may be used to unscrew rotors.

REWIND STARTER. Refer to blower section for service of rewind starter used on blowers.

To service rewind starter on trimmers, remove engine housing (6—Fig. HL46-5). Remove rope handle and allow rope to wind into starter. Remove pulley retainer (9) and remove starter components as needed. Wear appropriate safety eyewear and gloves when working with or around rewind spring (7) as spring may uncoil uncontrolled.

Before assembling starter, lubricate center post of housing and side of spring with light grease. Install rewind spring (7) in a clockwise direction from outer end. Rope length should be 42 inches (107 cm). Assemble starter while passing rope through housing rope outlet and attach rope handle to rope. To place tension on starter rope, rotate pulley clockwise so notch in pulley is aligned with rope outlet, then hold pulley to prevent pulley rotation. Pull rope back into housing while positioning rope in pulley notch. Turn rope pulley three turns clockwise. Allow pulley to turn counterclockwise until notch aligns with rope outlet. Disengage rope from notch then release pulley and allow rope to wind on pulley. Check starter operation. Rope handle should be held against housing by spring tension, but it must be possible to rotate pulley at least $\frac{1}{4}$ turn clockwise when rope is pulled out fully.

HOMELITE

ENGINE SERVICE

Model	Bore	Stroke	Displacement
HBC-38	1.5625 in.	1.281 in.	2.46 cu. in.
	(39.7 mm)	(32.5 mm)	(40 cc)
HBC-40	1.5625 in.	1.281 in.	2.46 cu. in.
	(39.7 mm)	(32.5 mm)	(40 cc)

ENGINE INFORMATION

The Homelite two-stroke, air-cooled engines covered in this section are used on Homelite string trimmers and brush cutters.

MAINTENANCE

LUBRICATION. The engine on all models is lubricated by mixing oil with gasoline. Homelite oil is recommended and should be mixed at ratio designated on container. If Homelite oil is not used, manufacturer specifies that only oils designed for two-stroke engines with a fuel:oil ratio of 32:1 or more should be used.

An antioxidant fuel stabilizer (such as Sta-Bil) should be added to the fuel if Homelite oil is not used. Homelite oil contains an antioxidant fuel stabilizer.

SPARK PLUG. Recommended spark plug is Champion DJ7Y. Spark plug electrode gap should be 0.025 inch (0.6 mm). Tighten spark plug to 120-180 in.-lbs. (13.6-20.3 N·m).

CARBURETOR. Model HBC-38 is equipped with a Zama C1Q diaphragm carburetor and Model HBC-40 is equipped with a Walbro WT diaphragm carburetor. Refer to following sections for service.

Walbro WT. To adjust carburetor, turn idle mixture screw (18—Fig. HL47-1) 1¼ turns out from a lightly seated position. Turn high-speed mixture screw (20) counterclockwise until stopped. Back out idle speed screw (6) until it does not contact throttle lever. Turn idle speed screw back in so it just contacts throttle lever, then turn in four more turns. Run engine until normal operating temperature is reached. Adjust idle mixture screw so engine accelerates cleanly without hesitation. Run engine at full throttle under load (string must be fully extended). Turn high-speed mixture screw in until highest engine speed is attained. Do not set high-speed mixture

too lean as engine may be damaged. Set idle speed screw so engine idles smoothly, but trimmer head or blade does not rotate.

Carburetor disassembly and reassembly is evident after inspection of carburetor and referral to Fig. HL47-1. Do not lose detent ball (15) when withdrawing choke shaft (17). Clean and inspect all components. Do not use wires or drill bits to clean fuel passages as calibration of carburetor could be affected if passages are enlarged. Inspect diaphragms (2, 4 and 30) for defects that may affect operation. Examine fuel inlet valve and seat. Inlet valve (25) is renewable, but carburetor body must be renewed if seat is damaged or excessively worn. Discard carburetor body if mixture screw seats are damaged or excessively worn. Clean fuel screen (7).

Check metering lever height as shown in Fig. HL47-2 using Walbro tool 500-13. Metering lever should just touch leg on tool. Bend lever to obtain correct lever height.

Zama C1Q. To adjust carburetor, turn idle mixture screw (19—Fig. HL47-3) and high-speed mixture screw (17) ⅞ turn out from a lightly seated position. Back out idle speed screw (28) until it does not contact throttle lever. Turn idle speed screw back in so it just contacts throttle lever, then turn in four more turns. Run engine until normal operating temperature is reached. Adjust idle mixture screw so engine accelerates cleanly without hesitation. Run engine at full throttle under load (string must be fully extended). Adjust high-speed mixture screw so highest engine speed is attained. Do not set high-speed mixture too lean as engine may be damaged. Set idle speed screw so engine idles smoothly, but trimmer head or blade does not rotate.

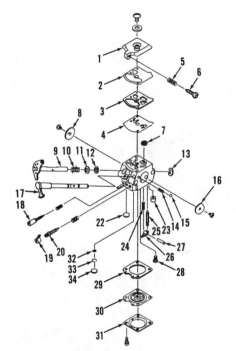

Fig. HL47-1—Exploded view of Walbro WT carburetor.

1. Cover
2. Surge diaphragm
3. Gasket
4. Fuel pump diaphragm
5. Spring
6. Idle speed screw
7. Screen
8. Throttle plate
9. Throttle shaft
10. Spring
11. Washer
12. Seal
13. "E" ring
14. Spring
15. Detent ball
16. Choke plate
17. Choke shaft
18. Idle mixture screw
19. Cap
20. High-speed mixture screw
22. Welch plug
23. Check valve seat
24. Spring
25. Fuel inlet valve
26. Metering lever
27. Pin
28. Screw
29. Gasket
30. Metering diaphragm
31. Cover
32. Check valve
33. Retainer
34. Welch plug

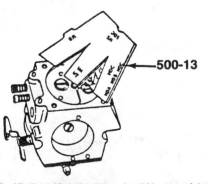

Fig. HL47-2—Metering lever should just touch leg of Walbro tool 500-13. Bend lever to obtain correct lever height.

Illustrations courtesy Homelite Div. of Textron, Inc.

Carburetor disassembly and reassembly is evident after inspection of carburetor and referral to Fig. HL47-3. Do not lose detent ball (7) when withdrawing choke shaft (21). Clean and inspect all components. Do not use wires or drill bits to clean fuel passages as calibration of carburetor may be affected if passages are enlarged. Inspect diaphragms (2 and 25) for defects that may affect operation. Examine fuel inlet valve and seat. Inlet valve (12) is renewable, but carburetor body must be renewed if seat is damaged or excessively worn. Discard carburetor body if mixture screw seats are damaged or excessively worn.

To reassemble carburetor, reverse disassembly procedure. Metering lever should be level with chamber floor as shown in Fig. HL47-4. Bend metering lever as needed.

IGNITION. A solid state ignition is used on all models. The ignition module is attached to the side of the engine cylinder. Air gap between ignition module and flywheel is adjustable and should be 0.008-0.012 inch (0.2-0.3 mm). Loosen ignition module mounting screws and adjust module position to set air gap. Tighten ignition module screws to 45-55 in.-lbs. (5.1-6.2 N·m).

REPAIRS

TIGHTENING TORQUES. Recommended tightening torques are as follows:

Carburetor . . . . .25-35 in.-lbs.
(2.8-3.9 N·m)
Clutch hub . . . . .150-200 in.-lbs.
(17-22.6 N·m)
Crankcase . . . . .60-80 in.-lbs.
(6.8-9.0 N·m)
Flywheel . . . . .200-250 in.-lbs.
(22.6-28.2 N·m)
Ignition module . . . . .45-55 in.-lbs.
(5.1-6.2 N·m)

Intake manifold . . . . .30-40 in.-lbs.
(3.4-4.5 N·m)
Spark plug . . . . .120-180 in.-lbs.
(13.6-20.3 N·m)

CYLINDER, PISTON, PIN AND RINGS. The cylinder (19—Fig. HL47-5) may be removed using the following procedure. Remove trimmer drive shaft and clutch unit from engine. Unbolt and remove starter housing (5), muffler shield (4), air shroud (1), fuel tank (2) and support pad (3). Remove muffler and carburetor from cylinder. Secure crankshaft from turning and remove flywheel nut and flywheel (14) from crankshaft. Remove flywheel shroud (13) and ignition module (20). Unscrew four screws in bottom of crankcase (10) and remove cylinder. Be careful when removing cylinder as crankshaft assembly will be loose in crankcase. Care should be taken not to damage mating surfaces of cylinder and crankcase. Remove retaining rings (15), push piston pin (16) out of piston (17) and separate piston from connecting rod.

The cylinder bore is chrome plated. Inspect cylinder bore and discard cylinder if excessively worn or damaged. Cylinder may not be bored for oversized pistons and oversize cylinders are not available.

The piston is equipped with a single piston ring. Oversize pistons and rings are not available.

Piston is equipped with a piston ring locating pin in the piston ring groove. In-

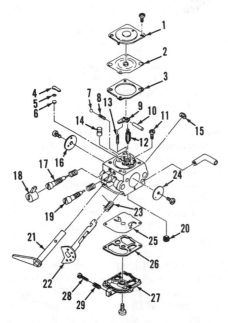

Fig. HL47-3—Exploded view of Zama C1Q carburetor.

1. Cover	17. High-speed mixture
2. Metering diaphragm	screw
3. Gasket	18. Cap
4. Welch plug	19. Idle mixture screw
5. Retainer	20. Screen
6. Check valve	21. Choke shaft
7. Detent ball	22. Throttle shaft
8. Spring	23. Spring
9. Metering lever	24. Throttle plate
10. Pin	25. Fuel pump
11. Screw	diaphragm
12. Fuel inlet valve	26. Gasket
13. Spring	27. Cover
14. Check valve nozzle	28. Idle speed screw
15. "E" ring	29. Spring
16. Choke plate	

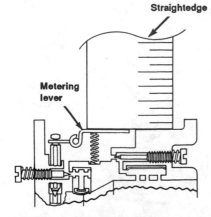

Fig. HL47-4—Metering lever should be level with chamber floor on Zama C1Q carburetor. Bend metering lever as needed.

Fig. HL47-5—Exploded view of engine.

1. Shroud	7. Seal	12. Seal	17. Piston
2. Fuel tank	8. Bearing	13. Flywheel shroud	18. Piston ring
3. Plate	9. Crankshaft & connecting	14. Flywheel	19. Cylinder
4. Muffler shield	rod assy.	15. Retaining rings	20. Ignition module
5. Recoil starter housing	10. Crankcase	16. Piston pin	21. Muffler
6. Crankcase plate	11. Snap ring		

stall piston ring so end gap indexes with locating pin in ring groove.

To reassemble, reverse the disassembly procedure. Piston should be assembled to connecting rod so piston ring end gap faces intake port side of cylinder. Lightly oil cylinder and piston ring before sliding cylinder over piston.

CONNECTING ROD, CRANKSHAFT AND CRANKCASE. Crankshaft assembly (9—Fig. HL47-5) is free after separating cylinder from crankcase as outlined in CYLINDER, PISTON, PIN AND RINGS section.

Inspect components and renew any that are damaged or excessively worn.

Connecting rod, bearing and crankshaft are a unit assembly. Do not attempt to disassemble.

Install seals (7 and 12) with lip to inside. Cylinder and crankcase mating surfaces should be flat and free of nicks and scratches. Clean mating surfaces, then coat with a suitable sealer before assembly.

Bearings, seals and snap ring must be positioned correctly on crankshaft before final assembly. Snap ring (11—Fig. HL47-5) must engage groove in crankcase and cylinder. Tighten crankcase screws to 60-80 in.-lbs. (6.8-9.0 N·m).

CLUTCH. Power is transmitted through the three-shoe clutch shown in Fig. HL47-6. Clutch shoes (9) are available only as a set. When assembling shoes, hook spring (8) ends together between any two shoes. Tighten clutch hub to 150-200 in.-lbs. (17-22.6 N·m).

To remove clutch drum (7), detach drive shaft tube from housing (1). Detach housing (1) from engine. On Model HBC-40, separate clutch carrier (4) from housing. Reach through slot in clutch drum (7) and detach snap ring (6). Press clutch drum and bearing(s) out of housing or carrier. Detach snap ring (3) and press clutch drum out of bearing(s).

REWIND STARTER. To service rewind starter, remove starter housing (7—Fig. HL47-7). Pull starter rope and hold rope pulley with notch in pulley adjacent to rope outlet. Pull rope back through outlet so that it engages notch in pulley and allow pulley to completely unwind. Unscrew pulley retaining screw (3) and remove rope pulley being careful not to dislodge rewind spring in housing. Wear appropriate safety eyewear and gloves before detaching rewind spring from housing as spring may uncoil uncontrolled.

Rewind spring is wound in counterclockwise direction in starter housing. Rope is wound on rope pulley in counterclockwise direction as viewed with pulley in housing. To place tension on rewind spring, pass rope through rope outlet in housing and install rope handle. Pull rope out and hold rope pulley so notch on pulley is adjacent to rope outlet. Pull rope back through outlet between notch in pulley and housing. Turn rope pulley counterclockwise to place tension on spring. Pull rope out of notch, release pulley and allow rope to wind onto pulley. Check starter action. Do not place more tension on rewind spring than is necessary to draw rope handle up against housing.

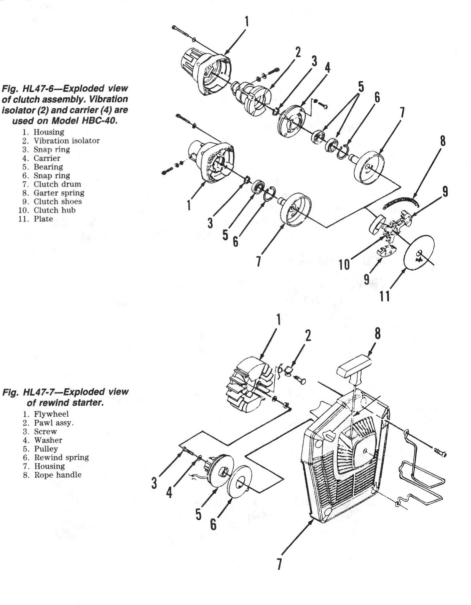

Fig. HL47-6—Exploded view of clutch assembly. Vibration isolator (2) and carrier (4) are used on Model HBC-40.

1. Housing
2. Vibration isolator
3. Snap ring
4. Carrier
5. Bearing
6. Snap ring
7. Clutch drum
8. Garter spring
9. Clutch shoes
10. Clutch hub
11. Plate

Fig. HL47-7—Exploded view of rewind starter.

1. Flywheel
2. Pawl assy.
3. Screw
4. Washer
5. Pulley
6. Rewind spring
7. Housing
8. Rope handle

Illustrations courtesy Homelite Div. of Textron, Inc.

HUSQVARNA

ENGINE SERVICE

Model	Bore	Stroke	Displacement
36	36 mm	32 mm	36 cc
	(1.42 in.)	(1.26 in.)	(2.20 cu. in.)
140	40 mm	32 mm	40 cc
	(1.57 in.)	(1.26 in.)	(2.44 cu. in.)
165	48 mm	36 mm	65 cc
	(1.89 in.)	(1.42 in.)	(3.96 cu. in.)
244	42 mm	32 mm	44 cc
	(1.65 in.)	(1.26 in.)	(2.68 cu. in.)
250	44 mm	32 mm	49 cc
	(1.73 in.)	(1.26 in.)	(3.0 cu. in.)

ENGINE INFORMATION

These engines are used on Husqvarna Series 36R, 140R, 165R, 165RX, 244R, 244RX and 250RX trimmers and brush cutters. Refer to adjoining Husqvarna engine sections for engine service information on other Husqvarna models.

MAINTENANCE

LUBRICATION. Engine lubrication is obtained by mixing gasoline with an oil designed for two-stroke, air-cooled engines. Refer to trimmer service section for manufacturer's recommended fuel:oil mixture ratio.

SPARK PLUG. Recommended spark plug is a Champion RCJ7Y or equivalent. Specified electrode gap for all models is 0.5 mm (0.020 in.).

CARBURETOR. All models are equipped with a Tillotson diaphragm-type carburetor (Figs. HQ101 and HQ102). Service and adjustment procedure is similar for both carburetors.

Initial adjustment of idle mixture screw (24) is one turn out from a lightly seated position. Initial adjustment of high-speed mixture screw (23) is ¾ turn out.

Final adjustments are made with trimmer line fully extended or blade assembly installed. Engine must be at operating temperature and running. Turn idle speed screw (11) in until trimmer head or blade just begins to rotate. Adjust idle mixture screw to obtain maximum idle speed, then turn idle mixture screw ⅙ turn counterclockwise. Adjust idle speed screw until trimmer head or

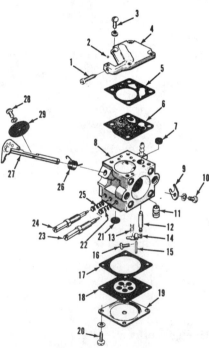

Fig. HQ101—Exploded view of Tillotson carburetor used on some models.

1. Screw
2. Pump cover
3. Gasket
4. Fuel pump diaphragm
5. Welch plug
6. Screw
7. Clip
8. Body
9. Ball
10. Spring
11. Idle speed screw
12. Collar
13. Spring
14. Choke plate
15. Screw
16. Choke shaft
17. Spring
18. Throttle plate
19. Throttle shaft
20. Screw
21. Spring
22. Spring
23. High-speed mixture screw
24. Idle mixture screw
25. Screw
26. Pin
27. Gasket
28. Metering diaphragm
29. Cover
30. Screw
31. Metering lever
32. Fuel inlet valve
33. Spring
34. Welch plug
35. Welch plug
36. Retainer
37. Screen

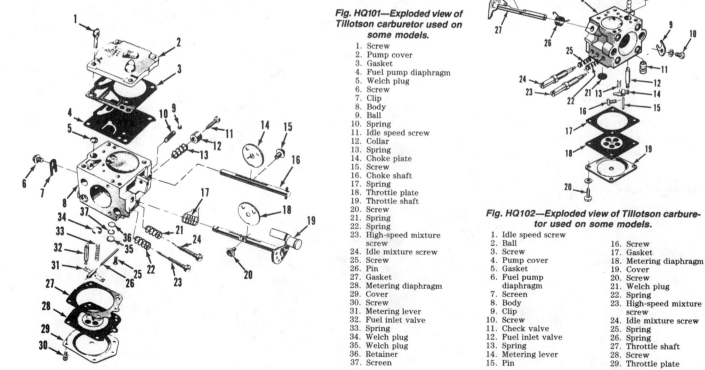

Fig. HQ102—Exploded view of Tillotson carburetor used on some models.

1. Idle speed screw
2. Ball
3. Screw
4. Pump cover
5. Gasket
6. Fuel pump diaphragm
7. Screen
8. Body
9. Clip
10. Screw
11. Check valve
12. Fuel inlet valve
13. Spring
14. Metering lever
15. Pin
16. Screw
17. Gasket
18. Metering diaphragm
19. Cover
20. Screw
21. Welch plug
22. Spring
23. High-speed mixture screw
24. Idle mixture screw
25. Spring
26. Spring
27. Throttle shaft
28. Screw
29. Throttle plate

blade stops rotating (approximately 2500 rpm). Operate trimmer at full throttle and adjust high-speed mixture screw to obtain maximum engine rpm, then turn high-speed mixture $\frac{1}{6}$ turn counterclockwise. Engine speed must not exceed 12,500 rpm.

Carburetor disassembly and reassembly is evident after inspection of carburetor and referral to Figs. HQ101 and HQ102. Clean and inspect all components. Wire or drill bits should not be used to clean passages as fuel flow may be altered if passages are enlarged. Inspect diaphragms for defects that may affect operation. Examine fuel inlet valve and seat. Inlet valve is renewable, but carburetor body must be renewed if seat is damaged or excessively worn.

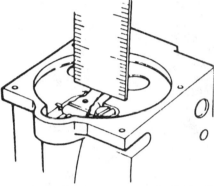

Fig. HQ103—Metering lever must be flush with carburetor body. Bend lever as needed.

Discard carburetor body if mixture screw seats are damaged or excessively worn. Screens should be clean. Be sure throttle plate fits shaft and carburetor bore properly. Apply Loctite to throttle plate retaining screws. Adjust metering lever height so metering lever tip is flush with body as shown in Fig. HQ103.

IGNITION SYSTEM. The engine is equipped with an electronic ignition system. Ignition system performance is considered satisfactory if a spark will jump across a 3 mm ($\frac{1}{8}$ in.) electrode gap on a test spark plug. If no spark is produced, check on/off switch, wiring and ignition module air gap. Air gap between ignition module and flywheel magnet should be 0.35-0.40 mm (0.014-0.016 in.). If switch, wiring and module air gap are satisfactory, but spark is not present, renew ignition module.

REPAIRS

CYLINDER, PISTON, PIN AND RINGS. The piston is accessible after removing cylinder. Remove piston pin retainers and use a suitable puller to extract pin from piston.

The piston is equipped with one piston ring. Ring rotation is prevented by a locating pin in each piston ring groove.

Piston ring end gap should not exceed 0.6 mm (0.024 in.).

Piston and cylinder are coded by stamped letters on piston crown and top of cylinder. Code letters are ''A,'' ''B'' and ''C.'' Install piston in cylinder with a corresponding letter code.

Cylinder should be inspected and any aluminum transfer from piston (especially at exhaust port area) should be removed with fine emery cloth. Inspect cylinder for scoring or excessive wear and renew as necessary.

Lubricate piston and cylinder bore with oil prior to assembly. Install piston so arrow on piston crown points towards exhaust port. Be sure piston ring gaps are correctly indexed with locating pins in piston ring grooves when installing cylinder.

CRANKSHAFT, CONNECTING ROD AND CRANKCASE. Crankshaft, connecting rod and rod bearing are a unit assembly; individual components are not available. The crankshaft is supported by ball bearings at both ends. A renewable needle bearing is located in the small end of the connecting rod.

To remove crankshaft and connecting rod assembly, refer to Figs. HQ104 and HQ105. Remove cooling shroud, recoil starter assembly, muffler, carburetor

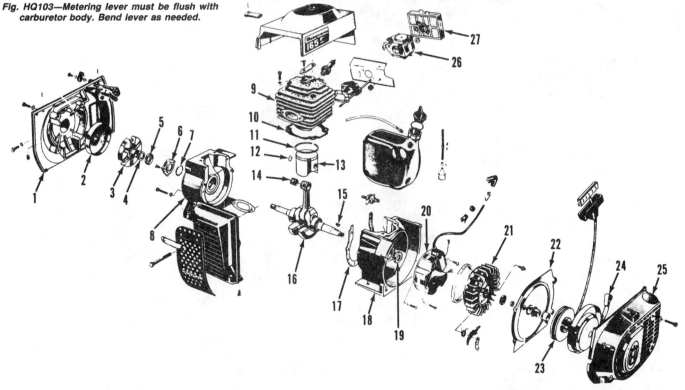

Fig. HQ104—Exploded view of Model 165 engine. All other engines are similar except for crankcase shown in Fig. HQ105.

1. Cover	6. Seal plate	11. Piston ring
2. Clutch drum	7. ''O'' ring	12. Retainer
3. Clutch assy.	8. Crankcase half	13. Piston
4. Shim	9. Cylinder	14. Bearing
5. Seal	10. Gasket	15. Key

16. Crankshaft assy.	20. Ignition system
17. Gasket	21. Flywheel
18. Crankcase half	22. Shroud
19. Seal	23. Pulley

24. Rewind spring
25. Cover
26. Carburetor
27. Air cleaner

and flywheel. Remove centrifugal clutch assembly. Note that clutch hub assembly or clutch hub retaining nut has left-hand threads. Remove cylinder retaining bolts and carefully work cylinder away from crankcase and piston. Remove crankcase retaining bolts and carefully separate crankcase halves. Remove crankshaft and connecting rod assembly. It may be necessary to slightly heat crankcase halves to remove or install the ball bearing main bearings.

To reassemble engine, install ball bearings on crankshaft making certain they are seated against shoulders of crankshaft. Heat crankcase halves slightly and install crankshaft assembly making certain bearings seat completely in bearing bores. Tighten crankcase retaining bolts in a criss-cross pattern. Lubricate seals (5) and seal "O" ring (7) prior to installation.

CLUTCH. Refer to Figs. HQ106 or HQ107 for an exploded view of clutch. Clutch hub retaining nut (5—Fig. HQ106) has left-hand threads. On Model 165 engine, clutch hub (3—Fig. HQ107) has left-hand threads. Clutch hub, shoes and springs are available only as a unit assembly. Clutch drum bearings are not available separately, only with housing.

Early Model 140 engines were equipped with a clutch housing (1—Fig. HQ106) with a bearing bore to accept a 9 mm thick, 32 mm diameter bearing. Drive shaft used on these models has a 46 mm long shoulder that seats directly against bearing and requires no shim between bearing and drive shaft shoulder.

Late production engines are equipped with a 14 mm thick, 35 mm diameter bearing. Bearings on these models are retained in clutch housing (1) by a snap ring. The drive shaft used on these models has a 44 mm shoulder that the bearing seats against and a 2 mm shim is installed between the bearing and drive shaft shoulder. Do not attempt to interchange parts between early and late models.

REWIND STARTER. Refer to Figs. HQ108 or HQ109 for an exploded view of starter. To disassemble starter, detach starter housing from engine. Remove rope handle and allow rope to wind into starter. Unscrew center screw and remove rope pulley. Wear appropriate safety eyewear and gloves before detaching rewind spring from housing as spring may uncoil uncontrolled.

To assemble starter, lubricate center post of housing and spring side with light grease. Install rewind spring so coil windings are clockwise from outer end on Model 165 or counterclockwise on all other models. Assemble starter while passing rope through housing rope outlet and attach rope handle to rope. To place tension on starter rope, pull rope out of housing. Engage rope in notch on pulley and turn pulley two turns clockwise on Model 165 or counterclockwise on all other models to place tension on spring. Hold pulley and disengage rope from pulley notch. Release pulley and allow rope to wind on pulley. Check starter operation. Rope handle should be held against housing by spring tension, but it must be possible to rotate pulley at least an additional $1/2$ turn when rope is pulled out fully.

It may be necessary to pull starter rope slightly as starter housing assembly is installed to engage flywheel starter pawls with pulley.

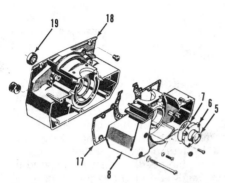

Fig. HQ105—Exploded view of crankcase assembly used on all engines except Model 165.

5. Seal
6. Seal plate
7. "O" ring
8. Crankcase half
17. Gasket
18. Crankcase half
19. Seal

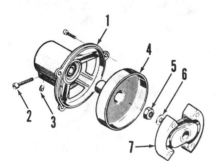

Fig. HQ106—Exploded view of clutch assembly used on all engines except Model 165.

1. Clutch housing
2. Clamp bolt
3. Locating screw
4. Clutch drum
5. Nut (L.H.)
6. Washer
7. Clutch assy.

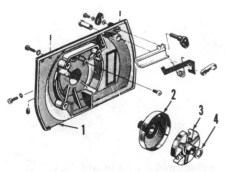

Fig. HQ107—Exploded view of clutch assembly used on Model 165 engine.

1. Cover
2. Clutch drum
3. Clutch assy.
4. Shim

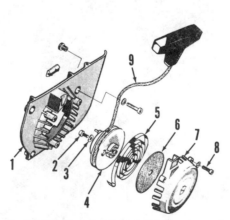

Fig. HQ108—Exploded view of rewind starter used on all engines except Model 165.

1. Cover
2. Screw
3. Washer
4. Pulley
5. Rewind spring
6. Plate
7. Housing
8. Screw
9. Rope

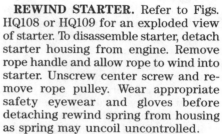

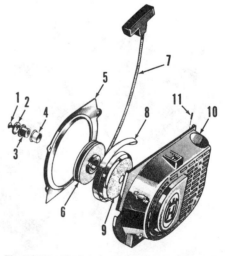

Fig. HQ109—Exploded view of rewind starter used on Model 165 engine.

1. Screw
2. Washer
3. Bearing
4. Bearing sleeve
5. Cover
6. Pulley
7. Rope
8. Rewind spring
9. Plate
10. Cover
11. Pin

HUSQVARNA

ENGINE SERVICE

Model	Bore	Stroke	Displacement
18	28 mm	30 mm	18.5 cc
	(1.10 in.)	(1.18 in.)	(1.13 cu. in.)

ENGINE INFORMATION

This engine is used on Husqvarna Model 18RL trimmer. Refer to adjoining Husqvarna engine sections for engine service information on other Husqvarna models.

MAINTENANCE

LUBRICATION. Engine lubrication is obtained by mixing gasoline with an oil designed for two-stroke, air-cooled engines. Refer to trimmer service section for manufacturer's recommended fuel:oil mixture ratio.

SPARK PLUG. Recommended spark plug is a NGK BM6A or equivalent. Specified electrode gap for all models is 0.7 mm (0.028 in.).

CARBURETOR. The engine is equipped with a Walbro WT diaphragm-type carburetor. Refer to Fig. HQ201 for an exploded view of carburetor. Initial adjustment of idle mixture screw (13) and high-speed mixture screw (12) is one turn open. Final adjustment is performed with engine at normal operating temperature and cutter line at desired length. Turn idle speed screw (20) in until trimmer head or blade just begins to rotate. Adjust idle mixture screw so engine idles smoothly and accelerates cleanly without hesitation. Readjust idle speed screw so trimmer head or blade stops turning. Adjust high-speed mixture screw for best engine performance under load. Do not adjust high-speed mixture screw too lean as engine may be damaged.

Carburetor disassembly and reassembly is evident after inspection of carburetor and referral to Fig. HQ201. Clean and inspect all components. Inspect diaphragms (2 and 23) for defects that may affect operation. Examine fuel inlet valve and seat. Inlet valve (5) is renewable, but carburetor body must be renewed if seat is damaged or excessively worn. Discard carburetor body if mixture screw seats are damaged or excessively worn. Clean fuel screen (24).

Check metering lever height as shown in Fig. HQ202 using Walbro tool 500-13. Metering lever should just touch leg on tool. Bend lever to obtain correct lever height.

IGNITION SYSTEM. The engine is equipped with a breaker-point-type ignition system. The ignition condenser and breaker points are located behind the flywheel. To adjust breaker-point gap, the flywheel must be removed. Breaker-point gap should be 0.35 mm (0.014 in.). Points should be adjusted so points begin to open when match mark on flywheel aligns with ''M'' or ''P'' mark cast on crankcase.

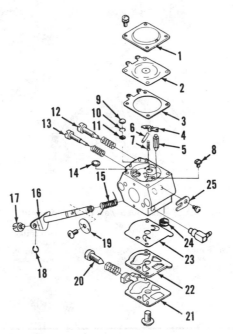

Fig. HQ201—Exploded view of Walbro WT carburetor.

1. Cover
2. Metering diaphragm
3. Gasket
4. Metering lever
5. Fuel inlet valve
6. Pin
7. Spring
8. Screw
9. Welch plug
10. Retainer
11. Screen
12. High-speed mixture screw
13. Idle mixture screw
14. Welch plug
15. Spring
16. Throttle shaft
17. Swivel
18. ''E'' ring
19. Throttle plate
20. Idle speed screw
21. Cover
22. Gasket
23. Fuel pump diaphragm
24. Fuel inlet screen
25. Retainer

REPAIRS

PISTON, PIN AND RINGS. The piston is equipped with two piston rings. Ring rotation is prevented by a locating pin in each piston ring groove.

Piston and rings are available only in standard diameter.

Install piston so arrow on piston crown points towards exhaust port. Be sure piston ring gaps are correctly indexed with locating pins in piston ring grooves when installing cylinder.

CYLINDER. The engine is equipped with a plated cylinder. Renew cylinder if bore is excessively worn, scored or otherwise damaged. Cylinder is available only in standard size.

CRANKSHAFT, CONNECTING ROD AND CRANKCASE. Crankshaft, connecting rod and rod bearing are a unit assembly; individual components are not available. The crankshaft is supported by ball bearings at both ends.

To remove crankshaft and connecting rod assembly (see Fig. HQ203), first disengage trimmer drive shaft from engine. Remove cooling shroud, recoil starter assembly, muffler, carburetor and flywheel. Remove centrifugal clutch assembly. Remove cylinder retaining bolts and work cylinder away from crankcase and piston. Remove crankcase retaining bolts and carefully separate crankcase halves. Remove crankshaft and connect-

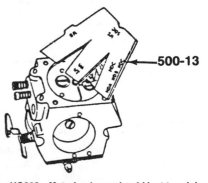

Fig. HQ202—Metering lever should just touch leg of Walbro tool 500-13. Bend lever to obtain correct lever height.

ing rod assembly. It may be necessary to slightly heat crankcase halves to remove or install the ball bearing main bearings.

A renewable needle bearing is located in the small end of the connecting rod.

To install crankshaft, reverse removal procedure. Install seals with lip towards inside of crankcase.

CLUTCH. The engine is equipped with a two-shoe clutch. The clutch shoe assembly is mounted on the flywheel. The clutch drum rides in the drive housing, which may be the fan housing on some engines.

To remove clutch drum, first unbolt and remove drive housing (1—Fig. HQ204) from engine. Reach through slot and detach snap ring (4), then press clutch drum (5) and bearing (3) out of housing. Heating housing will ease removal. Detach snap ring (2) and press clutch drum shaft out of bearing (3). Clutch shoes (7) are available only as a pair.

Reverse removal procedure to install clutch drum.

REWIND STARTER. Refer to Fig. HQ205 for an exploded view of starter. To disassemble starter, detach starter housing (10) from engine. Remove rope handle and allow rope to wind into starter. Unscrew center screw (2) and remove rope pulley (7). Wear appropriate safety eyewear and gloves before detaching rewind spring (8) from housing as spring may uncoil uncontrolled.

To assemble starter, lubricate center post of housing and spring side with light grease. Install rewind spring so coil windings are clockwise from outer end. Assemble starter while passing rope through housing rope outlet and attach rope handle to rope. To place tension on starter rope, pull rope out of housing. Engage rope in notch on pulley and turn pulley clockwise to place tension on spring. Hold pulley and disengage rope from pulley notch. Release pulley and allow rope to wind on pulley. Check starter operation. Rope handle should be held against housing by spring tension, but it must be possible to rotate pulley at least 1/2 turn clockwise when rope is pulled out fully.

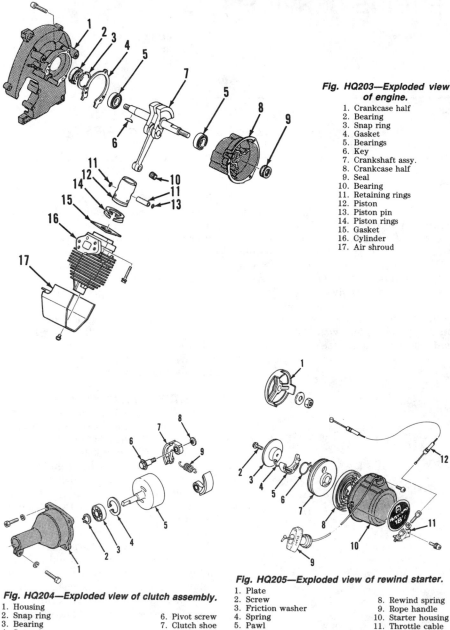

Fig. HQ203—Exploded view of engine.
1. Crankcase half
2. Bearing
3. Snap ring
4. Gasket
5. Bearings
6. Key
7. Crankshaft assy.
8. Crankcase half
9. Seal
10. Bearing
11. Retaining rings
12. Piston
13. Piston pin
14. Piston rings
15. Gasket
16. Cylinder
17. Air shroud

Fig. HQ204—Exploded view of clutch assembly.
1. Housing
2. Snap ring
3. Bearing
4. Snap ring
5. Clutch drum
6. Pivot screw
7. Clutch shoe
8. Washer
9. Spring

Fig. HQ205—Exploded view of rewind starter.
1. Plate
2. Screw
3. Friction washer
4. Spring
5. Pawl
6. Friction spring
7. Pulley
8. Rewind spring
9. Rope handle
10. Starter housing
11. Throttle cable bracket
12. Throttle cable

HUSQVARNA

ENGINE SERVICE

Model	Bore	Stroke	Displacement
22	30 mm	30 mm	21.2 cc
	(1.18 in.)	(1.18 in.)	(1.29 cu. in.)
25	32 mm	30 mm	24.1 cc
	(1.26 in.)	(1.18 in.)	(1.47 cu. in.)
125	34 mm	28 mm	25.4 cc
	(1.34 in.)	(1.10 in.)	(1.55 cu. in.)
132	38 mm	28 mm	31.8 cc
	(1.50 in.)	(1.10 in.)	(1.94 cu. in.)

ENGINE INFORMATION

These engines are used on Husqvarna Series 22, 25, 125 and 132 trimmers and brush cutters. Refer to adjoining Husqvarna engine sections for engine service information on other Husqvarna models.

MAINTENANCE

LUBRICATION. Engine lubrication is obtained by mixing gasoline with an oil designed for two-stroke, air-cooled engines. Refer to trimmer service section for manufacturer's recommended fuel:oil mixture ratio.

SPARK PLUG. Recommended spark plug is a NGK BM6A or equivalent on Model 22 and 25 engines, or a NGK BPM6Y on Model 125 and 132 engines. Specified electrode gap for all models is 0.6-0.7 mm (0.024-0.028 in.).

CARBURETOR. Later Model 22 and 25 engines are equipped with a Walbro WY diaphragm carburetor and Model 125 and 132 engines are equipped with a Walbro WYK diaphragm carburetor. Early Model 22 and 25 engines are equipped with a slide-valve-type carburetor. Refer to following sections for service information.

Walbro WY and WYK. Both carburetors use a barrel-type throttle rather than a throttle plate. Idle fuel for the carburetor flows up into the throttle barrel where it is fed into the air stream. On some models, the idle fuel flow can be adjusted by turning an idle mixture limiter plate (P—Fig. HQ301). Initial setting is in center notch. Rotating the plate clockwise will lean the idle mixture. Inside the limiter plate is an idle mixture needle (N—Fig. HQ302) that is preset at the factory (a plug covers the

needle). If removed, use the following procedure to determine correct position. Back out needle (N) until unscrewed. Screw in needle five turns on Model WY or 15 turns on Model WYK. Rotate idle mixture plate (P—Fig. HQ301) to center notch. Run engine until normal operating temperature is attained. Adjust idle speed screw (I) so engine idles at 3000 rpm. Rotate idle mixture needle (N—Fig. HQ302) and obtain highest rpm (turning needle clockwise leans the mixture), then turn needle ¼ turn counterclockwise. Readjust idle speed screw. Note that idle mixture limiter plate and needle are available

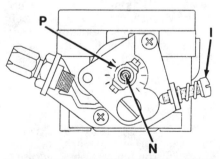

Fig. HQ301—On Walbro WY and WYK carburetors, idle speed screw is located at (I), idle mixture limiter plate is located at (P) and idle mixture needle is located at (N). A plug covers the idle mixture needle.

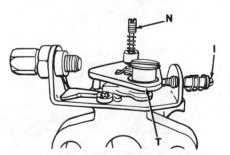

Fig. HQ302—View of idle mixture needle (N) used on Walbro WY and WYK carburetors.

only as an assembly with throttle barrel.

High-speed mixture is controlled by a fixed main jet (20—Fig. HQ303).

To overhaul carburetor, refer to exploded view in Fig. HQ303 and note the

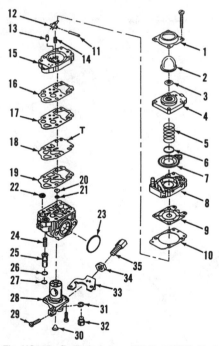

Fig. HQ303—Exploded view of Walbro WYK. Model WY is similar.

1. Cover
2. Primer bulb
3. Check valve
4. Plate
5. Spring
6. Retainer
7. Start diaphragm
8. Start diaphragm body
9. Metering diaphragm
10. Gasket
11. Pin
12. Metering lever
13. Fuel inlet valve
14. Spring
15. Fuel pump body
16. Gasket
17. Fuel pump plate
18. Fuel pump diaphragm
19. Gasket
20. Main jet
21. "O" ring
22. Fuel screen
23. "O" ring
24. Spring
25. Start valve
26. "O" ring
27. "O" ring
28. Throttle barrel assy.
29. Idle speed screw
30. Plug
31. "E" ring
32. Swivel
33. Bracket
34. Nut
35. Adjuster

following: On models with a plastic body, clean only with solvents approved for use with plastic. Do not use wire or drill bits to clean fuel passages. Do not disassemble throttle barrel assembly. Examine fuel inlet valve and seat. Inlet valve (13) is renewable, but fuel pump body (15) must be renewed if seat is excessively worn or damaged. Clean fuel screen (22). Inspect diaphragms for tears and other damage. When installing plates and gaskets (16 through 19), note that tabs (T) on ends will ''stairstep'' when correctly installed. Adjust metering lever height to obtain 1.5 mm (0.059 in.) between carburetor body surface and lever as shown in Fig. HQ304.

Slide-Valve Type Carburetor. The carburetor used on early Model 22 and

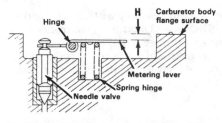

Fig. HQ304—Metering lever height (H) must be 1.5 mm (0.059 in.) on Walbro WY and WYK carburetors.

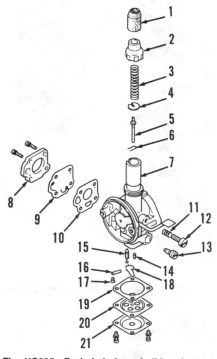

Fig. HQ305—Exploded view of slide-valve-type carburetor used on early Models 22 and 25.

1. Boot	11. Spring
2. Cap	12. Idle speed screw
3. Spring	13. Mixture screw
4. Retainer	14. Spring
5. Jet needle	15. Fuel inlet valve
6. Clip	16. Pin
7. Throttle slide	17. Screw
8. Cover	18. Metering lever
9. Fuel pump diaphragm	19. Gasket
	20. Metering diaphragm
10. Gasket	21. Cover

25 engines is a diaphragm-type carburetor with a slide-valve-type throttle rather than a throttle plate. The carburetor has an integral fuel pump.

Fuel mixture is adjusted by turning mixture screw (13—Fig. HQ305). Midrange mixture is determined by the position of the clip (6) on jet needle (5). Normal position of clip is in the middle groove. The mixture will be leaner if clip is installed in the top groove, or richer if clip is installed in the bottom groove.

Before removing carburetor from engine, unscrew cap (2) and withdraw throttle slide (7) assembly. When overhauling carburetor, refer to Fig. HQ305 and note the following: Examine fuel inlet valve and seat. Inlet valve (15) is renewable, but carburetor body must be renewed if seat is excessively worn or damaged. Inspect mixture screw and seat. Renew carburetor body if seat is excessively worn or damaged. Inspect diaphragms for tears and other damage. When installing throttle slide (7), be sure groove in side of throttle slide indexes with pin in bore of carburetor body.

IGNITION SYSTEM. The engine is equipped with an electronic ignition system. All later models are equipped with a one-piece ignition module that includes the ignition coil. Early Models 22 and 25 are equipped with a two-piece ignition system.

The ignition system is considered satisfactory if a spark will jump across the 3 mm ($\frac{1}{8}$ in.) gap of a test spark plug. If no spark is produced, check on/off switch, wiring and ignition module/coil air gap. Air gap between ignition module/coil and flywheel magnet should be 0.3 mm (0.012 in.).

REPAIRS

PISTON, PIN AND RINGS. The piston is accessible after removing cylinder. Remove piston pin retainers and use a suitable puller to extract pin from piston.

The piston is equipped with two piston rings. Ring rotation is prevented by a locating pin in each piston ring groove.

Piston and rings are available only in standard diameter.

Install piston so arrow on piston crown points toward exhaust port. Be sure piston ring gaps are correctly indexed with locating pins in piston ring grooves when installing cylinder.

CYLINDER. The engine is equipped with a plated cylinder. Renew cylinder if bore is excessively worn, scored or otherwise damaged. Cylinder is available only in standard size.

CRANKSHAFT, CONNECTING ROD AND CRANKCASE. Crankshaft, connecting rod and rod bearing are a unit assembly; individual components are not available. The crankshaft is supported by ball bearings at both ends. A renewable needle bearing is located in the small end of the connecting rod.

To remove crankshaft and connecting rod assembly (see Fig. 306), separate engine from trimmer drive shaft. Remove cooling shroud, flywheel housing, recoil starter assembly, muffler, carburetor and fuel tank. Remove nuts retaining flywheel and recoil starter pawl carrier to crankshaft and remove flywheel and pawl carrier. Remove cylinder mounting screws and work cylinder off crankcase and piston. Remove crankcase retaining bolts and separate crankcase halves. Remove crankshaft and connecting rod assembly. Heat crankcase if necessary to aid removal of main bearings.

To reassemble engine, reverse disassembly procedure. Install seals (14 and 18) with lip toward inside of crankcase.

CLUTCH. The upper end of the drive shaft is threaded into the clutch drum hub on early models. To service clutch, detach drive housing (4—Fig. HQ307) from engine. Clutch shoes (9) are available only as a set.

To service clutch drum (7), remove gear head from drive shaft housing. Detach drive shaft housing tube from drive housing (1). To remove clutch drum on models with a threaded drive shaft, insert a tool through slot of clutch drum so it cannot rotate, then turn square end (trimmer end) of drive shaft so drum unscrews from drive shaft. On models with a removable drive shaft, reach through slot in clutch drum and detach snap ring (6). If necessary, remove bearings (5) from housing.

REWIND STARTER. Refer to Figs. HQ308 or HQ309 for an exploded view of starter. To disassemble starter, detach starter housing (9) from engine. Remove rope handle and allow rope to wind into starter. Unscrew center screw (5) and remove rope pulley (7). Wear appropriate safety eyewear and gloves before detaching rewind spring (8) from housing as spring may uncoil uncontrolled.

To assemble starter, lubricate center post of housing and spring side with light grease. Install rewind spring so coil windings are clockwise from outer end on Models 22 and 25 or counterclockwise on Models 125 and 132. Assemble starter while passing rope through housing rope outlet and attach rope handle to rope. To place tension on starter rope, pull rope out of housing. Engage rope in notch on pulley and turn pulley to place tension in spring. Hold pulley and disengage rope from pulley notch. Release pulley and allow rope to wind on pulley. Check starter operation.

Rope handle should be held against housing by spring tension, but it must be possible to rotate pulley an additional $1/2$ turn when rope is pulled out fully.

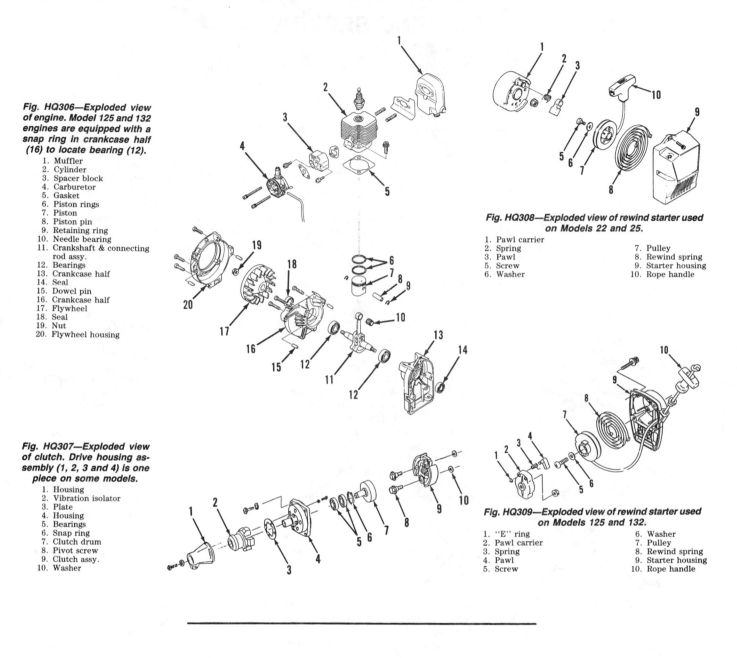

Fig. HQ306—Exploded view of engine. Model 125 and 132 engines are equipped with a snap ring in crankcase half (16) to locate bearing (12).

1. Muffler
2. Cylinder
3. Spacer block
4. Carburetor
5. Gasket
6. Piston rings
7. Piston
8. Piston pin
9. Retaining ring
10. Needle bearing
11. Crankshaft & connecting rod assy.
12. Bearings
13. Crankcase half
14. Seal
15. Dowel pin
16. Crankcase half
17. Flywheel
18. Seal
19. Nut
20. Flywheel housing

Fig. HQ308—Exploded view of rewind starter used on Models 22 and 25.

1. Pawl carrier
2. Spring
3. Pawl
5. Screw
6. Washer
7. Pulley
8. Rewind spring
9. Starter housing
10. Rope handle

Fig. HQ307—Exploded view of clutch. Drive housing assembly (1, 2, 3 and 4) is one piece on some models.

1. Housing
2. Vibration isolator
3. Plate
4. Housing
5. Bearings
6. Snap ring
7. Clutch drum
8. Pivot screw
9. Clutch assy.
10. Washer

Fig. HQ309—Exploded view of rewind starter used on Models 125 and 132.

1. "E" ring
2. Pawl carrier
3. Spring
4. Pawl
5. Screw
6. Washer
7. Pulley
8. Rewind spring
9. Starter housing
10. Rope handle

HUSQVARNA

ENGINE SERVICE

Model	Bore	Stroke	Displacement
26	....	....	26 cc (1.29 cu. in.)
32	....	....	32 cc (1.95 cu. in.)

ENGINE INFORMATION

These engines are used on Husqvarna Model 26LC, 26RLC, 32LC, 32R, 32RL and 32RLC trimmers. Refer to adjoining Husqvarna engine sections for engine service information on other Husqvarna models.

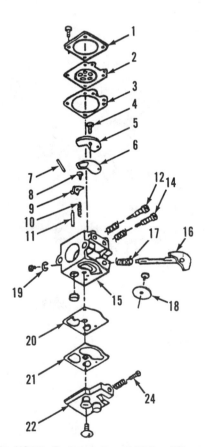

Fig. HQ401—Exploded view of Walbro WA carburetor.

1. Cover
2. Metering diaphragm
3. Gasket
4. Screw
5. Circuit plate
6. Gasket
7. Pin
8. Screw
9. Metering lever
10. Spring
11. Fuel inlet valve
12. High-speed mixture screw
14. Idle mixture screw
15. Carburetor body
16. Throttle shaft
17. Spring
18. Throttle plate
19. "E" ring
20. Screen
21. Fuel pump diaphragm
22. Gasket
23. Cover
24. Idle speed screw

MAINTENANCE

LUBRICATION. Engine lubrication is obtained by mixing gasoline with an oil designed for two-stroke, air-cooled engines. Refer to trimmer service section for manufacturer's recommended fuel:oil mixture ratio.

SPARK PLUG. Recommended spark plug is a Champion CJ14 or equivalent. Specified electrode gap for all models is 0.63 mm (0.025 in.).

CARBURETOR. The engine is equipped with a Walbro WA diaphragm-type carburetor. Initial adjustment of idle and high-speed mixture screws is one turn out from a lightly seated position. Final adjustments are performed with trimmer line at recommended length or blade installed. Engine must be at operating temperature and running. Adjust idle speed screw (24—Fig. HQ401) so trimmer head or blade does not rotate (approximately 3000 rpm). Adjust idle mixture screw (14) so engine idles smoothly and accelerates without hesitation. Readjust idle speed as necessary. Operate unit at full throttle and adjust high-speed mixture screw (12) to obtain maximum engine rpm, then turn high-speed mixture screw 1/6 turn counterclockwise. Do not adjust high-speed mixture too lean as engine may be damaged.

When overhauling carburetor, refer to exploded view in Fig. HQ401. Examine fuel inlet valve and seat. Inlet valve (11) is renewable, but carburetor body must be renewed if seat is excessively worn or damaged. Inspect mixture screws and seats. Renew carburetor body if seats are excessively worn or damaged. Clean fuel screen (20). Inspect diaphragms for tears and other damage.

Check metering lever height as shown in Fig. HQ402. Metering lever should be flush with circuit plate. Bend lever to obtain correct lever height.

IGNITION SYSTEM. The engine is equipped with an electronic ignition system. Ignition system performance is considered satisfactory if a spark will jump across a 3 mm (1/8 in.) electrode gap on a test spark plug. If no spark is produced, check on/off switch, wiring and ignition module air gap. Air gap between ignition module and flywheel magnet should be 0.25-0.36 mm (0.010-0.014 in.). If switch, wiring and module air gap are satisfactory, but spark is not present, renew ignition module.

REPAIRS

PISTON, PIN AND RING. The piston (7—Fig. HQ403) is accessible after removing cylinder (10). Remove piston pin retainers (5) and use a suitable puller to extract pin (6) from piston.

The piston is equipped with a single piston ring (8). Ring rotation is prevented by a locating pin in the piston ring groove. Piston is available in standard size only.

Be sure piston ring end gap is correctly indexed with locating pin in piston ring groove when installing cylinder.

CYLINDER. The cylinder is available in standard size only. Renew cylinder if damaged or excessively worn.

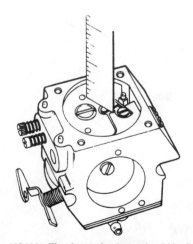

Fig. HQ402—Tip of metering lever should be flush with circuit plate. Bend metering lever as needed.

CRANKSHAFT AND CONNECTING ROD. The crankshaft (13—Fig. HQ403) is supported at flywheel end only by two ball bearings (15 and 18). The stamped steel connecting rod (11) has a caged roller bearing at both ends. Connecting rod and bearings are serviced only as an assembly.

To remove crankshaft and connecting rod, first separate engine from trimmer drive shaft housing. Remove clutch housing, recoil starter assembly, flywheel housing, muffler and carburetor. Remove spark plug and place a piston locking tool or end of a rope in spark plug hole to lock piston and connecting rod. Remove flywheel nut and withdraw flywheel from crankshaft. Remove fuel tank and crankcase shroud assembly (1). Remove cylinder retaining screws and work cylinder off crankcase and piston. Remove connecting rod (11) from crankpin. Detach snap ring (19) and carefully press crankshaft out of bearings. Drive or press bearings out of crankcase, remove snap rings (16) and remove seal (17).

When reinstalling crankshaft, install seal (17) in bearing bore of crankcase so cupped side of seal is toward inside of crankcase. Outer main bearing (18) has a single shielded side that must be out toward flywheel side of engine after installation. Press bearings (15 and 18) in until seated against snap rings. Install spacer (14) on crankshaft main bearing journal and press crankshaft into main bearings.

REED VALVE. A reed valve (3—Fig. HQ403) is located on the inner face of the crankcase cover. Inspect reed petal and discard if torn, broken, creased or otherwise damaged.

CLUTCH. The engine is equipped with a two-shoe clutch (10—Fig. HQ404). Clutch hub, shoes and spring are available only as a unit assembly. The clutch drum is contained in housing (13). Drum and housing are available only as a unit assembly.

REWIND STARTER. Refer to Fig. HQ404 for an exploded view of rewind starter. To disassemble starter, detach clutch housing (13) and starter housing (8) from engine. Remove rope handle (14) and allow rope to wind into starter. Unscrew pulley retainer (7) and remove rope pulley (5). Wear appropriate safety eyewear and gloves before detaching rewind spring (6) from housing as spring may uncoil uncontrolled.

To assemble starter, lubricate center post of housing and spring side with light grease. Install rewind spring so coil windings are clockwise from outer end. Rope length should be 107 cm (42 in.).

Assemble starter while passing rope through housing rope outlet and attach rope handle to rope. To place tension on starter rope, pull rope out of housing. Engage rope in notch on pulley and turn pulley clockwise to place tension on rewind spring. Hold pulley and disengage rope from pulley notch. Release pulley and allow rope to wind on pulley. Check starter operation. Rope handle should be held against housing by spring tension, but it must be possible to rotate pulley at least $\frac{1}{4}$ turn clockwise when rope is pulled out fully.

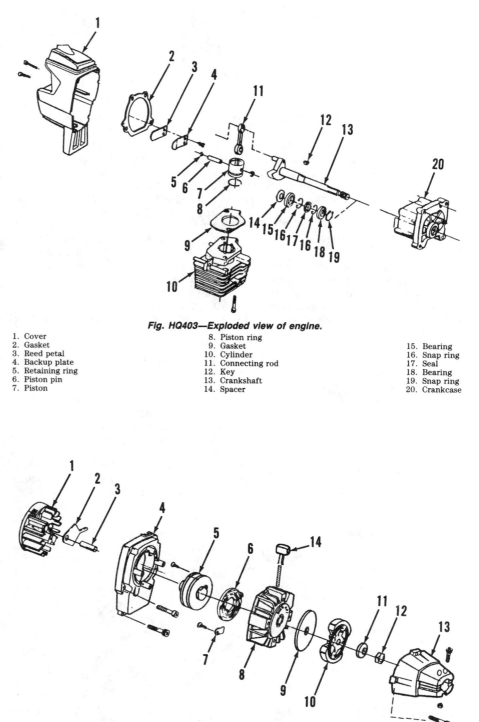

Fig. HQ403—Exploded view of engine.

1. Cover	8. Piston ring	15. Bearing
2. Gasket	9. Gasket	16. Snap ring
3. Reed petal	10. Cylinder	17. Seal
4. Backup plate	11. Connecting rod	18. Bearing
5. Retaining ring	12. Key	19. Snap ring
6. Piston pin	13. Crankshaft	20. Crankcase
7. Piston	14. Spacer	

Fig. HQ404—Exploded view of clutch and rewind starter assemblies. Counterweight (2) is not used on all models.

1. Flywheel	6. Rewind spring	11. Belleville washer
2. Counterweight	7. Retainer	12. Nut
3. Spacer	8. Starter housing	13. Housing
4. Shroud	9. Plate	14. Rope handle
5. Pulley	10. Clutch assy.	

HUSQVARNA

ENGINE SERVICE

Model	Bore	Stroke	Displacement
39	40 mm	32 mm	40 cc
	(1.57 in.)	(1.26 in.)	(2.4 cu. in.)
240	42 mm	32 mm	44 cc
	(1.65 in.)	(1.26 in.)	(2.7 cu. in.)
245	42 mm	32 mm	44 cc
	(1.65 in.)	(1.26 in.)	(2.7 cu. in.)

ENGINE INFORMATION

These engines are used on Husqvarna Model 39R, 240R, 245R and 245RX trimmers and brush cutters. Refer to adjoining Husqvarna engine sections for engine service information on other Husqvarna models.

MAINTENANCE

LUBRICATION. Engine lubrication is obtained by mixing gasoline with an oil designed for two-stroke, air-cooled engines. Refer to trimmer service section for manufacturer's recommended fuel:oil mixture ratio.

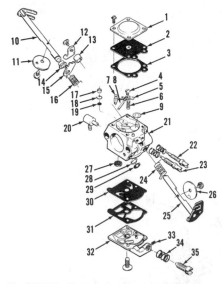

Fig. HQ501—Exploded view of typical Walbro WT carburetor.

1. Cover	19. Screen
2. Metering diaphragm	20. Fuel fitting
3. Gasket	21. Carburetor body
4. Screw	22. Idle mixture screw
5. Metering lever	23. High-speed mixture
6. Spring	screw
7. Fuel inlet valve	24. Spring
8. Pin	25. Throttle shaft
9. Welch plug	26. Throttle plate
10. Choke shaft	27. Fuel inlet screen
11. Choke plate	28. Washer
12. Arm	29. ''E'' ring
13. Spacer	30. Fuel pump diaphragm
14. Spacer	31. Gasket
15. Lever	32. Cover
16. Spring	33. Screw
17. Welch plug	34. Spring
18. Retainer	35. Idle speed screw

SPARK PLUG. Recommended spark plug is a Champion RCJ7Y or equivalent. Specified electrode gap for all models is 0.5 mm (0.020 in.).

CARBURETOR. All models are equipped with a Walbro WT diaphragm carburetor. Initial adjustment of idle mixture screw (22—Fig. HQ501) and high-speed mixture screw (23) is one turn out from a lightly seated position. Final adjustments are performed with trimmer line at recommended length or blade installed. Engine must be at operating temperature and running. Adjust idle speed screw (35) to approximately 2500 rpm (trimmer head or blade should not rotate). Adjust idle mixture screw so engine runs at maximum idle speed and accelerates without hesitation. Readjust idle speed. Operate unit at full throttle and adjust high-speed mixture screw to obtain maximum engine rpm, then turn counterclockwise until engine starts to four-cycle. Engine speed must not exceed 12,500 rpm.

Carburetor disassembly and reassembly is evident after inspection of carburetor and referral to Fig. HQ501. Clean and inspect all components. Inspect diaphragms (2 and 30) for defects that may affect operation. Examine fuel inlet valve (7) is renewable, but carburetor body (21) must be renewed if seat is damaged or

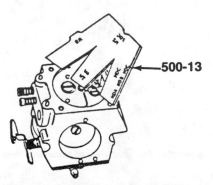

Fig. HQ502—Metering lever should just touch leg of Walbro tool 500-13. Bend lever to obtain correct lever height.

excessively worn. Discard carburetor body if mixture screw seats are damaged or excessively worn. Clean fuel screen (27).

Check metering lever height as shown in Fig. HQ502 using Walbro tool 500-13. Metering lever should just touch leg on tool. Bend lever to obtain correct lever height.

IGNITION SYSTEM. The engine is equipped with an electronic ignition system. Ignition system performance is considered satisfactory if a spark will jump across a 3 mm (1/8 in.) electrode gap on a test spark plug. If no spark is produced, check on/off switch, wiring and ignition module air gap. Air gap between ignition module and flywheel magnet should be 0.3 mm (0.012 in.). If switch, wiring and module air gap are satisfactory, but spark is not present, renew ignition module.

REPAIRS

PISTON, PIN AND RING. The piston (3—Fig. HQ503) is accessible after removing cylinder (1). Remove piston pin retainers (5) and use a suitable puller to extract pin (4) from piston.

Piston and piston ring are available only in standard size.

Install piston on connecting rod so arrow on piston crown will point toward exhaust port when the cylinder is installed.

The piston is equipped with a single piston ring. Piston ring rotation is prevented by a locating pin in the piston ring groove. Make certain ring end gap is correctly positioned around locating pin before installing piston in cylinder.

CYLINDER. Inspect cylinder and renew if scratched, scored or otherwise damaged. Cylinder is available in standard size only with a fitted piston.

CRANKSHAFT, CONNECTING ROD AND CRANKCASE. Crankshaft and connecting rod are a unit assembly. Crankshaft main bearings (9—Fig. HQ503) are supported in interlocking bearing carriers (7).

To remove crankshaft and connecting rod, first separate engine from trimmer drive shaft. Remove engine cover, fuel tank and recoil starter assembly. Remove spark plug and install a piston locking tool in spark plug hole to prevent crankshaft from turning. Remove clutch housing and clutch assembly. Remove nut retaining flywheel and remove flywheel from crankshaft. Remove cylinder mounting screws and separate cylinder (1) from crankcase (11) and piston. Remove piston pin retainers (5), piston pin (4) and piston (3) from connecting rod. Remove main bearing carrier mounting screws and withdraw crankshaft and connecting rod from crankcase. Withdraw bearing carriers (7), seals (8) and bearings (9) from crankshaft ends.

When assembling engine, install seals (8) so lip is toward bearing. Make sure mating surfaces of bearing carriers (7), lower crankcase (11) and cylinder (1) are clean and dry. Place a thin bead of a suitable form-in-place gasket compound onto sealing areas of lower crankcase (11) and cylinder (1). Tighten cylinder screws to 11 N·m (97 in.-lbs.). Make sure crankshaft rotates freely.

CLUTCH. The upper end of the drive shaft is threaded into the clutch drum

hub (2—Fig. HQ504). To service clutch, detach drive housing (1) from engine. Clutch shoes and hub (3) are available only as a unit assembly.

To service clutch drum, remove gear head from drive shaft housing. Detach drive shaft housing tube from drive housing. Hold drive shaft while unscrewing clutch drum. Housing and bearing are available only as a unit assembly.

REWIND STARTER. Refer to Fig. HQ505 for an exploded view of rewind starter. To disassemble starter, detach starter housing (9) from engine. Remove rope handle and allow rope to wind into starter. Unscrew center screw (5) and remove rope pulley (7). Wear appropriate safety eyewear and gloves before detaching rewind spring (8) from housing as spring may uncoil uncontrolled.

To assemble starter, lubricate center post of housing and spring side with light grease. Install rewind spring so coil windings are clockwise from outer end. Assemble starter while passing rope through housing rope outlet and attach rope handle to rope. To place tension on starter rope, pull rope out of housing. Engage rope in notch on pulley and turn pulley two turns clockwise to place tension on rewind spring. Hold pulley and disengage rope from pulley notch. Release pulley and allow rope to wind on pulley. Check starter operation. Rope handle should be held against housing by spring tension, but it must be possible to rotate pulley at least $\frac{1}{2}$ turn clockwise when rope is pulled out fully.

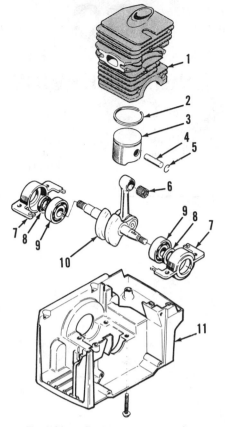

Fig. HQ503—Exploded view of engine.

1. Cylinder	7. Bearing carrier
2. Piston ring	8. Seal
3. Piston	9. Main bearings
4. Piston pin	10. Crankshaft &
5. Retaining ring	connecting rod assy.
6. Bearing	11. Crankcase

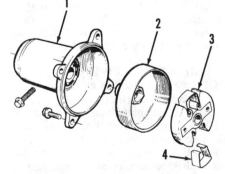

Fig. HQ504—Exploded view of clutch assembly.

1. Housing	3. Clutch assy.
2. Clutch drum	4. Spring

Fig. HQ505—Exploded view of rewind starter

1. Flywheel
2. Spring
3. Pawl
4. Pin
5. Screw
6. Washer
7. Pulley
8. Rewind spring
9. Starter housing
10. Rope handle

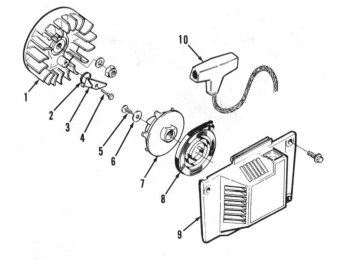

IDC

ENGINE SERVICE

Model	Bore	Stroke	Displacement
IDC	1.31 in.	1.25 in.	1.7 cu. in.
	(33.3 mm)	(31.8 mm)	(28.5 cc)
IDC	1.37 in.	1.25 in.	1.9 cu. in.
	(34.8 mm)	(31.8 mm)	(31.0 cc)

ENGINE INFORMATION

The IDC two-stroke, air-cooled gasoline engines are used by several manufacturers of string trimmers and brush cutters. The engine is equipped with a cantilever-type crankshaft that is supported in two ball bearings at the flywheel end.

MAINTENANCE

LUBRICATION. Engine lubrication is obtained by mixing gasoline with an oil designed for two-stroke, air-cooled engines. Refer to trimmer or blower service section for manufacturer's recommended fuel:oil mixture ratio.

SPARK PLUG. Recommended spark plug is a Champion DJ8J or equivalent. Specified electrode gap for all models is 0.025 inch (0.6 mm). Tighten spark plug to 150 in.-lbs. (17 N·m).

CARBURETOR. The engine may be equipped with a Walbro or Zama diaphragm-type carburetor. Refer to following section for service information.

Walbro WT And WTA. Refer to Fig. ID101 for an exploded view of carburetor. Initial adjustment of idle mixture screw (17) and high-speed mixture screw (19) is 1½ turns open. Final adjustment is performed with engine at normal operating temperature and cutter line at desired length. Be sure engine air filter is clean before adjusting carburetor.

Set idle speed screw so engine idles at 2800-3000 rpm. Adjust idle mixture screw so engine idles smoothly and accelerates cleanly without hesitation. Readjust idle speed screw, if necessary, so trimmer head does not rotate when engine is idling. Adjust high-speed mixture screw for best engine performance under load. Maximum speed should be 8000 rpm on Model 200 blower, 7500 rpm on Model 300 blower and 6800-7200 on trimmers. Do not adjust high-speed mixture screw too lean as engine may be damaged.

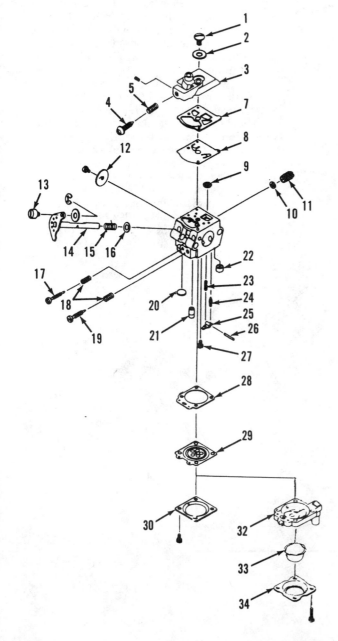

Fig. ID101—Exploded view of Walbro WT carburetor. Model WTA is similar. Some models are equipped with a governor valve (11) and some models are equipped with primer (33).

1. Screw
2. Washer
3. Cover
4. Idle speed screw
5. Spring
7. Gasket
8. Fuel pump diaphragm
9. Screen
10. "O" ring
11. Governor valve
12. Throttle plate
13. Swivel
14. Throttle shaft
15. Spring
16. Washer
17. Idle mixture screw
18. Spring
19. High-speed mixture screw
20. Welch plug
21. Nozzle
22. Check valve
23. Spring
24. Fuel inlet valve
25. Metering lever
26. Pin
27. Screw
28. Gasket
29. Metering diaphragm
30. Cover
32. Cover
33. Primer bulb
34. Bulb retainer

Carburetor disassembly and reassembly is evident after inspection of carburetor and referral to Fig. ID101. Clean and inspect all components. Inspect diaphragms for defects that may affect operation. Examine fuel inlet valve and seat. Inlet valve is renewable, but carburetor body must be renewed if seat is damaged or excessively worn. Discard carburetor body if mixture screw seats are damaged or excessively worn. Clean fuel screen.

Check metering lever height as shown in Fig. ID102 using Walbro tool 500-13. Metering lever should just touch leg on tool. Bend lever to obtain correct lever height.

Some carburetors are equipped with a governor valve (11—Fig. ID101) that enriches the mixture at high-speed to prevent overspeeding. The governor valve is not adjustable.

Some carburetors are equipped with primer bulb (33—Fig. ID101). Inspect primer bulb and reject if cracked, hardened or otherwise damaged.

Zama C1U. Refer to Fig. ID103 for an exploded view of the Zama C1U carburetor used on some engines. Initial adjustment of idle mixture screw (15) and high-speed mixture screw (17) is 1½ turns open. Set idle speed screw (28) so engine idles at 2800-3000 rpm. Be sure engine air filter is clean before adjusting carburetor.

Final adjustment is performed with engine at normal operating temperature. Before final adjustment on trimmer models, cutter line should be desired length. Adjust idle mixture screw so engine idles smoothly and accelerates cleanly without hesitation. Adjust idle speed screw so trimmer head does not rotate when engine is idling. Adjust high-speed mixture screw for best engine performance under load. Maximum speed should be 8000 rpm on Model 200 blower, 7500 rpm on Model 300 blower and 6800-7200 on trimmers.

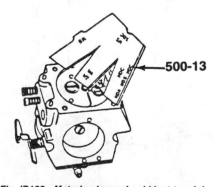

Fig. ID102—Metering lever should just touch leg of Walbro tool 500-13. Bend lever to obtain correct lever height.

Do not adjust high-speed mixture screw too lean as engine may be damaged.

Carburetor disassembly and reassembly is evident after inspection of carburetor and referral to Fig. ID103. Clean and inspect all components. Exercise care when removing Welch plug (12). To remove plug, pierce towards the end of the "tail" portion with a suitable punch, but do not insert punch deeply as underlying body metal may be damaged. Apply sealant to new plug. Inspect diaphragms for defects that may affect operation. Examine fuel inlet valve and seat. Inlet valve is renewable, but carburetor body must be renewed if seat is damaged or excessively worn. Discard carburetor body if mixture screw seats are damaged or excessively worn. Clean fuel screen.

To reassemble carburetor, reverse disassembly procedure. Clearance (C—Fig. ID104) between metering lever and a straightedge positioned across gasket surface of carburetor body should be 0-0.03 mm (0-0.012 in.). Bend metering lever as needed.

IGNITION SYSTEM. The engine is equipped with a solid-state ignition system. The ignition module/coil is mounted on the engine cylinder. Air gap between ignition coil legs and flywheel magnet should be 0.010-0.015 in. (0.25-0.38 mm). Tighten module retaining screws to 28 in.-lbs. (3 N·m).

REPAIRS

COMPRESSION PRESSURE. For optimum performance, cylinder compression pressure should be 90-120 psi (621-828 kPa). Compression pressure should be checked with engine at operating temperature and throttle and choke valves wide open.

TIGHTENING TORQUES. Recommended tightening torques are as follows:

Carburetor . . . . .40 in.-lbs. (4.5 N·m)
Clutch hub . . . . .150 in.-lbs. (17 N·m)
Crankcase cover . . . . .15 in.-lbs. (1.7 N·m)
Cylinder . . . . .120 in.-lbs. (13 N·m)
Flywheel . . . . .150 in.-lbs. (17 N·m)
Ignition module . . . . .28 in.-lbs. (3 N·m)
Spark plug . . . . .150 in.-lbs. (17 N·m)
Starter housing . . . . .40 in-lbs. (4 N·m)

PISTON, RINGS AND CONNECTING ROD. Piston, piston ring, bearings and

connecting rod are serviced only as an assembly. Assembly is offered in standard size only. The stamped steel connecting rod (34—Figs. ID105 or ID106) has a caged roller bearing at both ends. The piston (35) is equipped with a single piston ring. To remove piston and connecting rod, refer to CRANKSHAFT section for removal procedure.

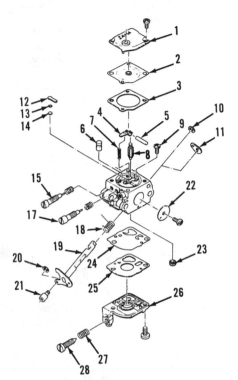

Fig. ID103—Exploded view of Zama C1U carburetor.

1. Cover
2. Metering diaphragm
3. Gasket
4. Metering lever
5. Pin
6. Nozzle
7. Spring
8. Fuel inlet valve
9. Screw
10. "E" ring
11. Arm
12. Welch plug
13. Retainer
14. Screen
15. Idle mixture screw
17. High-speed mixture screw
18. Spring
19. Throttle shaft
20. "E" ring
21. Swivel
22. Throttle plate
23. Fuel inlet screen
24. Fuel pump diaphragm
25. Gasket
26. Cover
27. Spring
28. Idle speed screw

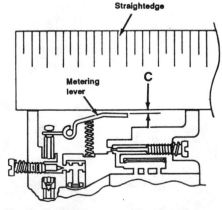

Fig. ID104—Metering lever should be bent so clearance (C) is 0-0.3 mm (0.0-0.012 in.).

Maximum piston ring side clearance in piston ring groove is 0.005-in. (0.13 mm). Piston ring end gap is 0.085-in. (2.16 mm). Note notched portion of piston that must be towards crankshaft counterweight. See Fig. ID107. Install piston ring so end gap is opposite exhaust port.

CYLINDER. The cylinder is available in standard size only. Renew cylinder if damaged or excessively worn. Tighten cylinder retaining screws to 120 in.-lbs. (13 N·m).

CRANKSHAFT AND CRANKCASE. The crankshaft (9—Figs. ID105 or ID106) is supported at flywheel end only by two ball bearings (13 and 17). Connecting rod is a slip fit on stub crankpin journal. Crankpin journal must be smooth, round and free from scores or damage.

To remove crankshaft, first remove engine cover, fuel tank, clutch housing (models so equipped) and recoil starter assembly. Remove clutch assembly from flywheel. On blower models, separate engine from blower housing. On all models, remove spark plug and install locking bolt or insert end of a rope in spark plug hole to lock piston and crankshaft. Remove flywheel retaining nut and remove flywheel (18) and key (33) from crankshaft. Remove ignition module. Remove air cleaner, carburetor (4) and muffler (40). Remove cylinder mounting screws and pull cylinder (39) off piston. Unbolt and remove crankcase cover (6). Slide connecting rod off crankpin and remove piston and connecting rod assembly. Unbolt and remove cover (20). Carefully press crankshaft out of bearings in crankcase (11). Drive bearings (13 and 17) from crankcase housing. Remove snap rings (14 and 16) and drive seal (15) out of crankcase housing.

To reinstall crankshaft, install seal (15) in bearing bore of crankcase 0.875-in. (22.23 mm) from flywheel side of crankcase. Press against flat surface of seal so cupped side of seal enters crankcase first. Install snap rings (14 and 16). One main bearing (17) has a single shielded side that must be out toward flywheel side of engine after installation. Press bearings (13 and 17) in until seated

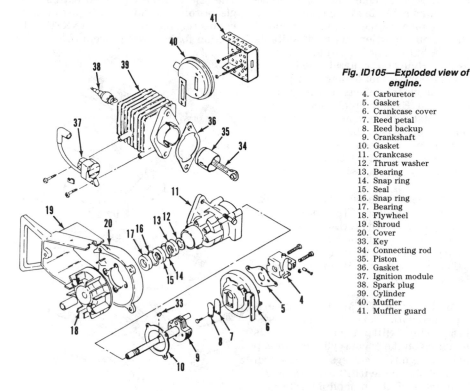

Fig. ID105—Exploded view of engine.

4. Carburetor
5. Gasket
6. Crankcase cover
7. Reed petal
8. Reed backup
9. Crankshaft
10. Gasket
11. Crankcase
12. Thrust washer
13. Bearing
14. Snap ring
15. Seal
16. Snap ring
17. Bearing
18. Flywheel
19. Shroud
20. Cover
33. Key
34. Connecting rod
35. Piston
36. Gasket
37. Ignition module
38. Spark plug
39. Cylinder
40. Muffler
41. Muffler guard

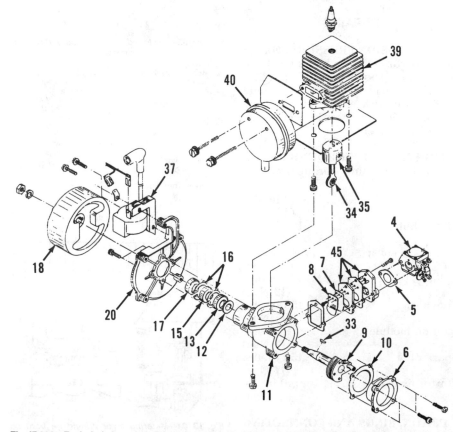

Fig. ID106—Exploded view of engine. Refer to Fig. ID105 for legend except for reed block assembly (45).

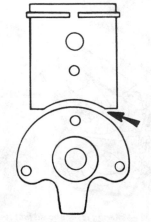

Fig. ID107—The piston skirt is notched on one side to clear crankshaft counterweight.

against snap rings. Install thrust washer (12) on crankshaft main bearing journal and press crankshaft into main bearings. Rotate crankshaft until crankpin is at cylinder side and install connecting rod and piston assembly with notched portion of piston skirt toward crankshaft counterweight (Fig. ID107). Install crankcase cover and tighten screws in a crossing pattern to 15 in.-lbs. (1.7 N·m). Reassemble remainder of engine.

REED VALVE. On all models except Model 200 and 210 blowers, a reed valve assembly is attached to the crankcase cover (6—Fig. ID105). On Model 200 and 210 blowers, the reed valve assembly is attached to the side of the crankcase as shown in Fig. ID106. Install reed petal and backup plate as shown in Fig. ID108.

CLUTCH. Some engines are equipped with a clutch. Note that clutch drum (30—Fig. ID109) is retained by a screw (29S) that is located in square drive hole of clutch drum shaft. Screw is coated with thread locking compound and may be difficult to unscrew. When assembling clutch, tighten hub (28) to 150 in.-lbs. (17 N·m).

REWIND STARTER. Refer to Figs. ID110 or ID111 for an exploded view of rewind starter. To disassemble starter, detach starter housing from engine. Remove rope handle and allow rope to wind into starter. Unscrew pulley retaining screw (8—Fig. ID110) or retainer (25—Fig. ID112) and remove rope pulley. Wear appropriate safety eyewear and gloves before detaching rewind

spring from housing as spring may uncoil uncontrolled.

To assemble starter, lubricate center post of housing and spring side with light grease. Install rewind spring so coil windings are clockwise from outer end. Assemble starter while passing rope through housing rope outlet and attach rope handle to rope. To place tension on starter rope, pull rope out of housing. Engage rope in notch on pulley and turn pulley one turn clockwise. Hold pulley and disengage rope from pulley notch. Release pulley and allow rope to wind on pulley. Check starter operation. Rope handle should be held against housing by spring tension, but it must be possible to rotate pulley at least $1/4$ turn clockwise when rope is pulled out fully.

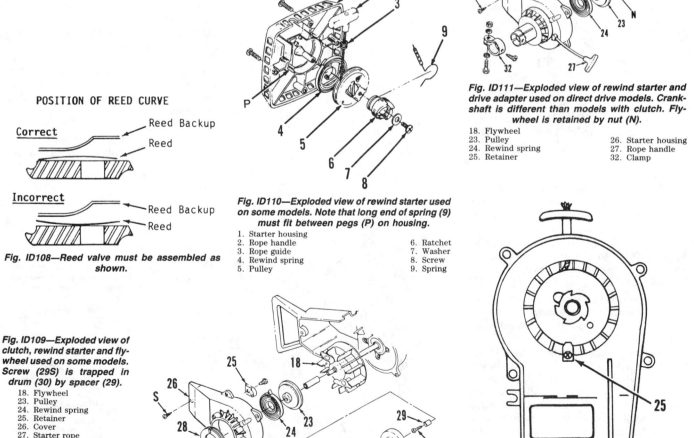

POSITION OF REED CURVE

Correct — Reed Backup / Reed

Incorrect — Reed Backup / Reed

Fig. ID108—Reed valve must be assembled as shown.

Fig. ID110—Exploded view of rewind starter used on some models. Note that long end of spring (9) must fit between pegs (P) on housing.

1. Starter housing
2. Rope handle
3. Rope guide
4. Rewind spring
5. Pulley
6. Ratchet
7. Washer
8. Screw
9. Spring

Fig. ID111—Exploded view of rewind starter and drive adapter used on direct drive models. Crankshaft is different than models with clutch. Flywheel is retained by nut (N).

18. Flywheel
23. Pulley
24. Rewind spring
25. Retainer
26. Starter housing
27. Rope handle
32. Clamp

Fig. ID109—Exploded view of clutch, rewind starter and flywheel used on some models. Screw (29S) is trapped in drum (30) by spacer (29).

18. Flywheel
23. Pulley
24. Rewind spring
25. Retainer
26. Cover
27. Starter rope
28. Clutch hub assy.
29. Spacer
30. Clutch drum
31. Clutch housing
32. Clamp

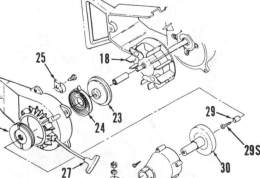

Fig. ID112—View showing location of rewind starter pulley retainer (25) used on some models.

KAWASAKI

ENGINE SERVICE

Model	Bore	Stroke	Displacement
KE18	28.9 mm (1.14 in.)	27.9 mm (1.10 in.)	18.4 cc (1.12 cu. in.)
KE24	32.0 mm (1.26 in.)	30.0 mm (1.18 in.)	24.1 cc (1.47 cu. in.)
TD18	28.9 mm (1.14 in.)	27.9 mm (1.10 in.)	18.4 cc (1.12 cu. in.)
TD24	32.0 mm (1.26 in.)	30.0 mm (1.18 in.)	24.1 cc (1.47 cu. in.)
TD33	36.8 mm (1.45 in.)	30.9 mm (1.22 in.)	33.3 cc (2.03 cu. in.)
TD40	40.0 mm (1.57 in.)	32.0 mm (1.26 in.)	40.2 cc (2.45 cu. in.)

ENGINE INFORMATION

Kawasaki two-stroke air-cooled gasoline engines are used by several manufacturers of string trimmers and brush cutters.

MAINTENANCE

SPARK PLUG. Recommended spark plug for all models except Model TD40 is a NGK BM6A. Recommended spark plug for Model TD40 is a NGK B7S. Specified electrode gap is 0.6 mm (0.025 in.) for all models.

CARBURETOR. Engines may be equipped with a DPK series diaphragm type carburetor (Fig. KA10), a Walbro WA diaphragm type carburetor (Fig. KA13) or a float type carburetor (Fig. KA15). Refer to the appropriate paragraphs for model being serviced.

DPK Series Carburetor. Initial setting of the main fuel mixture needle is 1½ turns out from a lightly seated position.

Make final adjustments with trimmer line at proper length or blade assembly installed. Engine should be at operating temperature and running. Operate engine at wide open throttle and turn main fuel mixture needle until engine begins to run smoothly as needle is turned IN, then back needle out 1/8 turn. Normal range of adjustment is 1-2 turns out from a lightly seated position.

Adjust idle speed screw so engine idles just below clutch engagement speed.

Midrange mixture is determined by the position of clip (7—Fig. KA10) on jet needle (8). There are three grooves located at the upper end of the jet needle (Fig. KA11) and normal position of clip (7—Fig. KA10) is in the middle groove. The mixture will be leaner if clip is installed in the top groove or richer if clip is installed in the bottom groove.

DPK carburetor is equipped with an integral fuel pump (16, 17 and 18). During servicing inspect fuel pump and metering diaphragms for pin holes, tears or other damage. Diaphragms should be flexible. Metal button must be tight on metering diaphragm. When assembling the carburetor note that the

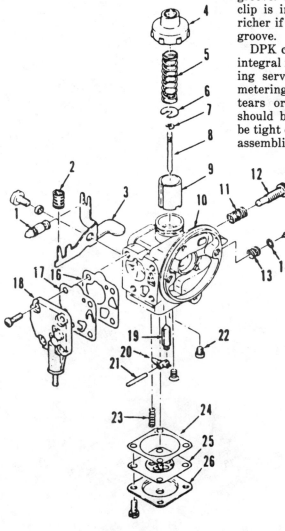

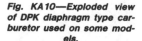

Fig. KA10—Exploded view of DPK diaphragm type carburetor used on some models.

1. Tickler valve
2. Spring
3. Lever
4. Cap
5. Spring
6. Retainer
7. Clip
8. Jet needle
9. Throttle slide
10. Body
11. Spring
12. Idle speed screw
13. Spring
14. "O" ring
15. Main fuel mixture needle
16. Pump gasket
17. Pump diaphragm
18. Pump cover
19. Inlet needle valve
20. Metering lever
21. Pin
22. Jet
23. Spring
24. Gasket
25. Diaphragm
26. Cover

metering diaphragm lever should be 2.1-2.4 mm (0.08-0.09 in.) below the carburetor body (Fig. KA12).

Walbro WA Series Carburetor. Initial setting of the Walbro WA series carburetor is one turn out from a lightly seated position for both mixture needles.

Make final adjustments with engine at operating temperature and running. Operate trimmer engine at full throttle and turn high speed mixture needle (16—Fig. KA13) until engine begins to run smoothly as needle is turned IN, then back needle out 1/8 turn. Allow engine to idle and adjust idle mixture needle (14) until engine idles smoothly and will accelerate without hesitation. Adjust idle speed screw (1) so engine idles just below clutch engagement speed.

During servicing inspect fuel pump and metering diaphragms for pin holes, tears or other damage. Diaphragms should be flexible. Metal button must be tight on metering diaphragm. When assembling the carburetor, the metering diaphragm lever should be flush with floor of cavity as shown in Fig. KA14. If necessary, adjust by carefully bending diaphragm lever.

Float Type Carburetor. Adjustment of the float type carburetor is lim-ited to float level adjustment and adjustment of the "E" clip to vary fuel needle adjustment.

To adjust float level, remove float bowl assembly (25—Fig. KA15). Invert carburetor throttle body and measure float level as shown in Fig. KA16. Dimension "D" should be 2.5 mm (0.09 in.). Carefully bend float lever to obtain correct float level.

Install "E" clip on fuel needle at the position marked (C) in Fig. KA17. Installation of "E" clip at positions (A or B) on fuel needle results in a leaner

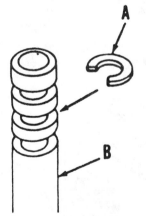

Fig. KA11—View of needle and clip used on DPK series diaphragm carburetor. Install clip (A) in middle groove for normal operation.

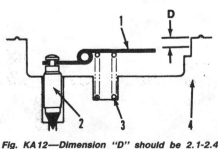

Fig. KA12—Dimension "D" should be 2.1-2.4 mm (0.08-0.09 in.).
1. Fuel lever   3. Spring
2. Fuel needle   4. Carburetor body

Fig. KA13—Exploded view of Walbro diaphragm type carburetor used on some models.

1. Idle speed screw	
2. Spring	18. Body
3. Screw	19. Clip
4. Pump cover	20. Screw
5. Gasket	21. Fuel inlet needle
6. Pump diaphragm	22. Spring
7. Screw	23. Pin
8. Throttle plate	24. Fuel lever
9. "E" clip	25. Screw
10. Cable clamp	26. Gasket
11. Throttle shaft	27. Gasket
12. Spring	28. Circuit plate
13. Spring	29. Screw
14. Low speed needle	30. Gasket
15. Spring	31. Main diaphragm
16. High speed needle	32. Cover
17. Screen	33. Screw

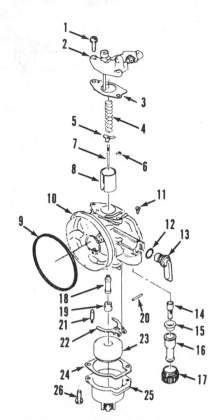

Fig. KA15—Exploded view of float type carburetor used on some models.

1. Screw	14. Strainer
2. Cover	15. Gasket
3. Gasket	16. Fitting
4. Spring	17. Nut
5. Spring seat	18. Jet
6. Clip	19. Jet
7. Fuel needle	20. Pin
8. Slide	21. Fuel inlet needle
9. Gasket	22. Float hinge
10. Body	23. Float
11. Screw	24. Gasket
12. "O" ring	25. Fuel bowl
13. Shut-off	26. Screw

Fig. KA14—Metering valve lever should be flush with carburetor body.

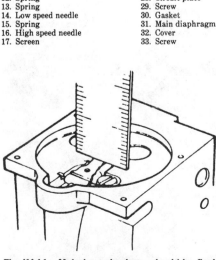

Fig. KA16—Dimension "D" should be 2.5 mm (0.09 in.) for correct float level setting.

fuel:air mixture and installation of "E" clip at the positions marked (D or E) results in a richer fuel:air mixture.

IGNITION SYSTEM. Models TD18, TD24 and TD33 may be equipped with a breaker point type ignition or a transistorized ignition system. Model TD40 is equipped with a transistorized ignition system. Refer to appropriate paragraphs for model being serviced.

Breaker Point Type Ignition. Breaker point set and condenser are attached to crankcase behind the recoil starter pulley. To adjust the point gap, remove recoil starter assembly. Rotate flywheel so that points are at maximum opening. Point gap should be 0.3-0.4 mm (0.012-0.016 in.). Loosen set screw retaining breaker point plate and use a screwdriver in supporting groove to rotate plate slightly to adjust point gap (Fig. KA18).

To adjust ignition timing, rotate flywheel until "F" mark (line stamped on blades) is aligned with the crankcase mark (Fig. KA19). Ignition points should be just beginning to open with flywheel at this position. Shift breaker point plate as required to adjust timing.

Transistorized Ignition System. Transistorized ignition system is operating satisfactorily if spark will jump across the 3 mm (1/8 in.) gap of a test spark plug. If no spark is produced, check on/off switch and wiring.

The coil may be tested with an ohmmeter as follows: Set ohmmeter to the R x 1 scale and connect the red ohmmeter lead to the primary lead wire (Fig. KA20). Connect the black ohmmeter lead wire to the coil core. Specified resistance of the primary winding is 0.5 ohms for 18.4 cc (1.12 cu. in.) engines, 0.6-0.7 ohms for 24.1 and 33.3 cc (1.47 and 2.03 cu. in.) engines and 0.9 ohms for 40.2 cc (2.45 cu. in.) engines. Connect the red ohmmeter lead to the spark plug wire and connect the black ohmmeter lead to the coil core (Fig. KA21). Specified resistance of the secondary coil windings is 9.7 ohms for 18.4 cc (1.12 cu. in.) engines, 7-8 ohms for 24.1 and 33.3 cc (1.47 and 2.03 cu. in.) engines and 11.5 ohms for 40.2 cc (2.45 cu. in.) engines. Renew coil if any faults are noted.

The igniter may be tested with an ohmmeter as follows: Set ohmmeter to the R x 10K scale and connect the black ohmmeter lead to the igniter case and connect the red ohmmeter lead to the igniter lead tab (Fig. KA22). Ohmmeter needle should deflect from infinity to slightly more than zero ohms. Reverse the ohmmeter leads and the ohmmeter needle should again deflect from infinity to slightly more than zero ohms. The ohmmeter needle should not return all the way back to zero ohms after deflecting to infinity. Renew igniter if any faults are noted.

LUBRICATION. All models are lubricated by mixing a good quality two-stroke air-cooled engine oil with gasoline. Refer to TRIMMER SERVICE section for correct fuel/oil mixture ratio recommended by trimmer manufacturer.

CARBON. Manufacturer recommends disassembling engine at 100 hour intervals of use and cleaning carbon from exhaust port, cylinder and from top of piston.

REPAIRS

COMPRESSION PRESSURE. For optimum performance, compression pressure should be as follows with engine at operating temperature and throttle and choke wide open. Crank engine until maximum pressure is observed.

18.4 cc (1.12 cu. in.) engine:
Low . . . . 793 kPa
(115 psi)
High . . . . 1000 kPa
(145 psi)

24.1 cc (1.47 cu. in.) engine:
Low . . . . 965 kPa
(140 psi)
High . . . . 1172 kPa
(170 psi)

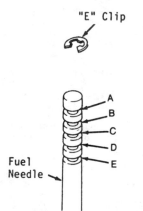

Fig. KA17—Refer to text for correct placement of fuel clip for model being serviced.

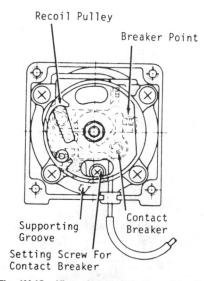

Fig. KA18—View showing location of ignition components. Refer to text.

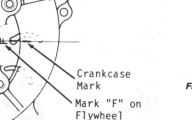

Fig. KA19—Align "F" timing mark on flywheel with timing mark on crankcase. Refer to text.

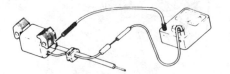

Fig. KA20—To test coil primary side, refer to text for proper test sequence.

Fig. KA21—To test coil secondary side, refer to text for proper test sequence.

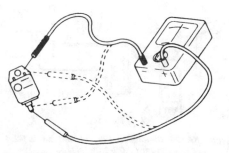

Fig. KA22—Refer to text for correct connection sequence for igniter tests using an ohmmeter.

33.3 cc (2.03 cu. in.) engine:
Low . . . . 1103 kPa
(160 psi)
High . . . . 1310 kPa
(190 psi)

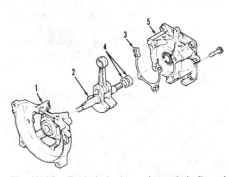

Fig. KA23—Exploded view of crankshaft and connecting rod assembly used on Models KE18, TD18, KE24, TD24 and TD33.

1. Crankcase half
2. Crankshaft & connecting rod assy.
3. Gasket
4. Shims
5. Crankcase half

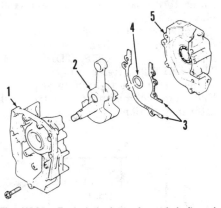

Fig. KA24—Exploded view of crankshaft and connecting rod assembly used on Model TD40.

1. Crankcase half
2. Crankshaft & connecting rod assy.
3. Gaskets
4. Shim
5. Crankcase half

40.2 cc (2.47 cu. in.) engine:
Low . . . . Not Available

High . . . . Not Available

A compression reading of 620 kPa (90 psi) or lower for any model indicates a need for repairs.

TIGHTENING TORQUES. Recommended tightening torque specifications are as follows:

Clutch pin to flywheel:
KE18, TD18,
KE24 & TD24 . . . . . . 8-10 N·m
(69-85 in.-lbs.)
TD33, TD40 . . . . . . 13-14 N·m
(120-137 in.-lbs.)

Crankcase:
KE18, TD18, KE24,
TD24 & TD33 . . . . . . .3-4 N·m
(30-34 in.-lbs.)
TD40 . . . . .5-7 N·m
(52-61 in.-lbs.)

Cylinder to crankcase:
KE18, TD18, KE24,
TD24 & TD33 . . . . . . .3-4 N·m
(30-34 in.-lbs.)
TD40 . . . . .7-9 N·m
(61-78 in.-lbs.)

Flywheel:
KE18, TD18,
KE24 & TD24 . . . . . . 8-10 N·m
(69-85 in.-lbs.)

TD33 & TD40 . . . . . 30-34 N·m
(260-304 in.-lbs.)

Spark plug:
All models . . . . 12-16 N·m
(103-146 in.-lbs.)

CRANKSHAFT AND CONNECTING ROD. Refer to Fig. KA23 for an exploded view of crankshaft and connecting rod assembly used on 18.4, 24.1 and 33.3 cc (1.12, 1.47 and 2.03 cu. in.) engines or to Fig. KA24 for 40.2 cc (2.45 cu. in.) engine. On all models, crankshaft is pressed together at connecting rod journal, therefore crankshaft and connecting rod must be renewed as an assembly. Crankshaft is supported by ball bearings at both ends. For exploded views of engine assemblies refer to Fig. KA25 for Models KE18 and TD18, to Fig. KA26 for Models KE24, TD24 and TD33 and to Fig. KA27 for Model TD40.

To remove crankshaft assembly refer to appropriate exploded view and remove engine cooling shroud and recoil starter assembly. On Models KE18, TD18 and TC40, unscrew starter pulley retaining nut and pry starter pulley off of crankshaft. On Models KE24, TD24 and TD33, the starter pulley is threaded onto crankshaft and is removed by unscrewing. On all models, remove flywheel, carburetor, muffler and cylinder. Split crankcase and remove crankshaft. Remove piston.

Fig. KA25 — Exploded view of TD18 engine. KE18 engine is similar.

1. Clutch shoe	18. Ring
2. Clutch bolt	19. Gasket
3. Spring	20. Cylinder
4. Clutch shoe	21. Spark plug
5. Ignition switch	22. Shim
6. Shroud	23. Shim
7. Nut	24. Bearing
8. Ignition coil	25. Seal
9. Flywheel	26. Gasket
10. Crankcase half	27. Crankcase half
11. Seal	28. Point & condenser (as equipped)
12. Bearing	29. Felt
13. Key	30. Pulley
14. Crankshaft & connecting rod assy.	31. Washer
15. Retainer	32. Nut
16. Piston pin	33. Gasket
17. Piston	34. Starter housing

Inspect crankshaft assembly for damage or excessive wear. Inspect main bearings and roller bearing (as equipped) in small end of connecting rod. Renew parts as required.

To reassemble, crankshaft end play must be correctly set. Shims are available for Models KE18, TD18, KE24, TD24 and TD33 in the sizes listed in chart in Fig. KA28. Shims are avail-able for Model TD40 in the sizes listed in chart in Fig. KA29. Note that all shim sizes are measured in millimeters only. All measurements and dimensions must be in millimeters to correctly set crankshaft end play.

On Models KE18, TD18, KE24, TD24 and TD33, correct crankshaft end play is 0.05-0.268 mm (0.002-0.011 in.). Refer to Fig. KA30 and measure dimensions "A", "B" and "C" as illustrated. Make certain gasket is installed on one surface only when measurements are taken. Add dimension "A" to dimension "B". Subtract dimension "C" from the total of "A" plus "B". This will result in dimension "D". Refer to the chart in Fig. KA28 for the correct shim or combination of shims to correctly set crankshaft end play.

On Model TD40 correct crankshaft end play is 0.045-0.305 mm (0.002-0.012 in.). Refer to Fig. KA31 and measure dimensions "A", "B" and "C" as illustrated. Make certain gasket is installed on one surface only when measurements are made. Add dimension "A" to dimension "B". Subtract dimension "C" from the total of "A" plus "B". This will result in dimension "D". Refer to the chart in Fig. KA29 for the correct shim or combination of shims to correctly set crankshaft end play.

Crankcase bolts should be tightened to specified torque in a criss-cross pattern for Models KE18, TD18, KE24, TD24 and TD33. Refer to Fig. KA32 for Model TD40 bolt tightening sequence. Ends of gasket may have to be trimmed after installation.

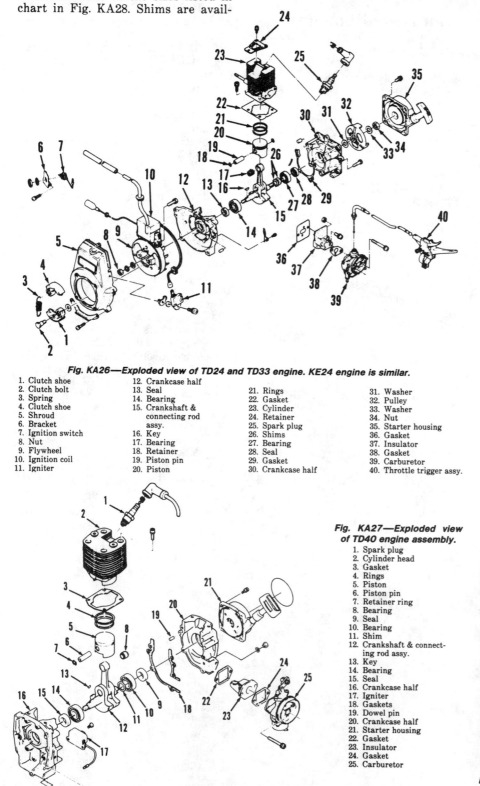

Fig. KA26—Exploded view of TD24 and TD33 engine. KE24 engine is similar.

1. Clutch shoe
2. Clutch bolt
3. Spring
4. Clutch shoe
5. Shroud
6. Bracket
7. Ignition switch
8. Nut
9. Flywheel
10. Ignition coil
11. Igniter
12. Crankcase half
13. Seal
14. Bearing
15. Crankshaft & connecting rod assy.
16. Key
17. Bearing
18. Retainer
19. Piston pin
20. Piston
21. Rings
22. Gasket
23. Cylinder
24. Retainer
25. Spark plug
26. Shims
27. Bearing
28. Seal
29. Gasket
30. Crankcase half
31. Washer
32. Pulley
33. Washer
34. Nut
35. Starter housing
36. Gasket
37. Insulator
38. Gasket
39. Carburetor
40. Throttle trigger assy.

Fig. KA27—Exploded view of TD40 engine assembly.

1. Spark plug
2. Cylinder head
3. Gasket
4. Rings
5. Piston
6. Piston pin
7. Retainer ring
8. Bearing
9. Seal
10. Bearing
11. Shim
12. Crankshaft & connect-ing rod assy.
13. Key
14. Bearing
15. Seal
16. Crankcase half
17. Igniter
18. Gaskets
19. Dowel pin
20. Crankcase half
21. Starter housing
22. Gasket
23. Insulator
24. Gasket
25. Carburetor

Shim No.	Shim Thickness (mm)
①	0.1
②	0.2
③	0.4
④	0.6

Clearance (D)	Shim No.
-0.11 ~ under +0.03	None
+0.03 ~ under +0.13	①
+0.13 ~ under +0.23	②
+0.23 ~ under +0.33	② + ①
+0.33 ~ under +0.43	③
+0.43 ~ under +0.53	③ + ①
+0.53 ~ under +0.63	④

Fig. KA28—Refer to text for procedure to determine correct shim thickness and number. Note all dimensions are in millimeters.

Shim No.	Shim Thickness (mm)
①	0.1
②	0.2
③	0.4
④	0.6

TA 40	TA 51
Clearance (D)	**Thickness Of Shim**
-0.10 ~ -0.09	None
-0.08 ~ 0.01	①
0.02 ~ 0.13	②
0.14 ~ 0.22	① + ②
0.23 ~ 0.34	③
0.35 ~ 0.43	① + ②
0.44 ~ 0.54	④
0.55 ~ 0.64	① + ④
0.65 ~ 0.76	② + ④
0.77 ~ 0.84	① + ② + ⑥

Fig. KA29—Refer to text for procedure to determine correct shim thickness and number. Note all dimensions are in millimeters.

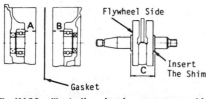

Fig. KA30—Illustration showing measurement locations to determine correct thickness and number of shims required on Models KE18, TD18, KE24, TD24 and TD33. Refer to text.

PISTON, PIN AND RINGS. Piston for Models KE18 and TD18 is equipped with one piston ring. Piston for Models KE24, TD24, TD33 and TD40 is equipped with two piston rings. On all models, piston is equipped with a locating pin (Fig. KA33) in piston ring groove (grooves) to prevent ring rotation. A needle bearing is installed in connecting rod pin bearing bore of all models except Models KE18 and TD 18. On Models KE18 and TD18, piston pin rides directly in connecting rod bore.

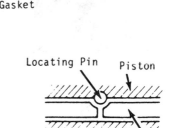

Fig. KA31—Illustration showing measurement locations to determine correct thickness and number of shims required on Model TD40. Refer to text.

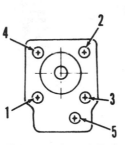

Fig. KA32—Tighten crankcase bolts in sequence shown to specified torque.

To remove piston from all models, remove cooling shroud and recoil starter assembly. Remove carburetor and muffler. Remove all bolts retaining cylinder to crankcase and carefully work cylinder off of crankcase and piston. Remove retaining rings (3 and 6—Fig. KA34) and press pin (5) out of piston pin bore. Piston (4) may now be removed. Remove bearing (7) (as equipped) from connecting rod piston pin bearing bore.

When installing piston on connecting rod, arrow on piston top must point toward flywheel side of engine and piston pin must move smoothly in piston pin bearing installed in connecting rod.

Correct piston ring end gap is 0.7 mm (0.03 in.). Correct ring groove clearance for top ring is 0.17 mm (0.007 in.). Correct ring groove clearance for second ring of models so equipped is 0.15 mm (0.006 in.).

Correct piston to cylinder clearance is 0.15 mm (0.006 in.) for all models.

CYLINDER. Cylinder may be unbolted and removed from crankcase after shroud, muffler, carburetor and starter housing are removed.

Renew cylinder if bore is scored, cracked or if piston to cylinder clearance with new piston installed exceeds 0.15 mm (0.006 in.).

CLUTCH. Refer to Fig. KA35 for an exploded view of clutch shoe installation. Tighten clutch pin bolts (1) to specified torque. If clutch engages at low idle speeds, clutch spring (2) may be stretched or damaged. Clutch shoes, spring and drum should be inspected for excessive wear or damage any time clutch drum is removed. Renew parts as required.

Locating Pin   Piston
Ring

Fig. KA33—Piston ring or rings on all models are held in position by locating pin.

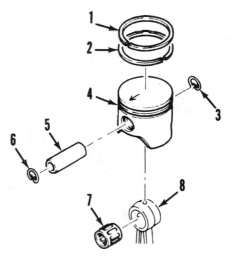

Fig. KA34—Exploded view of typical piston assembly. Note Models KE18 and TD18 are equipped with one ring only and connecting rod is not equipped with needle bearing (7).

1. Top ring
2. Second ring
3. Retainer
4. Piston
5. Piston pin
6. Retainer
7. Needle bearing
8. Connecting rod

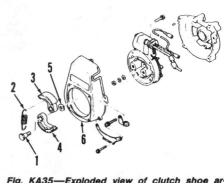

Fig. KA35—Exploded view of clutch shoe arrangement typical of most models.

1. Clutch pin (bolt)
2. Clutch spring
3. Clutch shoe
4. Clutch shoe
5. Washer
6. Shroud

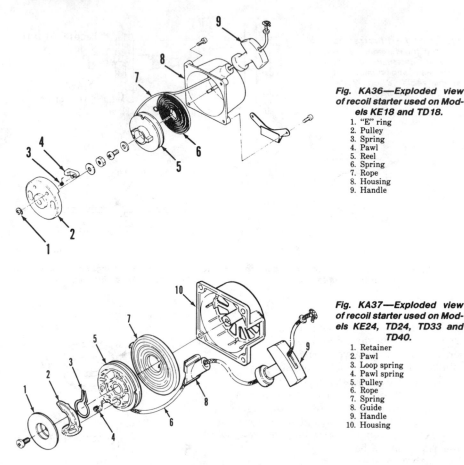

Fig. KA36—Exploded view of recoil starter used on Models KE18 and TD18.

1. "E" ring
2. Pulley
3. Spring
4. Pawl
5. Reel
6. Spring
7. Rope
8. Housing
9. Handle

Fig. KA38—Loop spring must be installed as shown.

Fig. KA37—Exploded view of recoil starter used on Models KE24, TD24, TD33 and TD40.

1. Retainer
2. Pawl
3. Loop spring
4. Pawl spring
5. Pulley
6. Rope
7. Spring
8. Guide
9. Handle
10. Housing

RECOIL STARTER. All models are equipped with a recoil type starter. Refer to appropriate paragraph for model being serviced.

Models KE18 And TD18. Refer to Fig. KA36 for an exploded view of starter assembly. To disassemble starter, remove starter assembly from engine. Pull rope 6 inches (15.2 cm) out of housing (8). Align notch in pulley (5) with rope hole in housing. While holding pulley and rope hole in alignment, pull slack rope back through rope hole in side housing. Hold rope in notch while slowly allowing pulley to unwind relieving spring (6) tension.

Remove the center screw and washer, then slowly lift pulley off center post of housing. Do not dislodge rewind spring. Use care if spring must be removed. Do not allow spring to uncoil uncontrolled.

Inspect rope and spring. Lubricate center post of housing with light grease prior to reassembly. Reassembly is reverse of disassembly procedure. Wind all but 6 inches (15.2 cm) of rope onto pulley before installing pulley in starter housing. Wrap rope around pulley in a clockwise direction as viewed from pawl side of pulley. Press down on pulley while turning to engage pulley with spring hook. Install retaining screw and washer. Recommended preload is three turns clockwise. Check rewind spring for bottoming after assembly by pulling rope all the way out of starter. Pulley

should still be able to rotate clockwise. If pulley will not rotate any further with rope pulled out, release one turn of preload.

Models KE24, TD24, TD33 And TD40. Refer to Fig. KA37 for an exploded view of starter assembly. To disassemble starter, first remove starter assembly from engine. Slide rope guide (8) out of starter housing (10) and slip rope (6) into slot on pulley. Hold rope in notch while slowly allowing pulley to unwind relieving spring (7) tension.

Remove the center screw, retainer (1), pawl (2) and springs (3 and 4). Slowly lift pulley off starter housing post while using a small screwdriver to release pulley from spring hook. Use care if spring must be removed. Do not allow spring to uncoil uncontrolled.

Inspect rope, pawl and springs for breakage or excessive wear and renew as needed. Lubricate center post of housing with light grease prior to reassembly. Reassembly is reverse of disassembly procedure. Install spring in a counterclockwise direction from outer end. Wind all but 6 inches (15.2 cm) of rope onto pulley before installing pulley in starter housing. Wrap rope around pulley in a counterclockwise direction as viewed from pawl side of pulley. Press down on pulley while turning to engage pulley with spring hook. Reinstall retaining screw, retainer, pawl, pawl spring and loop spring. Make sure loop spring is installed properly as shown in Fig. KA38. Preload the rewind spring three turns. Recheck to be sure pulley rewinds completely when released.

KIORITZ
ENGINE SERVICE

Model	Bore	Stroke	Displacement
Kioritz	26.0 mm (1.02 in.)	26.0 mm (1.02 in.)	13.8 cc (0.84 cu. in.)
Kioritz	28.0 mm (1.10 in.)	26.0 mm (1.02 in.)	16.0 cc (0.98 cu. in.)
Kioritz	32.2 mm (1.27 in.)	26.0 mm (1.02 in.)	21.2 cc (1.29 cu. in.)
Kioritz	28.0 mm (1.10 in.)	37.0 mm (1.46 in.)	30.1 cc (1.84 cu. in.)
Kioritz	40.0 mm (1.56 in.)	32.0 mm (1.26 in.)	40.2 cc (2.45 cu. in.)

ENGINE INFORMATION

Kioritz two-stroke air-cooled gasoline engines are used by several manufacturers of string trimmers and brush cutters.

MAINTENANCE

SPARK PLUG. Recommended spark plug is a Champion CJ8, or equivalent. Specified electrode gap for all models is 0.6-0.7 mm (0.024-0.28 in.).

CARBURETOR. Kioritz engines may be equipped with a Walbro diaphragm type carburetor with a built in fuel pump (Fig. KZ50) or a Zama diaphragm type carburetor (Fig. KZ52). Refer to appropriate paragraph for model being serviced.

Walbro Diaphragm Type Carburetor. Initial adjustment of fuel mixture needles from a lightly seated position is $1\frac{1}{8}$ turn open for low speed mixture needle (18—Fig. KZ50) and $1\frac{1}{4}$ turn open for high speed mixture needle (17).

Final adjustments are made with trimmer line at recommended length. Engine should be at operating temperature and running. Turn idle speed screw (31) to obtain 2500-3000 rpm, or just below clutch engagement speed. Adjust low speed mixture needle (18) to obtain consistent idling and smooth acceleration. Readjust idle speed screw (31) as required. Open throttle fully and adjust high speed mixture needle (17) to obtain highest engine rpm, then turn high speed mixture needle counterclockwise 1/8 turn.

To disassemble carburetor, remove the four screws retaining cover (1) to carburetor body. Remove cover (1), diaphragm (2) and gasket (3). Remove screw (4), pin (5), fuel inlet lever (6), spring (8) and fuel inlet needle (7). Remove screw (9) and remove circuit plate (10), check valve (11) and gasket (12). Remove screw (29), cover (28), gasket (27) and diaphragm (26). Remove inlet screen (24). Remove high and low speed mixture needles and springs. Remove throttle plate (13) and shaft (20) as required.

Carefully inspect all parts. Diaphragms should be flexible and free of cracks or tears. When reassembling, fuel inlet lever (6) should be flush with carburetor body (Fig. KZ51). Carefully bend fuel inlet lever to obtain correct setting.

Zama Diaphragm Type Carburetor. Initial adjustment of low speed (16—Fig. KZ52) and high speed (17) mixture needles is one turn open from a lightly seated position.

Final adjustments are made with trimmer line at recommended length. Engine should be at operating temperature and running. Turn idle speed screw (27) to obtain 2500-3000 rpm, or just below clutch engagement speed. Adjust low speed mixture needle (16) to obtain consistent idling and smooth acceleration. Readjust idle speed screw (27) as required. Open throttle fully and adjust high speed mixture needle (17) to obtain highest engine rpm, then turn high speed mixture needle counterclockwise 1/8 turn.

To disassemble carburetor, remove screw (26), pump cover (25), gasket (24) and diaphragm (23). Remove fuel inlet screen (22). Remove the two screws (1)

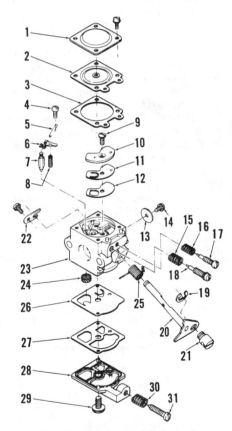

Fig. KZ50—Exploded view of Walbro carburetor used on some models.

1. Cover	17. High speed mixture needle
2. Metering diaphragm	
3. Gasket	18. Idle mixture needle
4. Metering lever screw	19. "E" clip
5. Metering lever pin	20. Throttle shaft
6. Metering lever	21. Swivel
7. Fuel inlet valve	22. Throttle shaft clip
8. Metering lever spring	23. Body
9. Circuit plate screw	24. Inlet screen
10. Circuit plate	25. Return spring
11. Check valve	26. Fuel pump diaphragm
12. Gasket	27. Gasket
13. Throttle valve	28. Cover
14. Shutter screw	29. Cover screw
15. Spring	30. Spring
16. Spring	31. Idle speed screw

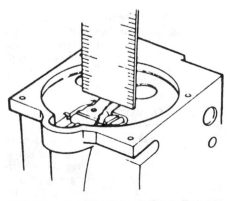

Fig. KZ51—Fuel inlet lever should be flush with carburetor body.

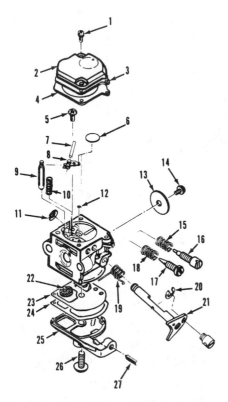

Fig. KZ52—Exploded view of Zama diaphragm carburetor used on some models.

1. Screw
2. Cover
3. Diaphragm
4. Gasket
5. Screw
6. Fuel metering lever disc
7. Pin
8. Fuel inlet lever
9. Fuel inlet needle
10. Spring
11. "E" ring
12. Disc
13. Throttle plate
14. Screw
15. Spring
16. Low speed mixture needle
17. High speed mixture needle
18. Spring
19. Spring
20. "E" ring
21. Throttle shaft
22. Screen
23. Diaphragm
24. Gasket
25. Cover
26. Screw
27. Idle speed screw

and remove cover (2), diaphragm (3) and gasket (4). Remove screw (5), pin (7), metering disc (6), fuel inlet lever (8), fuel inlet needle (9) and spring (10). Remove fuel mixture needles and springs. Remove "E" clip (11), throttle plate (13) and throttle shaft (21) as required.

Inspect all parts for wear or damage. Diaphragms should be flexible with no cracks or wrinkles. Fuel inlet lever (8) with metering disc (6) removed, should be flush with carburetor fuel chamber floor (Fig. KZ51).

IGNITION SYSTEM. Engines may be equipped with a magneto type ignition with breaker points and condenser or a CDI (capacitor-discharge) ignition system which requires no regular maintenance and has no breaker points. Ignition module (CDI) is located outside of flywheel. Refer to appropriate paragraph for model being serviced.

Breaker Point Ignition System. Breaker points may be located behind recoil starter or behind flywheel. Note location of breaker points and refer to following paragraphs for service.

To inspect or service magneto ignition with **breaker points and condenser located behind recoil starter and cover,** first remove fan cover. Refer to Fig. KZ53 and check pole gap between flywheel and ignition coil laminations. Gap should be 0.35-0.40 mm (0.014-0.016 in.). To adjust pole gap, loosen two retaining screws in coil (threads of retaining screws should be treated with Loctite or equivalent), place correct gage between flywheel and coil laminations. Pull coil to flywheel by hand as shown, then tighten screws and remove feeler gage.

Breaker points are accessible after removal of starter case, nut and pawl carrier. Nut and pawl carrier both have left-hand threads.

To adjust point gap and ignition timing, disconnect stop switch wire from stop switch. Connect one lead from a timing tester (Kioritz 990510-00031) or equivalent to stop switch wire. Ground remaining timing tester lead to engine body. Position flywheel timing mark as shown in Fig. KZ54 and set breaker point gap to 0.3-0.4 mm (0.012-0.014 in.). Rotate flywheel and check timing with timing tester. Readjust as necessary. Be accurate when setting breaker point gap. A gap greater than 0.4 mm (0.014 in.) will advance timing; a gap less than 0.3 mm (0.012 in.) will retard timing.

With point gap and flywheel correctly set, timing will be 23° BTDC.

To inspect or service magneto ignition with **breaker points and condenser located behind flywheel,** first remove starter case. Disconnect wire from stop switch and connect to timing tester (Kioritz 990510-00031) or equivalent. Ground remaining lead from timing tester to engine body. Position flywheel timing mark as shown in Fig. KZ55. If timing is not correct, loosen

retaining screw on breaker points through flywheel slot openings. Squeeze screwdriver in crankcase groove to adjust point gap. Breaker point gap should be 0.3-0.4 mm (0.012-0.016 in.) with flywheel at TDC.

If breaker points require renewal, flywheel must be removed. When installing breaker points note that stop lead (black) from condenser must pass under coil. White wire from coil must pass between condenser bracket and oiler felt. Push wire down to avoid contact with flywheel.

Ignition coil air gap between coil and flywheel should be 0.4 mm (0.016 in.). Retaining screws should be treated with Loctite or equivalent.

Be accurate when setting breaker point gap. A gap greater than 0.4 mm (0.016 in.) will advance timing; a gap less than 0.3 mm (0.012 in.) will retard timing.

With point gap and flywheel correctly set, timing will be 30° BTDC. Tighten flywheel nut.

Primary and secondary ignition coil resistance may be checked with an ohmmeter without removing coil.

To check primary coil resistance, connect ohmmeter to disconnected ignition coil primary lead and ground remaining lead to engine. Primary coil resistance should register 0.5-0.8 ohms.

To check secondary coil resistance connect one lead of ohmmeter to spark plug cable and remaining lead to ground on engine. Secondary coil resistance should register 5-10 ohms.

CD Ignition System. CD ignition system requires no regular maintenance and has no moving parts except for magnets cast in flywheel.

Ignition timing is fixed at 30° BTDC and clearance between CDI module laminations and flywheel should be 0.3 mm (0.012 in.). To check ignition timing, refer to Fig. KZ56. If timing is not correct, CDI module must be renewed.

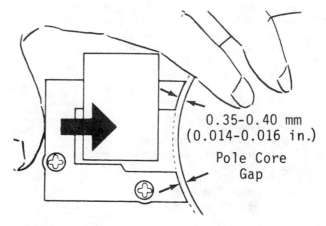

Fig. KZ53—Illustration showing correct pole core gap. Refer to text.

0.35-0.40 mm (0.014-0.016 in.)
Pole Core Gap

Ignition coil may be checked by connecting one ohmmeter lead to spark plug cable and remaining lead to coil primary lead; ohmmeter should register 0.0-0.2 ohms for all models. Connect ohmmeter lead to coil primary lead (red) wire and remaining ohmmeter lead to either the coil exciter lead (grounded wire), if so equipped, or to coil laminations. Ohmmeter should register 0.5-1.5k ohms for models with exciter lead or 1.5-3.0k ohms for remaining models. Connect one ohmmeter lead to exciter lead, of models so

equipped, and remaining ohmmeter lead to coil laminations; ohmmeter should register 120-200 ohms.

CARBON. Muffler and cylinder exhaust ports should be cleaned periodically to prevent loss of power due to carbon build-up. Remove muffler cover and baffle plate and scrape muffler free of carbon. With muffler cover removed, position engine so piston is at top dead center and carefully remove carbon from exhaust ports with wooden scraper. Be careful not to damage the edges

of exhaust ports or to scratch piston. Do not attempt to run engine without muffler baffle plate or cover.

LUBRICATION. Engine lubrication is obtained by mixing a good quality two-stroke air-cooled engine oil with gasoline. Refer to TRIMMER SERVICE section for fuel/oil mixture ratio recommended by trimmer manufacturer.

REPAIRS

COMPRESSION PRESSURE. For optimum performance, minimum compression pressure should be 621 kPa (90 psi). Compression test should be performed with engine cold and throttle and choke plates at wide open positions.

TIGHTENING TORQUES. Recommended tightening torque specifications are as follows:

Spark plug:
All models . . . . 14-15 N·m
(168-180 in.-lbs.)
Cylinder cover:
All models so equipped   1.5-1.9 N·m
(13-17 in.-lbs.)
Cylinder:
13.8, 16.0
& 21.2 cc engine . . . . .5.7-6.0 N·m
(50-55 in.-lbs.)
All other engines . . . .7.0-8.0 N·m
(65-75 in.-lbs.)
Crankcase:
All models . . . . .4.5-5.7 N·m
(40-50 in.-lbs.)

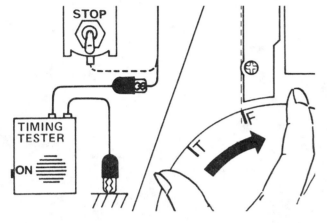

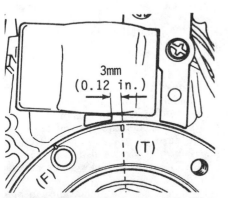

Fig. KZ54—Illustration showing proper timing mark setting for engines with breaker points located behind recoil starter and cover. Refer to text.

Fig. KZ55—Illustration showing proper timing mark setting for engines with breaker points located behind flywheel. Refer to text.

Fig. KZ56—Align top dead center mark (T) on flywheel with laminations as shown to check timing on models with CD ignition. Refer to text.

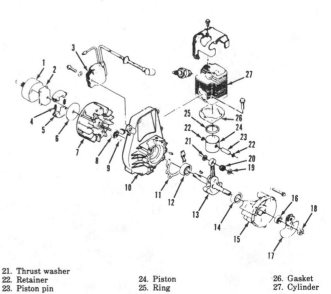

Fig. KZ57—Exploded view of engine similar to the 13.8, 16.0 and 21.2 cc (0.84, 0.98 and 1.29 cu. in.) displacement engines.

1. Clutch drum
2. Hub
3. Ignition module
4. Clutch springs
5. Clutch shoes
6. Plate
7. Flywheel
8. Seal
9. Key
10. Crankcase
11. Gasket
12. Bearing
13. Crankshaft & connecting rod assy.
14. Bearing
15. Crankcase cover
16. Seal
17. Ratchet assy.
18. Nut
19. Thrust washer
20. Bearing
21. Thrust washer
22. Retainer
23. Piston pin
24. Piston
25. Ring
26. Gasket
27. Cylinder

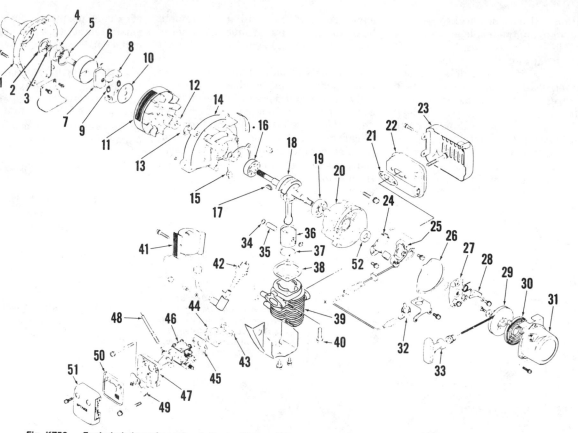

Fig. KZ58 — Exploded view of engine similar to 30.1 and 40.2 cc (1.84 and 2.45 cu. in.) displacement engines.

1. Fan cover
2. Stopper
3. Snap ring
4. Ball bearing
5. Snap ring
6. Clutch drum
7. Clutch hub
8. Clutch shoe
9. Clutch spring
10. Side plate
11. Flywheel/fan

12. Spacer
13. Seal
14. Crankcase
15. Crankcase packing
16. Ball bearing
17. Woodruff key
18. Crankshaft/connecting rod assy.
19. Ball bearing
20. Crankcase half
21. Gasket

22. Muffler
23. Cover
24. Condenser
25. Breaker points
26. Gasket
27. Pawl carrier
28. Pawl
29. Starter hub
30. Spring
31. Starter housing
32. Stop switch

33. Handle
34. Snap ring
35. Piston pin
36. Piston
37. Piston ring
38. Gasket
39. Cylinder
40. Screw
41. Coil assy.
42. Spark plug

43. Gasket
44. Insulator
45. Gasket
46. Carburetor
47. Case
48. Throttle cable
49. Choke shutter
50. Air filter
51. Cover
52. Seal

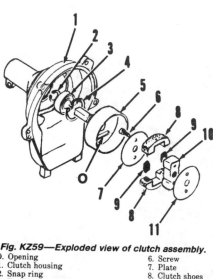

Fig. KZ59—Exploded view of clutch assembly.

O. Opening
1. Clutch housing
2. Snap ring
3. Bearing
4. Snap ring
5. Clutch drum

6. Screw
7. Plate
8. Clutch shoes
9. Clutch springs
10. Hub
11. Plate

CRANKSHAFT AND CONNECTING ROD. The crankshaft and connecting rod are serviced as an assembly only and crankshaft and connecting rod are not available separately.

To remove crankshaft and connecting rod assembly remove fan housing and clutch assembly. Remove carburetor, muffler and fuel tank. Remove starter assembly, flywheel and ignition module. Carefully remove cylinder (27—Fig. KZ57). Remove retaining rings (22) and use a suitable piston pin puller to remove pin (23). Note thrust washers (19 and 21) are installed on some engines and will fall when piston pin and piston are removed. Separate crankcase halves and remove crankshaft and connecting rod assembly. Carefully press ball bearings (12 and 14) off crankshaft as required. If bearings remain in crankcase, it may be necessary to heat crankcase halves slightly to remove bearings.

Inspect all parts for wear or damage. Standard connecting rod side clearance on crankpin journal is 0.55-0.60 mm (0.022-0.026 in.). If side clearance is 0.7 mm (0.028 in.) or more, crankshaft and connecting rod assembly must be renewed. Crankcase runout should not exceed 0.05 mm (0.002 in.). It may be necessary to heat crankcase halves slightly to install ball bearings (12 and 14).

PISTON, PIN AND RINGS. Rings are pinned to prevent ring rotation on all models. Piston may be equipped with one or two compression rings according to model and application.

Standard ring end gap is 0.3 mm (0.012 in.). If ring end gap is 0.5 mm (0.02 in.) or more, renew rings and/or cylinder.

Standard ring side clearance in piston groove is 0.06 mm (0.0024 in.). If ring side clearance is 0.10 mm (0.004 in.)

or more, renew ring and/or piston.

When installing piston, rings must be correctly positioned over pins in ring grooves. Install piston on connecting rod with arrow on top of piston towards exhaust side of engine. Make certain piston pin retaining rings are correctly seated in piston pin bore of piston. Use care when installing piston into cylinder that cylinder does not rotate.

CYLINDER. The cylinder bore has a chrome plated surface and must be renewed if plating is worn through or scored excessively. Worn spots will appear dull and may be easily scratched while chrome plating will be bright and much harder.

CLUTCH. Refer to Fig. KZ59 for an exploded view of centrifugal clutch assembly used on 13.8, 16.0 and 21.2 cc (0.84, 0.98 and 1.29 cu. in.) engines. Snap ring (4) is removed from snap ring bore through opening (O) in clutch drum. Drive clutch drum (5) out and remove snap ring (2). Remove ball bearing (3). Check shoes for wear or oil, check clutch springs for fatigue and renew parts as necessary. If removal of clutch hub is necessary, it is screwed on crankshaft with left-hand threads.

To remove clutch from all other engines, remove fan cover. Remove screw retaining clutch drum to crankshaft. Remove ball bearing from clutch drum. Check shoes for wear or oil, check clutch springs for fatigue and renew parts as necessary.

KOMATSU

ENGINE SERVICE

Model	Bore	Stroke	Displacement
G1E	28 mm	28 mm	17.2 cc
	(1.10 in.)	(1.10 in.)	(1.05 cu. in.)
G2E	34 mm	28 mm	25.4 cc
	(1.36 in.)	(1.10 in.)	(1.55 cu. in.)

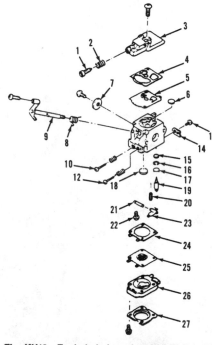

Fig. KU10—Exploded view of typical Walbro WA carburetor. Some models are equipped with a remote purge bulb that connects to plate (26).

1. Idle speed screw
2. Spring
3. Cover
4. Gasket
5. Fuel pump diaphragm
6. Inlet screen
7. Throttle plate
8. Spring
9. Throttle shaft
10. Idle mixture screw
12. High-speed mixture screw
13. Screw
14. Retainer
15. Check valve screen
16. Snap ring
17. Welch plug
18. Welch plug
19. Fuel inlet valve
20. Spring
21. Pin
22. Screw
23. Metering lever
24. Gasket
25. Metering diaphragm
26. Plate
27. Cover

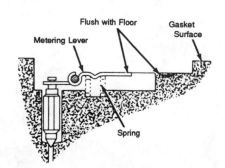

Fig. KU11—Metering lever should be flush with chamber floor as shown.

ENGINE INFORMATION

The Komatsu G1E and G2E two-stroke, air-cooled gasoline engines are used by several manufacturers of string trimmers and brush cutters. The engines are equipped with cantilever-type crankshafts that are supported in two ball bearings at the flywheel end. Refer to following sections for other Komatsu engine models.

MAINTENANCE

LUBRICATION. Engine lubrication is obtained by mixing gasoline with an oil designed for two-stroke, air-cooled engines. Refer to trimmer or blower service section for manufacturer's recommended fuel:oil mixture ratio.

SPARK PLUG. Recommended spark plug is a Champion RCJ8 or equivalent. Specified electrode gap for all models is 0.6-0.7 mm (0.024-0.028 in.). Tighten spark plug to 19.5-21.6 N·m (173-191 in.-lbs.).

CARBURETOR. The engine is equipped with a Walbro WA diaphragm-type carburetor. Some models are equipped with a remote air purge bulb that is connected to plate (26—Fig. KU10). Operating the air purge bulb (may be called a primer) fills the carburetor with fuel for faster fuel movement during starting.

Initial adjustment of idle mixture screw (10) is 1¼ turns out from a lightly seated position on trimmers and brush cutters, or 1½ turns out on blowers. Initial adjustment of high-speed mixture screw (12) is one turn out on trimmers and brush cutters, or 1½ turns out on blowers.

Final adjustments are performed with trimmer line at recommended length or blade installed. Engine must be at operating temperature and running. Be sure engine air filter is clean before adjusting carburetor.

Turn idle speed screw (1) in until trimmer head or blade just begins to rotate, or to 2700 rpm on blowers. Adjust idle mixture screw (10) to obtain maximum idle speed possible, then turn idle mixture screw ¹/₆ turn counterclockwise. Readjust idle speed. Operate unit at full throttle and adjust high-speed mixture screw (12) to obtain maximum engine rpm, then turn high-speed mixture screw ¹/₆ turn counterclockwise.

When overhauling carburetor, refer to exploded view in Fig. KU10. Examine fuel inlet valve and seat. Inlet valve (19) is renewable, but carburetor body must be renewed if seat is excessively worn or damaged. Inspect mixture screws and seats. Renew carburetor body if seats are excessively worn or damaged. Clean fuel inlet screen (6). Inspect diaphragms (5 and 25) for tears and other damage.

Metering lever (23) should be flush with chamber floor as shown in Fig. KU11. Bend lever to obtain correct lever height.

IGNITION SYSTEM. The engine is equipped with an electronic ignition system. The ignition system is considered satisfactory if a spark will jump across the 3 mm (¹/₈ in.) gap of a test spark plug. If no spark is produced, check on/off switch, wiring and clearance between ignition module and flywheel. Ignition module air gap should be 0.25 mm (0.010 in.). If switch, wiring and module air gap are satisfactory, but spark is not present, renew ignition module. Tighten ignition module retaining screws to 2.0-2.4 N·m (18-21 in.-lbs.). Apply Loctite to screws.

REPAIRS

COMPRESSION PRESSURE. For optimum performance, compression pressure should be 586 kPa (85 psi) and not less than 393 kPa (57 psi). Compression pressure should be checked with engine at operating temperature and with throttle and choke wide open.

TIGHTENING TORQUES. Recommended tightening torques are as follows:

Clutch shaft . . . . .12.0-13.6 N·m
(140-160 in.-lbs.)
Crankcase cover . . . . .2.9-3.3 N·m
(26-34 in.-lbs.)
Crankpin screw . . . . .3.0-3.8 N·m
(35-45 in.-lbs.)
Cylinder . . . . .5.9-6.8 N·m
(53-60 in.-lbs.)
Flywheel . . . . .13.7-15.7 N·m
(122-139 in.-lbs.)
Ignition module . . . . .2.0-2.4 N·m
(18-21 in.-lbs.)
Spark plug . . . . .19.7-24.5 N·m
(175-215 in.-lbs.)

PISTON, PIN AND RINGS. To remove piston, first remove fan housing, cylinder shroud, muffler and ignition module. Unscrew two retaining screws and remove cylinder by pulling straight up, otherwise the piston and ring may be damaged. Ring rotation is prevented by a locating pin in the piston ring groove. Remove piston pin retainers and use a suitable puller to remove piston pin. Remove piston from connecting rod.

Specified piston skirt diameter is 27.93 mm (1.099 in.) with a wear limit of 27.80 mm (1.094 in.). Specified piston ring groove width is 1.40 mm (0.055 in.) with a wear limit of 1.52 mm (0.059 in.). Piston ring end gap should be 0.10-0.25 mm (0.004-0.010 in.) and no more than 0.5 mm (0.019 in.). Specified piston ring width is 1.10 mm (0.043 in.) with a wear limit of 1.00 mm (0.039 in.). Specified piston ring thickness is 1.44 mm (0.057 in.) with a wear limit of 1.30 mm (0.051 in.).

The piston pin rides directly in connecting rod and piston. Specified piston pin diameter is 7.993 mm (0.315 in.) with a wear limit of 7.98 mm (0.314 in.).

Piston and ring are available in standard size only.

Install piston on rod so arrow on piston crown points toward exhaust port (Fig. KU12). Install piston pin so closed end is toward exhaust port. Be sure piston ring gap is correctly indexed with locating pin in piston ring groove when installing cylinder. Tighten cylinder retaining screws to 5.9-6.8 N·m (53-60 in.-lbs.).

CYLINDER. The cylinder bore is chrome plated. Renew cylinder if bore is excessively worn or bore surface is cracked, flaking or otherwise damaged. Specified cylinder bore is 28.01 mm (1.102 in.) with a wear limit of 28.07 mm (1.105 in.). Tighten cylinder retaining screws to 5.9-6.8 N·m (53-60 in.-lbs.).

CRANKSHAFT AND CONNECTING ROD. The crankshaft is supported at flywheel end only by two ball bearings. To remove crankshaft and connecting rod, remove fan housing (5—Fig. KU13)

and recoil starter assembly, cooling shroud (4) and ignition module (3). Disconnect fuel line and remove fuel tank. Remove air filter assembly (35), carburetor (31), muffler cover (1) and muffler (2). Remove flywheel retaining nut and pull flywheel (9) off crankshaft. Remove cylinder mounting bolts and pull cylinder (27) straight off piston. Remove piston pin retaining rings (22), then tap piston pin (23) out of piston and remove piston (24). Remove crankcase cover mounting screws and carefully separate crankcase cover (30) from crankcase (11). Remove connecting rod retaining screw (21), noting that screw has left-hand threads. Remove washer (20), thrust washers (16) and connecting rod (17) from crankpin, being careful not to lose 13 loose bearing rollers (18). To separate crankshaft (15) from crankcase, heat crankcase to 100° C (212° F) and press out crankshaft. Remove bearings (10 and 13) and oil seal (12) from crankcase.

Specified connecting rod big end diameter is 15.64 mm (0.616 in.) with a wear limit of 15.80 mm (0.622 in.). Specified connecting rod small end diameter

is 8.05 mm (0.317 in.) with a wear limit of 8.20 mm (0.322 in.).

Specified crankpin diameter is 9.547 mm (0.376 in.) with a wear limit of 9.53 mm (0.375 in.). Specified crankshaft main bearing journal diameter is 12.009 mm (0.473 in.) with a wear limit of 11.99 mm (0.472 in.).

Minimum rod bearing (18) roller diameter is 2.98 mm (0.117 in.) and minimum allowable length is 6.50 mm (0.256 in.).

Fig. KU12—Install piston so arrow on piston crown points toward exhaust port.

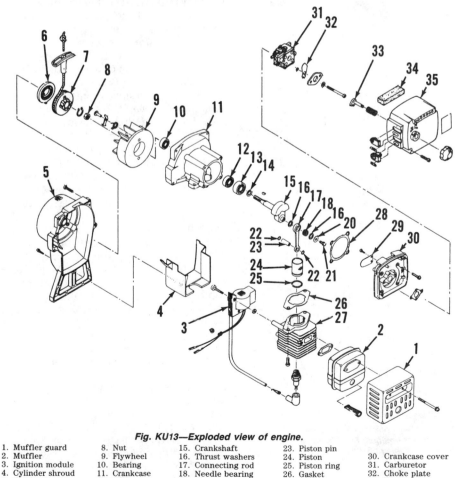

Fig. KU13—Exploded view of engine.

1. Muffler guard	15. Crankshaft	23. Piston pin
2. Muffler	16. Thrust washers	24. Piston
3. Ignition module	17. Connecting rod	25. Piston ring
4. Cylinder shroud	18. Needle bearing	26. Gasket
5. Fan housing	20. Washer	27. Cylinder
6. Rewind spring	21. Screw (L.H.)	28. Gasket
7. Pulley	22. Retaining rings	29. Reed valve
8. Nut		30. Crankcase cover
9. Flywheel		31. Carburetor
10. Bearing		32. Choke plate
11. Crankcase		33. Choke shaft
12. Seal		34. Air filter element
13. Bearing		35. Air cleaner cover
14. Washer		

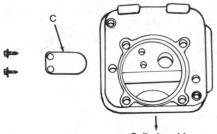

Fig. KU14—Install reed valve (C) so cut-off corner is toward cylinder side of crankcase cover.

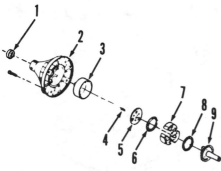

Fig. KU15—Exploded view of clutch assembly used on some models.

1. Spacer
2. Clutch housing
3. Clutch drum
4. Screw
5. Plate
6. Spring
7. Clutch shoes
8. Spring
9. Clutch shaft

Fig. KU16—Exploded view of clutch assembly used on some models.

1. Sleeve
2. Spacer
3. Snap ring
4. Clutch housing
5. Clutch drum
6. Spring
7. Clutch shoes
8. Clutch shaft

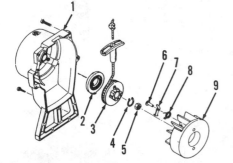

Fig. KU17—Exploded view of rewind starter used on trimmer engines. Pawl components (6, 7 and 8) are available only as an assembly on flywheel.

1. Housing
2. Rewind spring
3. Pulley
4. Snap ring
5. Nut
6. Post
7. Pawl
8. Spring
9. Flywheel

To assemble crankshaft, install spacer (14) and press bearing (13) onto crankshaft. Install seal (12) in crankcase so lip will be toward inside of engine. Heat crankcase to 100°C (212°F) and install bearing (10) with numbered side out. Install crankshaft and bearing in crankcase.

When installing connecting rod on crankpin, be sure 13 bearing rollers (18) are in place. Note that crankpin screw (21) has left-hand threads. Tighten crankpin screw to 3.0-3.8 N·m (35-45 in.-lbs.

REED VALVE. A reed valve (29—Fig. KU13) is located on the inside of the crankcase cover (30). Renew reed valve if cracked, broken or warped. Install reed valve so cut-off corner (C—Fig. KU14) is toward cylinder side of cover.

CLUTCH. Two clutch designs have been used. See Figs. KU15 and KU16. Clutch shoes are available only as a set. On models so equipped, be sure hole in side of sleeve (1—Fig. KU16) is aligned with hole in clutch housing. Tighten clutch shaft (8) to 12.0-13.6 N·m (140-160 in.-lbs.)

REWIND STARTER. Trimmers. Refer to Fig. KU17 for an exploded view of rewind starter used on trimmers. To disassemble starter, detach starter housing (1) from engine. Remove rope handle and allow rope to wind into starter. Remove snap ring (4) and remove rope pulley (3). Wear appropriate safety eyewear and gloves before detaching rewind spring (2) from housing as spring may uncoil uncontrolled.

To assemble starter, lubricate center post of housing and spring side with light grease. Install rewind spring so coil windings are clockwise from outer end. Assemble starter while passing rope through housing rope outlet and attach rope handle to rope. To place tension on starter rope, pull rope out of housing. Engage rope in notch on pulley and turn pulley four turns clockwise. Hold pulley and disengage rope from pulley notch. Release pulley and allow rope to wind on pulley. Check starter operation. Rope handle should be held against housing by spring tension, but it must be possible to rotate pulley at least $1/4$ turn clockwise when rope is pulled out fully.

Blowers. The rewind starter on engines used on blowers is located between the flywheel and the crankcase. Rewind spring case (1—Fig. KU18) is attached to the crankcase. To disassemble starter, the engine must be removed from blower housing. Push rope outlet into housing then pass rope handle through opening. Remove engine. Re-

move fan (9) and flywheel (6). Either remove rope handle or insert rope in rope pulley notch and allow rewind spring to unwind. Wear appropriate safety eyewear and gloves before detaching pulley (3) from rewind spring (2) as spring may uncoil uncontrolled. Note that hub of spring case (1) is slotted. Push in fingers of hub and disengage pulley from hub; rewind spring will be free when pulley is separated from spring.

To assemble starter, lubricate hub of spring case and spring side with light grease. Wind spring in case in a counterclockwise direction from outer end. Rope length should be 90 cm (35½ in.). Assemble spring case and pulley, but do not install on engine. To place tension on starter rope, pull rope out, engage rope in notch on pulley and turn pulley 2½ turns counterclockwise. Hold pulley and disengage rope from pulley notch. Release pulley and allow rope to wind on pulley. It should be possible to turn pulley 2 more turns counterclockwise with rope fully extended. Install spring case on crankcase being sure notches on spring case and ribs on crankcase are aligned. Reassemble blower and check starter operation.

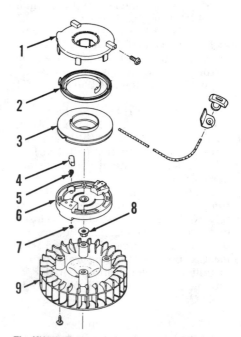

Fig. KU18—Exploded view of rewind starter used on blower engines.

1. Spring case
2. Rewind spring
3. Pulley
4. Pawl
5. Spring
6. "E" ring
7. Flywheel
8. Nut
9. Fan

KOMATSU

ENGINE SERVICE

Model	Bore	Stroke	Displacement
G2D	32 mm	28 mm	22.5 cc
	(1.26 in.)	(1.10 in.)	(1.37 cu. in.)
G2K	34 mm	28 mm	25.4 cc
	(1.34 in.)	(1.10 in.)	(1.55 cu. in.)
G2KC	32 mm	28 mm	22.5 cc
	(1.26 in.)	(1.10 in.)	(1.37 cu. in.)
G3K	36 mm	33 mm	33.6 cc
	(1.42 in.)	(1.32 in.)	(2.05 cu. in.)
G4K	40 mm	33 mm	41.5 cc
	(1.58 in.)	(1.32 in.)	(2.53 cu. in.)
Blower	40 mm	33 mm	41.5 cc
	(1.58 in.)	(1.32 in.)	(2.53 cu. in.)

ENGINE INFORMATION

Komatsu two-stroke, air-cooled gasoline engines are used by several manufacturers of string trimmers, brush cutters and blowers. Blower engine may be equipped with an electric starter. Refer to preceding Komatsu section for information on other engines.

MAINTENANCE

LUBRICATION. Engine lubrication is obtained by mixing gasoline with an oil designed for two-stroke, air-cooled engines. Refer to trimmer or blower service section for manufacturer's recommended fuel:oil mixture ratio.

SPARK PLUG. Recommended spark plug for Models G2D and G2K is Champion CJ8 or equivalent. Recommended

spark plug for Models G3K and G4K is Champion CJ8Y or equivalent. Recommended spark plug for blower engine is Champion RJ6C or equivalent. A resistor-type spark plug may be required to meet local ordinances. Electrode gap for all models should be 0.6-0.7 mm (0.024-0.028 in.). Tighten spark plug to 19.5-21.6 N·m (173-191 in.-lbs.).

CARBURETOR. Various types of carburetors have been used. Refer to the appropriate following section for carburetor service.

Walbro HDA. The Walbro HDA is used on some blower engines. Initial setting of idle mixture screw (5—Fig. KU51) is 1¼ turns out on HDA-26B carburetor and 1⅜ turns out on HDA-70 carburetor. Initial and final setting of high-speed mixture screw (4) is fully closed.

Note: Priming system will not operate properly if high-speed mixture screw is open. Final adjustment is performed with engine running at normal operating temperature. All blower tubing must be attached. Adjust idle speed screw (1) so engine idles at 2000 rpm. Adjust idle mixture screw to obtain highest idle speed, then readjust idle speed screw to 2000 rpm. If full-throttle engine speed exceeds 8000 rpm, open high-speed mixture screw no more than ¼ turn.

Carburetor disassembly and reassembly is evident after inspection of carburetor and referral to Fig. KU51. On models so equipped, do not lose detent ball (12) when withdrawing choke shaft (2). Clean and inspect all components. Inspect diaphragms for defects that may affect operation. Examine fuel inlet valve and seat. Inlet valve (15) is renewable, but carburetor body must be renewed if seat is damaged or excessively worn. Discard carburetor body if mixture screw seats are damaged or excessively worn. Screens should be clean. Be sure throttle and choke plates fit shaft and carburetor bore properly. Apply Loctite to throttle and choke plate retaining screws. Adjust metering lever height to obtain 0.13 mm (0.005 in.) between carburetor body surface and lever as shown in Fig. KU52.

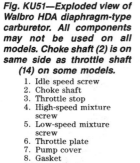

Fig. KU51—Exploded view of Walbro HDA diaphragm-type carburetor. All components may not be used on all models. Choke shaft (2) is on same side as throttle shaft (14) on some models.

1. Idle speed screw
2. Choke shaft
3. Throttle stop
4. High-speed mixture screw
5. Low-speed mixture screw
6. Throttle plate
7. Pump cover
8. Gasket
9. Pump diaphragm
10. Inlet screen
11. Choke plate
12. Choke detent ball
13. Spring
14. Throttle shaft
15. Fuel inlet valve
16. Welch plug
17. Spring
18. Metering lever
19. Pin
20. Screw
21. Gasket
22. Metering diaphragm
23. Plate
24. Primer bulb
25. Cover

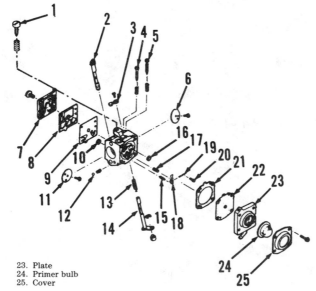

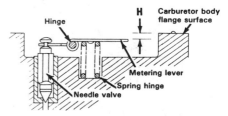

Fig. KU52—Metering lever height (H) must be set on diaphragm-type carburetors. Refer to text for specified height.

Walbro WY, WYJ and WYK. Some engines may be equipped with a Walbro WY, WYJ or WYK carburetor. This is a diaphragm-type carburetor that uses a barrel-type throttle rather than a throttle plate.

Idle fuel for the carburetor flows up into the throttle barrel where it is fed into the air stream. On some models, the idle fuel flow can be adjusted by turning an idle mixture limiter plate (P—Fig. KU53). Initial setting is in center notch. Rotating the plate clockwise will lean the idle mixture. Inside the limiter plate is an idle mixture needle (N—Fig. KU54) that is preset at the factory (a plug covers the needle). If removed, use the following procedure to determine correct position. Back out needle (N) until unscrewed. Screw in needle 5 turns on Model WY or 15 turns on Models WYJ and WYK. Rotate idle mixture plate (P—Fig. KU53) to center notch. Run engine until normal operating temperature is attained. Adjust idle speed screw (I) so engine idles at 2300 rpm on Model G4K engines or 2900 rpm on other models. Rotate idle mixture needle (N—Fig. KU54) and obtain highest rpm (turning needle clockwise leans the mixture), then turn needle 1/4 turn counterclockwise. Readjust idle speed screw. Note that idle limiter plate and needle are available only as an assembly with throttle barrel (25—Fig. KU55).

Most models are equipped with a removable fixed jet (16—Fig. KU55), however, some WYK models may be equipped with an adjustable high-speed mixture screw (22). Initial setting of the high-speed mixture screw is 1½ turns out from a lightly seated position. Adjust screw to obtain best performance with engine under load. Do not adjust mixture too lean as engine may be damaged.

To overhaul carburetor, refer to exploded view in Fig. KU55 and note the following: On models with a plastic body, clean only with solvents approved for use with plastic. Do not disassemble throttle barrel assembly (25). Examine fuel inlet valve and seat. Inlet valve (9) is renewable, but fuel pump body (11) must be renewed if seat is excessively worn or damaged. On models so equipped, inspect high-speed mixture screw and seat. Renew carburetor body if seat is excessively worn or damaged. Clean fuel inlet screen (18). Inspect diaphragms for tears and other damage. When installing plates and gaskets (12 through 15), note that tabs (T) on ends will "stairstep" when correctly installed. Adjust metering lever height to obtain 1.5 mm (0.059 in.) between carburetor body surface and lever as shown in Fig. KU52.

Nikki Carburetor. The Nikki carburetor is a diaphragm-type carburetor that has an integral fuel pump. When depressed, a lever attached to the metering diaphragm cover forces the metering diaphragm up thereby opening the fuel inlet valve. With the lever depressed, actuating the primer bulb at the fuel tank forces additional fuel into the carburetor to aid starting. Note that there is a check valve in the fuel tank pickup that functions with the primer pump.

Initial setting for high-speed mixture screw (13—Fig. KU56) is 2½ turns out. Midrange mixture is determined by the position of the clip on jet needle (6). There are three grooves in upper end of the jet needle (Fig. KU57) and normal position of clip is in the middle groove. The mixture will be leaner if clip is installed in the top groove, or richer if clip is installed in the bottom groove.

Before removing carburetor from engine, unscrew cap (2—Fig. KU56) and withdraw throttle slide (7) assembly.

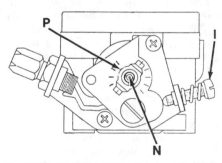

Fig. KU53—On Walbro WY carburetor, idle speed screw is located at (I), idle mixture limiter plate is located at (P) and idle mixture needle is located at (N). A plug covers the idle mixture needle.

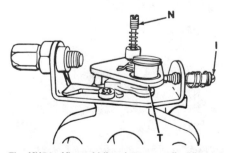

Fig. KU54—View of idle mixture needle (N) used on Walbro WY carburetor.

Fig. KU55—Exploded view of Walbro WYK. Models WY and WYJ are similar.

1. Cover
2. Primer bulb
3. Check valve
4. Plate
5. Metering diaphragm
6. Gasket
7. Pin
8. Metering lever
9. Fuel inlet valve
10. Spring
11. Fuel pump body
12. Gasket
13. Fuel pump plate
14. Fuel pump diaphragm
15. Gasket
16. Main jet
17. "O" ring
18. Fuel screen
19. "O" ring
20. Washer
21. Spring
22. High-speed mixture screw
23. Body
24. "O" ring
25. Throttle barrel assy.
26. Idle speed screw
27. Plug
28. Swivel
29. "E" ring
30. Bracket
31. Nut
32. Cable adjuster

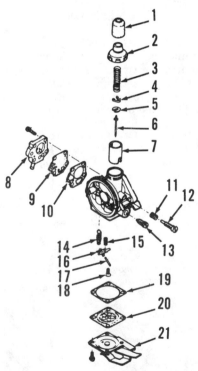

Fig. KU56—Exploded view of Nikki carburetor.

1. Cover
2. Cap
3. Spring
4. Retainer
5. Clip
6.
7. Throttle slide
8. Fuel pump cover
9. Fuel pump diaphragm
10. Gasket
11. Spring
12. Idle speed screw
13. High-speed mixture screw
14. Fuel inlet valve
15. Spring
16. Metering lever
17. Pin
18. Screw
19. Gasket
20. Metering diaphragm
21. Cover

When overhauling carburetor, refer to Fig. KU56 and note the following: Examine fuel inlet valve and seat. Inlet valve (14) is renewable, but carburetor body must be renewed if seat is excessively worn or damaged. Inspect mixture screw and seat. Renew carburetor body if seat is excessively worn or damaged. Inspect diaphragms for tears and other damage. Adjust metering lever height to obtain 1.6 mm (0.063 in.) between carburetor body surface and lever as shown in Fig. KU52. When installing throttle slide, be sure groove in side of throttle slide (7—Fig. KU56) indexes with pin in bore of carburetor body.

TK Diaphragm Carburetor. The TK diaphragm carburetor is equipped with an integral diaphragm-type fuel pump. Operating enrichment lever (3—Fig. KU58) opens enrichment valve (1) for additional fuel when starting engine.

Adjust idle speed screw (12) so engine idles just below clutch engagement speed. Initial setting of high-speed mixture screw (15) is 1½ turns out from a lightly seated position. Perform final adjustments with trimmer line at proper length or blade installed and engine at operating temperature. Be sure engine air filter is clean before adjusting carburetor.

Operate engine at wide-open throttle and turn high-speed mixture screw in so engine begins to run smoothly, then back out screw ⅛ turn. Normal range of adjustment is 1-2 turns out from a lightly seated position. Midrange mixture is determined by the position of clip (7—Fig. KU58) on jet needle (8). There are three grooves in upper end of the jet needle (Fig. KU57) and normal position of clip is in the middle groove. The mixture will be leaner if clip is installed in the top groove, or richer if clip is installed in the bottom groove.

Before removing carburetor from engine, unscrew cap (4—Fig. KU58) and

withdraw throttle slide (9) assembly. When overhauling carburetor, refer to Fig. KU58 and note the following: Examine fuel inlet valve and seat. Inlet valve (19) is renewable, but carburetor body (10) must be renewed if seat is excessively worn or damaged. Inspect mixture screw and seat. Renew carburetor body if seat is excessively worn or damaged. Inspect diaphragms for tears and other damage. Adjust metering lever height to obtain 1.4-1.7 mm (0.055-0.067 in.) between carburetor body surface and lever as shown in Fig. KU52. When installing throttle slide, be sure groove in side of throttle slide (9—Fig. KU58) indexes with pin in bore of carburetor body.

TK Float Carburetor. Refer to Fig. KU59 for an exploded view of carburetor. Idle mixture is not adjustable. High-speed mixture is controlled by removable fixed jet (12). Midrange mixture is determined by the position of clip (3) on jet needle (4). There are three grooves in upper end of the jet needle (Fig. KU57) and normal position of clip is in

the middle groove. The mixture will be leaner if clip is installed in the top groove, or richer if clip is installed in the bottom groove.

Before removing carburetor from engine, unscrew cap and withdraw throttle slide (5—Fig. KU59) assembly. When overhauling carburetor, refer to Fig. KU59 and note the following: Examine fuel inlet valve and seat. The inlet seat is not renewable and carburetor body must be renewed if seat is excessively worn or damaged. When installing throttle slide, be sure groove in side of throttle slide (5) indexes with pin in bore of carburetor body.

IGNITION SYSTEM. The engine is equipped with an electronic ignition system. Model G2KC is equipped with a one-piece ignition module that includes the ignition coil. On all other models, a two-piece ignition system is used. On blower engines, the ignition module is adjacent to the flywheel and the ignition coil is attached to the blower housing. On other two-piece systems,

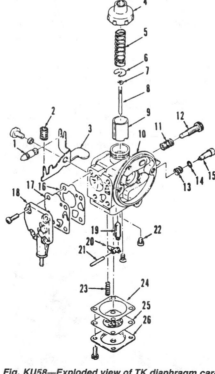

Fig. KU57—Install jet needle clip (A) in center groove on jet needle (B).

Fig. KU58—Exploded view of TK diaphragm carburetor.

1.	Enrichment valve	15.	High-speed mixture screw
2.	Spring	16.	Gasket
3.	Enrichment lever	17.	Fuel pump diaphragm
4.	Cap	18.	Cover
5.	Spring	19.	Fuel inlet valve
6.	Retainer	20.	Metering lever
7.	Clip	21.	Pin
8.	Jet needle	22.	Needle jet
9.	Throttle slide	23.	Spring
10.	Body	24.	Gasket
11.	Spring	25.	Metering diaphragm
12.	Idle speed screw	26.	Cover
13.	Spring		
14.	"O" ring		

Fig. KU59—Exploded view of TK float-type carburetor.

1.	Spring	9.	Float lever
2.	Seat	10.	Pin
3.	Clip	11.	Needle jet
4.	Jet needle	12.	Main jet
5.	Throttle slide	13.	Float
6.	Body	14.	Gasket
7.	Fuel inlet valve	15.	Fuel bowl

the ignition coil is adjacent to the flywheel and the ignition module is mounted on the crankcase.

The ignition system is considered satisfactory if a spark will jump across the 3 mm (1/8 in.) gap of a test spark plug. If no spark is produced, check on/off switch, wiring and air gap between ignition module/coil and flywheel magnet. Air gap on early Models G2D and G2K should be 0.3 mm (0.012 in.). Ignition module air gap on blower engine should be 0.3-0.4 mm (0.012-0.016 in.). Ignition module/coil air gap on all other models should be 0.4 mm (0.016 in.). On models with the ignition coil attached to the inside of the fan cover, it is necessary to remove the cylinder to set the air gap. Refer to REPAIRS section for ignition coil specifications.

REPAIRS

COMPRESSION PRESSURE. Refer to following table for desired compression pressure readings:

Model G2D	.....	490 kPa
		(71 psi)
Minimum	.....	297 kPa
		(43 psi)
Model G2K	.....	586 kPa
		(85 psi)
Minimum	.....	393 kPa
		(57 psi)
Model G2KC	.....	441 kPa
		(64 psi)
Minimum	.....	294 kPa
		(43 psi)
Model G3K	.....	686 kPa
		(99 psi)
Minimum	.....	490 kPa
		(71 psi)

Model G4K:

Early models	.....	586 kPa
		(85 psi)
Minimum	.....	393 kPa
		(57 psi)
Later models	.....	686 kPa
		(99 psi)
Minimum	.....	490 kPa
		(71 psi)
Blower engine	.....	490 kPa
		(71 psi)
Minimum	.....	343 kPa
		(50 psi)

TIGHTENING TORQUES. Recommended tightening torque specifications are as follows:

Blower fan	.....	6.6-7.8 N·m
		(52-69 in.-lbs.)

Carburetor:

Model G2D	.....	1.9-2.9 N·m
		(17-26 in.-lbs.)
All other models	.....	2.9-4.4 N·m
		(26-39 in.-lbs.)

Clutch shoe:

Model G2D	.....	4.9-6.6 N·m
		(43-52 in.-lbs.)

Models G2K & G2KC	.....	4.9-7.8 N·m
		(43-69 in.-lbs.)
Models G3K & G4K	.....	10.8-16.6 N·m
		(96-147 in.-lbs.)

Crankcase:

Model G2D	.....	3.4-4.4 N·m
		(30-39 in.-lbs.)
Blower engine	.....	2.9-4.4 N·m
		(26-39 in.-lbs.)
All other models	.....	2.5-3.9 N·m
		(22-35 in.-lbs.)

Cylinder:

Models G2D & G2K	.....	3.4-4.4 N·m
		(30-39 in.-lbs.)
All other models	.....	4.9-7.8 N·m
		(43-69 in.-lbs.)

Flywheel (rotor):

Model G2D	.....	15.7-17.6 N·m
		(139-156 in.-lbs.)
Model G4K	.....	19.6-29.4 N·m
		(173-260 in.-lbs.)
Blower engine	.....	19.6-29.4 N·m
		(173-260 in.-lbs.)
All other models	.....	11.7-17.6 N·m
		(104-156 in.-lbs.)

Ignition module:

Model G2D	.....	1.9-2.5 N·m
		(17-26 in.-lbs.)
Models G2K, G3K & G4K	.....	1.5-2.5 N·m
		(14-22 in.-lbs.)
Blower engine	.....	1.4-1.8 N·m
		(13-16 in.-lbs.)

Spark plug	.....	19.5-21.6 N·m
		(173-191 in.-lbs.)

IGNITION SYSTEM. Model G2KC is equipped with a one-piece ignition module that includes the ignition coil. On all other models, a two-piece ignition system is used. On blower engines, the ignition module is adjacent to the flywheel and the ignition coil is attached to the blower housing. On other two-piece systems, the ignition coil is adjacent to the flywheel and the ignition module is mounted on the crankcase.

Refer to following table for ignition coil test specifications. All values are in ohms.

Model	Primary	Secondary
G2D	0.68-0.88	5525-7475
G2K		
Early	0.43-0.63	5355-7245
Later	0.48-0.58	5355-7245
G2KC	0.44-0.59	4560-6840
G3K	0.48-0.58	5355-7245
G4K		
Early	0.43-0.63	5670-6930
Later	0.48-0.58	5355-7245
Blower engine	0.11-0.15	1600-2400

To check ignition module on blower engine, disconnect primary (red) lead of module and check resistance between primary lead and crankcase. Ohmmeter should indicate infinite resistance. To check ignition module on other models so equipped, manufacturer recommends using an ohmmeter and checking resistance readings of a good unit then comparing values on unit being checked. Due to inherent variance and accuracy of testers, providing specific values may be misleading. If a tester is not available, replace suspected unit with a unit known to be good.

PISTON, PIN AND RINGS. The piston is equipped with two piston rings. Ring rotation is prevented by a locating pin in each piston ring groove.

To remove piston, first remove air cleaner, carburetor, muffler, cylinder cover and fan housing. Remove cylinder mounting screws and pull cylinder straight off piston. Remove retaining rings (6—Fig. KU60) and push piston pin (5) out of piston using suitable pin removal tool. Be careful not to apply side thrust to connecting rod during pis-

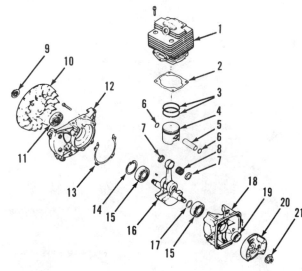

Fig. KU60—Exploded view of typical engine assembly.
1. Cylinder
2. Gasket
3. Piston rings
4. Piston
5. Piston pin
6. Retaining rings
7. Thrust washers
8. Bearing
9. Nut
10. Flywheel
11. Seal
12. Crankcase half
13. Gasket
14. Snap ring
15. Bearings
16. Crankshaft assy.
17. Shim
18. Crankcase half
19. Seal
20. Starter plate
21. Nut

ton pin removal. Thrust washers (7) around piston pin control connecting rod thrust and will be loose when piston pin is removed.

Piston and rings are available only in standard diameter.

Piston-to-cylinder clearance should be 0.060 mm (0.0023 in.) on Models G2D and G2K, 0.025-0.065 mm (0.0010-0.0025 in.) on Model G2KC and 0.045 mm (0.0018 in.) on Models G3K, G4K and blower engine. Maximum allowable piston clearance on all models is 0.2 mm (0.010 in.).

Refer to following table for standard piston diameter and wear limit.

Model	Piston Diameter	Wear Limit
G2D, G2KC	32.0 mm (1.260 in.)	31.9 mm (1.256 in.)
G2K	34.0 mm (1.338 in.)	33.86 mm (1.333 in.)
G3K	36.0 mm (1.417 in.)	35.86 mm (1.412 in.)
G4K	40.0 mm (1.575 in.)	39.86 mm (1.569 in.)
Blower engine	40.0 mm (1.575 in.)	39.86 mm (1.569 in.)

Refer to following table for standard piston pin diameter and wear limit.

Model	Piston Pin Diameter	Wear Limit
G2D, G2KC	8.0 mm (0.315 in.)	7.98 mm (0.314 in.)
G3K	9.0 mm (0.354 in.)	8.98 mm (0.353 in.)
G4K	11.0 mm (0.433 in.)	10.98 mm (0.432 in.)
Blower engine	11.0 mm (0.433 in.)	10.98 mm (0.432 in.)

Refer to following table for standard piston pin bore diameter in piston.

Model	Piston Pin Bore Dia.	Wear Limit
G2D, G2KC	8.0 mm (0.315 in.)	8.04 mm (0.317 in.)
G3K	9.0 mm (0.354 in.)	9.04 mm (0.356 in.)
G4K	11.0 mm (0.433 in.)	11.04 mm (0.435 in.)

Piston ring end gap should be 0.1-0.3 mm (0.004-0.012 in.) on all models, with a maximum allowable gap of 0.7 mm (0.028 in.). Piston ring width should be 1.5 mm (0.059 in.) on all models, with a minimum ring width of 1.4 mm (0.055 in.). Specified piston ring groove width on Model G4K and blower engine is 1.55 mm (0.061 in.) with a wear limit of 1.65 mm (0.065 in.). Specified piston ring groove width on all other models is 1.5

mm (0.059 in.) with a wear limit of 1.6 mm (0.063 in.).

Install piston so arrow on piston crown points toward exhaust port. See Fig. KU61. Be sure piston ring gaps are correctly indexed with locating pins in piston ring grooves when installing cylinder. Lubricate cylinder bore and piston with oil. Position cylinder so it will be in its installed position, then push cylinder straight down over piston. Twisting cylinder may damage piston rings and cylinder.

CYLINDER. All engines are equipped with a chrome plated cylinder bore. When separating cylinder from crankcase, pull straight up on cylinder to avoid damage to piston or piston rings.

Refer to following table for standard cylinder bore diameter and wear limit.

Model	Cylinder Diameter	Wear Limit
G2D, G2KC	32.0 mm (1.260 in.)	32.06 mm (1.262 in.)
G2K	34.0 mm (1.338 in.)	34.04 mm (1.340 in.)
G3K	36.0 mm (1.417 in.)	36.04 mm (1.419 in.)
G4K	40.0 mm (1.575 in.)	40.04 mm (1.576 in.)
Blower engine	40.0 mm (1.575 in.)	40.04 mm (1.576 in.)

Reject cylinder if excessively worn or if chrome plating is flaking, scored or otherwise damaged.

Tighten cylinder mounting screws on Models G2D & G2K to 3.4-4.4 N·m (30-39 in.-lbs.). Tighten cylinder mounting screws on all other models to 4.9-7.8 N·m (43-69 in.-lbs.).

CRANKSHAFT, CONNECTING ROD AND CRANKCASE. Crankshaft, connecting rod and rod bearing are a unit assembly; individual components are not available. The crankshaft is supported by ball bearings at both ends. Thrust washers (7—Fig. KU60) around piston pin control connecting rod thrust.

To remove crankshaft and connecting rod assembly, separate engine from drive unit. Remove fuel tank, air cleaner, carburetor, muffler, fan housing and starter housing. Remove clutch assembly (if so equipped). Remove flywheel retaining nut (9) and pull flywheel off crankshaft. Remove starter pulley nut (21) and use puller to remove pulley from crankshaft. Remove cylinder mounting screws and withdraw cylinder from piston. Remove piston pin retainers (6), push piston pin (5) out of piston and remove piston (4), thrust washers (7) and needle bearing (8) from connecting rod. Remove crankcase mounting

screws. Remove key from crankshaft, then tap lightly on one end of crankshaft to separate crankcase halves. Remove crankshaft (16). Pry oil seals (11 and 19) from crankcase halves, then press bearings (15) out pto side and starter side of crankcase halves (12 and 18).

With crankshaft ends supported in lathe centers or equivalent, maximum allowable crankshaft runout measured at main bearing journals is 0.07 mm (0.0028 in.). Excessive crankshaft runout can be corrected by a shop experienced in servicing unit-type crankshaft assemblies.

Use a suitable tool and press to install main bearings in crankcase halves. Install seals (11 and 19) with lip toward inside of crankcase. Cut off excess height of crankcase gasket (13) that extends above cylinder mating surface.

Specified crankshaft end play is 0.1-0.3 mm (0.004-0.012 in.) with a maximum allowable end play of 0.4 mm (0.016 in.). End play is adjusted by installing or removing shims (17).

Tighten crankcase screws on Model G2D to 3.4-4.4 N·m (30-39 in.-lbs.). Tighten crankcase screws on all other models to 2.5-3.9 N·m (22-35 in.-lbs.).

CLUTCH. Refer to Fig. KU62 for an exploded view of clutch assembly. On all

Fig. KU61—When installing piston, arrow on piston crown must point toward exhaust port.

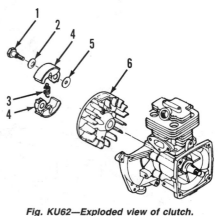

Fig. KU62—Exploded view of clutch.
1. Clutch bolt
2. Spring washer
3. Spring
4. Clutch shoes
5. Washer
6. Flywheel

models except G2D, the clutch shoes are mounted on the flywheel. On Model G2D, the clutch shoes are mounted on a clutch plate attached to the end of the crankshaft. To remove clutch, disconnect throttle cable and separate engine from drive housing. Use a suitable puller to remove clutch plate or flywheel (if necessary).

Clutch shoes are available only in pairs. Install components on clutch bolts as shown in Fig. KU63. Note position of washers. Open ends of clutch spring hooks should face inward. Install clutch

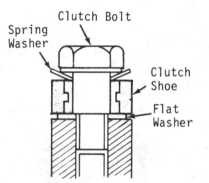

Fig. KU63—Assemble bolt, washers and clutch shoe as shown.

Fig. KU64—Install clutch shoes so arrows on shoes are visible.

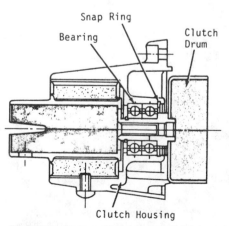

Fig. KU65—Cross-sectional view of clutch housing and drum assembly.

shoes so arrows (Fig. KU64) face outward. Apply a light coat of grease to stud portion of clutch bolt that contacts clutch shoe.

Tighten clutch shoe retaining screws to 4.9-6.6 N·m (43-52 in.-lbs.) on Model G2D, to 4.9-7.8 N·m (43-69 in.-lbs.) on Models G2K and G2KC, and to 10.8-16.6 N·m (96-147 in.-lbs.) on Models G3K and G4K.

Refer to Fig. KU65 for drawing showing clutch drum and bearing assembly, except on Models G2KC. To remove clutch drum on all models except G2KC, dislodge snap ring by working through slots in face of clutch drum. Press against drum shaft to separate drum and bearings from housing. Do not pry

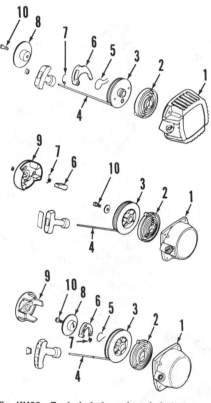

Fig. KU66—Exploded view of rewind starter assemblies. Top starter is used on G2D engine, middle starter is used on G2K, G2KC and G3K engines, and lower starter is used on G4K and blower engines.

1. Housing
2. Rewind spring
3. Pulley
4. Rope
5. Friction spring
6. Ratchet
7. Spring
8. Friction plate
9. Starter plate
10. Screw

Fig. KU67—Starter ratchet must be installed in pulley hole marked "R."

or apply force to drum portion. On Models G2KC, except models with a gear reduction, detach snap ring on end of clutch shaft, then remove clutch drum.

REWIND STARTER. Refer to Fig. KU66 for an exploded view of rewind starter. To disassemble starter, detach starter housing (1) from engine. Remove rope handle and allow rope to wind into starter. Unscrew center screw (10) and remove rope pulley (3). Wear appropriate safety eyewear and gloves before detaching rewind spring (2) from housing as spring may uncoil uncontrolled.

To remove starter plate (9), unscrew retaining nut and use a suitable puller to remove plate from crankshaft.

To assemble starter, lubricate center post of housing and spring side with light grease. Install rewind spring so coil windings are counterclockwise from outer end. Assemble starter while passing rope through housing rope outlet and attach rope handle to rope. To place tension on starter rope, pull rope out of housing. Engage rope in notch on pulley and turn pulley counterclockwise. Hold pulley and disengage rope from pulley notch. Release pulley and allow rope to wind on pulley. Check starter operation. Rope handle should be held against housing by spring tension, but it must be possible to rotate pulley at least $1/4$ turn counterclockwise when rope is pulled out fully.

On Models G2K, G2KC and G3K, ratchet (6) is installed in hole marked "R" (Fig. KU67).

ELECTRIC STARTER. The engine on blowers may be equipped with an electric starter. A battery pack provides electricity to drive the starter and a generating coil adjacent to the flywheel provides charging current for the battery.

The starter motor (2—Fig. KU68) drives the engine through a set of gears (8 and 12) in a gear case attached to the crankcase. Refer to Fig. KU68 for an exploded view of gear case and starter. Starter motor must be serviced as a unit assembly; individual components are not available.

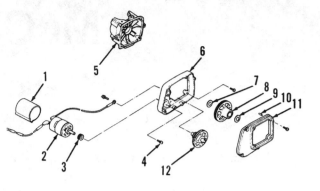

Fig. KU68—Exploded view of electric starter assembly.
1. Cover
2. Starter motor
3. Pinion
4. Screw
5. Crankcase half
6. Gear case
7. Washer
8. Gear
9. Washer
10. Dowel
11. Cover
12. Gear

McCULLOCH

ENGINE SERVICE

Model	Bore	Stroke	Displacement
McCulloch	32.2 mm*	25.4 mm	21.2 cc*
	(1.27 in.)	(1.02 in.)	(1.29 cu. in.)

*Engine on 2500 and 2500AV has a bore of 35 mm (1.38 in.) and a displacement of 25 cc (1.52 cu. in.).

ENGINE INFORMATION

The McCulloch two-stroke, air-cooled engine covered in this section is used on McCulloch string trimmers, brush cutters and blowers.

MAINTENANCE

LUBRICATION. Engine lubrication is obtained by mixing gasoline with an oil designed for two-stroke, air-cooled engines. Refer to service section for trimmer or blower for manufacturer's recommended fuel:oil mixture ratio.

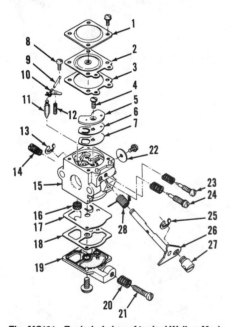

Fig. MC101—Exploded view of typical Walbro Model WA carburetor. Governor valve (14) is not used on some carburetors.

1. Cover	16. Inlet screen
2. Metering diaphragm	17. Fuel pump
3. Gasket	diaphragm
4. Screw	18. Gasket
5. Circuit plate	19. Cover
6. Check valve	20. Spring
7. Gasket	21. Idle speed screw
8. Screw	22. Throttle plate
9. Metering lever pin	23. Idle mixture screw
10. Metering lever	24. High-speed mixture
11. Fuel inlet valve	screw
12. Spring	25. "E" ring
13. "E" ring	26. Throttle shaft
14. Governor valve	27. Swivel
15. Body	28. Spring

SPARK PLUG. Recommended spark plug is a Champion DJ8J or equivalent. Specified electrode gap for all models is 0.63 mm (0.025 in.). Tighten spark plug to 11.9-14.6 N·m (105-130 in.-lbs.).

CARBURETOR. All models are equipped with a diaphragm-type carburetor manufactured by either Walbro or Zama. Refer to following sections for carburetor service.

Walbro Model WA. Refer to Fig. MC101 for an exploded view of carburetor. Initial adjustment of idle mixture screw (23) and high-speed mixture screw (24) is one turn open. Final adjustment is performed with engine at normal operating temperature and cutter line at desired length. Adjust low-speed mixture screw so engine idles smoothly and accelerates cleanly without hesitation. Adjust high-speed mixture screw for best engine performance under load. Do not adjust high-speed mixture screw too lean as engine may be damaged.

When overhauling carburetor, refer to exploded view in Fig. MC101. Examine fuel inlet valve and seat. Inlet valve (11)

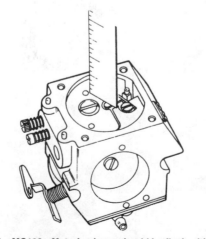

Fig. MC102—Metering lever should be flush with circuit plate as shown on Walbro WA carburetor. Bend lever to obtain correct lever height.

is renewable, but carburetor body (15) must be renewed if seat is excessively worn or damaged. Inspect mixture screws and seats. Renew carburetor body if seats are excessively worn or damaged. Clean fuel screen. Inspect diaphragms (2, 6 and 17) for tears and other damage. Circuit plate (5) must be flat.

Metering lever (10) should be flush with circuit plate (5) as shown in Fig. MC102. Bend lever to obtain correct lever height.

On some models, the carburetor is equipped with a governor valve (14—Fig. MC101) that enriches the mixture at high-speed to prevent overspeeding. The governor valve is not adjustable.

Walbro Model WT. Refer to Fig. MC103 for an exploded view of carburetor. Initial adjustment of idle mixture screw (15) and high-speed mixture screw (14) is one turn open. Final adjustment is performed with engine at normal operating temperature and cutter line at desired length. Adjust low-speed mixture screw so engine idles smoothly and accelerates cleanly without hesitation. Adjust high-speed mixture screw for best engine performance under load. Do not adjust high-speed mixture screw too lean as engine may be damaged.

Carburetor disassembly and reassembly is evident after inspection of carburetor and referral to Fig. MC103. Clean and inspect all components. Inspect diaphragms (2 and 21) for defects that may affect operation. Examine fuel inlet valve and seat. Inlet valve (6) is renewable, but carburetor body (18) must be renewed if seat is damaged or excessively worn. Discard carburetor body if mixture screw seats are damaged or excessively worn. Clean fuel screen (23).

Check metering lever height as shown in Fig. MC104 using Walbro tool 500-13. Metering lever should just touch leg on tool. Bend lever to obtain correct lever height.

On some models, the carburetor is equipped with a governor valve (30—Fig. MC103) that enriches the mixture

Illustrations courtesy McCulloch Corp.

at high-speed to prevent overspeeding. The governor valve is not adjustable.

Some models are equipped with a primer bulb (27). Inspect primer bulb and reject if cracked, hardened or otherwise damaged.

Zama Model C1S or C1U. Refer to Fig. MC105 or MC106 for an exploded view of carburetor. Initial adjustment of idle mixture screw (19) and high-speed mixture screw (18) is 1-1¼ turns out from a lightly seated position.

Final adjustment is performed with engine at normal operating temperature. Before final adjustment on trimmer models, cutter line should be at recommended length. Adjust idle speed screw (20 or 20A) to obtain desired idle speed. Adjust idle mixture screw (19) so engine idles smoothly and accelerates cleanly without hesitation. Open throttle to wide-open position and adjust high-speed mixture screw (18) to obtain highest engine rpm, then turn high-

speed mixture screw ⅛ turn counter-clockwise.

Carburetor disassembly and reassembly is evident after inspection of carburetor and referral to Figs. MC105 or MC106. Clean and inspect all components. Exercise care when removing Welch plug by piercing plug with a punch. Insert punch in center of plug, but do not insert punch deeply as underlying body metal may be damaged. When removing key-shaped Welch plug (14—Fig. MC106) on Model C1U, pierce

"tail" portion with a suitable punch. Apply sealant to new plug. Do not use wire or drill bits to clean fuel passages. Inspect diaphragms for defects that may affect operation. Examine fuel inlet valve and seat. Inlet valve (11) is renewable, but carburetor body must be renewed if seat is damaged or excessively worn. Discard carburetor body if mixture screw seats are damaged or excessively worn. Clean fuel screen (26). Model C1U may be equipped with a primer bulb (2—Fig. MC106). Inspect

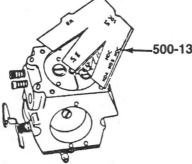

Fig. MC104—Metering lever should just touch leg of Walbro tool 500-13. Bend lever to obtain correct lever height.

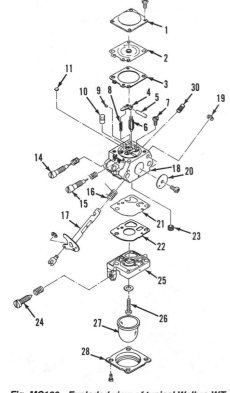

Fig. MC103—Exploded view of typical Walbro WT carburetor. Some models are not equipped with a governor valve (30).

1. Cover	17. Throttle shaft
2. Metering diaphragm	18. Carburetor body
3. Gasket	19. "E" ring
4. Metering lever	20. Throttle plate
5. Pin	21. Fuel pump
6. Fuel inlet valve	diaphragm
7. Screw	22. Gasket
8. Spring	23. Fuel inlet screen
9. Welch plug	24. Idle speed screw
10. Check valve	25. Cover
11. Welch plug	26. Screw
14. High-speed mixture	27. Primer bulb
screw	28. Cover
15. Idle mixture screw	30. Governor valve
16. Spring	

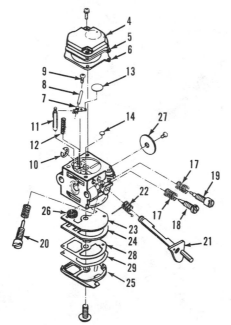

Fig. MC105—Exploded view of typical Zama C1S carburetor.

4. Cover	
5. Metering diaphragm	
6. Gasket	
7. Fuel metering lever	19. Idle mixture screw
8. Pin	20. Idle speed screw
9. Screw	21. Throttle shaft
10. "E" ring	22. Spring
11. Fuel inlet valve	23. Fuel pump
12. Spring	diaphragm
13. Fuel metering lever	24. Retainer
disc	25. Pump cover
14. Welch plug	26. Screen
17. Spring	27. Throttle plate
18. High-speed mixture	28. Gasket
screw	29. Surge diaphragm

Fig. MC106—Exploded view of typical Zama C1U carburetor. Primer bulb assembly may be located as shown by parts (1, 2, 3 and 4) or (1A, 2A, 3A and 25A) depending on application. On later models, or on models with a replacement primer bulb, spring (3 or 3A) is not used.

1. Cover	14. Welch plug
1A. Cover	15. Retainer
2. Primer bulb	16. Check valve
2A. Primer bulb	17. Spring
3. Spring	18. High-speed
3A. Spring	mixture screw
4. Primer base	19. Idle mixture screw
4A. Cover	20. Idle speed screw
5. Metering	20A. Idle speed screw
diaphragm	21. Throttle shaft
6. Gasket	22. Spring
7. Metering lever	23. Fuel pump
8. Pin	diaphragm
9. Screw	24. Gasket
10. "E" ring	25. Cover
11. Fuel inlet valve	25A. Primer base
12. Spring	26. Fuel inlet screen
13. Check valve	27. Throttle plate
nozzle	28. Carburetor body

primer bulb and reject if cracked, hardened or otherwise damaged.

To reassemble carburetor, reverse disassembly procedure. Note the two types of metering levers in Fig. MC107. Adjust clearance "A" to 0-0.03 mm (0-0.012 inch).

IGNITION SYSTEM. The engine is equipped with an electronic ignition system. Ignition system performance is considered satisfactory if a spark will jump across a 3 mm (⅛ in.) electrode gap on a test spark plug. If no spark is produced, check on/off switch, wiring and ignition module air gap. Air gap between ignition module and flywheel magnet should be 0.25 mm (0.010 in.).

If switch, wiring and module air gap are satisfactory, but spark is not present, renew ignition module.

Three variations of the ignition system have been used, with each variation identified by the color of the ignition module (28—Fig. MC108). The module may be orange, black or cream. The flywheel and module combination must be correct or ignition timing will be wrong.

Later models may be equipped with the black or cream ignition module. A flywheel stamped with a "S" must be used with a black ignition module. A flywheel stamped with "FL" must be used with a cream ignition module.

Early models may be equipped with a black or orange ignition module. Some

replacement flywheels for early models had two keyways marked "S" and "W." On models with a black ignition module, the key must engage the "S" keyway in the flywheel. On models with an orange ignition module, the key must engage the "W" keyway in the flywheel. See Fig. MC109.

REPAIRS

TIGHTENING TORQUES. Recommended tightening torque specifications are as follows:

Crankcase . . . . .4.0-4.8 N·m
(35-43 in.-lbs.)
Crankshaft nut . . . . .17.0-19.0 N·m
(150-168 in.-lbs.)
Cylinder . . . . .8.0-9.1 N·m
(71-81 in.-lbs.)
Spark plug . . . . .12.2-15.2 N·m
(108-135 in.-lbs.)

PISTON, PIN AND RINGS. The piston (20—Fig. MC108) is accessible after removing cylinder (23). Remove piston pin retainers (18) and use a suitable puller to extract pin (19) from piston. Note that some models are equipped with thrust washers on each side of connecting rod bearing (17) that will be loose when pin is removed.

Install piston on connecting rod so arrow on piston crown will point toward the exhaust port when the cylinder is installed.

The piston is equipped with a single piston ring. Piston ring rotation is prevented by a locating pin in the pis-

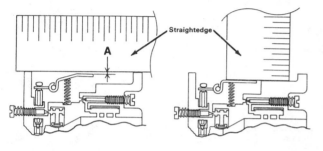

Fig. MC107—Note shape of metering lever and refer to drawing for correct metering lever height. Stepped-type metering lever should be bent so height (A) is 0-0.3 mm (0.000-0.012 in.). Straight-type metering lever should be flush with chamber floor as shown.

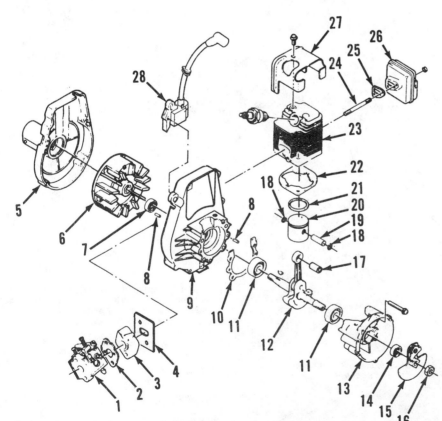

Fig. MC108—Exploded view of typical McCulloch engine. Cylinder (23) is rotated 180 degrees on some models, depending upon application.

1. Carburetor	6. Flywheel	12. Crankshaft &
2. Gasket	7. Seal	connecting rod assy.
3. Insulator	8. Pins	13. Crankcase cover
4. Gasket/insulator	9. Crankcase	14. Seal
shield	10. Gasket	15. Ratchet assy.
5. Fan housing	11. Bearings	16. Nut

17. Bearing	23. Cylinder
18. Retainer	24. Stud
19. Piston pin	25. Gasket
20. Piston	26. Muffler
21. Piston ring	27. Cylinder cover
22. Gasket	28. Ignition module

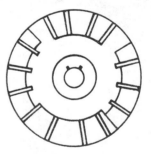

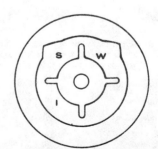

Fig. MC109—Early model flywheels may have two keyways. Engage "S" keyway if ignition module is black, or engage "W" keyway if ignition module is orange.

ton ring groove. Make certain ring end gap is correctly positioned around locating pin before installing piston in cylinder.

Standard piston diameter is 32.1 mm (1.264 in.). If piston diameter is 32.08 mm (1.263 in.) or less, renew piston. Oversize pistons are not available.

Standard piston pin bore diameter is 8.0 mm (0.3149 in.). If piston pin bore diameter is 8.3 mm (0.3268 in.) or more, renew piston.

Standard piston pin diameter is 8.0 mm (0.3149 in.). If piston pin diameter is 7.98 mm (0.3142 in.) or less, renew piston pin.

Standard ring side clearance in piston groove is 0.06 mm (0.0024 in.). If ring side clearance is 0.10 mm (0.004 in.) or more, renew ring and/or piston.

CYLINDER. The cylinder bore is chrome plated. Renew cylinder if plating of bore is worn through, scored or otherwise damaged. Worn spots will appear dull and may be easily scratched, while chrome plating will be bright and much harder.

CRANKSHAFT AND CONNECTING ROD. The crankshaft and connecting rod are serviced as an assembly; individual components are not available.

To remove crankshaft and connecting rod assembly, remove fan housing and clutch assembly. Remove carburetor, muffler and fuel tank. Remove starter assembly, flywheel and ignition module. Carefully remove cylinder (23—Fig. MC108). Remove retaining rings (18) and use a suitable piston pin puller to remove pin (19) and separate piston (20) from connecting rod. Unbolt and separate crankcase halves (9 and 13) and remove crankshaft assembly (12). When separating crankcase halves, main bearings (11) may remain on crankshaft or in crankcase. If bearing remains in crankcase, it may be necessary to heat crankcase slightly to loosen bearing for removal.

To install crankshaft assembly, reverse removal procedure. If necessary, heat crankcase halves to ease installation of bearings. Inner face of bearing should

be 11 mm (0.43 in.) from crankcase mating surface.

CLUTCH. Some models are equipped with the two-shoe clutch assembly shown in Fig. MC110. With clutch housing (1) separated from engine, press against shaft end of drum (5) to dislodge bearing (4) and drum from housing. Remove snap ring (3) and press bearing off drum shaft. Unscrew clutch hub (6) from crankshaft for access to clutch shoes (7) and springs (8). Springs are available as a pair. Clutch shoes are available only as an assembly with hub and springs.

When assembling unit, note that washer (2) is installed with concave side toward snap ring (3). Lightly oil outside of bearing (4) and press drum and bearing assembly into housing until bearing is seated.

REWIND STARTER. Refer to Fig. MC111 for an exploded view of rewind starter. To disassemble starter, remove starter from engine. Pull rope handle so rope is aligned with notch on pulley (3). Place rope in notch, pull rope slack into housing then allow pulley to unwind. Wear appropriate safety eyewear and gloves before disengaging pulley from starter housing (5) as rewind spring may uncoil uncontrolled. Place shop towel around pulley, remove screw (1) and lift pulley out of housing; spring (4) should remain in starter housing. If spring must be removed from housing, position housing so spring side is down and against floor, then tap housing to dislodge spring.

Before assembling starter, lubricate center post of housing and spring side of pulley with light grease. Install rewind spring (4) in a counterclockwise direction from outer end. Assemble starter while passing rope through housing rope outlet and attach rope handle to rope. To place tension on starter rope, rotate pulley counterclockwise so notch in pulley is aligned with rope outlet, then hold pulley to prevent pulley rotation. Pull rope back into housing while positioning rope in pulley notch. Turn rope pulley counterclockwise un-

til spring is tight. Allow pulley to turn clockwise until notch aligns with rope outlet. Disengage rope from notch then release pulley and allow rope to wind on pulley. Check starter operation. Rope handle should be held against housing by spring tension, but it must be possible to rotate pulley at least $\frac{1}{4}$ turn counterclockwise when rope is pulled out fully.

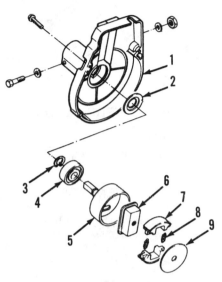

Fig. MC110—Exploded view of clutch assembly used on some models.

1. Housing	
2. Washer	6. Clutch hub
3. Snap ring	7. Clutch shoes
4. Bearing	8. Clutch springs
5. Clutch drum	9. Washer

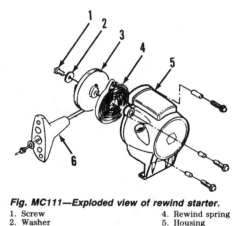

Fig. MC111—Exploded view of rewind starter.

1. Screw	4. Rewind spring
2. Washer	5. Housing
3. Pulley	6. Rope handle

McCULLOCH

ENGINE SERVICE

Model	Bore	Stroke	Displacement
McCulloch	32.2 mm	25.4 mm	21.2 cc
	(1.27 in.)	(1.02 in.)	(1.29 cu. in.)

This engine is used on McCulloch Models EAGER BEAVER SUPER, EAGER BEAVER SUPER-SL, MAC 65 and MAC 65-SL.

ENGINE INFORMATION

The McCulloch engine covered in this section is a two-stroke, air-cooled, single-cylinder engine.

MAINTENANCE

LUBRICATION. Engine lubrication is obtained by mixing gasoline with an oil designed for two-stroke, air-cooled engines. Refer to service section for trimmer for manufacturer's recommended fuel:oil mixture ratio.

SPARK PLUG. Recommended spark plug is a Champion DJ8J or equivalent. Specified electrode gap for all models is 0.63 mm (0.025 in.). Tighten spark plug to 11.9-14.6 N·m (105-130 in.-lbs.).

CARBURETOR. All models are equipped with a diaphragm-type carburetor manufactured by Walbro. Models MAC 65 and EAGER BEAVER SUPER are equipped with a Walbro Model WA, while Models MAC 65-SL and EAGER BEAVER SUPER-SL are equipped with a Walbro Model WT. Refer to following sections for carburetor service.

Walbro Model WA. Refer to Fig. MC201 for an exploded view of carburetor. Initial adjustment of idle mixture screw (24) and high-speed mixture screw (26) is one turn open. Final adjustment is performed with engine at normal operating temperature and cutter line at desired length. Adjust idle speed screw (21) to obtain desired idle speed. Adjust low-speed mixture screw (24) so engine idles smoothly and accelerates cleanly without hesitation.

Adjust high-speed mixture screw (26) for best engine performance under load. Do not adjust high-speed mixture screw too lean as engine may be damaged.

When overhauling carburetor, refer to exploded view in Fig. MC201. Examine fuel inlet valve and seat. Inlet valve (11) is renewable, but carburetor body (15) must be renewed if seat is excessively worn or damaged. Inspect mixture screws and seats. Renew carburetor body if seats are excessively worn or damaged. Clean fuel screen (16). Inspect diaphragms (2, 6 and 17) for tears and other damage. Circuit plate (5) must be flat.

Metering lever (10) should be flush with circuit plate (5) as shown in Fig. MC202. Bend lever to obtain correct lever height.

Walbro Model WT. Refer to Fig. MC203 for an exploded view of carburetor. Initial adjustment of idle mixture screw (14) and high-speed mixture screw (16) is one turn open. Final adjustment is performed with engine at normal operating temperature and cutter line at desired length. Adjust idle speed screw (25) to obtain desired idle speed. Adjust low-speed mixture screw (14) so engine idles smoothly and accelerates cleanly without hesitation. Adjust high-speed mixture screw (16) for best engine performance under load. Do not adjust high-speed mixture screw too lean as engine may be damaged.

Carburetor disassembly and reassembly is evident after inspection of carburetor and referral to Fig. MC203. Clean and inspect all components. Inspect diaphragms (2 and 21) for defects that may affect operation. Examine fuel inlet valve and seat. Inlet valve (7) is renewable, but carburetor body must be renewed if seat is damaged or excessively worn. Discard carburetor body if mixture screw seats are damaged or excessively worn. Clean fuel screen (23).

Check metering lever height as shown in Fig. MC204 using Walbro tool 500-13. Metering lever should just touch leg on tool. Bend lever to obtain correct lever height.

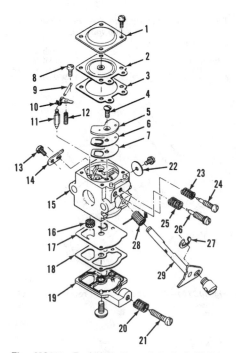

Fig. MC201—Exploded view of typical Walbro Model WA carburetor.

1. Cover	17. Fuel pump
2. Metering diaphragm	diaphragm
3. Gasket	18. Gasket
4. Screw	19. Cover
5. Circuit plate	20. Spring
6. Check valve	21. Idle speed screw
7. Gasket	22. Throttle plate
8. Screw	23. Spring
9. Metering lever pin	24. Idle mixture screw
10. Metering lever	25. Spring
11. Fuel inlet valve	26. High-speed mixture
12. Spring	screw
13. Screw	27. "E" ring
14. Retainer	28. Spring
15. Body	29. Throttle shaft
16. Inlet screen	

Fig. MC202—Metering lever should be flush with circuit plate (5) as shown on Walbro WA carburetor. Bend lever to obtain correct lever height.

Illustrations courtesy McCulloch Corp.

IGNITION SYSTEM. The engine is equipped with an electronic ignition system. Ignition system performance is considered satisfactory if a spark will jump across a 3 mm ($\frac{1}{8}$ in.) electrode gap on a test spark plug. If no spark is produced, check on/off switch, wiring and ignition module air gap. Air gap between ignition module and flywheel magnet should be 0.3 mm (0.012 in.). If switch, wiring and module air gap are satisfactory, but spark is not present, renew ignition module.

REPAIRS

TIGHTENING TORQUES. Recommended tightening torque specifications are as follows:

Crankcase . . . . .4.0-4.8 N·m
(35-43 in.-lbs.)
Crankshaft nut . . . . . . .17.0-19.0 N·m
(150-168 in.-lbs.)
Cylinder . . . . .8.0-9.1 N·m
(71-81 in.-lbs.)
Spark plug . . . . .12.2-15.2 N·m
(108-135 in.-lbs.)

PISTON, PIN AND RING. The piston (6—Fig. MC205) is accessible after removing cylinder (3). Remove piston pin retainers (9) and use a suitable puller to extract pin (7) from piston.

Install piston on connecting rod so arrow on piston crown will point toward exhaust port when the cylinder is installed.

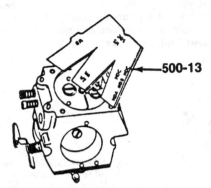

Fig. MC204—Metering lever should just touch leg of Walbro tool 500-13. Bend lever to obtain correct lever height.

The piston is equipped with a single piston ring (5). Piston ring rotation is prevented by a locating pin in the piston ring groove. Make certain ring end gap is correctly positioned around locating pin before installing piston in cylinder.

Standard piston diameter is 32.1 mm (1.268 in.). If piston diameter is 32.08 mm (1.263 in.) or less, renew piston. Oversize pistons are not available.

Standard piston pin bore diameter is 8.0 mm (0.315 in.). If piston pin bore diameter is 8.03 mm (0.316 in.) or more, renew piston.

Standard piston pin diameter is 8.0 mm (0.315 in.). If piston pin diameter is 7.98 mm (0.3142 in.) or less, renew piston pin.

Standard ring side clearance in piston groove is 0.06 mm (0.0024 in.). If ring side clearance is 0.10 mm (0.004 in.) or more, renew piston.

CYLINDER. Inspect cylinder and renew if scratched, scored or otherwise damaged. Cylinder is available in standard size only.

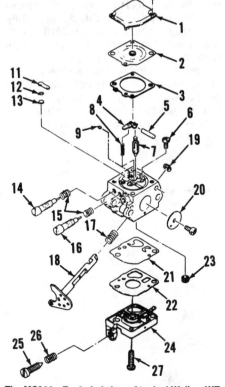

Fig. MC203—Exploded view of typical Walbro WT carburetor.

1. Cover	16. High-speed mixture
2. Metering diaphragm	screw
3. Gasket	17. Spring
4. Metering lever	18. Throttle shaft
5. Pin	19. "E" ring
6. Screw	20. Throttle plate
7. Fuel inlet valve	21. Fuel pump
8. Spring	diaphragm
9. Welch plug	22. Gasket
11. Welch plug	23. Fuel inlet screen
12. Retainer	24. Cover
13. Screen	25. Idle speed screw
14. Idle mixture screw	26. Spring
15. Spring	27. Screw

Fig. MC205—Exploded view of engine.

1. Muffler	8. Connecting rod	14. Gasket	20. Bearing housing	26. Spacer
2. Cylinder cover	9. Snap rings (2)	15. Dowel pin	21. Snap ring	27. Carburetor
3. Cylinder	10. Crankcase cover	16. Crankcase	22. Flywheel	28. Gasket
4. Gasket	11. Crankshaft	17. Seal	23. Washer	29. Insulator
5. Piston ring	12. Keys	18. Washer	24. Coupling	30. Gasket/insulator
6. Piston	13. Main bearing	19. Fan	25. Ignition module	shield
7. Piston pin				

CRANKSHAFT AND CONNECTING ROD. The engine is equipped with a half-crankshaft (11—Fig. MC205) that is supported by bearing (13) and a sealed bearing in bearing plate (20).

To remove crankshaft and connecting rod, remove recoil starter housing, fuel tank, carburetor (27), muffler (1), cylinder cover (2) and spark plug. Install a piston stop tool or insert end of a rope through spark plug hole to lock piston and crankshaft. Remove coupling (24) and pull flywheel (22) off crankshaft. Remove ignition module (25) and spacer (26). Remove cylinder mounting screws

and pull cylinder (3) from piston. Remove retaining rings (9) and separate piston pin (7) and piston (6) from connecting rod. Remove snap ring (21) and bearing plate (20). Remove fan (19) from crankshaft. Remove crankcase cover (10) from crankcase (16) and withdraw crankshaft and connecting rod from crankcase. Press main bearing (13) and seal (17) from crankcase.

Bearing plate (20) is available only as an assembly. Bearings in connecting rod (8) are not available separately. Inspect components for damage and excessive wear and renew as needed.

REWIND STARTER. The engine is equipped with the rewind starter shown in Fig. MC206. To disassemble starter, disconnect throttle cable (14) and detach trigger housing (11) from starter housing (6). Disconnect stop switch wire (3) from engine. Separate starter housing from engine. Remove rope handle (4) and allow rope to wind into starter. Wear appropriate safety eyewear and gloves when working with or around rewind spring (7) as spring may uncoil uncontrolled. Remove screw (10) and pulley retainer (9) and remove starter pulley (8). Spring (7) should remain in starter housing (6). If spring must be removed from housing, position housing so spring side is down and against floor, then tap housing to dislodge spring.

Before assembling starter, lubricate center post of housing and side of spring with light grease. Assemble starter while passing rope through housing rope outlet and attach rope handle to rope. To place tension on starter rope, rotate pulley clockwise so notch in pulley is aligned with rope outlet, then hold pulley to prevent pulley rotation. Pull rope back into housing while positioning rope in pulley notch. Turn rope pulley clockwise until spring is tight. Allow pulley to turn counterclockwise until notch aligns with rope outlet. Disengage rope from notch then release pulley and allow rope to wind on pulley. Check starter operation. Rope handle should be held against housing by spring tension, but it must be possible to rotate pulley at least $1/4$ turn clockwise when rope is pulled out fully.

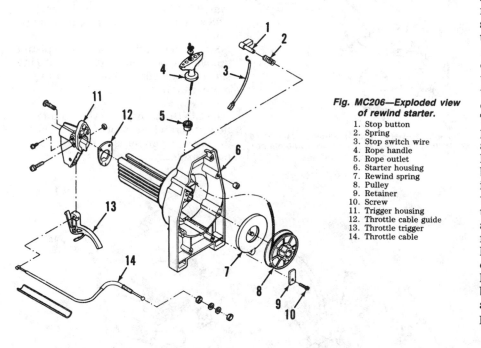

Fig. MC206—Exploded view of rewind starter.

1. Stop button
2. Spring
3. Stop switch wire
4. Rope handle
5. Rope outlet
6. Starter housing
7. Rewind spring
8. Pulley
9. Retainer
10. Screw
11. Trigger housing
12. Throttle cable guide
13. Throttle trigger
14. Throttle cable

McCULLOCH

ENGINE SERVICE

Model	Bore	Stroke	Displacement
McCulloch	...	...	30 cc
			(1.83 cu. in.)
McCulloch	...	...	38 cc
			(2.32 cu. in.)

These engines are used on McCulloch Models PRO SCAPER III, IV and V.

ENGINE INFORMATION

The McCulloch engines covered in this section are two-stroke, air-cooled, single-cylinder engines.

MAINTENANCE

LUBRICATION. Engine lubrication is obtained by mixing gasoline with an oil designed for two-stroke, air-cooled engines. Refer to trimmer service section for manufacturer's recommended fuel:oil mixture ratio.

SPARK PLUG. Recommended spark plug is a Champion RDJ8J or equivalent. Specified electrode gap for all models is 0.63 mm (0.025 in.). Tighten spark plug to 11.9-14.6 N·m (105-130 in.-lbs.).

CARBURETOR. All models are equipped with a Tillotson diaphragm-type carburetor. Refer to Fig. MC301 for an exploded view of carburetor.

Initial adjustment of low-speed mixture screw (13) is one turn open from a lightly seated position. Final adjustment is made with engine running at normal operating temperature. Adjust idle speed screw (17) to obtain desired idle speed. String trimmer head or blade should not turn when engine is running at idle speed. Adjust low-speed mixture screw so engine idles smoothly and accelerates cleanly without hesitation.

Disassembly is evident after inspection of unit and referral to Fig. MC301. Clean fuel screen (21). Inspect spring (7) and renew if stretched or damaged. Inspect diaphragms (2 and 20) for tears, cracks and other damage. Renew mixture screws if tips are broken or grooved. Carburetor body must be renewed if mixture screw seats are damaged or excessively worn. Fuel inlet valve seat in carburetor body is not renewable; body must be renewed if seat is damaged or excessively worn.

Check height of metering lever (4) when assembling carburetor. Lever must be flush with chamber floor as shown in Fig. MC302. Bend lever adjacent to spring to obtain correct lever position.

IGNITION SYSTEM. The engine is equipped with an electronic ignition system. Ignition system performance is considered satisfactory if a spark will jump across a 3 mm (1/8 in.) electrode gap on a test spark plug. If no spark is produced, check on/off switch, wiring and ignition module air gap. Air gap between ignition module and flywheel magnet should be 0.25-0.30 mm (0.010-0.012 in.). If switch, wiring and module air gap are satisfactory, but spark is not present, renew ignition module.

REPAIRS

PISTON, PIN AND RINGS. Piston (5—Fig. MC303) is accessible after removing cylinder (2) from crankcase. Remove retaining rings (7) and push piston pin (6) out of piston. Separate piston from connecting rod.

The piston is fitted with two compression rings (4). A locating pin in each piston ring groove prevents ring rotation. Make certain that piston ring gaps are correctly positioned around locating pins when installing cylinder and that ring end gaps face exhaust port side of cylinder.

The piston pin (6) rides in a needle bearing (8) in the connecting rod small end. Bearing is available separately from rod.

Piston is available in standard size only.

CYLINDER. The cylinder bore is chrome plated. Renew cylinder if plating in bore is worn through, scored or otherwise damaged. Worn spots will appear dull and may be easily scratched, while chrome plating will be bright and much harder.

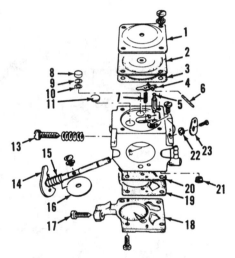

Fig. MC301—Exploded view of Tillotson HU carburetor.

1. Cover	14. Throttle shaft
2. Metering diaphragm	15. Spring
3. Gasket	16. Throttle plate
4. Metering lever	17. Idle speed adjust
5. Fuel inlet valve	screw
6. Pin	18. Cover
7. Spring	19. Gasket
8. Welch plug	20. Fuel pump
9. Retainer	diaphragm
10. Screen	21. Screen
11. Welch plug	22. "E" ring
13. Idle mixture screw	23. Arm

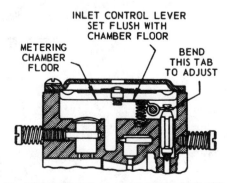

Fig. MC302—Metering lever should be flush with chamber floor as shown above.

CRANKSHAFT AND CONNECTING ROD. The crankshaft and connecting rod are serviced as an assembly; individual components are not available.

To remove crankshaft assembly, first separate engine from trimmer drive shaft housing. Remove recoil starter assembly, muffler, fuel tank and carburetor. Remove spark plug and install a piston locking tool or insert end of a rope through spark plug hole to lock piston and crankshaft. Remove nuts (9 and 20) and withdraw clutch assembly (11—Fig. MC303) and flywheel (19) from crankshaft. Unbolt and remove cylinder (2). Remove retaining rings (7) and piston pin (6) to separate piston from connecting rod. Carefully separate crankcase halves (13 and 17) and remove crankshaft assembly from crankcase. Remove main bearings (15) and seals (12 and 18) as necessary.

To install crankshaft and connecting rod, reverse the removal procedure.

REED VALVE. All models are equipped with a reed valve induction system. Inspect reed valve petals and seats on reed valve plate (22—Fig. MC303). Renew reed valve assembly if petals or seats are damaged.

CLUTCH. Individual components for the clutch (11—Fig. MC303) are not available. Clutch must be serviced as a unit assembly.

REWIND STARTER. To disassemble starter, remove starter housing (8—Fig. MC304) from crankcase. Slide pinion (4) forward and detach spring (5). Pull starter rope and hold rope pulley with notch in pulley adjacent to rope outlet of housing. Pull rope back through rope outlet so it engages notch in pulley and allow pulley to completely unwind. Remove screw (1), washers (2 and 3) and pinion (4). Detach rope handle and remove pulley (6) while being careful not to dislodge rewind spring (7) in housing

(8). Wear appropriate safety eyewear and gloves when working with or around rewind spring (7) as spring may uncoil uncontrolled.

Install rewind spring (7) in housing so coil direction is counterclockwise from outer end. Assemble starter while passing rope through housing rope outlet and attach rope handle to rope. To place tension on starter rope, rotate pulley counterclockwise so notch in pulley is aligned with rope outlet, then hold pulley to prevent pulley rotation. Pull rope back into housing while positioning rope in pulley notch. Turn rope pulley counterclockwise until spring is tight. Allow pulley to turn clockwise until notch aligns with rope outlet. Disengage rope from notch, then release pulley and allow rope to wind on pulley. Check starter operation. Do not place more tension on rewind spring than is necessary to draw rope handle up against housing. Install spring (5) and check starter action.

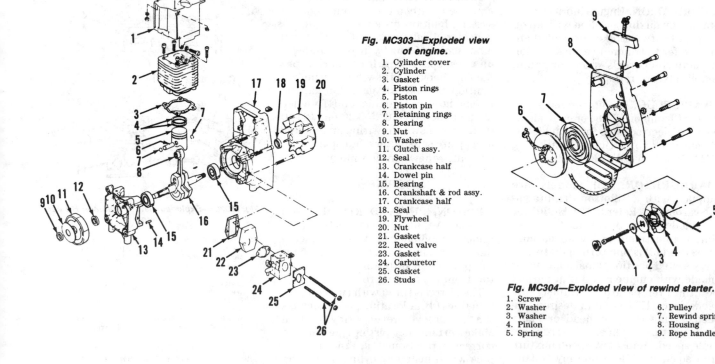

Fig. MC303—Exploded view of engine.
1. Cylinder cover
2. Cylinder
3. Gasket
4. Piston rings
5. Piston
6. Piston pin
7. Retaining rings
8. Bearing
9. Nut
10. Washer
11. Clutch assy.
12. Seal
13. Crankcase half
14. Dowel pin
15. Bearing
16. Crankshaft & rod assy.
17. Crankcase half
18. Seal
19. Flywheel
20. Nut
21. Gasket
22. Reed valve
23. Gasket
24. Carburetor
25. Gasket
26. Studs

Fig. MC304—Exploded view of rewind starter.
1. Screw
2. Washer
3. Washer
4. Pinion
5. Spring
6. Pulley
7. Rewind spring
8. Housing
9. Rope handle

MITSUBISHI

ENGINE SERVICE

Model	Bore	Stroke	Displacement
T110	30 mm	30 mm	21.2 cc
	(1.18 in.)	(1.18 in.)	(1.29 cu. in.)
TMX-21	30 mm	30 mm	21.2 cc
	(1.18 in.)	(1.18 in.)	(1.29 cu. in.)
T140	32 mm	30 mm	24.1 cc
	(1.26 in.)	(1.18 in.)	(1.47 cu. in.)
TM-24	32 mm	30 mm	24.1 cc
	(1.26 in.)	(1.18 in.)	(1.47 cu. in.)
T180	36 mm	32 mm	32.5 cc
	(1.42 in.)	(1.26 in.)	(1.98 cu. in.)
T200	39 mm	34 mm	40.6 cc
	(1.54 in.)	(1.34 in.)	(2.48 cu. in.)

ENGINE INFORMATION

Mitsubishi two-stroke, air-cooled gasoline engines are used by several manufacturers of string trimmers, brush cutters and blowers.

MAINTENANCE

LUBRICATION. Engine lubrication is obtained by mixing gasoline with an oil designed for two-stroke, air-cooled engines. Refer to equipment service section for manufacturer's recommended fuel:oil mixture ratio.

SPARK PLUG. Recommended spark plug is a NGK BM6A or equivalent. Specified electrode gap for all models is 0.6 mm (0.024 in.).

CARBURETOR. Various types of carburetors have been used. Refer to the appropriate following section for carburetor service.

Walbro WY and WYJ. Some engines may be equipped with a Walbro WY or WYJ carburetor. This is a diaphragm-type carburetor that uses a barrel-type throttle rather than a throttle plate.

Idle fuel for the carburetor flows up into the throttle barrel where it is fed into the air stream. On some models, the idle fuel flow can be adjusted by turning an idle mixture limiter plate (P—Fig. MI51). Initial setting is in center notch. Rotating the plate clockwise will lean the idle mixture. Inside the limiter plate is an idle mixture needle (N—Fig. MI52) that is preset at the factory. If removed, use the following procedure to determine correct position. Back out needle (N) until unscrewed. Screw in needle 5

turns on Model WY or 15 turns on Model WYJ. Rotate idle mixture plate (P—Fig. MI51) to center notch. Run engine until normal operating temperature is attained. Adjust idle speed screw (I) so trimmer head or blade does not rotate. Rotate idle mixture needle (N—Fig. MI52) and obtain highest rpm (turning needle clockwise leans the mixture), then turn needle ¼ turn counterclockwise. Readjust idle speed screw. Note that idle mixture plate and needle are available only as an assembly with throttle barrel.

The high-speed mixture is controlled by a removable fixed jet (16—Fig. MI53).

To overhaul carburetor, refer to exploded view in Fig. MI53 and note the following: On models with a plastic body, clean only with solvents approved for use with plastic. Do not disassemble throttle barrel assembly. Examine fuel inlet valve and seat. Inlet valve (9) is renewable, but fuel pump body (11) must be renewed if seat is excessively worn or damaged. Clean fuel screen (18). Inspect diaphragms for tears and other damage. When installing plates and gaskets (12 through 15) note that tabs (T) on ends will "stairstep" when correctly installed. Adjust metering lever height to obtain 1.5 mm (0.059 in.) between carburetor body surface and lever as shown in Fig. MI54.

Throttle Slide-Type Carburetor. Some models are equipped with the diaphragm carburetor shown in Fig. MI55. A throttle slide (11—Fig. MI56) is used in place of a throttle plate.

Initial adjustment of high-speed mixture screw (4—Fig. MI55) is 2½ turns out from a lightly seated position. Final adjustment is performed with trimmer line fully extended or blade assembly installed. Engine should be at operating temperature and running. Operate trimmer at full throttle and adjust high-speed mixture screw to obtain maximum engine output with smooth acceleration. Turning mixture screw counterclockwise enriches mixture.

Normal position of jet needle clip (6—Fig. MI56) is in the center groove on jet needle (7). When installing metering diaphragm lever, adjust metering lever height to obtain 0.5 mm (0.020 in.) be-

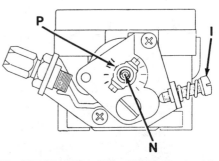

Fig. MI51—On Walbro WY or WYJ carburetor, idle speed screw is located at (I), idle mixture limiter plate is located at (P) and idle mixture needle is located at (N). A plug covers the idle mixture needle.

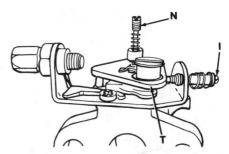

Fig. MI52—View of idle mixture needle (N) used on Walbro WY and WYJ carburetors.

tween carburetor body surface and lever as shown in Fig. MI54.

IGNITION SYSTEM. Models T110, T140, T180, TMX-21, TM-24 and later Model T200 are equipped with an electronic ignition system. Early Model T200 is equipped with a breaker-point-type ignition system.

Ignition system performance is considered satisfactory if a spark will jump across a 3 mm (1/8 in.) electrode gap on a test spark plug. If no spark is produced, check on/off switch, wiring and ignition module air gap. Air gap on models with an ignition module should be 0.3-0.4 mm (0.012-0.016 in.). If switch, wiring and module air gap are satisfactory, but spark is not present, renew ignition module.

Breaker points and condenser on early Model T200 are located behind flywheel. Breaker point gap should be 0.28-0.38 mm (0.011-0.015 in.). Air gap between ignition coil and flywheel should be 0.41-0.50 mm (0.016-0.020 in.). Points should be adjusted so points begin to open as match mark on flywheel aligns with "M" or "P" mark cast on crankcase.

REPAIRS

CYLINDER, PISTON, PIN AND RINGS. The piston is accessible after removing cylinder. Remove piston pin retainers and use a suitable puller to extract pin from piston.

The piston is equipped with two piston rings. Ring rotation is prevented by a locating pin in each piston ring groove. Piston is available in standard size only.

Standard piston ring end gap is 0.1-0.3 mm (0.004-0.012 in.) for all models. If ring end gap exceeds 0.7 mm (0.028 in.), renew rings and/or cylinder.

CRANKSHAFT, CONNECTING ROD AND CRANKCASE. See Fig. MI57 for an exploded view of the T200 engine. Crankshaft, connecting rod and rod bearing are a unit assembly; individual components are not available. The crankshaft is supported by ball bearings at both ends. A renewable needle bearing is located in the small end of the connecting rod.

To remove crankshaft, separate the engine from trimmer drive shaft or blower housing. Remove all cooling shrouds and rewind starter assembly. Remove muffler and carburetor. Remove ignition module or coil. Remove flywheel and clutch (if used) from crankshaft. Remove all cylinder retaining bolts, then carefully separate cylinder from crankcase. Cylinder should be pulled straight off piston with no twisting motion. Remove all crankcase retaining bolts, separate crankcase halves

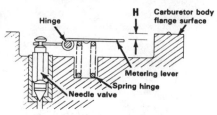
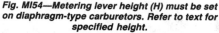

Fig. MI54—Metering lever height (H) must be set on diaphragm-type carburetors. Refer to text for specified height.

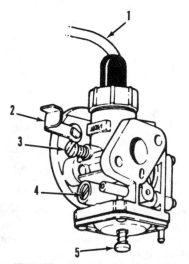

Fig. MI55—View of slide-valve-type diaphragm carburetor used on some models.

1. Throttle cable	4. High-speed mixture screw
2. Choke lever	
3. Idle speed screw	5. Primer button

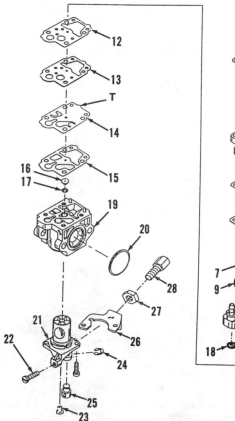

Fig. MI53—Exploded view of Walbro WYJ. Model WY is similar.

1. Cover
2. Primer bulb
4. Plate
5. Metering diaphragm
6. Gasket
7. Metering lever
8. Pin
9. Fuel inlet valve
10. Spring
11. Fuel pump body
12. Gasket
13. Fuel pump plate
14. Fuel pump diaphragm
15. Gasket
16. Main jet
17. "O" ring
18. Fuel screen
19. Body
20. "O" ring
21. Throttle barrel assy.
22. Idle speed screw
23. Plug
24. "E" ring
25. Swivel
26. Bracket
27. Nut
28. Adjuster

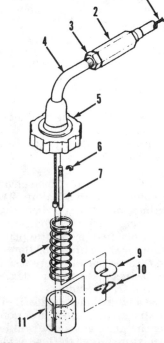

Fig. MI56—Exploded view of throttle slide assembly.

1. Inner throttle cable
2. Cable adjusting nut
3. Jam nut
4. Housing
5. Cap
6. Clip
7. Jet needle
8. Spring
9. Spring seat
10. Spring seat retainer
11. Throttle slide

and remove crankshaft. Heat crankcase if necessary to aid removal of main bearings.

Side clearance at rod big end should be 0.16-0.35 mm (0.006-0.014 in.) for all models. Standard crankshaft main bearing journal diameter is 12 mm (0.472 in.) for Models T110, T140, T180, TMX-21 and TM-24 and 15 mm (0.591 in.) for Model T200. If diameter is 0.05 mm (0.002 in.) less than standard diameter, renew crankshaft.

CLUTCH. Refer to Fig. MI58 for an exploded view of centrifugal clutch used on most models. All models are equipped with two clutch shoes and one clutch spring. The clutch drum is connected to the drive shaft. On some models the drive shaft is threaded into the clutch drum.

Clutch shoes are available only as a set. Install clutch shoes so side marked "M" is visible.

Refer to Figs. MI59 and MI60 for exploded view of typical clutch drum assemblies. Reach through slot in clutch drum to detach snap ring (4—Fig. MI59 or 8—Fig. MI60) and remove drum and

bearing from housing. Inside diameter of clutch drum is 54-56 mm (2.13-2.20 in.) for Models T110, T140, TMX-21 and TM-24, and 76-78 mm (2.99-3.07 in.) for Models T180 and T200.

REWIND STARTER. Refer to Figs. MI61 or MI62 for an exploded view of starter. To disassemble starter, detach starter housing from engine. Remove rope handle and allow rope to wind into starter. Unscrew center screw and remove rope pulley. Wear appropriate safety eyewear and gloves before

Fig. MI57—Exploded view of T200 engine. Other models are similar. Snap ring (10) is not used on all models. Points and condenser (7) are used on early models.

1. Air cleaner assy.
2. Carburetor
3. Clutch assy.
4. Ignition coil
5. Nut
6. Flywheel
7. Points & condenser
8. Crankcase
9. Seal
10. Snap ring
11. Bearing
12. Key
13. Retainer
14. Cylinder
15. Gasket
16. Piston rings
17. Piston
18. Piston pin
19. Bearing
20. Crankshaft assy.
21. Gasket
22. Bearing
23. Shim
24. Crankcase
25. Seal
26. Pulley
27. Nut
28. Housing
29. Screw
30. Friction plate
31. Pawl
32. Brake spring
33. Pulley
34. Rewind spring

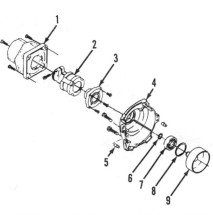

Fig. MI60—Exploded view of clutch drum assembly used on some models.

1. Housing
2. Vibration isolator
3. Support
4. Housing
5. Dowel pin
6. Snap ring
7. Bearing
8. Snap ring
9. Clutch drum

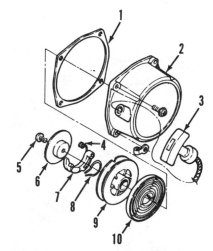

Fig. MI61—Exploded view of rewind starter used on some models.

1. Gasket
2. Housing
3. Rope handle
4. Spring
5. Screw
6. Friction plate
7. Pawl
8. Brake spring
9. Pulley
10. Rewind spring

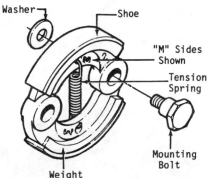

Fig. MI58—Exploded view of clutch shoe assembly used on some models.

Washer
Shoe
"M" Sides Shown
Tension Spring
Mounting Bolt
Weight

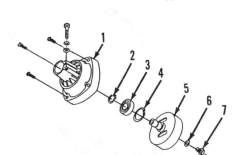

Fig. MI59—Exploded view of clutch drum assembly used on some models.

1. Housing
2. Snap ring
3. Bearing
4. Snap ring
5. Clutch drum
6. Washer
7. Screw

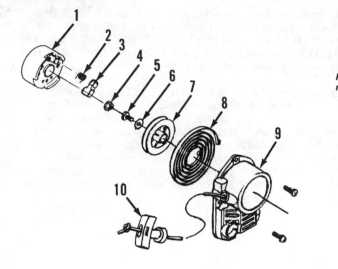

Fig. MI62—Exploded view of rewind starter used on some models.

1. Flywheel
2. Spring
3. Pawl
4. Nut
5. Screw
6. Washer
7. Pulley
8. Rewind spring
9. Housing
10. Rope handle

detaching rewind spring from housing as spring may uncoil uncontrolled.

To assemble starter, lubricate center post of housing and spring side with light grease. Install rewind spring so coil windings are counterclockwise from outer end. Assemble starter while passing rope through housing rope outlet and attach rope handle to rope. To place tension on starter rope, pull rope out of housing. Engage rope in notch on pulley and turn pulley counterclockwise. Hold pulley and disengage rope from pulley notch. Release pulley and allow rope to wind on pulley. Check starter operation. Rope handle should be held against housing by spring tension, but it must be possible to rotate pulley at least $1/4$ turn counterclockwise when rope is pulled out fully.

PISTON POWERED PRODUCTS

ENGINE SERVICE

Model	Bore	Stroke	Displacement
31 cc	1.37 in.	1.25 in.	1.9 cu. in.
	(34.8 mm)	(31.8 mm)	(31 cc)

ENGINE INFORMATION

Engine serial number decal is located on aluminum crankcase plate as shown in Fig. P10. Engines are equipped with Walbro diaphragm type carburetor. Cylinder head and cylinder is a single cast unit which may be separated from crankcase.

MAINTENANCE

SPARK PLUG. Recommended spark plug is a Champion DJ8J, or equivalent. Specified electrode gap is 0.025 inch (0.51 mm).

AIR CLEANER. Engine air filter should be cleaned and re-oiled at 10 hour intervals of normal use. If operating in dusty conditions, clean and re-oil more frequently.

To remove air filter, remove the two air filter housing retaining screws (S— Fig. P11) and lift filter housing from engine. Remove foam element (1) and clean housing and carburetor compart-

ment thoroughly. Wash element in mild solution of detergent and water. Rinse thoroughly, wrap element in a dry cloth and squeeze water out. Allow element to air dry. Re-oil element with SAE 30 engine oil and squeeze excess oil out. Install element in housing and install housing on engine.

CARBURETOR. The "all position" Walbro diaphragm type carburetor is equipped with an idle speed adjustment screw and a low speed mixture needle. High speed mixture is controlled by a fixed jet. All adjustment procedures must be performed with trimmer line at proper length or blade installed.

Initial adjustment of low speed mixture needle (21—Fig. P14) is 1-1/2 turns open from a lightly seated position. To initially adjust idle speed screw (4), turn idle speed screw out counterclockwise until throttle lever contacts boss on carburetor, then turn screw in clockwise direction until screw just contacts throttle lever. Turn screw clockwise two full turns from this position.

Final carburetor adjustment is made with engine running and at operating temperature. Operate engine at idle speed (adjust idle speed screw in 1/8 turn increments as necessary) and turn low speed mixture needle slowly clockwise until engine falters. Note this position and turn low speed mixture needle

counterclockwise until engine begins to run unevenly. Note this position and set low speed mixture needle halfway between first (lean) and last (rich) positions. Squeeze throttle trigger. If engine falters or hesitates on acceleration, turn low speed mixture needle counterclockwise 1/16 turn and repeat acceleration test. Continue until smooth acceleration is obtained. Adjust idle speed as necessary to maintain idle speed just below clutch engagement speed.

To disassemble carburetor, refer to Fig. P14. Remove the four screws (18) and remove diaphragm cover (17), diaphragm (16) and gasket (15). Remove screw (14) and carefully lift metering valve (12) and pin (13) from carburetor.

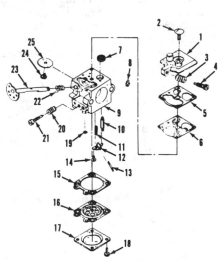

Fig. P14—Exploded view of Walbro diaphragm type carburetor.

1. Cover	14. Screw
2. Screw	15. Gasket
3. Spring	16. Diaphragm
4. Idle speed screw	17. Cover
5. Gasket	18. Screw
6. Diaphragm	19. Welch plug
7. Screen	20. Spring
8. "E" clip	21. Low speed mixture
9. Body	needle
10. Fuel inlet needle	22. Spring
11. Spring	23. Throttle shaft
12. Fuel inlet lever	24. Screw
13. Pin	25. Throttle plate

Fig. P10—View showing engine serial number location.

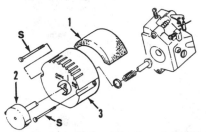

Fig. P11—View showing location of air filter retaining screws (S). Foam pad (1) is used as air filter element. Refer to text for cleaning procedure.

1. Air filter
2. Choke knob
3. Air filter housing

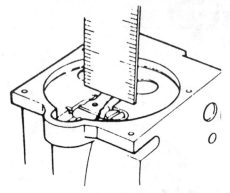

Fig. P15—Metering lever (fuel inlet lever) must be flush with fuel chamber floor as shown. Carefully bend lever to obtain correct adjustment.

Use care not to lose spring (11). Remove screw (2), cover (1), gasket (5), pump diaphragm (6), screen (7), low speed mixture needle (21) and spring (20). Remove screw (24) and throttle plate (25). Remove "E" clip (8) and throttle shaft (23). Welch plugs (19) may be removed as necessary and if new plugs are available.

Clean all metallic parts in a good quality carburetor cleaner. Rinse with clean water and use compressed air to dry. Metering lever should be flush with carburetor body (Fig. P15). Gently bend metering lever to obtain correct adjustment. Diaphragm is installed with rivet head toward metering valve lever.

IGNITION SYSTEM. Ignition module for the solid state ignition system is mounted on cylinder (37—Fig. P17). To service the module, remove the five screws retaining rewind starter

assembly to engine and note location of the single screw with lag type threads. On some models, it will be necessary to remove plastic engine cover and fuel tank. Air gap between module and flywheel is 0.010-0.015 inch (0.25-0.38 mm).

LUBRICATION. Engine is lubricated by mixing gasoline with a good quality two-stroke air-cooled engine oil. Refer to TRIMMER SERVICE section for correct fuel/oil ratio recommended by trimmer manufacturer.

CARBON. Muffler and exhaust ports should be cleaned after every 50 hours of operation if engine is operated continuously at full load. If operated at light or medium load, the cleaning interval can be extended to 100 hours.

REPAIRS

COMPRESSION PRESSURE. For optimum performance cylinder compression pressure should be 90-120 psi (621-828 kPa). Compression pressure should be checked with engine at operating temperature and throttle and choke valves wide open.

TIGHTENING TORQUES. Recommended tightening torque specifications are as follows:

Crankcase plate to crankcase	120 in.-lbs. (13 N·m)
Cylinder to crankcase	120 in.-lbs. (13 N·m)
Carburetor	40 in.-lbs. (4 N·m)
Reed plate	15 in.-lbs. (1 N·m)
Flywheel nut	150 in.-lbs. (17 N·m)
Ignition module	28 in.-lbs. (3 N·m)
Starter housing screws	40 in.-lbs. (4 N·m)
Muffler	56 in.-lbs. (6 N·m)
Air cleaner cover	40 in.-lbs. (4 N·m)
Spark plug	150 in.-lbs. (17 N·m)

CRANKSHAFT. Cantilevered design crankshaft (9—Fig. P17) is supported on flywheel side by two ball bearing type main bearings (13 and 17). Crankshaft must be a press fit in ball bearing type main bearings. Connecting rod is a slip fit on stub crankpin journal. Crankpin journal must be smooth, round and free from scores or damage.

To remove crankshaft, from models equipped with clutch, first remove clutch housing (31—Fig. P18). Unscrew the clutch drum retaining screw (29S) located at bottom of squared drive shaft adapter hole of clutch drum (30) then remove drum. Threads of the slotted head screw are coated with thread locking material and may be difficult to remove. Unscrew clutch hub assembly (28) and shoes from end of crankshaft. On all models, remove the five screws retaining rewind starter housing (26—Fig. P18 or P18A), then remove housing. Note location of the single screw with lag type threads (S). Disconnect spark plug and remove stand assembly (19—Fig. P17). Remove flywheel retaining nut from direct drive models. Remove flywheel (18) and key (33) from all models. Remove fuel tank assembly and fuel line. Remove the three muffler

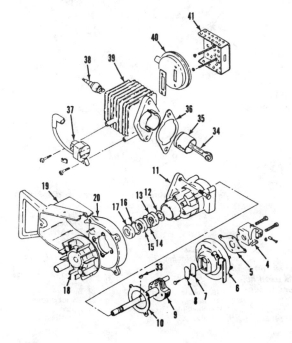

Fig. P17—Exploded view of Piston Powered Product engine.

4.	Carburetor
5.	Gasket
6.	Crankcase plate
7.	Reed plate
8.	Reed backup
9.	Crankshaft
10.	Gasket
11.	Crankcase
12.	Thrust washer
13.	Bearing
14.	Snap ring
15.	Seal
16.	Snap ring
17.	Bearing
18.	Flywheel
19.	Shroud
20.	Cover
33.	Key
34.	Connecting rod
35.	Piston
36.	Gasket
37.	Ignition module
38.	Spark plug
39.	Cylinder
40.	Muffler
41.	Muffler guard

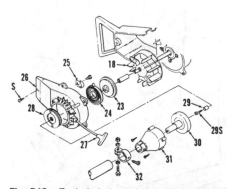

Fig. P18—Exploded view of the clutch, rewind starter and flywheel used on some models. Screw (29S) is trapped in drum (30) by spacer (29).

23. Pulley	28. Clutch hub assy.
24. Rewind spring	29. Spacer
25. Retainer	30. Clutch drum
26. Cover	31. Clutch housing
27. Handle	32. Clamp

mounting screws and muffler assembly. Remove air cleaner housing. Remove the two carburetor mounting screws, carburetor (4) and gasket (5). Remove the four crankcase plate mounting screws and crankcase plate assembly (6). Remove the two cylinder mounting screws and carefully work cylinder (39) away from piston. Rotate crankshaft until crankpin is at cylinder side of crankcase and slide connecting rod off crankpin to remove connecting rod and piston assembly. Remove the four screws retaining crankcase cover (20) to crankcase and remove cover. Carefully press crankshaft (9—Fig. P17) out of bearings in crankcase (11). Remove thrust washer (12) from crankshaft. Drive bearings (13 and 17) from crankcase housing, remove snap rings (14 and 16) and drive seal (15) out of crankcase housing.

(15) in bearing bore of crankcase 0.875 inch (22.23 mm) from flywheel side of crankcase. Press against flat surface of seal so that cupped side of seal enters crankcase first. Install snap rings (14 and 16). One main bearing (17) has a single shielded side which must be out toward flywheel side of engine after installation. Press bearings (13 and 17) in until seated against snap rings. Install thrust washer (12) on crankshaft main bearing journal and press crankshaft into main bearings. Rotate crankshaft until crankpin is at cylinder side and install connecting rod and piston assembly with cut-out portion of piston skirt toward crankshaft counterweight (Fig. P21). Install gasket (36—Fig. P17) and crankcase cover (20), then tighten screws to specified torque (Fig. P19). Make certain ring gap is correctly positioned at ring locating pin and carefully work cylinder (39—Fig. P17) over piston until seated against crankcase. Tighten screws to specified torque. Install fuel tank and rubber tank mounts

(as equipped). Install crankcase plate assembly, carburetor, air cleaner and muffler. Install key (33) and flywheel (18), tightening flywheel nut to specified torque. Install rewind starter assembly and clutch (as equipped).

PISTON, RINGS AND CONNECTING ROD. Piston and connecting rod are serviced as an assembly only. Stamped steel connecting rod utilizes caged needle bearings at piston pin and crankpin journal end. Caged bearings are not available separately. Piston ring on single ring piston has a locating pin in ring groove. Piston ring side clearance must not exceed 0.005 inch (0.13 mm). Piston ring width is 0.052 inch (1.32 mm). Piston ring end gap must not exceed 0.085 inch (2.16 mm). Piston standard diameter is 1.375-1.3805 inch (34.93-35.05 mm). Piston skirt is cut-out on crankshaft counterweight side to provide clearance.

CYLINDER. Cylinder must be smooth and free of scratches or flaking. Clean carbon carefully as necessary. Standard cylinder bore diameter is 1.3790-1.3805 inches (35.03-35.05 mm). Check cylinder size by installing a new piston ring squarely in cylinder and measuring ring end gap. If ring end gap exceeds 0.085 inch (2.16 mm), renew cylinder.

CRANKCASE, BEARINGS AND SEAL. Seal (15—Fig. P17) is pressed into crankcase bearing bore 0.875 inch (22.23 mm) from flywheel side. Press seal from flat surface of seal and into bearing bore from flywheel side of crankcase. Install snap rings (14 and 16) and press main bearings in until seated against snap rings. Note one main bearing has a shielded side that must be out toward flywheel side of crankcase.

REED VALVE. Crankcase plate (6—Fig. P17) utilizes a single reed (7) and reed back-up plate (8) held in position by two screws. Reed and reed back-up plate must be installed as shown in Fig. P20.

POSITION OF REED CURVE

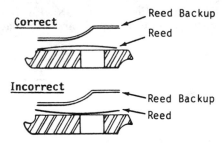

Fig. P20—Reed must be installed as shown.

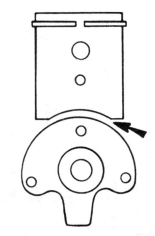

Fig. P21—Piston skirt is cut out on one side to clear crankshaft counterweight.

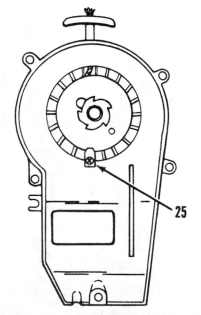

Fig. P22—View showing location of rewind starter pulley retainer (25). Refer to text.

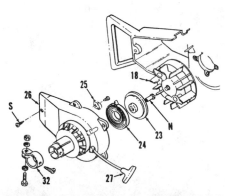

Fig. P18A—Exploded view of rewind starter and drive adapter used on direct drive models. Crankshaft is different than models with clutch and flywheel is retained by nut (N). Refer to Fig. P18 for legend.

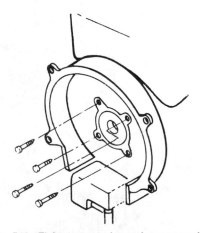

Fig. P19—Tighten screws in crankcase cover in a criss-cross pattern.

REWIND STARTER. Rewind starter dogs and springs are attached to flywheel assembly. To disassemble rewind starter, remove handle (27—Fig. P18 or P18A) and allow rope to wind onto rope pulley until all spring tension is removed. Remove retainer screw and retainer (25—Fig. P22), then carefully lift out pulley. CAUTION: Rewind spring will uncoil rapidly and come out of rewind housing. Use care during this procedure. Before reassembly, lightly coat rewind spring and inner side of pulley with grease. Wind rope entirely onto pulley. Maximum length of rope is 33 inches (89 cm). Hook outer hook on spring to spring retainer in rewind housing and carefully begin coiling spring inside housing using housing and thumb to trap spring coils. With spring wound in housing, place pulley on top of spring and use a hooked wire to work spring into position so pulley will slip all the way down into housing and engage spring. Wind spring just tight enough to provide tension to hold handle against rewind housing and push rope through rope hole in housing. Install handle and tie knot to retain rope in handle.

POULAN

ENGINE SERVICE

Model	Bore	Stroke	Displacement
Poulan	…	…	22.2 cc (1.35 cu. in.)
Poulan	…	…	26.2 cc (1.60 cu. in.)
Poulan	…	…	28 cc (1.72 cu. in.)

ENGINE INFORMATION

These engines are used on Poulan, Weed Eater and Yard Pro trimmers and blowers. Refer to adjoining Poulan engine section for engine service information on other Poulan engine models.

MAINTENANCE

LUBRICATION. Engine lubrication is obtained by mixing gasoline with an oil designed for two-stroke, air-cooled engines. Refer to trimmer or blower service section for manufacturer's recommended fuel:oil mixture ratio.

SPARK PLUG. Recommended spark plug is a Champion CJ14 for trimmer engines or a Champion CJ8 for blower engines. Specified electrode gap for all models is 0.6-0.65 mm (0.024-0.026 in.).

CARBURETOR. The engine is equipped with a Walbro WA diaphragm-type carburetor. Some models are equipped with a primer system that uses a plunger pump to force fuel into the intake passage prior to starting.

Initial adjustment of idle and high-speed mixture screws is ¾ to 1¼ turns out from a lightly seated position (blower engine carburetor is not equipped with an idle mixture screw). Final adjustments are performed with trimmer line at recommended length or blade installed on trimmer models. Engine must be at operating temperature and running. Adjust idle speed screw (31—Fig. PN50) so engine idles at approximately 3000 rpm (on trimmers with a clutch, trimmer head or blade should not rotate). On trimmer engines, adjust idle mixture screw (18) so engine idles smoothly and accelerates without hesitation. Readjust idle speed. Operate unit at full-throttle and adjust high-speed mixture screw (17) to obtain maximum engine rpm, then turn high-speed mixture screw counterclockwise until engine just begins to run rough.

When overhauling carburetor, refer to exploded view in Fig. PN50. Examine fuel inlet valve and seat. Inlet valve (7) is renewable, but carburetor body must be renewed if seat is excessively worn or damaged. Inspect mixture screws and seats. Renew carburetor body if seats are excessively worn or damaged. Clean fuel screen (24). Inspect diaphragms (2, 11 and 26) for tears and other damage.

Check metering lever height as shown in Fig. PN51. Metering lever should be flush with circuit plate. Bend lever to obtain correct lever height.

IGNITION SYSTEM. The engine is equipped with an electronic ignition system. Ignition system performance is considered satisfactory if a spark will jump across a 3 mm (⅛ in.) electrode gap on a test spark plug. If no spark is produced, check on/off switch, wiring and ignition module air gap. Air gap between ignition module and flywheel magnet should be 0.25-0.36 mm (0.010-0.014 in.). If switch, wiring and module air gap are satisfactory, but spark is not present, renew ignition module.

REPAIRS

COMPRESSION PRESSURE. For optimum performance, compression pressure should be 621 kPa (90 psi). Compression pressure should be checked with engine at operating temperature and with throttle and choke wide-open.

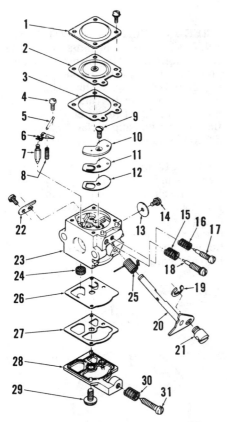

Fig. PN50—Exploded view of Walbro WA carburetor.

1. Cover
2. Metering diaphragm
3. Gasket
4. Screw
5. Pin
6. Metering lever
7. Fuel inlet valve
8. Spring
9. Screw
10. Circuit plate
11. Check valve
12. Gasket
13. Throttle plate
14. Screw
15. Spring
16. Spring
17. High-speed mixture screw
18. Idle mixture screw
19. "E" clip
20. Throttle shaft
21. Swivel
22. Clip
23. Body
24. Inlet screen
25. Return spring
26. Fuel pump diaphragm
27. Gasket
28. Cover
29. Screw
30. Spring
31. Idle speed screw

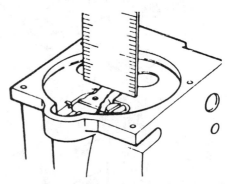

Fig. PN51—Metering lever should be flush with carburetor body.

TIGHTENING TORQUES. Recommended tightening torques are as follows:

Clutch drum . . . . 3.4-4.0 N·m
(30-35 in.-lbs.)
Clutch hub . . . . 18-20 N·m
(156-180 in.-lbs.)
Crankcase . . . . 5.1-5.7 N·m
(45-50 in.-lbs.)
Cylinder . . . . 7.0-7.3 N·m
(60-65 in.-lbs.)
Flywheel . . . . 18-20 N·m
(156-180 in.-lbs.)
Ignition module . . . . 3.4-4.0 N·m
(30-35 in.-lbs.)
Spark plug . . . . 14-15 N·m
(124-134 in.-lbs.)

PISTON, PIN AND RINGS. The piston is equipped with a single piston ring. A locating pin in the piston ring groove prevents ring rotation.

The piston is accessible after separating cylinder from crankcase. Remove both piston pin retaining rings (25—Fig. PN52). Use suitable piston pin removal tool (No. 31069) while applying heat to top of piston to remove piston pin (26) from piston. If pin removal tool is not available, use a press to press pin from piston. Do not attempt to drive the pin out of piston.

Standard ring end gap is 0.3 mm (0.012 in.). Standard ring side clearance in piston groove is 0.06 mm (0.0024 in.). If ring side clearance is 0.10 mm (0.004 in.) or more, renew piston.

When installing piston, ring ends must be correctly positioned around locating pin in piston ring groove. Install piston on connecting rod so piston ring locating pin will be positioned as shown in Fig. PN53. Closed end of piston pin must be toward exhaust side of engine. Apply heat to top of piston when installing piston pin. Apply engine oil to piston and cylinder prior to assembly. Do not rotate cylinder when installing cylinder over piston.

CYLINDER. The cylinder bore is chrome plated. Renew cylinder if plating in bore is worn through, scored or otherwise damaged. Worn spots will appear dull and may be easily scratched, while chrome plating will be bright and much harder.

CRANKSHAFT AND CONNECTING ROD. The crankshaft and connecting rod are serviced as an assembly; individual components are not available.

To remove crankshaft and connecting rod assembly, separate engine assembly from engine covers, fuel tank and cooling shrouds. Remove carburetor (7—Fig. PN52), fuel lines and carburetor housing (8). Remove muffler. Remove flywheel and ignition module. Remove drive shaft coupling or clutch hub from crankshaft. Remove cylinder retaining screws and slide cylinder off piston. Remove piston pin retainers (25) and use suitable piston pin removal tool to push

pin out of piston. Remove mounting screws from crankcase halves and separate crankcase halves. Remove crankshaft and connecting rod assembly (17) and thrust washers (16 and 19). Use tools 31033 and 31087 to remove bearings (15 and 20) and seals (13 and 22) from crankcase halves.

The piston pin bushing (23) in connecting rod is renewable. Use service tools 31069, 31077 and 31092, or equivalent tools, to remove bushing. Side of bearing with numbers should face away from flywheel side of crankshaft.

Install main bearings using tools 31033 and 31088. Numbered side of bearing must be toward inside of crankcase half. Install seals using tools 31033 and 31087 with seal lip toward bearing.

Install washers (16 and 19) so shoulder is toward crankcase. Apply sealer 30054 to mating surfaces of crankcase halves prior to assembly. Tighten crankcase screws evenly to 5.1-5.7 N·m (45-50 in.-lbs.).

REED VALVE. A reed valve (11—Fig. PN52) is located on the inner face of the carburetor housing (8). Inspect reed petal and discard if torn, broken, creased or otherwise damaged. Sharp edge of retaining screw washer must be against reed petal. Tip of reed petal should be flat against housing surface; maximum allowable standoff is 0.13 mm (0.005 in.).

CLUTCH. A two-shoe clutch (Fig. PN54) is used on some engines. Before removing clutch drum (1), be sure to unscrew hidden screw in center of clutch drum shaft. Unscrew the clutch hub by inserting a suitable spanner wrench in holes of clutch shoes. Clutch shoes and hub are available only as a unit assem-

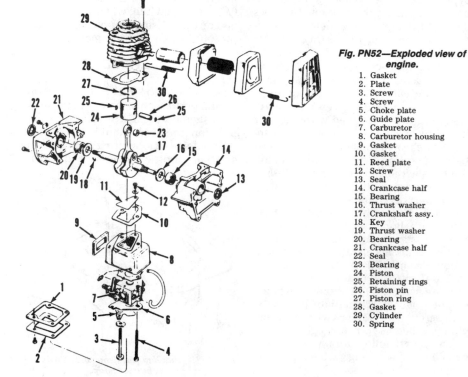

Fig. PN52—Exploded view of engine.

1. Gasket
2. Plate
3. Screw
4. Screw
5. Choke plate
6. Guide plate
7. Carburetor
8. Carburetor housing
9. Gasket
10. Gasket
11. Reed plate
12. Screw
13. Seal
14. Crankcase half
15. Bearing
16. Thrust washer
17. Crankshaft assy.
18. Key
19. Thrust washer
20. Bearing
21. Crankcase half
22. Seal
23. Bearing
24. Piston
25. Retaining rings
26. Piston pin
27. Piston ring
28. Gasket
29. Cylinder
30. Spring

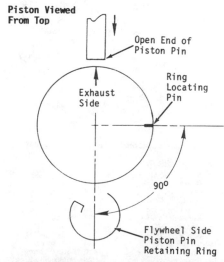

Fig. PN53—Install piston on connecting rod so piston ring locating pin is to the right when looking toward exhaust side of engine. Closed end of piston pin must be toward exhaust side after installation.

bly. On models with two washers, install washer 15377 between hub and crankcase and washer 15381 between hub and drum as shown in Fig. PN54.

Fig. PN54—Exploded view of clutch assembly used on some models. Note location of thrust washers. Clutch drum is retained by a screw located in shaft of clutch drum (1).

1. Clutch drum
2. Thrust washer (15381)
3. Clutch hub & shoe assy.
4. Thrust washer (15377)

REWIND STARTER. Refer to Fig. PN55 for an exploded view of rewind starter. To disassemble starter, detach starter housing from engine. Remove rope handle and allow rope to wind into starter. Remove screw (6) and rope pulley. Wear appropriate safety eyewear and gloves before detaching rewind spring from housing as spring may uncoil uncontrolled.

To assemble starter, lubricate center post of housing and spring side with light grease. Install rewind spring (3) so coil windings are counterclockwise from outer end. Rope length should be 86 cm (34 in.). Assemble starter while passing rope through housing rope outlet and attach rope handle to rope. To place tension on starter rope, pull rope out of housing. Engage rope in notch on pulley and turn pulley three turns counterclockwise. Hold pulley and disengage rope from pulley notch. Release pulley and allow rope to wind on pulley. Check starter operation. Rope handle should be held against housing by spring tension, but it must be possible to rotate pulley at least ½ turn counterclockwise when rope is pulled out fully.

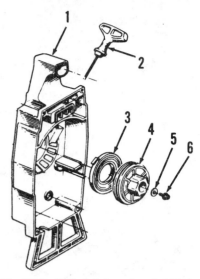

Fig. PN55—Exploded view of rewind starter.

1. Housing
2. Rope handle
3. Rewind spring
4. Pulley
5. Washer
6. Screw

POULAN

ENGINE SERVICE

Model	Bore	Stroke	Displacement
Poulan	…	…	22 cc (1.34 cu. in.)
Poulan	…	…	26 cc (1.59 cu. in.)
Poulan	…	…	30 cc (1.83 cu. in.)

ENGINE INFORMATION

These engines are used on Poulan and Weed Eater trimmers and blowers. Refer to adjoining Poulan engine section for engine service information on other Poulan engine models.

MAINTENANCE

LUBRICATION. Engine lubrication is obtained by mixing gasoline with an oil designed for two-stroke, air-cooled engines. Refer to trimmer service section for manufacturer's recommended fuel:oil mixture ratio.

SPARK PLUG. Recommended spark plug is a Champion CJ14 or equivalent. Specified electrode gap for all models is 0.635 mm (0.025 in.).

CARBURETOR. The engine is equipped with a Walbro WA diaphragm-type carburetor. Initial adjustment of idle and high-speed mixture screws is one turn out from a lightly seated position (blower engine carburetor is not equipped with an idle mixture screw). Final adjustments are performed with trimmer line at recommended length or blade installed on trimmer engines. Engine must be at operating temperature and running. Adjust idle speed screw (2—Fig. PN101) so engine idles at approximately 3000 rpm (on trimmers with a clutch, trimmer head or blade should not rotate). On trimmer engines, adjust idle mixture screw (10) so engine idles smoothly and accelerates without hesitation. Readjust idle speed. Operate unit at full-throttle and adjust high-speed mixture screw (11) to obtain maximum engine rpm, then turn high-speed mixture screw counterclockwise until engine just begins to run rough.

When overhauling carburetor, refer to exploded view in Fig. PN101. Examine fuel inlet valve and seat. Inlet valve (12) is renewable, but carburetor body must be renewed if seat is excessively worn or damaged. Inspect mixture screws and

seats. Renew carburetor body if seats are excessively worn or damaged. Clean fuel screen (5). Inspect diaphragms (4 and 21) for tears and other damage.

Check metering lever height as shown in Fig. PN102. Metering lever should be flush with circuit plate. Bend lever to obtain correct lever height.

IGNITION SYSTEM. The engine is equipped with an electronic ignition system. Ignition system performance is considered satisfactory if a spark will jump across a 3 mm (¹⁄₈ in.) electrode gap on a test spark plug. If no spark is produced, check on/off switch, wiring and ignition module air gap. Air gap between ignition module and flywheel magnet should be 0.25-0.36 mm (0.010-0.014 in.). If switch, wiring and module air gap are satisfactory, but spark is not present, renew ignition module.

REPAIRS

PISTON, PIN AND RING. The piston (22—Fig. PN103) is accessible after removing cylinder (25) from crankcase (17). Remove piston pin retainers (19) and use a suitable puller to extract pin (20) from piston.

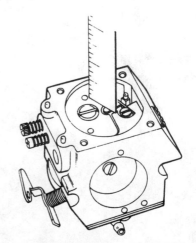

Fig. PN102—Tip of metering lever should be flush with circuit plate. Bend metering lever as needed.

Fig. PN101—Exploded view of Walbro WA carburetor.

1. Cover
2. Idle speed screw
3. Gasket
4. Fuel pump diaphragm
5. Screen
6. "E" ring
7. Throttle plate
8. Throttle shaft
9. Spring
10. Idle mixture screw
11. High-speed mixture screw
12. Fuel inlet valve
13. Spring
14. Metering lever
15. Pin
16. Screw
17. Gasket
18. Circuit plate
19. Screw
20. Gasket
21. Metering diaphragm
22. Cover

The piston is equipped with a single piston ring. Ring rotation is prevented by a locating pin in the piston ring groove. Piston is available in standard size only.

Be sure piston ring end gap is correctly indexed with locating pin in piston ring groove when installing cylinder. Lubricate piston and cylinder bore with oil prior to reassembly.

CYLINDER. The cylinder is available in standard size only. Renew cylinder if damaged or excessively worn.

CRANKSHAFT AND CONNECTING ROD. The crankshaft (10—Fig. PN103) is supported at flywheel end only by two ball bearings (12 and 15). The stamped steel connecting rod (21) has a caged roller bearing at both ends. Connecting rod and bearings are serviced only as an assembly.

To remove crankshaft and connecting rod, separate engine assembly from engine covers, fuel tank and cooling shrouds. Remove carburetor and muffler. Remove spark plug and insert piston stop tool in spark plug hole or insert end of a rope through plug hole to lock piston and crankshaft. Remove flywheel retaining nut and remove flywheel from crankshaft. Remove cylinder mounting screws and slide cylinder off piston. Unbolt and remove reed block (6) from crankcase (17). Separate connecting rod from crankpin. Detach snap ring (16) and carefully press crankshaft out of bearings. Drive or press bearings (12 and 15) out of crankcase, remove snap rings (13) and remove seal (14).

When reinstalling crankshaft, install seal (14) in bearing bore of crankcase so cupped side of seal is toward inside of crankcase. Outer main bearing (15) has a single shielded side that must be out toward flywheel side of engine after installation. Press bearings (12 and 15) in until seated against snap rings. Install spacer (11) on crankshaft main bearing journal and press crankshaft into main bearings.

REED VALVE. A reed valve (8—Fig. PN103) is located on the inner face of the reed block (6). Inspect reed petal and discard if torn, broken, creased or otherwise damaged.

CLUTCH. Some engines may be equipped with a two-shoe clutch (10—Fig. PN104). Clutch hub, shoes and spring are available only as a unit assembly. The clutch drum is contained in housing (13). Drum and housing are available only as a unit assembly.

REWIND STARTER. Refer to Figs. PN104, PN105 or PN106 for an exploded view of rewind starter. To disassemble starter, detach starter housing from engine. Remove rope handle and allow rope to wind into starter. Unscrew pulley retainer or pulley retaining screw and remove rope pulley. Wear appropriate safety eyewear and gloves before

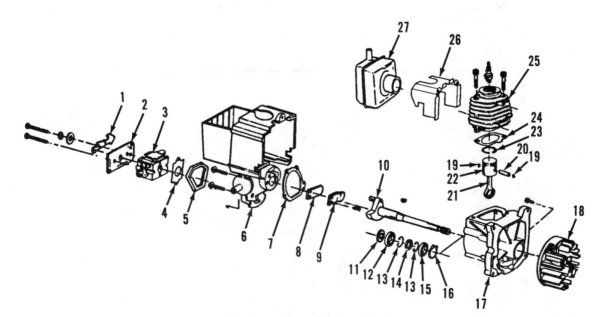

Fig. PN103—Exploded view of engine.

1. Choke shutter	6. Reed block	11. Spacer
2. Plate	7. Gasket	12. Inner bearing
3. Carburetor	8. Reed valve	13. Snap rings
4. Gasket	9. Reed stop	14. Seal
5. Seal	10. Crankshaft	15. Outer bearing

16. Snap ring	20. Piston pin
17. Crankcase	21. Connecting rod
18. Flywheel	22. Piston
19. Retaining rings	23. Piston ring

24. Gasket
25. Cylinder
26. Air baffle
27. Muffler

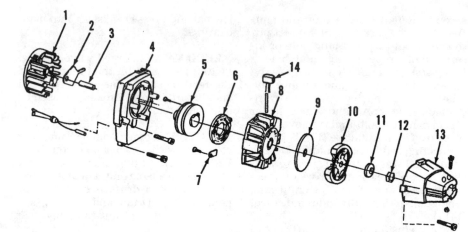

Fig. PN104—Exploded view of clutch and rewind starter assemblies used on trimmers. Counterweight (2) is not used on all models.

1. Flywheel
2. Counterweight
3. Spacer
4. Shroud
5. Starter pulley
6. Rewind spring
7. Retainer
8. Starter housing
9. Plate
10. Clutch assy.
11. Belleville washer
12. Nut
13. Housing
14. Rope handle

detaching rewind spring from housing as spring may uncoil uncontrolled.

To assemble starter, lubricate center post of housing and spring side with light grease. Install rewind spring so coil windings are counterclockwise from outer end. Rope length should be 107 cm (42 in.). Assemble starter while passing rope through housing rope outlet and attach rope handle to rope. To place tension on starter rope, pull rope out of housing. Engage rope in notch on pulley and turn pulley counterclockwise to place tension on rewind spring. Hold pulley and disengage rope from pulley notch. Release pulley and allow rope to wind on pulley. Check starter operation. Rope handle should be held against housing by spring tension, but it must be possible to rotate pulley at least an additional $1/4$ turn when rope is pulled out fully.

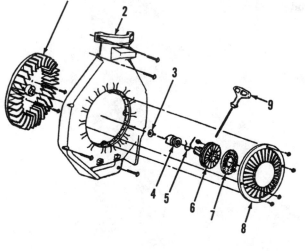

Fig. PN105—Exploded view of rewind starter used on some blower engines.

1. Retainer
2. Starter pulley
3. Rewind spring
4. Housing
5. Rope handle

Fig. PN106—Exploded view of rewind starter used on some blower engines.

1. Blower fan
2. Blower housing
3. Screw
4. Ratchet
5. Spring
6. Starter pulley
7. Rewind spring
8. Housing
9. Rope handle

Illustrations courtesy Poulan/Weed Eater

SACHS-DOLMAR

ENGINE SERVICE

Model	Bore	Stroke	Displacement
Sachs-Dolmar	37.0 mm (1.46 in.)	31.0 mm (1.22 in.)	33.0 cc (2.01 cu. in.)
Sachs-Dolmar	40.0 mm (1.57 in.)	31.0 mm (1.22 in.)	40.0 cc (2.44 cu. in.)

ENGINE INFORMATION

Sachs-Dolmar two-stroke air-cooled gasoline engines are used on Sachs-Dolmar string trimmers and brush cutters.

MAINTENANCE

SPARK PLUG. Recommended spark plug is a NGK BM7 A, or equivalent. Specified electrode gap for all models is 0.6-0.7 mm (0.024-0.028 in.).

CARBURETOR. All models are equipped with a Walbro WT series diaphragm type carburetor with a built in fuel pump (Fig. SD50).

Initial setting of low (26) and high (25) speed mixture needles is two turns open from a lightly seated position.

Final adjustments are made with trimmer line at recommended length or blade assembly installed. Engine should be at operating temperature and running. Adjust low speed mixture needle (26) so that engine idles and accelerates smoothly. Adjust idle speed screw (1) to obtain 2900-3000 engine rpm, or just below idle speed. Use an accurate digital tachometer and adjust high speed mixture needle (25) to obtain 10,800-11,000 engine rpm. Recheck engine idle speed and acceleration.

IGNITION SYSTEM. All models are equipped with an electronic ignition system. Ignition system is considered satisfactory if spark will jump across the 3 mm (1/8 in.) gap of a test spark plug. If no spark is produced, check on/off switch and wiring. If switch and wiring are satisfactory and spark is not present, renew ignition module.

Air gap between ignition module and flywheel should be 0.2-0.3 mm (0.008-0.010 in.).

LUBRICATION. All models are lubricated by mixing gasoline with a good quality two-stroke air-cooled gasoline engine oil. Refer to TRIMMER SERVICE section for correct fuel/oil mixture

ratio recommended by trimmer manufacturer.

REPAIRS

TIGHTENING TORQUES. Recommended tightening torque specifications are as follows:

Carburetor . . . . 10 N·m (7.0 ft.-lbs.)

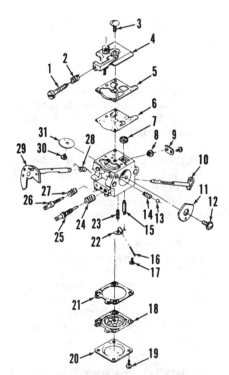

Fig. SD50—Exploded view of Walbro WT diaphragm type carburetor used on all models.

1. Idle speed screw
2. Spring
3. Screw
4. Pump cover
5. Gasket
6. Diaphragm
7. Screen
8. "E" ring
9. Clip
10. Choke shaft
11. Choke plate
12. Screw
13. Ball
14. Spring
15. Fuel inlet needle
16. Pin
17. Screw
18. Diaphragm
19. Screw
20. Cover
21. Gasket
22. Fuel inlet lever
23. Spring
24. Spring
25. High speed mixture needle
26. Low speed mixture needle
27. Spring
28. Spring
29. Throttle shaft
30. Screw
31. Throttle plate

Clutch nut . . . . 25 N·m (18.5 ft.-lbs.)

Flywheel . . . . 20 N·m (15.0 ft.-lbs.)

Spark plug . . . . 15 N·m (11.0 ft.-lbs.)

Cylinder bolts . . . . .6 N·m (4.5 ft.-lbs.)

Crankcase bolts . . . . .6 N·m (4.5 ft.-lbs.)

Muffler bolts . . . . 10 N·m (7.0 ft.-lbs.)

CRANKSHAFT AND CONNECTING ROD. To remove crankshaft, remove all covers and shrouds. Remove clutch, ignition system, fuel tank, clutch flange and cylinder. Use care when separating cylinder from crankcase and pull cylinder straight off piston. Remove crankcase retaining screws and carefully separate crankcase halves. The manufacturer does not recommend separating connecting rod (12 – Fig. SD52) from crankshaft (14) or removing the 12 connecting rod needle bearings (13). Remove seals (7 and 19) and snap rings (8 and 18). Heat crankcase until needle bearings (9 and 17) can be easily removed.

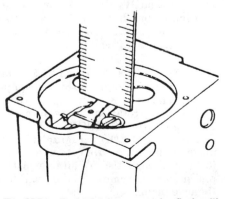

Fig. SD51—Fuel inlet lever must be flush with carburetor body. Carefully bend fuel inlet lever to adjust.

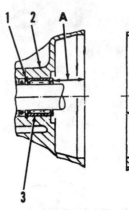

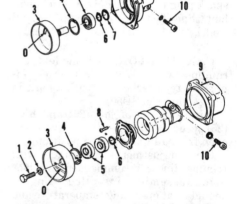

Fig. SD52—Exploded view of engine crankcase, crankshaft and cylinder assembly.

A. Arrow
1. Cylinder
2. Gasket
3. Ring
4. Piston
5. Piston pin
6. Retaining ring
7. Seal
8. Snap ring
9. Main bearing
10. Shim
11. Key
12. Connecting rod
13. Needle bearings
14. Crankshaft
15. Key
16. Shim
17. Main bearing
18. Snap ring
19. Seal
20. Clutch flange
21. Bolts
22. Rivet
23. Crankcase half
24. Gasket
25. Crankcase

Fig. SD53—Cross-section view of main bearings installed in crankcase. Refer to text.

A. 16 mm (0.63 in.)
B. 15.7 mm (0.62 in.)
1. Snap ring
2. Crankcase half (clutch side)
3. Main bearing
4. Crankcase half
5. Snap ring
6. Main bearing

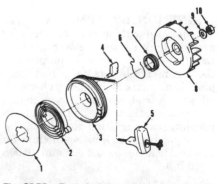

Fig. SD54—Exploded view of the centrifugal clutch assemblies.

O. Opening
1. Bolt
2. Washer
3. Clutch drum
4. Snap ring
5. Bearings
6. Snap ring
7. Snap ring
8. Screw
9. Clutch housing
10. Clamp bolt

To install needle bearings, heat crankcase until bearings can be installed in crankcase housings. Bearing cage is hardened on one side marked "xxx". If bearing cage edge is not marked, test with a file. Hardened side of bearing is installed toward crankshaft counterweight. Note that bearing (3—Fig. SD53) is installed 16 mm (0.63 in.) from gasket surface and bearing (6) is installed 15.7 mm (0.62 in.) from gasket surface. Bearing cages should not contact snap rings (1 and 5). Depth of main bearings and thickness of shims (10 and 16—Fig. SD52) control crankshaft end play. Correct crankshaft end play is 0.2-0.6 mm (0.79-2.36 in.). Vary shim (10 and 16) thickness or change position of bearing (9 or 17) in crankcase bearing bores as required to obtain correct crankshaft end play.

PISTON, PIN AND RINGS. The single ring aluminum piston is equipped with a locating pin in ring groove to prevent ring rotation. To remove piston, refer to CRANKSHAFT AND CONNECTING ROD paragraphs to remove cylinder. Remove retaining rings (6—Fig. SD52). Use a suitable piston pin puller to remove piston pin (5). Remove piston (4).

Make certain ring end gap is correctly positioned at locating pin before installing piston in cylinder. Arrow (A) on piston top must point toward exhaust side of engine after installation on connecting rod.

CYLINDER. To remove cylinder assembly refer to the CRANKSHAFT AND CONNECTING ROD paragraphs. Inspect cylinder for scoring or excessive wear and renew if damaged.

CLUTCH. Engines may be equipped with one of the clutch assemblies shown in Fig. SD54. To disassemble, remove snap ring (4) through opening (O) in clutch drum. Press drum assembly from clutch housing. Remove all necessary snap rings and remove bearings as required.

REWIND STARTER. Rewind starter assembly shown in Fig. SD55 is used on all models. To disassemble, remove fan housing and flywheel (8). Carefully remove brake spring (6) and snap ring (7). Remove starter pawl ratchet (4). Remove pulley (3), starter rope and handle (5), rewind spring (2) and disc (1) as an assembly keeping disc (1) and pulley (3) tight together during removal to prevent rewind spring from unwinding. Carefully allow tension of rewind spring to be released.

Fig. SD55—Exploded view of the rewind starter assembly.

1. Disc
2. Rewind spring
3. Pulley
4. Ratchet
5. Rope & handle assy.
6. Brake spring
7. Snap ring
8. Flywheel
9. Washer
10. Nut

SHINDAIWA

ENGINE SERVICE

Model	Bore	Stroke	Displacement
Shindaiwa	30.0 mm	28.0 mm	19.8 cc
	(1.18 in.)	(1.10 in.)	(1.21 cu. in.)
Shindaiwa	31.0 mm	28.0 mm	21.1 cc
	(1.22 in.)	(1.10 in.)	(1.29 cu. in.)
Shindaiwa	32.0 mm	30.0 mm	24.1 cc
	(1.26 in.)	(1.18 in.)	(1.47 cu. in.)
Shindaiwa	36.0 mm	33.0 mm	33.6 cc
	(1.42 in.)	(1.30 in.)	(2.05 cu. in.)
Shindaiwa	39.0 mm	33.0 mm	39.4 cc
	(1.54 in.)	(1.30 in.)	(2.40 cu. in.)

ENGINE INFORMATION

Shindaiwa two-stroke air-cooled gasoline engines are used by several manufacturers of string trimmers and brush cutters.

MAINTENANCE

SPARK PLUG. Recommended spark plug for all engines is a Champion CJ 8, or equivalent. Specified electrode gap for all engines is 0.6 mm (0.025 in.).

CARBURETOR. Shindaiwa 19.8 cc (1.21 cu. in.) displacement engine is equipped with a Walbro WA series diaphragm type carburetor (Fig. SH45), 21.1 cc (1.29 cu. in.) engine is equipped with a Walbro WZ series variable venturi carburetor (Fig. SH47) and all other engines are equipped with diaphragm type carburetors with a piston type throttle valve manufactured by TK (Fig. SH50). Refer to the appropriate paragraph for model being serviced.

Walbro WA Series Carburetor. Refer to Fig. SH45 for an exploded view of the Walbro WA series carburetor. Initial adjustment of low speed mixture needle (12) is 1-1/4 turns open from a lightly seated position. Initial adjust-

ment of high speed mixture needle (13) is 1-1/16 turns open from a lightly seated position.

Final carburetor adjustment is made with trimmer line at recommended

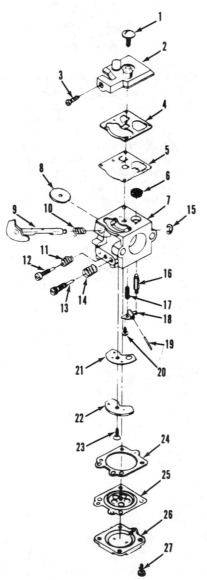

length, engine at operating temperature and running. Turn low speed mixture needle (12) clockwise until engine falters. Note this position and turn low speed mixture screw counterclockwise until engine begins to falters. Note this position and turn low speed mixture needle screw until it is halfway between first (lean) and last (rich) positions. Adjust idle speed screw (3) so that engine idles at 2500-3000 rpm. Operate engine at full rpm and adjust high speed mixture needle (13) using the same procedure outlined for low speed mixture needle. Turn high speed mixture needle in 1/8 turn increments. A properly adjusted carburetor will give high rpm with some unburned residue from muffler.

To disassemble carburetor, remove pump cover retaining screw (1), pump cover (2), diaphragm (5) and gasket (4). Remove inlet screen (6). Remove the four metering cover screws (27), metering cover (26), diaphragm (25) and gasket (24). Remove screw (20), pin (19), fuel lever (18), spring (17) and fuel inlet needle (16). Remove screw (23), circuit plate (22) and gasket (21). Remove high and low speed mixture needles and

Fig. SH45—Exploded view of Walbro WA diaphragm type carburetor used on some models.

1. Screw	14. Spring
2. Pump cover	15. "E" clip
3. Idle speed screw	16. Fuel inlet needle
4. Gasket	17. Spring
5. Pump diaphragm	18. Fuel inlet lever
6. Screen	19. Pin
7. Body	20. Screw
8. Throttle plate	21. Gasket
9. Throttle shaft	22. Circuit plate
10. Spring	23. Screw
11. Spring	24. Gasket
12. Low speed mixture	25. Diaphragm
needle	26. Cover
13. High speed mixture	27. Screw
needle	

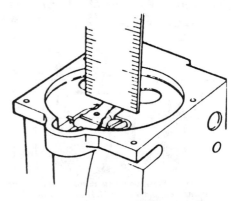

Fig. SH46—Fuel inlet lever should be flush with carburetor body.

Fig. SH47—Exploded view of Walbro WZ variable venturi carburetor used on some models.

1. Screw
2. Plate
3. Primer bulb
4. Screw
5. Cover
6. Gasket
7. Plate
8. Diaphragm
9. Gasket
10. Fuel inlet needle
11. Spring
12. Fuel inlet lever
13. Pin
14. Gasket
15. Diaphragm
16. Cover
17. Screw
18. Bracket
19. Screw
20. Nut
21. Bolt
22. Gasket
23. Body
24. Throttle valve assy.
25. Low speed mixture needle
26. Throttle cable swivel
27. Screw
28. Bracket
29. Spring
30. Idle speed screw
31. "E" ring
32. Metal sleeve support
33. Plate
34. Spring
35. Air filter
36. Cover
37. Wick
38. Gasket
39. Plate
40. Cap
41. Sleeve
42. High speed mixture needle
43. Spring

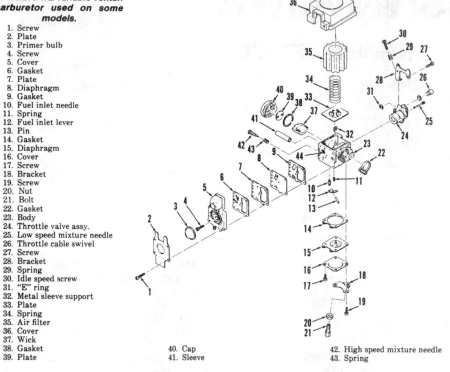

low speed mixture needle clockwise leans fuel mixture.

To disassemble Walbro WZ series carburetor, remove air filter cover (36), filter element (35), spring (34) and plate (33). Remove the four screws (1), metal plate (2) and primer bulb (3). Remove screw (4) and separate pump cover (5), gasket (6), plate (7), pump diaphragm (8) and gasket (9) from carburetor body (23). Remove fuel strainer screen from port (44) in carburetor body. Remove the four screws (17), cover (16), diaphragm (15) and gasket (14). Use a small screwdriver to "pop" pin (13) from plastic retainers, then remove pin, fuel inlet lever (12), fuel needle (10) and spring (11). Remove high speed mixture needle (42) and spring (43). Remove metal sleeve (41) and pull throttle valve assembly (24) from body as required. Do not disassemble throttle valve. Clear plastic end cap (40) is bonded to the plastic carburetor body at the factory and should not be removed.

Clean carburetor in a cleaning solution approved for the all plastic carburetor body. Inspect all parts for wear or damage. Tip of fuel inlet needle should be smooth and free of grooves. Fuel inlet lever spring (11) free length should be 8.7 mm (0.34 in.). When reassembling carburetor, fuel inlet lever (12) should be adjusted to obtain 1.5 mm (0.059 in.) between carburetor body surface and top of lever (D—Fig. SH48).

springs. Remove throttle plate (8) and throttle shaft (9) as required.

Clean parts thoroughly and inspect all diaphragms for wrinkles, cracks or tears. Diaphragms should be flexible and soft. Fuel inlet lever (18) should be flush with carburetor body (Fig. SH46).

Walbro WZ Series Carburetor. Refer to Fig. SH47 for an exploded view of the Walbro WZ series carburetor. Initial setting for low speed adjustment screw (25) is at the middle of the five notches. Initial setting for the high speed mixture needle (42) is 1-1/2 turns open from a lightly seated position.

Final adjustment is made with string trimmer line at recommended length or blade assembly installed. Engine must be at operating temperature and running. Operate engine at full rpm and

adjust high speed mixture needle to obtain approximately 11000 rpm. Release throttle and allow engine to idle. Adjust idle speed screw (30) to obtain 3000-3300 rpm. If idle rpm cannot be obtained at idle speed screw, turn low speed mixture needle one notch at a time to obtain 3000-3300 rpm. Turning low speed mixture needle counterclockwise richens fuel mixture and turning

TK Series Carburetor. Refer to Fig. SH50 for an exploded view of the TK diaphragm type carburetor. Initial setting for the low speed mixture needle

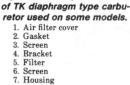

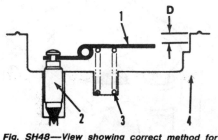

Fig. SH48—View showing correct method for measuring dimension (D). Refer to text.

1. Fuel inlet lever
2. Fuel inlet needle
3. Spring
4. Carburetor body

Fig. SH50—Exploded view of TK diaphragm type carburetor used on some models.

1. Air filter cover
2. Gasket
3. Screen
4. Bracket
5. Filter
6. Screen
7. Housing
8. Throttle valve
9. Fuel needle
10. Clip
11. Spring seat
12. Spring
13. Cap
14. Nut
15. Throttle cable adjuster
16. Spring
17. Idle speed screw
18. Low speed mixture needle
19. Spring
20. Spring
21. High speed mixture needle
22. "O" ring
23. Tube
24. Body
25. Spring
26. Fuel inlet needle
27. Fuel inlet lever
28. Pin
29. Screw
30. Gasket
31. Diaphragm
32. Cover
33. Screw
34. Sealing rings
35. Fuel pump plate
36. Gasket
37. Diaphragm
38. Fuel pump cover
39. Screws
40. Stud
41. Choke lever
42. Choke plate
43. Washer
44. Nut

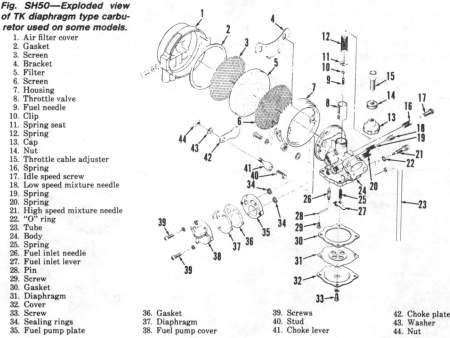

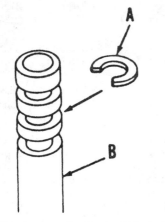

Fig. SH51—Fuel needle clip should be installed in the center groove.

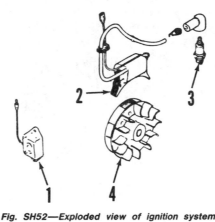

Fig. SH52—Exploded view of ignition system component parts.

1. Igniter
2. Coil
3. Spark plug
4. Flywheel (rotor)

Fig. SH53—Connect red ohmmeter lead to iron laminations and black lead to primary lead to check coil primary side resistance.

Fig. SH54—Connect red ohmmeter lead to iron laminations and black lead to spark plug lead to check coil secondary side resistance.

(18) is 3/4 turn open from a lightly seated position. Initial setting for the high speed mixture needle (21) is 2 turns open from a lightly seated position.

Final adjustments are made with trimmer head line at recommended length or blade assembly installed. Engine should be at operating temperature and running. Idle speed screw (17) should be adjusted to obtain 2500-3000 engine rpm. Trimmer head or blade should not rotate at this speed. Adjust low speed mixture needle to obtain maximum rpm at idle, then turn screw to richen mixture slightly. Readjust idle speed screw (17) to obtain 2500-3000 engine rpm at idle. Operate engine at full throttle and adjust high speed mixture needle to obtain maximum engine rpm, then turn screw counterclockwise 1/6 turn to richen fuel mixture slightly.

To disassemble carburetor, unscrew cap (13) and remove throttle valve assembly. Remove carburetor from engine. Remove fuel pump retaining screws (39) and separate pump cover (38), diaphragm (37) and gasket (36) from pump plate (35). Remove sealing rings (34). Remove the four metering cover screws (33). Remove metering cover (32), diaphragm (31) and gasket (30). Remove screw (29), pin (28), fuel inlet lever (27), fuel inlet needle (26) and spring (25). Remove low speed mixture needle (18) and high speed mixture needle (21).

Clean and inspect all parts for wear or damage. Inspect fuel inlet needle and renew if needle tip is worn, grooved or damaged. Fuel inlet lever spring (25) should have a free length of 9.5 mm (0.35 in.). Diaphragms should be soft and flexible. Install fuel inlet lever (27) and carefully bend lever to obtain 2.1 mm (0.08 in.) distance (D—Fig. SH48) between carburetor body surface and fuel inlet lever. Clip (10—Fig. SH50)

should be installed in middle groove of fuel needle (Fig. SH51).

IGNITION SYSTEM. All engines are equipped with transistorized ignition system. Ignition system is considered satisfactory if spark will jump across the 3 mm (1/8 in.) gap of a test spark plug. If no spark is produced, check on/off switch and wiring. If switch and wiring are satisfactory, remove coil assembly (2—Fig. SH52). Connect ohmmeter as shown in Fig. SH53 and check coil primary side resistance. Ohmmeter should register approximately 0.830 ohms. Connect ohmmeter as shown in Fig. SH54 and check coil secondary side resistance. Ohmmeter should register approximately 5600 ohms. If coil appears satisfactory, install a new igniter unit (1). Clearance between coil and flywheel (rotor) should be 0.30-0.35 mm (0.12-0.14 in.).

LUBRICATION. All models are lubricated by mixing gasoline with a good quality two-stroke air-cooled engine oil. Refer to TRIMMER SERVICE section for correct fuel/oil mixture ratio recommended by trimmer manufacturer.

REPAIRS

COMPRESSION PRESSURE. For optimum performance, compression pressure for all 19.8, 21.1 and 24.1 cc (1.21, 1.29 and 1.47 cu. in.) engines should be 586-896 kPa (85-130 psi) or 620-965 kPa (90-140 psi) for all 33.6 and 39.4 cc (2.05 and 2.40 cu. in.) engines. Compression test should be performed with engine at operating temperature and throttle and choke wide open. A compression reading of 379 kPa (55 psi) or lower for engines with 24.1 cc (1.47 cu. in.) or smaller displacement or a compression reading of 517 kPa (75 psi) for 33.6 cc (2.05 cu. in.)

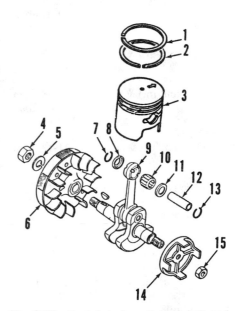

Fig. SH55—Exploded view of crankshaft and connecting rod assembly.

1. Ring
2. Ring
3. Piston
4. Nut
5. Washer
6. Flywheel
7. Retainer
8. Thrust washer
9. Connecting rod & crankshaft assy.
10. Bearing
11. Thrust washer
12. Piston pin
13. Retainer
14. Rewind pulley
15. Nut

or larger engines indicates a need for repair.

TIGHTENING TORQUES. Recommended tightening torque specifications are as follows:

Clutch pin to flywheel:
24.1 cc
(1.47 cu. in.) & below . . 7-10 N·m
(60-90 in.-lbs.)
33.6 cc
(2.05 cu. in.) & above . . 12-14 N·m
(113-130 in.-lbs.)

Illustrations courtesy Shindaiwa Inc.

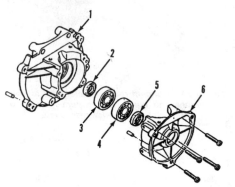

Fig. SH56—Exploded view of crankcase assembly.

1. Crankcase half
2. Seal
3. Bearing
4. Bearing
5. Seal
6. Crankcase half

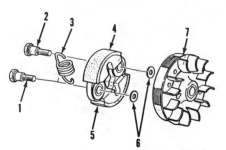

Fig. SH57—Exploded view of clutch assembly used on some models.

1. Clutch bolt
2. Clutch bolt
3. Clutch spring
4. Clutch shoe
5. Clutch shoe
6. Washers
7. Flywheel (rotor)

Crankcase:
24.1 cc
(1.47 cu. in.) & below . . 4-5 N·m
(35-44 in.-lbs.)
33.6 cc
(2.05 cu. in.) & above . . 7-8 N·m
(60-70 in.-lbs.)
Cylinder:
24.1 cc
(1.47 cu. in.) & below . . 4-5 N·m
(35-44 in.-lbs.)
33.6 cc
(2.05 cu. in.) & above . . 7-8 N·m
(60-70 in.-lbs.)
Flywheel:
24.1 cc
(1.47 cu. in.) & below . . 11-13 N·m
(104-122 in.-lbs.)
33.6 cc
(2.05 cu. in.) & above . . .19-24 N·m
(170-218 in.-lbs.)
Ignition coil:
24.1 cc
(1.47 cu. in.) & below . . 4-5 N·m
(35-44 in.-lbs.)
33.6 cc
(2.05 cu. in.) & above . . 5-5.5 N·m
(44-52 in.-lbs.)
Spark plug:
All models . . . . 19-22 N·m
(170-190 in.-lbs.)

CRANKSHAFT AND CONNECTING ROD. Refer to Fig. SH55 for an exploded view of crankshaft and connecting rod assembly. Refer also to Fig. SH56 for an exploded view of crankcase showing ball bearing main bearings and crankshaft seals. Crankshaft and connecting rod are considered an assembly and are not serviced separately. Do not remove connecting rod from crankshaft.

To remove crankshaft, remove all cooling shrouds, recoil starter assembly, fuel tank, carburetor, muffler, ignition module and clutch assembly. Remove bolts retaining cylinder to crankcase and carefully work cylinder off of crankcase and piston. Use care not to damage piston or connecting rod. Remove all crankcase bolts and carefully separate crankcase halves.

Do not use any type of tool inserted in crankcase split to separate crankcase.

If necessary, heat crankcase at main bearing areas to allow easier separation. Remove retaining rings and use a piston pin puller to remove piston pin. Remove piston and thrust washers. Note thrust washers are installed between piston and connecting rod at piston pin to control connecting rod thrust. Thrust washers must be installed. Remove piston pin bearing from connecting rod piston pin bore. Press bearings from crankshaft as required.

To reassemble, coat crankcase halves with a silicon type sealer and heat crankcase halves slightly to aid reassembly. Piston is installed so arrow stamped on top of piston will be toward exhaust side of cylinder.

PISTON, PIN AND RINGS. Piston for all models is equipped with two rings which are prevented from rotating on piston by a locating pin installed in each piston ring groove. Make certain ring end gaps are aligned with locating pins prior to installation of piston into cylinder. To remove piston, refer to CRANKSHAFT AND CONNECTING ROD paragraphs. Note location of thrust washers (8 and 11—Fig. SH55) to control connecting rod thrust.

Refer to the following chart for standard piston diameters and wear limits.

Engine	Standard	Limit
19.8 cc	29.975 mm	29.90 mm
(1.21 cu. in.)	(1.180 in.)	(1.177 in.)
21.1 cc	30.970 mm	30.90 mm
(1.29 cu. in.)	(1.219 in.)	(1.217 in.)
24.1 cc	31.970 mm	31.90 mm
(1.47 cu. in.)	(1.259 in.)	(1.256 in.)
33.6 cc	35.970 mm	35.90 mm
(2.05 cu. in.)	(1.416 in.)	(1.413 in.)
39.4 cc	38.950 mm	38.88 mm
(2.40 cu. in.)	(1.534 in.)	(1.531 in.)

Refer to the following chart for standard piston pin bore diameter in piston.

Engine	Standard	Limit
19.8 cc	8.0 mm	8.03 mm
(1.21 cu. in.)	(0.3150 in.)	(0.3161 in.)
21.1 cc	8.0 mm	8.03 mm
(1.29 cu. in.)	(0.3150 in.)	(0.3161 in.)
24.1 cc	9.0 mm	9.03 mm
(1.47 cu. in.)	(0.3540 in.)	(0.3555 in.)
33.6 cc	10.0 mm	10.03 mm
(2.05 cu. in.)	(0.3937 in.)	(0.3949 in.)
39.4 cc	10.0 mm	10.03 mm
(2.40 cu. in.)	(0.3937 in.)	(0.3949 in.)

Ring end gap for all engines should be 1-3 mm (0.004-0.012 in.). Minimum ring end gap is 0.6 mm (0.24 in.).

Piston ring width should be 1.5 mm (0.059 in.) and not less than 1.37 mm (0.054 in.) for all models.

Piston ring thickness for 19.8 and 21.1 cc (1.21 and 1.47 cu. in.) engines should be 1.3 mm (0.051 in.) and not less than 1.1 mm (0.043 in.). Piston ring thickness for 24.1 and 33.6 cc (1.47 and 2.05 cu. in.) engines should be 1.5 mm (0.059 in.) and not less than 1.3 mm (0.051 in.). Piston ring thickness for 39.4 cc (2.40 cu. in.) engine should be 1.7 mm (0.067 in.) and not less than 1.5 mm (0.059 in.).

Ring clearance in piston ring groove for 19.8, 21.1 and 24.1 cc (1.21, 1.29 and 1.47 cu. in.) engines should be 0.04-0.08 mm (0.0016-0.0031 in.) and not more than 0.20 mm (0.008 in.). Ring clearance in piston ring groove for 33.6 and 39.4 cc (2.05 and 2.40 in.) engines should be 0.02-0.06 mm (0.0008-0.0024 in.).

Piston to cylinder clearance for 19.8, 21.1, 24.1 and 33.6 cc (1.21, 1.29, 1.47 and 2.05 cu. in.) engines should be 0.025-0.060 mm (0.001-0.0024 in.). Piston to cylinder clearance for 39.4 cc (2.40 in.) engine should be 0.045-0.080 mm (0.0018-0.0030 in.).

Piston pin diameter for 19.8 and 21.1 cc (1.21 and 1.29 cu. in.) engines should be 8.0 mm (0.3150 in.) and not less than 7.98 mm (0.3142 in.). Piston pin diameter for 24.1 cc (1.47 cu. in.) engine should be 9.0 mm (0.3543 in.) and not

Illustrations courtesy Shindaiwa Inc.

less than 8.98 mm (0.3535 in.). Piston pin diameter for 33.6 and 39.4 cc (2.05 and 2.40 cu. in.) engines should be 10.0 mm (0.3937 in.) and not less than 9.98 mm (0.3929 in.).

CYLINDER. All engines are equipped with a chrome plated cylinder bore. Refer to the following chart for standard cylinder bore diameters and wear limits.

Engine	Standard	Limit
19.8 cc	30.0 mm	30.1 mm
(1.21 cu. in.)	(1.181 in.)	(1.185 in.)
21.1 cc	31.0 mm	31.1 mm
(1.29 cu. in.)	(1.220 in.)	(1.224 in.)
24.1 cc	32.0 mm	32.1 mm
(1.47 cu. in.)	(1.260 in.)	(1.264 in.)
33.6 cc	36.0 mm	36.1 mm
(2.05 cu. in.)	(1.417 in.)	(1.421 in.)
39.4 cc	39.0 mm	39.1 mm
(2.40 cu. in.)	(1.535 in.)	(1.539 in.)

On all engines, renew cylinder if taper exceeds 0.01 mm (0.0004 in.) or if cylinder out-of-round exceeds 0.03 mm (0.0012 in.).

CLUTCH. Refer to Fig. SH57 for an exploded view of clutch assembly used on all engines except 33.6 and 39.4 cc (2.05 and 2.40 cu. in.) engines. Clutch assembly for the 33.6 and 39.4 cc (2.05 and 2.40 cu. in.) engines is similar except that four clutch shoes are used instead of two.

To remove clutch assembly, remove fan cover and bolts. Remove bolts (1 and 2) and remove clutch shoe assembly. New clutch shoe lining thickness is 2.0 mm (0.079 in.). Renew shoes if lining thickness is less than 0.08 mm (0.003 in.).

Clutch drum is retained in clutch housing by a snap ring. Remove snap ring and press drum out of the clutch housing bearings. It may be necessary to heat housing slightly to remove clutch drum and bearings as an assembly.

RECOIL STARTER. All models are equipped with a recoil type starter. To disassemble starter, remove starter assembly from crankcase. Remove starter handle and allow rope to rewind onto pulley. Remove retaining screw and friction plate. Remove friction spring and ratchet return spring. Make certain rewind spring tension has been fully released and carefully separate pulley from starter case. Use pliers to remove rewind spring as required. Lubricate spring prior to reassembly. Preload rewind spring 2-3 turns to make sure handle will be returned to the housing.

STIHL

ENGINE SERVICE

Model	Bore	Stroke	Displacement
O15	38.0 mm	28.0 mm	32.0 cc
	(1.50 in.)	(1.10 in.)	(1.96 cu. in.)

ENGINE INFORMATION

Stihl O15 series engines are used on Stihl string trimmers and brushcutters. Refer to following sections for other Stihl engine models.

MAINTENANCE

SPARK PLUG. Recommended spark plug for O15 series engine is a Bosch WKA175T6, or equivalent. Specified electrode gap should be 0.5 mm (0.020 in.).

CARBURETOR. A Walbro Model HDC diaphragm carburetor is used on O15 series engine. Initial adjustment of idle and high speed mixture needles from a lightly seated position is 3/4 turn open. Adjust idle speed screw until engine idles just below clutch engagement speed. Final adjustment should be made with engine at operating temperature and running. Adjust high speed mixture needle to obtain optimum performance with trimmer line at recommended length or blade assembly installed. Adjust idle mixture needle to obtain smooth idle and good acceleration.

Refer to Fig. SL50 for an exploded view of Walbro Model HDC carburetor. Use caution when disassembling carburetor not to lose ball (13) and spring (14) as choke shaft is removed.

Clean and inspect all parts. Inspect diaphragms for defects which may affect operation. Examine fuel inlet needle and seat. The needle is renewable, but carburetor body must be renewed if needle seat is excessively worn or damaged. Sharp objects should not be used to clean orifices or passages as fuel flow may be altered. Compressed air should not be used to clean main nozzle as check valve may be damaged. A check valve repair kit is available to renew a damaged valve. Fuel mixture needles must be renewed if grooved or broken. Inspect mixture needle seats in carburetor body and renew body if seats are damaged or excessively worn. Screens should be clean.

To reassemble carburetor, reverse disassembly procedure. Fuel metering lever should be flush with a straightedge laid across carburetor body as shown in Fig. SL51. Make certain lever spring correctly contacts locating dimple on lever before measuring lever height. Carefully bend lever to obtain correct height.

Fig. SL50—Exploded view of Walbro Model HDC diaphragm type carburetor.

1. Pump cover
2. Gasket
3. Fuel pump diaphragm & valves
4. Throttle plate
5. Body
6. Return spring
7. Throttle shaft
8. Choke shaft
9. Idle speed screw
10. Idle mixture needle
11. High speed mixture needle
12. Choke plate
13. Choke friction ball
14. Spring
15. Gasket
16. Fuel inlet valve
17. Spring
18. Diaphragm lever
19. Circuit plate
20. Gasket
21. Metering diaphragm
22. Cover
23. Check valve screen
24. Retainer

IGNITION SYSTEM. Model O15 engine may be equipped with a conventional flywheel magneto ignition system or a breakerless transistor ignition system. Refer to the appropriate paragraph for model being serviced.

Flywheel Magneto Ignition. Ignition breaker point gap should be 3.5-4.0 mm (0.014-0.016 in.). Ignition timing is not adjustable except by adjusting breaker point gap. Ignition timing should occur when piston is 2.2 mm (0.09 in.) BTDC. Magneto edge gap ("E" gap) shown in Fig. SL52 should be 3.0-7.5 mm (0.12-0.29 in.). Magneto edge gap may be adjusted slightly by loosening flywheel nut and rotating flywheel on crankshaft as there is a small clearance between flywheel groove and crankshaft key.

Air gap between ignition coil and flywheel should be 0.5 mm (0.020 in.). Ignition coil windings may be checked using an ohmmeter. Primary winding should have 0.8-1.3 ohms resistance and secondary winding should have 7200-8800 ohms.

Transistor Ignition System. Some models are equipped with a Bosch breakerless transistor ignition system. Ignition should occur when piston is 2.2 mm (0.087 in.) BTDC. Ignition timing may be adjusted slightly by loosening

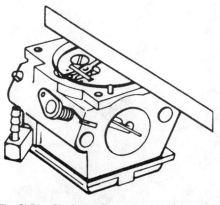

Fig. SL51—Diaphragm lever should just touch a straightedge placed across carburetor body as shown.

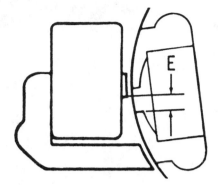

Fig. SL52—Magneto edge gap (E) should be 3.0-7.5 mm (0.12-0.29 in.).

flywheel nut and rotating flywheel on crankshaft as there is a small clearance between flywheel groove and crankshaft key.

Recommended air gap between ignition coil armature legs and flywheel is 0.15-0.2 mm (0.006-0.008 in.). Loosen ignition coil mounting screws and move ignition coil to adjust air gap.

LUBRICATION. The engine is lubricated by mixing gasoline with a good quality two-stroke air-cooled engine oil. Refer to TRIMMER SERVICE section for correct fuel/oil mixture ratio recommended by trimmer manufacturer.

REPAIRS

CRANKSHAFT AND SEALS. The crankshaft is supported in needle bearings (10 and 12—Fig. SL53) held between the cylinder and front crankcase half. Care should be taken when removing cylinder as crankshaft will be loose in crankcase and connecting rod may slide off bearing rollers (7) allowing them to fall into crankcase.

Large diameter needle bearing (10), retaining ring (9) and seal (8) on later models must be installed on flywheel end of crankshaft while smaller diameter bearing retaining ring and seal must be installed on clutch end. Some models are also equipped with thrust washers (T) located between crankshaft bearings and crankshaft. Bearings, retaining rings and seals on early models have the same outer diameter and may be installed on either end of crankshaft. Retaining rings (9 and 13) must fit in ring grooves of crankcase and cylinder. Tighten cylinder-to-crankcase screws to 7 N·m (60 in.-lbs.).

Before reassembling crankcase halves, apply a light coat of nonhardening sealant to crankcase mating surfaces.

CONNECTING ROD. To remove connecting rod, remove crankshaft as

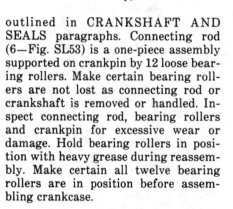

Fig. SL53—Exploded view of engine. Thrust washers (T) are used on late models.

T. Thrust washer	14. Oil seal
1. Cylinder	15. Crankcase
2. Piston ring	16. Gasket
3. Piston pin	17. Handle assy.
4. Pin retainer	18. Oil pick-up
5. Piston	
6. Connecting rod	
7. Bearing rollers (12)	
8. Oil seal	
9. Retaining ring	
10. Needle bearing	
11. Crankshaft	
12. Needle bearing	
13. Retaining ring	

outlined in CRANKSHAFT AND SEALS paragraphs. Connecting rod (6—Fig. SL53) is a one-piece assembly supported on crankpin by 12 loose bearing rollers. Make certain bearing rollers are not lost as connecting rod or crankshaft is removed or handled. Inspect connecting rod, bearing rollers and crankpin for excessive wear or damage. Hold bearing rollers in position with heavy grease during reassembly. Make certain all twelve bearing rollers are in position before assembling crankcase.

CYLINDER, PISTON, PIN AND RINGS. Cylinder and front crankcase are one-piece. Crankshaft and bearings are loose when the cylinder is removed. Care must be taken not to damage mating surfaces of crankcase halves during disassembly.

Cylinder head is integral with cylinder. Piston is equipped with a single piston ring and the piston pin rides directly in the piston and small end of connecting rod. Cylinder bore is chrome plated and should be inspected for damage or excessive wear. Cylinder (1—Fig. SL53) and front crankcase half (15) are available only as a complete assembly.

Piston pin (3) must be installed with closed end of pin toward "A" side of piston crown shown in Fig. SL54 and piston must be installed with "A" side toward exhaust port in cylinder. Piston and piston pin are available in standard sizes only.

Refer to CRANKSHAFT AND SEALS paragraphs for assembly of crankcase and cylinder.

REWIND STARTER. Refer to Fig. SL55 for exploded view of pawl type rewind starter used on all models. Care should be taken if it is necessary to remove rewind spring (3) to prevent spring from uncoiling uncontrolled.

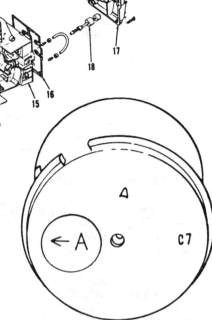

Fig. SL54—Install piston on connecting rod with "A" on piston crown towards exhaust port in cylinder.

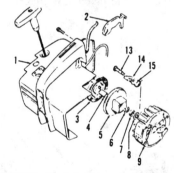

Fig. SL55—Exploded view of rewind starter.

1. Rear housing	7. Flywheel nut
2. Trigger interlock	8. Washer
3. Rewind spring	9. Flywheel
4. Bushing	13. Stud
5. Rope pulley	14. Pawl
6. "E" ring	15. Spring

Rewind spring must be wound in clockwise direction in housing. Wind starter rope in clockwise direction around rope pulley (5) as viewed with pulley installed in starter housing. Turn rope pulley 3-4 turns in clockwise direction before passing rope through rope outlet to place tension on rewind spring. To check spring tension, pull starter rope to full length. It should be possible to rotate rope pulley in clockwise direction with rope fully extended.

Starter pawl studs (13) are driven into flywheel. To renew pawl stud or spring, remove flywheel, then drive stud out of flywheel. Apply "Loctite" to stud before installation.

STIHL
ENGINE SERVICE

Model	Bore	Stroke	Displacement
O20*	38.0 mm	28.0 mm	32.0 cc
	(1.50 in.)	(1.10 in.)	(1.96 cu. in.)
O41	44.0 mm	40.0 mm	61.0 cc
	(1.73 in.)	(1.57 in.)	(3.72 cu. in.)

* Some O20 engines have a displacement of 35.0 cc (2.13 cu. in.).

ENGINE INFORMATION

Stihl O20 and O41 series engines are used on Stihl string trimmers and brushcutters. Refer to preceding and following sections for other Stihl engine models.

MAINTENANCE

SPARK PLUG. Recommended spark plug for all models is a Bosch WSR6F, or equivalent. Specified electrode gap should be 0.5 mm (0.020 in.).

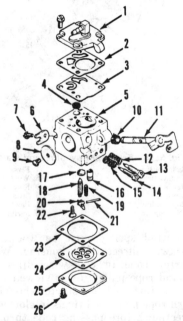

Fig. SL60—Exploded view of diaphragm type carburetor used on all models.

1. Pump cover
2. Gasket
3. Diaphragm
4. Screen
5. Body
6. Clip
7. Screw
8. Throttle plate
9. Screw
10. Spring
11. Throttle shaft
12. Spring
13. High speed mixture needle
14. Low speed mixture needle
15. Spring
16. Check valve
17. Welch plug
18. Fuel inlet needle
19. Spring
20. Fuel inlet lever
21. Pin
22. Screw
23. Gasket
24. Diaphragm
25. Cover
26. Screw

CARBURETOR. A diaphragm type carburetor is used on all models (Fig. SL60). Initial adjustment of low and high speed mixture needles for O20 engine is 1-1/4 turns open from a lightly seated position. Initial adjustment of O41 engine low and high speed mixture needles from a lightly seated position is 1-1/4 turns open for low speed mixture needle and 7/8 turn open for the high speed mixture needle.

To disassemble carburetor, refer to Fig. SL60. Clean filter screen (4). Welch plugs (18 and 24—Fig. SL61) may be removed by drilling plug with a suitable size drill bit, then pry out as shown in Fig. SL62. Care must be taken not to drill into carburetor body.

Inspect inlet lever spring (19—Fig. SL60) and renew if stretched or damaged. Inspect diaphragms for tears, cracks or other damage. Renew low and high speed mixture needles if needle points are grooved or broken. Carburetor body must be renewed if needle seats are damaged. Fuel inlet needle has a rubber tip which seats directly on a machined orifice in carburetor body. Inlet needle or carburetor body should be renewed if worn excessively.

Adjust position of inlet control lever so lever is flush with diaphragm chamber floor as shown in Fig. SL63. Bend lever adjacent to spring to obtain correct position.

IGNITION SYSTEM. Engine may be equipped with a conventional magneto type ignition system, a Bosch capacitor discharge ignition system or a Sems transistorized ignition system. Refer to the appropriate paragraph for model being serviced.

Magneto Ignition System. Ignition breaker point gap should be set at 3.5-4.0 mm (0.014-0.016 in.). Ignition timing is adjusted by loosening stator mounting screws and rotating stator plate. Ignition timing should occur when piston is 2.0-2.3 mm (0.08-0.087 in.) BTDC for O20 engine or 2.4-2.6 mm (0.095-0.102 in.) BTDC for O41 engine.

Ignition coil air gap should be 4-6 mm (0.16-0.24 in.) for O20 engine or 0.2-0.3 mm (0.008-0.012 in.) for O41 engine.

Ignition coil primary and secondary windings may be checked using an ohmmeter. Primary winding resistance should register 1.5-1.9 ohms for O20 engine, 1.9-2.5 ohms for O41 engine with Bosch date code 523 or 1.2-1.7

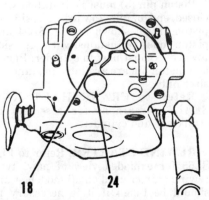

Fig. SL61—View showing location of Welch plugs (18 and 24).

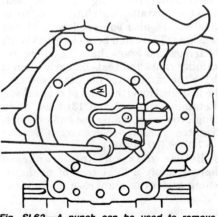

Fig. SL62—A punch can be used to remove Welch plugs after drilling a hole in plug. Refer to text.

ohms for O41 engine with Bosch date code 524.

Bosch Breakerless Ignition System. Ignition module air gap should be 0.2-0.3 mm (0.008-0.012 in.). Ignition should occur when piston is 2.5 mm (0.098 in.) BTDC.

Sems Breakerless Ignition System. Ignition module air gap should be 0.2-0.3 mm (0.008-0.012 in.). Ignition should occur when piston is 2.5 mm (0.098 in.) BTDC.

Ignition module primary and secondary windings may be checked using an ohmmeter. Primary winding resistance should be 0.4-0.5 ohms. Secondary winding resistance should be 2.7-3.3k ohms.

LUBRICATION. All Models are lubricated by mixing gasoline with a good quality two-stroke air-cooled engine oil. Refer to TRIMMER SERVICE section for correct fuel/oil mixture ratio recommended by trimmer manufacturer.

REPAIRS

TIGHTENING TORQUES. Recommended tightening torque specifications are as follows:

Clutch nut . . . . 39 N·m
                  (29 ft.-lbs.)
Clutch hub . . . . 34 N·m
                  (25.3 ft.-lbs.)
Clutch hub carrier (O20) . . . 28 N·m
                  (21 ft.-lbs.)
Flywheel nut:
  O20 . . . . 24 N·m
                  (18 ft.-lbs.)
  O41 . . . . 35 N·m
                  (26 ft.-lbs.)

CRANKSHAFT AND SEALS. All models are equipped with a split type crankcase from which cylinder may be removed separately (Fig. SL64 and SL65). It may be necessary to heat crankcase halves slightly to remove main bearings if they remain in crankcase during disassembly.

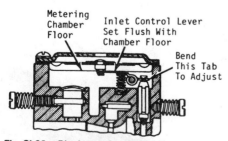

Fig. SL63—Diaphragm lever should be flush with fuel chamber floor as shown.

CONNECTING ROD. The connecting rod and crankshaft are considered an assembly and individual parts are not available separately. Do not remove connecting rod from crankshaft.

Connecting rod big end rides on a roller bearing and should be inspected for excessive wear or damage. If rod, bearing or crankshaft is damaged, complete crankshaft and connecting rod assembly must be renewed.

CYLINDER, PISTON, PIN AND RINGS. The aluminum alloy piston is equipped with two piston rings. The floating piston pin is retained in the piston with a snap ring at each end. The

pin bore of the piston is unbushed; the connecting rod has a caged needle roller piston pin bearing.

Cylinder bore and cylinder head are cast as one-piece. The cylinder assembly is available only with a fitted piston. Pistons and cylinders are grouped into different size ranges with approximately 0.0005 mm (0.0002 in.) difference between each range. Each group is marked with letters "A" to "E". Letter "A" denotes smallest size with "E" being largest. The code letter is stamped on the top of the piston and on the top of the cylinder. The code letter of the piston and the cylinder must be the same for proper fit of a new piston

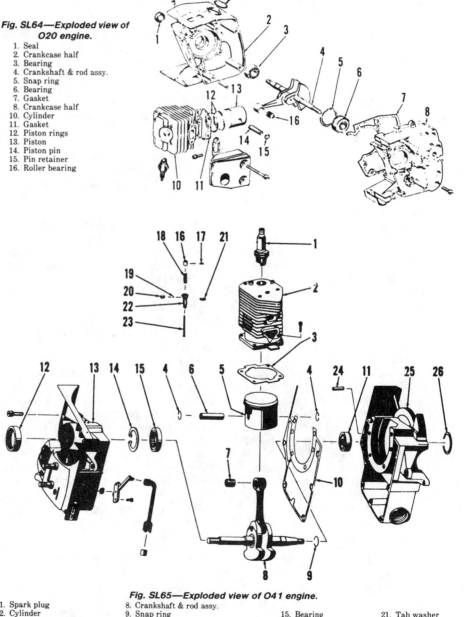

Fig. SL64—Exploded view of O20 engine.

1. Seal
2. Crankcase half
3. Bearing
4. Crankshaft & rod assy.
5. Snap ring
6. Bearing
7. Gasket
8. Crankcase half
10. Cylinder
11. Gasket
12. Piston rings
13. Piston
14. Piston pin
15. Pin retainer
16. Roller bearing

Fig. SL65—Exploded view of O41 engine.

1. Spark plug	8. Crankshaft & rod assy.	15. Bearing	21. Tab washer
2. Cylinder	9. Snap ring	16. Knob	22. Housing
3. Head gasket	10. Gasket	17. Pin	23. Plunger
4. Snap ring	11. Bearing	18. Spring	24. Pin
5. Piston	12. Seal	19. Pin	25. Crankcase half
6. Piston pin	13. Crankcase half	20. Spring	26. Snap ring
7. Bearing	14. Snap ring		

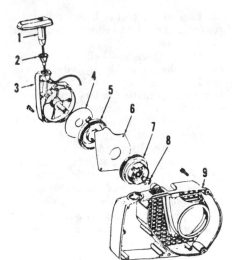

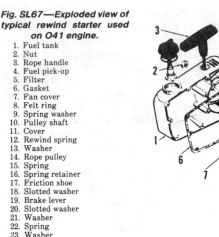

1. Fuel tank
2. Nut
3. Rope handle
4. Fuel pick-up
5. Filter
6. Gasket
7. Fan cover
8. Felt ring
9. Spring washer
10. Pulley shaft
11. Cover
12. Rewind spring
13. Washer
14. Rope pulley
15. Spring
16. Spring retainer
17. Friction shoe
18. Slotted washer
19. Brake lever
20. Slotted washer
21. Washer
22. Spring
23. Washer
24. "E" ring

Fig. SL66—Exploded view of pawl type starter used on O20 engine.

1. Rope handle
2. Bushing
3. Housing
4. Washer
5. Rewind spring
6. Cover
7. Rope pulley
8. "E" ring
9. Fan housing

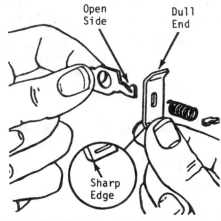

Fig. SL68—Illustration showing proper method of assembly of friction shoe plates to starter brake lever.

in a new cylinder. However, new pistons are available for installation in used cylinders. Used cylinders with code letters "A" or "B" may use piston with code letter "A". Used cylinder with code letters "A", "B" or "C" may use piston with code letter "B". Used cylinder with code letters "B", "C" or "D" may use piston with code letter "C". Used cylinder with code letters "C", "D" or "E" may use piston with code letter "D". Used cylinder with code letters "D" or "E" may use piston with code letter "E".

Cylinder bore on all models is chrome plated. Cylinder should be renewed if chrome plating is flaking, scored or worn away.

To reinstall piston on connecting rod, install one snap ring in piston. Lubricate the piston pin needle bearing with motor oil, then slide bearing into pin bore of connecting rod. Install piston on rod so that arrow on piston crown points toward exhaust port. Push piston pin in far enough to install second snap ring.

After piston and rod assembly is attached to crankshaft, rotate crankshaft to top dead center and support piston with a wood block that will fit between piston skirt and crankcase when cylinder gasket is in place. A notch should be cut in the wood block so that it will fit around the connecting rod. Lubricate piston and rings with motor oil, then compress rings with compressor that can be removed after cylinder is pushed down over piston. On some models it may be necessary to remove the cylinder and install an additional gasket between the cylinder and crankcase if piston strikes top of cylinder.

REWIND STARTER. Friction shoe type and pawl type starters have been used. Refer to Fig. SL66 for an exploded view of starter assembly used on O20 engine and to Fig. SL67 for an exploded view of starter assembly used on O41 engine. Refer to Fig. SL68 for proper method of assembly of friction shoe plates to starter brake lever on O41 engine starter.

To place tension on rope of starter shown in Fig. SL66 for O20 engine, pull starter rope, then hold rope pulley to prevent spring from rewinding rope on pulley. Pull rope back through rope outlet and wrap two additional turns of rope on pulley without moving pulley. Release pulley and allow rope to rewind. Rope handle should be pulled against housing, but spring should not be completely wound when rope is pulled to greatest length.

To place tension on O41 engine starter rope, pull rope out of handle until notch in pulley is adjacent to rope outlet, then hold pulley to prevent rope from rewinding. Pull rope back through outlet and out of notch in pulley. Turn rope pulley two turns clockwise and release rope back through notch. Check starter operation. Rope handle should be held against housing by spring tension, but spring should not be completely wound when rope is pulled to greatest length.

STIHL

ENGINE SERVICE

Model	Bore	Stroke	Displacement
O8S	47.0 mm (1.85 in.)	32.0 (1.26 in.)	56.0 cc (3.39 cu. in.)

ENGINE INFORMATION

Stihl O8S series engines are used on Stihl string trimmers and brushcutters. Refer to preceding sections for other Stihl engine models.

MAINTENANCE

SPARK PLUG. Recommended spark plug for O8S engine is a Bosch W175T7, or equivalent. Specified electrode gap should be 0.5 mm (0.020 in.).

CARBURETOR. O8S engine is equipped with a Tillotson diaphragm type carburetor. Initial adjustment of idle and high speed mixture needles is one turn open from a lightly seated position.

Final adjustments are made with trimmer line at recommended length or blade assembly installed. Engine should be at operating temperature and running. Adjust low speed mixture needle and idle speed screw until engine idles just below clutch engagement speed. Adjust high speed mixture needle to obtain optimum performance under load. Do not adjust high speed mixture needle too lean as engine may be damaged.

To disassemble carburetor, refer to Fig. SL70. Remove and clean filter screen (4). Welch plugs (18 and 24—Fig. SL71) can be removed by drilling plug with a suitable size drill bit, then pry out as shown in Fig. SL72. Care must be taken not to drill into carburetor body.

Inspect inlet lever spring (19—Fig. SL70) and renew if stretched or damaged. Inspect diaphragms for tears, cracks or other damage. Renew idle and high speed mixture needles if needle points are grooved or broken. Carburetor body must be renewed if needle seats are damaged. Fuel inlet needle has a rubber tip which seats directly on a machined orifice in carburetor body. Inlet needle or carburetor body should be renewed if worn excessively.

Inlet control lever should be adjusted so that control lever is flush with fuel chamber floor as shown in Fig. SL73. Carefully bend lever adjacent to spring to obtain correct position.

GOVERNOR. Model O8S is equipped with an air vane type governor. The governor linkage is attached to the carburetor choke shaft lever. Maximum speed is controlled by the air vane governor closing the choke plate.

Governed speed is adjusted by changing the tension of the governor spring. The adjusting plate is mounted to the engine behind the starter housing as shown in Fig. SL74. After maximum governed speed is adjusted at factory, position of spring is secured by a lead seal. If necessary to readjust governor, new position of governor spring should be sealed or wired securely. Maximum no-load governed speed is 8000 rpm.

IGNITION SYSTEM. OS8 engine is equipped with a conventional magneto type ignition system.

Coil air gap should be 0.5 mm (0.020 in.). Ignition breaker point gap should be 3.5-4.0 mm (0.014-0.016 in.). Ignition timing is adjusted by loosening stator mounting screws and rotating stator plate. Ignition should occur when piston is 1.9-2.1 mm (0.075-0.083 in.) BTDC.

Coil primary and secondary windings may be checked using an ohmmeter. Primary winding resistance should be 1.9-2.5 ohms for Bosch coil with date code 523 or 1.2-1.7 ohms for Bosch coil with date code 524. Secondary winding resistance should be 5.0-6.7k ohms for

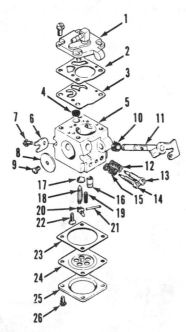

Fig. SL70—Exploded view of diaphragm type carburetor.

1. Pump cover	14. Low speed mixture
2. Gasket	needle
3. Diaphragm	15. Spring
4. Screen	16. Check valve
5. Body	17. Welch plug
6. Clip	18. Fuel inlet needle
7. Screw	19. Spring
8. Throttle plate	20. Fuel inlet lever
9. Screw	21. Pin
10. Spring	22. Screw
11. Throttle shaft	23. Gasket
12. Spring	24. Diaphragm
13. High speed mixture	25. Cover
needle	26. Screw

Fig. SL71—View showing location of Welch plugs (18 and 24).

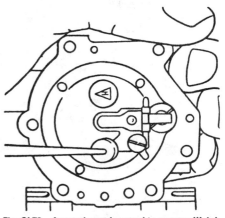

Fig. SL72—A punch can be used to remove Welch plugs after drilling a hole in plug. Refer to text.

Bosch coil with date code 523 or 5.0-6.7k ohms for Bosch coil with date code 524.

LUBRICATION. All Models are lubricated by mixing gasoline with a good quality two-stroke air-cooled engine oil. Refer to TRIMMER SERVICE section for correct fuel/oil mixture ratio recommended by trimmer manufacturer.

REPAIRS

TIGHTENING TORQUES. Recommended tightening torque specifications are as follows:

Clutch nut . . . . 34 N·m
(25 ft.-lbs.)
Flywheel nut . . . . 29 N·m
(21.7 ft.-lbs.)
Spark plug . . . . 24 N·m
(18 ft.-lbs.)
Cylinder screws . . . . 10 N·m
(7.2 ft.-lbs.)

CRANKSHAFT AND SEALS. All models are equipped with a split type crankcase from which cylinder may be removed separately (Fig. SL75). Crankshaft is supported at both ends in ball type main bearings and crankshaft end play is controlled by shims (11) installed between the bearing (10) and shoulders on the crankshaft on early models, or between bearing and

crankcase on later models. Shims are available in a variety of thicknesses. Correct crankshaft end play is 0.2-0.3 mm (0.0008-0.012 in.). It may be necessary to heat crankcase halves slightly to remove main bearings if they remain in crankcase during disassembly.

CONNECTING ROD. The connecting rod and crankshaft are considered an assembly and individual parts are not available separately. Do not remove connecting rod from crankshaft.

Connecting rod big end rides on a roller bearing and should be inspected for excessive wear or damage. If rod, bearing or crankshaft is damaged, complete crankshaft and connecting rod assembly must be renewed.

CYLINDER, PISTON, PIN AND RINGS. The aluminum alloy piston is equipped with two piston rings. The floating piston pin is retained in the piston with a snap ring at each end. The pin bore of the piston is unbushed; the connecting rod has a caged needle roller piston pin bearing.

Cylinder bore and cylinder head are cast as one-piece. The cylinder is available only with a fitted piston. Pistons and cylinders are grouped into different size ranges with approximately 0.0005 mm (0.0002 in.) difference between each range. Each group is marked

with letters "A" to "E". Letter "A" denotes smallest size with "E" being largest. The code letter is stamped on the top of the piston and on the top of the cylinder on all models. The code letter of the piston and the cylinder must be the same for proper fit of a new piston in a new cylinder. However, new pistons are available for installation in used cylinders. Used cylinders with code letters "A" or "B" may use piston with code letter "A". Used cylinder with code letters "A", "B" or "C" may use piston with code letter "B". Used cylinder with code letters "B", "C" or "D" may use piston with code letter "C". Used cylinder with code letters "C", "D" or "E" may use piston with code letter "D". Used cylinder with code letters "D" or "E" may use piston with code letter "E".

Cylinder bore on all models is chrome plated. Cylinder should be renewed if chrome plating is flaking, scored or worn away.

To reinstall piston on connecting rod, install one snap ring in piston. Lubricate the piston pin needle bearing with motor oil, then slide bearing into pin bore of connecting rod. Install piston on rod so that arrow on piston crown points toward exhaust port. Push piston pin in far enough to install second snap ring.

After piston and rod assembly is attached to crankshaft, rotate crankshaft to top dead center and support piston with a wood block that will fit between piston

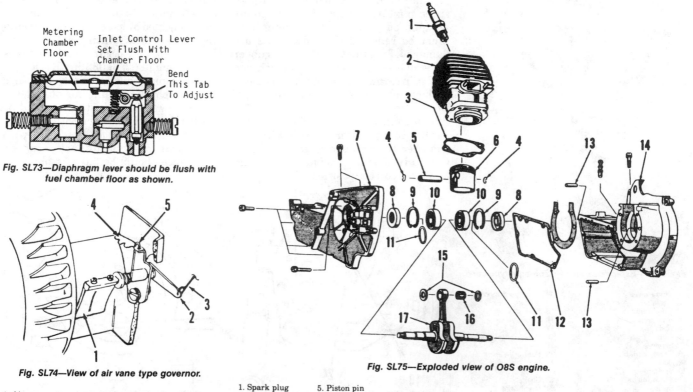

Metering Chamber Floor
Inlet Control Lever Set Flush With Chamber Floor
Bend This Tab To Adjust

Fig. SL73—Diaphragm lever should be flush with fuel chamber floor as shown.

Fig. SL74—View of air vane type governor.

1. Air vane
2. Lever
3. Throttle link
4. Notched plate
5. Governor spring

Fig. SL75—Exploded view of O8S engine.

1. Spark plug	5. Piston pin			
2. Cylinder	6. Piston	9. Snap ring	12. Gasket	15. Washer
3. Head gasket	7. Crankcase half	10. Ball bearing	13. Dowel pin	16. Bearing
4. Snap ring	8. Seal	11. Shim	14. Crankcase half	17. Crankshaft & rod assy.

Illustrations courtesy Stihl Inc.

*Fig. SL76—Exploded view of
    pawl type starter.*

1. Fuel tank
2. Nut
3. Rope handle
4. Fuel pick-up
5. Filter
6. Gasket
7. Fan cover
8. Felt ring
9. Spring washer
10. Pulley shaft
11. Cover
12. Rewind spring
13. Washer
14. Rope pulley
15. Spring
16. Spring retainer
17. Friction shoe
18. Slotted washer
19. Brake lever
20. Slotted washer
21. Washer
22. Spring
23. Washer
24. "E" ring

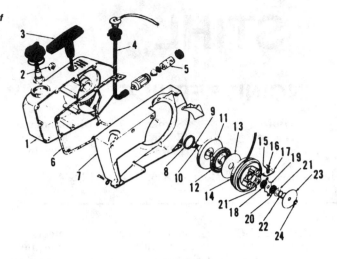

*Fig. SL77—Illustration showing proper method of
assembly of friction shoe plates to starter brake
lever.*

skirt and crankcase when cylinder gasket is in place. A notch should be cut in the wood block so that it will fit around the connecting rod. Lubricate piston and rings with motor oil, then compress rings with compressor that can be removed after cylinder is pushed down over piston. On some models it may be necessary to remove the cylinder and install an additional gasket between the cylinder and crankcase if piston strikes top of cylinder.

REWIND STARTER. O8S engine is equipped with a pawl type rewind starter assembly similar to Fig. SL76.

To place tension on engine starter rope, pull rope out of handle until notch in pulley is adjacent to rope outlet, then hold pulley to prevent rope from rewinding. Pull rope back through outlet and out of notch in pulley. Turn rope pulley two turns clockwise and release rope back through notch. Check starter operation.

Rope handle should be held against housing by spring tension, but spring should not be completely wound when rope is pulled to greatest length.

Refer to Fig. SL77 for correct assembly of starter shoes on brake lever. Make certain assembly is installed as shown in exploded views and leading edges of friction shoes are sharp or shoes may not properly engage drum.

STIHL

ENGINE SERVICE

Model	Bore	Stroke	Displacement
Stihl	34.8 mm	31.8 mm	30.2 cc
	(1.37 in.)	(1.25 in.)	(1.9 cu. in.)

This engine is used on Stihl Models FS36, FS40 and FS44.

ENGINE INFORMATION

The Stihl engine covered in this section is a two-stroke, air-cooled, single-cylinder engine.

MAINTENANCE

LUBRICATION. Engine lubrication is obtained by mixing gasoline with an oil designed for two-stroke, air-cooled engines. Refer to trimmer or blower service section for manufacturer's recommended fuel:oil mixture ratio.

SPARK PLUG. Recommended spark plug is AC CSR45, NGK BMR6A or equivalent. Specified electrode gap is 0.7-0.8 mm (0.028-0.031 in.). Tighten spark plug to 19 N·m (168 in.-lbs.).

CARBURETOR. The engine is equipped with a Walbro WT diaphragm-type carburetor. Refer to Fig. SL101 for an exploded view of carburetor. Initial adjustment of idle mixture screw (22) and high-speed mixture screw (20) is one turn open. Final adjustment is performed with engine at normal operating temperature and cutter line at desired length. Be sure air cleaner is clean before performing adjustments.

Adjust idle speed screw (32) clockwise until trimmer head begins to rotate, then turn screw counterclockwise one half turn. Trimmer head must not rotate when engine is at idle speed. Adjust idle mixture screw so engine idles smoothly and accelerates cleanly without hesitation. Readjust idle speed screw if necessary. Adjust high-speed mixture screw for best engine performance under load. Do not adjust high-speed mixture screw too lean as engine may be damaged.

Carburetor disassembly and reassembly is evident after inspection of carburetor and referral to Fig. SL101. Do not lose detent ball (18) when withdrawing choke shaft. Clean and inspect all components. Inspect diaphragms (2 and 28)

for defects that may affect operation. Examine fuel inlet valve and seat. Inlet valve (5) is renewable, but carburetor body must be renewed if seat is damaged or excessively worn. Discard carburetor body if mixture screw seats are damaged or excessively worn. Clean fuel screen (27).

Press nozzle (11) into body until inner face is flush with bore as shown in Fig. SL102. Install choke plate (C) as shown in Fig. SL103. Install throttle plate (T) so hole (H) is toward metering chamber as shown in Fig. SL104. Apply Loc-

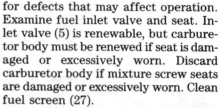

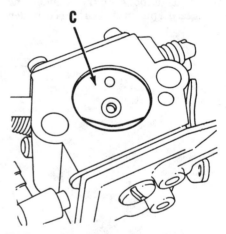

Fig. SL103—View showing correct installation of choke plate (C).

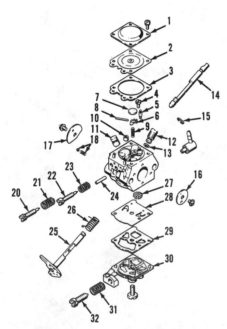

Fig. SL101—Exploded view of Walbro WT diaphragm carburetor.

1. Cover
2. Metering diaphragm
3. Gasket
4. Screw
5. Fuel inlet valve
6. Metering lever
7. Welch plug
8. Pin
9. Spring
10. Check valve
11. Fuel nozzle
12. Governor valve
13. "O" ring
14. Choke shaft
15. "E" ring
16. Throttle plate
17. Choke plate
18. Detent ball & spring
20. High-speed mixture screw
21. Spring
22. Idle speed mixture screw
23. Spring
24. Tube
25. Throttle shaft
26. Spring
27. Screen
28. Fuel pump diaphragm
29. Gasket
30. Fuel pump cover
31. Spring
32. Idle speed screw

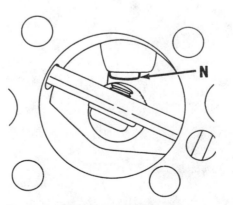

Fig. SL102—Install fuel nozzle (N) so inner face is flush with venturi bore.

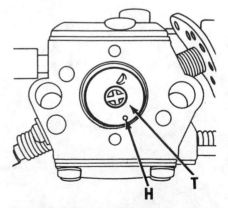

Fig. SL104—View showing correct installation of throttle plate (T). Hole (H) in plate must point toward metering chamber cover.

tite to choke and throttle plate retaining screws. Check metering lever height as shown in Fig. SL105 using Walbro tool 500-13. Metering lever should just touch leg on tool. Bend lever to obtain correct lever height. Install cover (1) so hole (H) is towards fuel inlet side of carburetor as shown in Fig. SL106.

The carburetor is equipped with a governor valve (12—Fig. SL101) that enriches the mixture at high speed to prevent overspeeding. The governor valve is not adjustable.

IGNITION SYSTEM. The engine is equipped with an electronic ignition system. Ignition system performance is considered satisfactory if a spark will jump across a 3 mm ($1/8$ in.) electrode gap on a test spark plug. If no spark is produced, check on/off switch, wiring and ignition module air gap. Air gap between ignition module and flywheel magnet should be 0.1-0.5 mm (0.004-0.020 in.). If switch, wiring and module air gap are satisfactory, but spark is not present, renew ignition module.

Tighten ignition module screws to 3.5 N·m (31 in.-lbs.).

Ignition timing should be 1.3-1.9 mm (0.05-0.07 in.) before top dead center at 6000 rpm. Ignition timing is not adjustable.

REPAIRS

TIGHTENING TORQUES. Recommended tightening torques values are as follows:

Carburetor	3.5 N·m (31 in.-lbs.)
Clutch hub	17 N·m (150 in.-lbs.)
Crankcase cover	5.5 N·m (49 in.-lbs.)
Cylinder	14 N·m (124 in.-lbs.)
Ignition module	3.5 N·m (31 in.-lbs.)
Muffler	6.5 N·m (57 in.-lbs.)
Spark plug	19 N·m (168 in.-lbs.)

PISTON, RINGS AND CONNECTING ROD. Piston and connecting rod (15—Fig. SL107) are serviced only as a unit assembly. The stamped steel connecting rod is equipped with a non-renewable roller bearing in the big end. Piston ring rotation is prevented by a locating pin in the piston ring groove (Fig. SL108). Oversize pistons and piston rings are not available.

To remove piston and connecting rod assembly, first remove engine shroud, fuel tank, carburetor and muffler. Remove cylinder mounting screws and pull cylinder off piston. Unbolt and remove crankcase cover/reed block assembly (1—Fig. SL107). Pull connecting rod off crankshaft pin and remove piston and connecting rod assembly.

When installing piston and rod on crankpin, be sure cutaway portion of piston skirt is toward crankshaft counterweight (see Fig. SL109).

CYLINDER. The engine is equipped with a cylinder that has an impregnated bore. Inspect cylinder for excessive wear, scoring and other damage. The cylinder is available only with a piston and rod assembly.

When installing cylinder, be sure piston ring end gap properly surrounds

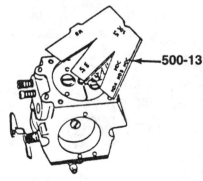

Fig. SL105—Leg of Walbro tool 500-13 should just touch metering lever.

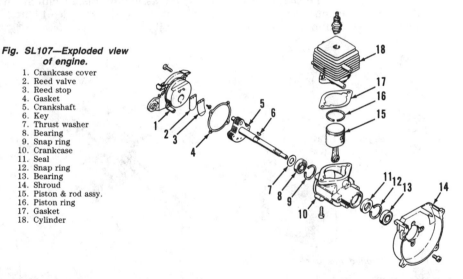

Fig. SL107—Exploded view of engine.

1. Crankcase cover
2. Reed valve
3. Reed stop
4. Gasket
5. Crankshaft
6. Key
7. Thrust washer
8. Bearing
9. Snap ring
10. Crankcase
11. Seal
12. Snap ring
13. Bearing
14. Shroud
15. Piston & rod assy.
16. Piston ring
17. Gasket
18. Cylinder

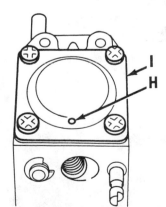

Fig. SL106—Install cover (1) so hole (H) is toward fuel inlet.

Fig. SL108—A pin prevents piston ring from rotating in ring groove. Ring end gap must be positioned around pin as shown.

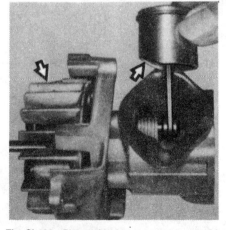

Fig. SL109—Piston skirt is cut away on one side to clear crankshaft counterweight and must be installed as shown.

locating pin in piston ring groove (Fig. SL108). Lubricate piston and cylinder bore with oil prior to assembly. The lower section of cylinder is tapered so piston ring is automatically compressed as cylinder is pushed over the piston.

CRANKSHAFT AND CRANKCASE. The crankshaft (5—Fig. SL107) is a cantilever design that is supported by two ball bearings (8 and 13).

To remove crankshaft, separate clutch housing and drive tube from engine. Be sure to unscrew hidden screw in center of clutch drum shaft and remove clutch drum. Use a suitable spanner wrench to unscrew clutch hub from crankshaft. See CLUTCH section. Remove crankcase cover (1), cylinder and piston. Remove flywheel and key from crankshaft. Press crankshaft out of main bearings. Heat crankcase to 212° F (100° C) to aid removal of bearings from crankcase.

When assembling crankcase, install snap ring (9) then install seal (4) so seal is against snap ring with lip toward inside of crankcase. Note that bearing (8) is open on both sides and that bearing should be pressed against snap ring (9). Install snap ring (12) and press bearing (13) against snap ring so shielded side faces outward. Install thrust washer (7) on crankshaft, then press crankshaft into main bearings. Install piston and rod assembly on crankshaft. Be sure cutaway portion of piston skirt is toward crankshaft counterweight (see Fig. SL109). Tighten crankcase cover screws to 5.5 N·m (49 in.-lbs.).

REED VALVE. A reed valve (2—Fig. SL107) is located on the inner face of the crankcase cover (1). Inspect reed petal and discard if torn, broken, creased or otherwise damaged.

CLUTCH. A two-shoe clutch (Fig. SL110) is used. The clutch hub (4) is threaded onto the crankshaft and retains the flywheel. Before removing clutch drum (5), be sure to unscrew hidden screw in center of clutch drum shaft. Unscrew the clutch hub by inserting a suitable spanner wrench in holes of clutch shoes. Clutch springs are available and must be renewed as a pair. Clutch shoes and hub are available only as a unit assembly. Install clutch on crankshaft so "OFF" on side of clutch hub is visible.

REWIND STARTER. Refer to Fig. SL111 for an exploded view of rewind starter. To disassemble starter, detach starter housing from engine. Remove rope handle and allow rope to wind into starter. Remove snap ring (5) and remove rope pulley (7). Wear appropriate safety eyewear and gloves before detaching rewind spring (8) from housing (9) as spring may uncoil uncontrolled.

To assemble starter, lubricate center post of housing and spring side with light grease. Install rewind spring so coil windings are clockwise from outer end. Rope length should be 96 cm (38 in.). Assemble starter while passing rope through housing rope outlet and attach rope handle to rope. To place tension on starter rope, pull rope out of housing. Engage rope in notch on pulley and turn pulley four turns clockwise. Hold pulley and disengage rope from pulley notch. Release pulley and allow rope to wind on pulley. Check starter operation. Rope handle should be held against housing by spring tension, but it must be possible to rotate pulley at least 1/2 turn clockwise when rope is pulled out fully.

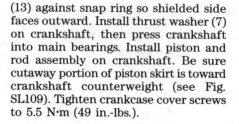

Fig. SL111—Exploded view of rewind starter.

1. Flywheel
2. Spring
3. Pawl
4. Stud
5. Snap ring
6. Washer
7. Spool
8. Rewind spring
9. Starter housing
10. Rope handle
11. Rope guide

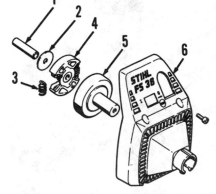

Fig. SL110—Exploded view of clutch assembly.

1. Spacer
2. Washer
3. Clutch spring
4. Clutch shoe & hub assy.
5. Clutch drum
6. Clutch housing

STIHL

ENGINE SERVICE

Model	Bore	Stroke	Displacement
Stihl	29 mm	26 mm	17.1 cc
	(1.14 in.)	(1.02 in.)	(1.04 cu. in.)
Stihl	31 mm	26 mm	19.6 cc
	(1.22 in.)	(1.02 in.)	(1.20 cu. in.)
Stihl	32 mm	28 mm	22.5 cc
	(1.26 in.)	(1.10 in.)	(1.37 cu. in.)
Stihl	34 mm	28 mm	25.4 cc
	(1.36 in.)	(1.10 in.)	(1.55 cu. in.)
Stihl	37 mm	32 mm	34.4 cc
	(1.46 in.)	(1.26 in.)	(2.10 cu. in.)

These engines are used on Stihl Models FS48, FS52, FS56, FS60, FS62, FS62AVE, FS62AVRE, FS65, FS66, FS66AVE, FS66AVRE, FS80, FS81, FS81AVE, FS81AVRE, FS86AVE, FS86AVRE, FR106 and FS106.

ENGINE INFORMATION

The Stihl engines covered in this section are two-stroke, air-cooled, single-cylinder engines.

MAINTENANCE

LUBRICATION. Engine lubrication is obtained by mixing gasoline with an oil designed for two-stroke, air-cooled engines. Refer to trimmer or blower service section for manufacturer's recommended fuel:oil mixture ratio.

SPARK PLUG. Recommended spark plug is NGK BMR7A or equivalent. Specified electrode gap is 0.6 mm (0.024 in.). Tighten spark plug to 20 N·m (177 in.-lbs.).

CARBURETOR. Engines with 34.4 cc displacement are equipped with a Zama C1Q carburetor. All other engines are equipped with a Walbro WT carburetor. Refer to following sections for service information.

Walbro WT. Refer to Fig. SL201 for an exploded view of carburetor. Initial adjustment of idle mixture screw (11) and high-speed mixture screw (13) is one turn open. Final adjustment is performed with engine at normal operating temperature and cutter line at desired length. Be sure engine air filter is clean before performing carburetor adjustments.

Turn idle speed screw (34) clockwise until trimmer head rotates, then turn counterclockwise one half turn. Trimmer head must not rotate when engine is at idle speed. Adjust idle mixture screw so engine idles smoothly and accelerates cleanly without hesitation. Readjust idle speed screw if necessary. Open throttle to wide-open position and adjust high-speed mixture screw (13). Engine speed must not exceed 10,000 rpm. If an accurate tachometer is not available, do not adjust high-speed mixture needle beyond initial setting. Do not adjust high-speed mixture screw too lean as engine may be damaged.

The carburetor is equipped with an accelerator pump that forces additional fuel into the carburetor bore when the throttle shaft is rotated. The pump piston (26—Fig. SL201) rests against a flat on the throttle shaft. Shaft rotation moves the piston against fuel in a passage.

Carburetor disassembly and reassembly is evident after inspection of carburetor and referral to Fig. SL201. Do not lose detent ball (15) when withdrawing choke shaft. Accelerator pump piston (26) is released when throttle shaft is withdraw. Clean and inspect all components. Inspect diaphragms (2 and 30) for defects that may affect operation. Ex-

Fig. SL201—Exploded view of Walbro WT carburetor.

1. Cover
2. Metering diaphragm
3. Gasket
4. Nozzle
5. Pin
6. Metering lever
7. Fuel inlet valve
8. Screw
9. Spring
10. Welch plug
11. Idle mixture screw
12. Spring
13. High-speed mixture screw
14. Spring
15. Detent ball & spring
17. Choke plate
18. Swivel
19. Throttle shaft
20. "E" ring
21. Spring
22. "E" ring
23. Choke shaft
24. Handle
25. Throttle plate
26. Accelerator piston
27. "O" ring
28. Spring
29. Screen
30. Fuel pump diaphragm
31. Gasket
32. Cover
33. Spring
34. Idle speed screw

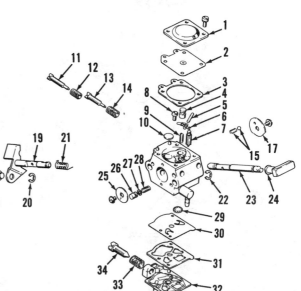

amine fuel inlet valve and seat. Inlet valve (7) is renewable, but carburetor body must be renewed if seat is damaged or excessively worn. Discard carburetor body if mixture screw seats are damaged or excessively worn. Clean fuel screen (29).

Press nozzle (4) into body until inner face is flush with venturi bore as shown in Fig. SL202. Install choke plate as

shown in Fig. SL203. Install throttle plate so hole is toward metering chamber cover as shown in Fig. SL204. Apply Loctite to choke and throttle plate retaining screws. Check metering lever height as shown in Fig. SL205 using Walbro tool 500-13. Metering lever should just touch leg on tool. Bend lever to obtain correct lever height. Install cover (1—Fig. SL201) so hole is toward fuel inlet side of carburetor as shown in Fig. SL206.

Zama C1Q. Refer to Fig. SL207 for an exploded view of carburetor. Initial adjustment of idle mixture screw (12) and high-speed mixture screw (13) is 1 turn out from a lightly seated position.

Final adjustment is performed with engine at normal operating temperature. Be sure that air cleaner is clean before attempting to adjust carburetor. Before final adjustment on trimmer models, cutter line should be desired length. Turn idle speed screw (16) until cutting tool begins to rotate, then turn screw back out one half turn. Tool must not rotate when engine is at idle speed. Adjust idle mixture screw (12) so engine idles smoothly and accelerates cleanly without hesitation. Readjust idle speed screw if necessary. Open throttle to wide-open position and adjust high-speed mixture screw (13). Engine speed must not exceed 10,000 rpm. If an accurate tachometer is not available, do not adjust high-speed mixture needle beyond initial setting. Do not adjust high-speed mixture screw too lean as engine may be damaged.

Carburetor disassembly and reassembly is evident after inspection of carburetor and referral to Fig. SL207. Do not lose detent ball (18) when withdrawing choke shaft. Clean and inspect all components. Inspect diaphragms (2 and 29) for defects that may affect operation.

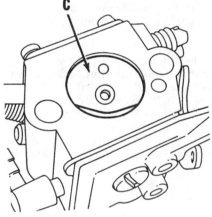

Fig. SL202—Install fuel nozzle (N) so inner face is flush with venturi bore.

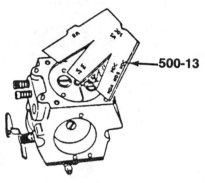

Fig. SL205—Leg of Walbro tool 500-13 should just touch metering lever.

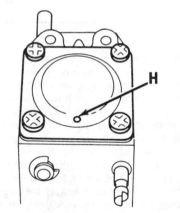

Fig. SL206—Install cover so hole (H) is toward fuel inlet.

Fig. SL203—View showing correct installation of choke plate (C).

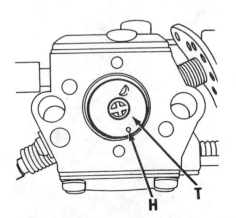

Fig. SL204—View showing correct installation of throttle plate (T). Hole (H) in plate should face metering chamber cover.

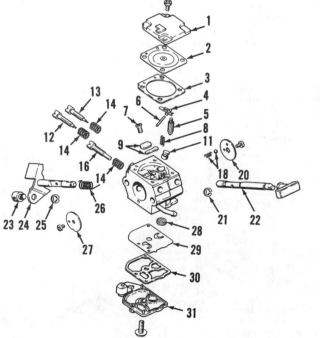

Fig. SL207—Exploded view of Zama C1Q carburetor.

1. Cover
2. Metering diaphragm
3. Gasket
4. Metering lever
5. Fuel inlet valve
6. Pin
7. Screw
8. Spring
9. Welch plugs
11. Nozzle
12. Idle mixture screw
13. High-speed mixture screw
14. Springs
16. Idle speed screw
18. Detent ball & spring
20. Choke plate
21. "E" ring
22. Choke shaft
23. Swivel
24. Throttle shaft
25. "E" ring
26. Spring
27. Throttle plate
28. Screen
29. Fuel pump diaphragm
30. Gasket
31. Cover

Examine fuel inlet valve and seat. Inlet valve (5) is renewable, but carburetor body must be renewed if seat is damaged or excessively worn. Discard carburetor body if mixture screw seats are damaged or excessively worn. Clean fuel screen (28).

To reassemble carburetor, reverse disassembly procedure. Metering lever should be level with chamber floor as shown in Fig. SL208. Bend metering lever as needed.

IGNITION SYSTEM. Some engines are equipped with a one-piece ignition module that includes the ignition coil. On other engines, a two-piece ignition system is used with the ignition coil adjacent to the flywheel and the ignition module mounted on the crankcase.

Ignition coil air gap should be 0.2-0.5 mm (0.008-0.020 in.) on Models FS52, FS62, FS66, FS81, FS86.

REPAIRS

PISTON, PIN AND RINGS. The piston (5—Fig. SL209) is equipped with two piston rings (3). Ring rotation is prevented by a locating pin in each piston ring groove (Fig. SL210). Piston and rings are available only in standard diameter.

To remove piston, first remove fan housing, engine cover, carburetor and muffler. Remove cylinder mounting screws and pull cylinder off the piston. Pry piston pin retainers (4—Fig. SL209) from piston and push piston pin (6) out of piston. Hold piston securely when removing pin to avoid applying side force to connecting rod. Remove piston and needle bearing (12) from connecting rod.

When reassembling, heat piston to about 60° C (140° F) to ease installation of piston pin. Install piston on connecting rod so mark on piston crown points toward exhaust port. Be sure piston ring gaps are correctly indexed with locating pins in piston ring grooves as shown in Fig. SL210. Lubricate piston and cylinder with oil prior to assembly. Use suitable clamping strap to compress piston rings. Align cylinder so it is correctly positioned on crankcase, then push cylinder straight down over piston. Tighten cylinder mounting screws evenly to 5 N·m (44 in.-lbs.).

CYLINDER. The engine is equipped with a cylinder that has an impregnated bore. Renew cylinder if bore is excessively worn, scored or otherwise damaged. Cylinder is available only in standard size with a piston.

CRANKSHAFT, CONNECTING ROD AND CRANKCASE. Crankshaft, connecting rod and rod bearing are a unit assembly; individual components are not available. The crankshaft is supported by ball bearings at both ends.

To remove crankshaft, first remove spark plug and install a piston locking screw in spark plug hole to lock piston and crankshaft. Separate engine from clutch housing. Remove clutch assembly and flywheel from crankshaft. Remove recoil starter housing and unscrew locknut and starter pawl carrier (17.1 cc, 19.6 cc and 19.8 cc engines have left-hand threads) from end of crankshaft. Remove muffler, carburetor, fuel tank and ignition unit. Remove mounting screws from crankcase halves (9 and 15—Fig. SL209). Use a plastic hammer to tap crankshaft out of main bearings and crankcase halves. Remove oil seals (8). Heat crankcase to approximately 130° C (235° F) to aid removal and installation of bearings (10) in crankcase.

Install seals (8—Fig. SL209) with lip toward inside of crankcase. Shims (11) are available in thicknesses of 0.1 and 0.2 mm to adjust crankshaft end play. Maximum allowable end play is 0.3 mm (0.012 in.). There is no gasket between crankcase halves. Apply a suitable gasket sealer to crankcase half mating surfaces.

CLUTCH. The engine is equipped with a two-shoe clutch. The clutch shoe assembly is mounted on the flywheel (1—Fig. SL211). The clutch drum (8) rides in the drive housing (11), which

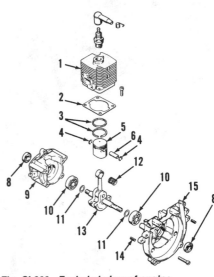

Fig. SL209—Exploded view of engine.

1. Cylinder	9. Crankcase half
2. Gasket	10. Bearing
3. Piston rings	11. Shim
4. Retaining rings	12. Bearing
5. Piston	13. Crankshaft assy.
6. Piston pin	14. Dowel pin
8. Seal	15. Crankcase half

Fig. SL210—Piston ring end gaps must be positioned around locating pins in ring grooves as shown.

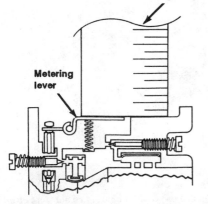

Fig. SL208—Metering lever should be level with chamber floor. Bend metering lever as needed.

Fig. SL211—Exploded view of clutch assembly. On some models, the face of drum (8) is slotted to allow access to snap ring (9).

1. Flywheel
2. Washer
3. Nut
4. Clutch shoes
5. Spring
6. Washer
7. Shoulder bolt
8. Clutch drum
9. Snap ring
10. Bearing
11. Housing
12. Snap ring

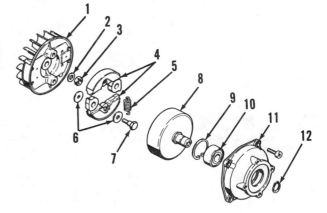

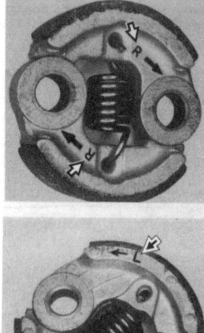

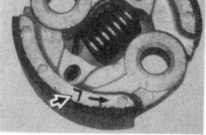

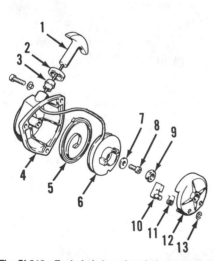

may be the fan housing on some engines.

To remove clutch drum on models with slots in clutch face, reach through slot and detach snap ring (9), then press clutch drum and bearing (10) out of housing. Heating housing will ease removal. On other engines, detach snap ring (12) and press clutch drum shaft out of bearing (10). Detach snap ring (9), heat housing to approximately 280° F (140° C) and remove bearing (10). Reverse removal procedure to install clutch drum.

Clutch shoes (4) are available as a pair. Prior to removing clutch shoes, note whether side marked "R" or "L" (Fig. SL212) faces outward so that shoes may be reinstalled in same position. Tighten clutch mounting screws to 8 N·m (6 ft.-lbs.).

REWIND STARTER. Refer to Figs. SL213 or SL214 for an exploded view of starter. To disassemble starter, detach starter housing (4) from engine. Remove rope handle and allow rope to wind into starter. Unscrew center screw (8) and remove rope pulley (6). Wear appropriate safety eyewear and gloves before detaching rewind spring (5) from housing as spring may uncoil uncontrolled.

To remove starter plate (12), unscrew retaining nut (8) then unscrew plate from crankshaft. Note that nut and plate have left-hand threads on 17.1 cc, 19.6 cc and 19.8 cc engines. Before removing pawl (10) from starter plate, note whether pawl is located in hole marked "R" or "L" so it can be rein-

stalled in same position (Fig. SL215 or SL216).

To assembly starter, install pawl (10) in hole marked "R" (Fig. SL215) or "L" (Fig. SL216) in starter plate. Legs of torsion spring (11) must locate against carrier plate and pawl as shown. Lubricate center post of housing and spring side with light grease. Install rewind spring so coil windings are positioned as shown in Figs. SL213 or SL214. Assemble starter while passing rope through housing rope outlet and attach rope handle to rope. To place tension on starter rope, pull rope out of housing. Engage rope in notch on pulley and rotate pulley against spring tension seven turns. Hold pulley and disengage rope from pulley notch. Release pulley and allow rope to wind on pulley. Check starter operation. Rope handle should be held against housing by spring tension, but it must be possible to rotate pulley at least an additional ½ turn when rope is pulled out fully.

Fig. SL212—Install clutch shoes so "L" or "R" on shoe is visible, depending on direction of crankshaft rotation.

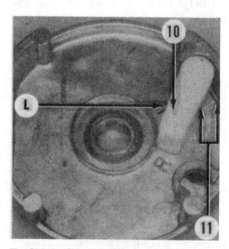

Fig. SL215—On 17.1 cc, 19.6 cc and 19.8 cc engines, install pawl (10) in starter plate hole marked "L." Be sure that legs of spring (11) are against pawl and plate as shown.

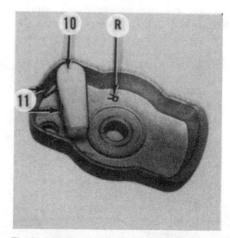

Fig. SL216—On 22.5 cc, 25.4 cc and 34.4 cc engines, install pawl (10) in starter plate hole marked "R." Note position of spring (11).

Fig. SL213—Exploded view of rewind starter used on 17.1 cc, 19.6 cc and 19.8 cc engines. Nut (9) and plate (12) have left-hand threads.

1. Rope handle
2. Cover
3. Rope guide
4. Starter housing
5. Rewind spring
6. Pulley
7. Washer
8. Screw
9. Nut
10. Pawl
11. Spring
12. Carrier plate
13. "E" ring

Fig. SL214—Exploded view of rewind starter used on 22.5 cc, 25.4 cc and 34.4 cc engines.

1. Rope handle
2. Cover
3. Rope guide
4. Starter housing
5. Rewind spring
6. Pulley
7. Washer
8. Screw
9. Nut
10. Pawl
11. Spring
12. Carrier plate
13. "E" ring

Illustrations courtesy Stihl Inc.

STIHL

ENGINE SERVICE

Model	Bore	Stroke	Displacement
Stihl	28 mm	26 mm	16.0 cc
	(1.10 in.)	(1.02 in.)	(0.96 cu. in.)

This engine is used on Stihl Models FS50 and FS51.

ENGINE INFORMATION

The Stihl engine covered in this section is a two-stroke, air-cooled, single-cylinder engine.

MAINTENANCE

LUBRICATION. Engine lubrication is obtained by mixing gasoline with an oil designed for two-stroke, air-cooled engines. Refer to trimmer or blower service section for manufacturer's recommended fuel:oil mixture ratio.

SPARK PLUG. Recommended spark plug is a NGK BMR6 or equivalent. Specified electrode gap for all models is 0.6-0.7 mm (0.024-0.028 in.).

CARBURETOR. The engine is equipped with a Teikei diaphragm-type carburetor. Refer to Fig. SL301 for an exploded view of carburetor.

Initial adjustment of fuel mixture needles from a lightly seated position is $1\frac{1}{4}$ turns open for the idle mixture screw and $\frac{3}{4}$ turn open for the high-speed mixture screw. Final adjustments are performed with trimmer line at recommended length or blade assembly installed. Engine must be at operating temperature and running. Be sure engine air filter is clean before performing carburetor adjustments.

Operate trimmer engine at full throttle and adjust high-speed mixture needle to obtain 9000 rpm. If an accurate tachometer is not available, do not adjust high-speed mixture needle beyond initial setting. Operate trimmer engine at idle speed and adjust idle mixture screw until a smooth idle is obtained and engine does not hesitate during acceleration. Adjust idle speed screw so engine idles just below clutch engagement speed.

Carburetor overhaul is evident after inspection and referral to Fig. SL301. Clean all parts in suitable solvent. Examine fuel inlet valve and seat. Inlet valve (14) is renewable, but carburetor

body must be renewed if seat is excessively worn or damaged. Inspect mixture screws and seats. Renew carburetor body if seats are excessively worn or damaged. Inspect diaphragms (6 and 19) for tears and other damage.

The metering lever (16) must be 2.0 mm (0.08 in.) below gasket surface as shown in Fig. SL302.

IGNITION SYSTEM. The engine is equipped with an electronic ignition system. The ignition system is considered satisfactory if a spark will jump across the 3 mm ($\frac{1}{8}$ in.) gap of a test spark plug. If no spark is produced, check on/off switch, wiring and ignition module air gap. Ignition module air gap should be 0.2-0.3 mm (0.008-0.010 in.). The cylinder must be removed for access to module and flywheel so air gap can be set. Tighten ignition module retaining screws to 2.0 N·m (18 in.-lbs.). If switch, wiring and module air gap are satisfactory, but spark is not present, renew ignition module.

REPAIRS

TIGHTENING TORQUES. Recommended tightening torques are as follows:

Clutch shoe	8 N·m
	(71 in.-lbs.)
Crankcase cover	3.5 N·m
	(31 in.-lbs.)
Crankpin screw	2.0 N·m
	(18 in.-lbs.)
Cylinder	4.0 N·m
	(35 in.-lbs.)
Flywheel	15.0 N·m
	(133 in.-lbs.)
Ignition module	2.0 N·m
	(18 in.-lbs.)

FLYWHEEL. Note that flywheel nut has left-hand threads. Tighten nut to 15.0 N·m (133 in.-lbs.).

PISTON, PIN AND RINGS. To remove piston, remove muffler, carburetor and cylinder cover. Unscrew two retaining

screws and remove cylinder by pulling straight up. Remove piston pin retain-

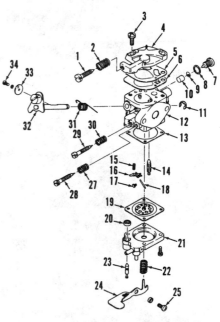

Fig. SL301—Exploded view of Teikei diaphragm carburetor.

1. Idle speed screw		18. Pin
2. Spring		19. Diaphragm
3. Screw		20. Seat
4. Pump cover		21. Cover
5. Gasket		22. Spring
6. Diaphragm		23. Plunger
7. Plug		24. Primer lever
8. "O" ring		25. Screw
9. Screen		27. Spring
10. Felt		28. High-speed mixture
11. "E" ring		screw
12. Body		29. Idle mixture screw
13. Gasket		30. Spring
14. Fuel inlet valve		31. Spring
15. Spring		32. Throttle shaft
16. Metering lever		33. Throttle plate
17. Screw		34. Screw

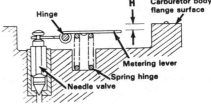

Fig. SL302—Height (H) of metering lever should be 2.0 mm (0.08 in.).

ers and use a suitable puller to remove piston pin. Hold piston securely when removing pin to avoid applying side force to connecting rod. Remove piston from connecting rod.

Piston and ring are available in standard size only.

Fig. SL303—Install piston on rod so arrow on piston crown points toward exhaust port.

Fig. SL304—Piston ring end gaps must be positioned around locating pins in ring grooves as shown.

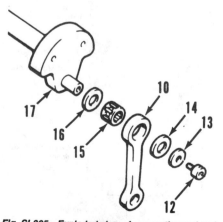

Fig. SL305—Exploded view of connecting rod and crankshaft assembly.

10. Connecting rod
12. Screw
13. Washer
14. Shim
15. Bearing
16. Shim
17. Crankshaft

When reassembling, heat piston to about 60° C (140° F) to ease installation of piston pin. Install piston on connecting rod so arrow on piston crown points toward exhaust port (Fig. SL303). Be sure piston ring gaps are correctly indexed with locating pins in piston ring grooves as shown in Fig. SL304. Lubricate piston and cylinder with oil prior to assembly. Use suitable clamping strap to compress piston rings. Align cylinder so it is correctly positioned on crankcase, then push cylinder straight down over piston. Tighten cylinder retaining screws to 4.0 N·m (35 in.-lbs.).

CYLINDER. The cylinder bore is chrome plated. Renew cylinder if bore is excessively worn or bore surface is cracked, flaking or otherwise damaged. Tighten cylinder retaining screws to 4.0 N·m (35 in.-lbs.).

CRANKSHAFT AND CONNECTING ROD. The crankshaft is supported at flywheel end by two ball bearings. To remove crankshaft, disconnect throt-

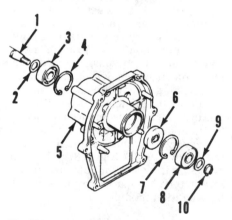

Fig. SL306—Exploded view of main bearing assembly.

1. Crankshaft
2. Shim
3. Bearing
4. Snap ring
5. Crankcase half
6. Seal
7. Snap ring
8. Bearing
9. Shim
10. Snap ring

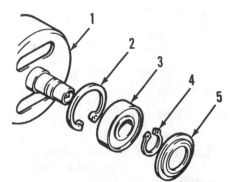

Fig. SL307—Exploded view of clutch drum and bearing assembly.

1. Clutch drum
2. Snap ring
3. Bearing
4. Snap ring
5. Washer

tle cable and remove fan housing mounting screws. Hold starter rope handle while removing fan housing and trimmer drive tube. Turn flywheel and recoil starter rope to release tension of rewind spring. Remove spark plug and install locking screw in spark plug hole to lock piston and crankshaft. Unbolt and remove clutch assembly from flywheel. Remove flywheel nut (left-hand threads) and pull flywheel off crankshaft. Remove snap ring, rope pulley and rewind spring housing. Remove muffler, carburetor, cylinder and piston. Remove fuel tank and fuel tank bracket. Remove crankcase cover. Install piston pin in small end of connecting rod and position a wooden block on top of crankcase to prevent crankshaft from turning. Remove connecting rod retaining screw (12—Fig. SL305), washer (13) and shim (14). Remove connecting rod (10), needle bearing (15) and second shim (16) from crankpin. Remove snap ring (10—Fig. SL306) and shim (9) from end of crankshaft (1). Use plastic mallet to tap crankshaft out of main bearings. Heat crankcase to 212° F (100° C) and tap lightly on wood block to remove bearings (3 and 8) from crankcase. Remove snap rings (4 and 7) and press oil seal (6) out of crankcase.

When installing crankshaft in crankcase and main bearings, vary thickness of shims (2 and 9—Fig. SL306) to obtain 0.1-0.3 mm (0.004-0.012 in.) end play. Install shim (16—Fig. SL305) on crankpin. Apply Loctite 242 to connecting rod retaining screw (12). Tighten crankpin screw to 2.0 N·m (18 in.-lbs.). Tighten crankcase cover screws to 3.5 N·m (31 in.-lbs.).

REED VALVE. A reed valve is located on the inside of the crankcase cover. Renew reed valve if cracked, broken or warped.

CLUTCH. The engine is equipped with a two-shoe clutch. The clutch shoe assembly is mounted on the flywheel. The clutch drum rides in the fan housing.

To remove clutch drum, remove fan housing mounting screws. Hold tension on starter rope while removing fan housing and trimmer drive tube from engine. Remove clamp screw and locating screw from fan housing and pull drive tube out of housing. Reach through slot in drum and detach snap ring (1—Fig. SL307), then press clutch drum and bearing (3) out of fan housing. Reverse removal procedure to install clutch drum. Rotate starter rope pulley three turns clockwise to pretension starter rewind spring before installing fan housing.

Clutch shoes are available as a pair. Install clutch shoes so sides marked "R" are visible as shown in Fig. SL308. Tighten clutch shoe screws to 8 N·m (71 in.-lbs.).

REWIND STARTER. The starter is located between the flywheel and the crankcase. The rewind spring is contained in a case that is attached to the crankcase. To remove starter assembly, remove fan housing from engine. Remove spark plug and install locking tool in spark plug hole to lock piston and crankshaft. Remove flywheel nut (left-hand threads) and pull flywheel off crankshaft. Remove starter pawls (1—Fig. SL309) and torsion springs (2) from flywheel if necessary. Pawls and springs must be renewed in pairs. Remove snap ring retaining rope pulley and remove pulley. Remove rewind spring housing mounting screws and remove spring and housing as an assembly.

When reassembling, position rope pulley on spring housing so that spring loop engages slot in pulley as shown in Fig. SL310. Rope length should be 70 cm (27½ in.) long. Wind rope around pulley in a clockwise direction as viewed from flywheel side of pulley. Place tension on rewind spring before engaging flywheel with pulley. Rotate rope rotor and flywheel three turns clockwise to pretension starter spring, then install fan housing. When properly installed, rope handle should be held against housing by spring tension.

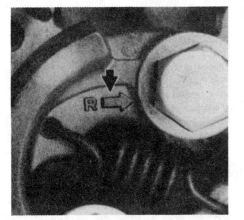

Fig. SL308—Install clutch shoes so "R" on shoe is visible.

Fig. SL309—Starter pawls (1) are located on back side of flywheel.

Fig. SL310—Starter rewind spring loop must engage slot in rope pulley.

STIHL

ENGINE SERVICE

Model	Bore	Stroke	Displacement
Stihl	35 mm	31 mm	29.8 cc
	(1.38 in.)	(1.22 in.)	(1.82 cu. in.)
Stihl	38 mm	31 mm	35.2 cc
	(1.50 in.)	(1.22 in.)	(2.15 cu. in.)
Stihl	40 mm	31 mm	39.0 cc
	(1.57 in.)	(1.22 in.)	(2.38 cu. in.)

These engines are used on Stihl Models FS160, FS180, FS220 and FS280.

ENGINE INFORMATION

The Stihl engines covered in this section are two-stroke, air-cooled, single-cylinder engines.

MAINTENANCE

LUBRICATION. Engine lubrication is obtained by mixing gasoline with an oil designed for two-stroke, air-cooled engines. Refer to trimmer service section for manufacturer's recommended fuel:oil mixture ratio.

SPARK PLUG. Recommended spark plug is NGK BPMR7A or equivalent. Specified electrode gap is 0.5 mm (0.020 in.). Tighten spark plug to 20 N·m (177 in.-lbs.).

CARBURETOR. The engine is equipped with a Zama C1S diaphragm-type carburetor. Refer to Fig. SL401 for an exploded view of carburetor. Initial adjustment of idle mixture screw (15) and high-speed mixture screw (16) is one turn out from a lightly seated position. Final adjustment is performed with engine at normal operating temperature. Be sure engine air filter is clean. Before final adjustment on trimmer models, cutter line should be desired length.

Adjust idle mixture screw (15) so engine idles smoothly and accelerates cleanly without hesitation. Adjust idle speed screw (27) so engine idles just below clutch engagement speed. Open throttle to wide-open position and adjust high-speed mixture screw (16). Engine speed must not exceed 12,500 rpm. If an accurate tachometer is not available, do not adjust high-speed mixture screw beyond initial setting. Do not set high-speed adjustment screw too lean as engine damage may result. The ignition system on engines with 39 cc displacement has an engine speed limiting circuit that prevents engine speeds in excess of 13,200 rpm.

Carburetor disassembly and reassembly is evident after inspection of carburetor and referral to Fig. SL401. Do not lose detent ball (12) when withdrawing choke shaft. Clean and inspect all components. Inspect diaphragms (2 and 23) for defects that may affect operation. Examine fuel inlet valve and seat. Inlet valve (6) is renewable, but carburetor body must be renewed if seat is damaged or excessively worn. Discard carburetor body if mixture screw seats are damaged or excessively worn. Clean fuel screen (22).

Metering lever should be level with chamber floor as shown in Fig. SL402. Bend metering lever as needed.

IGNITION SYSTEM. Engines with 39 cc displacement are equipped with an ignition coil and a separate ignition module. On all other engines the ignition module and ignition coil are a molded assembly.

Air gap between ignition module/coil and flywheel magnet should be 0.15-0.25 mm (0.006-0.010 in.). Tighten module/coil retaining screws to 3.0 N·m (26 in.-lbs.).

The ignition system on engines with 39 cc displacement incorporates an engine speed limiter that prevents engine speed from exceeding 13,200 rpm.

Ignition coil primary windings resistance should be 0.8-1.3 ohms, and secondary windings resistance should be 7200-8800 ohms.

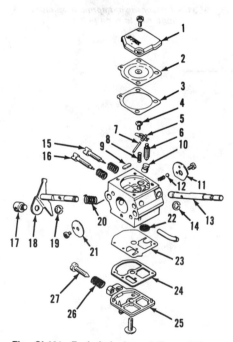

Fig. SL401—Exploded view of Zama C1S carburetor.

1. Cover		16. High-speed mixture
2. Metering diaphragm		screw
3. Gasket		17. Swivel
4. Screw		18. Throttle shaft
5. Metering lever		19. "E" ring
6. Fuel inlet valve		20. Spring
7. Pin		21. Throttle plate
8. Spring		22. Screen
9. Welch plug		23. Fuel pump
10. Nozzle		diaphragm
11. Choke plate		24. Gasket
12. Detent ball		25. Cover
13. Choke shaft		26. Spring
14. "E" ring		27. Idle speed screw
15. Idle mixture screw		

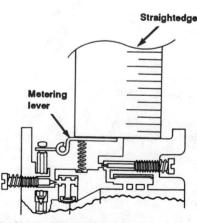

Fig. SL402—Metering lever should be level with chamber floor. Bend metering lever as needed.

REPAIRS

TIGHTENING TORQUES. Recommended tightening torques are as follows:

Carburetor . . . . .4 N·m
(35 in.-lbs.)
Clutch shoe . . . . .12 N·m
(106 in.-lbs.)
Crankcase . . . . .8.5 N·m
(75 in.-lbs.)
Cylinder . . . . .8 N·m
(71 in.-lbs.).
Flywheel . . . . .24 N·m
(212 in.-lbs.)
Ignition module . . . . .3 N·m
(26 in.-lbs.)
Spark plug . . . . .20 N·m
(177 in.-lbs.)
Starter cup . . . . .10 N·m
(88 in.-lbs.)

INTAKE MANIFOLD. The intake manifold clamp must be positioned so the clamp opening is 70 degrees from vertical as shown in Fig. SL403. When

Fig. SL403—Position clamp (1) on intake manifold (2) so gap at clamp ends is 70 degrees from vertical as shown.

Fig. SL404—Wind a string around flange of intake manifold and pull string through opening in tank housing during installation of housing.

inserting manifold through tank assembly, wrap a string around manifold flange as shown in Fig. SL404. Place ends of string through intake opening in fuel tank housing and pull string while pressing tank housing against manifold during assembly so flange on manifold does not fold back.

PISTON, PIN AND RINGS. The piston is equipped with two piston rings. Ring rotation is prevented by a locating pin in each piston ring groove. Piston and rings are available only in standard diameter.

To remove piston, remove engine shroud, muffler, air cleaner and carburetor. Remove metal sleeve from rubber intake manifold tube. Remove throttle cable clamp and disconnect ignition wires at spade terminals. Unbolt and remove clutch housing and trimmer drive shaft from engine. Remove rewind starter assembly. Remove fuel tank housing mounting screws, push manifold tube out of tank housing and remove housing from engine. Remove cylinder mounting screws and pull cylinder off piston. Pry piston pin retaining rings (6—Fig. SL405) from piston (4). Push piston pin (5) out of piston. If piston pin is stuck, lightly tap pin out of piston while holding piston securely to avoid applying side force to connecting rod. Remove piston and needle bearing (7) from connecting rod.

When reassembling, heat piston to about 60° C (140° F) to ease installation of piston pin. Install piston on connecting rod so arrow (Fig. SL406) on piston crown points toward exhaust port. Be sure piston ring gaps are correctly indexed with locating pins in piston ring grooves as shown in Fig. SL407. Lubricate piston and cylinder bore with oil.

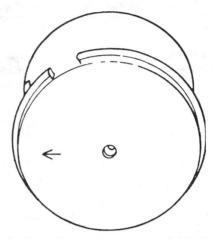

Fig. SL406—Install piston so arrow points toward exhaust port.

Fig. SL407—Piston ring end gaps must be positioned around locating pins in ring grooves as shown.

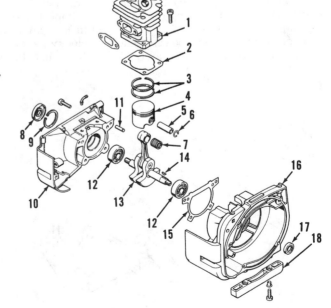

Fig. SL405—Exploded view of engine.

1. Cylinder
2. Gasket
3. Piston rings
4. Piston
5. Piston pin
6. Retaining ring
7. Bearing
8. Seal
9. Snap ring
10. Crankcase half
11. Dowel pin
12. Bearing
13. Crankshaft assy.
14. Key
15. Gasket
16. Crankcase half
17. Seal
18. Support

Use a suitable clamping strap to compress piston rings. Align cylinder so it is correctly positioned on crankcase, then push cylinder straight down over piston. Complete installation by reversing removal procedure.

CYLINDER. The engine is equipped with a cylinder that has an impregnated bore. Renew cylinder if bore is excessively worn, scored or otherwise damaged. Cylinder is available only in standard size with a piston. Tighten cylinder screws to 8 N·m (71 in.-lbs.).

CONNECTING ROD, CRANKSHAFT AND CRANKCASE. The crankshaft is supported by ball bearings at both ends. Connecting rod, crankpin and crankshaft are a pressed-together assembly and available only as a unit.

To remove crankshaft assembly, remove cylinder as previously outlined. Position a piece of wood between bottom of piston skirt and crankcase to prevent crankshaft from turning. Remove clutch assembly from flywheel. Remove flywheel mounting nut and pull flywheel from crankshaft using a suitable puller tool. Remove ignition module and trigger unit, if so equipped. Remove starter cup locknut, then unscrew starter cup from crankshaft. Remove piston pin and piston from connecting rod. Remove crankcase retaining screws and press crankshaft out of starter side crankcase half (10—Fig. SL405) first and then out of flywheel side crankcase half (16). Pry out seals (8 and 17) and remove snap ring (9). Heat crankcase halves to approximately 150° C (300° F), then tap lightly against wood block to remove main bearings (12).

Connecting rod big end rides on a roller bearing and should be inspected for excessive wear and damage. If rod, bearing or crankshaft is damaged, complete crankshaft and connecting rod assembly must be renewed.

When installing main bearings, heat crankcase halves to approximately 150°

C (300° F) and seat bearing against snap ring (9—Fig. SL405) or against shoulder of crankcase half (16). It may be necessary to use a soldering iron to heat main bearing inner race to ease insertion of crankshaft. Install oil seals so lip is toward inside of crankcase. Tighten crankcase screws to 8.5 N·m (75 in.-lbs.).

CLUTCH. The engine is equipped with a two-shoe clutch. The clutch shoe assembly is mounted on the flywheel (1—Fig. SL408). The clutch drum (8) rides in the drive housing (11).

To remove clutch drum, first remove engine shroud and air cleaner assembly. Disconnect throttle cable and remove throttle cable clamp. Disconnect ignition wires at spade terminals. Unbolt and remove clutch housing and trimmer drive tube from engine. Detach snap ring (12) and press clutch drum shaft out of bearing (10). Detach snap ring (9) and press bearing (10) from housing. Reverse removal procedure to install clutch drum.

Clutch shoes are available as a pair. Install clutch shoes so arrows on shoes point in a counterclockwise direction as shown in Fig. SL409. Install clutch spring (6) so, when assembly is mounted on flywheel, the spring hook ends will be toward flywheel (1).

REWIND STARTER. Refer to Fig. SL410 for an exploded view of rewind starter. To disassemble starter, detach starter housing (3) from engine. Remove rope handle and allow rope to wind into starter. Detach retaining clip (8) and remove rope pulley (5). Wear appropriate safety eyewear and gloves before detaching rewind spring (4) from housing as spring may uncoil uncontrolled. To remove starter cup (10), unscrew retaining nut (9) then unscrew cup from crankshaft.

Rope length should be 96 cm (37¾ in.). Wind rewind spring in counterclockwise direction from outer end. Note that clip (8) retains pulley (5) and

pawl (6) and that peg on pawl must be inside clip as shown in Fig. SL411. Closed end of clip (C—Fig. SL411) points

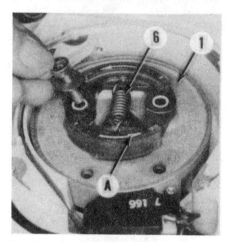

Fig. SL409—Install clutch shoes so arrow (A) points in counterclockwise direction. Hook ends of spring (6) must be toward flywheel (1).

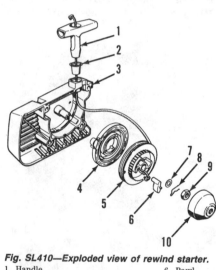

Fig. SL410—Exploded view of rewind starter.
1. Handle
2. Rope outlet
3. Starter housing
4. Rewind spring
5. Pulley
6. Pawl
7. Washer
8. Clip
9. Nut
10. Starter cup

Fig. SL411—Closed end of clip (C) should point in a counterclockwise direction and peg on pawl must be positioned inside the clip.

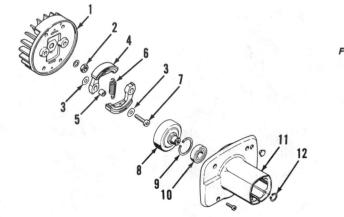

Fig. SL408—Exploded view of clutch assembly.
1. Flywheel
2. Nut
3. Washer
4. Clutch shoe
5. Bushing
6. Spring
7. Screw
8. Clutch drum
9. Snap ring
10. Bearing
11. Drive housing
12. Snap ring

in a counterclockwise direction when installed correctly. Assemble starter while passing rope through housing rope outlet and attach rope handle to rope. To place tension on starter rope, pull rope out of housing. Engage rope in notch on pulley and turn pulley counterclockwise seven turns. Hold pulley and disengage rope from pulley notch. Release pulley and allow rope to wind on pulley. Check starter operation. Rope handle should be held against housing by spring tension, but it must be possible to rotate pulley at least $\frac{1}{2}$ turn counterclockwise when rope is pulled out fully.

Tighten starter cup to 10 N·m (7 ft.-lbs.) and locknut to 24 N·m (18 ft.lbs.).

STIHL

ENGINE SERVICE

Model	Bore	Stroke	Displacement
Stihl	44 mm	34 mm	51.7 cc
	(1.73 in.)	(1.34 in.)	(3.16 cu. in.)
Stihl	46 mm	34 mm	56.5 cc
	(1.81 in.)	(1.34 in.)	(3.45 cu. in.)

These engines are used on Stihl Models BG17, BR320, BR400, FS360, FS420, SG17, SR320 and SR400.

ENGINE INFORMATION

The Stihl engines covered in this section are two-stroke, air-cooled, single-cylinder engines.

MAINTENANCE

LUBRICATION. Engine lubrication is obtained by mixing gasoline with an oil

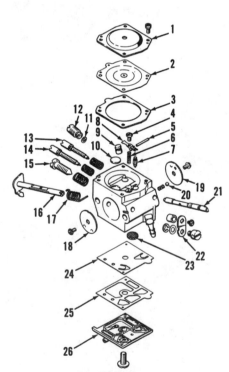

Fig. SL501—Exploded view of Walbro HD carburetor.

1. Cover	14. Idle mixture screw
2. Metering diaphragm	15. Idle speed screw
3. Gasket	16. Throttle shaft
4. Screw	17. Spring
5. Pin	18. Throttle plate
6. Spring	19. Choke plate
7. Fuel inlet valve	20. Detent ball
8. Metering lever	21. Choke shaft
9. Nozzle	22. Throttle lever
10. Welch plug	23. Screen
11. "O" ring	24. Fuel pump
12. Governor	diaphragm
13. High-speed mixture	25. Gasket
screw	26. Cover

designed for two-stroke, air-cooled engines. Refer to trimmer or blower service section for manufacturer's recommended fuel:oil mixture ratio.

SPARK PLUG. Recommended spark plug is NGK BPMR7A or equivalent. Specified electrode gap is 0.5 mm (0.020 in.). Tighten spark plug to 25 N·m (221 in.-lbs.).

CARBURETOR. The engine is equipped with a Walbro HD diaphragm carburetor. Refer to Fig. SL501 for an exploded view of carburetor. Initial setting of idle mixture screw and high-speed mixture screw is one turn out from a lightly seated position. Final adjustment is performed with engine at normal operating temperature. Be sure that air filter is clean before adjusting carburetor.

To perform final adjustment on trimmer and brush cutters, proceed as follows. Cutter line should be desired length. Adjust idle mixture screw (14—Fig. SL501) so engine idles smoothly and accelerates cleanly without hesitation. Adjust idle speed screw (15) so engine idles just below clutch engagement speed. Open throttle to wide-open position and adjust high-speed mixture screw (13). Engine must not exceed 12,500 rpm. If an accurate tachometer is not available, do not adjust high-speed mixture screw beyond initial setting. Do not set high-speed adjustment screw too lean as engine damage may result. The carburetor on trimmer or brush cutter engines with 56.5 cc displacement is equipped with a governor valve (12) that enriches the mixture at high-speed to prevent overspeeding.

To perform final adjustment on blowers, proceed as follows. Adjust idle mixture screw (14—Fig. SL501) so engine idles smoothly and accelerates cleanly without hesitation. Open throttle to wide-open position and adjust high-speed mixture screw (13) to obtain

highest engine speed, then turn high-speed mixture screw counterclockwise until engine speed drops 150 rpm. Do not set adjustment screw too lean as engine damage may result.

Carburetor disassembly and reassembly is evident after inspection of carburetor and referral to Fig. SL501. On models so equipped, do not lose detent ball (20) when withdrawing choke shaft. Clean and inspect all components. Wires or drill bits should not be used to clean passages as fuel flow may be altered. Inspect diaphragms (2 and 24) for defects that may affect operation. Examine fuel inlet valve and seat. Inlet valve (7) is renewable, but carburetor body must be renewed if seat is damaged or excessively worn. Discard carburetor body if mixture screw seats are damaged or excessively worn. Screen should be clean.

Press nozzle (9) into body until inner face is flush with venturi wall as shown in Fig. SL502. Install throttle plate so holes (H—Fig. SL503) are toward fuel pump cover. Install choke plate so notch (N—Fig. SL504) is toward fuel pump cover. The metering lever should be

Fig. SL502—Install nozzle (arrow) so face is flush with carburetor bore.

Illustrations courtesy Stihl Inc.

flush with body surface as shown in Fig. SL505. Bend metering lever as needed.

IGNITION SYSTEM. The engine is equipped with a one-piece, solid state ignition system. The ignition module and ignition coil are a molded assembly.

Ignition coil air gap should be 0.2-0.3 mm (0.008-0.012 in.) on trimmers and brush cutters, and 0.15-0.25 mm (0.006-0.010 in.) on blowers. Tighten ignition coil retaining screws to 8.0 N·m (71 in.-lbs.). Ignition timing should be 2.4-3.0 mm (0.095-0.118 in.) BTDC on trimmers and brush cutters. Ignition timing on blowers should be 2.2-2.9 mm (0.08-0.11 in.) BTDC. Ignition timing is not adjustable.

Ignition coil primary windings resistance on trimmers and brush cutters should be 0.7-1.0 ohm, and secondary windings resistance should be 7700-10,300 ohms.

Ignition coil primary windings resistance on blowers should be 0.8-1.3 ohms, and secondary windings resistance should be 7200-8800 ohms.

REPAIRS

TIGHTENING TORQUES. Recommended tightening torques are as follows:
Carburetor:
Trimmer . . . . .5 N·m (44 in.-lbs.)
Blower . . . . .4.5 N·m (40 in.-lbs.)
Clutch shoe . . . . .12 N·m (106 in.-lbs.)
Crankcase . . . . .8 N·m (71 in.-lbs.)
Cylinder . . . . .8 N·m (71 in.-lbs.)
Flywheel:
Trimmer . . . . .30 N·m (22 ft.-lbs.)
Blower . . . . .25 N·m (221 in.-lbs.)

Ignition module . . . . .8 N·m (71 in.-lbs.)
Spark plug . . . . .25 N·m (221 in.-lbs.)
Starter cup . . . . .15 N·m (133 in.-lbs.)
Starter cup nut . . . . .25 N·m (221 in.-lbs.)

INTAKE MANIFOLD. The intake manifold clamp on trimmers and brush cutters must be positioned so the clamp screw is parallel to the cylinder fins as shown in Fig. SL506. Tighten screw so opening between clamp ends is 8-9 mm ($^5/_{16}$-$^3/_8$ in.). When inserting manifold through tank assembly, wrap a string around manifold and thread ends of string through opening in tank housing. Pull string while pushing tank housing against manifold so flange on manifold does not fold back.

PISTON, PIN AND RINGS. The piston is equipped with two piston rings. Ring rotation is prevented by a locating pin in each piston ring groove. Piston and rings are available only in standard diameter.

To remove piston, remove engine shrouds, carburetor and muffler. On trimmer and brush cutter models, disconnect throttle cable and ignition wires from engine. Unbolt and remove clutch housing and drive tube from engine. Remove fuel tank housing. On blower models, remove power unit from support frame. On all models, remove cylinder mounting screws and pull cylinder off piston. Pry retaining rings (6—Fig. SL507) from piston and push piston pin (5) out of piston. If pin is stuck, tap lightly with a brass drift while holding piston securely to avoid applying side thrust to connecting rod. Remove piston and needle bearing (7) from connecting rod.

Install piston on connecting rod so arrow (Fig. SL508) on piston crown points

toward exhaust port. Heat the piston to approximately 60° C (140° F) to ease installation of piston pin. Be sure piston ring gaps are correctly indexed with locating pins in piston ring grooves as shown in Fig. SL509. Lubricate piston and cylinder bore with oil. Use a suitable clamping strap to compress piston rings. Align cylinder so it is correctly positioned on crankcase, then push cylinder straight down over piston. Complete installation by reversing removal procedure.

CYLINDER. The engine is equipped with a cylinder that has an impregnated bore. Renew cylinder if bore is excessively worn, scored or otherwise damaged. Cylinder is available only in standard size with a piston. Tighten cylinder screws to 8 N·m (71 in.-lbs.).

CONNECTING ROD, CRANKSHAFT AND CRANKCASE. The crankshaft (14—Fig. SL507) is supported by ball bearings (13) at both ends. Connecting rod, crankpin and crankshaft are a pressed-together assembly and available only as a unit.

To remove crankshaft assembly, first separate engine from clutch housing

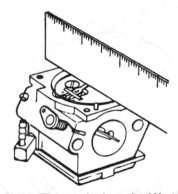

Fig. SL505—The metering lever should just touch a straightedge laid across the carburetor body. Bend lever as needed.

Fig. SL506—Install intake manifold clamp on trimmers and brush cutters so clamp screw (1) is parallel to cylinder fins as shown.

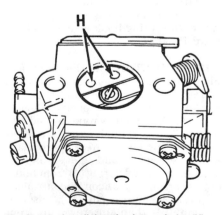

Fig. SL503—Install throttle plate so holes (H) are toward fuel pump cover.

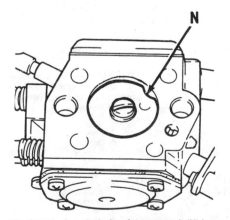

Fig. SL504—Install choke plate so notch (N) is toward fuel pump cover.

and drive tube on trimmer and brush cutter models, or from blower housing on blower models. Remove cylinder as outlined above. Position a piece of wood between bottom of piston skirt and crankcase to prevent piston and crankshaft from moving. Remove clutch assembly (trimmers and brush cutters)

and flywheel (all models). A suitable puller will be required to remove flywheel. Unscrew starter cup locknut, then unscrew starter cup from crankshaft. Remove piston from connecting rod. Remove screws securing the crankcase halves and press crankshaft out of first one crankcase half and then the other half. Pry out oil seals (8 and 16) and remove snap ring (12). Press bearings (13) from crankcase halves (9 and 15).

Connecting rod big end rides on a roller bearing and should be inspected for excessive wear and damage. If rod, bearing or crankshaft is damaged, complete crankshaft and connecting rod assembly must be renewed.

When installing main bearings, heat crankcase halves to approximately 80° C (180° F) and seat bearing against snap ring (12—Fig. SL507) or against shoulder of crankcase half (15). Install bearing with shouldered side toward snap ring (12). It may be necessary to heat main bearing to ease insertion of crankshaft. Install oil seals so lip is toward inside of crankcase. Tighten crankcase screws to 8 N·m (71 in.-lbs.).

Fig. SL507—Exploded view of engine used on trimmers and brush cutters. Blower engine is similar.

1. Cylinder
2. Gasket
3. Piston rings
4. Piston
5. Piston pin
6. Retaining ring
7. Bearing
8. Seal
9. Crankcase half
10. Dowel pin
11. Gasket
12. Snap ring
13. Bearings
14. Crankshaft assy.
15. Crankcase half
16. Seal

CLUTCH. The engine on trimmers and brush cutters is equipped with a two-shoe clutch. The clutch shoe assembly is mounted on the flywheel (1—Fig. SL510). The clutch drum (9) rides in the clutch housing (11).

To remove clutch drum, disconnect throttle cable and ignition wires from engine. Remove clutch housing mounting screws and remove clutch housing and drive tube as an assembly. Remove clutch housing clamp bolt and set screw and withdraw drive tube from housing. Detach snap ring (13) and press clutch drum shaft out of bearing (12). Detach snap ring (10) and remove bearing (12). Reverse removal procedure to install clutch drum.

Clutch shoes (3) are available as a pair. Install clutch shoes so arrows on shoes point in a counterclockwise direction as shown in Fig. SL511. Install clutch spring (5) so when assembly is mounted on flywheel the spring hook ends will be toward flywheel.

Fig. SL508—Install piston on connecting rod so arrow points toward exhaust port.

Fig. SL509—Piston ring end gaps must be positioned around locating pins in ring grooves as shown.

REWIND STARTER. Refer to Fig. SL512 for an exploded view of rewind starter. To disassemble starter, detach starter housing (3) from engine. Remove rope handle and allow rope to wind into starter. Detach retaining clip (8) and remove rope pulley (5). Wear appropriate safety eyewear and gloves before detaching rewind spring (4) from housing as spring may uncoil uncontrolled.

To remove starter cup (10), unscrew locknut (9), then unscrew cup from crankshaft.

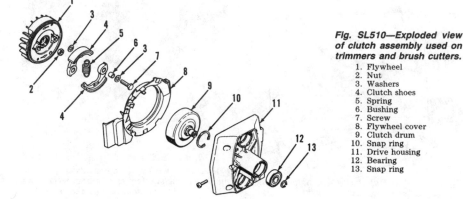

Fig. SL510—Exploded view of clutch assembly used on trimmers and brush cutters.

1. Flywheel
2. Nut
3. Washers
4. Clutch shoes
5. Spring
6. Bushing
7. Screw
8. Flywheel cover
9. Clutch drum
10. Snap ring
11. Drive housing
12. Bearing
13. Snap ring

Rope length should be 96 cm (37³/₄ in.). Wind rewind spring in counterclockwise direction from outer end. Note that clip (8) retains pulley and pawl (6) and that peg on pawl must be inside clip as shown in Fig. SL513. Closed end of clip (Fig. SL513) points in a counterclockwise direction when installed correctly. Assemble starter while passing rope through housing rope outlet and attach rope handle to rope. To place tension on starter rope, pull rope out of housing. Engage rope in notch on pulley and turn pulley counterclockwise seven turns. Hold pulley and disengage rope from pulley notch. Release pulley and allow rope to wind on pulley. Check starter operation. Rope handle should be held against housing by spring tension, but it must be possible to rotate pulley at least ¹/₂ turn counterclockwise when rope is pulled out fully.

Tighten starter cup to 10 N·m (88 in.-lbs.) and locknut to 25 N·m (18 ft.-lbs.).

Fig. SL511—Install clutch shoes so arrows point in counterclockwise direction. Hook ends of spring (5) must be toward flywheel.

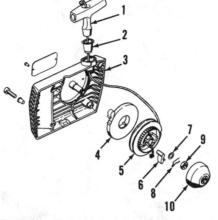

Fig. SL512—Exploded view of rewind starter used on trimmers and brush cutters. Starter on blowers is similar.

1. Handle	6. Pawl
2. Rope outlet	7. Washer
3. Starter housing	8. Clip
4. Rewind spring	9. Nut
5. Pulley	10. Starter cup

Fig. SL513—Closed end of starter clip (arrow) should point in a counterclockwise direction. Pawl pin must be located inside the clip.

Illustrations courtesy Stihl Inc.

TANAKA (TAS)

ENGINE SERVICE

Model	Bore	Stroke	Displacement
Tanaka	27 mm	28 mm	16.0 cc
	(1.06 in.)	(1.10 in.)	(0.94 cu. in.)
Tanaka	30 mm	28 mm	20.0 cc
	(1.18 in.)	(1.10 in.)	(1.22 cu. in.)
Tanaka	31 mm	28 mm	21.0 cc
	(1.22 in.)	(1.10 in.)	(1.28 cu. in.)
Tanaka	31 mm	30 mm	22.6 cc
	(1.22 in.)	(1.18 in.)	(1.38 cu. in.)
Tanaka	33 mm	30 mm	26.0 cc
	(1.30 in.)	(1.18 in.)	(1.59 cu. in.)
Tanaka	36 mm	30 mm	31.0 cc
	(1.42 in.)	(1.18 in.)	(1.86 cu. in.)
Tanaka	38 mm	30 mm	34.0 cc
	(1.50 in.)	(1.18 in.)	(2.07 cu. in.)
Tanaka	38 mm	33 mm	37.4 cc
	(1.50 in.)	(1.30 in.)	(2.28 cu. in.)
Tanaka	40 mm	32 mm	40.0 cc
	(1.57 in.)	(1.26 in.)	(2.44 cu. in.)
Tanaka	38 mm	38 mm	43.0 cc
	(1.50 in.)	(1.50 in.)	(2.62 cu. in.)
Tanaka	41 mm	38 mm	50.2 cc
	(1.61 in.)	(1.50 in.)	(3.06 cu. in.)

Fig. TA101—Exploded view of Walbro HDA carburetor.

1. Cover
2. Fuel pump diaphragm
3. Gasket
4. Screen
5. Throttle plate
6. Throttle shaft
7. Throttle stop
8. Choke shaft
9. Idle speed screw
10. Idle mixture screw
11. High-speed mixture screw
12. Choke plate
13. Detent ball
14. Spring
15. Fuel inlet valve
16. Metering lever
17. Pin
18. Screw
19. Gasket
20. Metering diaphragm
21. Plate
22. Cover

These engines are used on Tanaka equipment, as well as equipment of other manufacturers. Refer to other Tanaka engine section for service information on engines used on Tanaka Models AST-5000, TBC-4000, TBC-4500 and TBC-5000.

ENGINE INFORMATION

Tanaka two-stroke, air-cooled gasoline engines are used by several manufacturers of string trimmers, brush cutters and blowers. Tanaka trimmer AST-7000 is equipped with an electric starter.

MAINTENANCE

LUBRICATION. Engine lubrication is obtained by mixing gasoline with an oil designed for two-stroke, air-cooled engines. Refer to trimmer or blower service section for manufacturer's recommended fuel:oil mixture ratio.

SPARK PLUG. Recommended spark plug is NGK BM6A or equivalent. Electrode gap should be 0.6 mm (0.024 in.).

CARBURETOR. Various types of carburetors have been used. Refer to the appropriate following section for carburetor service.

Walbro HDA. The Walbro HDA is used on some engines. Initial setting of idle and high-speed mixture screws is $1^{1}/_{8}$ turns out from a lightly seated position. Final adjustment is performed with engine running at normal operating temperature. Be sure engine air filter is clean before adjusting carburetor.

Adjust idle speed screw (9—Fig. TA101) so engine idles at 2500 rpm. Adjust idle mixture screw (10) to obtain highest idle speed, then turn screw $^{1}/_{6}$ turn counterclockwise and readjust idle speed screw to 2500 rpm. Adjust high-speed mixture screw (11) to obtain highest engine speed at full throttle, then turn screw $^{1}/_{6}$ turn counterclockwise. Do not adjust high-speed mixture screw too lean as engine may be damaged.

Carburetor disassembly and reassembly is evident after inspection of carburetor and referral to Fig. TA101. Clean and inspect all components. Wires or drill bits should not be used to clean passages as fuel flow may be altered. Inspect diaphragms (2 and 20) for defects that may affect operation. Examine fuel inlet valve and seat. Inlet valve (15) is renewable, but carburetor body must be renewed if seat is damaged or excessively worn. Discard carburetor body if mixture screw seats are damaged or excessively worn. Screens should be clean. Be sure throttle plate fits shaft and carburetor bore properly. Apply Loctite to throttle plate retaining screws. Adjust metering lever height so meter lever tip is flush with body as shown in Fig. TA102.

Walbro WA. Some engines are equipped with a Walbro WA diaphragm-type carburetor. Initial adjustment of idle and high-speed mixture screws is 1¼ turns out from a lightly seated position. Final adjustments are performed with trimmer line at recommended length or blade installed. Engine must be at operating temperature and running. Be sure engine air filter is clean before adjusting carburetor.

Adjust idle speed screw (11—Fig. TA103) so trimmer head or blade does not rotate. Adjust idle mixture screw (5) to obtain maximum idle speed possible, then turn idle mixture screw ⅙ turn counterclockwise. Readjust idle speed. Operate unit at full throttle and adjust high-speed mixture screw (4) to obtain maximum engine rpm, then turn high-speed mixture screw ⅙ turn counterclockwise.

When overhauling carburetor, refer to exploded view in Fig. TA103. Examine fuel inlet valve and seat. Inlet valve (14) is renewable, but carburetor body must be renewed if seat is excessively worn or damaged. Inspect mixture screws and seats. Renew carburetor body if seats are excessively worn or damaged. Clean fuel screen. Inspect diaphragms for tears and other damage.

Check metering lever height as shown in Fig. TA104 using Walbro tool 500-13. Metering lever should just touch leg on tool. Bend lever to obtain correct lever height.

Walbro WY and WYJ. Some engines may be equipped with a Walbro WY or WYJ carburetor. This is a diaphragm-type carburetor that uses a barrel-type throttle rather than a throttle plate.

Idle fuel for the carburetor flows up into the throttle barrel where it is fed into the air stream. On some models, the idle fuel flow can be adjusted by turning an idle mixture limiter plate (P—Fig.

TA105). Initial setting is in center notch. Rotating the plate clockwise will lean the idle mixture. Inside the limiter plate is an idle mixture needle (N—Fig. TA106) that is preset at the factory. If removed, use the following procedure to determine correct position. Back out needle (N) until unscrewed. Screw in needle five turns on Model WY or 15 turns on Model WYJ. Rotate idle mixture plate (P—Fig. TA105) to center notch. Run engine until normal operating temperature is attained. Adjust idle speed screw so trimmer head or blade does not rotate. Rotate idle mixture needle (N—Fig. TA106) and obtain highest rpm (turning needle clockwise leans the mixture), then turn needle ¼ turn counterclockwise. Readjust idle speed screw. Note that idle mixture plate and needle are available only as an assembly with throttle barrel (21—Fig. TA107).

The high-speed mixture is controlled by a removable fixed jet (16—Fig. TA107).

To overhaul carburetor, refer to exploded view in Fig. TA107 and note the following: On models with a plastic body, clean only with solvents approved for use with plastic. Do not use wire or drill bits to clean fuel passages as fuel flow may be altered. Do not disassemble throttle barrel assembly (21). Exam-

ine fuel inlet valve and seat. Inlet valve (9) is renewable, but fuel pump body (11) must be renewed if seat is excessively worn or damaged. Clean fuel screen. Inspect diaphragms for tears and other damage. When installing plates and gaskets (12 through 15) note that tabs (T) on ends will "stairstep" when correctly installed. Adjust metering lever height to obtain 1.5 mm (0.059 in.) between carburetor body surface and lever as shown in Fig. TA108.

Walbro WZ. Some engines may be equipped with a Walbro WZ carburetor. This is a diaphragm-type carburetor that uses a barrel-type throttle rather than a throttle plate.

Idle fuel for the carburetor flows up into the throttle barrel where it is fed

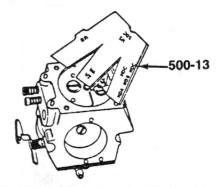

Fig. TA104—Metering lever should just touch leg of Walbro tool 500-13. Bend lever to obtain correct lever height.

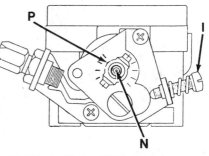

Fig. TA105—On Walbro WY or WYJ carburetor, idle speed screw is located at (I), idle mixture limiter plate is located at (P) and idle mixture needle is located at (N). A plug covers the idle mixture needle.

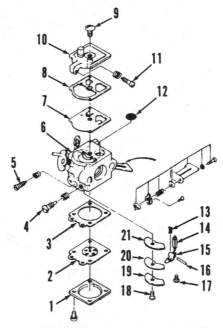

Fig. TA103—Exploded view of Walbro WA carburetor.

1. Cover	
2. Diaphragm	
3. Gasket	11. Idle speed screw
4. High-speed mixture	12. Screen
screw	13. Spring
5. Idle mixture screw	14. Fuel inlet valve
6. Body	15. Metering lever
7. Fuel pump	16. Pin
diaphragm	17. Screw
8. Gasket	18. Screw
9. Screw	19. Circuit plate
10. Cover	20. Diaphragm
	21. Gasket

Fig. TA102—Tip of metering lever should be flush with body. Bend metering lever as needed.

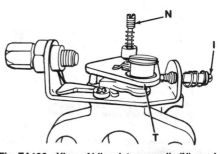

Fig. TA106—View of idle mixture needle (N) used on Walbro WY carburetor.

into the air stream. Idle fuel flow can be adjusted by turning idle mixture limiter plate (P—Fig. TA109). Initial setting is in center notch. Rotating the plate clockwise will lean the idle mixture. Inside the limiter plate is an idle mixture needle (N—Fig. TA106) that is preset at the factory (a plug covers the needle). If idle mixture needle is removed, use the following procedure to determine correct position. Back out needle (N) until unscrewed, then screw in needle six turns. Rotate idle mixture plate (P—Fig. TA109) to center notch. Run engine until normal operating temperature is attained. Adjust idle speed screw so trimmer head or blade does not rotate. Rotate idle mixture needle (N—Fig. TA106) and obtain highest rpm

(turning needle clockwise leans the mixture), then turn needle counterclockwise until rpm decreases 200-500 rpm. Readjust idle speed screw. Note that idle mixture plate and needle are available only as an assembly with throttle barrel.

Initial setting of high-speed mixture screw (21—TA110) is 1½ turns out from a lightly seated position. Adjust high-speed mixture screw to obtain highest engine speed, then turn screw ¼ turn counterclockwise. Do not adjust mixture too lean as engine may be damaged.

To overhaul carburetor, refer to exploded view in Fig. TA110 and note the following: Clean only with solvents approved for use with plastic. Do not disassemble throttle barrel assembly. Ex-

amine fuel inlet valve and seat. Inlet valve (13) is renewable, but carburetor body must be renewed if seat is excessively worn or damaged. Inspect high-speed mixture screw and seat. Renew carburetor body if seat is excessively worn or damaged. Clean fuel screen. Inspect diaphragms for tears and other damage. When installing plates and gaskets (24, 25 and 26) note that tabs (T) on ends will "stairstep" when correctly installed. Adjust metering lever height to obtain 1.5 mm (0.059 in.) between carburetor body surface and lever as shown in Fig. TA108.

Float-Type Carburetor. Two different float-type carburetors have been used (see Fig. TA111 and TA112). Service procedure for both carburetors is similar.

Idle mixture is not adjustable. Idle speed may be adjusted by turning adjusting screw (17). High-speed mixture is controlled by removable fixed jet (9). Midrange mixture is determined by the position of clip (4) on jet needle (5).

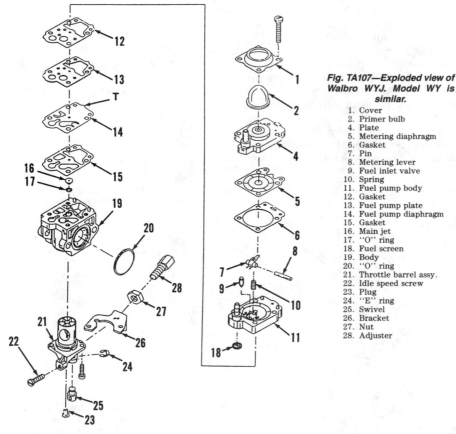

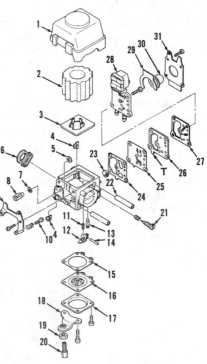

Fig. TA107—Exploded view of Walbro WYJ. Model WY is similar.

1. Cover
2. Primer bulb
4. Plate
5. Metering diaphragm
6. Gasket
7. Pin
8. Metering lever
9. Fuel inlet valve
10. Spring
11. Fuel pump body
12. Gasket
13. Fuel pump plate
14. Fuel pump diaphragm
15. Gasket
16. Main jet
17. "O" ring
18. Fuel screen
19. Body
20. "O" ring
21. Throttle barrel assy.
22. Idle speed screw
23. Plug
24. "E" ring
25. Swivel
26. Bracket
27. Nut
28. Adjuster

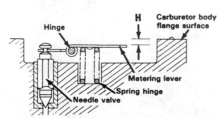

Fig. TA108—Metering lever height (H) must be set on diaphragm-type carburetors. Refer to text for specified height.

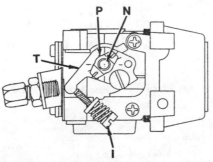

Fig. TA109—On Walbro WZ carburetor, idle speed screw is located at (I), idle mixture limiter plate is located at (P) and idle mixture needle is located at (N). A plug covers the idle mixture needle.

Fig. TA110—Exploded view of Walbro WZ carburetor.

1. Cover
2. Air cleaner element
3. Plate
4. Plate
5. Stop ring
6. Gasket
7. Thrust washer
8. Bracket
9. Bracket
10. Idle speed screw
11. Spring
12. Metering lever
13. Fuel inlet valve
14. Pin
15. Gasket
16. Metering diaphragm
17. Cover
18. Bracket
19. Nut
20. Cable adjuster
21. High-speed mixture screw
22. Sleeve
23. Screen
24. Gasket
25. Fuel pump diaphragm
26. Plate
27. Gasket
28. Fuel pump cover
29. Gasket
30. Primer bulb
31. Retainer

                                              Illustrations courtesy Tanaka Ltd.

There are three grooves in upper end of the jet needle and normal position of clip is in the middle groove. The mixture will be leaner if clip is installed in the top groove, or richer if clip is installed in the bottom groove.

Before removing carburetor from engine, unscrew cap (1) and withdraw throttle slide (6) assembly. When overhauling carburetor, refer to Fig. TA111 or TA112 and note the following: Examine fuel inlet valve and seat. Inlet valve (10) is renewable on all models. Inlet seat (21) is renewable on some models. On some models, the inlet seat is not renewable and carburetor body (7) must be renewed if seat is excessively worn or damaged. When installing throttle slide, be sure groove in side of throttle slide (6) indexes with pin in bore of carburetor body.

Rotary-Type Carburetor. Refer to Fig. TA113 for an exploded view of the rotary-type carburetor used on some models.

Idle mixture is not adjustable. High-speed mixture is controlled by removable fixed jet (9). Midrange mixture is determined by the position of clip (4) on jet needle (5). There are three grooves in upper end of the jet needle and normal position of clip is in the middle groove. The mixture will be leaner if clip is installed in the top groove, or richer if clip is installed in the bottom groove.

Before removing carburetor from engine, unscrew cap (1) and withdraw throttle slide (6) assembly. When overhauling carburetor, refer to Fig. TA113 and note the following: Remove reservoir (13), clip (14) and rubber cap (15). Pull check valve (12) out of reservoir. Remove check valve cap (10) and "O" ring (11).

Inspect components and renew if damaged or excessively worn. When installing throttle slide, be sure groove in side of throttle slide (6) indexes with pin in bore of carburetor body.

IGNITION SYSTEM. The engine may be equipped with a breaker-point-type ignition system or a solid-state-type ignition system. Refer to appropriate following paragraphs for service information.

Breaker-Point Ignition System. The ignition condenser and breaker-points are located behind the flywheel. To adjust or renew breaker-points, the flywheel must be removed. Breaker-point gap should be 0.35 mm (0.014 in.).

Ignition timing is adjusted by moving magneto stator plate. Breaker-points should open when "M" mark on flywheel is aligned with reference mark on crankcase (see Fig. TA114).

On models with external ignition coil, air gap between coil legs and flywheel should be 0.35 mm (0.014 in.). On models with ignition coil on stator plate (Fig. TA115), the metal core legs of the ignition coil should be flush with outer edge of the stator plate.

Solid-State Ignition System. All later models are equipped with a solid-state ignition system. The engine may be equipped with a one-piece ignition

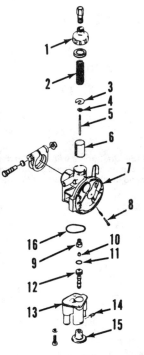

Fig. TA113—Exploded view of rotary-type carburetor used on some models.

1. Cap	9. Main jet
2. Spring	10. Cap
3. Seat	11. "O" ring
4. Clip	12. Check valve
5. Jet needle	13. Reservoir
6. Throttle slide	14. Clip
7. Body	15. Rubber cap
8. Mixture screw	16. Gasket

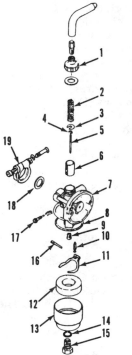

Fig. TA111—Exploded view of float-type carburetor used on some models.

1. Cap	11. Float lever
2. Spring	12. Float
3. Seat	13. Float bowl
4. Clip	14. Gasket
5. Jet needle	15. Screw
6. Throttle slide	16. Pin
7. Body	17. Idle speed screw
8. Gasket	18. Gasket
9. Main jet	19. Clamp
10. Fuel inlet valve	

Fig. TA112—Exploded view of float-type carburetor used on some models.

1. Cap	
2. Spring	
3. Seat	14. Gasket
4. Clip	15. Screw
5. Jet needle	16. Pin
6. Throttle slide	17. Idle speed screw
7. Body	18. Clamp
8. Gasket	19. Gasket
9. Main jet	20. Nozzle
10. Fuel inlet valve	21. Fuel inlet valve seat
11. Float lever	22. "O" ring
12. Float	23. Fuel inlet bolt
13. Float bowl	24. Nut
	25. Cable adjuster

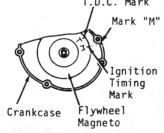

Fig. TA114—On models with breaker-points, align "M" mark on flywheel magneto with mark on crankcase as shown.

Illustrations courtesy Tanaka Ltd.

module that includes the ignition coil, or a two-piece ignition system that consists of a separate ignition module and ignition coil. The ignition coil or module may be mounted on the blower housing, crankcase or cylinder.

The ignition system is considered satisfactory if a spark will jump across the 3 mm (1/8 in.) gap of a test spark plug. If no spark is produced, check on/off switch, wiring and ignition module/coil air gap. Air gap between flywheel magnet and ignition module/coil should be 0.25-0.35 mm (0.010-0.014 in.).

REPAIRS

PISTON, PIN AND RINGS. The piston is equipped with two piston rings.

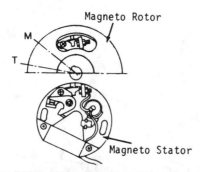

Fig. TA115—On models with ignition coil on stator plate, the metal core legs of the ignition coil should be flush with outer edge of the stator plate.

Ring rotation is prevented by a locating pin in each piston ring groove. Piston and rings are available only in standard diameter.

To remove piston, remove engine cover, starter housing and fuel tank. Remove air cleaner, carburetor and muffler. Remove cylinder mounting screws and pull cylinder off piston. Remove retaining rings (5—Fig. TA116), then use a suitable pin puller to push piston pin (6) out of piston. Remove piston (4) and bearing (7) from connecting rod.

Install piston so arrow on piston crown points toward exhaust port. On 50.2 cc engine, install piston so shaped portion of crown is toward intake. Lubricate piston and cylinder bore with oil. Be sure piston ring gaps are correctly indexed with locating pins in piston ring grooves when installing cylinder.

CYLINDER. Some engines are equipped with a chrome plated cylinder. Renew cylinder if bore is excessively worn, scored or otherwise damaged. Cylinder is available only in standard size.

CRANKSHAFT, CONNECTING ROD AND CRANKCASE. Crankshaft, connecting rod and rod bearing are a unit assembly; individual components are not available. The crankshaft is supported by ball bearings at both ends.

To remove crankshaft and connecting rod assembly, separate engine from trimmer drive housing. Remove engine cover, starter housing, fuel tank, air cleaner, carburetor and muffler. Remove spark plug and install the end of a starter rope in spark plug hole to lock piston and crankshaft. Remove nuts attaching flywheel and starter pulley to crankshaft. Use suitable puller to remove flywheel. Remove cylinder mounting screws and pull cylinder off piston. Remove crankshaft keys and crankcase retaining bolts. Carefully tap on one end of crankshaft to separate crankcase halves. Remove crankshaft and connecting rod assembly from crankcase. Use suitable puller to push piston pin from piston and separate piston from crankshaft. If main bearings (13) remain in crankcase, heat crankcase halves slightly to aid bearing removal. Drive seals (12) out of crankcase halves.

A renewable needle bearing (7) is located in the small end of the connecting rod. Maximum allowable side clearance at rod big end is 0.5 mm (0.020 in.).

Install seals (12—Fig. TA116) with lip toward inside of crankcase. On some engines, shims (16) are available to adjust crankshaft end play. Maximum allowable crankshaft end play is 0.1 mm (0.004 in.).

CLUTCH. 50.2 cc Engine. Trimmers with a 50.2 cc engine are equipped with the clutch shown in Fig. TA117. The upper end of the drive shaft is threaded into the clutch drum hub. To service clutch, disconnect throttle cable and stop switch wires from engine. Detach drive housing (1) from engine. To service clutch drum (4), remove gear head from drive shaft housing. Insert a tool through slot of clutch drum so it cannot rotate, then turn square end (trimmer end) of drive shaft so drum unscrews from drive shaft. Detach snap ring (3) then force drive shaft and bearing out toward large end of drive housing.

Clutch shoes (7) are available only as a set. Clutch springs are available only as a set.

All Other Engines. The engine is equipped with a two-shoe clutch (Fig. TA118). The clutch shoe assembly (11) is mounted on the flywheel. The clutch drum (6) rides in the drive housing (1), which may be the fan housing on some engines.

To remove clutch drum, first disconnect throttle cable and stop switch wires from engine. Separate trimmer drive housing assembly from engine. On models with slots in clutch face, reach through slot and detach snap ring (5—Fig. TA118), then press clutch drum (6) and bearing (4) out of housing. Heating housing will ease removal. On other en-

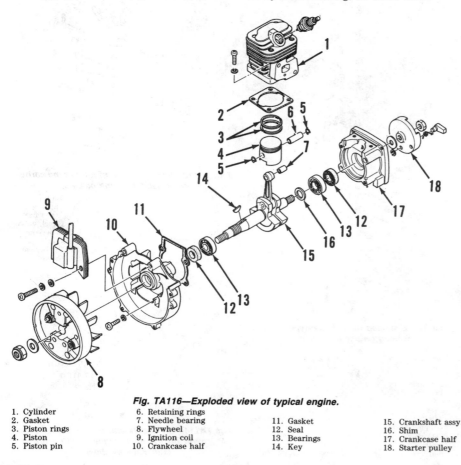

Fig. TA116—Exploded view of typical engine.

1. Cylinder	6. Retaining rings	11. Gasket
2. Gasket	7. Needle bearing	12. Seal
3. Piston rings	8. Flywheel	13. Bearings
4. Piston	9. Ignition coil	14. Key
5. Piston pin	10. Crankcase half	15. Crankshaft assy.
		16. Shim
		17. Crankcase half
		18. Starter pulley

Illustrations courtesy Tanaka Ltd.

gines, detach carrier (3—Fig. TA119) from drive housing (1) and press drum and bearing assembly out of carrier. Detach snap ring (4) and press clutch drum shaft out of bearings (5). Reverse removal procedure to install clutch drum.

Clutch shoes are available only as a pair.

REWIND STARTER. Refer to Figs. TA120, TA121 or TA122 for an exploded view of starter. To disassemble starter, detach starter housing from engine. Remove rope handle and allow rope to wind into starter. Unscrew center screw and remove rope pulley. Wear appropriate safety eyewear and gloves before detaching rewind spring from housing as spring may uncoil uncontrolled.

To assemble starter, lubricate center post of housing and spring side with light grease. Install rewind spring so coil windings are counterclockwise from outer end (clockwise on Tanaka Models TBC-160, TBC-202 and TBC-210). Assemble starter while passing rope through housing rope outlet and attach rope handle to rope. To place tension on starter rope, pull rope out of housing. Engage rope in notch on pulley and turn pulley counterclockwise (clockwise on Tanaka Models TBC-160, TBC-202 and

TBC-210). Hold pulley and disengage rope from pulley notch. Release pulley and allow rope to wind on pulley. Check starter operation. Rope handle should be held against housing by spring tension, but it must be possible to rotate pulley at least ¼ turn counterclockwise (clockwise on Tanaka Models TBC-160, TBC-202 and TBC-210) when rope is pulled out fully.

On engines with a plate attached to the crankshaft that carries a pawl, install pawl (P—Fig. TA123) in hole marked "R."

ELECTRIC STARTER. Engines with 20 cc or 21 cc displacement may be equipped with an electric starter. Refer to Fig. TA124 for a diagram of starter components. A battery pack of four or six 1.2v/1.2AH nicad batteries provides power to the starter motor. A relay is used to energize the starter when the start button is depressed. The batteries are charged by a circuit off the ignition coil. A rectifier converts alternating current to direct current for battery charging. The batteries can also be charged using 120v line current and a transformer as outlined in trimmer section.

To check motor operation, remove spark plug, disconnect four-wire connector to handle and use a jumper wire

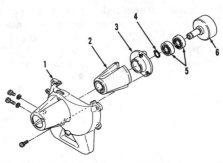

Fig. TA119—Exploded view of clutch drum and bearing assembly used on some models.

1. Housing	4. Snap ring
2. Isolator	5. Bearings
3. Carrier	6. Clutch drum

Fig. TA120—Exploded view of rewind starter used on some models.

1. Screw	
2. Washer	
3. Pulley	5. Housing
4. Rewind spring	6. Rope guide
	7. Handle

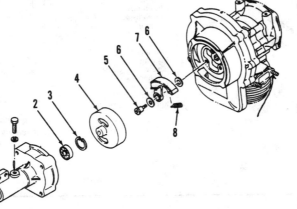

Fig. TA117—Exploded view of clutch assembly used on some models.

1. Housing
2. Bearing
3. Snap ring
4. Clutch drum
5. Shoulder screw
6. Washers
7. Clutch shoe
8. Spring

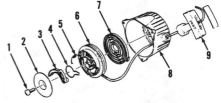

Fig. TA121—Exploded view of rewind starter used on some models.

1. Handle	
2. Housing	
3. Rewind spring	6. Washer
4. Pulley	7. Friction plate
5. Pawl	8. Washer
	9. Screw

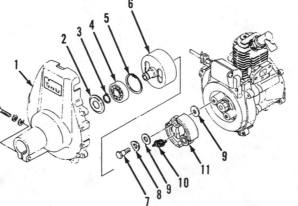

Fig. TA118—Exploded view of clutch assembly used on some models.

1. Clutch housing
2. Washer
3. Snap ring
4. Bearing
5. Snap ring
6. Clutch drum
7. Shoulder screw
8. Wave washer
9. Washer
10. Spring
11. Clutch shoe

Fig. TA122—Exploded view of rewind starter used on some models.

1. Screw	6. Pulley
2. Plate	7. Rewind spring
3. Pawl	8. Housing
4. Friction spring	9. Handle
5. Spring	

to connect terminals (1 and 4—Fig. TA125) of female connector. Starter motor should run; if not, check relay. If motor runs, but engine does not run, check drive gears. To check relay, remove cov-

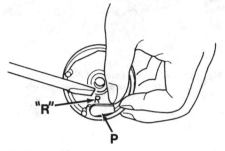

Fig. TA123—Install pawl (P) in hole marked "R."

er (1—Fig. TA124) and connect voltmeter test leads to motor terminals. Connect jumper wire between terminals (1 and 4—Fig. TA125). If no voltage is indicated at motor terminals, renew relay. If battery voltage is indicated at motor terminals, but motor does not turn, motor is faulty.

To check engine charging system, run engine and disconnect two-wire connector to battery pack and four-wire connector to handlebar. Check voltage at terminals (1 and 2—Fig. TA125) of female connector by connecting negative tester lead to terminal (1) and positive lead to terminal (2). With engine running at 6000 rpm, tester should indicate more than 1.1 volts. If voltage is lower than 1.1 volts, check wiring harness for

open circuit. Check air gap between flywheel magnet and ignition coil. If both items are satisfactory, renew ignition coil.

To check wiring harness, shut off engine and disconnect four-wire connector at engine fan cover. Connect voltmeter negative test lead to terminal (1—Fig. TA125) and positive test lead to terminal (4). Battery voltage should be indicated on tester. Connect negative test lead to terminal (1) and positive test lead to terminal (3). There should be no voltage indicated on tester. Renew wiring harness if either of these tests are failed.

To check battery pack, recharge battery pack then disconnect four-wire connector at handlebar. With engine stopped, connect negative lead of a voltmeter to terminal (1) of female connector and positive tester lead to terminal (2). Battery voltage reading should be at least 4.8 volts on 20 cc engine or 7.0 volts on 21 cc engine.

Starter motor must be serviced as a unit assembly; components are not available.

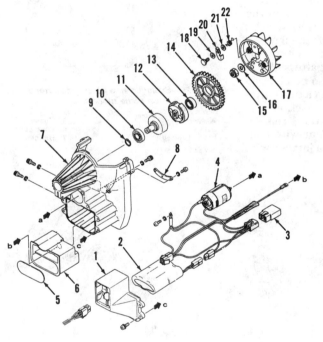

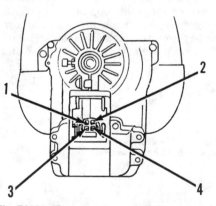

Fig. TA124—Exploded view of electric starter components on 21 cc engine. Components on 20 cc engine are similar.

1. Cover
2. Battery pack
3. Relay
4. Starter motor
5. Cushion
6. Case
7. Housing
8. Bracket
9. Snap ring
10. Bearing
11. Clutch drum
12. Clutch assy.
13. Bearing
14. Gear
15. Nut
16. Washer
17. Flywheel
18. Screw
19. Washer
20. Pawl
21. Washer
22. Spring

Fig. TA125—Tests may be performed on starter electrical system by attaching tester to connector terminals as outlined in text.

TANAKA (TAS)

ENGINE SERVICE

Model	Bore	Stroke	Displacement
Tanaka	30 mm	28 mm	20.0 cc
	(1.18 in.)	(1.10 in.)	(1.22 cu. in.)

These engines are used on Tanaka Models AST-5000, TBC-4000, TBC-4500 and TBC-5000.

ENGINE INFORMATION

These Tanaka two-stroke, air-cooled gasoline engines are used on Tanaka Models AST-5000, TBC-4000, TBC-4500 and TBC-5000. Tanaka trimmer AST-5000 is equipped with an electric starter.

MAINTENANCE

LUBRICATION. Engine lubrication is obtained by mixing gasoline with an oil designed for two-stroke, air-cooled engines. Refer to trimmer service section for manufacturer's recommended fuel:oil mixture ratio.

SPARK PLUG. Recommended spark plug is NGK BPM6A or equivalent. Electrode gap should be 0.6 mm (0.024 in.).

CARBURETOR. Various types of carburetors have been used. Refer to the appropriate following section for carburetor service.

Walbro WY, WYJ and WYL. Some engines may be equipped with a Walbro WY, WYJ or WYL carburetor. This is a diaphragm-type carburetor that uses a barrel-type throttle rather than a throttle plate.

Idle fuel for the carburetor flows up into the throttle barrel where it is fed into the air stream. On some models, the idle fuel flow can be adjusted by turning an idle mixture limiter plate (P—Fig. TA201). Initial setting is in center notch. Rotating the plate clockwise will lean the idle mixture. Inside the limiter plate is an idle mixture needle (N—Fig. TA202) that is preset at the factory. If

removed, use the following procedure to determine correct position. Back out needle (N) until unscrewed. Screw in needle five turns on Model WY or 15 turns on Models WYJ and WYL. Rotate idle mixture plate (P—Fig. TA201) to center notch. Run engine until normal operating temperature is attained. Adjust idle speed screw so trimmer head or blade does not rotate. Rotate idle mixture needle (N—Fig. TA202) and obtain highest rpm (turning needle clockwise leans the mixture), then turn needle $1/4$ turn counterclockwise. Readjust idle speed screw. Note that idle mixture plate and needle are available only as an assembly with throttle barrel (18—Fig. TA203).

The high-speed mixture is controlled by a removable fixed jet (14—Fig. TA203).

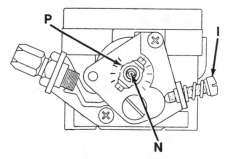

Fig. TA201—On Walbro WY, WYJ or WYL carburetor, idle speed screw is located at (I), idle mixture limiter plate is located at (P) and idle mixture needle is located at (N). A plug covers the idle mixture needle.

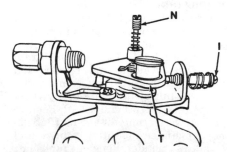

Fig. TA202—View of idle mixture needle (N) used on Walbro WY, WYJ and WYL carburetors.

Fig. TA203—Exploded view of Walbro WYJ. Models WY and WYL are similar.

1. Cover
2. Metering diaphragm
3. Gasket
4. Metering lever
5. Pin
6. Fuel inlet valve
7. Spring
8. Fuel pump body
9. Fuel screen
10. Gasket
11. Fuel pump plate
12. Fuel pump diaphragm
13. Gasket
14. Main jet
15. "O" ring
16. Body
17. "O" ring
18. Throttle barrel assy.
19. Idle speed screw
20. Plug
21. Swivel
22. "E" ring
23. Bracket
24. Nut
25. Cable adjuster

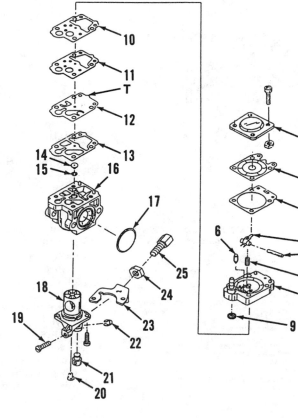

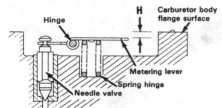

Fig. TA204—Metering lever height (H) must be set on diaphragm-type carburetors. Refer to text for specified height.

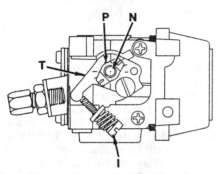

Fig. TA205—On Walbro WZ carburetor, idle speed screw is located at (I), idle mixture limiter plate is located at (P) and idle mixture needle is located at (N). A plug covers the idle mixture needle.

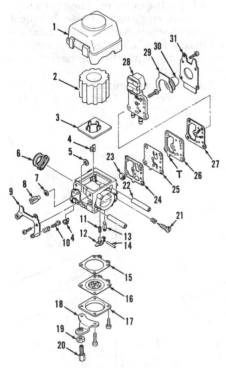

Fig. TA206—Exploded view of Walbro WZ carburetor.

1. Cover
2. Air cleaner element
3. Plate
4. Plate
5. Stop ring
6. Gasket
7. Thrust washer
8. Swivel
9. Bracket
10. Idle speed screw
11. Spring
12. Metering lever
13. Fuel inlet valve
14. Pin
15. Gasket
16. Metering diaphragm
17. Cover
18. Bracket
19. Nut
20. Cable adjuster
21. High-speed mixture screw
22. Sleeve
23. Screen
24. Gasket
25. Fuel pump diaphragm
26. Plate
27. Gasket
28. Fuel pump cover
29. Gasket
30. Primer bulb
31. Retainer

To overhaul carburetor, refer to exploded view in Fig. TA203 and note the following: On models with a plastic body, clean only with solvents approved for use with plastic. Do not disassemble throttle barrel assembly (18). Examine fuel inlet valve and seat. Inlet valve (6) is renewable, but fuel pump body (8) must be renewed if seat is excessively worn or damaged. Clean fuel screen. Inspect diaphragms for tears and other damage. When installing plates and gaskets (10 through 13), note that tabs (T) on ends will "stairstep" when correctly installed. Adjust metering lever height to obtain 1.5 mm (0.059 in.) between carburetor body surface and lever as shown in Fig. TA204.

Walbro WZ. Some engines may be equipped with a Walbro WZ carburetor. This is a diaphragm-type carburetor that uses a barrel-type throttle rather than a throttle plate.

Idle fuel for the carburetor flows up into the throttle barrel where it is fed into the air stream. Idle fuel flow can be adjusted by turning idle mixture limiter plate (P—Fig. TA205). Initial setting is in center notch. Rotating the plate clockwise will lean the idle mixture. Inside the limiter plate is an idle mixture needle (N—Fig. TA202) that is preset at the factory (a plug covers the needle). If idle mixture needle is removed, use the following procedure to determine correct position. Back out needle (N) until unscrewed, then screw in needle six turns. Rotate idle mixture plate (P—Fig. TA205) to center notch. Run engine until normal operating temperature is attained. Adjust idle speed screw so trimmer head or blade does not rotate. Rotate idle mixture needle (N—Fig. TA202) and obtain highest rpm (turning needle clockwise leans the mixture), then turn needle counterclockwise until rpm decreases 200-500 rpm. Readjust idle speed screw. Note that idle mixture plate and needle are available only as an assembly with throttle barrel.

Initial setting of high-speed mixture screw (21—Fig. TA206) is 1½ turns out from a lightly seated position. Adjust high-speed mixture screw to obtain highest engine speed, then turn screw ¼ turn counterclockwise. Do not adjust mixture too lean as engine may be damaged.

To overhaul carburetor, refer to exploded view in Fig. TA206 and note the following: Clean only with solvents approved for use with plastic. Do not disassemble throttle barrel assembly. Examine fuel inlet valve and seat. Inlet valve is renewable, but carburetor body must be renewed if seat is excessively worn or damaged. Inspect high-speed mixture screw and seat. Renew carbu-

retor body if seat is excessively worn or damaged. Clean fuel screen. Inspect diaphragms for tears and other damage. When installing plates and gaskets (24, 25 and 26), note that tabs (T) on ends will "stairstep" when correctly installed. Adjust metering lever height to obtain 1.5 mm (0.059 in.) between carburetor body surface and lever as shown in Fig. TA204.

IGNITION SYSTEM. The engine is equipped with an electronic ignition system. Ignition system performance is considered satisfactory if a spark will jump across a 3 mm (⅛ in.) electrode gap on a test spark plug. If no spark is produced, check on/off switch, wiring and ignition module air gap. Ignition module air gap should be 0.3 mm (0.012 in.). If switch, wiring and module air gap are satisfactory, but spark is not present, renew ignition module.

REPAIRS

PISTON, PIN AND RINGS. The piston is accessible after removing cylinder. Remove piston pin retainers (5—Fig. TA207) and use a suitable puller to extract pin from piston.

Piston and ring are available only in standard diameter.

Install piston on connecting rod so arrow on piston crown will point toward exhaust port when the cylinder is installed.

The piston is equipped with a single piston ring. Piston ring rotation is prevented by a locating pin in the piston ring groove. Make certain ring end gap is correctly positioned around locating pin before installing piston in cylinder.

CYLINDER. The cylinder bore is chrome plated. Renew cylinder if plating in bore is worn through, scored or otherwise damaged. Cylinder is available only in standard size.

CRANKSHAFT AND CONNECTING ROD. The engine is equipped with a half-crankshaft (13—Fig. TA207) that is supported by bearing (15) in crankcase (18) and a bearing (8—Fig. TA208) in fan housing (9).

To remove crankshaft and connecting rod, remove engine cover. Separate engine from trimmer drive housing. Unscrew clutch (7—Fig. TA208) from crankshaft. Unbolt and remove fan housing (9) and fuel tank. Remove flywheel mounting nut and pull flywheel (19—Fig. TA207) off crankshaft. Remove ignition coil, carburetor and muffler. Remove cylinder mounting screws and withdraw cylinder. Remove crankshaft key (14) and crankcase retaining bolts, then separate crankcase cover (8) from crankcase half (18). Remove snap ring (9), thrust washer (10), connecting rod (11) and bearing (12) from crankpin. Tap crankshaft (13) out of crankcase half. Drive seal (16) and bearing (15) from crankcase bore.

Crankcase is available only as an assembly. Bearings in connecting rod are available separately. Inspect components for damage and excessive wear and renew as needed.

CLUTCH. Some models are equipped with the two-shoe clutch assembly shown in Fig. TA208. With drive housing (3) separated from engine, press against shaft end of drum (6) to dislodge bearing (5) and drum from housing. Remove snap ring (4) and press bearing off drum shaft. Unscrew clutch (7) from crankshaft. Clutch shoes, hub and springs are available only as an assembly.

REWIND STARTER. Engines Without Electric Start. Refer to Fig. TA208 for an exploded view of rewind starter. To disassemble starter, detach starter housing (9) from engine. Remove rope handle and allow rope to wind into starter. Detach snap ring on engines so equipped, or unscrew pulley retainer (10), and remove rope pulley (12). Wear appropriate safety eyewear and gloves before detaching rewind spring (11) from housing as spring may uncoil uncontrolled.

To assemble starter, lubricate center post of housing and spring side with light grease. Install rewind spring so coil windings are clockwise from outer end. Assemble starter while passing rope through housing rope outlet and attach rope handle to rope. To place tension on starter rope, pull rope out of housing.

Engage rope in notch on pulley and turn pulley clockwise to place tension on spring. Hold pulley and disengage rope from pulley notch. Release pulley and allow rope to wind on pulley. Check starter operation. Rope handle should be held against housing by spring tension, but it must be possible to rotate pulley at least $1/4$ turn clockwise when rope is pulled out fully.

Engines With Electric Start. Refer to Fig. TA209 for an exploded view of starter. To disassemble starter, detach starter housing (14) from engine. Remove rope handle and allow rope to wind into starter. Unscrew center screw (7) and remove rope pulley (12). Wear appropriate safety eyewear and gloves before detaching rewind spring (13) from housing as spring may uncoil uncontrolled.

To assemble starter, lubricate center post of housing and spring side with light grease. Install rewind spring so coil windings are counterclockwise from outer end. Assemble starter while passing rope through housing rope outlet and attach rope handle to rope. To place tension on starter rope, pull rope out of housing. Engage rope in notch on pulley and turn pulley counterclockwise. Hold pulley and disengage rope from pulley notch. Release pulley and allow rope to wind on pulley. Check starter operation. Rope handle should be held against housing by spring tension, but it must be possible to rotate pulley at least $1/4$ turn counterclockwise when rope is pulled out fully.

ELECTRIC STARTER. Some engines may be equipped with an electric starter. Refer to Fig. TA210 for a diagram of starter components. A battery pack of four 1.2v/1.2AH nicad batteries provides power to the starter motor. A relay is

used to energize the starter when the start button is depressed. The batteries are charged by a circuit off the ignition coil. A rectifier converts alternating current to direct current for battery charging. The batteries can also be charged using 120v line current and a transformer as outlined in trimmer section.

To check motor operation, remove spark plug, disconnect four-wire connector to handle and use a jumper wire to connect terminals (1 and 4—Fig. TA211) of female connector. Starter motor should run; if not, check relay. If motor runs, but engine does not run, check drive gears. To check relay, remove cover (14—Fig. TA210) and connect voltmeter test leads to motor terminals. Connect jumper wire between terminals (1 and 4—Fig. TA211). If no voltage is indicated at motor terminals, renew wiring harness; relay is not available separately. If battery voltage is indicated at motor terminals, but motor does not turn, motor is faulty.

To check engine charging system, run engine and disconnect two-wire connector to battery pack and four-wire connector to handlebar. Check voltage at terminals (1 and 2—Fig. TA211) of female connector by connecting voltmeter negative lead to terminal (1) and positive lead to terminal (2). With engine running at 6000 rpm, tester should indicate more than 1.1 volts. If voltage is lower than 1.1 volts, check wiring harness for open circuit. Check air gap be-

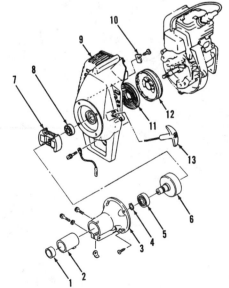

Fig. TA207—Exploded view of engine. Some engines are not equipped with snap ring (9) and thrust washer (10).

1. Cylinder
2. Gasket
3. Piston ring
4. Piston
5. Retaining rings
6. Piston pin
7. Bearing
8. Crankcase half
9. Snap ring
10. Thrust washer
11. Connecting rod
12. Bearing
13. Crankshaft
14. Key
15. Bearing
16. Seal
17. Gasket
18. Crankcase half
19. Flywheel

Fig. TA208—Exploded view of clutch and rewind starter assemblies used on engines not equipped with an electric starter. The clutch assembly is similar on all engines.

1. Collar
2. Rubber sleeve
3. Housing
4. Snap ring
5. Bearing
6. Clutch drum
7. Clutch assy.
8. Bearing
9. Starter housing
10. Retainer
11. Rewind spring
12. Pulley
13. Rope handle

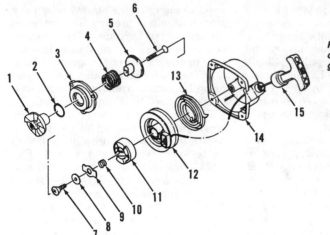

Fig. TA209—Exploded view of rewind starter used on engines with an electric starter.

1. Dog flange
2. "O" ring
3. Holder
4. Spring
5. Driver
6. Screw
7. Screw
8. Washer
9. Friction plate
10. Spring
11. Pawl
12. Pulley
13. Rewind spring
14. Starter housing
15. Rope handle

tween flywheel magnet and ignition coil. If both items are satisfactory, renew ignition coil.

To check wiring harness, shut off engine and disconnect four-wire connector. Connect voltmeter negative test lead to terminal (1—Fig. TA211) and positive lead to terminal (4). Battery voltage should be indicated on tester. Connect negative test lead to terminal (1) and positive test lead to terminal (3). There should be no voltage indicated on tester. Renew harness if either of these tests are failed.

To check battery pack, recharge battery pack then disconnect four-wire connector at handlebar. With engine stopped, connect negative lead of a voltmeter to terminal (1) of female connector and positive tester lead to terminal (2). Battery voltage reading should be at least 4.8 volts.

Starter motor (13—Fig. TA210) must be serviced as a unit assembly; components are not available.

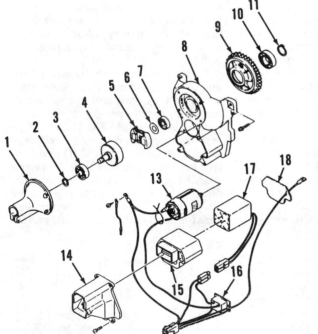

Fig. TA210—Exploded view of electric starter components.

1. Housing
2. Snap ring
3. Bearing
4. Clutch drum
5. Clutch assy.
6. Washer
7. Bearing
8. Housing
9. Gear
10. Bearing
11. Snap ring
13. Starter motor
14. Cover
15. Battery case
16. Relay
17. Battery pack
18. Cover

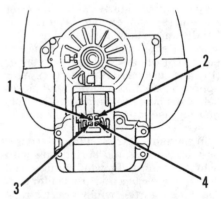

Fig. TA211—Tests may be performed on starter electrical system by attaching tester to connector terminals as outlined in text.

Illustrations courtesy Tanaka Ltd.

TECUMSEH

ENGINE SERVICE

Model	Bore	Stroke	Displacement
TC200	1.4375 in.	2.250 in.	2.0 cu. in.
	(36.51 mm)	(57.15 mm)	(32.8 cc)

ENGINE INFORMATION

Engine type and model numbers are stamped into blower housing base as indicated in Fig. T9. Always furnish engine model and type number when ordering parts. Tecumseh TC200 engine is used by several manufacturers of string trimmers and brushcutters.

MAINTENANCE

SPARK PLUG. Recommended spark plug is a Champion RCJ-8Y, or equivalent. Specified electrode gap is 0.030 inch (0.76 mm).

AIR CLEANER. Air cleaner element should be removed and cleaned at eight hour intervals of use. Polyurethane element may be washed in a mild detergent and water solution and squeezed until all dirt is removed. Rinse thoroughly. Wrap in clean dry cloth and squeeze until completely dry. Apply engine oil to element and squeeze out excess. Clean air cleaner body and cover and dry thoroughly.

CARBURETOR. Tecumseh TC200 engines used on string trimmers are equipped with diaphragm type carburetor with a single idle mixture needle. Initial adjustment of idle mixture needle is one turn open from a lightly seated position.

Final carburetor adjustment is made with engine at operating temperature

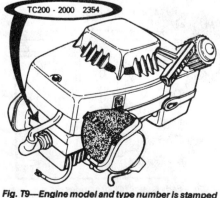

Fig. T9—Engine model and type number is stamped into blower housing base.

and running. Operate engine at idle speed and turn idle mixture needle slowly clockwise until engine falters. Note this position and turn idle mixture needle counterclockwise until engine begins to run unevenly. Note this position and turn adjustment screw until it is halfway between first (lean) and last (rich) positions.

To disassemble carburetor, refer to Fig. T11. Remove idle speed stop screw (9) and spring. Remove pump cover (10), gasket (11) and diaphragm (12). Remove cover

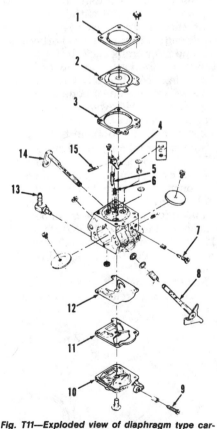

Fig. T11—Exploded view of diaphragm type carburetor used on TC200 engine.

1. Cover
2. Diaphragm
3. Gasket
4. Metering lever
5. Inlet needle valve
6. Spring
7. Idle mixture needle
8. Throttle shaft
9. Idle speed screw
10. Cover
11. Gasket
12. Diaphragm
13. Fuel inlet
14. Choke shaft
15. Pin

(1), diaphragm (2) and gasket (3). Carefully remove pin (15), metering lever (4), inlet needle valve (5) and spring (6). Remove screws retaining throttle plate to throttle shaft (8). Remove screws retaining choke plate to choke shaft (14). Remove "E" clip from throttle shaft and choke shaft and remove shafts. Remove all nonmetallic parts, idle mixture needle, fuel inlet screen and fuel inlet (13). Remove all Welch plugs.

Clean and inspect all parts. Do not allow parts to soak in cleaning solvent longer than 30 minutes.

To reassemble, install fuel inlet needle, metering lever spring and pin. Metering lever hooks onto the inlet needle and rests on the metering spring. Entire assembly is held in place by metering lever pin screw. Tip of metering lever must be 0.060-0.070 inch (1.52-1.78 mm) from the face of carburetor body (Fig. T12).

Install diaphragm gasket so tabs of gaskets align with the bosses on the carburetor body. After gasket is in place, install the diaphragm again aligning tabs to bosses. The head of the rivet in the diaphragm must be toward the carburetor body. Check the atmospheric vent hole in the diaphragm cover to make certain it is clean. Install cover on carburetor.

Install pump diaphragm with the corner holes aligning with the same holes in the carburetor body. Align pump gasket in the same manner and place pump cover onto carburetor.

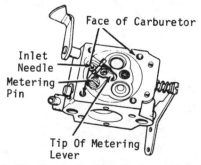

Fig. T12—Tip of metering valve lever should be 0.060-0.070 inch (1.52-1.78 mm) from the face of carburetor body.

Numbers on throttle plate should face to the outside when throttle is closed. Apply a small amount of Loctite grade 609 to fuel inlet before installation.

IGNITION SYSTEM. All Model TC200 engines are equipped with a solid state ignition module located outside the flywheel. Correct air gap between laminations of module and magnets of flywheel is 0.012 inch (0.30 mm). Use Tecumseh gage part number 670297.

GOVERNOR ADJUSTMENT. Model TC200 engine is equipped with an air vane type governor. Refer to ENGINE REPAIRS paragraphs for adjustment procedure.

LUBRICATION. Engine is lubricated by mixing gasoline with a good quality two-stroke air-cooled engine oil. Refer to TRIMMER SERVICE section for correct fuel/oil mixture ratio recommended by trimmer manufacturer.

CARBON. Muffler and exhaust ports should be cleaned after every 50 hours of operation if engine is operated continuously at full load. If operated at light or medium load, the cleaning interval can be extended to 100 hours.

REPAIRS

TIGHTENING TORQUES. Recommended tightening torque specifications are as follows:

Crankcase cover
to crankcase . . . . 70-100 in.-lbs.
(8-11 N · m)
Cylinder to crankcase . . 60-75 in.-lbs.
(7-8 N · m)
Carburetor . . . . 20-32 in.-lbs.
(2.3-3.6 N · m)
Flywheel nut . . . . 180-240 in.-lbs.
(20-27 N · m)
Ignition module . . . . 30-40 in.-lbs.
(3.4-4.5 N · m)
Starter retainer screw . . . . 45-55 in.-lbs.
(5.1-6.2 N · m)

CRANKSHAFT. To remove crankshaft, drain fuel tank, remove tank strap and disconnect fuel line at carburetor. Disconnect and remove spark plug. Remove the three screws retaining blower housing and rewind starter assembly and remove housing. Remove the two screws retaining ignition module. Use strap wrench to hold flywheel. Use flywheel puller (670299) to remove flywheel. Remove air cleaner assembly with carburetor, spacer, gaskets and screen. Mark and remove governor link from carburetor throttle lever. Remove the three 5/16 inch cap screws, then separate blower housing base from crankcase. Attach engine holder tool (670300) with the three blower housing base screws. Place tool in a bench vise. Remove muffler springs using tool fabricated from a 12 inch piece of heavy wire with a ¼ inch hook made on one end. Remove the four cylinder retaining nuts or Torx bolts, then pull cylinder off squarely and in line with piston. Use caution so rod does not bend. Install seal protector (670206) at magneto end of crankshaft and seal protector (670263) at pto end of crankshaft. Remove crankcase cover screws, then carefully separate crankcase cover from crankcase. Rotate crankshaft to top dead center and withdraw crankshaft through crankcase cover opening while sliding connecting rod off crankpin and over crankshaft. Refer to Fig. T18. Use care not to lose any of the 23 crankpin needle bearings which will be loose. Flanged side of connecting rod (Fig. T19) must be toward pto side of engine after installation. Handle connecting rod carefully to avoid bending.

Standard crankpin journal diameter is 0.5985-0.5990 inch (15.202-15.215 mm). Standard crankshaft pto side main bearing journal diameter is 0.6248-0.6253 inch (15.870-15.880 mm). Standard crankshaft magneto side main bearing journal diameter is 0.4998-0.5003 inch (12.69-12.71 mm). Crankshaft end play should be 0.004-0.012 inch (0.10-0.30 mm).

To install crankshaft, clean mating surfaces of crankcase, cylinder and

crankcase cover. Avoid scarring or burring mating surfaces.

Crankshaft main bearing in crankcase of early model engines did not have a retaining ring as shown in Fig. T20. Retaining ring was installed as a running change in late model engines. To install new caged bearing in crankcase, place bearing on installation tool (670302) with the numbered side of bearing away from tool. Press bearing into crankcase until tool is flush with crankcase housing. Install retaining ring (as equipped). Place seal for magneto side onto seal installation tool (670301) so metal case of seal enters tool first. Press seal in until tool is flush with crankcase. Use the same procedure to install bearing and seal in crankcase cover using bearing installation tool (670304) and seal installation tool (670303).

New crankpin needle bearings are on bearing strips. Heavy grease may be used to retain old bearings on crankpin journal as required. During reassembly, connecting rod must not be forced onto crankpin journal as rod failure or bending will result. Apply Loctite 515 to mating surfaces of crankcase during reassembly and use seal protectors when installing lip seals over ends of crankshaft. When installing cylinder over piston, install a wooden block with a slot cut out for connecting rod under piston to provide support and prevent connecting rod damage. Exhaust ports in cylinder are on the same side of engine as muffler resting boss. Make certain cylinder is correctly positioned, stagger ring end gaps and compress rings using a suitable ring compressor which can be removed after cylinder is installed over piston. Install cylinder and push cylinder onto crankcase studs to expose 1-2 threads of studs. Install the four nuts onto exposed threads of studs, then push cylinder further down to capture nuts on studs. Tighten nuts or Torx bolts in a criss-cross pattern to specified torque.

Install muffler using fabricated tool to install springs. Install blower housing

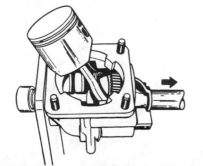

Fig. T18—Connecting rod must be carefully worked over crankpin during crankshaft removal. Do not lose the 23 loose crankpin needle bearings.

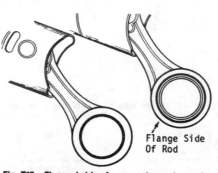

Fig. T19—Flanged side of connecting rod must face pto side of engine after installation.

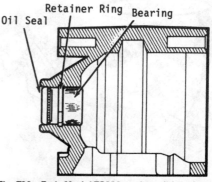

Fig. T20—Early Model TC200 engines did not have retaining ring shown. Retaining ring was installed as a running change in late model engines.

base and tighten the three screws to specified torque.

Refer to Fig. T26 to install governor air vane assembly. Speed adjustment lever is held in place by inserting screw into the blower housing base. Long end of governor spring hooks into the notch on neck of air vane. Short end hooks into the hole in speed adjustment lever. To decrease governed speed of engine, bend speed adjusting lever towards spark plug end of engine. To increase governed speed of engine, bend lever in the opposite direction. Throttle link is inserted into hole in the neck of the air vane and the hole closest to the throttle shaft in throttle plate.

Install carburetor, spacer, gaskets, screen and air cleaner body on engine. Tighten screws to specified torque. Install and adjust ignition module. Install blower housing/rewind starter assembly and tighten screws to specified torque. Install fuel tank.

PISTON, RINGS AND CONNECTING ROD. Standard piston diameter is 1.4327-1.4340 inch (36.39-36.42 mm). Standard width of both ring grooves is 0.050-0.051 inch (1.27-1.29 mm). Standard piston ring width is 0.46-0.47 inch (11.7-11.9 mm). Standard ring end gap is 0.004-0.014 inch (0.10-0.36 mm).

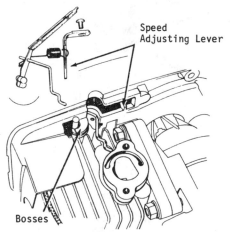

Fig. T26—View of air vane governor assembly used on Model TC200 engines. Refer to text.

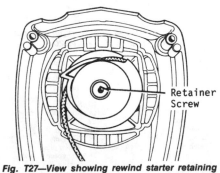
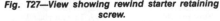

Fig. T27—View showing rewind starter retaining screw.

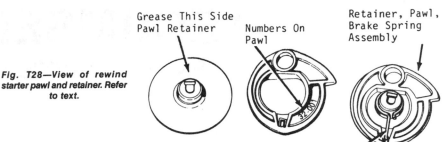

Fig. T28—View of rewind starter pawl and retainer. Refer to text.

CYLINDER. Cylinder must be smooth and free of scratches or flaking. Clean carbon carefully as necessary. Standard bore size is 1.4375 inches (36.513 mm).

TECUMSEH SPECIAL TOOLS. Tecumseh special tools are available to aid in engine disassembly and reassembly are listed by use and tool part number.

FLYWHEEL PULLER	670299
AIR GAP GAGE	670297
ENGINE HOLDER	670300
SEAL PROTECTOR (MAG. END)	670206
SEAL PROTECTOR (PTO END)	670263
SEAL INSTALLER (MAG END)	670301
SEAL INSTALLER (PTO END)	670303
BEARING INSTALLER (MAG END)	670302
BEARING INSTALLER (PTO END)	670304

REWIND STARTER. The rewind starter assembly is incorporated into blower housing. Blower housing design varies according to engine model and specification number. To release rewind spring tension, remove staple in starter handle and slowly let spring tension release by winding rope onto rope sheave. Remove the 5/16 inch retainer screw (Fig. T27). Remove pawl retainer and pawl (Fig. T28) and extract starter pulley. Use caution not to pull rewind spring out of housing at this time. Uncoiling spring can be very dangerous. If rewind spring is damaged or weak, use caution when removing spring from housing.

To reassemble, grease center post of housing and portion of housing where rewind spring will rest. Grip rewind spring firmly with needlenose pliers ahead of spring tail. Insert spring and hook tail into housing as shown in Fig. T29. Make certain spring is seated in housing before removing needlenose pliers from spring. Grease top of spring. Insert starter rope into starter pulley and tie a left handed knot in end of rope. With neck of starter pulley up, wind starter rope in a counterclockwise rotation. Place end of

rope in notch of pulley and place pulley in housing. Press down on pulley and rotate until pulley attaches to rewind spring. Refer to Fig. T30. Lubricate pawl retainer with grease and place the pawl, numbers up, onto retainer. Place brake spring on center of retainer with tab locating into pawl (Fig. T28). Tab on pawl retainer must align with notch in center post of housing and locating hole in pawl must mesh with boss on starter pulley (Fig. T31). Install retainer screw (Fig. T27) and torque to specified torque. Use starter rope to wind spring a minimum of 2 turns counterclockwise and a maximum of 3 turns. Feed starter rope through starter grommet and secure starter handle using a left hand knot.

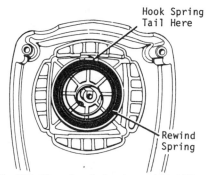

Fig. T29—View of rewind spring and housing.

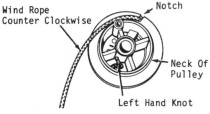

Fig. T30—View showing rewind starter rope as shown and as outlined in text.

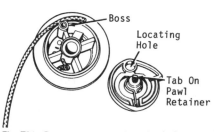

Fig. T31—Boss must engage locating hole on pawl retainer. Refer to text.

Illustrations courtesy Tecumseh Products Co.

TECUMSEH
ENGINE SERVICE

Model	Bore	Stroke	Displacement
AV520	2.09 in.	1.50 in.	5.2 cu. in.
	(53 mm)	(38 mm)	(85 cc)

ENGINE INFORMATION

Engine type and model number tags will be at one of a number of locations. Refer to Fig. T50. Always furnish engine model and type number when ordering parts. Model AV520 engines used on string trimmers and brushcutters are equipped with a diaphragm type carburetor and utilize a ball bearing type main bearing at magneto side and a needle type main bearing at pto side.

MAINTENANCE

SPARK PLUG. Recommended spark plug is a Champion RJ-17M, or equivalent. Specified electrode gap is 0.030 inch (0.76 mm).

AIR CLEANER. Refer to Fig. T51 for an exploded view of air cleaner used

on most models. Polyurethane element may be washed in a mild detergent and water solution and squeezed until all dirt is removed. Rinse thoroughly. Wrap in clean dry cloth, then squeeze until completely dry. Apply engine oil to element and squeeze out excess. Clean air cleaner body and cover and dry thoroughly.

CARBURETOR. Tecumseh Model AV520 engine is equipped with a diaphragm type carburetor shown in Fig. T52. Most models are equipped with carburetor shown utilizing fixed high speed metering and adjustable low speed mixture needle; however, some models may be equipped with both low speed and high speed mixture needles. Carburetor model number is stamped on carburetor flange (Fig. T53).

Initial adjustment of low speed and high speed (as equipped) mixture needles is one turn open from a lightly seated position.

Final carburetor adjustment is made with engine at operating temperature and running. Operate engine at idle speed and turn low speed mixture needle slowly clockwise until engine falters. Note this position and turn low speed mixture needle counterclockwise until engine begins to falter. Note this position and turn mixture needle until it is halfway between first (lean) and last (rich) positions. Operate engine at rated governed speed with trimmer line at correct length or brush blade installed and use the same procedure to

adjust the high speed mixture needle (as equipped) as used for the low speed mixture needle. Make adjustments on high speed mixture needle in 1/8 turn increments.

To disassemble carburetor, refer to Fig. T52. Remove throttle (29) and choke (8) plates and shafts. Remove low

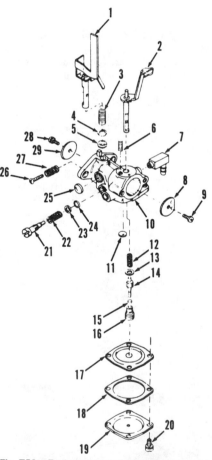

Fig. T52—Exploded view of diaphragm type carburetor used on Model AV520.

1. Throttle shaft
2. Choke shaft
3. Return spring
4. Steel washer
5. Felt washer
6. Choke positioning spring
7. Fuel fitting
8. Choke plate
9. Screw
10. Carburetor body
11. Welch plug
12. Valve spring
13. Gasket
14. Inlet needle
15. Neoprene seat
15. Neoprene seat
16. Seat fitting
17. Diaphragm
18. Gasket
19. Cover
20. Screw
21. Idle mixture needle
22. Spring
23. Washer
24. "O" ring
25. Welch plug
26. Idle speed screw
27. Spring
28. Screw
29. Throttle plate

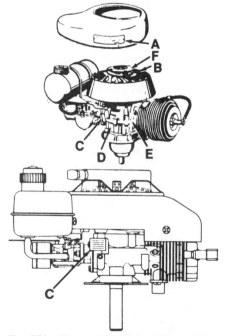

Fig. T50—The engine serial number and type number may be found at one of the locations indicated above.

A. Nameplate on air shroud
B. Model & type number plate
C. Metal tab on crankcase
D. Stamped on crankcase
E. Stamped on cylinder flange
F. Stamped on starter pulley

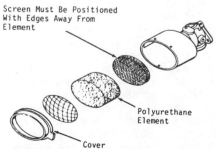

Screen Must Be Positioned With Edges Away From Element

Polyurethane Element

Cover

Fig. T51—View of air cleaner most commonly used on these engines. Refer to text for service procedures.

speed mixture needle, remove "O" ring on mixture needle and note design of screw. If equipped with high speed mixture needle, remove needle and discard "O" ring. Drill an off center hole in idle fuel chamber Welch plug (25), then pry out with suitable tool. Remove the four screws (20) retaining diaphragm cover (19) and remove cover, gasket (18) and diaphragm (17). Early type inlet needle seat fitting (16) is slotted and may be removed using a screwdriver. Late style inlet needle seat fitting (16) must be removed using a thin wall 9/32 inch socket. Inlet needle is spring loaded. Use care when removing not to lose spring (12). Remove and discard neoprene needle seat (15) located in inlet needle seat fitting (16). Remove fuel inlet fitting (7). Note presence of filter screen in fuel inlet fitting. Drill off center hole in Welch plug (11) and remove plug.

Make certain all "O" rings and non-metallic parts are removed, then soak carburetor parts in clean carburetor cleaner for 30 minutes. Rinse in clean water and use compressed air to dry. To reassemble, make certain fuel inlet fitting filter screen is clear and press fitting partially in, apply Loctite 515 to exposed portion of fitting and press fitting in until seated. Refer to Fig. T54 and install new Welch plugs (11 and 25 – Fig. T52). Install spring (12), needle (14), gasket (13), seat (15) and fitting (16). Make certain new diaphragm is the same style as the old diaphragm which was removed. Diaphragm rivet head

must always be toward inlet needle valve (Fig. T55). Refer to Fig. T56 to determine installation location of diaphragm and gasket, then install in proper sequence. Install cover (19 – Fig. T52). Place new "O" rings on fuel mixture needles and install needles until they are lightly seated, then back out one turn. Install choke shaft (2) and install choke plate (8) with flat of choke plate toward fuel inlet side of carburetor and mark on face of choke plate parallel with choke shaft. Install throttle shaft (1) and install throttle plate with short line stamped in plate to top of carburetor, parallel with throttle shaft, and facing out when throttle is closed.

IGNITION SYSTEM. Model AV520 engines may be equipped with a magneto type ignition system or a solid state ignition system. Refer to appropriate paragraph for model being serviced.

Magneto Ignition. Coil (12 – Fig. T57), condenser (15) and breaker point assembly (6) are located behind flywheel (1). To renew breaker points and condenser, remove rewind starter assembly (1 – Fig. T60) and blower housing (6). Remove nut (2), washer (3), starter cup (4) and screen (5). Use flywheel puller set (670215) to remove flywheel. DO NOT use knock off tool as main bearing damage will occur. Remove clip retainer (2 – Fig. T57), cover (3) and gasket (4). Disconnect wiring from breaker point assembly (6), remove screw (7) and lift out breaker point assembly. Remove screw (14) and lift out condenser. Install new condenser and breaker point assembly. Place one drop of engine oil on lubricating felt (9). Rotate engine until breaker point cam (5) opens breaker point set to maximum opening. Adjust breaker point plate until point gap is 0.020 inch

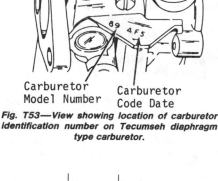

Fig. T53—View showing location of carburetor identification number on Tecumseh diaphragm type carburetor.

Fig. T54—Use a flat punch the same diameter or larger to install new Welch plugs.

Fig. T55—Rivet head on diaphragm must be toward fuel inlet needle.

Fig. T56—Gasket and diaphragm installation sequence is determined by letter "F" stamped on carburetor flange.

Fig. T57—Exploded view of magneto ignition system used on Model AV520 engine.

1. Flywheel
2. Retainer
3. Cover
4. Gasket
5. Cam
6. Breaker points
7. Screw
8. Breaker point plate
9. Lubricating felt
10. Stator assy.
11. Spark plug lead
12. Coil
13. Coil locking clip
14. Screw
15. Condenser

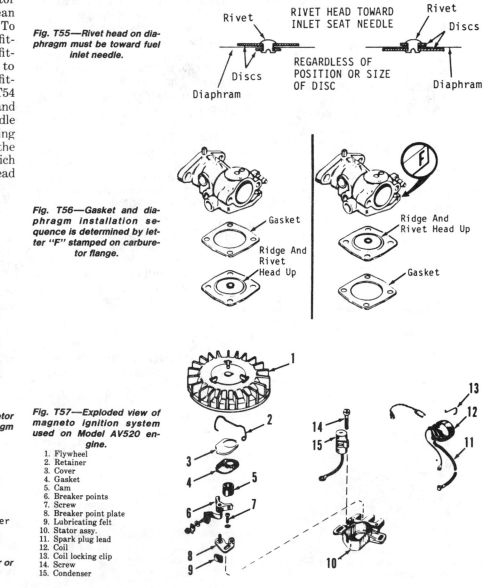

(0.51 mm). Tighten screw (7) to maintain setting. Stator assembly should be positioned so ignition breaker points just open when piston top is 0.070 inch (1.78 mm) before top dead center with points correctly gapped. Correct air gap between coil and flywheel is 0.015 inch (0.38 mm).

Solid-State Ignition. The Tecumseh solid-state ignition system does not use ignition points. The system's only moving part is the rotating flywheel with the charging magnets. As the flywheel magnet passes position (1A—Fig. T58), a low-voltage ac current is induced into input coil (2). The current passes through rectifier (3), which converts it to dc current. Then, it travels to the capacitor (4) where it is stored. The flywheel rotates approximately 180 degrees to position (1B). As it passes trigger coil (5), it induces a small electric charge into the coil. This charge passes through resistor (6) and turns on the SCR (silicon-controlled rectifier) switch (7). With SCR switch closed, the low-voltage current stored in capacitor

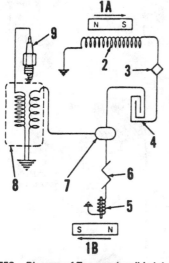

Fig. T58—Diagram of Tecumseh solid state ignition system. Items (3, 4, 5, 6 and 7) are encased in magneto assembly.

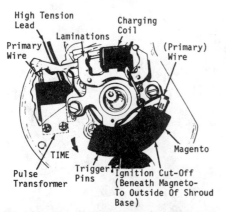

Fig. T59—View showing location of solid state ignition system component parts.

(4) travels to the pulse transformer (8). The voltage is stepped up instantaneously and the current is discharged across the electrodes of spark plug (9), producing a spark.

If system fails to produce a spark at spark plug, first make certain air gap between coil and flywheel is 0.005-0.008 inch (0.13-0.20 mm). Check the high-tension lead (Fig. T59). If condition of the high-tension lead is questionable, renew the pulse transformer and high-tension lead assembly. Check the condition of primary wire. Renew primary wire if insulation is faulty. The ignition charging coil (magneto), electronic triggering system and mounting plate are available only as an assembly. If necessary to renew this assembly, place the unit in position on the engine. Start the retaining screws, turn the mounting plate counterclockwise as far as possible, then tighten retaining screws to 5-7 ft.-lbs. (7-10 N·m).

GOVERNOR ADJUSTMENT. Model AV520 engine is equipped with an air vane type governor located on throttle shaft. Idle speed stop screw (26 Fig. T52) should be set to allow engine to idle at 2600 rpm. High speed stop screw (47—Fig. T60) should be set to limit engine maximum rpm to 4600-4800 rpm.

LUBRICATION. Engine is lubricated by mixing gasoline with a good quality two-stroke air-cooled engine oil. Refer to TRIMMER SERVICE section for correct mixture ratio recommended by trimmer manufacturer.

CARBON. Muffler and exhaust ports should be cleaned after every 50 hours of operation if engine is operated continuously at full load. If operated at light or medium load, the cleaning interval can be extended to 100 hours.

REPAIRS

TIGHTENING TORQUES. Recommended tightening torque specifications are as follows:

Crankcase base to
  crankcase . . . . 70-80 in.-lbs.
    (8-10 N·m)
Cylinder head . . . . . . 80-100 in.-lbs.
    (10-11 N·m)
Connecting rod . . . . . 70-80 in.-lbs.
    (8-10 N·m)
Flywheel nut . . . . . .264-324 in.-lbs.
    (30-37 N·m)
Ignition module . . . . .30-40 in.-lbs.
    (3.4-4.5 N·m)
Reed valve plate . . . . . 50-60 in.-lbs.
    (6-7 N·m)

Rewind retainer screw . 65-75 in.-lbs.
    (7-8 N·m)

CRANKSHAFT AND BEARINGS. To remove crankshaft and main bearings, remove rewind starter assembly (1—Fig. T60), blower housing (6) and fuel tank. Remove muffler, nut (2), washer (3), starter cup (4) and screen (5). Note location and condition of air vane governor. Use flywheel puller set (670215) to remove flywheel. DO NOT use knock off tool to remove flywheel. Remove ignition system component parts. Remove carburetor assembly (40) and reed plate assembly (38). Remove cylinder head (30) and gasket (29). Remove the two connecting rod cap screws and carefully remove connecting rod cap (19). Use care not to lose the connecting rod needle bearings (18). Push connecting rod and piston assembly out of cylinder. Remove piston pin retaining ring (24). Heat piston top slowly until piston pin (23) can be easily pushed out. Caged bearing (21) can be pressed out. Remove the four cap screws retaining base (13) plate to block and tap base plate to break gasket bond. Remove base plate/crankshaft assembly as a unit. If ball bearing main is noisy or damaged, slowly heat bearing area of base plate until ball bearing can be easily removed. Press bearing off of crankshaft. Insert tip of ice pick or similar tool into location shown in Fig. T61, then remove the wire retainer (10—Fig. T60). Remove retainer plate (11) and seal (12). Repeat procedure to remove wire retainer (34), retainer plate (35) and seal (36) in block. Press caged needle bearing (27) out of block.

Standard crankpin journal diameter is 0.8442-0.8450 inch (21.443-21.463 mm). Standard crankshaft pto side main bearing journal diameter is 0.9998-1.0003 inch (25.395-25.407 mm). Standard crankshaft magneto side main bearing journal diameter is 0.6691-0.6695 inch (16.995-17.005 mm). There should be zero crankshaft end play.

When installing ball bearing on magneto end of crankshaft, place a 1/4-in. (6.35 mm) dot of Loctite 609 in two places, 180 degrees apart, on crankshaft main bearing journal and press ball bearing into position. It may be necessary to heat base slightly when installing crankshaft so ball bearing will slip into bearing bore easily.

To install caged needle bearing in pto side of crankcase, heat crankcase slightly and press bearing into bearing bore.

To install crankshaft, install caged needle bearing and seal in cylinder block/crankcase assembly as outlined. Install ball bearing on crankshaft. In-

Illustrations courtesy Tecumseh Products Co.

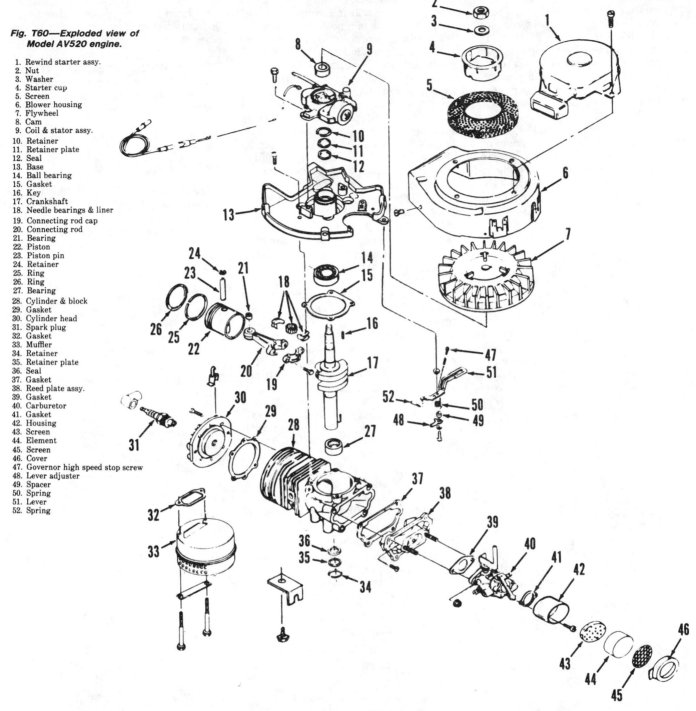

Fig. T60—Exploded view of Model AV520 engine.

1. Rewind starter assy.
2. Nut
3. Washer
4. Starter cup
5. Screen
6. Blower housing
7. Flywheel
8. Cam
9. Coil & stator assy.
10. Retainer
11. Retainer plate
12. Seal
13. Base
14. Ball bearing
15. Gasket
16. Key
17. Crankshaft
18. Needle bearings & liner
19. Connecting rod cap
20. Connecting rod
21. Bearing
22. Piston
23. Piston pin
24. Retainer
25. Ring
26. Ring
27. Bearing
28. Cylinder & block
29. Gasket
30. Cylinder head
31. Spark plug
32. Gasket
33. Muffler
34. Retainer
35. Retainer plate
36. Seal
37. Gasket
38. Reed plate assy.
39. Gasket
40. Carburetor
41. Gasket
42. Housing
43. Screen
44. Element
45. Screen
46. Cover
47. Governor high speed stop screw
48. Lever adjuster
49. Spacer
50. Spring
51. Lever
52. Spring

stall seal in base plate. Slightly heat base plate (13—Fig. T60) and install crankshaft and ball bearing assembly in base plate. Make certain to use seal protectors or tape to prevent seal damage. Place a thin bead of silicon type sealer to base plate gasket. Install crankshaft through caged needle bearing in cylinder block/crankcase assembly and carefully work crankshaft through seal and bearing until base plate contacts cylinder block/crankcase assembly. Use seal protector or tape to prevent seal damage. Install the four base plate retaining screws and tighten

to specified torque. Install rings on piston and connecting rod assembly, stagger ring end gaps. Install needle bearing connecting rod bearings on crankshaft journal and remove paper backing on new bearings or use heavy grease on used bearings to retain in position. Compress rings and carefully install piston and connecting rod assembly into cylinder and crankcase. Install connecting rod cap and tighten screws to specified torque. Place a thin bead of silicon sealer to reed plate gasket and install gasket and reed plate. Tighten screws to specified torque. Install car-

buretor and air cleaner assembly. Install ignition system components and adjust as required. Continue to reverse disassembly procedure for reassembly.

PISTON, PIN AND RINGS. Standard piston diameter is 2.0870-2.0880 inch (53.010-53.035 mm). Upper and lower ring groove width is 0.0645-0.0655 inch (1.638-1.763 mm). Standard piston ring width is 0.0615-0.0625 inch (1.562-1.587 mm). Standard ring end gap is 0.006-0.016 inch (0.15-0.40 mm). If rings are beveled on inner edge, beveled edge is installed toward top of piston (Fig.

T64). Stagger ring end gaps around circumference of piston.

An offset piston is used on some models and is identified by a "V" or "1111" hash marks stamped into top of piston. The older version piston arrowhead is 90° from a line of the piston pin bore. Newer version piston arrowhead points in a line parallel to the piston bore. Refer to Fig. T62. Newer version wrist pin bore diameter is smaller at the arrowhead side. Piston which is not offset will have no markings on piston top and may be installed on connecting rod either way. Refer to CONNECTING ROD paragraphs for correct piston to connecting rod installation procedure.

Standard piston pin diameter is 0.4997-0.4999 inch (12.692-12.697 mm).

CONNECTING ROD. The steel connecting rod used on Model AV520 is equipped with a caged needle bearing at piston pin bore and with loose needle bearings at crankpin bore. New crankpin bore needle bearings are held in place by a waxed strip. Use heavy grease to retain old crankpin bore needle bearings in place. When installing new caged bearing in piston pin bore, press on lettered side of bearing. Offset

piston is installed on connecting rod so that match marks on connecting rod will be toward magneto side when installed in crankcase. When assembling piston to connecting rod, "V" or "1111" hash marks will be to the left side of connecting rod with connecting rod match marks up (Fig. T62). Piston with no marks on top may be installed either way. To install piston on connecting rod, heat piston in oil until oil just begins to smoke. Install piston pin as shown in Fig. T63. Piston pin must slide into piston easily. Do not force.

CYLINDER, BLOCK AND CRANKSHAFT SEALS. Standard cylinder bore diameter is 2.093-2.094 inches (53.16-53.18 mm). Maximum clearance between piston and cylinder bore is 0.005-0.007 inch (0.13-0.18 mm). If clearance between piston and cylinder exceeds 0.007 inch (0.18 mm), or cylinder bore is scratched or scored, renew cylinder.

It is important to exercise extreme care when renewing crankshaft seals to prevent their being damaged during installation. If a protector sleeve is not available, use tape to cover any splines, keyways, shoulders or threads over which the seal must pass during installation. Seals should be installed with channel groove of seal toward inside (center) of engine.

REED VALVES. Model AV520 engines are equipped with reed type inlet valve (38—Fig. T60). Reed petals should

not stand out more than 0.010 inch (0.25 mm) from the reed plate and must not be bent, distorted or cracked. The reed plate must be smooth and flat.

TECUMSEH SPECIAL TOOLS. Tecumseh special tools available to aid in engine disassembly and reassembly are listed by use and tool part number.

FLYWHEEL PULLER 670215
BALL BEARING DRIVER . . .670258
DIAL INDICATOR 670241

REWIND STARTER. The rewind starter assembly (1—Fig. T60) is riveted to blower housing (6) during production. If rewind starter must be renewed, note position on blower housing and cut rivets and bolt new unit to blower housing.

To disassemble rewind starter, remove handle (1—Fig. T65) and allow spring to slowly unwind in housing. Remove retainer screw (10), retainer cup (9), starter dog (8), dog spring (6) and brake spring (7). Lift pulley and spring assembly from rewind housing. Turn spring and keeper assembly to remove.

To reassemble rewind starter, apply a light coat of grease to rewind spring and place rewind spring and keeper assembly into pulley. Turn to lock into position. Place pulley into starter housing. Install brake spring, starter dog and dog return spring. Replace retainer cup and retainer screw. Tighten screw to specified torque.

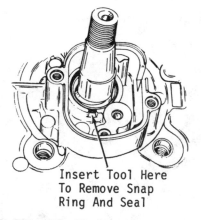

Insert Tool Here To Remove Snap Ring And Seal

Fig. T61—Wire retainer ring must be removed to remove retainer plate and seal. Refer to text.

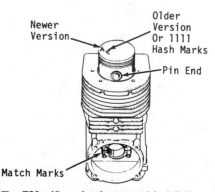

Fig. T62—View showing correct installation of connecting rod and piston assembly.

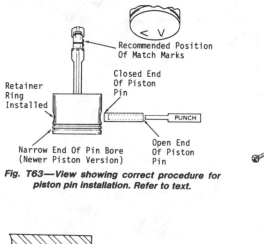

Fig. T63—View showing correct procedure for piston pin installation. Refer to text.

Inside Chamfer To Piston Top

Fig. T64—If inner ring edge is beveled, beveled side is installed toward top of piston.

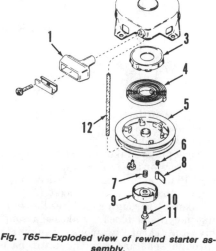

Fig. T65—Exploded view of rewind starter assembly.

1. Handle	7. Brake spring
2. Housing	8. Dog
3. Keeper	9. Retainer
4. Spring	10. Screw
5. Pulley	11. Centering pin
6. Dog spring	12. Rope

TML (TRAIL)

ENGINE SERVICE

Model	Bore	Stroke	Displacement
150528	1.44 in.	1.28 in.	2.1 cu. in.
	(36.5 mm)	(32.5 mm)	(35 cc)

ENGINE INFORMATION

TML (Trail) two-stroke air-cooled gasoline engine is used on TML trimmers and brush cutters. The die cast aluminum cylinder is an integral part of one crankcase half. The crankshaft is supported in caged roller bearings at each end. Engine is equipped with a one piece connecting rod which rides on roller bearings.

MAINTENANCE

SPARK PLUG. Recommended spark plug is a Champion CJ6, or equivalent. Specified electrode gap is 0.025 inch (0.6 mm).

CARBURETOR. TML engine is equipped with a Walbro diaphragm type carburetor (Fig. TL1). Initial adjustment of low speed mixture needle (12) is 1-1/4 turns open from a lightly seated position. Initial adjustment of high speed mixture needle (13) is 1-1/16 turns open from a lightly seated position.

Final carburetor adjustment is made with trimmer line at recommended length, engine at operating temperature and running. Turn low speed mixture needle (12) clockwise until engine falters. Note this position and turn low speed mixture needle counterclockwise until engine falters. Note this position and turn low speed mixture needle until it is halfway between first (lean) and last (rich) positions. Adjust idle speed screw (3) until engine idles at 2500-3000 rpm, or just below clutch engagement speed. Operate engine at full rpm and adjust high speed mixture needle (13) using the same procedure outlined for low speed mixture needle. Turn high speed mixture needle in 1/8 turn increments. A properly adjusted carburetor will give high rpm with some unburned residue from muffler.

To disassemble carburetor, remove pump cover retaining screw (1), pump cover (2), diaphragm (5) and gasket (4). Remove inlet screen (6). Remove the four metering cover screws (27), me-

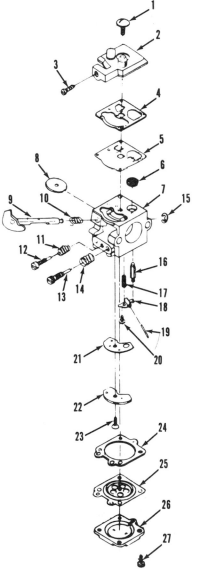

Fig. TL1—Exploded view of Walbro diaphragm type carburetor.

1. Screw
2. Pump cover
3. Idle screw
4. Gasket
5. Pump diaphragm
6. Inlet screen
7. Body
8. Throttle plate
9. Throttle shaft
10. Spring
11. Spring
12. Low speed mixture needle
13. High speed mixture needle
14. Spring
15. "E" clip
16. Fuel inlet needle
17. Spring
18. Fuel inlet lever
19. Pin
20. Screw
21. Gasket
22. Circuit plate
23. Screw
24. Gasket
25. Metering diaphragm
26. Cover
27. Screw

tering cover (26), diaphragm (25) and gasket (24). Remove screw (20), pin (19), fuel lever (18), spring (17) and fuel inlet needle (16). Remove screw (23), circuit plate (22) and gasket (21). Remove high and low speed mixture needles and springs. Remove throttle plate (8) and throttle shaft (9) as required.

Clean parts thoroughly and inspect all diaphragms for wrinkles, cracks or tears. Diaphragms should be flexible and soft. Fuel inlet lever (18) should be flush with carburetor body (Fig. TL2).

IGNITION SYSTEM. Engine is equipped with a solid state ignition system. Ignition system is considered satisfactory if spark will jump across the 3 mm (1/8 in.) gap of a test spark plug. If no spark is produced, check on/off switch, wiring and air gap. If switch, wiring and air gap are satisfactory, install a new ignition module (11—Fig. TL3).

Correct air gap for ignition module is 0.015 inch (0.38 mm). If ignition module screws are loosened or removed, apply Loctite 242 thread locking compound to screw threads prior to installation. Timing is not adjustable.

LUBRICATION. Manufacturer recommends mixing gasoline with a good quality two-stroke, air-cooled engine oil. Refer to TRIMMER SERVICE section for correct fuel/oil mixture ratio recommended by trimmer manufacturer.

CARBON. Muffler and exhaust ports should be cleaned after every 50 hours of operation if engine is operated continuously at full load. If operated at light or medium load, the cleaning interval can be extended to 100 hours.

REPAIRS

COMPRESSION PRESSURE. For optimum performance, compression pressure for a cold engine with throttle and choke wide open should be 120-140 psi (827-965 kPa). Minimum acceptable

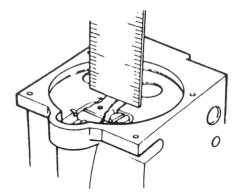

Fig. TL2 — Fuel inlet valve lever should be flush with carburetor surface.

compression pressure for a cold engine is 90 psi (620 kPa).

TIGHTENING TORQUES. Recommended tightening torque specifications are as follows:

Crankcase cover . . . . 70 in.-lbs.
                                      (8 N·m)

Flywheel nut . . . . 175 in.-lbs.
                                    (20 N·m)

Ignition module . . . . 25 in.-lbs.
                                    (3 N·m)

Carburetor . . . . 30 in.-lbs.
                                    (3.4 N·m)

CRANKSHAFT AND BEARINGS.
Crankshaft (17—Fig. TL3) is supported at each end in caged needle bearings clamped in bearing bores at crankcase split. To remove crankshaft, remove all cooling shrouds, recoil starter assembly, fuel tank, muffler and carburetor. Remove nut, flywheel and clutch. Remove the crankcase retaining bolts (20), then remove crankcase cover (19). Carefully remove crankshaft, pulling piston out of cylinder as crankshaft is removed. When handling crankshaft, hold connecting rod toward counterweight side to prevent the 11 connecting rod needle bearings from falling out. Remove all seals, bearings and thrust washers. Work connecting rod off small end of crankshaft using care to catch the 11 connecting rod needle bearings (18).

To reassemble, coat connecting rod needle bearings with heavy grease and install all 11 bearings on crankshaft connecting rod journal. Work connecting rod over small end of crankshaft and over bearings. Thrust washers are installed with chamfered side toward crankshaft web. Seals are installed with spring side toward the inner side of crankcase. Apply a thin coat of sili-

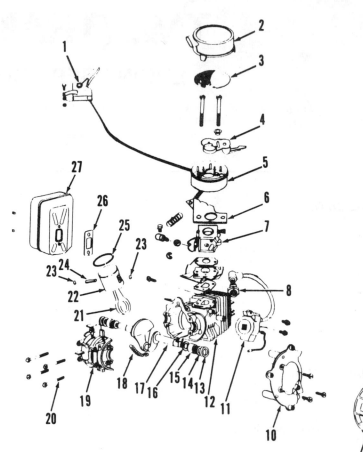

Fig. TL3 — Exploded view of 150528 engine.

1. Throttle cable assy.	8. Spark plug	15. Bearing
2. Air cleaner cover	9. Flywheel	16. Thrust washer
3. Filter	10. Base plate	17. Crankshaft
4. Choke	11. Ignition module	18. Needle bearings (11)
5. Housing	12. Cylinder/crankcase	19. Crankcase cover
6. Bracket	13. Seal	20. Crankcase cover bolts
7. Carburetor	14. Retaining ring	21. Connecting rod

22. Piston	
23. Retaining ring	
24. Piston pin	
25. Ring	
26. Gasket	
27. Muffler	

con sealer around crankcase mating edges and install crankcase cover. Make certain all bearings and seals are correctly positioned in crankcase bearing bores. Tighten crankcase cover bolts to specified torque.

PISTON, PIN AND RING. A single ring aluminum piston is used. Piston is equipped with a locating pin in piston ring groove to prevent ring from turning. To remove piston, refer to CRANKSHAFT AND BEARING paragraphs. After connecting rod has been removed, remove retaining rings (23—Fig. TL3) and press piston pin from piston. Remove piston.

Inspect piston for scratches, scoring or excessive wear. Renew piston as required.

CONNECTING ROD. The one piece connecting rod rides on 11 needle bearings at crankshaft journal. Piston pin rides directly in connecting rod piston pin bore. To remove connecting rod, refer to CRANKSHAFT AND BEARINGS paragraphs.

CYLINDER. The die-cast aluminum cylinder has a chrome plated bore and is an integral part of one crankcase half. To remove cylinder, refer to CRANKSHAFT AND BEARINGS paragraphs. Cylinder should be renewed if it is scored, chrome is flaking off or aluminum is showing. If in doubt as to whether a spot is where aluminum is showing, try to scratch the area carefully. Aluminum will scratch easily and chrome plating will not.

TWO-STROKE ENGINES

MIXING GASOLINE AND OIL

Most two-stroke engines are lubricated by oil mixed with the gasoline. The manufacturers carefully determine which type of oil and how much oil should be mixed with the gasoline to provide the most desirable operation, then list these mixing instructions. Often, two or more gasoline-to-oil ratios will be listed depending upon type of oil or severity of service.

You should always follow the manufacturer's recommended mixing instructions, because mixing the wrong amount of oil or using the wrong type of oil can cause extensive engine damage. Too much oil can cause lower power, spark plug fouling and excessive carbon buildup. Not enough oil will cause inadequate lubrication and will probably result in scuffing, seizure or other forms of engine damage.

Use only the gasoline type and octane rating recommended by manufacturer. Never use gasoline that has been stored for a long period of time.

Accurate measurement of gasoline and oil is necessary to assure correct lubrication. Proper quantities of gasoline and oil for some of the more common mixture ratios are shown in the accompanying chart.

When mixing, use a separate, approved, safety container that is large enough to hold the desired amount of fuel with additional space for mixing. Pour about half the required amount of gasoline into container, add the required amount of oil, then shake vigorously until completely mixed. Pour remaining amount of gasoline into container, then complete mixing by shaking. Serious engine damage can be caused by incomplete mixing. Never attempt to mix gasoline and oil in the unit's fuel tank.

Always observe safe handling practices when working with gasoline. Gasoline is extremely flammable. Do not smoke or allow sparks or open flame around fuel or in the presence of fuel vapors. Be sure area is well-ventilated. Observe fire prevention rules.

Ratio	Gasoline	Oil
14:1	0.9 Gal. (3.4 L)	8 oz. (235 mL)
16:1	1.0 Gal. (3.8 L)	8 oz. (235 mL)
20:1	1.25 Gal. (4.7 L)	8 oz. (235 mL)
25:1	1.5 Gal. (5.7 L)	8 oz. (235 mL)
30:1	1.9 Gal. (7.2 L)	8 oz. (235 mL)
32:1	2.0 Gal. (7.6 L)	8 oz. (235 mL)
40:1	2.5 Gal. (9.4 L)	8 oz. (235 mL)
50:1	3.1 Gal. (11.7 L)	8 oz. (235 mL)

Ratio	Gasoline	Oil
14:1	1 Gal. (3.8 L)	9.1 oz. (270 mL)
16:1	1 Gal. (3.8 L)	8.0 oz. (235 mL)
20:1	1 Gal. (3.8 L)	6.4 oz. (190 mL)
25:1	1 Gal. (3.8 L)	5.1 oz. (150 mL)
30:1	1 Gal. (3.8 L)	4.2 oz. (125 mL)
32:1	1 Gal. (3.8 L)	4.0 oz. (120 mL)
40:1	1 Gal. (3.8 L)	3.2 oz. (95 mL)
50:1	1 Gal. (3.8 L)	2.5 oz. (75 mL)

METRIC CONVERSION

Square centimeters x	.155	= Square inches
Square centimeters =	6.4515	x Square inches
Square meters	x 10.7641	= Square feet
Square meters	= .0929	x Square feet
Cubic centimeters	x .061025	= Cubic inches
Cubic centimeters	= 16.387	x Cubic inches
Cubic meters	x 35.3156	= Cubic feet
Cubic meters	= .0283	x Cubic feet
Cubic meters	x 1.308	= Cubic yards
Cubic meters	= .765	x Cubic yards
Liters	x 61.023	= Cubic inches
Liters	= .0164	x Cubic inches
Liters	x .2642	= U.S. gallons
Liters	= 3.7854	x U.S. gallons
Grams	x 15.4324	= Grains
Grams	= .0648	x Grains
Grams	x .03527	= Ounces avoirdupois
Grams	= 28.3495	x Ounces avoirdupois
Kilograms	x 2.2046	= Pounds
Kilograms	= .4536	x Pounds
Kilograms per square centimeter	x 14.2231	= Pounds per square inch

Kilograms per square centimeter =	.0703	x Pounds per square inch
Kilograms per cubic meter	x .06243	= Pounds per cubic foot
Kilograms per cubic meter	= 16.0189	x Pounds per cubic foot
Metric tons (1000 kilograms)	x 1.1023	= Tons (2000 pounds)
Metric tons (1000 kilograms)	= .9072	x Tons (2000 pounds)
Kilowatts	= .746	x Horsepower
Kilowatts	x 1.3405	= Horsepower
Millimeters	x .03937	= Inches
Millimeters	= 25.4	x Inches
Meters	x 3.2809	= Feet
Meters	= .3048	x Feet
Kilometers	x .62138	= Miles
Kilometers	= 1.6093	x Miles

METRIC CONVERSION

MM.	INCHES		±	MM.	INCHES		±	MM.	INCHES		±	MM.	INCHES		±	MM.	INCHES		±	MM.	INCHES		±
1	0.0394	1/32	+	51	2.0079	2.0	+	101	3.9764	3 31/32	+	151	5.9449	5 15/16	+	201	7.9134	7 29/32	+	251	9.8819	9 7/8	+
2	0.0787	3/32	−	52	2.0472	2 1/16	−	102	4.0157	4 1/32	−	152	5.9842	5 31/32	+	202	7.9527	7 15/16	+	252	9.9212	9 29/32	+
3	0.1181	1/8	−	53	2.0866	2 3/32	−	103	4.0551	4 1/16	−	153	6.0236	6 1/32	−	203	7.9921	8.0	−	253	9.9606	9 31/32	−
4	0.1575	5/32	+	54	2.1260	2 1/8	+	104	4.0945	4 3/32	+	154	6.0630	6 1/16	+	204	8.0315	8 1/32	+	254	10.0000	10.0	
5	0.1969	3/16	+	55	2.1654	2 5/32	+	105	4.1339	4 1/8	+	155	6.1024	6 3/32	+	205	8.0709	8 1/16	+	255	10.0393	10 1/32	+
6	0.2362	1/4		56	2.2047	2 7/32	−	106	4.1732	4 3/16	−	156	6.1417	6 5/32	−	206	8.1102	8 1/8	−	256	10.0787	10 3/32	−
7	0.2756	9/32	−	57	2.2441	2 1/4	−	107	4.2126	4 7/32	−	157	6.1811	6 3/16	+	207	8.1496	8 5/32	−	257	10.1181	10 1/8	−
8	0.3150	5/16	−	58	2.2835	2 9/32	+	108	4.2520	4 1/4	+	158	6.2205	6 7/32	+	208	8.1890	8 3/16	+	258	10.1575	10 5/32	+
9	0.3543	11/32	+	59	2.3228	2 5/16	+	109	4.2913	4 9/32	+	159	6.2598	6 1/4	+	209	8.2283	8 7/32	+	259	10.1968	10 3/16	+
10	0.3937	13/32	−	60	2.3622	2 3/8	−	110	4.3307	4 11/32	−	160	6.2992	6 5/16	−	210	8.2677	8 9/32	−	260	10.2362	10 1/4	−
11	0.4331	7/16	−	61	2.4016	2 13/32	−	111	4.3701	4 3/8	−	161	6.3386	6 11/32	−	211	8.3071	8 5/16	−	261	10.2756	10 9/32	−
12	0.4724	15/32	−	62	2.4409	2 7/16	−	112	4.4094	4 13/32	−	162	6.3779	6 3/8	+	212	8.3464	8 11/32	+	262	10.3149	10 5/16	+
13	0.5118	1/2	+	63	2.4803	2 15/32	+	113	4.4488	4 7/16	+	163	6.4173	6 13/32	+	213	8.3858	8 3/8	+	263	10.3543	10 11/32	+
14	0.5512	9/16	−	64	2.5197	2 17/32	−	114	4.4882	4 1/2	−	164	6.4567	6 15/32	−	214	8.4252	8 7/16	−	264	10.3937	10 13/32	−
15	0.5906	19/32	−	65	2.5591	2 9/16	−	115	4.5276	4 17/32	−	165	6.4961	6 1/2	−	215	8.4646	8 15/32	−	265	10.4330	10 7/16	−
16	0.6299	5/8	+	66	2.5984	2 19/32	+	116	4.5669	4 9/16	+	166	6.5354	6 17/32	+	216	8.5039	8 1/2	+	266	10.4724	10 15/32	+
17	0.6693	21/32	+	67	2.6378	2 5/8	+	117	4.6063	4 19/32	+	167	6.5748	6 9/16	+	217	8.5433	8 17/32	+	267	10.5118	10 1/2	+
18	0.7087	23/32	−	68	2.6772	2 11/16	−	118	4.6457	4 21/32	−	168	6.6142	6 5/8	−	218	8.5827	8 19/32	−	268	10.5512	10 9/16	−
19	0.7480	3/4	−	69	2.7165	2 23/32	−	119	4.6850	4 11/16	−	169	6.6535	6 21/32	−	219	8.6220	8 5/8	−	269	10.5905	10 19/32	−
20	0.7874	25/32	+	70	2.7559	2 3/4	+	120	4.7244	4 23/32	+	170	6.6929	6 11/16	+	220	8.6614	8 21/32	+	270	10.6299	10 5/8	+
21	0.8268	13/16	+	71	2.7953	2 25/32	+	121	4.7638	4 3/4	+	171	6.7323	6 23/32	+	221	8.7008	8 11/16	+	271	10.6693	10 21/32	+
22	0.8661	7/8	−	72	2.8346	2 27/32	−	122	4.8031	4 13/16	−	172	6.7716	6 25/32	−	222	8.7401	8 3/4	−	272	10.7086	10 23/32	−
23	0.9055	29/32	−	73	2.8740	2 7/8	−	123	4.8425	4 27/32	−	173	6.8110	6 13/16	−	223	8.7795	8 25/32	−	273	10.7480	10 3/4	−
24	0.9449	15/16	+	74	2.9134	2 29/32	+	124	4.8819	4 7/8	+	174	6.8504	6 27/32	+	224	8.8189	8 13/16	+	274	10.7874	10 25/32	+
25	0.9843	31/32	+	75	2.9528	2 15/16	+	125	4.9213	4 29/32	+	175	6.8898	6 7/8	+	225	8.8583	8 27/32	+	275	10.8268	10 13/16	+
26	1.0236	1 1/32	−	76	2.9921	3.0	−	126	4.9606	4 31/32	−	176	6.9291	6 15/16	−	226	8.8976	8 29/32	−	276	10.8661	10 7/8	−
27	1.0630	1 1/16	+	77	3.0315	3 1/32	+	127	5.0000	5.0		177	6.9685	6 31/32	−	227	8.9370	8 15/16	−	277	10.9055	10 29/32	−
28	1.1024	1 3/32	+	78	3.0709	3 1/16	+	128	5.0394	5 1/32	+	178	7.0079	7.0	+	228	8.9764	8 31/32	+	278	10.9449	10 15/16	+
29	1.1417	1 5/32	−	79	3.1102	3 1/8	−	129	5.0787	5 3/32	−	179	7.0472	7 1/16	−	229	9.0157	9 1/32	−	279	10.9842	10 31/32	−
30	1.1811	1 3/16	−	80	3.1496	3 5/32	−	130	5.1181	5 1/8	−	180	7.0866	7 3/32	−	230	9.0551	9 1/16	−	280	11.0236	11 1/32	−
31	1.2205	1 7/32	+	81	3.1890	3 3/16	+	131	5.1575	5 5/32	+	181	7.1260	7 1/8	+	231	9.0945	9 3/32	+	281	11.0630	11 1/16	+
32	1.2598	1 1/4	+	82	3.2283	3 7/32	+	132	5.1968	5 3/16	+	182	7.1653	7 5/32	+	232	9.1338	9 1/8	+	282	11.1023	11 3/32	+
33	1.2992	1 5/16	−	83	3.2677	3 9/32	−	133	5.2362	5 1/4	−	183	7.2047	7 7/32	−	233	9.1732	9 3/16	−	283	11.1417	11 5/32	−
34	1.3386	1 11/32	−	84	3.3071	3 5/16	−	134	5.2756	5 9/32	−	184	7.2441	7 1/4	−	234	9.2126	9 7/32	−	284	11.1811	11 3/16	−
35	1.3780	1 3/8	+	85	3.3465	3 11/32	+	135	5.3150	5 5/16	+	185	7.2835	7 9/32	+	235	9.2520	9 1/4	+	285	11.2204	11 7/32	+
36	1.4173	1 13/32	+	86	3.3858	3 3/8	+	136	5.3543	5 11/32	+	186	7.3228	7 5/16	+	236	9.2913	9 9/32	+	286	11.2598	11 1/4	+
37	1.4567	1 15/32	−	87	3.4252	3 7/16	−	137	5.3937	5 13/32	−	187	7.3622	7 3/8	−	237	9.3307	9 11/32	−	287	11.2992	11 5/16	−
38	1.4961	1 1/2	−	88	3.4646	3 15/32	−	138	5.4331	5 7/16	−	188	7.4016	7 13/32	−	238	9.3701	9 3/8	−	288	11.3386	11 11/32	−
39	1.5354	1 17/32	+	89	3.5039	3 1/2	+	139	5.4724	5 15/32	+	189	7.4409	7 7/16	+	239	9.4094	9 13/32	+	289	11.3779	11 3/8	+
40	1.5748	1 9/16	+	90	3.5433	3 17/32	+	140	5.5118	5 1/2	+	190	7.4803	7 15/32	+	240	9.4488	9 7/16	+	290	11.4173	11 13/32	+
41	1.6142	1 5/8	−	91	3.5827	3 19/32	−	141	5.5512	5 9/16	−	191	7.5197	7 17/32	−	241	9.4882	9 1/2	−	291	11.4567	11 15/32	−
42	1.6535	1 21/32	−	92	3.6220	3 5/8	−	142	5.5905	5 19/32	−	192	7.5590	7 9/16	−	242	9.5275	9 17/32	−	292	11.4960	11 1/2	−
43	1.6929	1 11/16	+	93	3.6614	3 21/32	+	143	5.6299	5 5/8	+	193	7.5984	7 19/32	+	243	9.5669	9 9/16	+	293	11.5354	11 17/32	+
44	1.7323	1 23/32	+	94	3.7008	3 11/16	+	144	5.6693	5 21/32	+	194	7.6378	7 5/8	+	244	9.6063	9 19/32	+	294	11.5748	11 9/16	+
45	1.7717	1 25/32	−	95	3.7402	3 3/4	−	145	5.7087	5 23/32	−	195	7.6772	7 11/16	−	245	9.6457	9 21/32	−	295	11.6142	11 5/8	−
46	1.8110	1 13/16	−	96	3.7795	3 25/32	−	146	5.7480	5 3/4	−	196	7.7165	7 23/32	−	246	9.6850	9 11/16	−	296	11.6535	11 21/32	−
47	1.8504	1 27/32	+	97	3.8189	3 13/16	+	147	5.7874	5 25/32	+	197	7.7559	7 3/4	+	247	9.7244	9 23/32	+	297	11.6929	11 11/16	+
48	1.8898	1 7/8	+	98	3.8583	3 27/32	+	148	5.8268	5 13/16	+	198	7.7953	7 25/32	+	248	9.7638	9 3/4	+	298	11.7323	11 23/32	+
49	1.9291	1 15/16	−	99	3.8976	3 29/32	−	149	5.8661	5 7/8	−	199	7.8346	7 27/32	−	249	9.8031	9 13/16	−	299	11.7716	11 25/32	−
50	1.9685	1 31/32	−	100	3.9370	3 15/16	−	150	5.9055	5 29/32	−	200	7.8740	7 7/8	−	250	9.8425	9 27/32	−	300	11.8110	11 13/16	

NOTE: The + or − sign indicates that the decimal equivalent is larger or smaller than the fractional equivalent.

Alpina North America
Box 112
Northport, WA 99157
(604) 367-9202

Black & Decker
10 North Park Drive
Hunt Valley, MD 21030
(301) 683-7975

Bunton
P.O. Box 33247
4303 Poplar Level Road
Louisville, KY 40232
(502) 966-0550

Deere & Company
John Deere Road
Moline, IL 61265
(309) 765-8000

Echo, Inc.
400 Oakwood Rd.
Lake Zurich, IL 60047
(708) 540-8400

The Green Machine
P.O. Box 4070
Medford, OR 97501
(503) 826-8900

Hoffco
358 N.W. F Street
Richmond, IN 47374
(317) 966-8161

Homelite
P.O. Box 7047
Charlotte, NC 28273
(704) 588-3200

Husqvarna Forest & Garden
9006-J Perimeter Woods Dr.
Charlotte, NC 28216
(704) 597-5000

IDC
Ryobi Outdoor Products
550 N. 54th St.
Chandler, AZ 85226
(602) 961-0034

Jonsered Power Products
1379 Jamike Ave.
Erlanger, KY 41018
(606) 525-9033

Lawn Boy
P.O. Box 152
Plymouth, WI 53073
(414) 893-1011

Maruyama
15436 N.E. 95th St.
Redmond, WA 98052
(206) 885-0811

McCulloch
P.O. Box 11990
Tucson, AZ 85734
(602) 574-1311

Olympyk
Tilton Equipment Co.
P.O. Box 68
Rye, NH 03870
(603) 964-6560

Poulan/Weed Eater
5020 Flournoy-Lucas Rd.
Shreveport, LA 71129
(318) 687-0100

Red Max
1505 Pavilion Place
Suite A
Norcross, GA 30093
(404) 381-5147

Robin
U.S. Importer - Carswell Import &
    Marketing Assoc.
3750 N. Liberty St.
Winston Salem, NC 27115
(919) 767-9432

Ryan
Ryobi Outdoor Products
550 N. 54th St.
Chandler, AZ 85226
(602) 961-0034

Ryobi Outdoor Products
550 N. 54th St.
Chandler, AZ 85226
(602) 961-0034

Sachs-Dolmar
Dolmar USA, Inc.
P.O. Box 78526
Shreveport, LA 71137
(318) 226-0081

Sears
Sears Tower
Chicago, IL 60684

Shindaiwa
11975 S.W. Herman Rd.
Tualatin, OR 97062
(503) 692-3070

Snapper
Macon Highway
McDonough, GA 30253
(404) 957-9141

Stihl
536 Viking Dr.
Virginia Beach, VA 23452
(804) 486-9100

Tanaka
22322 20th Ave. S.E.
Bothell, WA 98021
(206) 481-2000

Toro
8111 Lyndale Ave. South
Minneapolis, MN 55420
(612) 887-8801

Wards
Montgomery Ward Plaza
Chicago, IL 60671
(312) 467-2624

Western Auto
2107 Grand
Kansas City, MO 64108

Yazoo
P.O. Box 4449
Jackson, MS 39296
(601) 366-6421

MAINTENANCE LOG

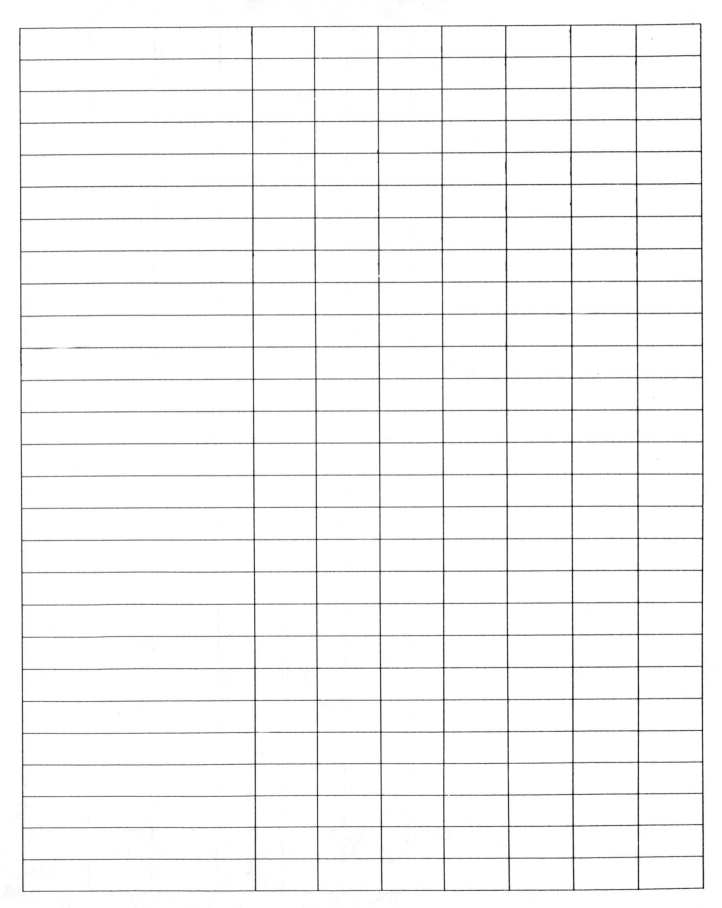

MAINTENANCE LOG

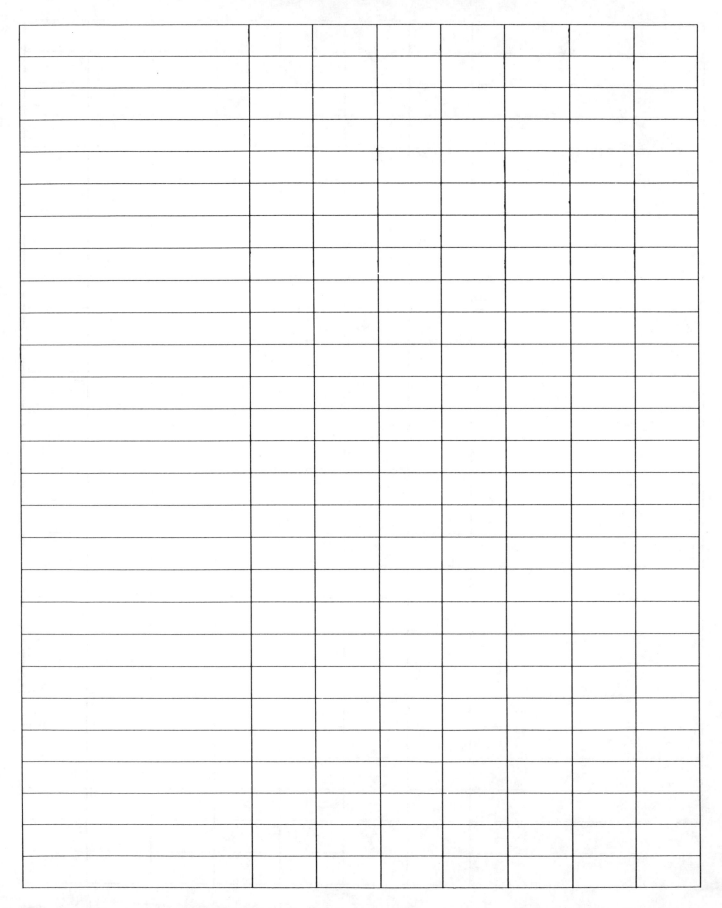

MAINTENANCE LOG

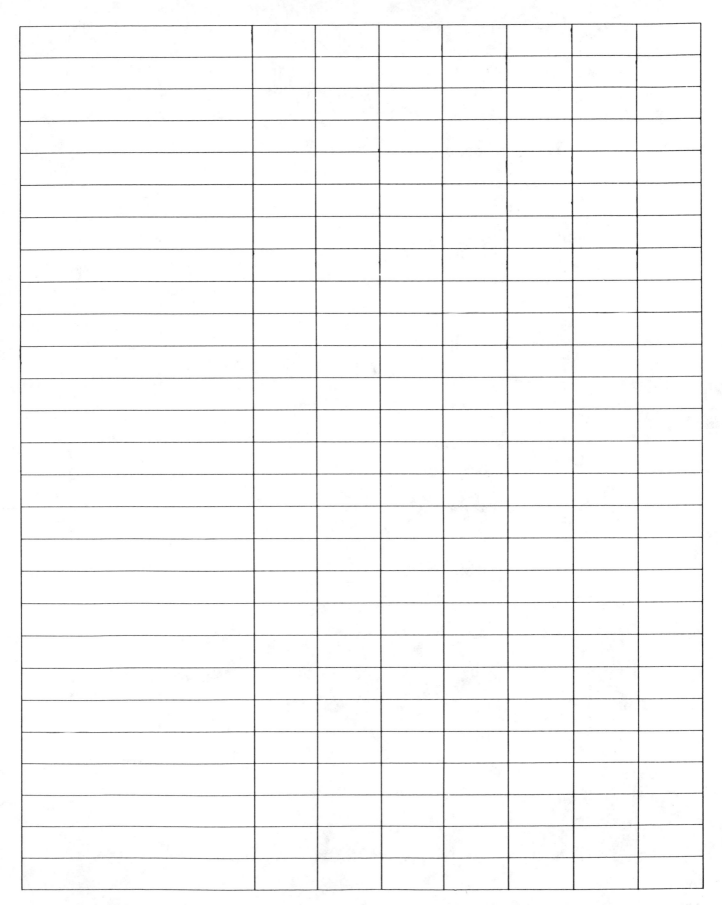

NOTES

NOTES

NOTES

NOTES

NOTES